DAYANITA SINGH

DAYANITA SINGH

DAYANITA SINGH
LET'S SEE

Steidl

I like visual novels, the novels that lurk in pictures,
with a contemporary consciousness of ruptures,
blockages, surprises, interruptions,
Steve Reich's rhythms and frictions.
In books, turning a page is more than a movement.

Walter Keller

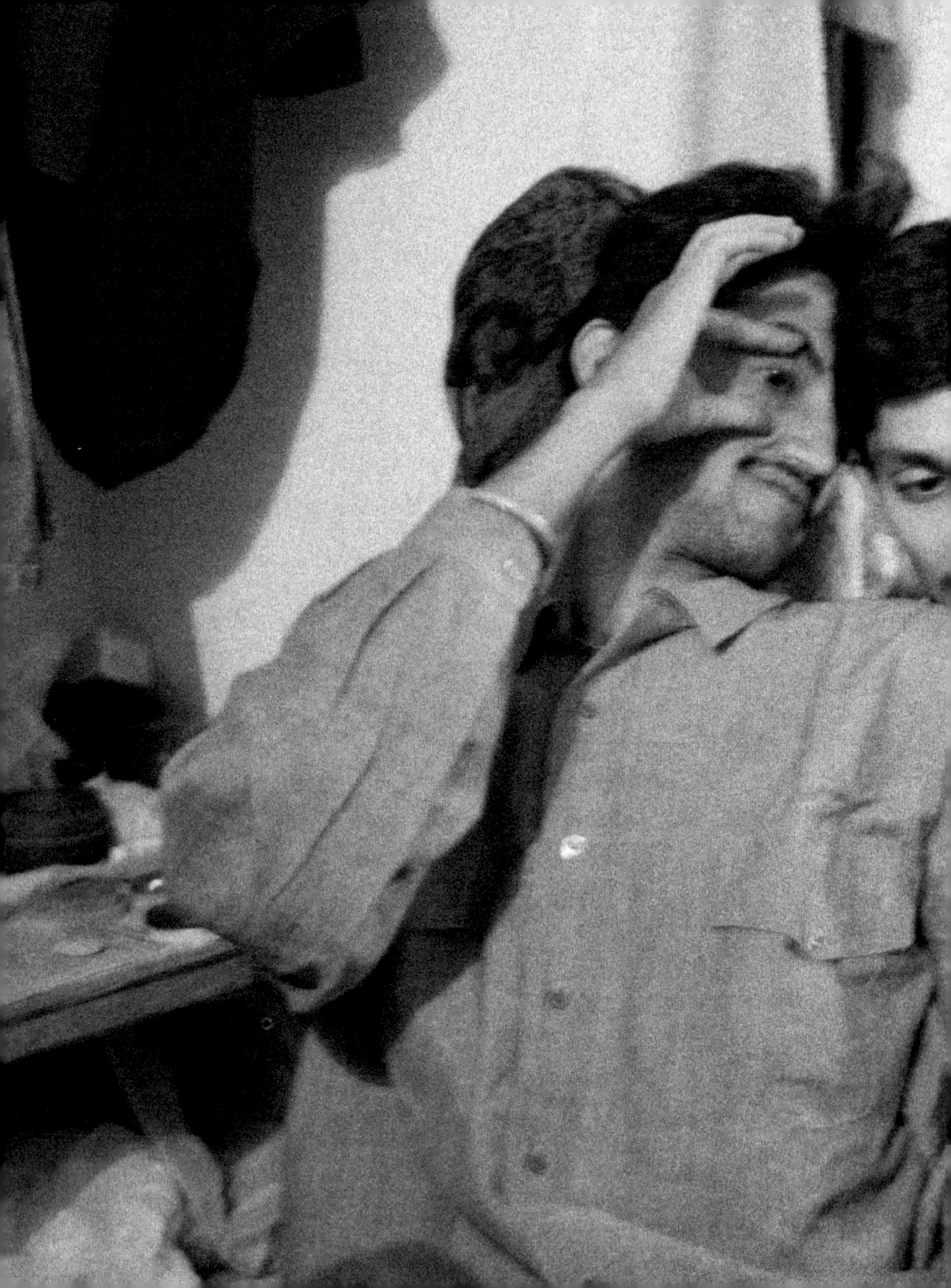

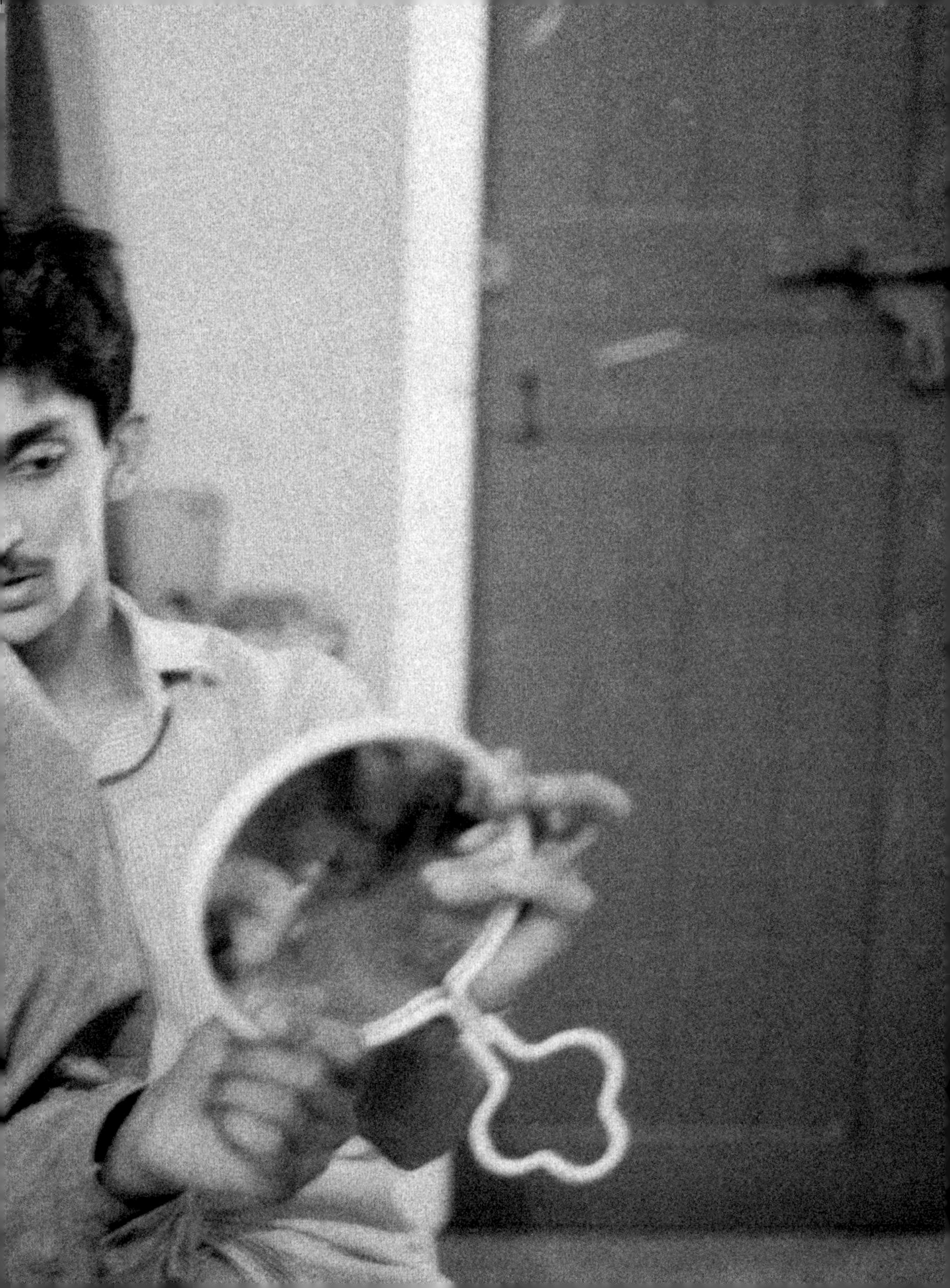

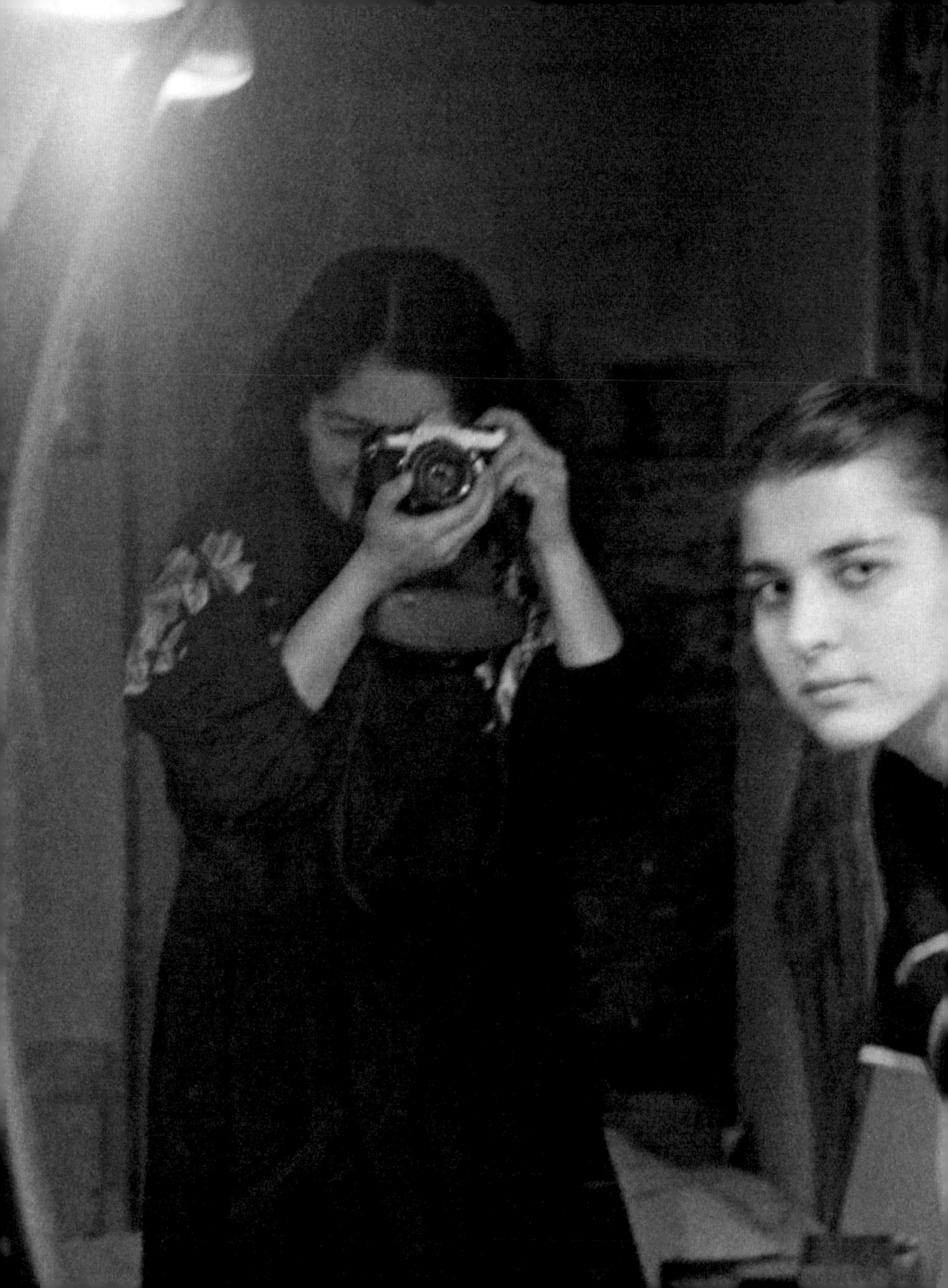

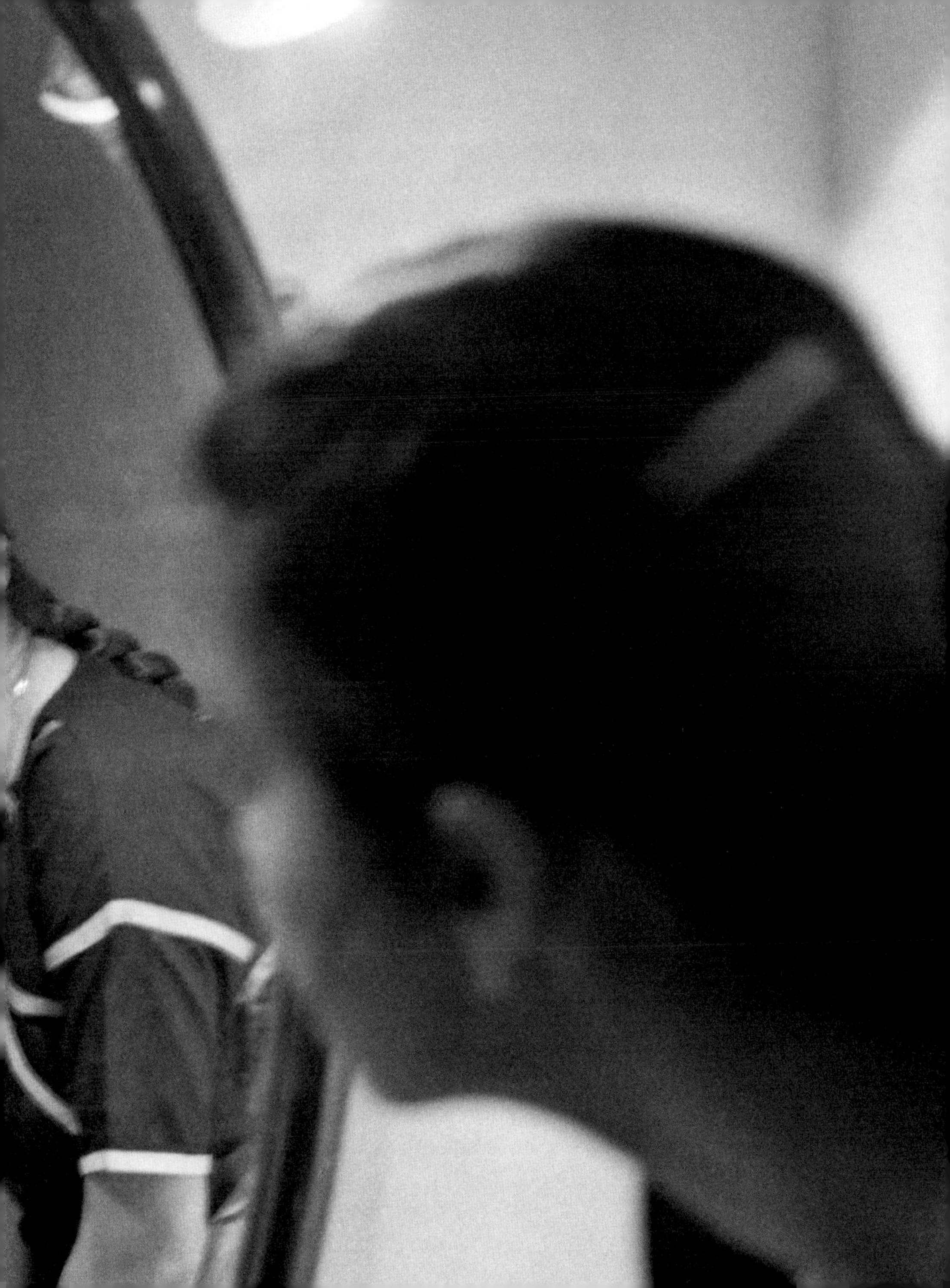

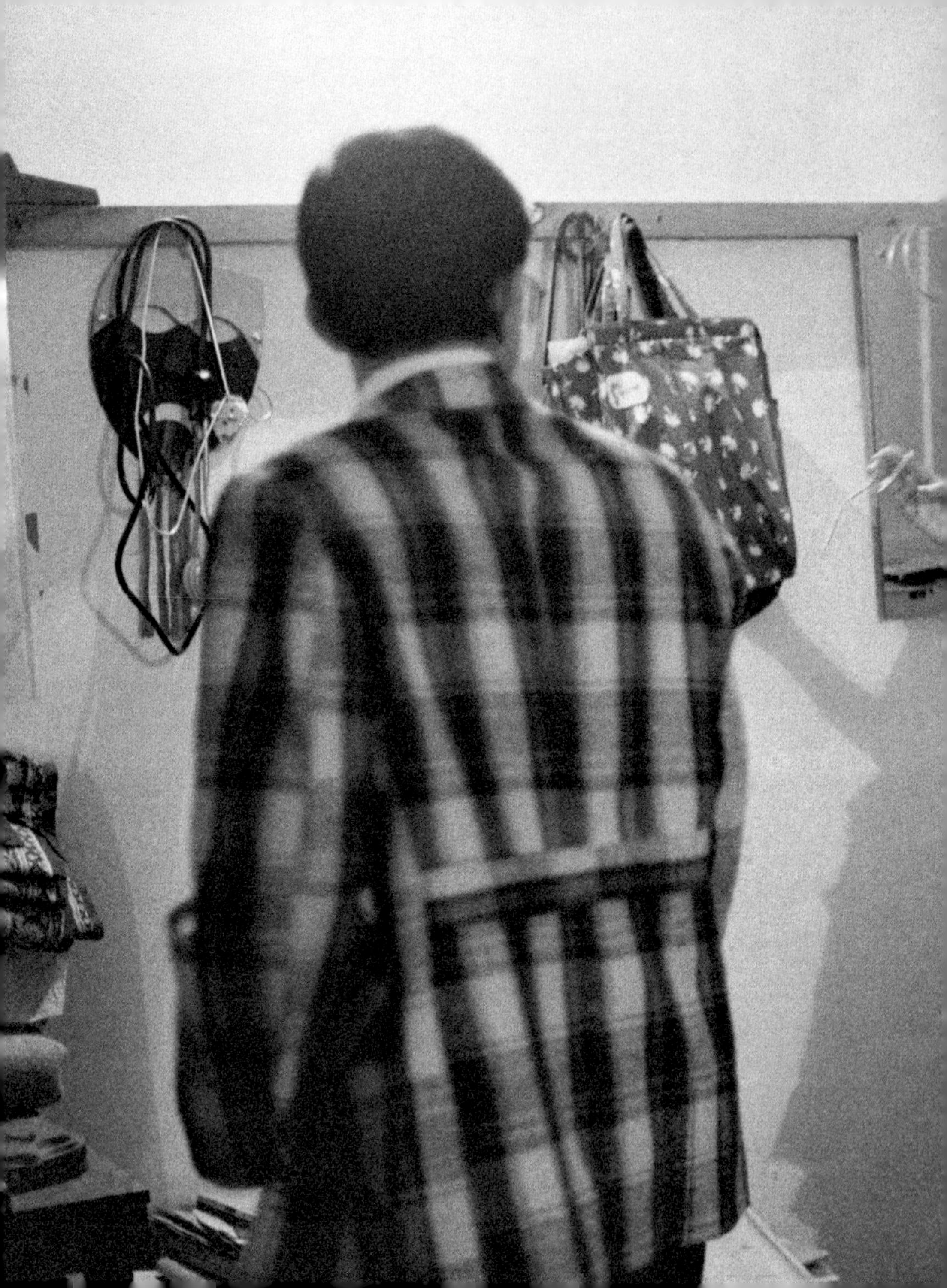

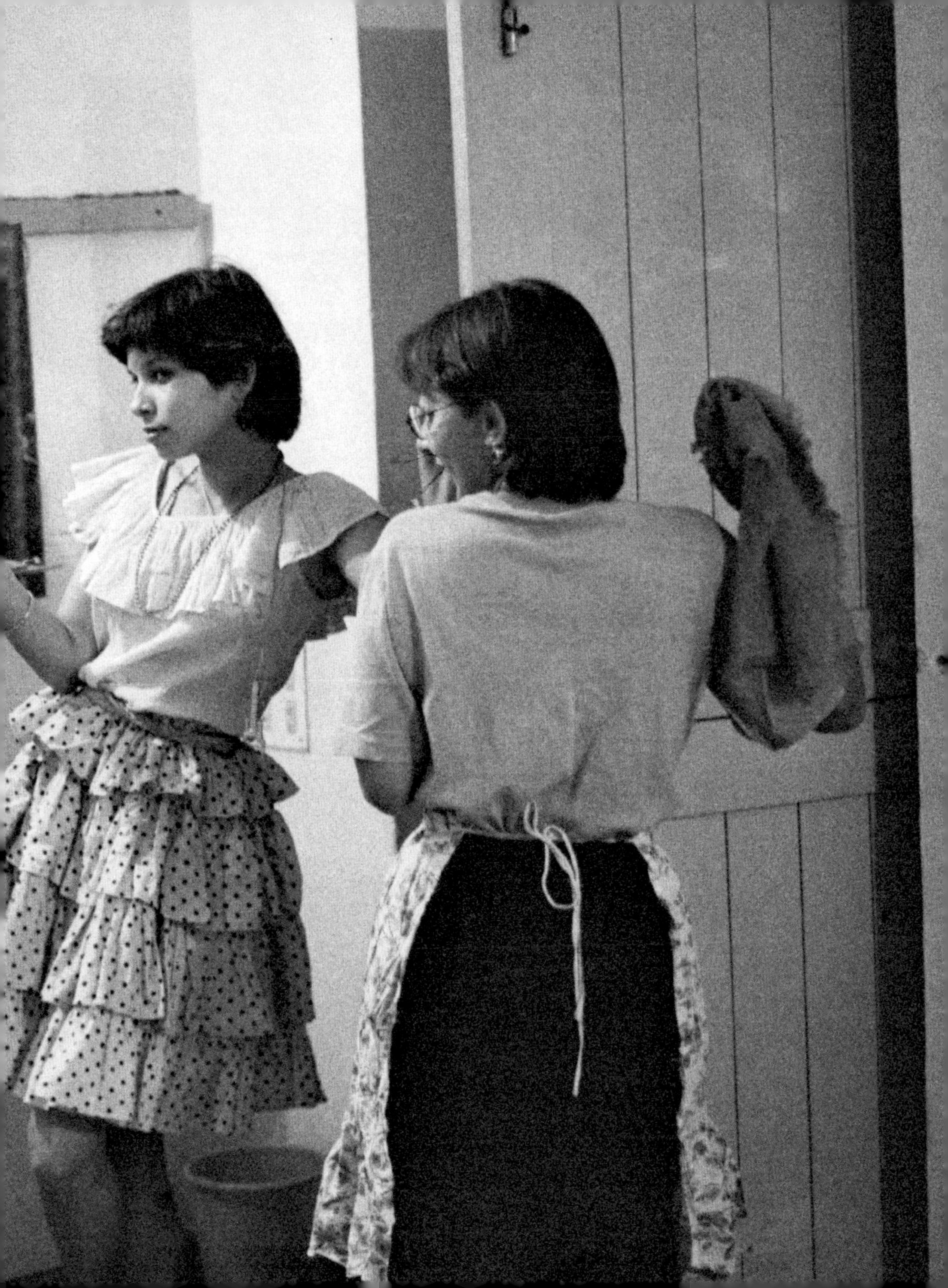

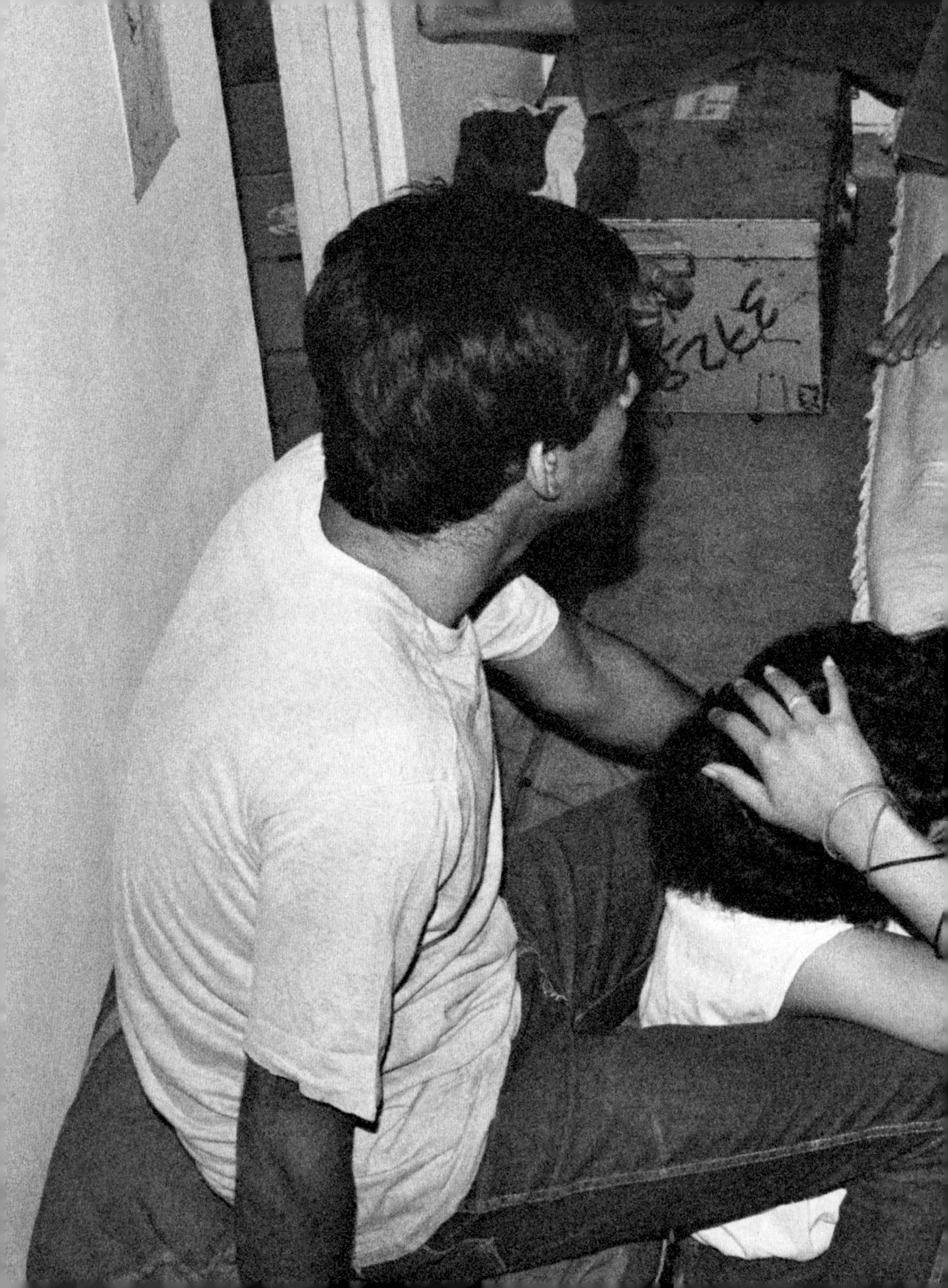

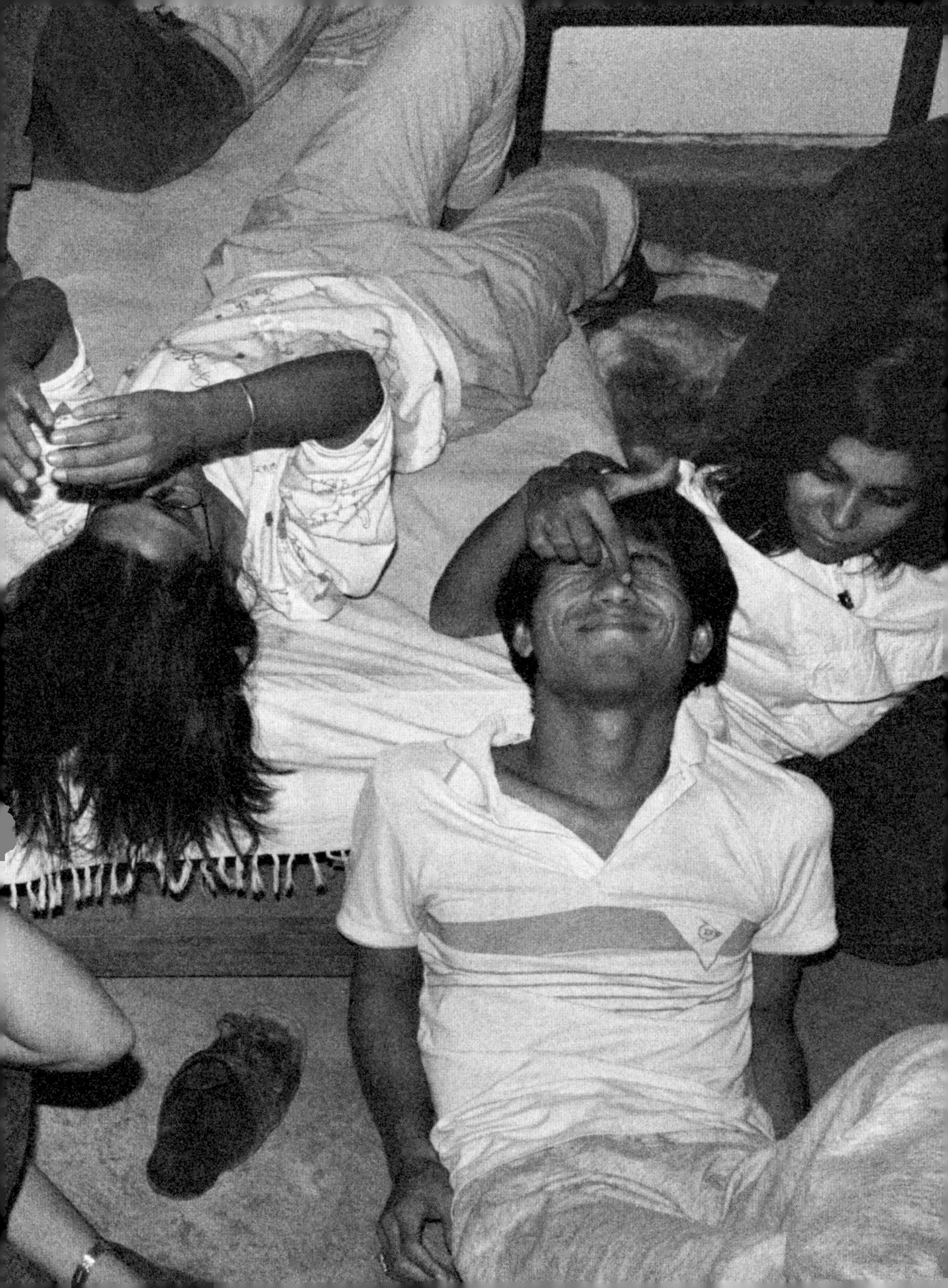

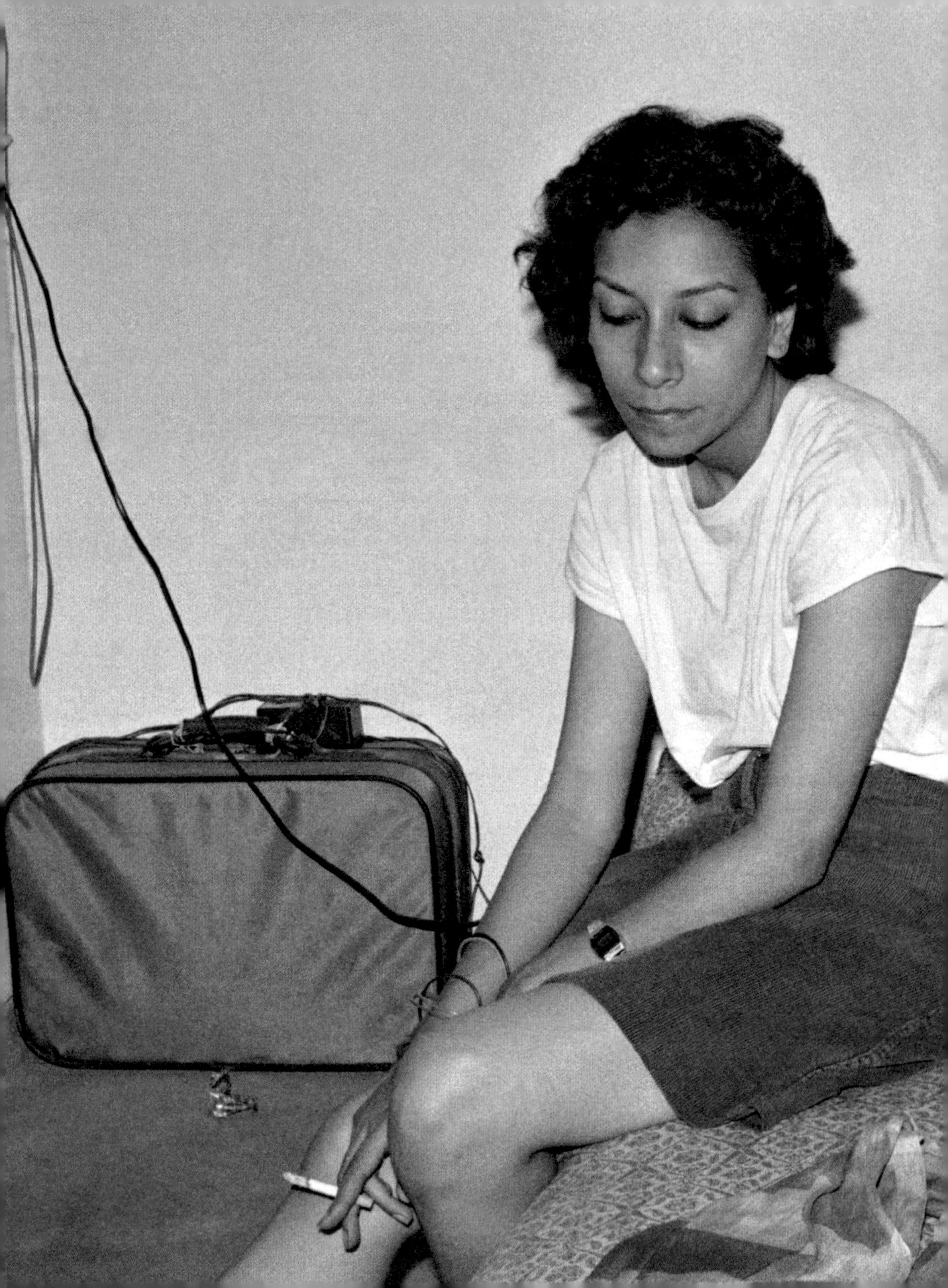

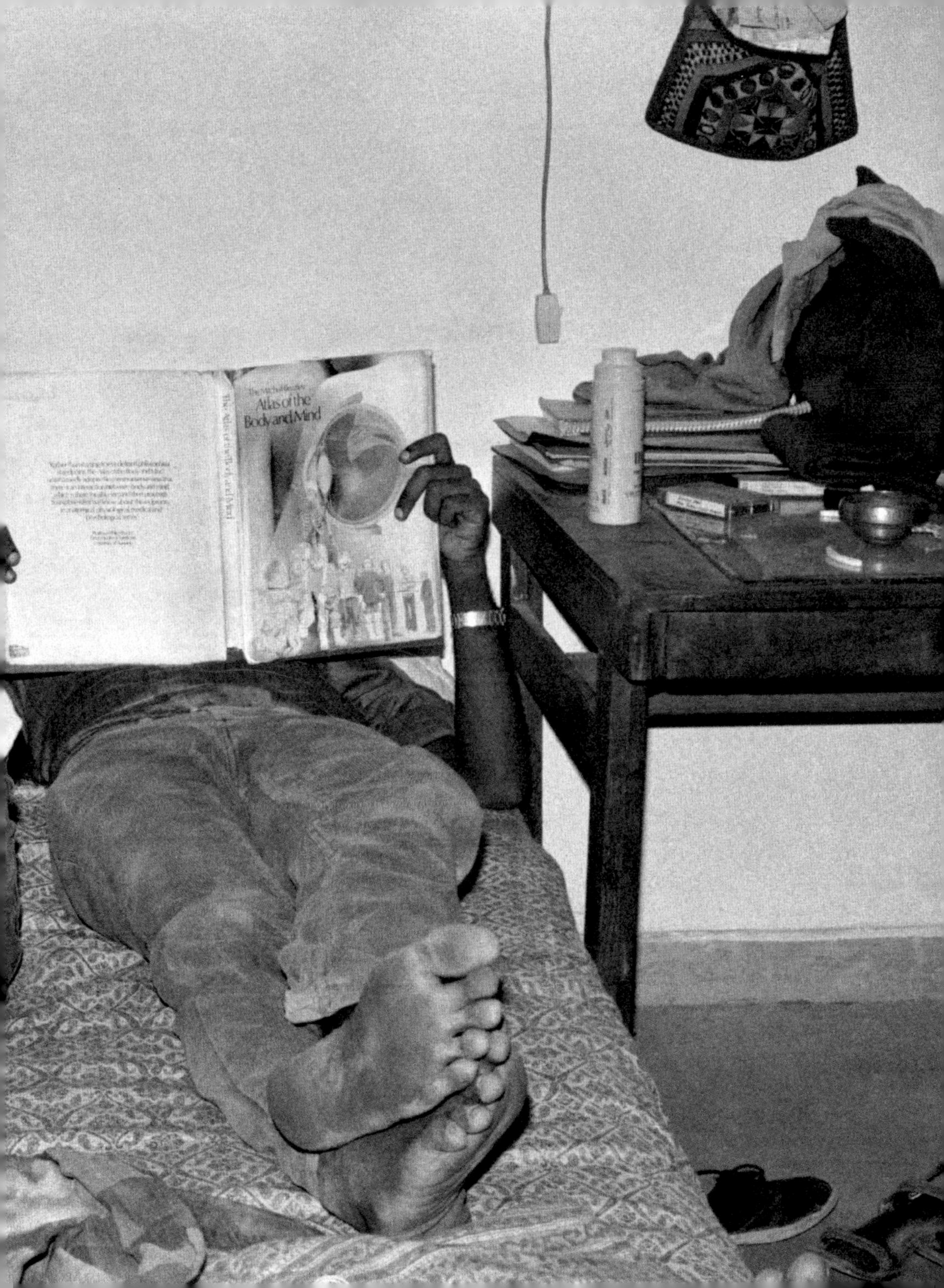
The Mitchell Beazley
Atlas of the
Body and Mind
The Atlas of the Body and Mind

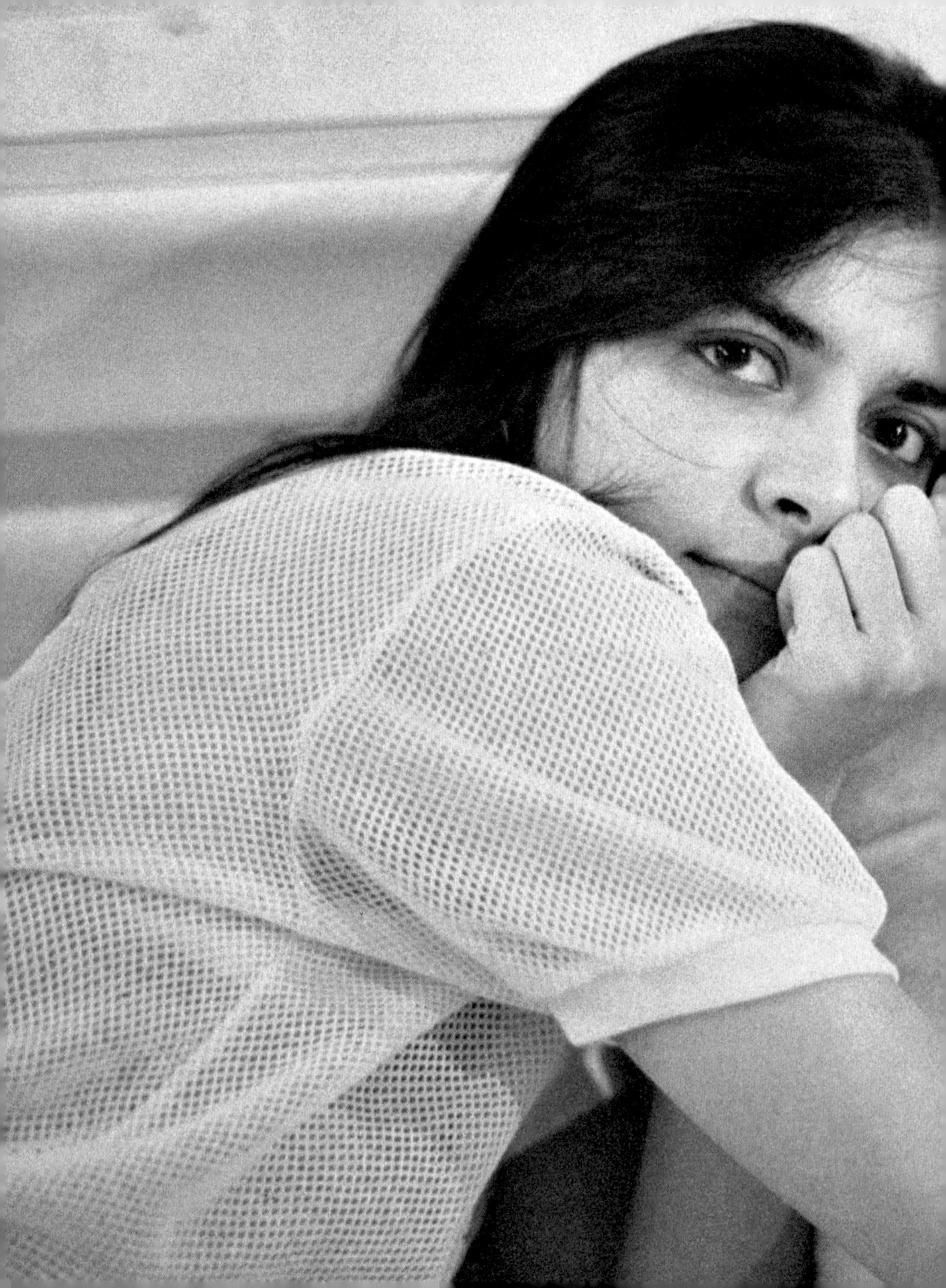

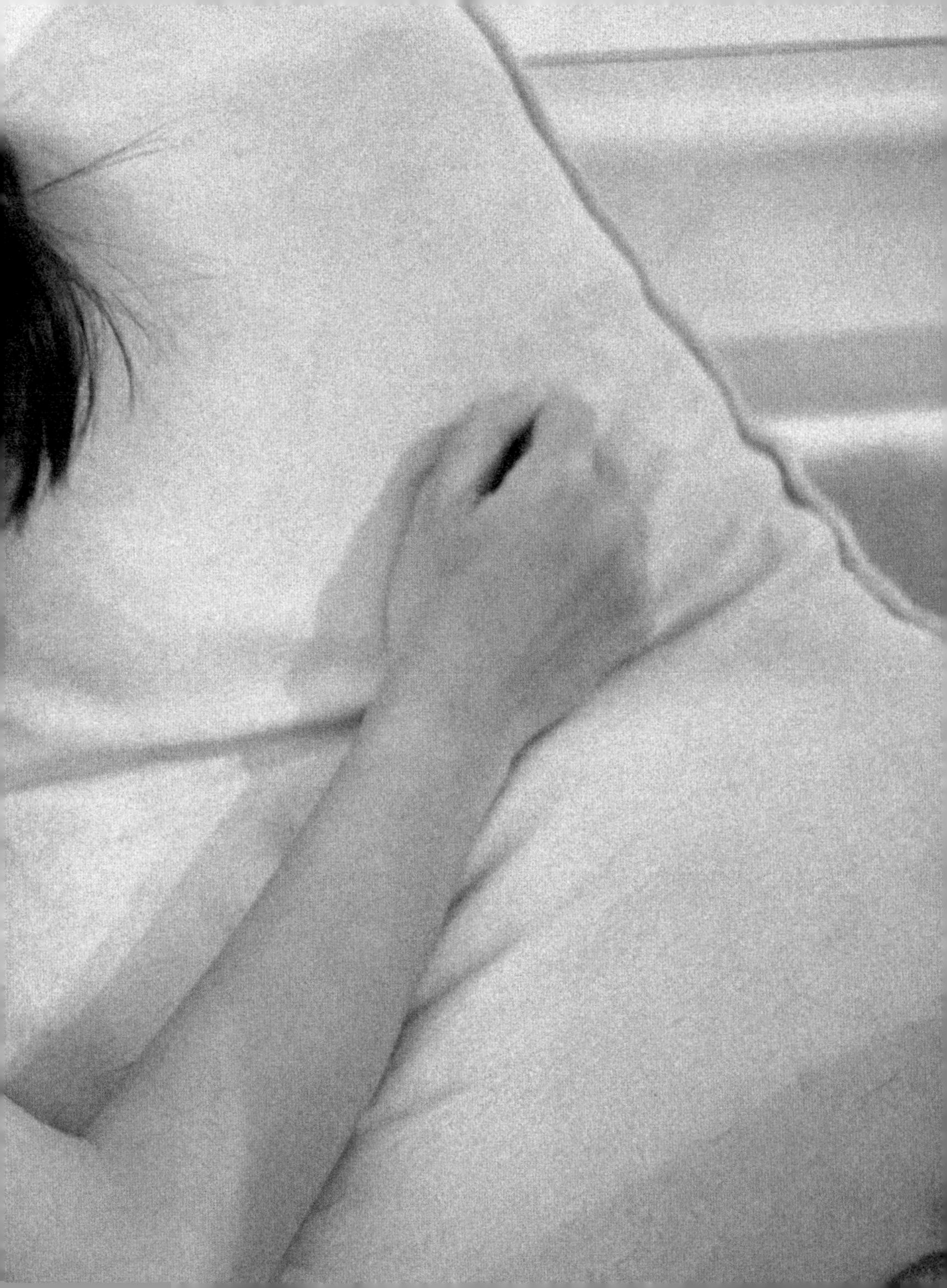

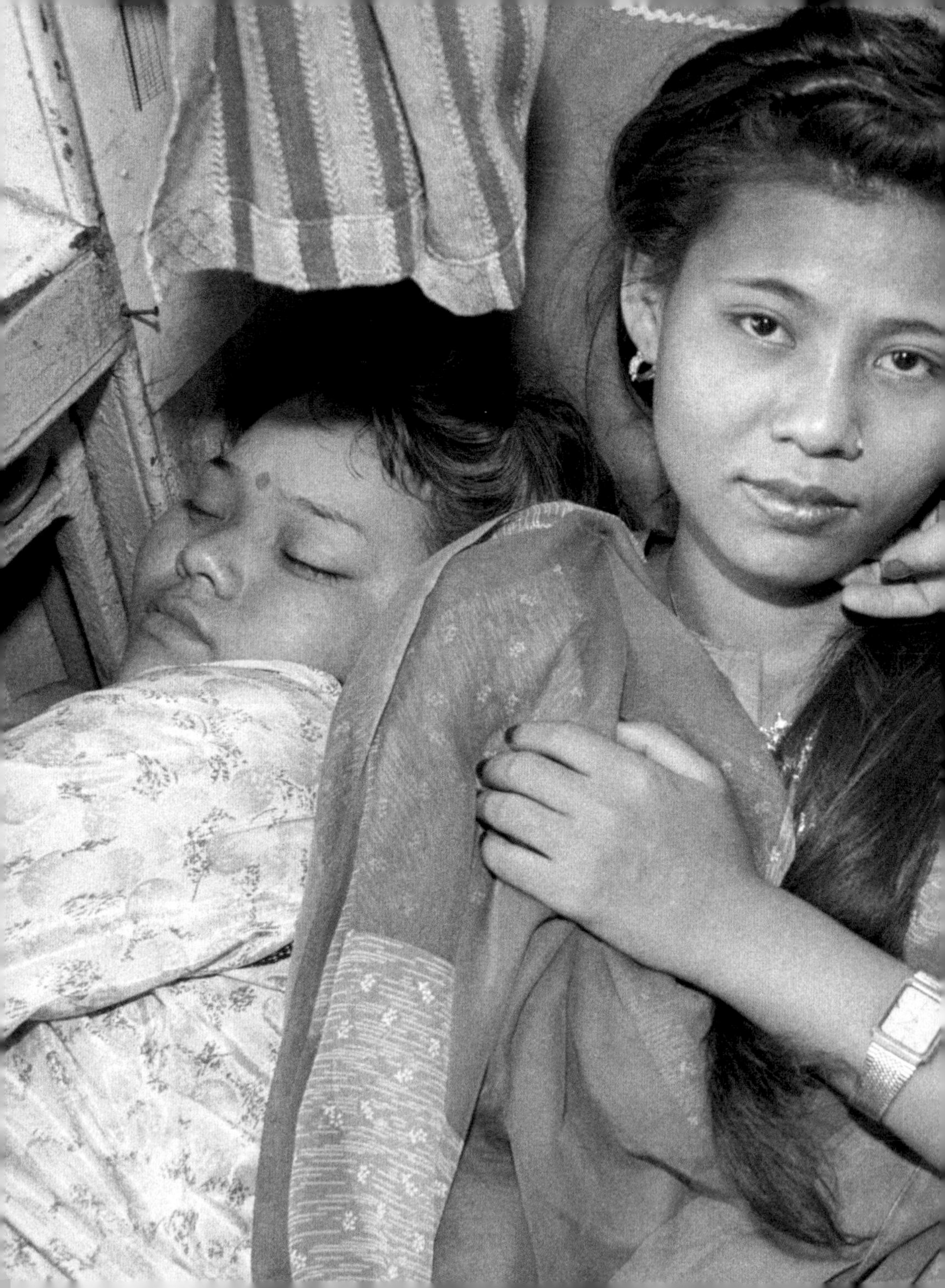

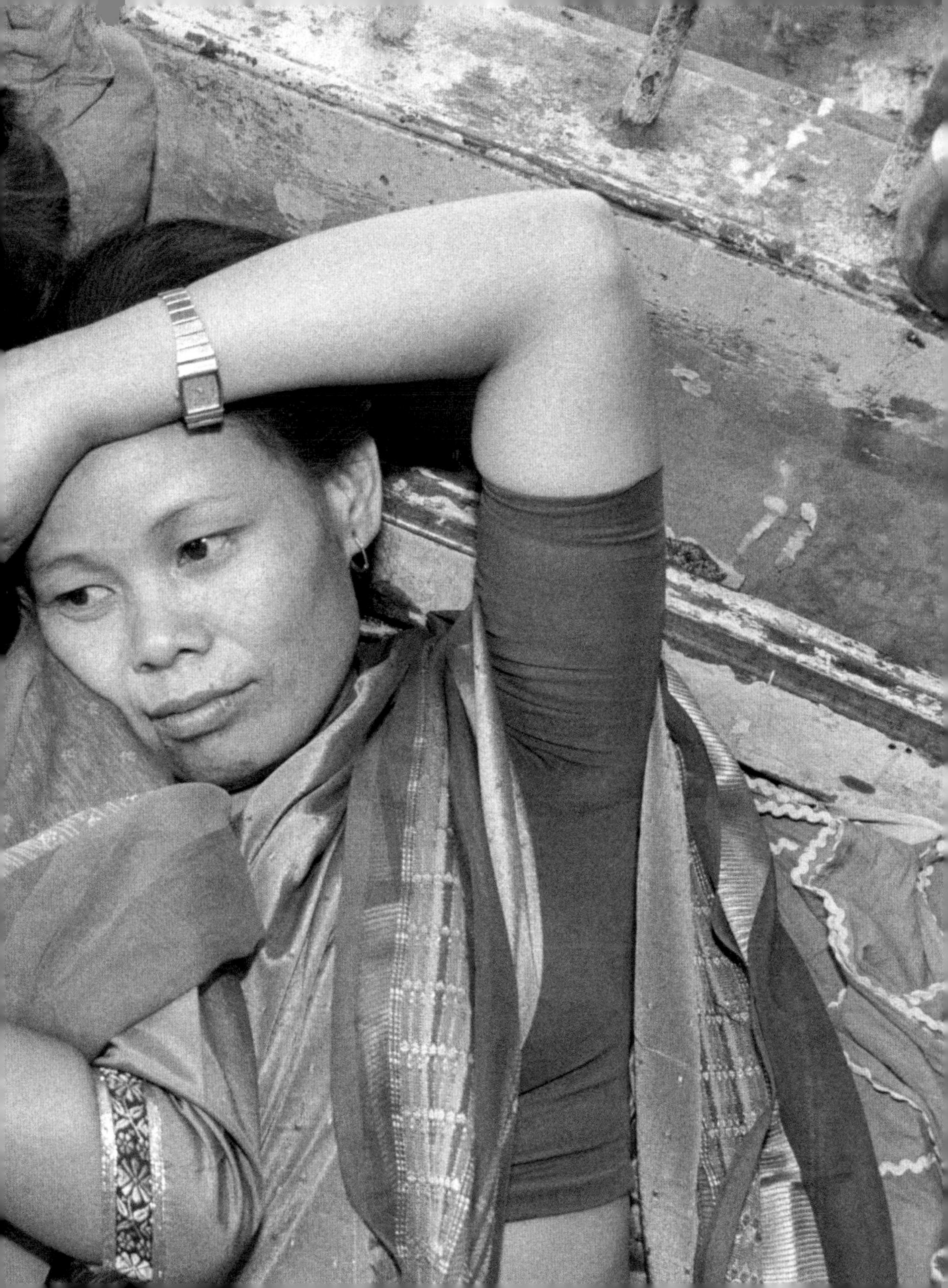

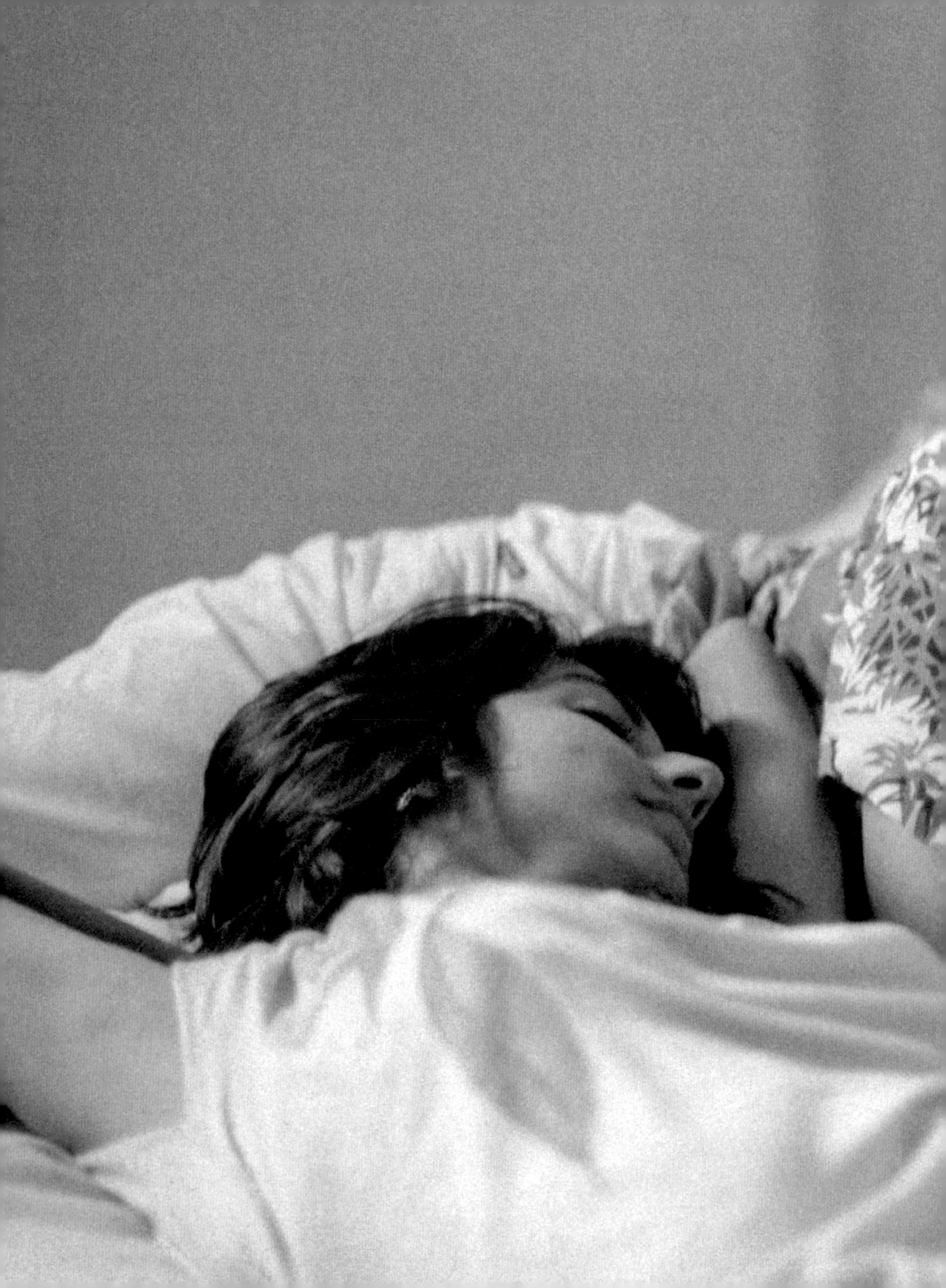

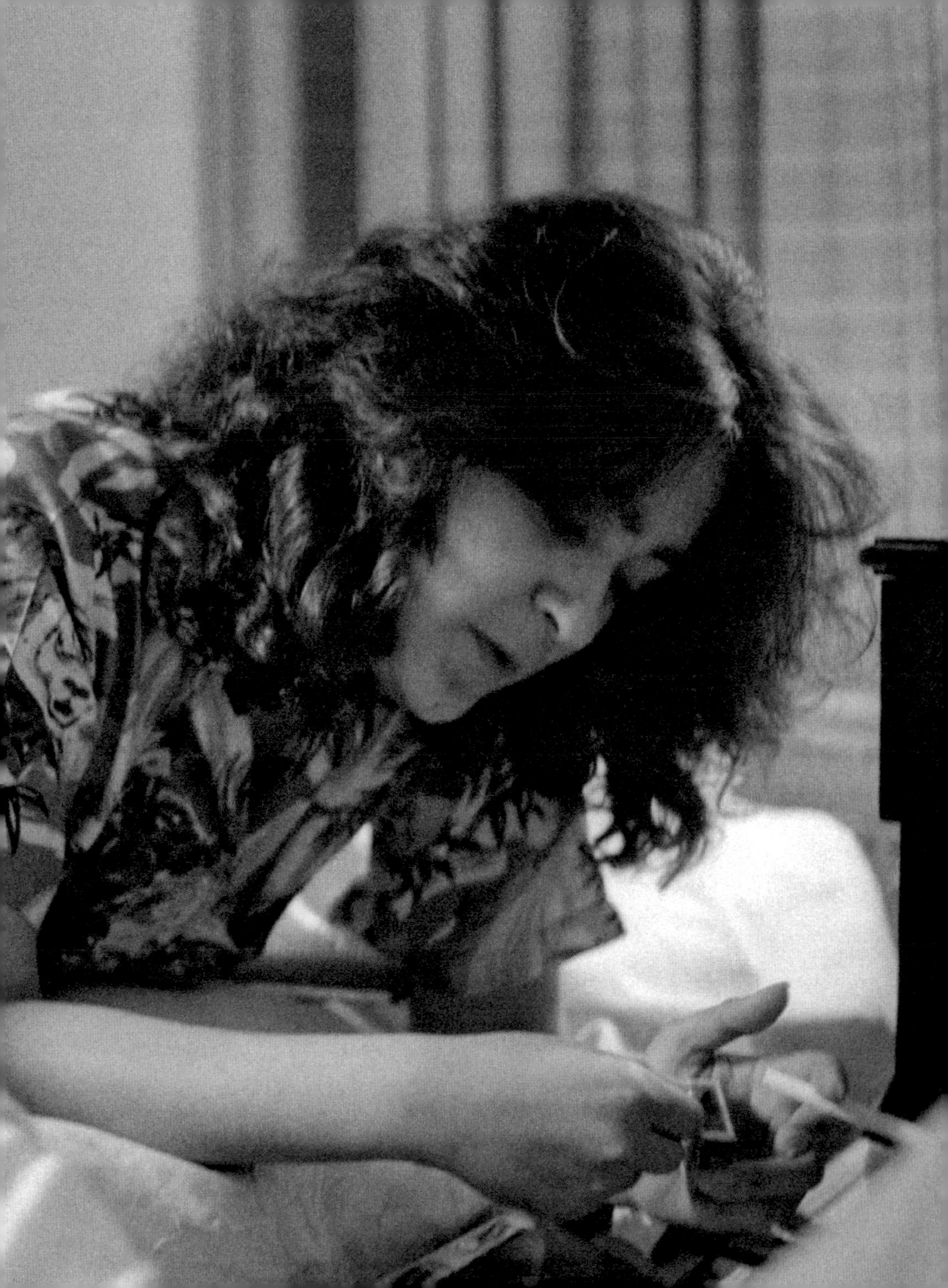

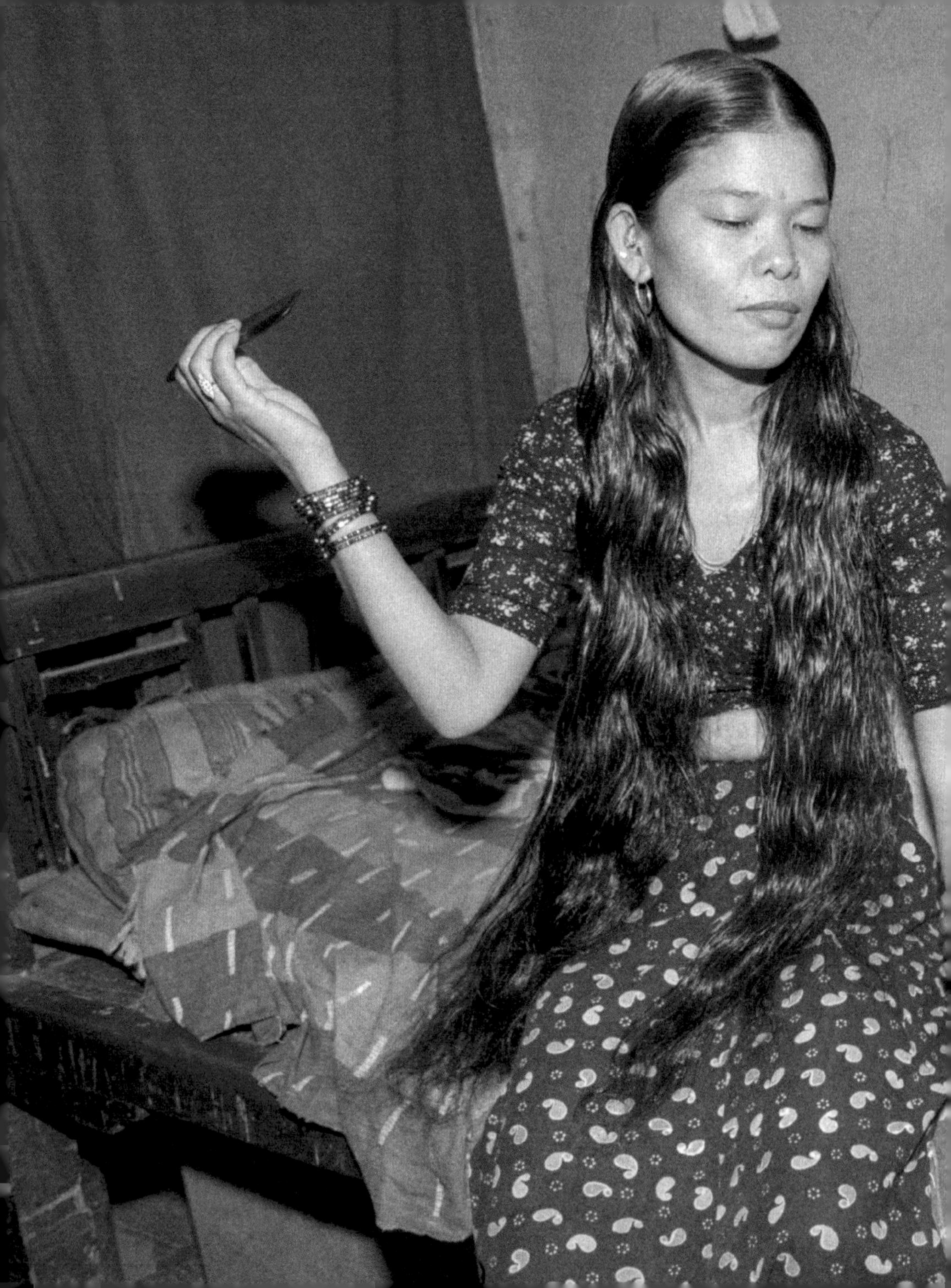

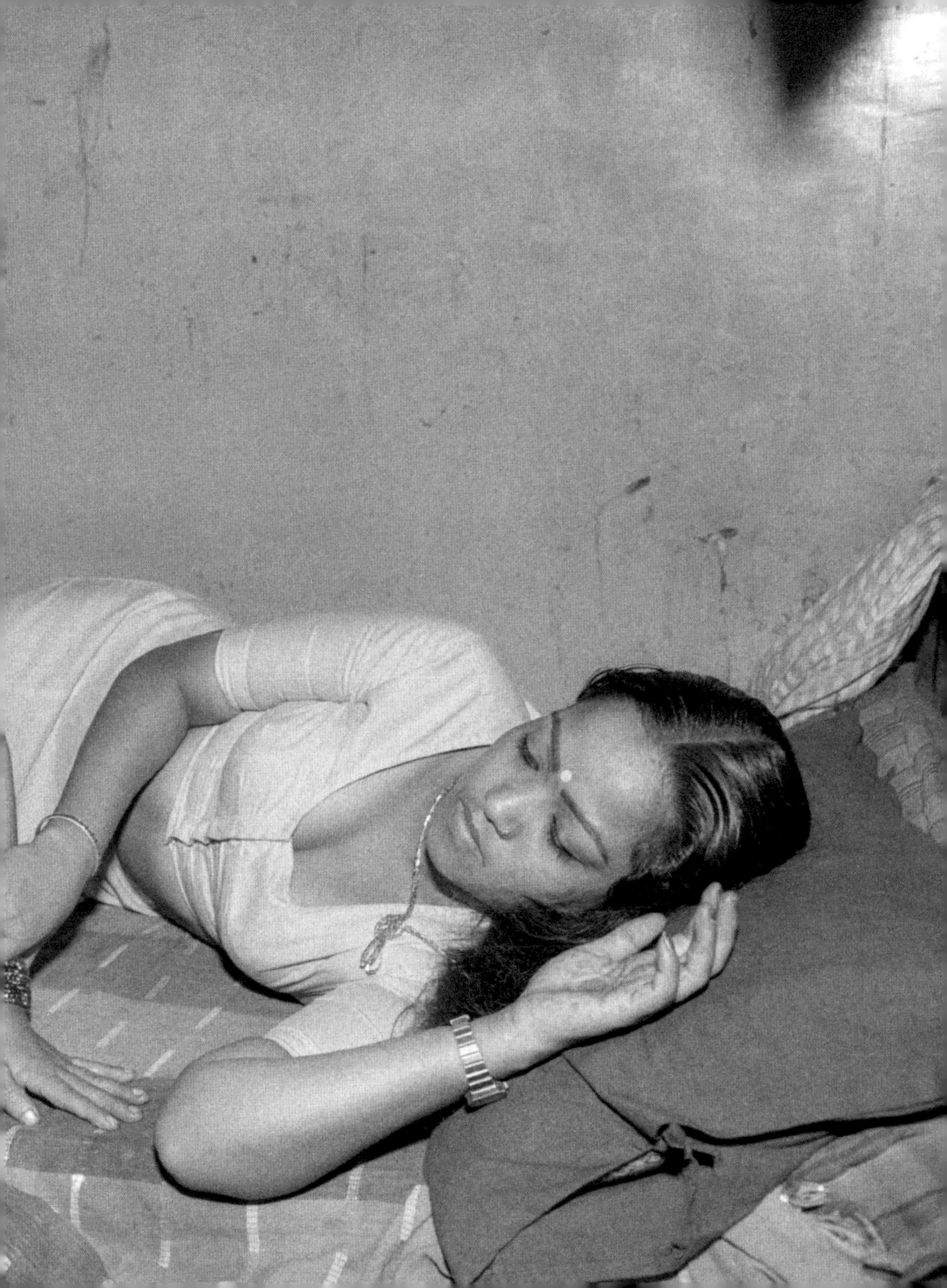

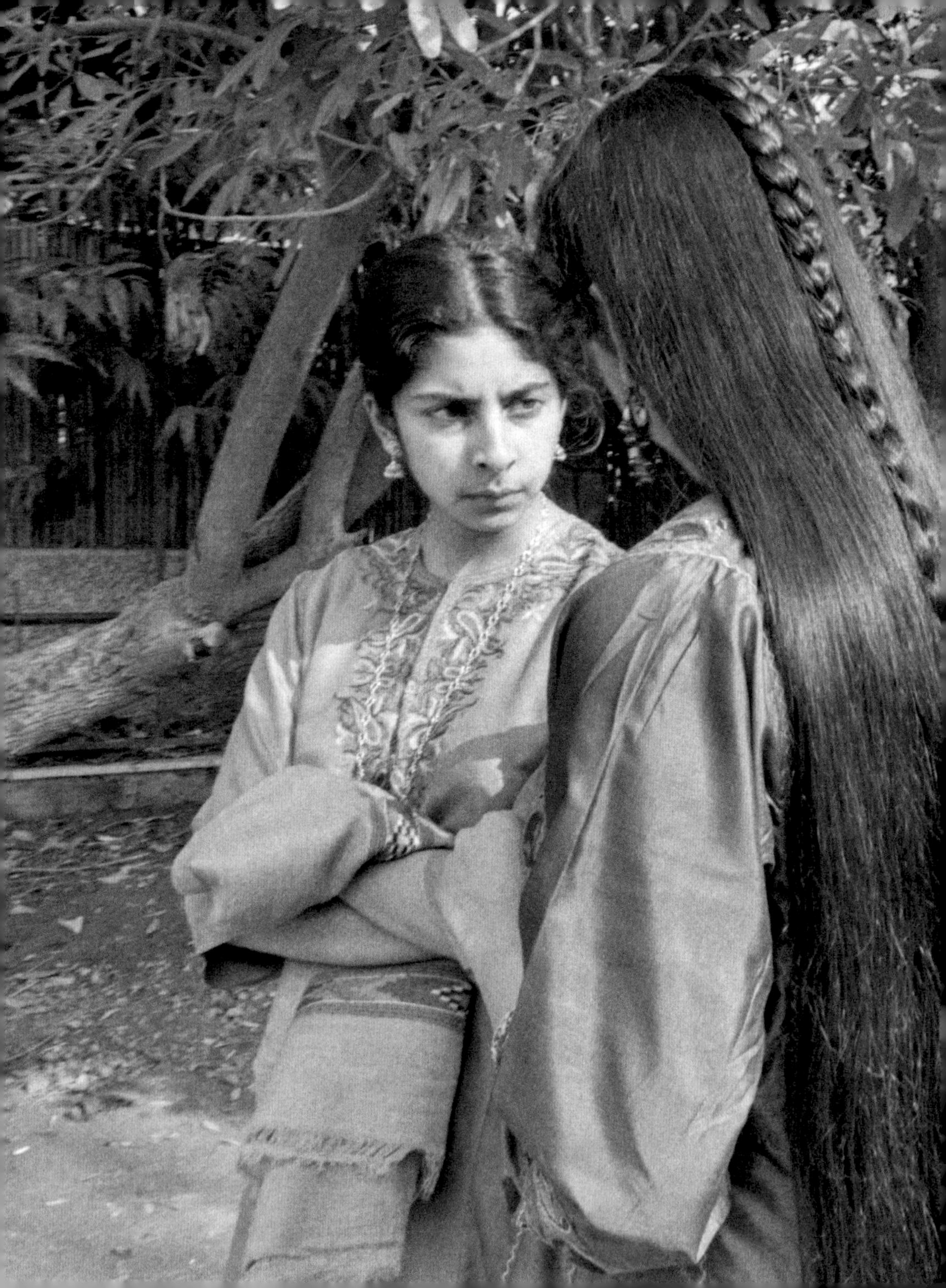

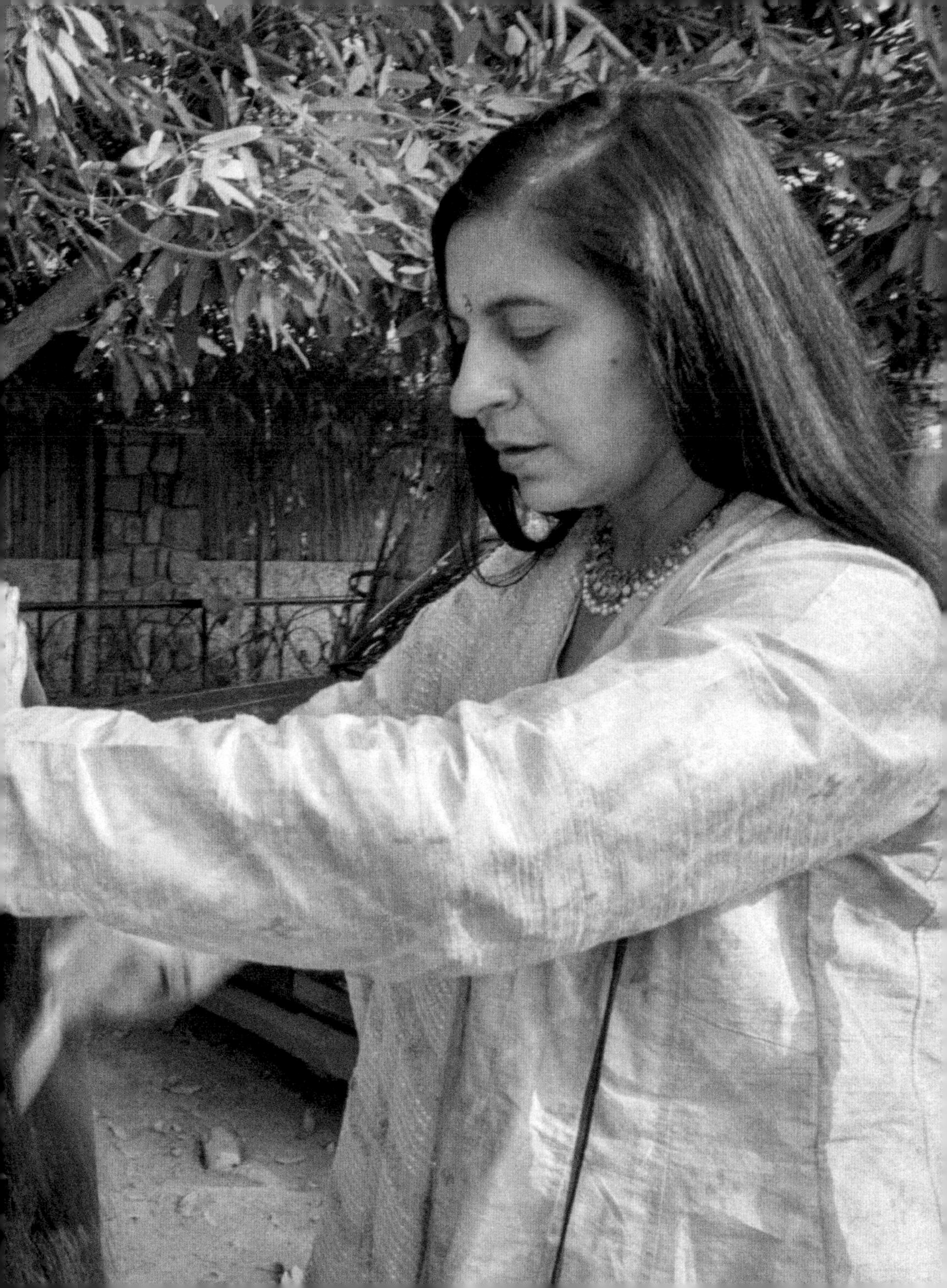

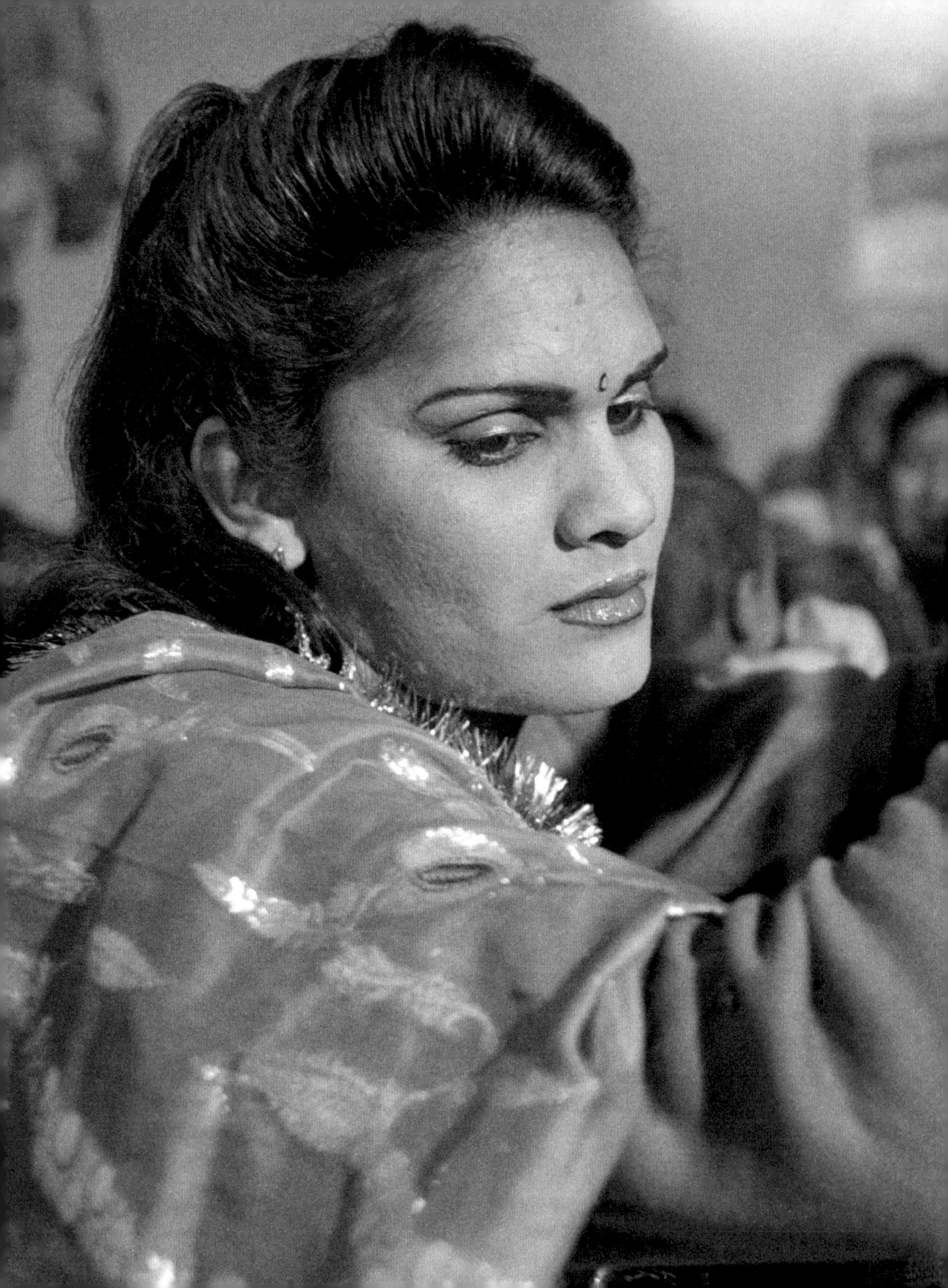

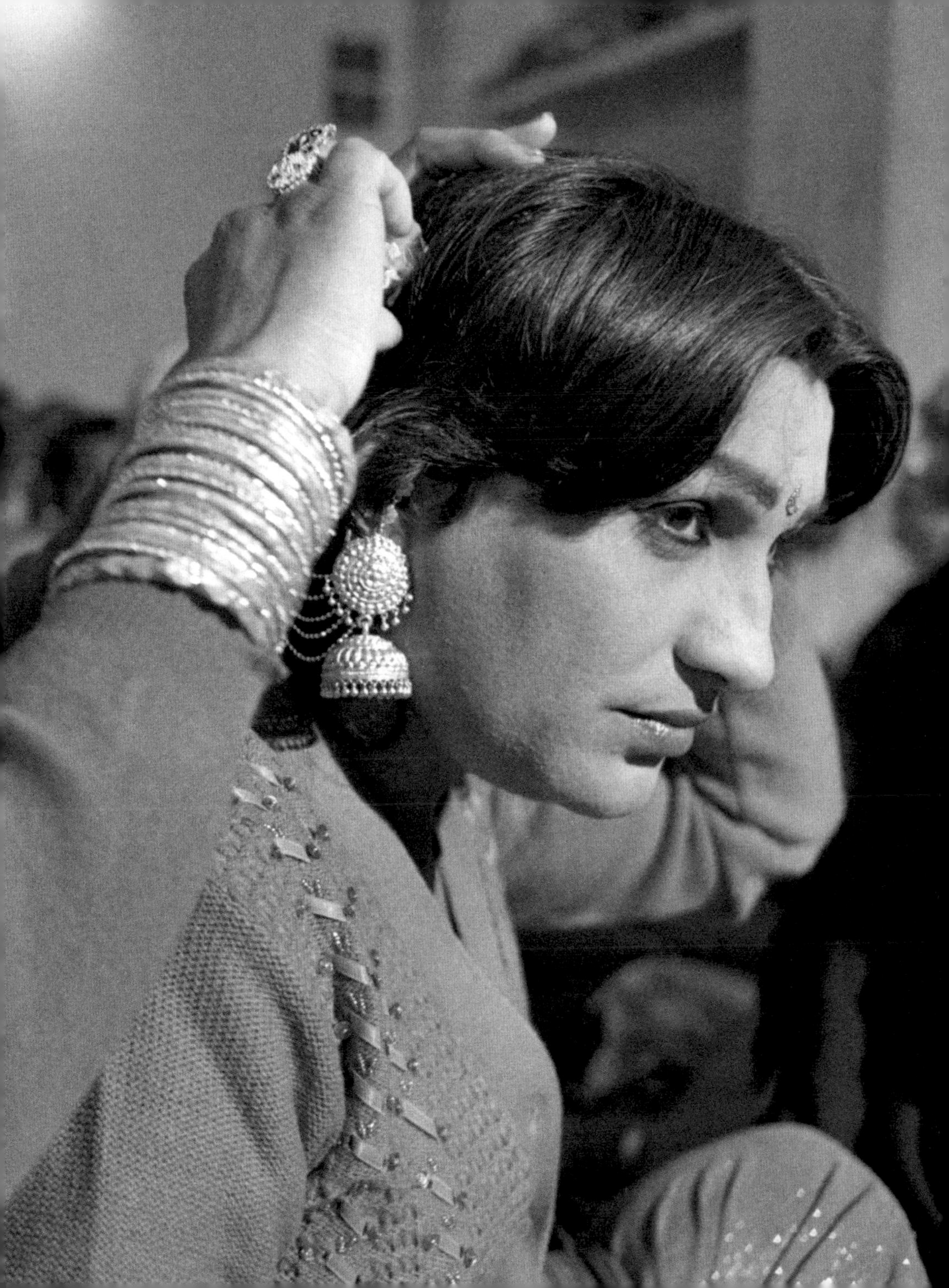

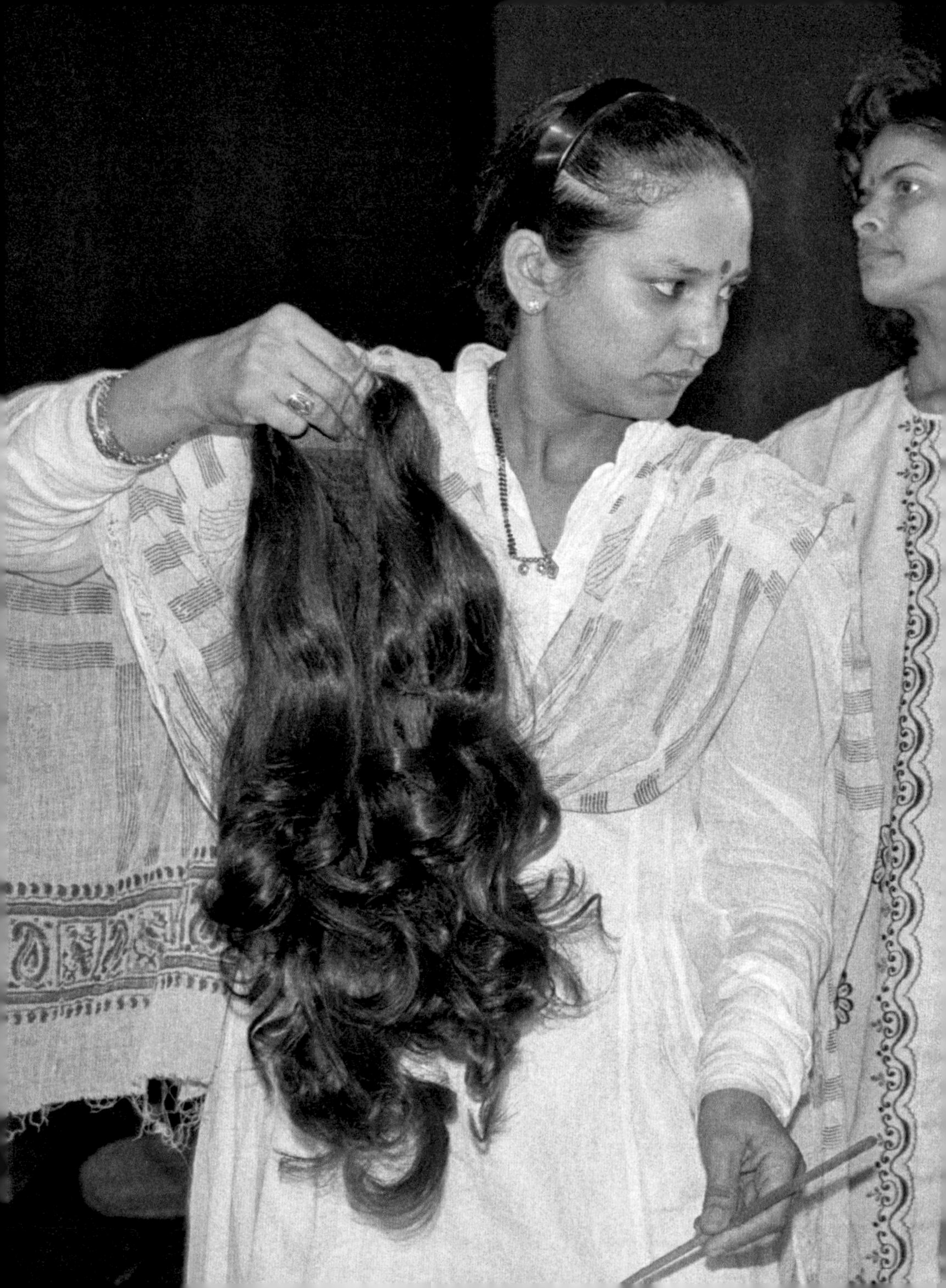

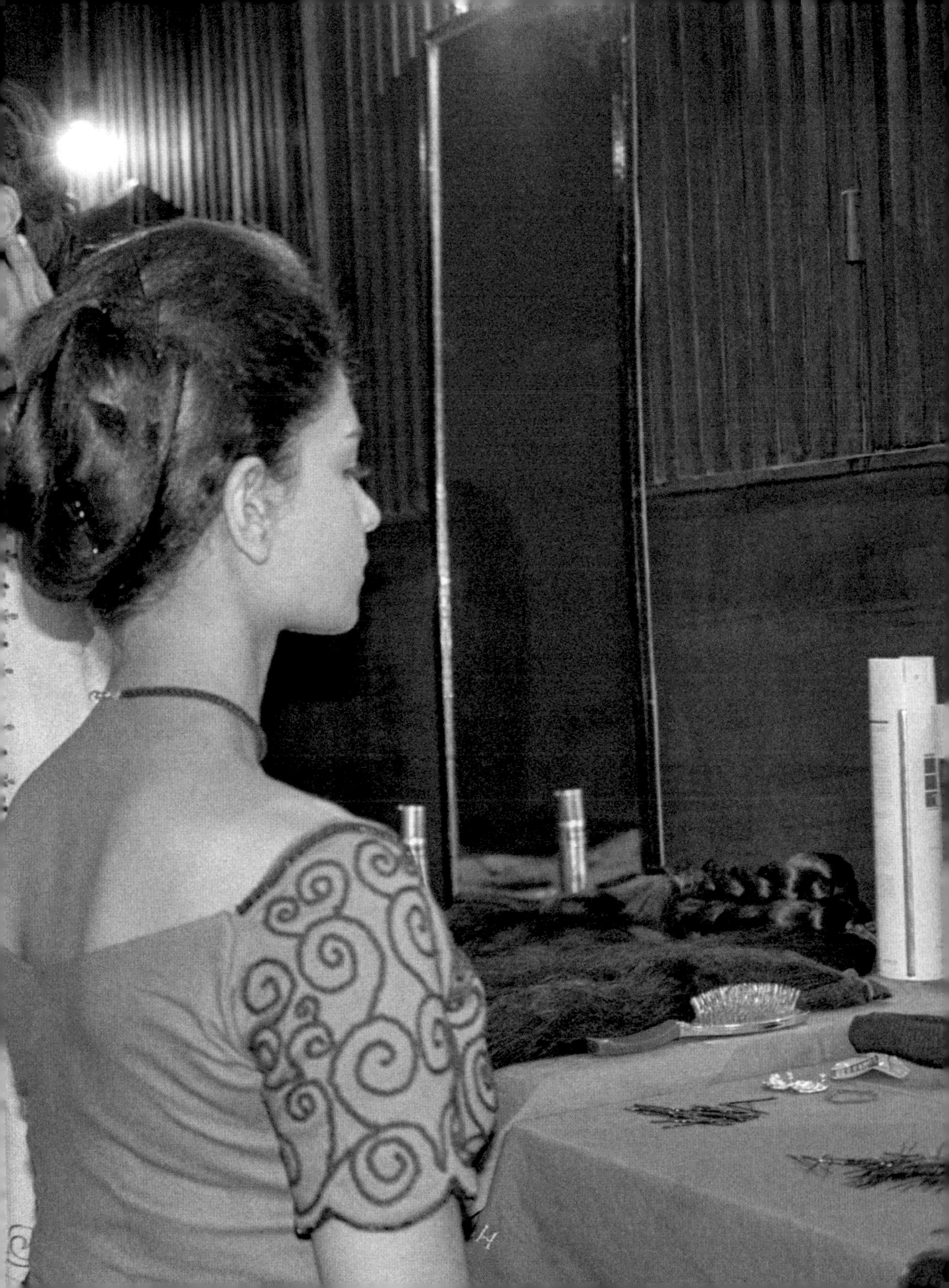

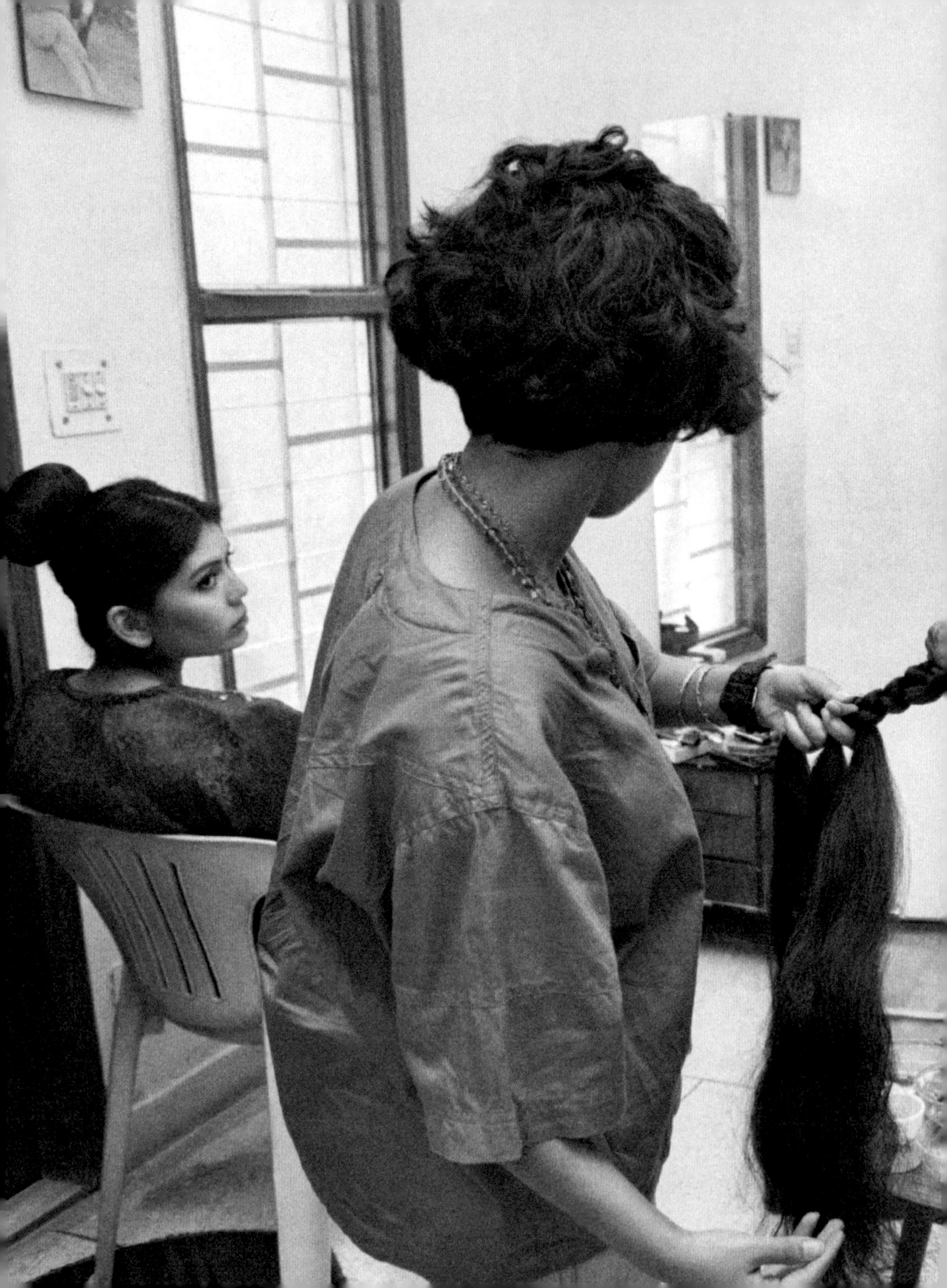

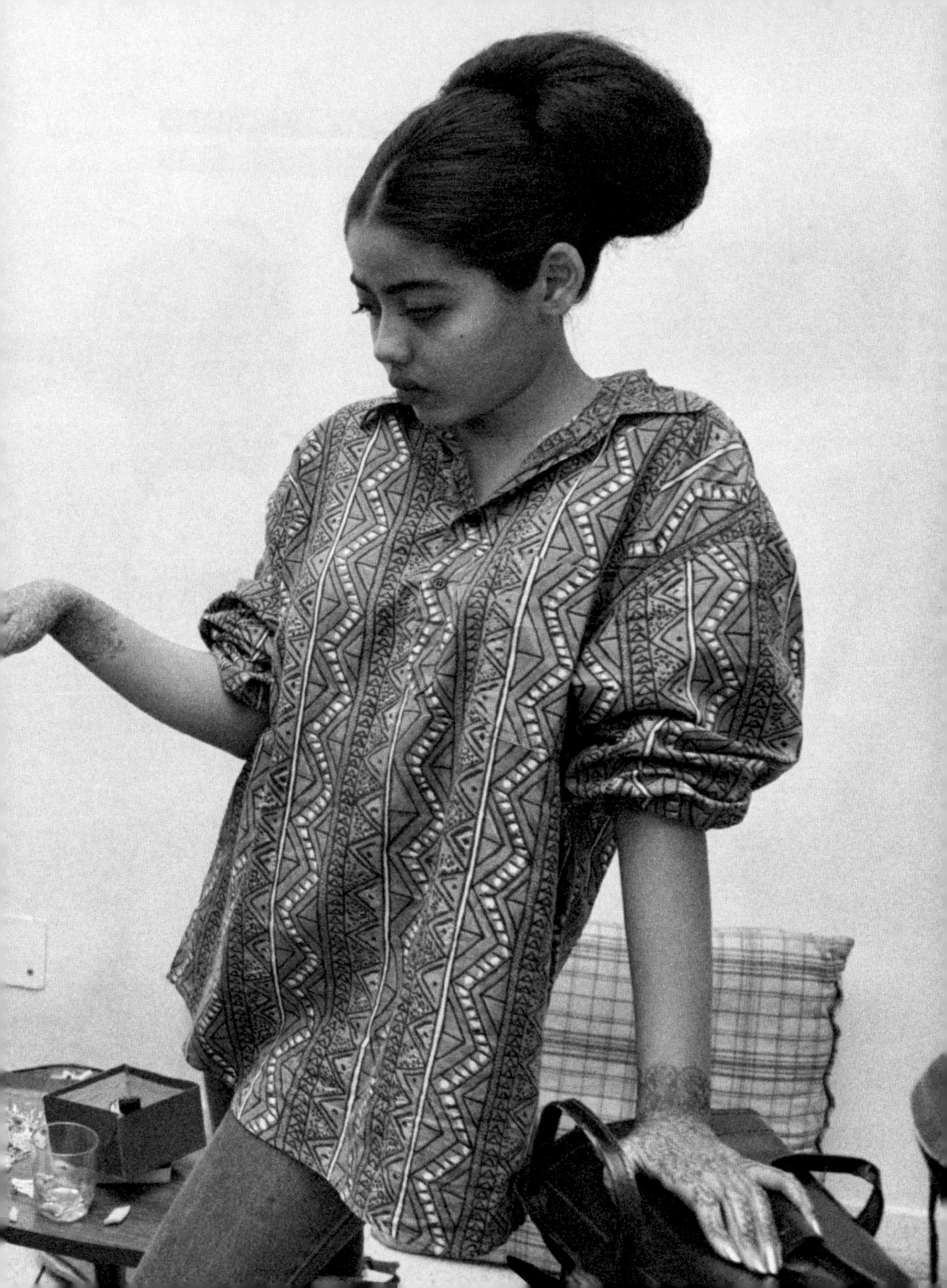

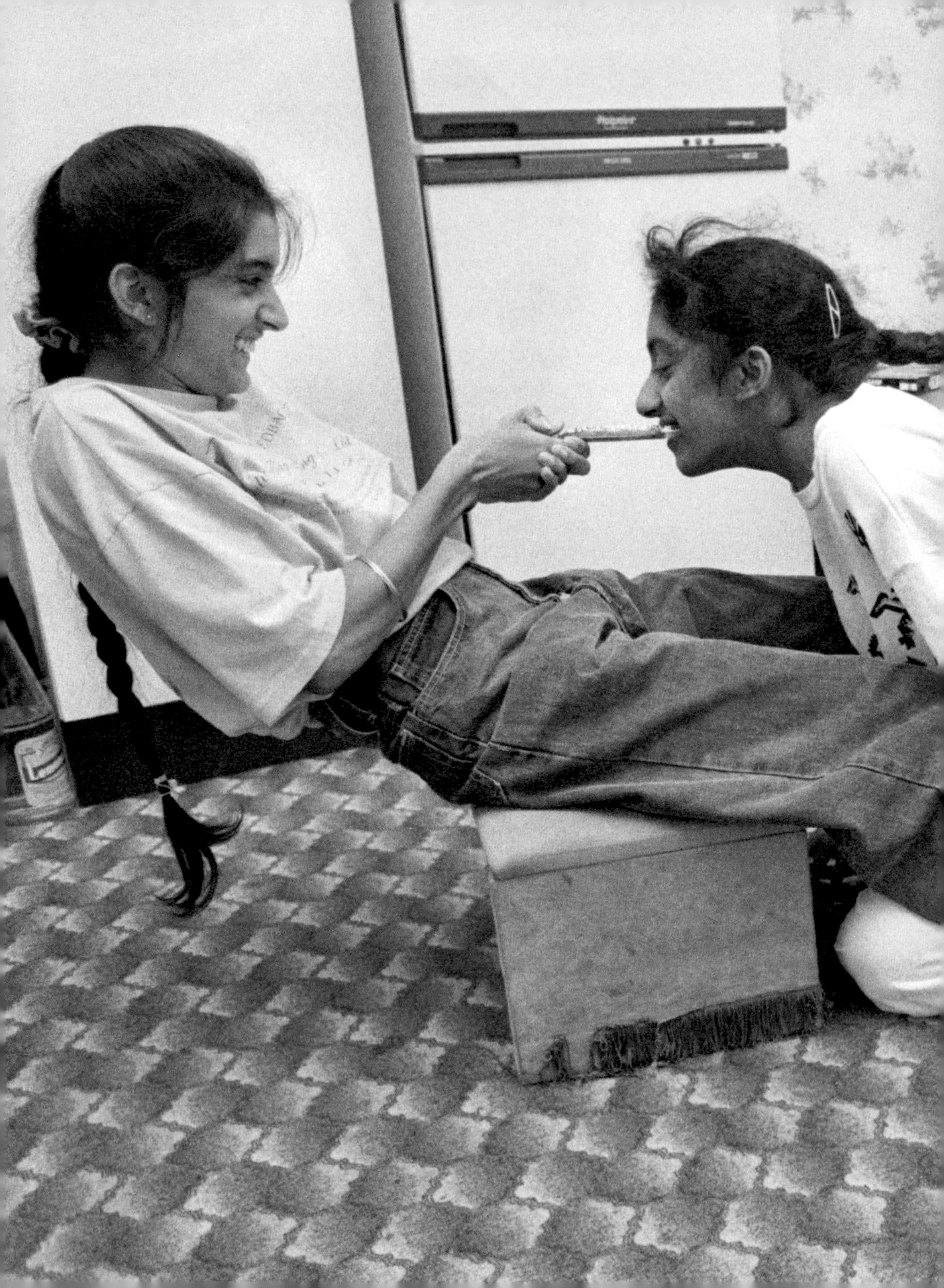

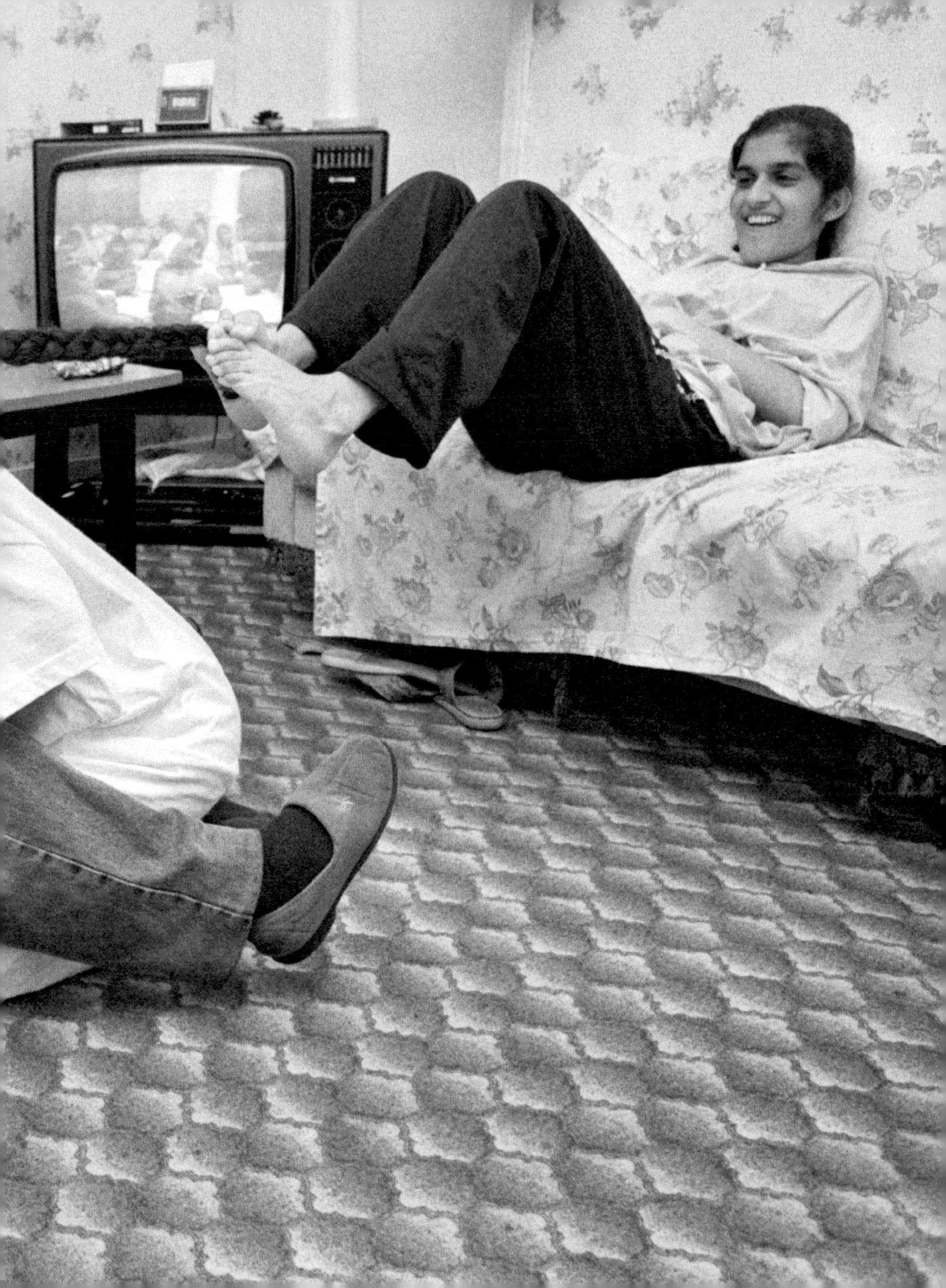

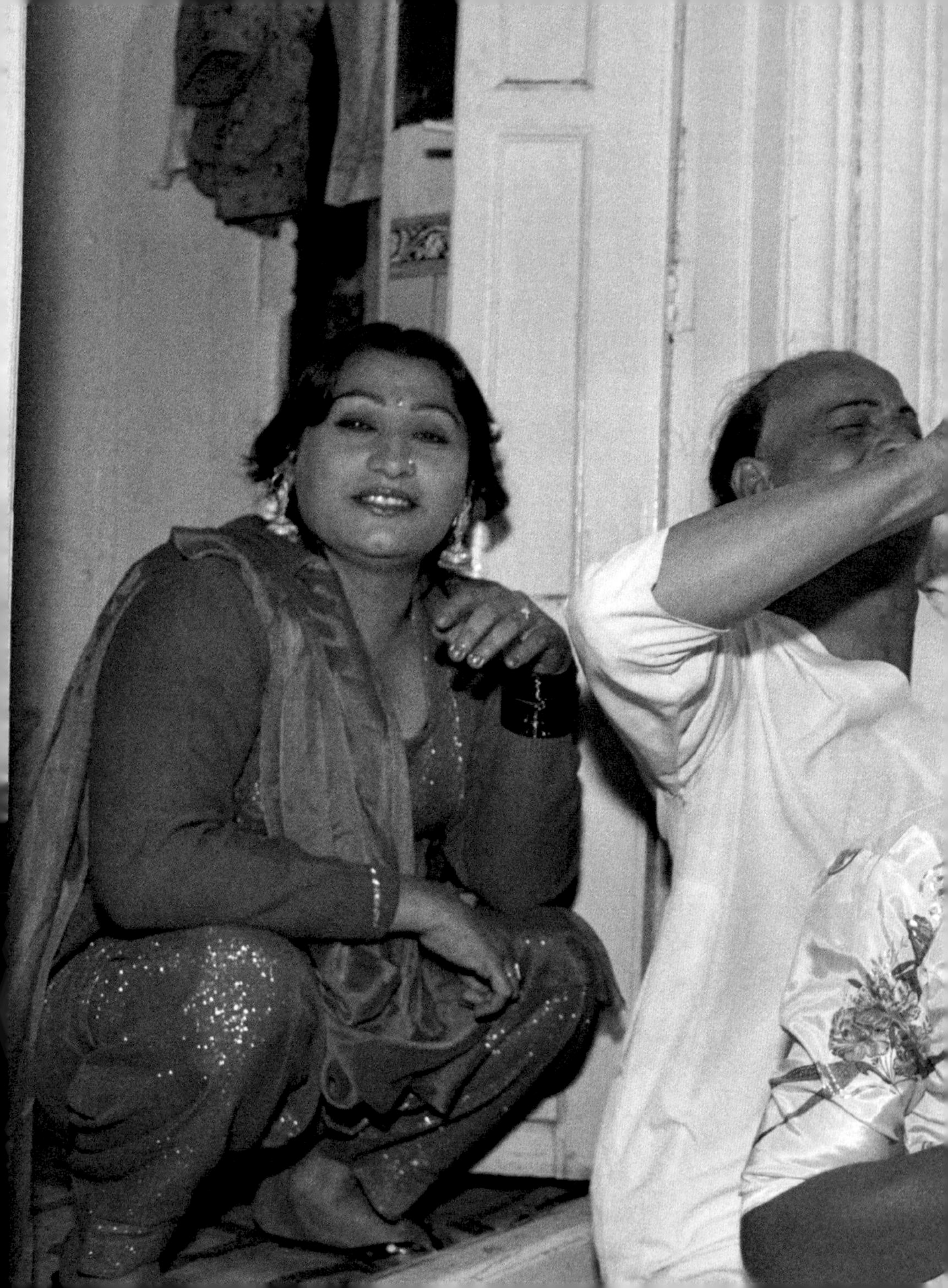

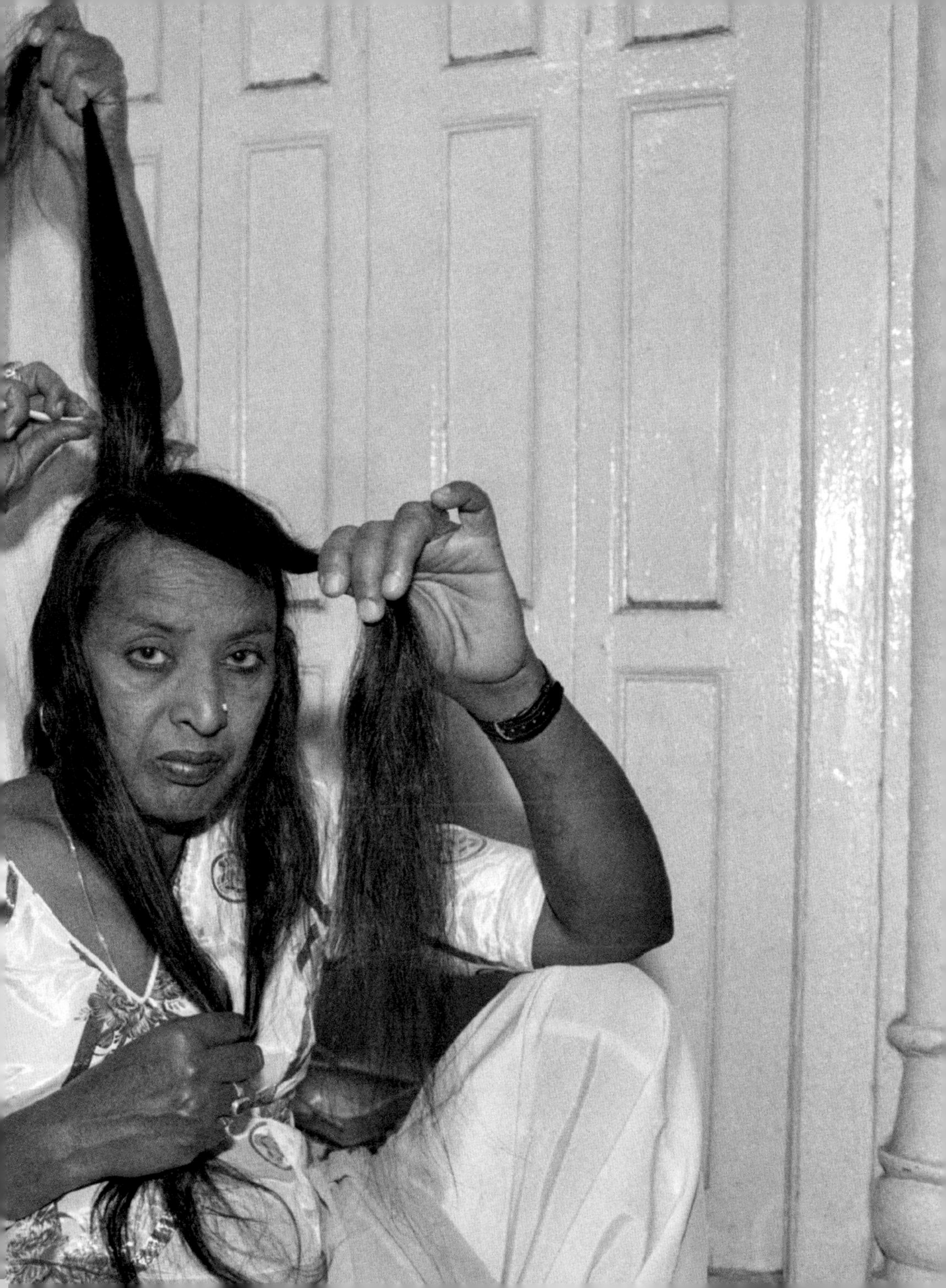

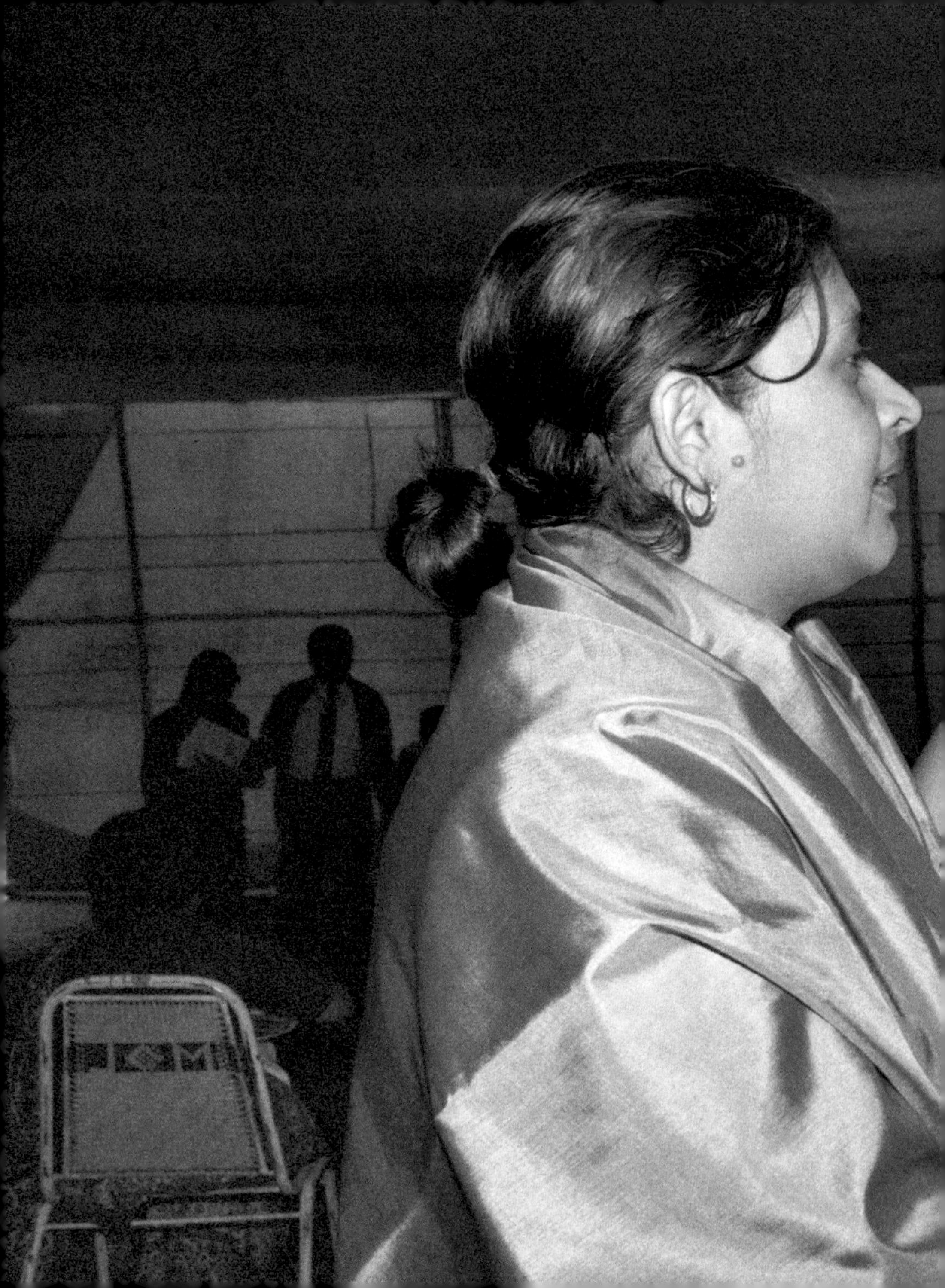

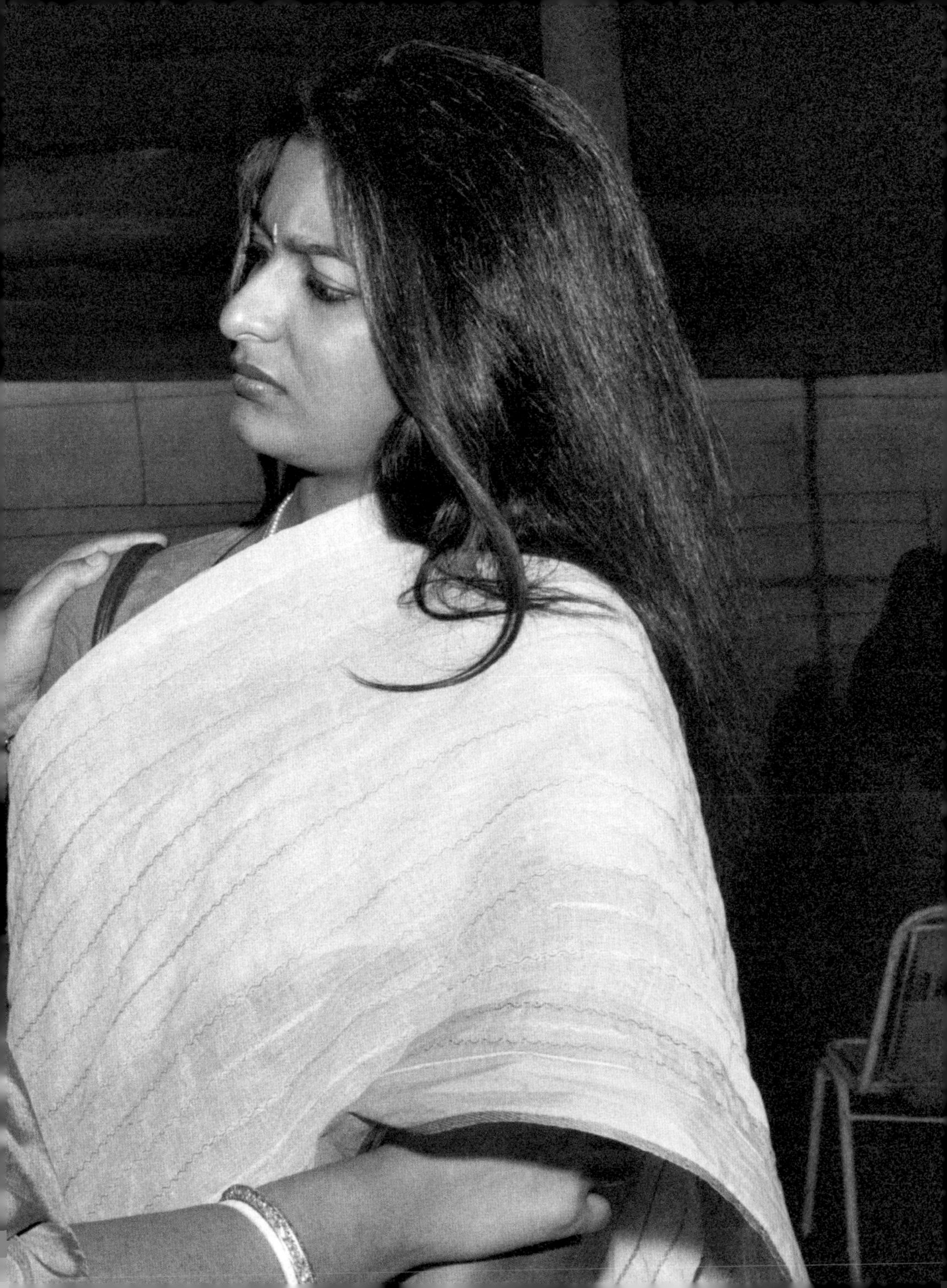

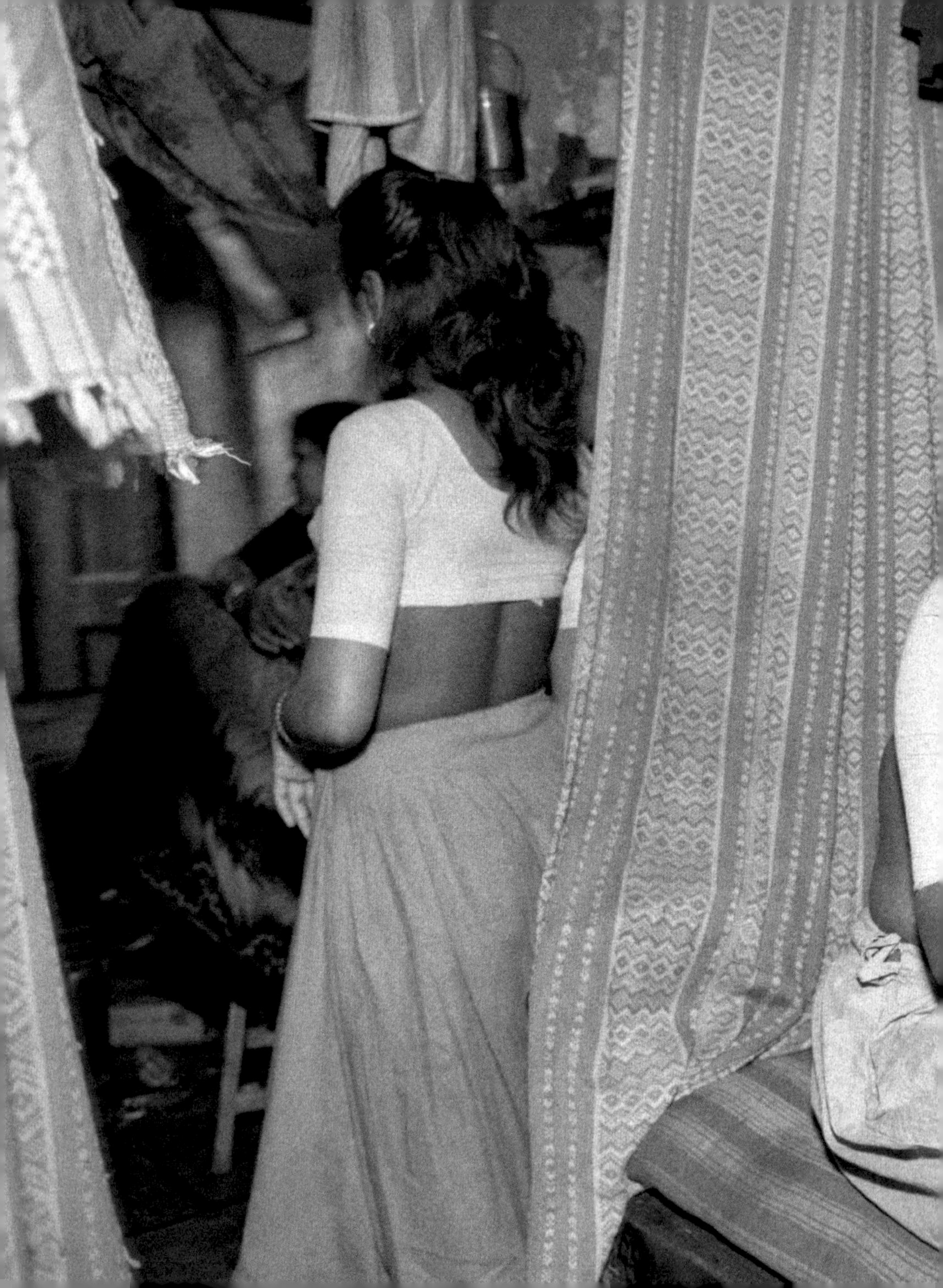

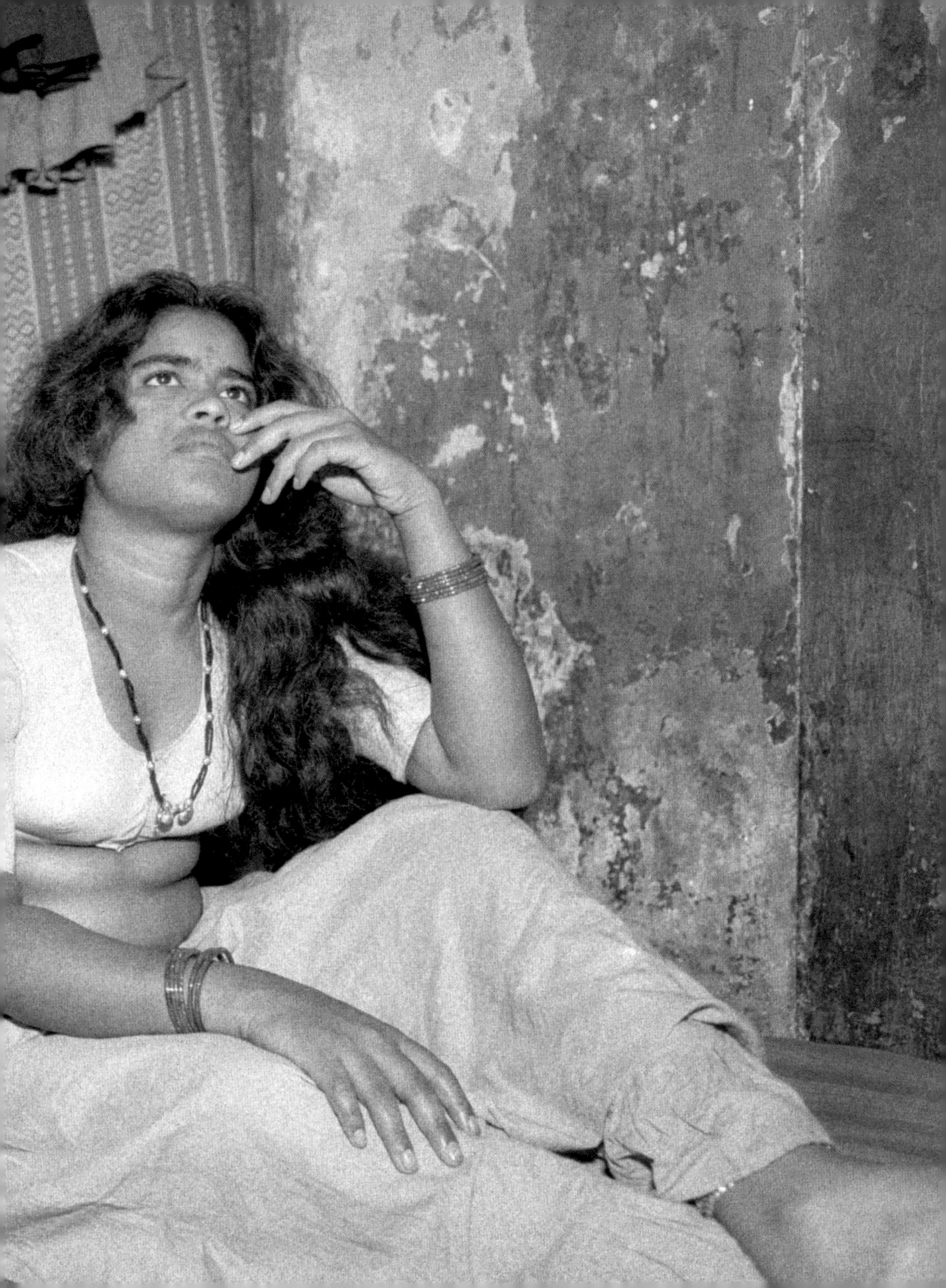

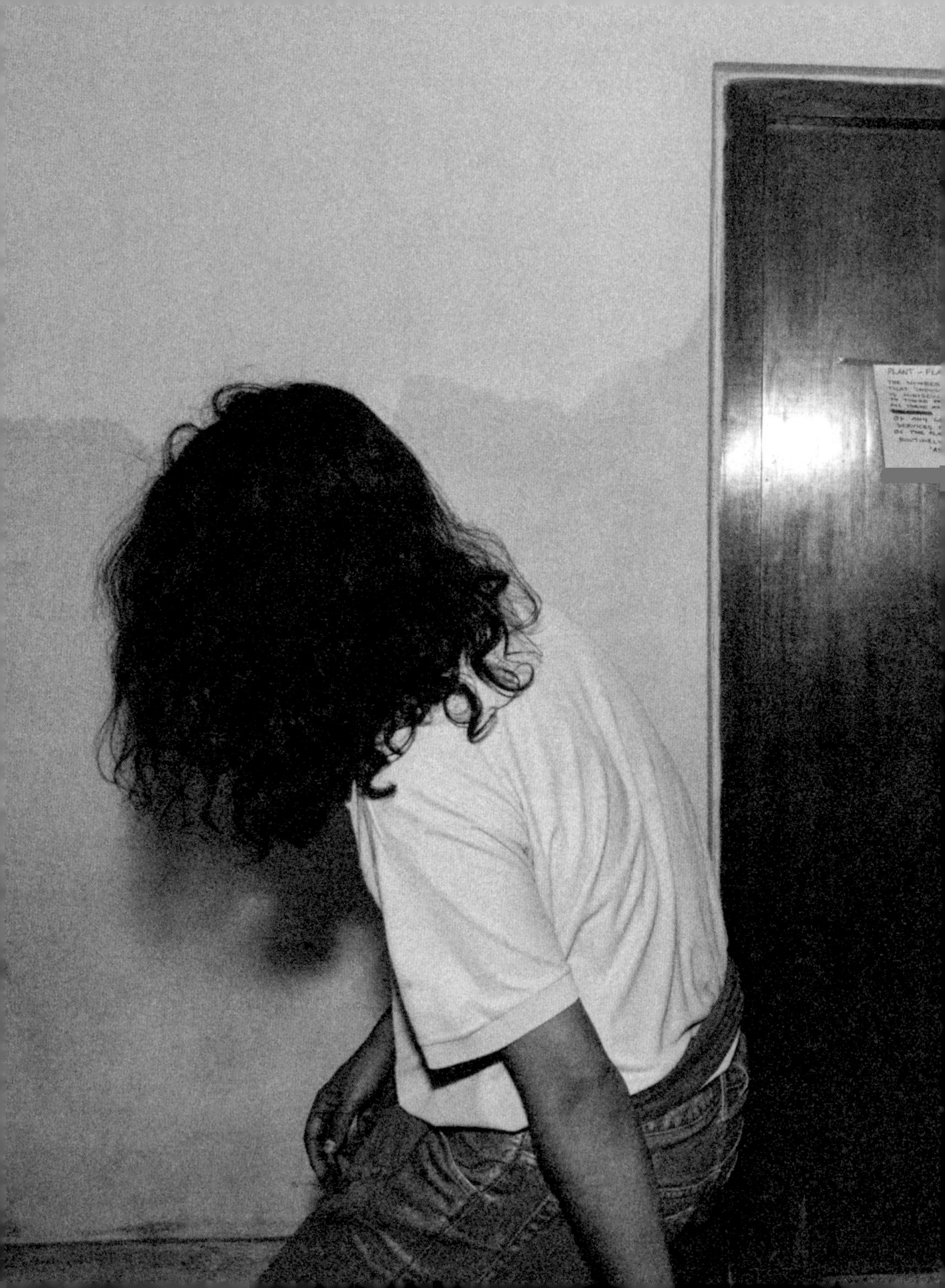

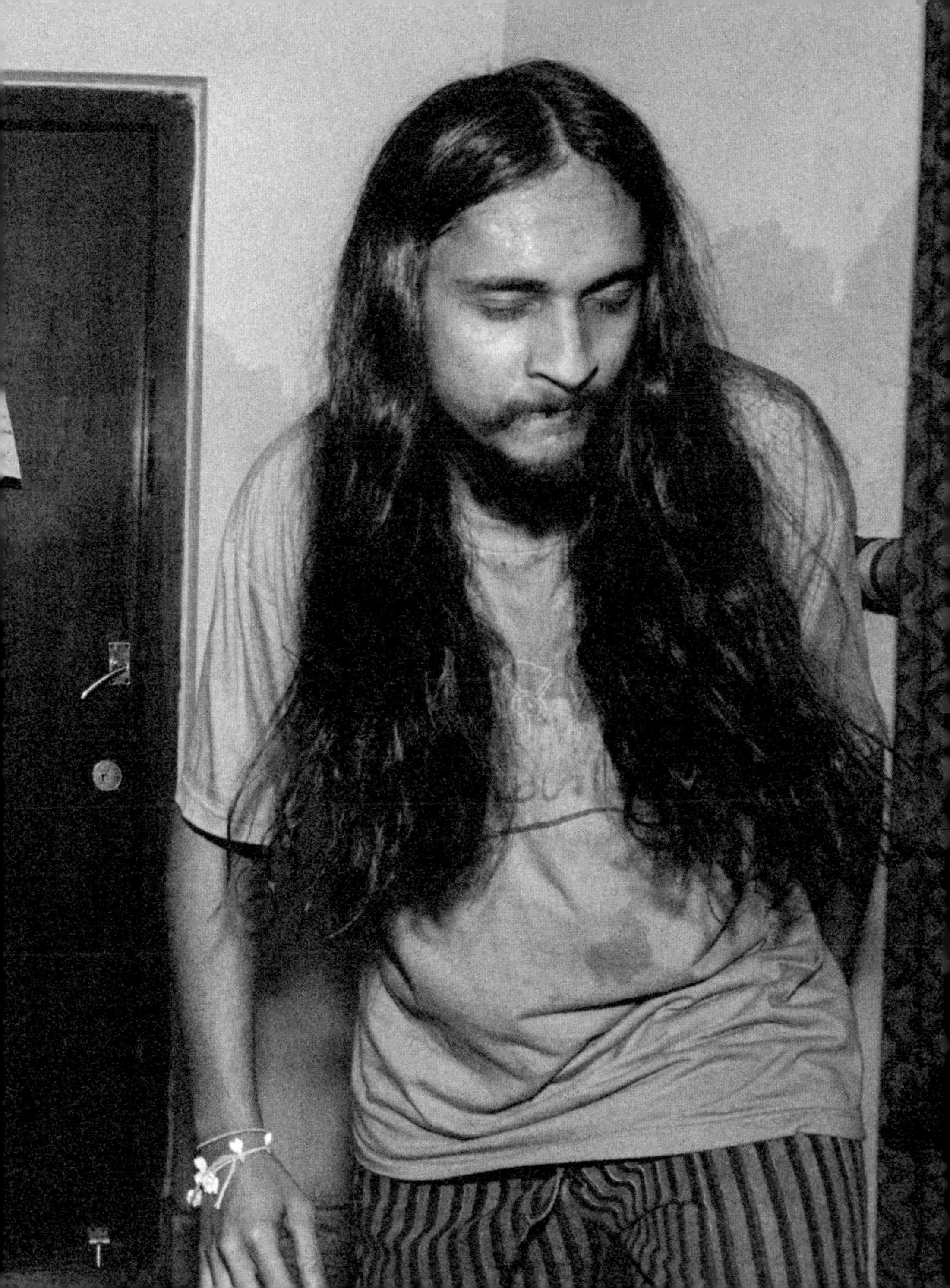

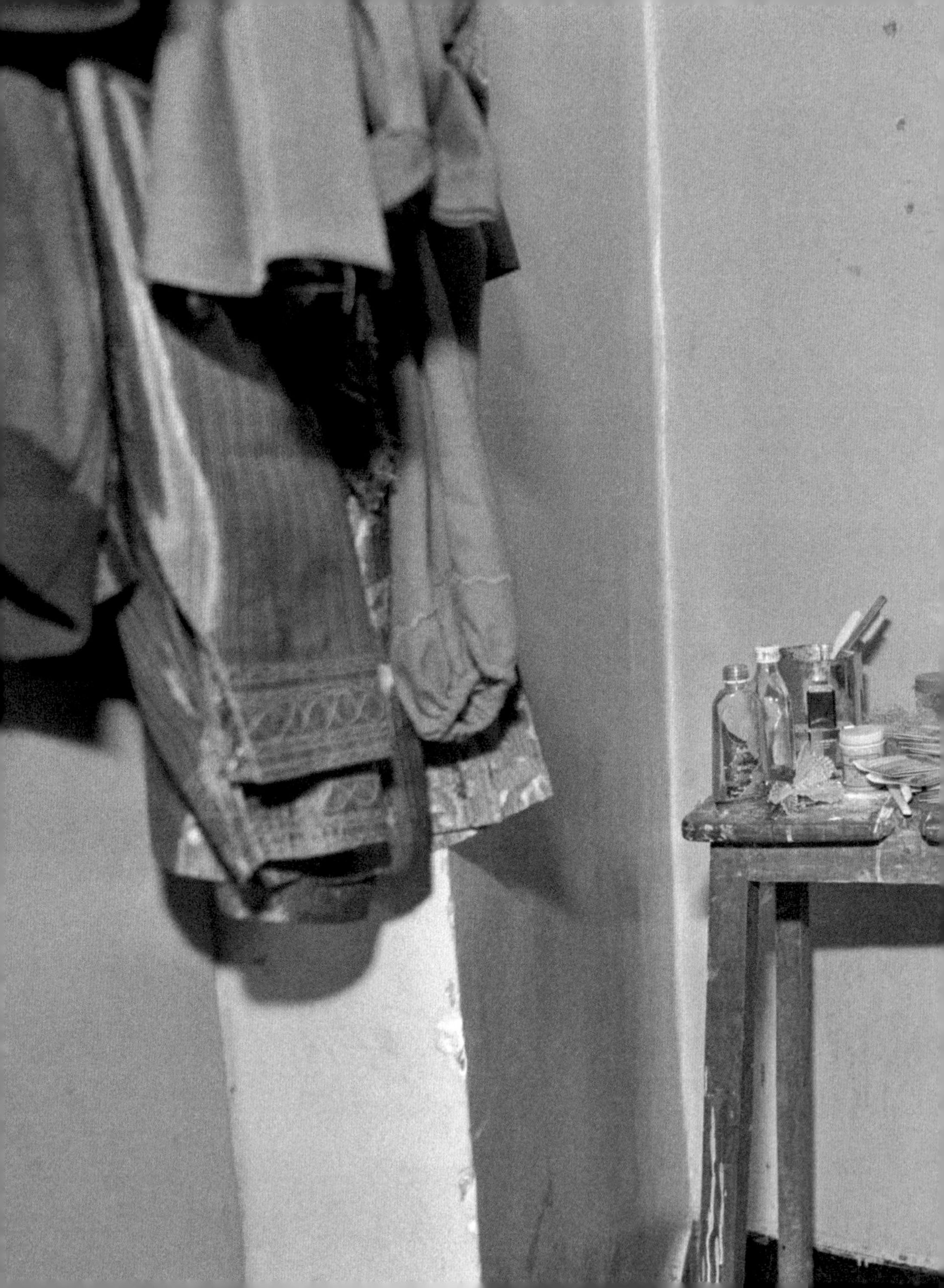

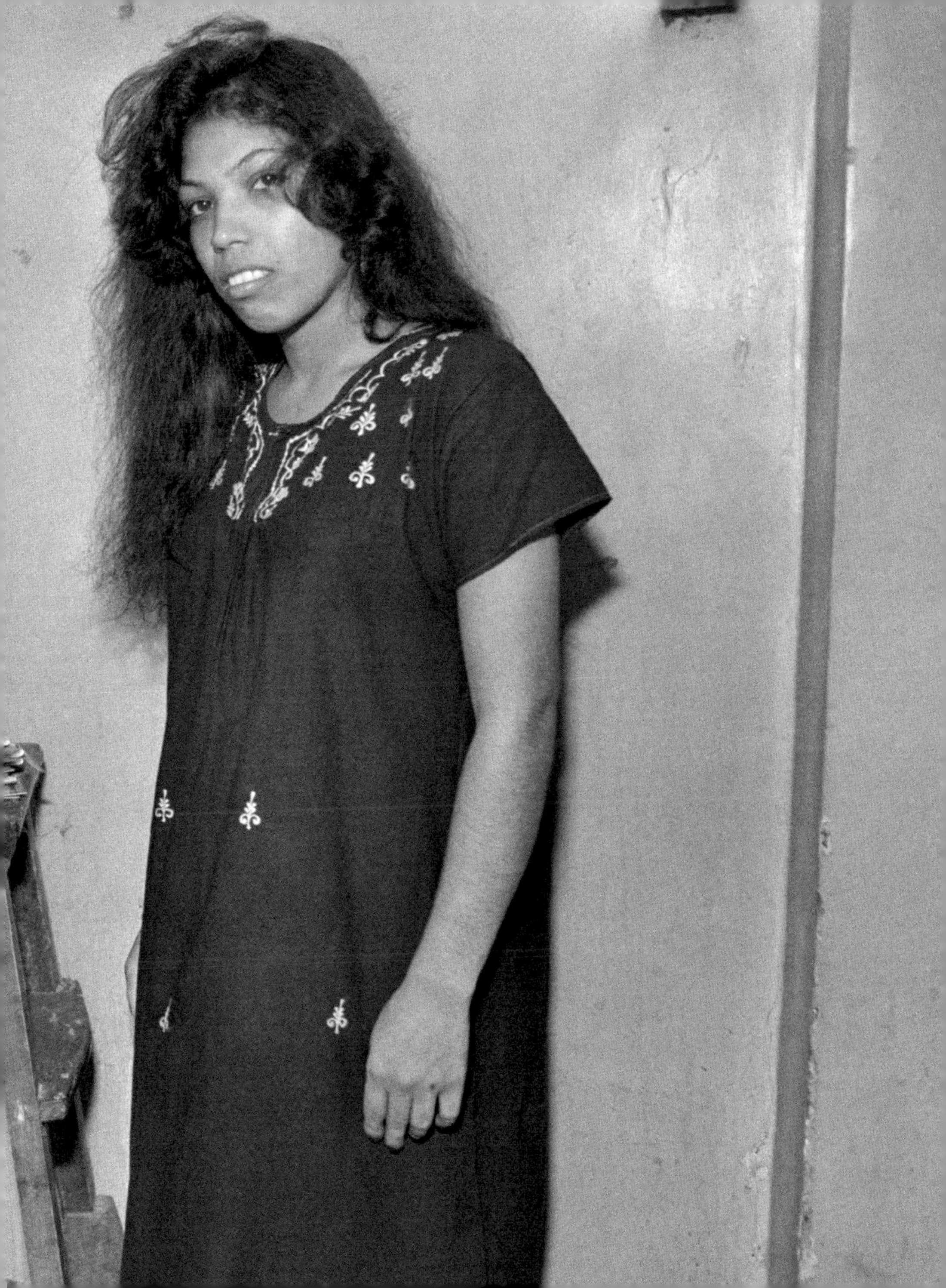

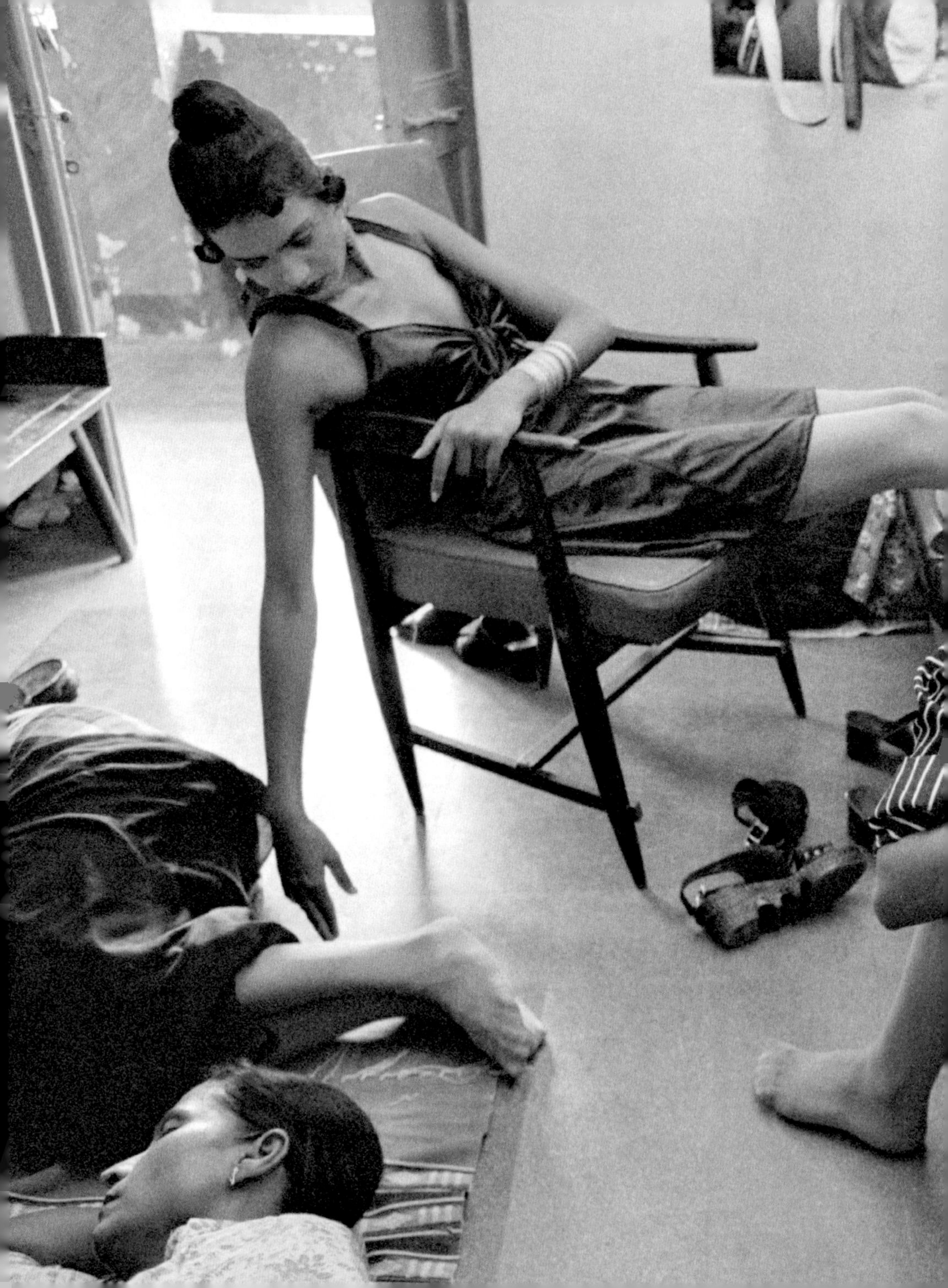

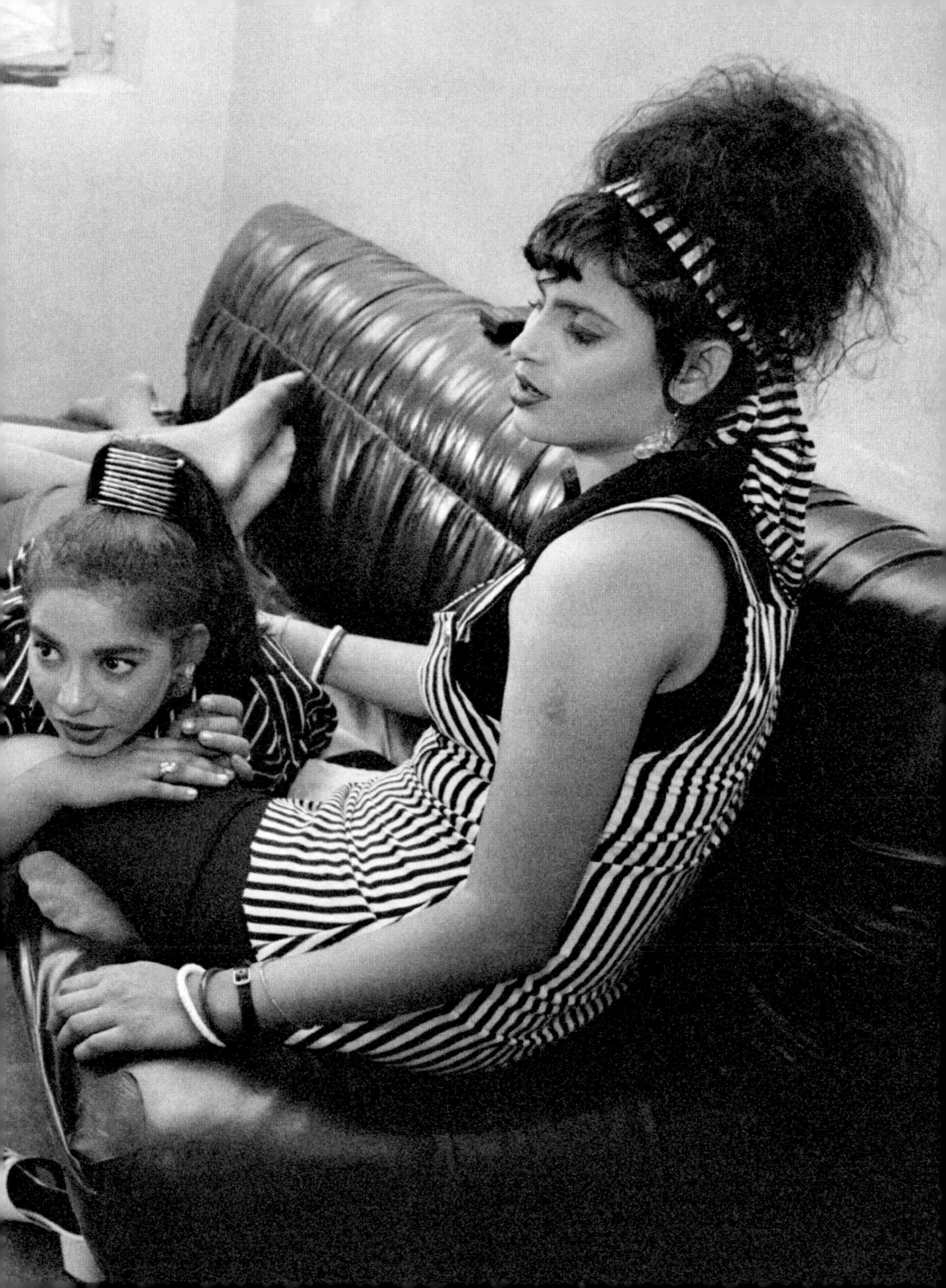

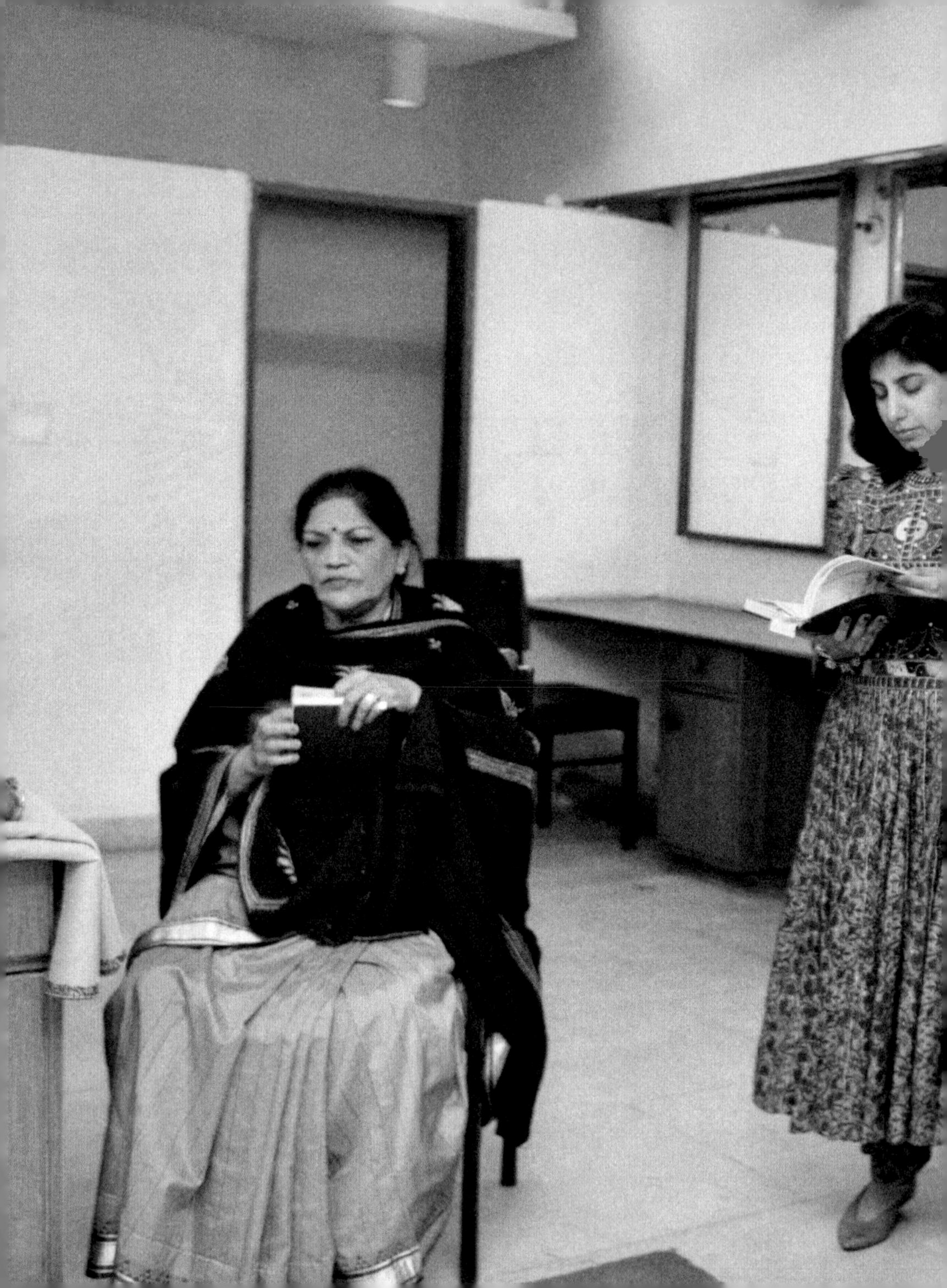

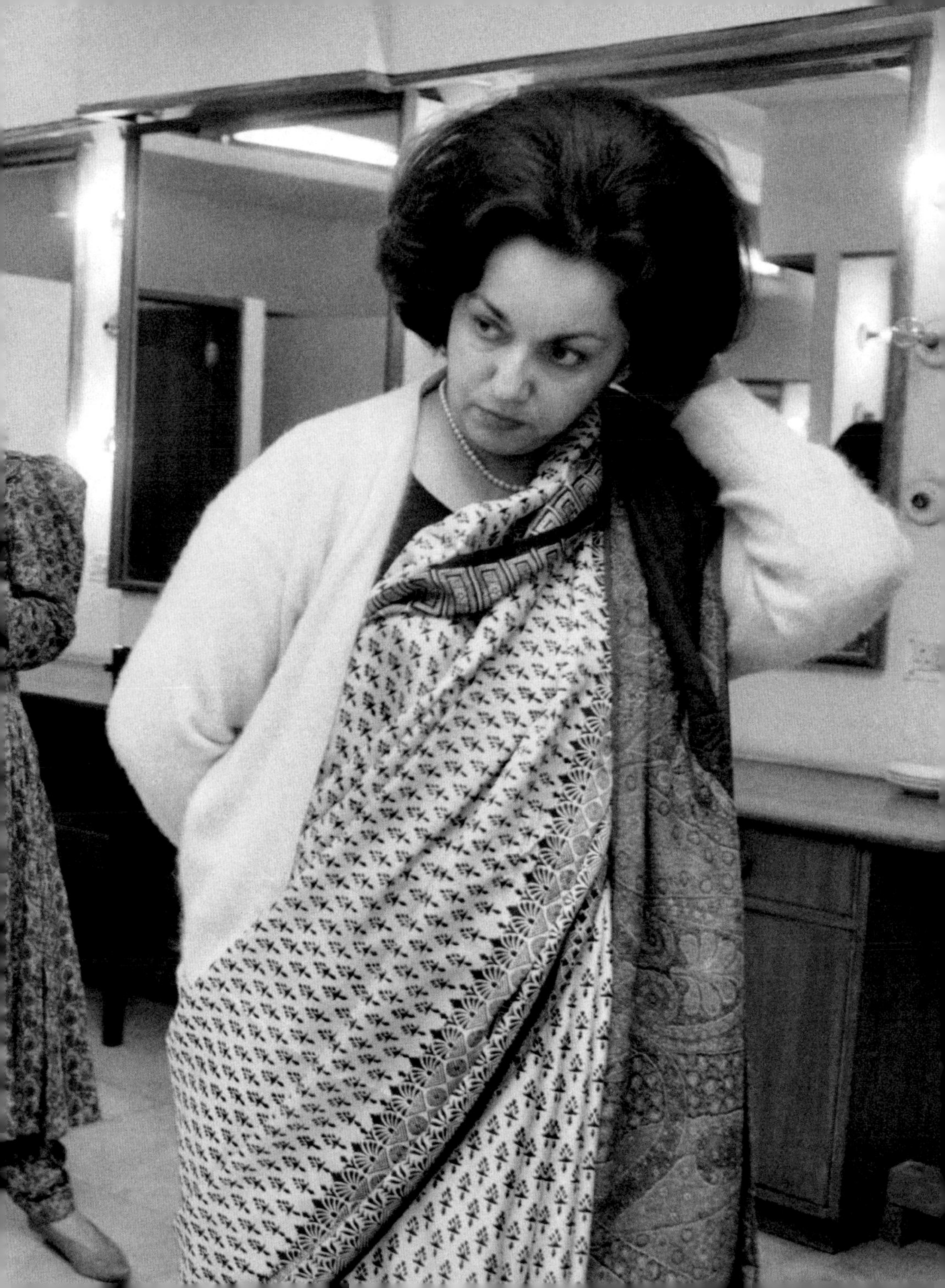

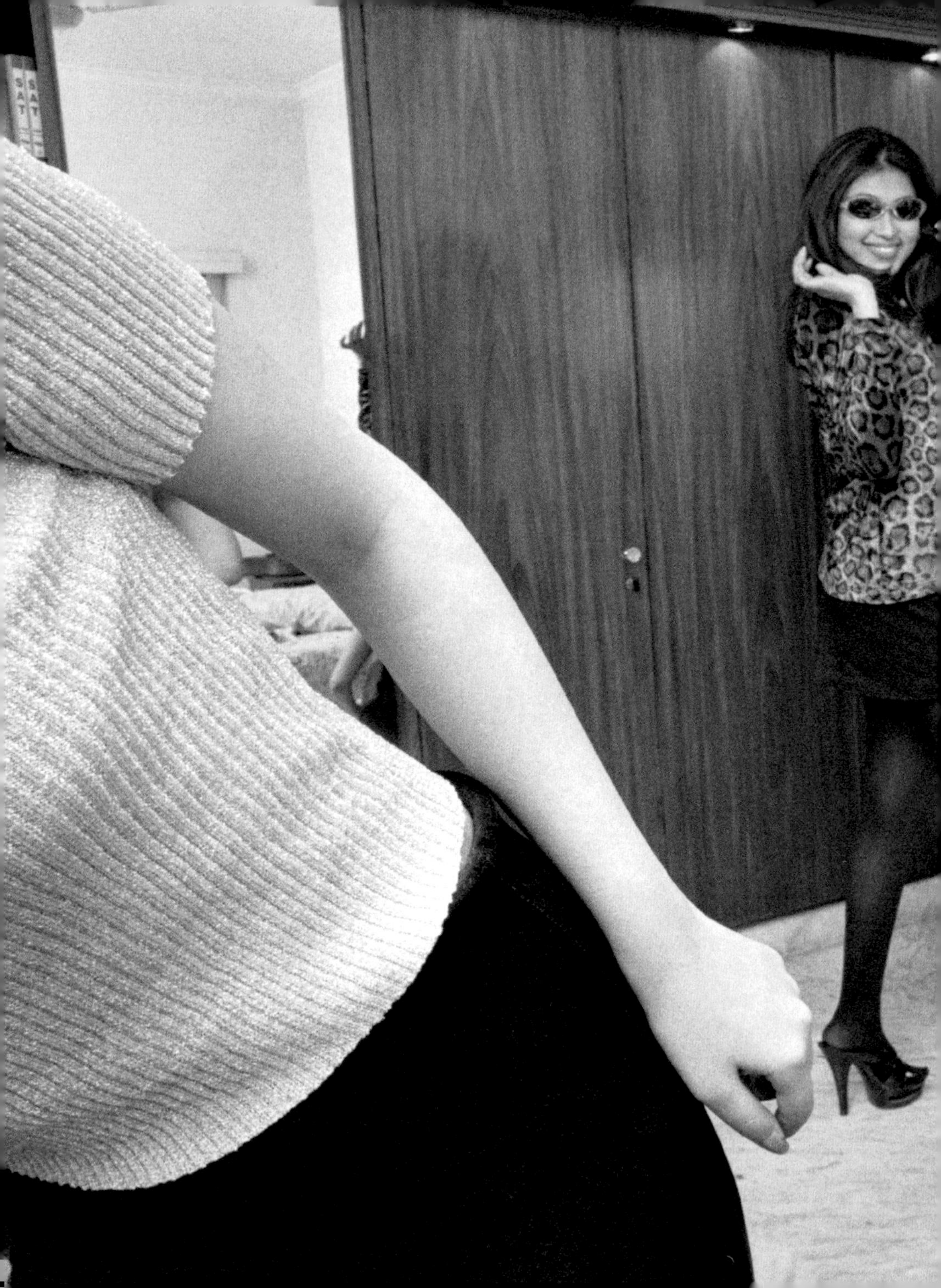

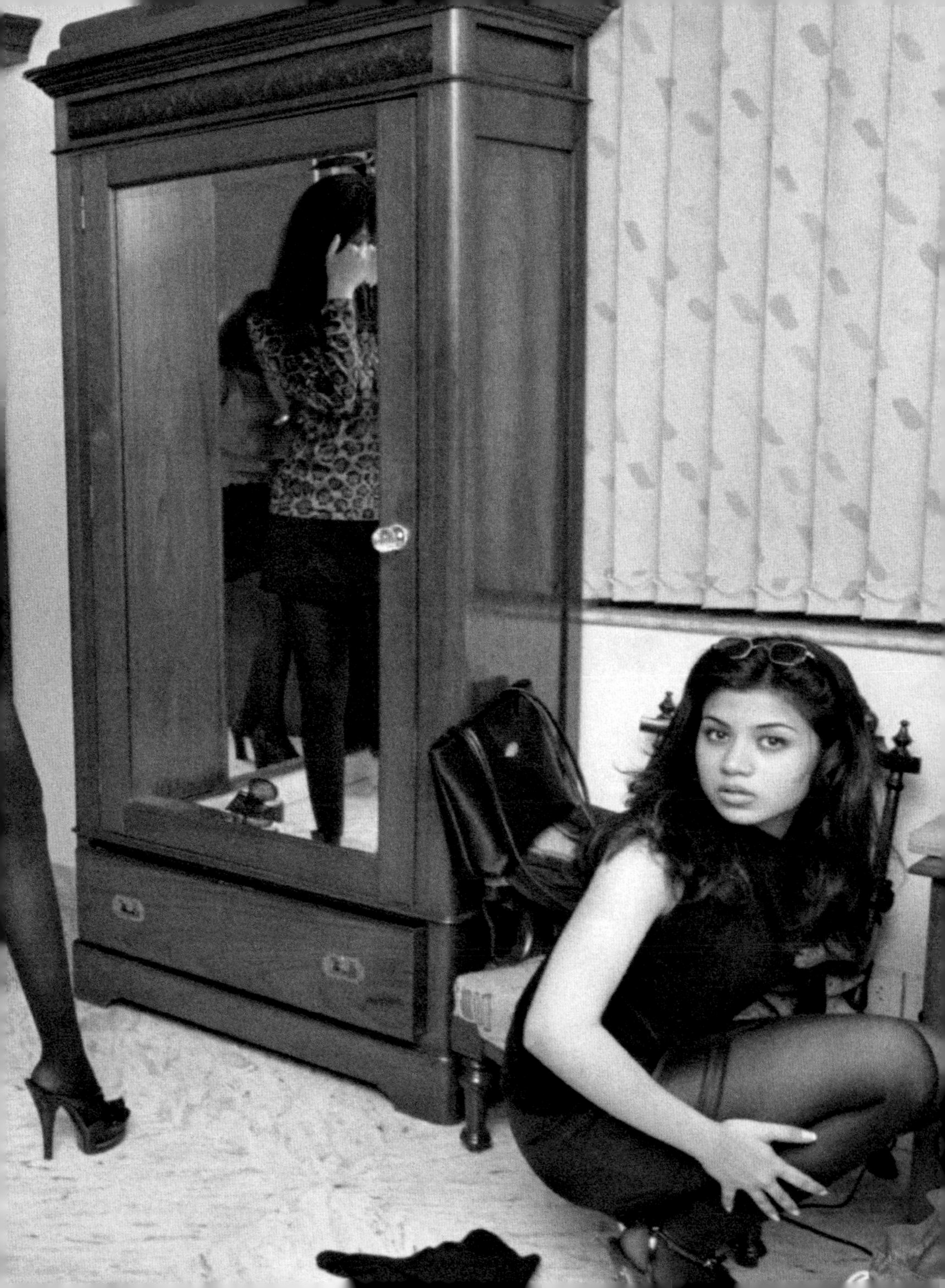

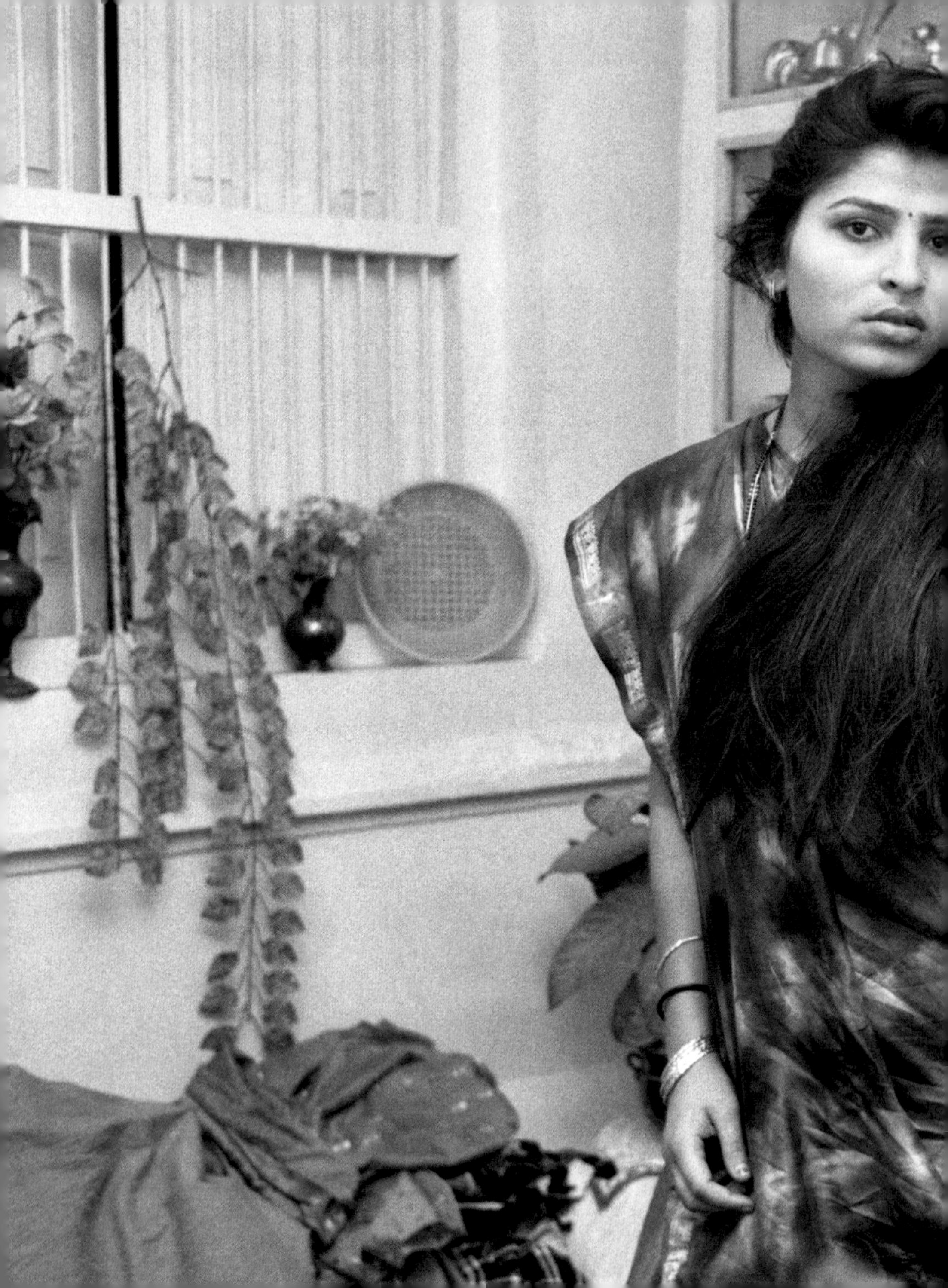

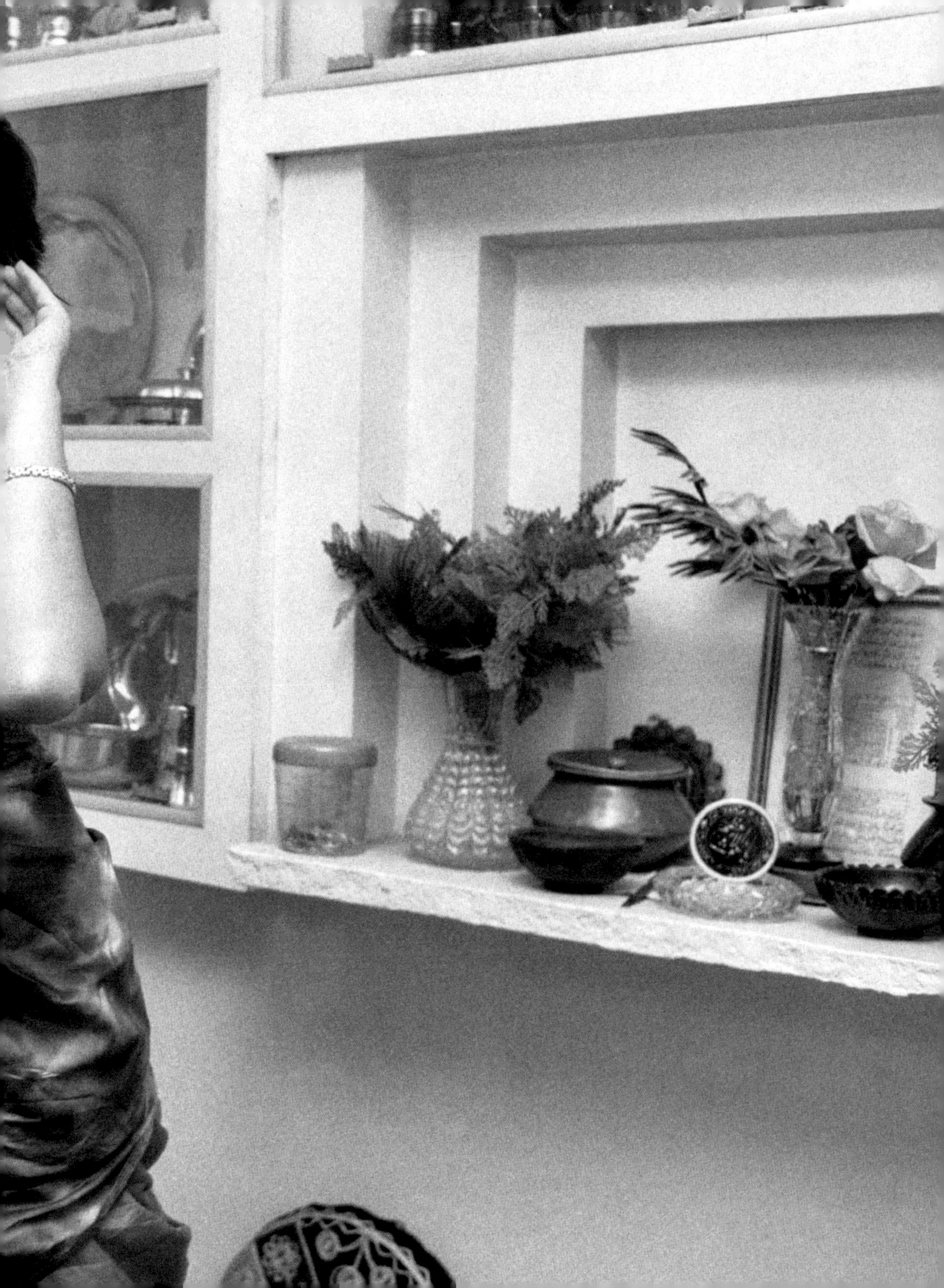

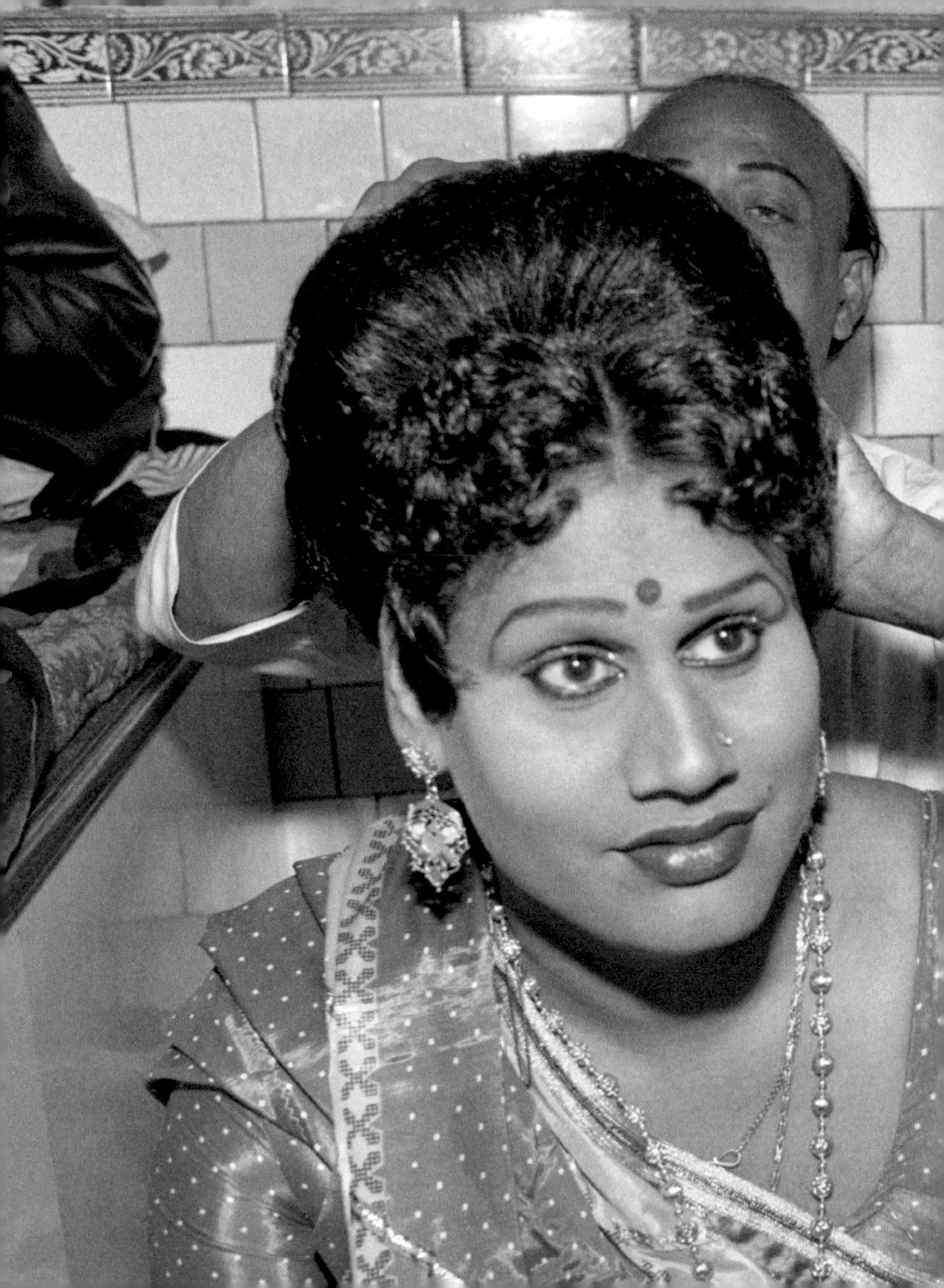

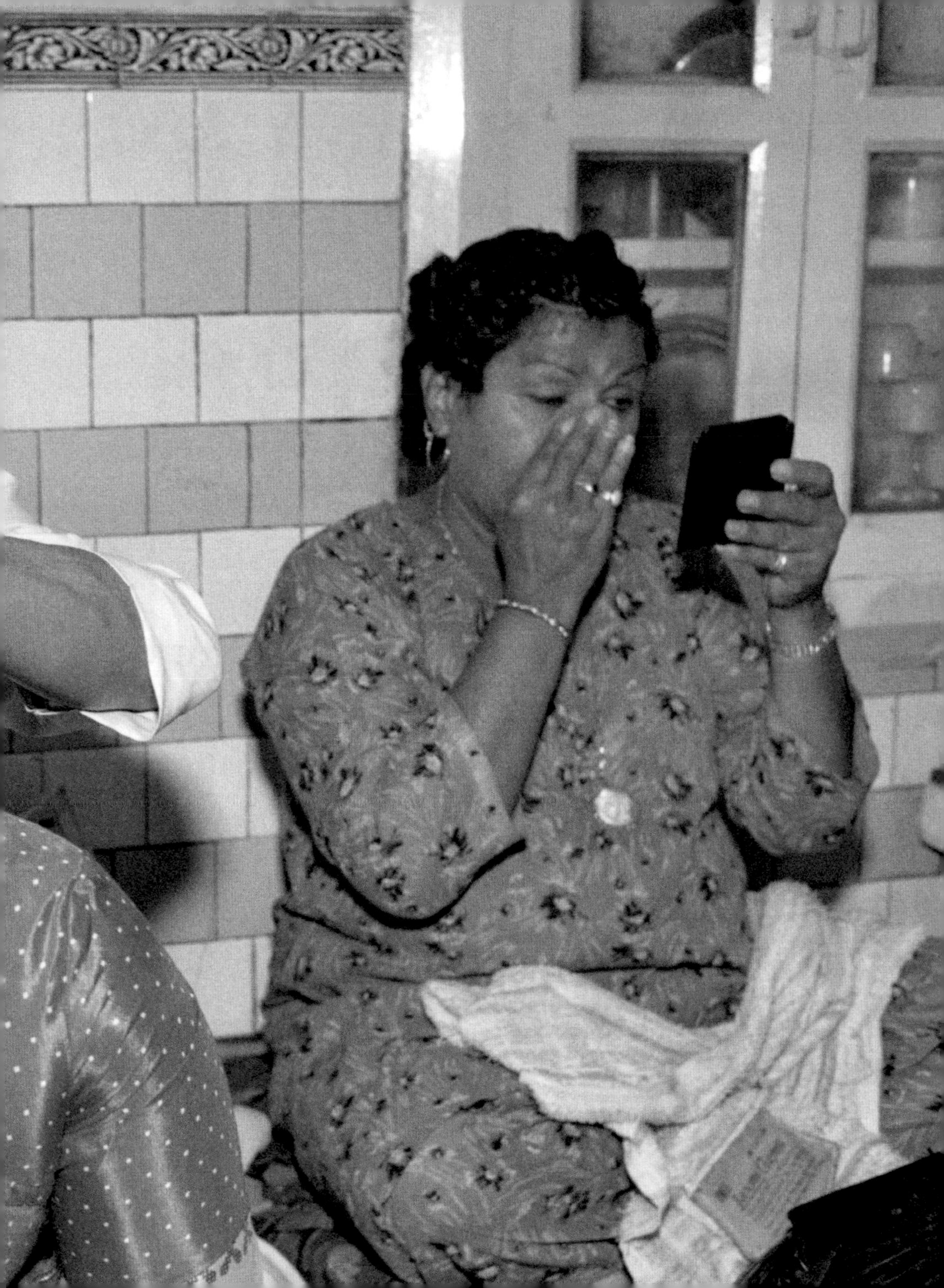

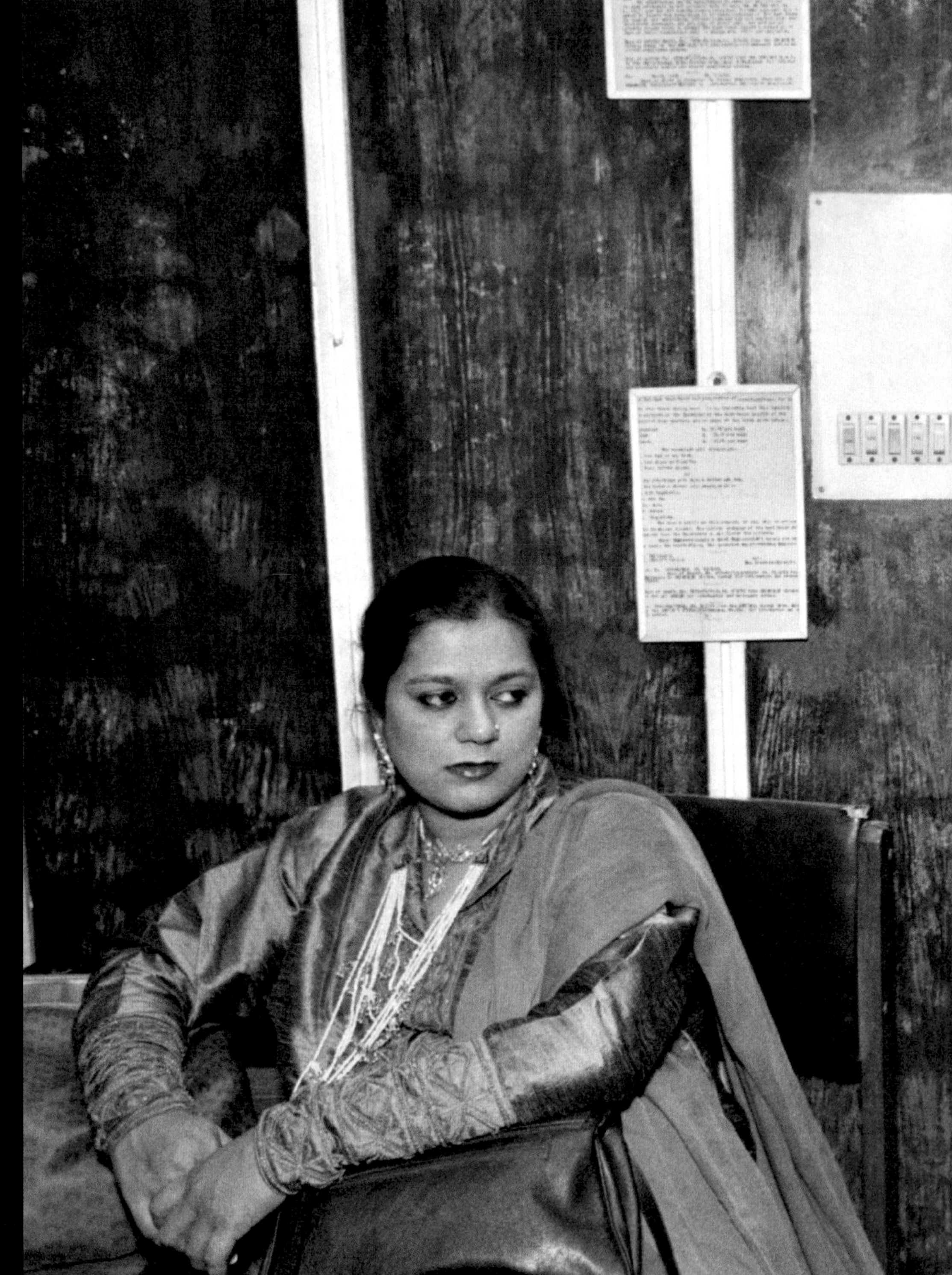

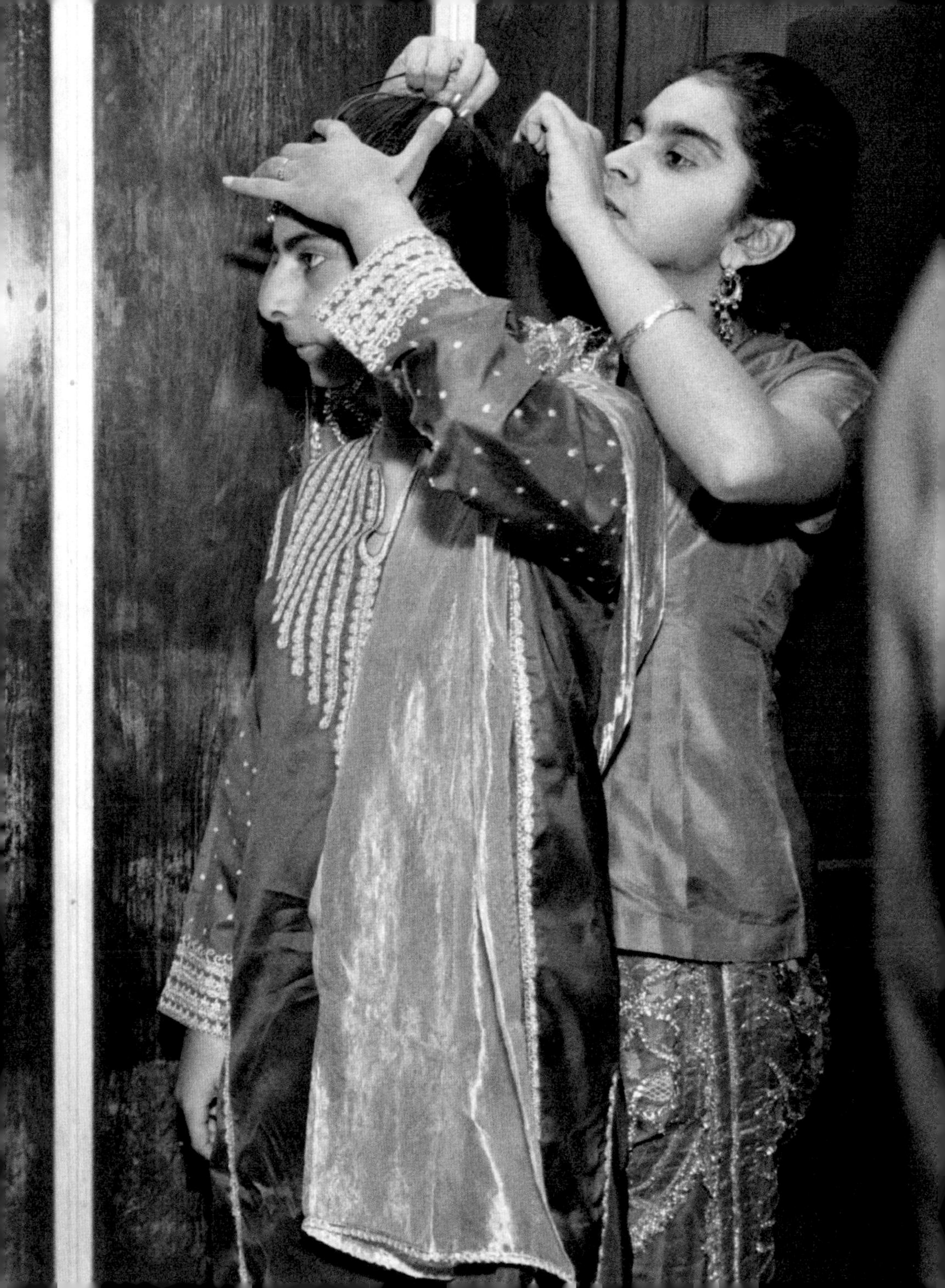

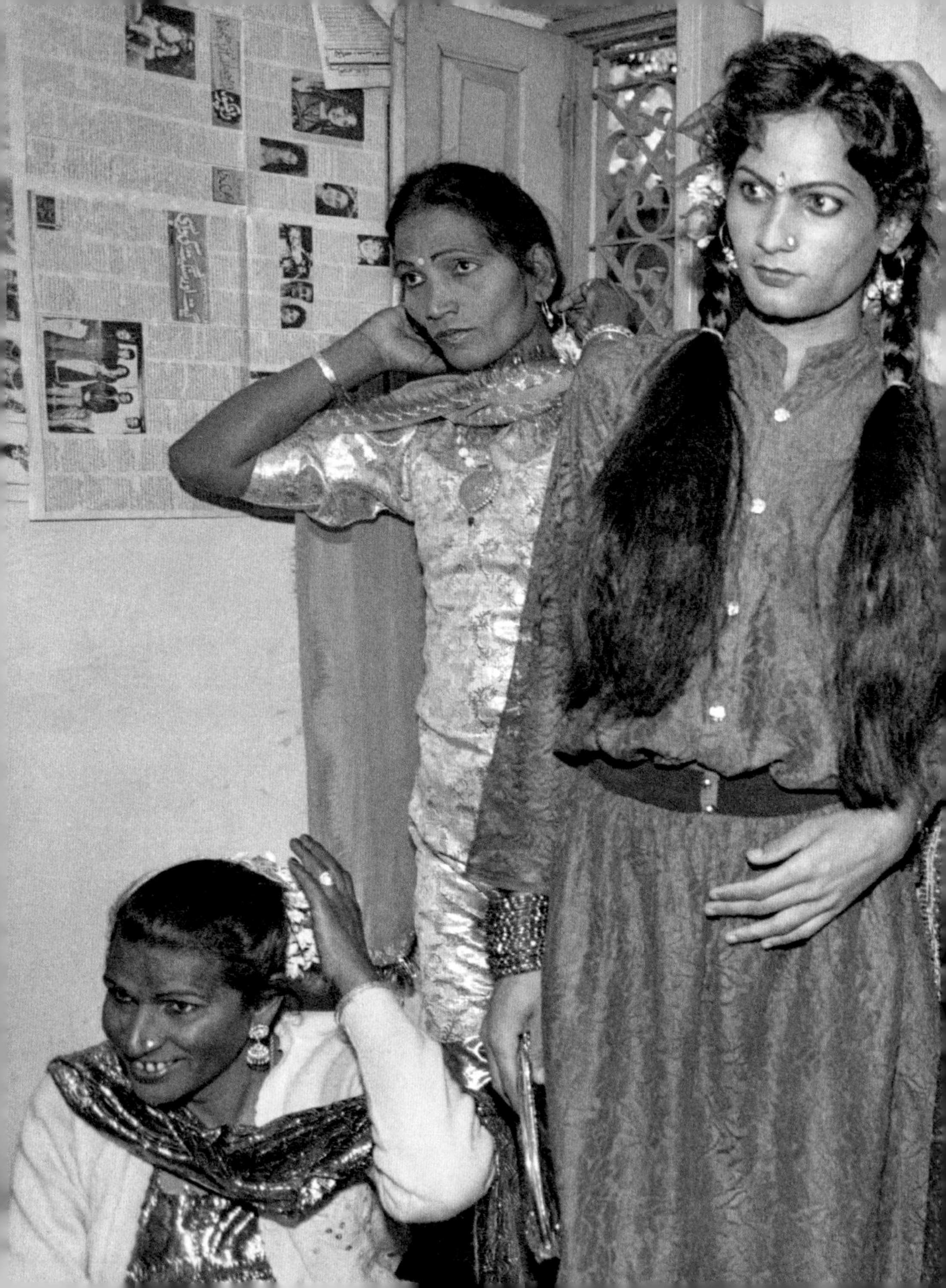

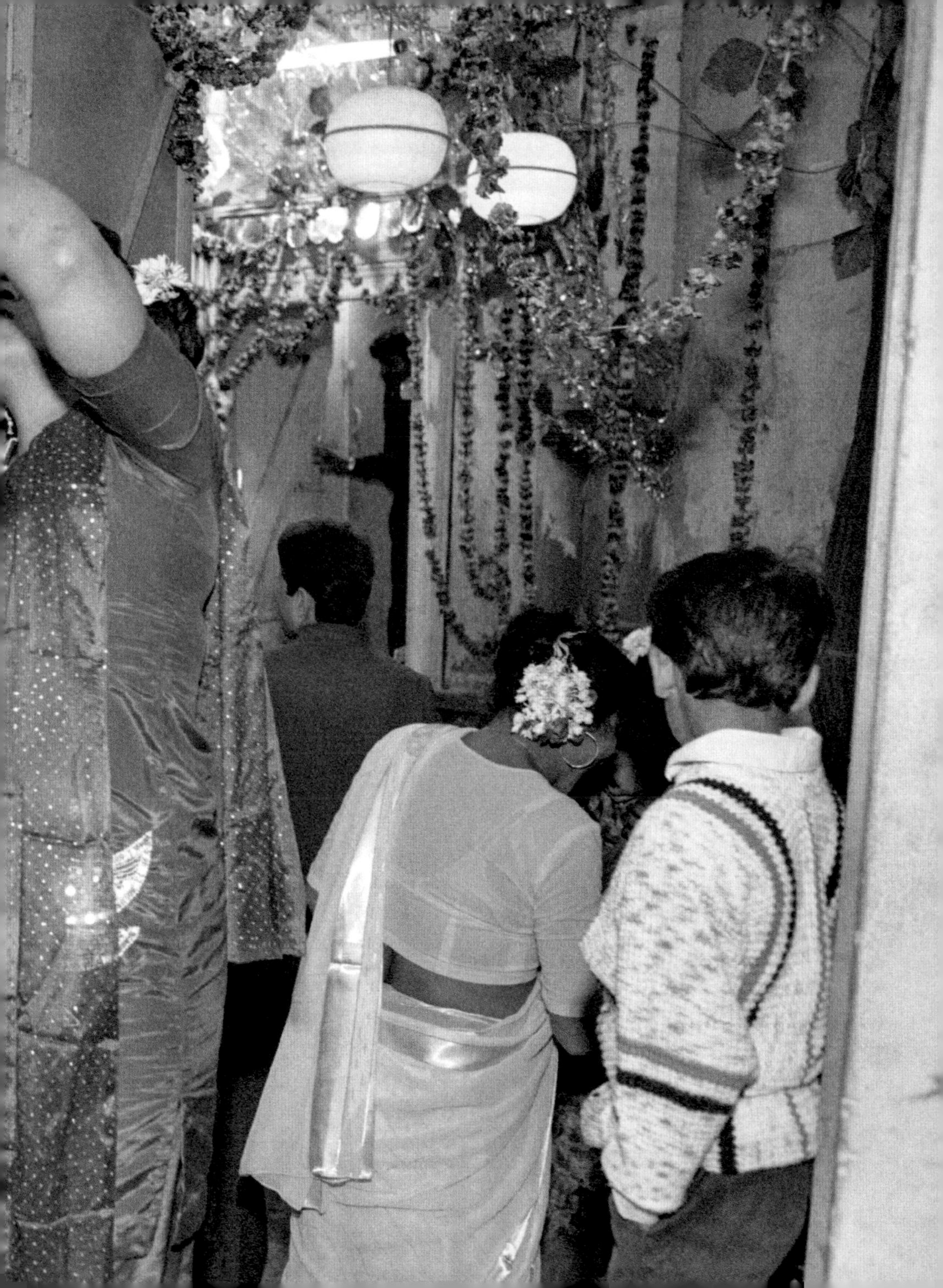

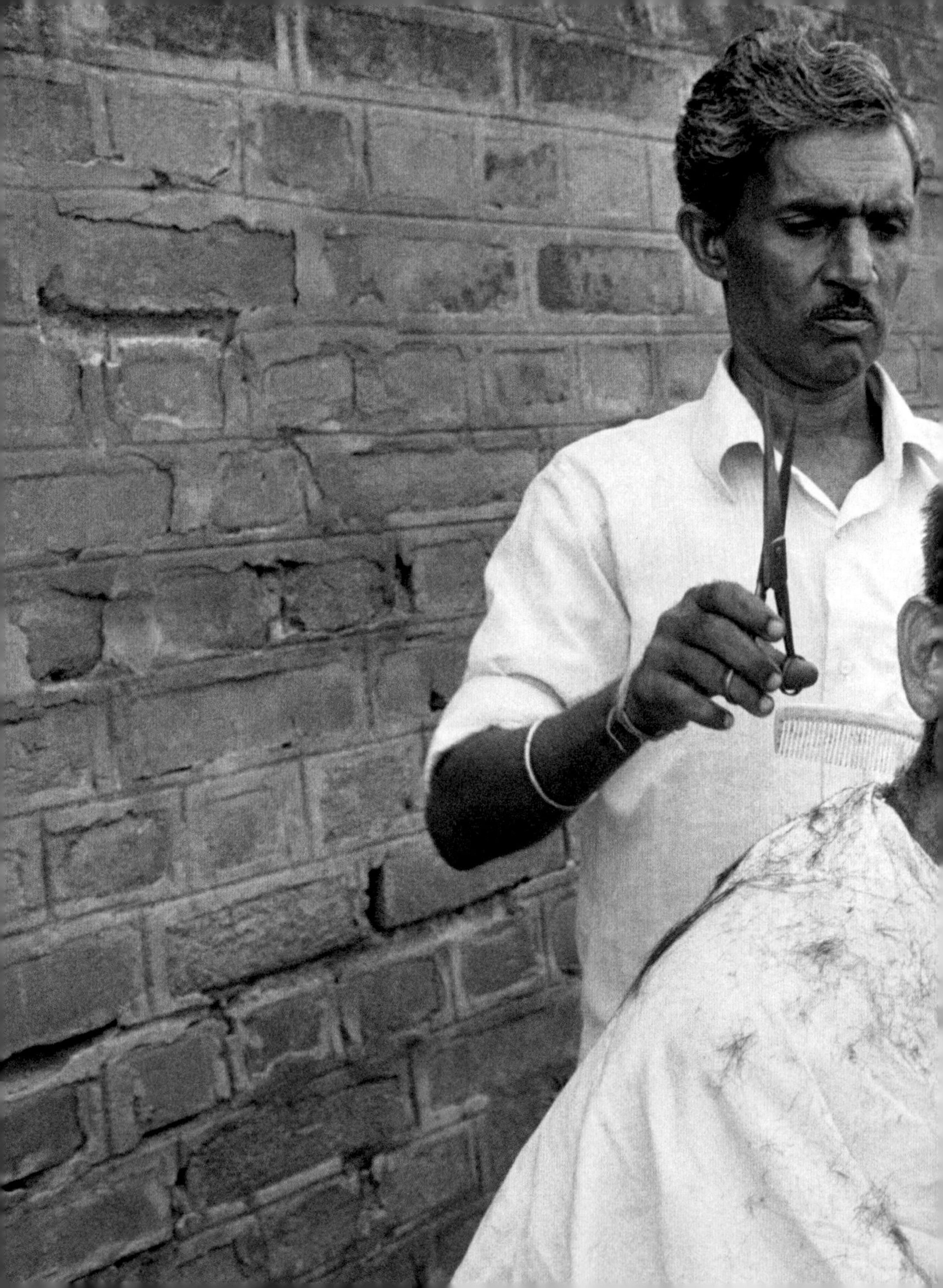

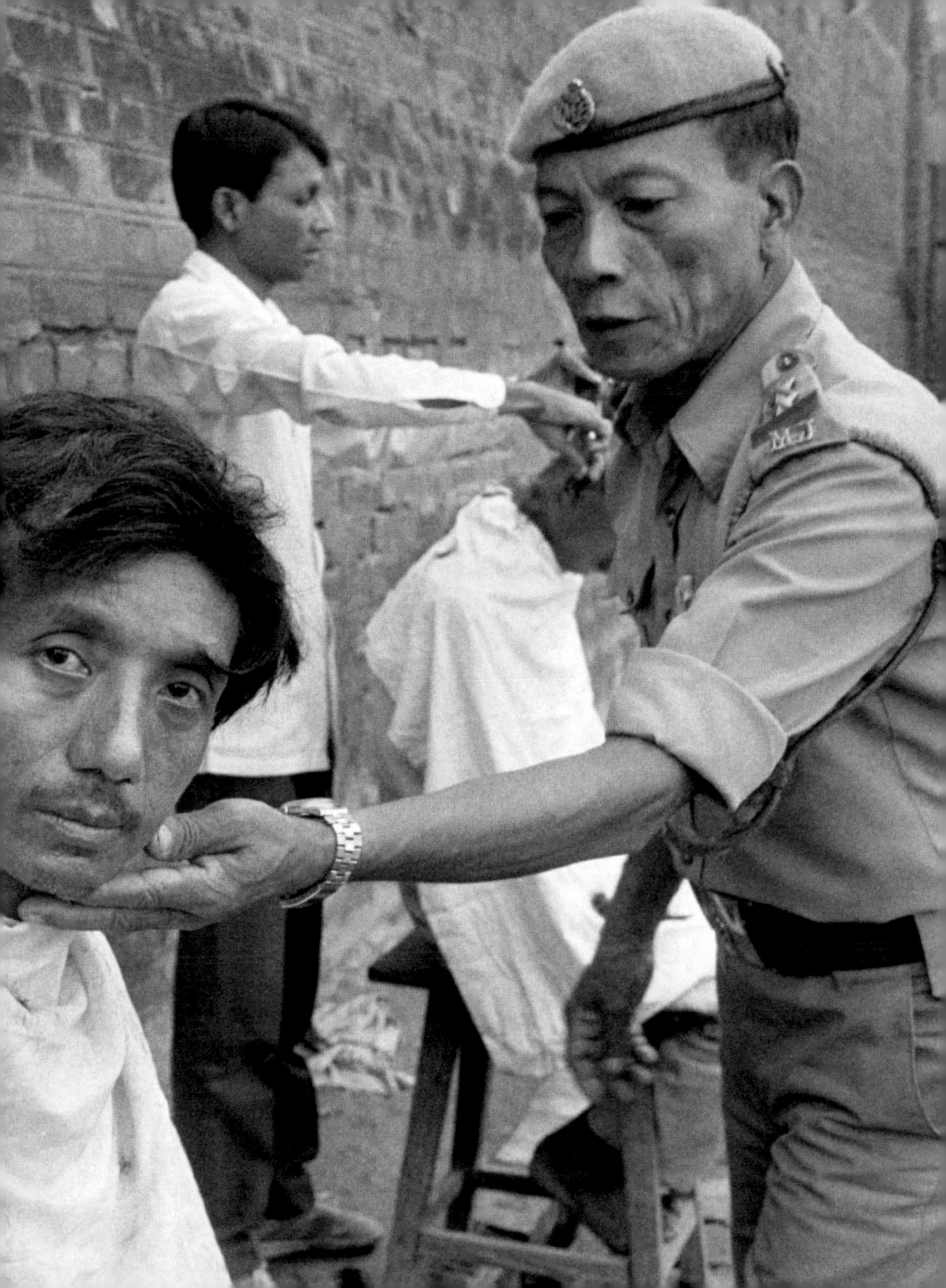

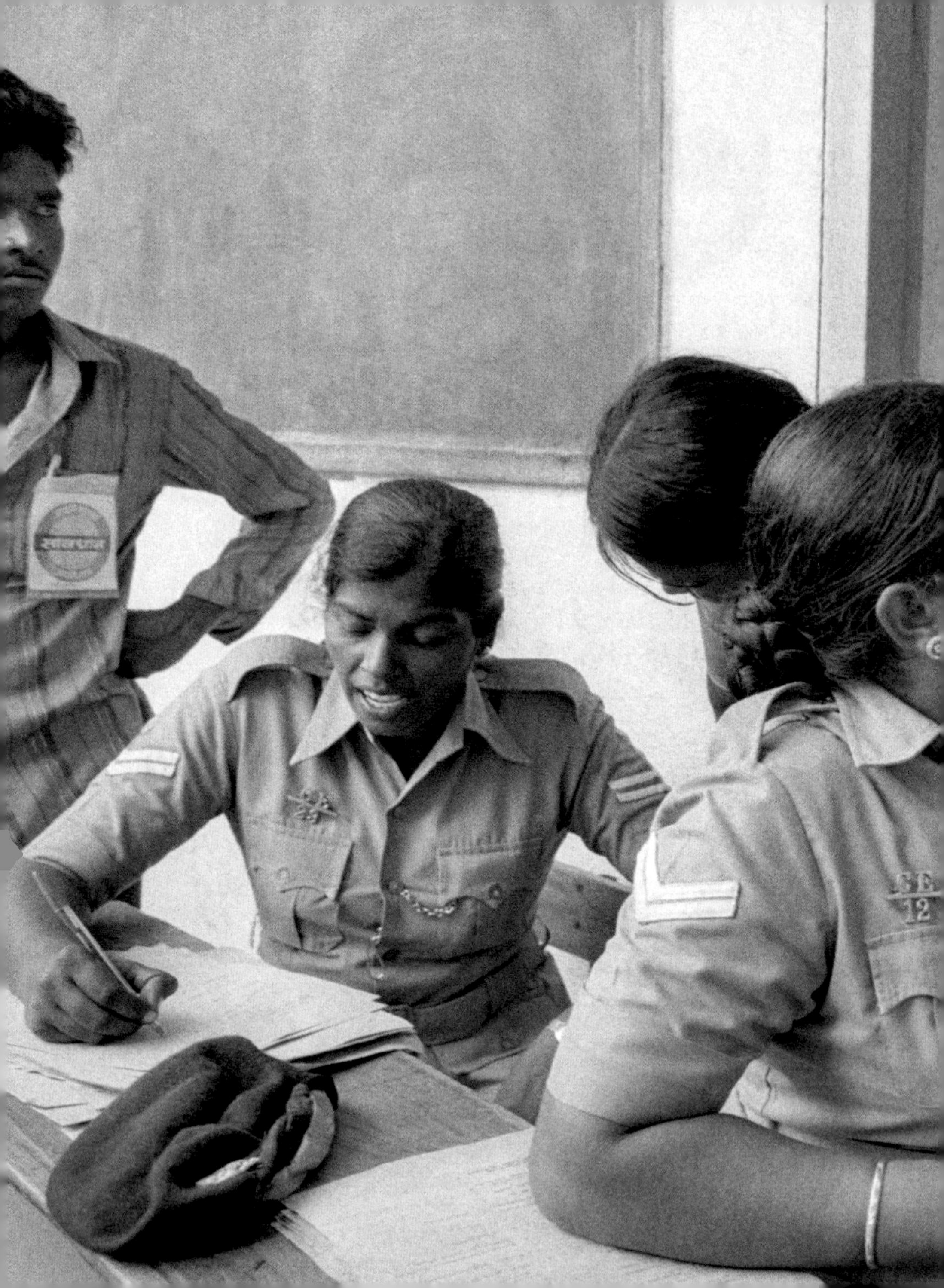

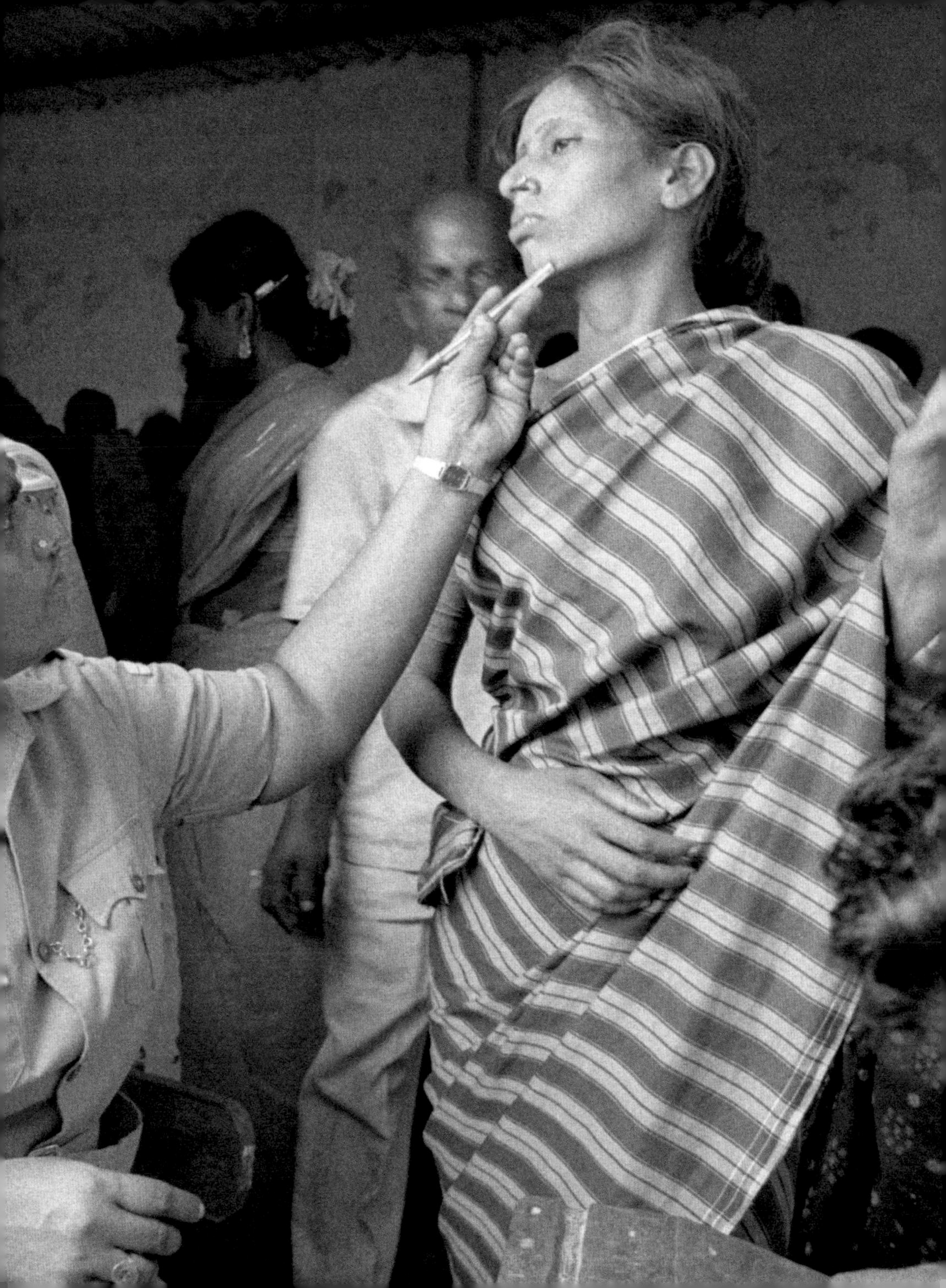

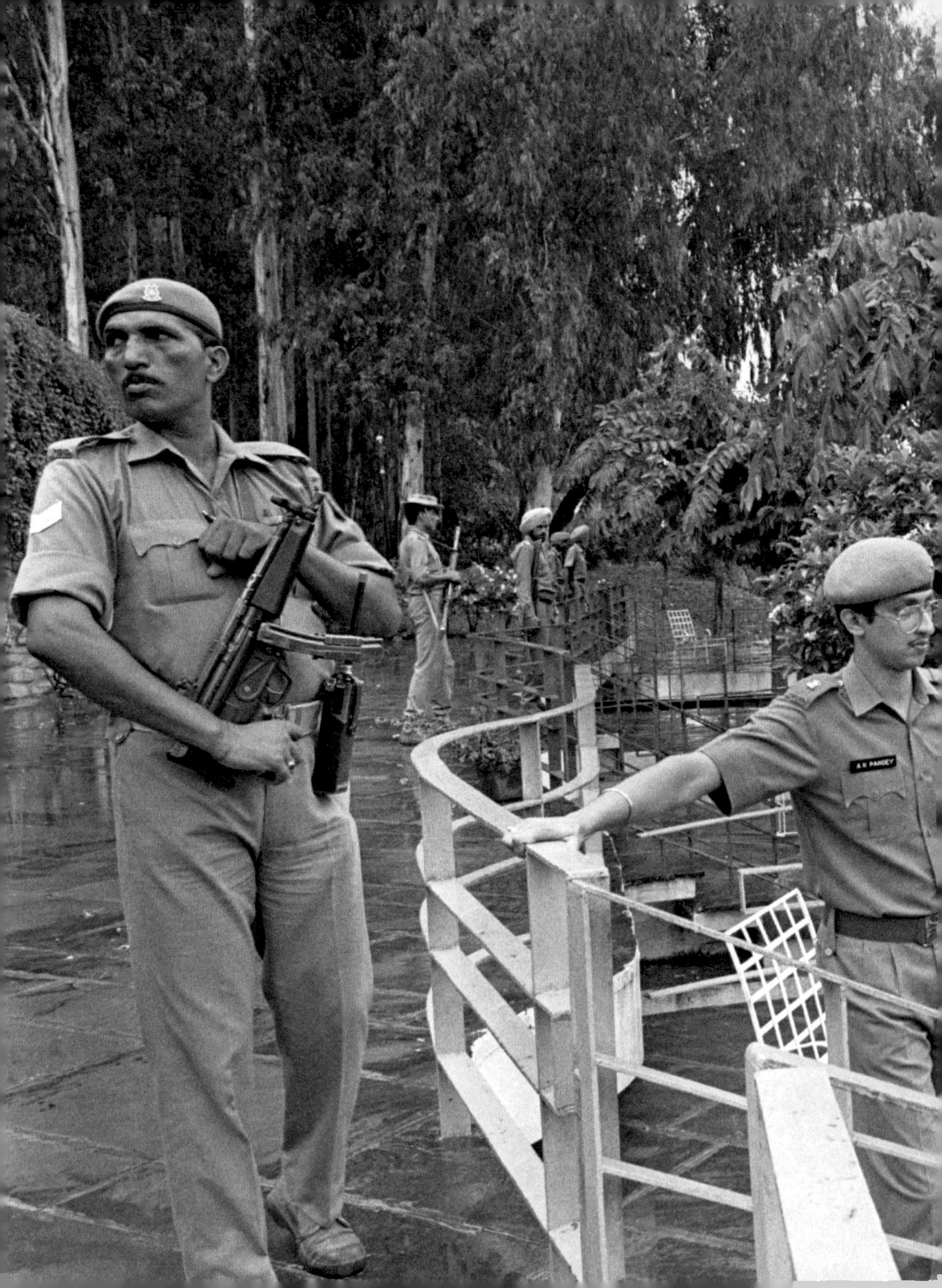

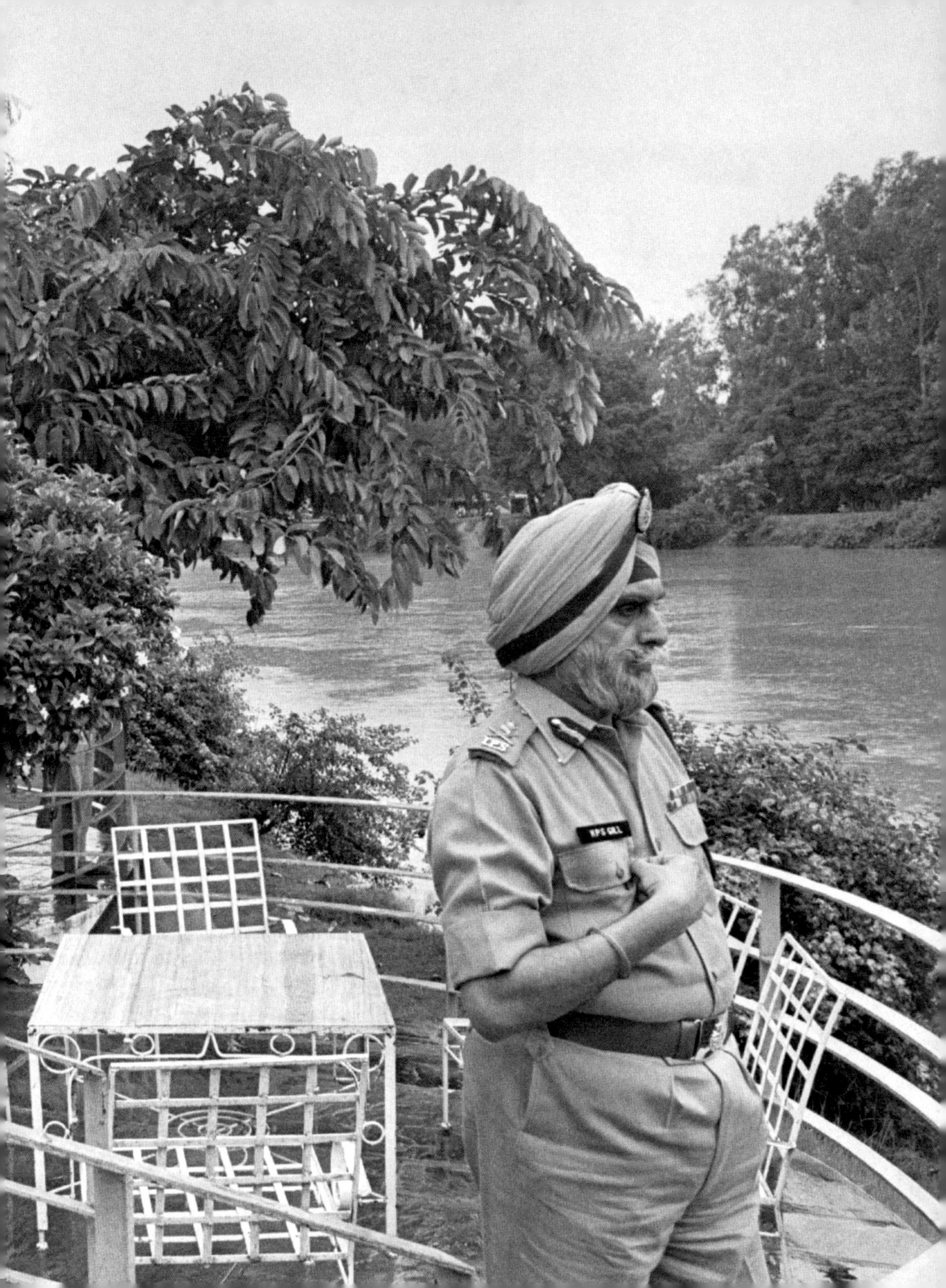

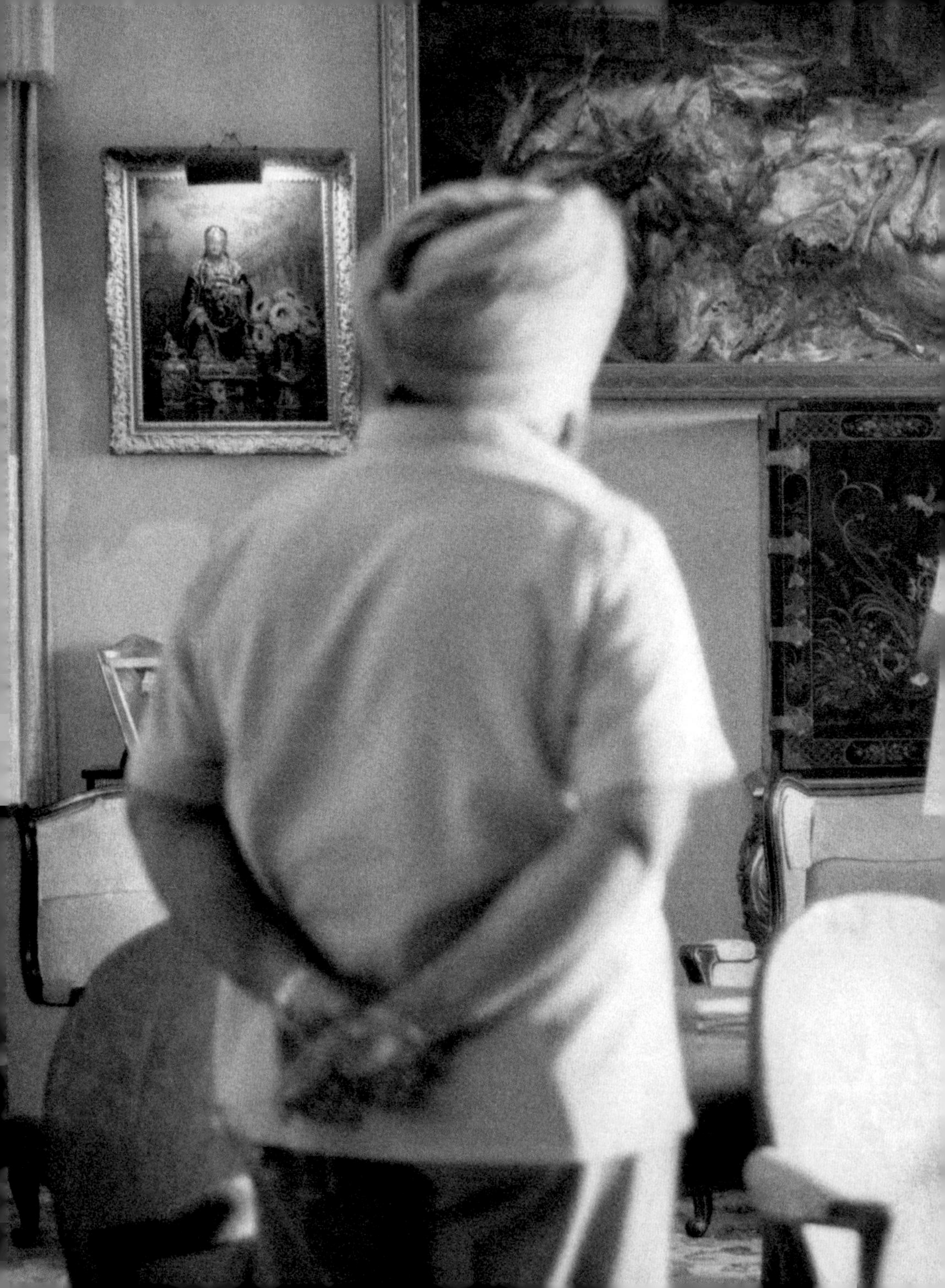

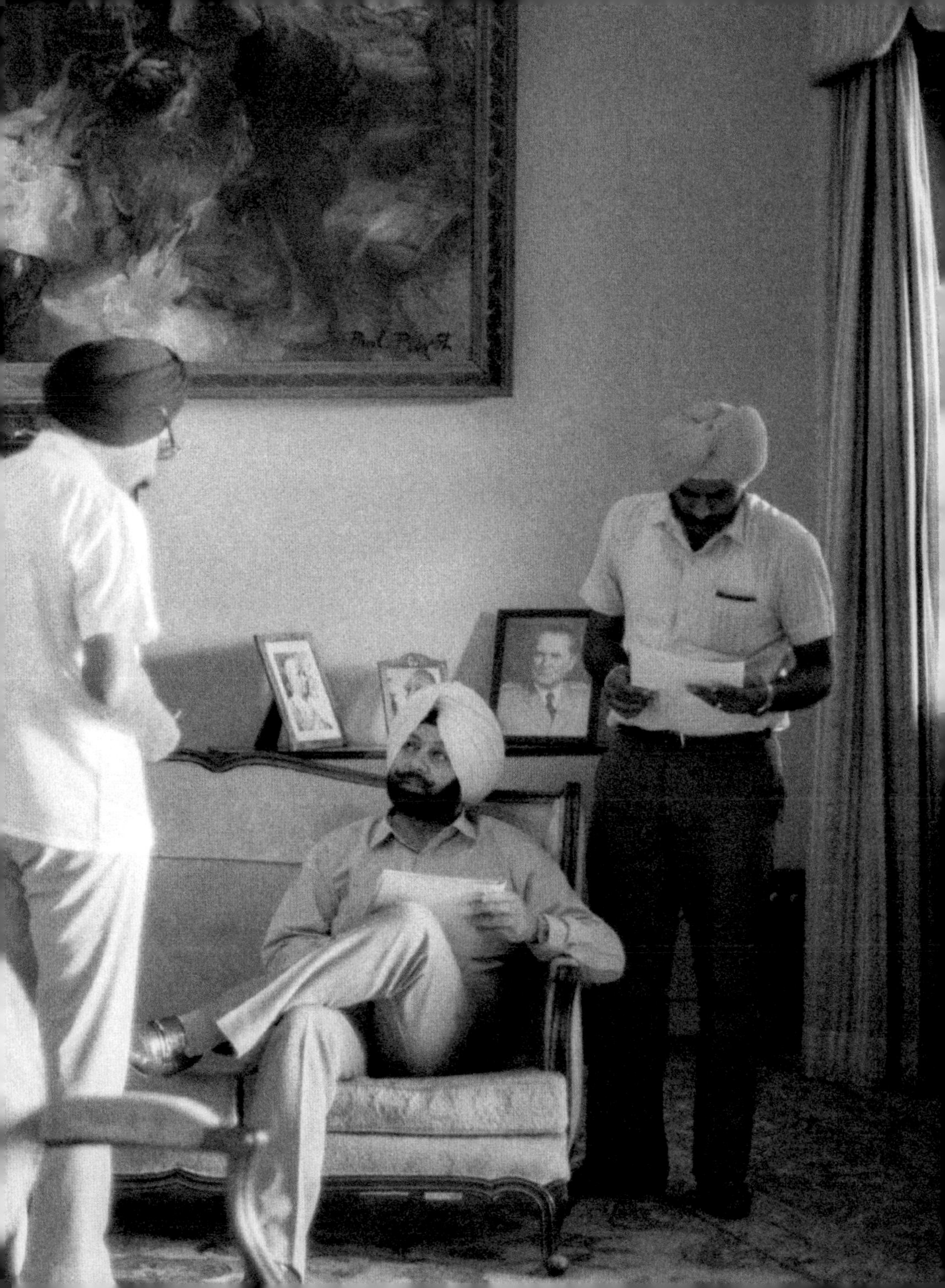

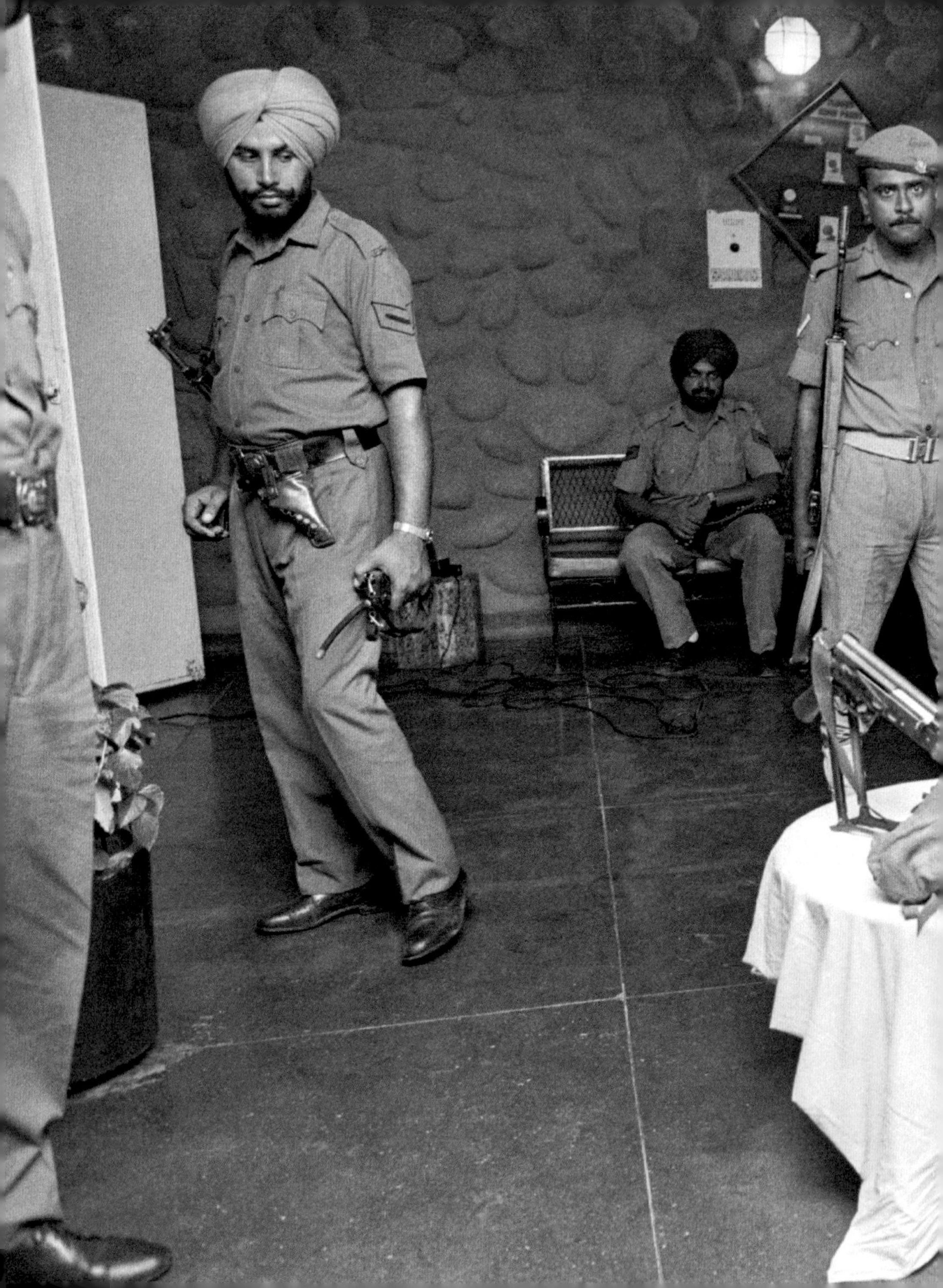

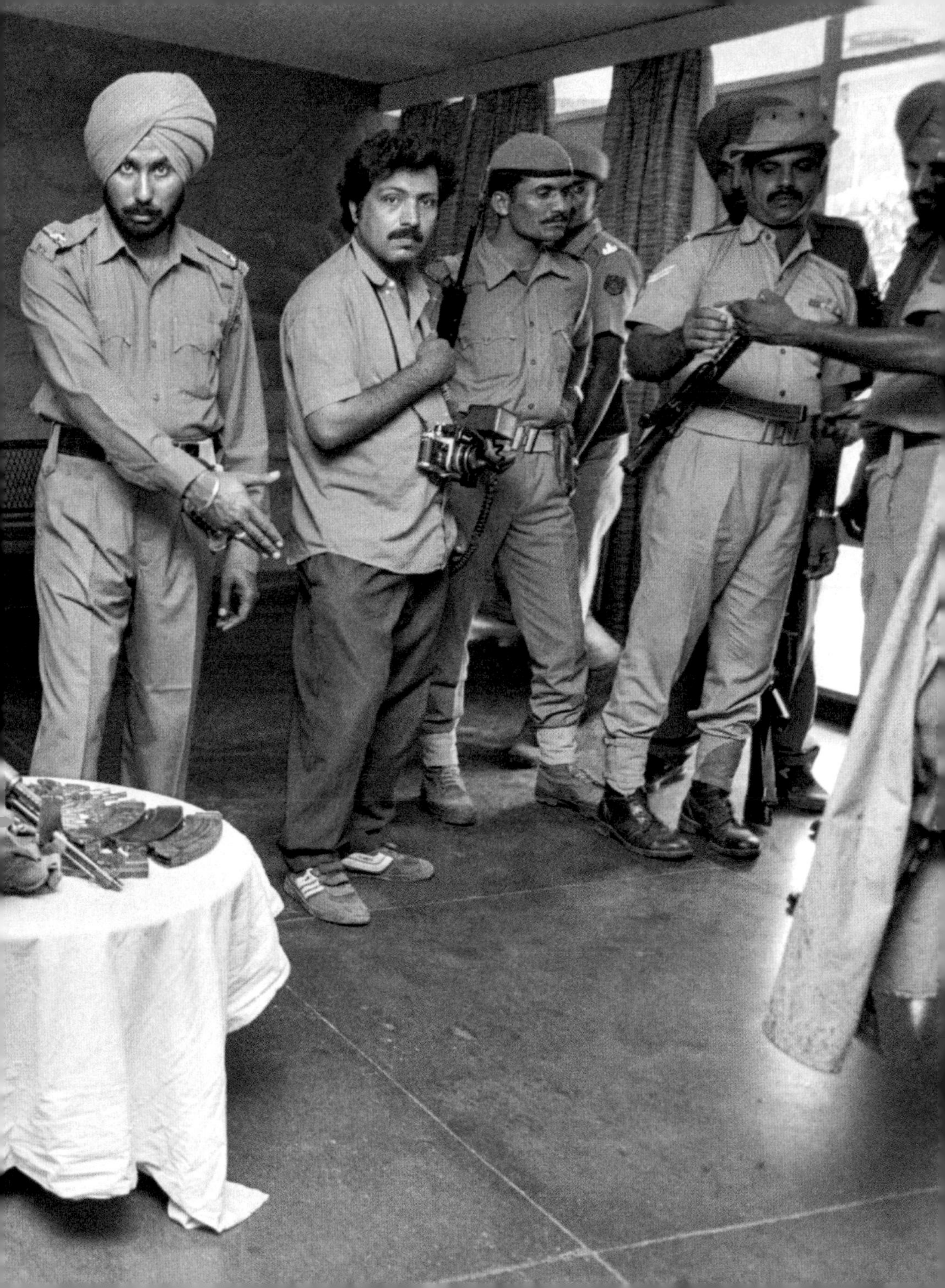

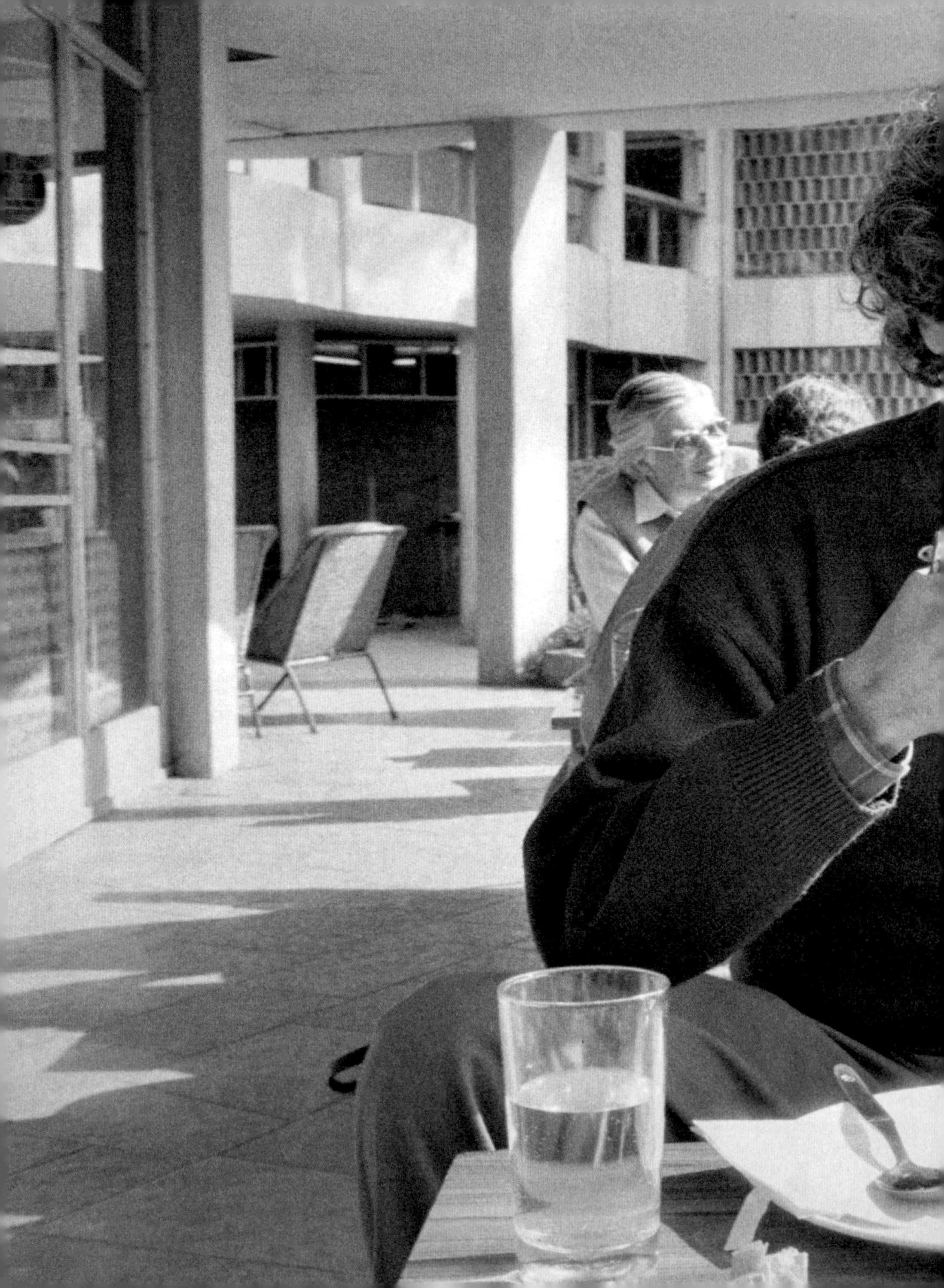

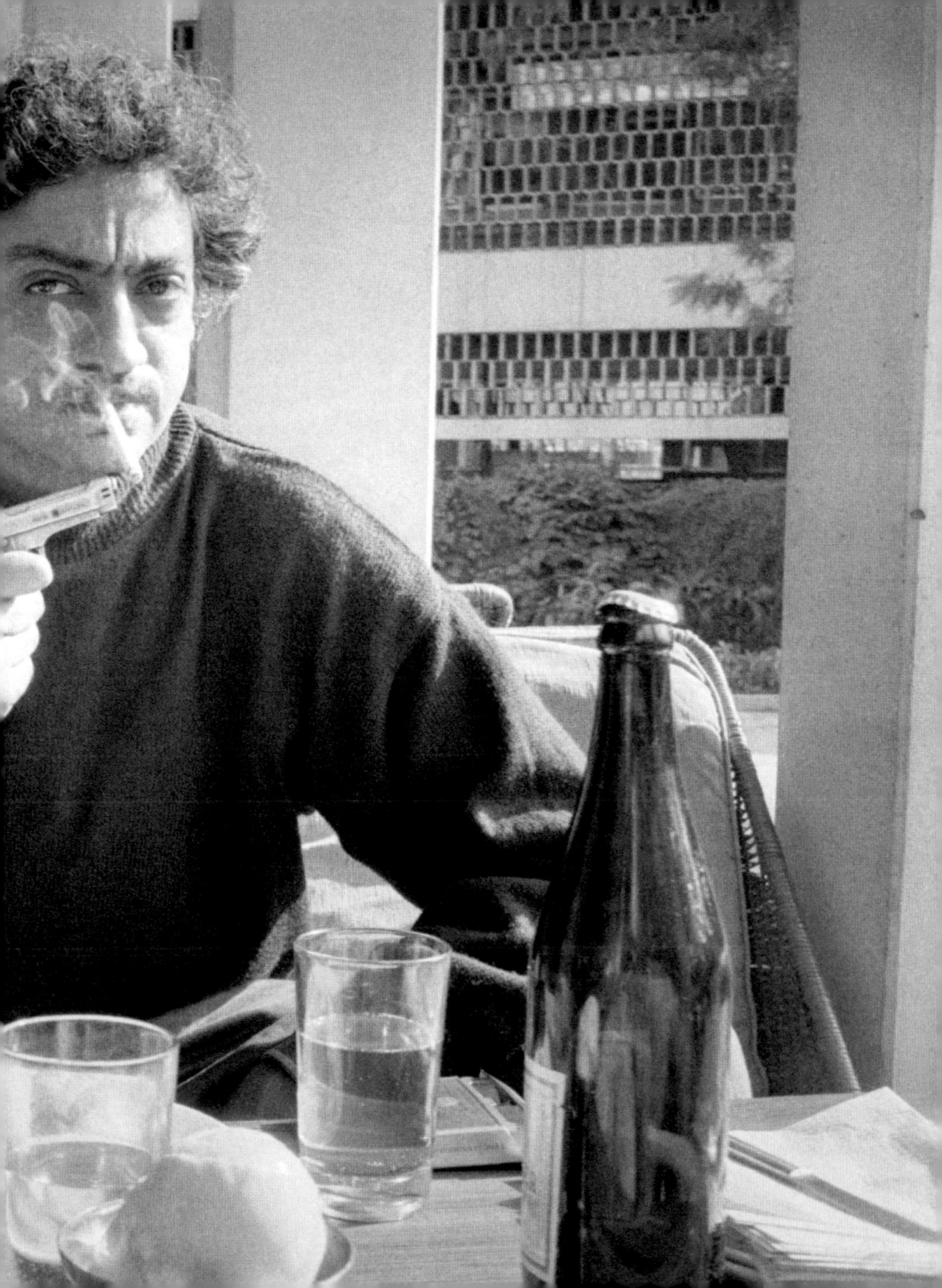

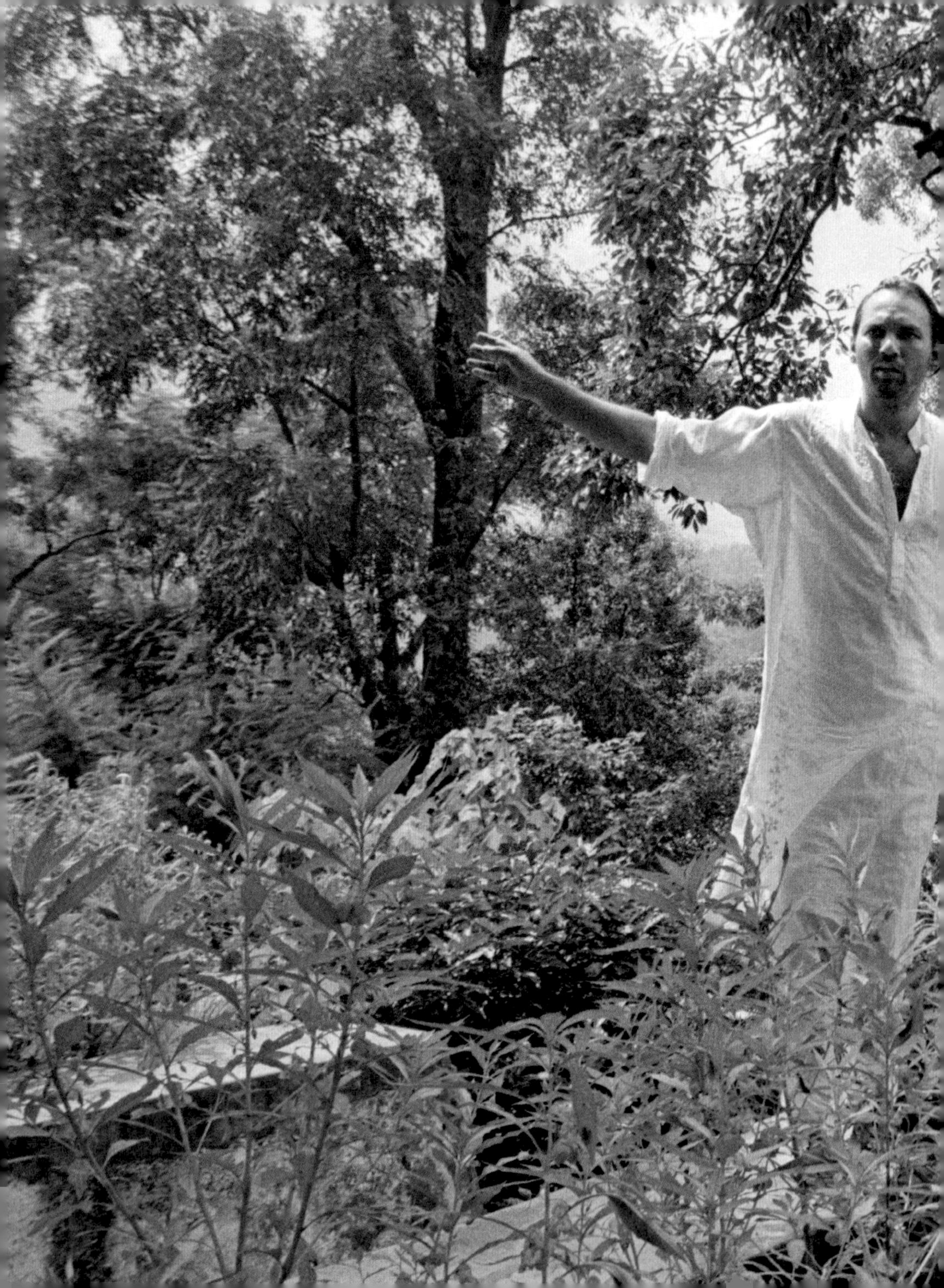

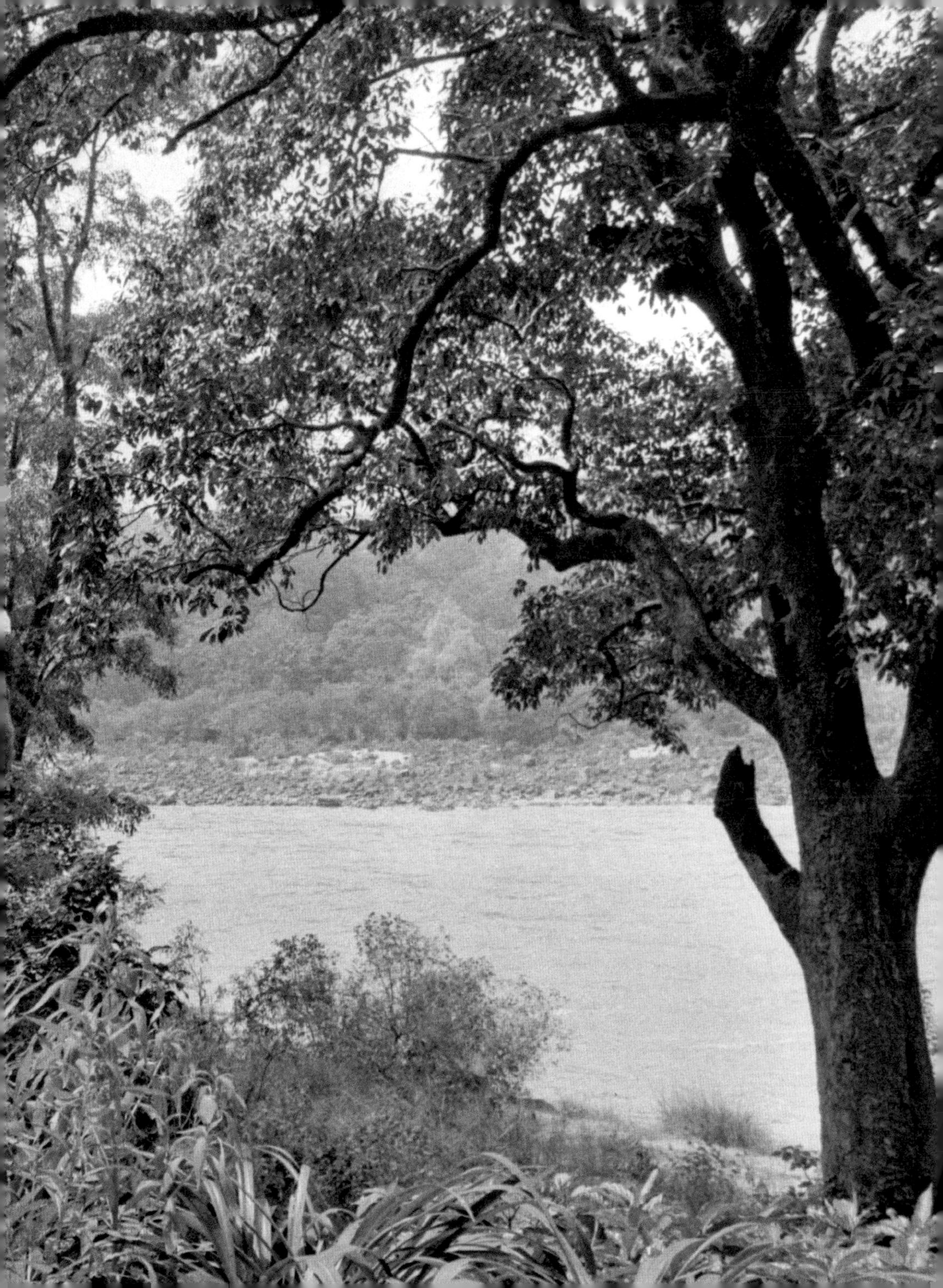

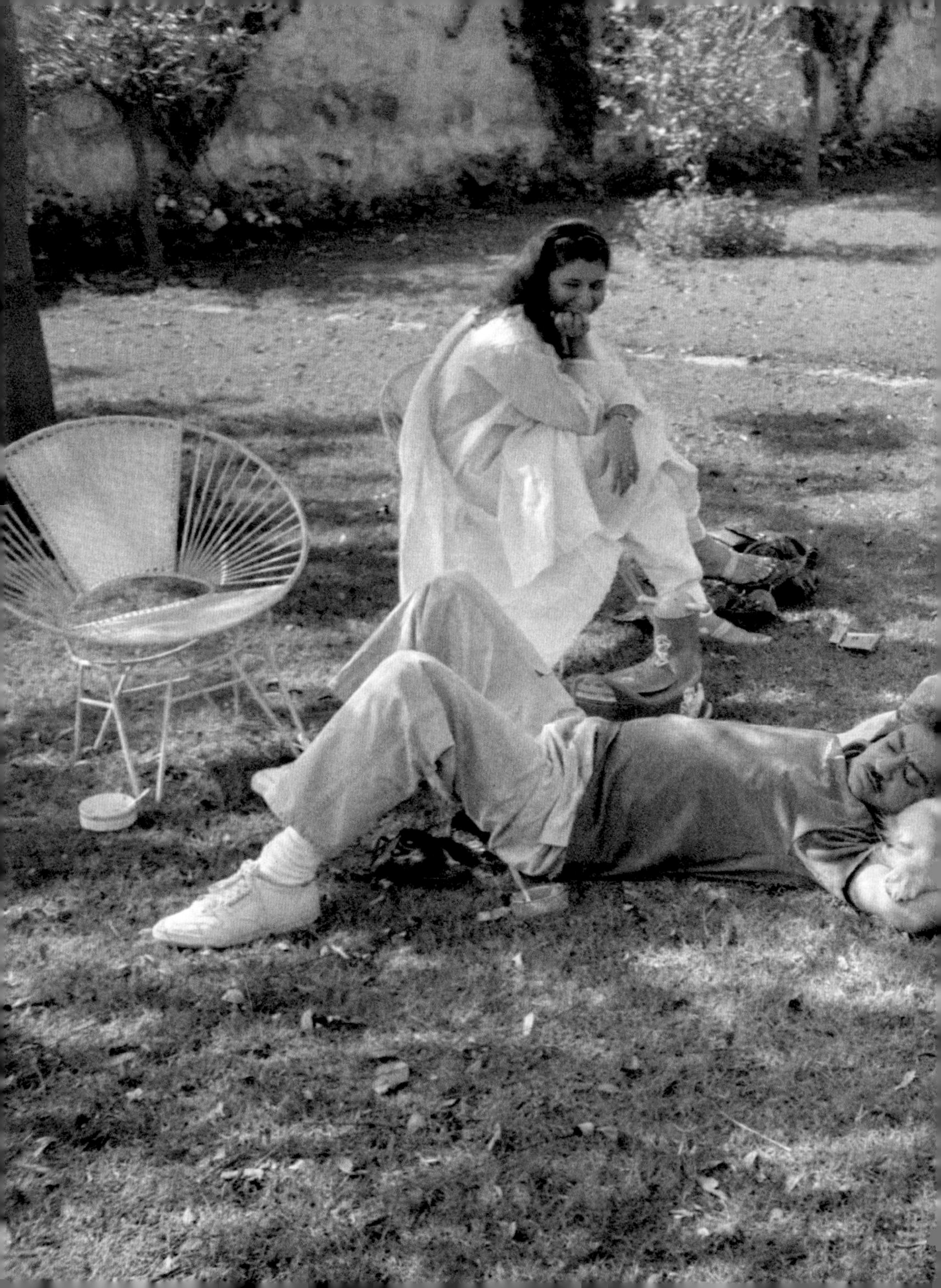

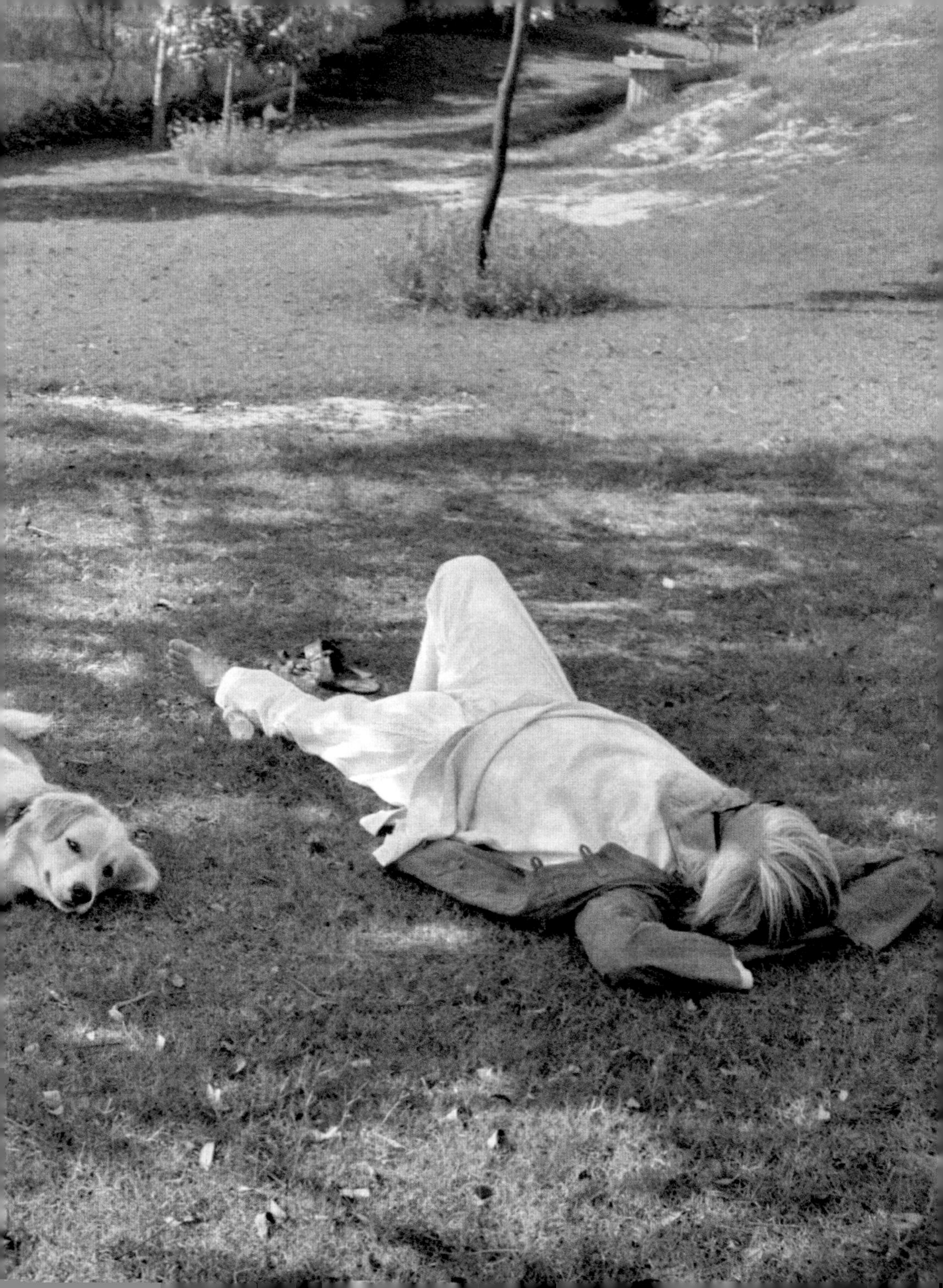

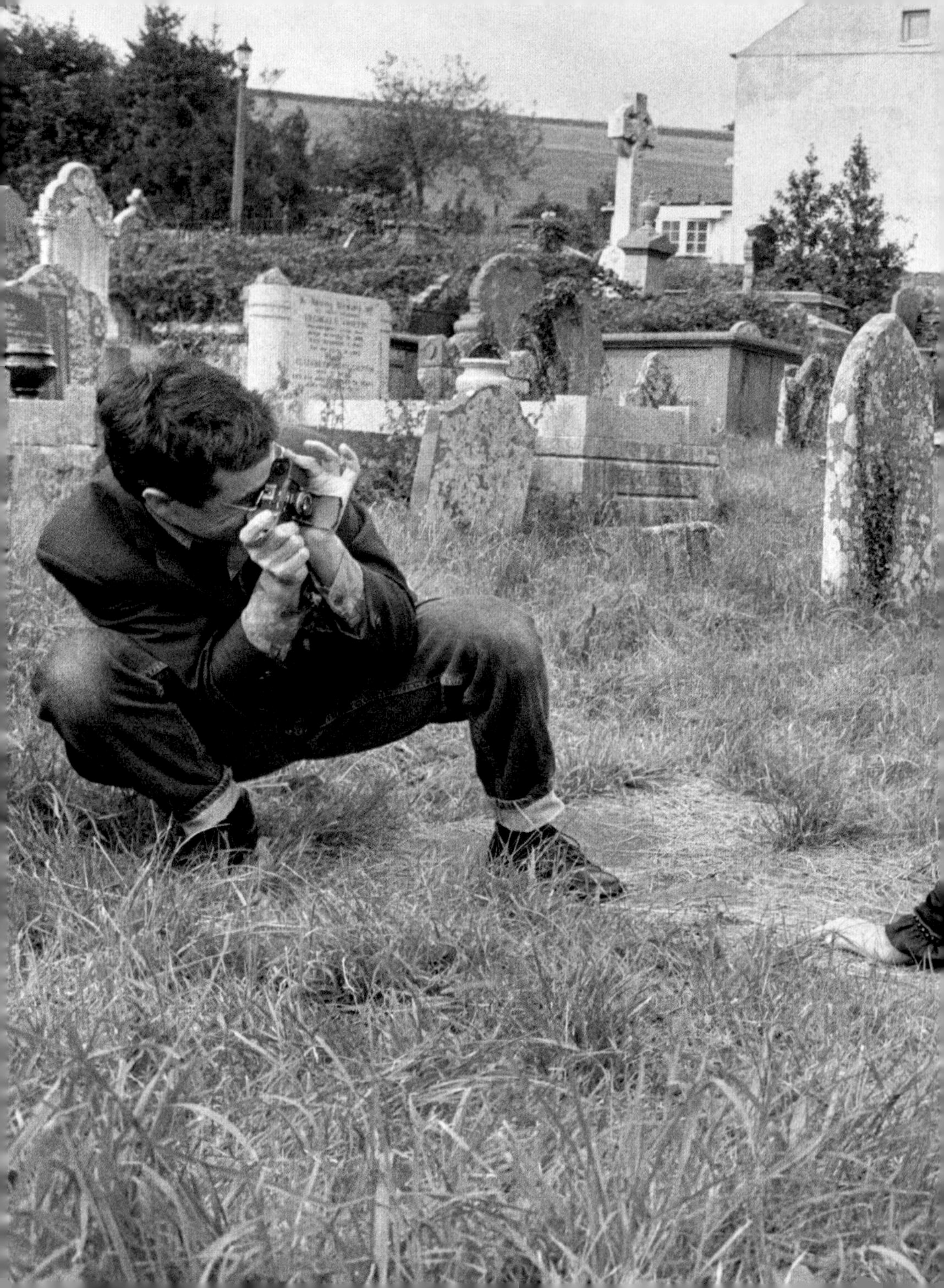

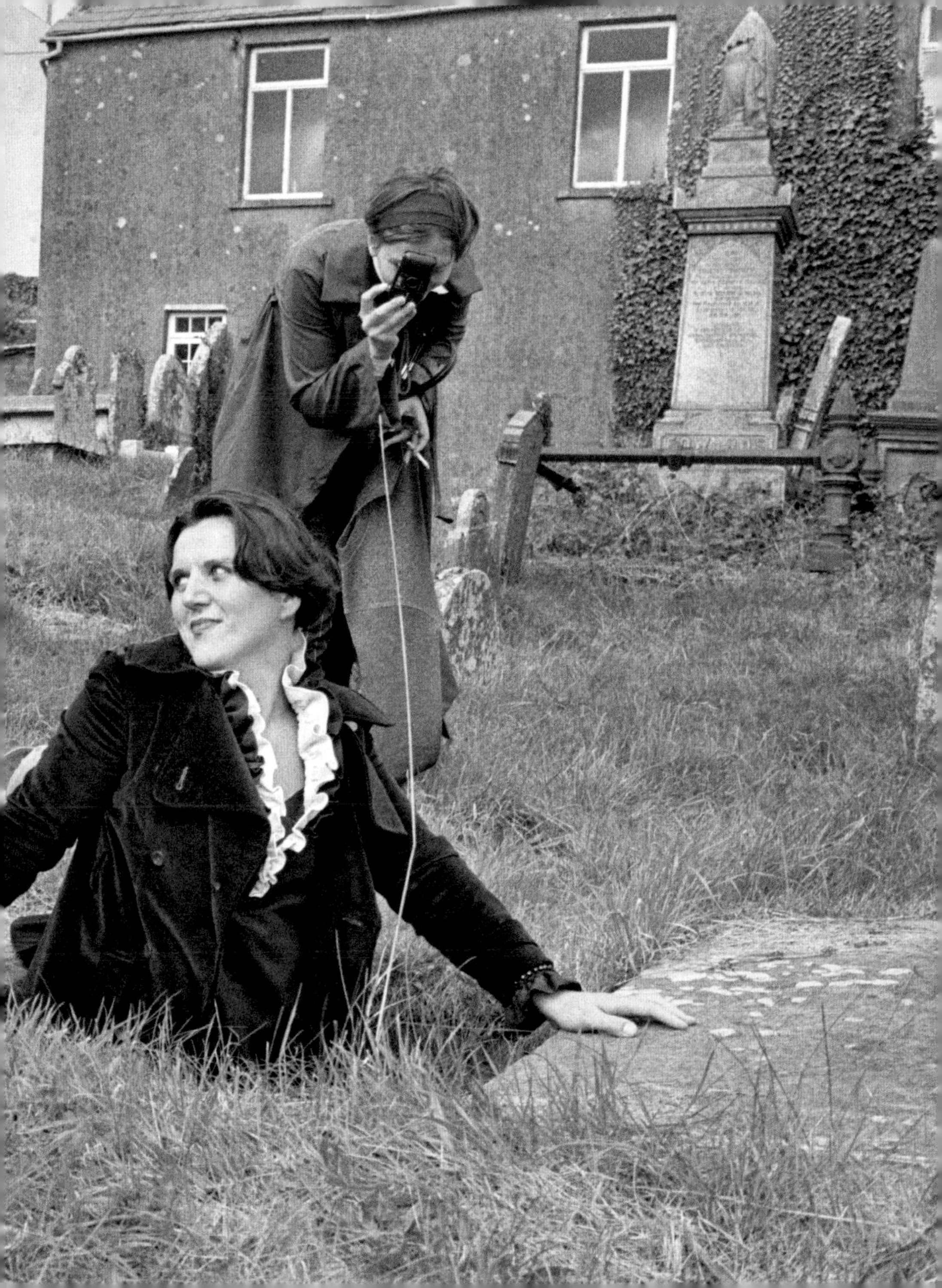

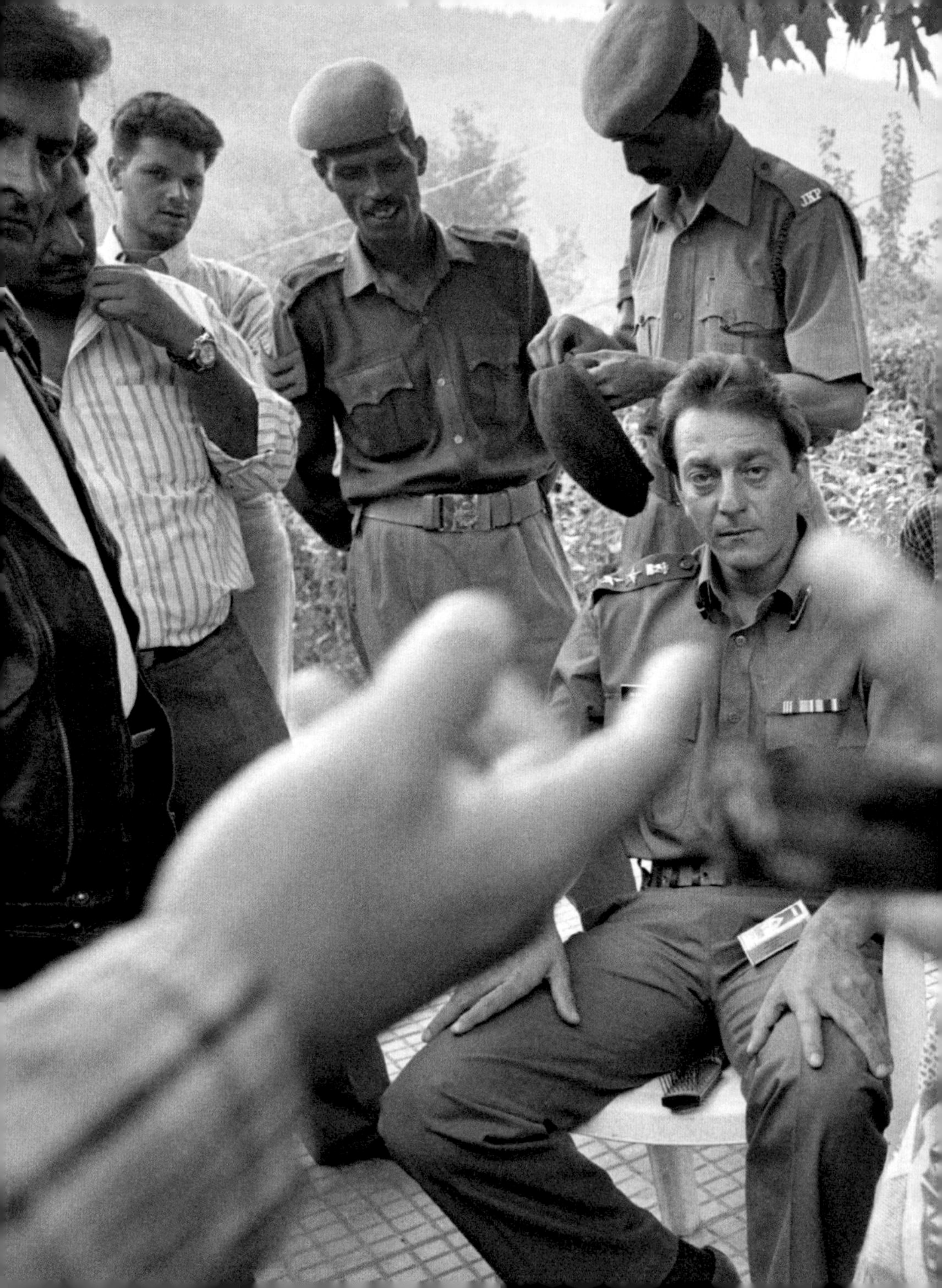

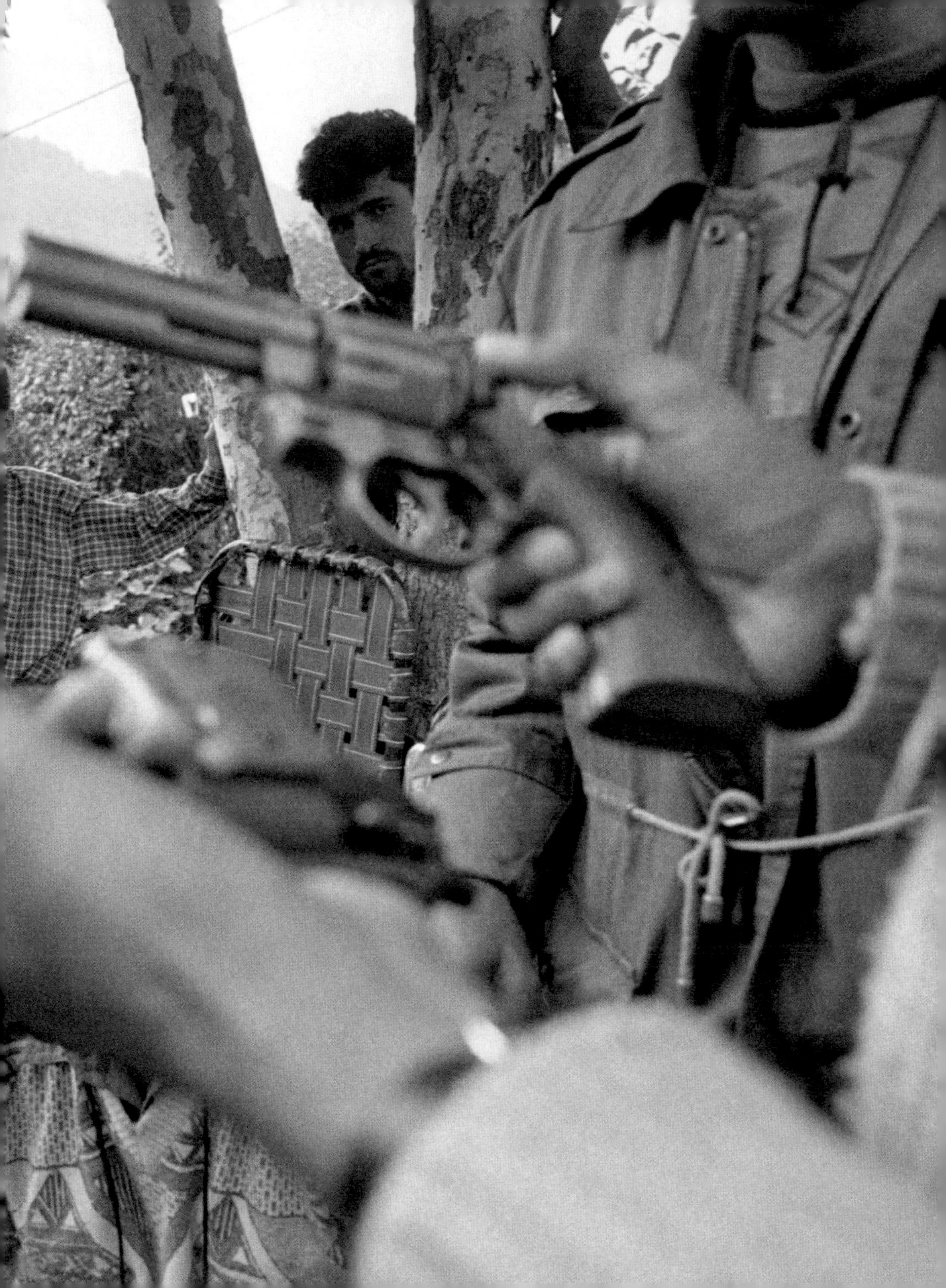

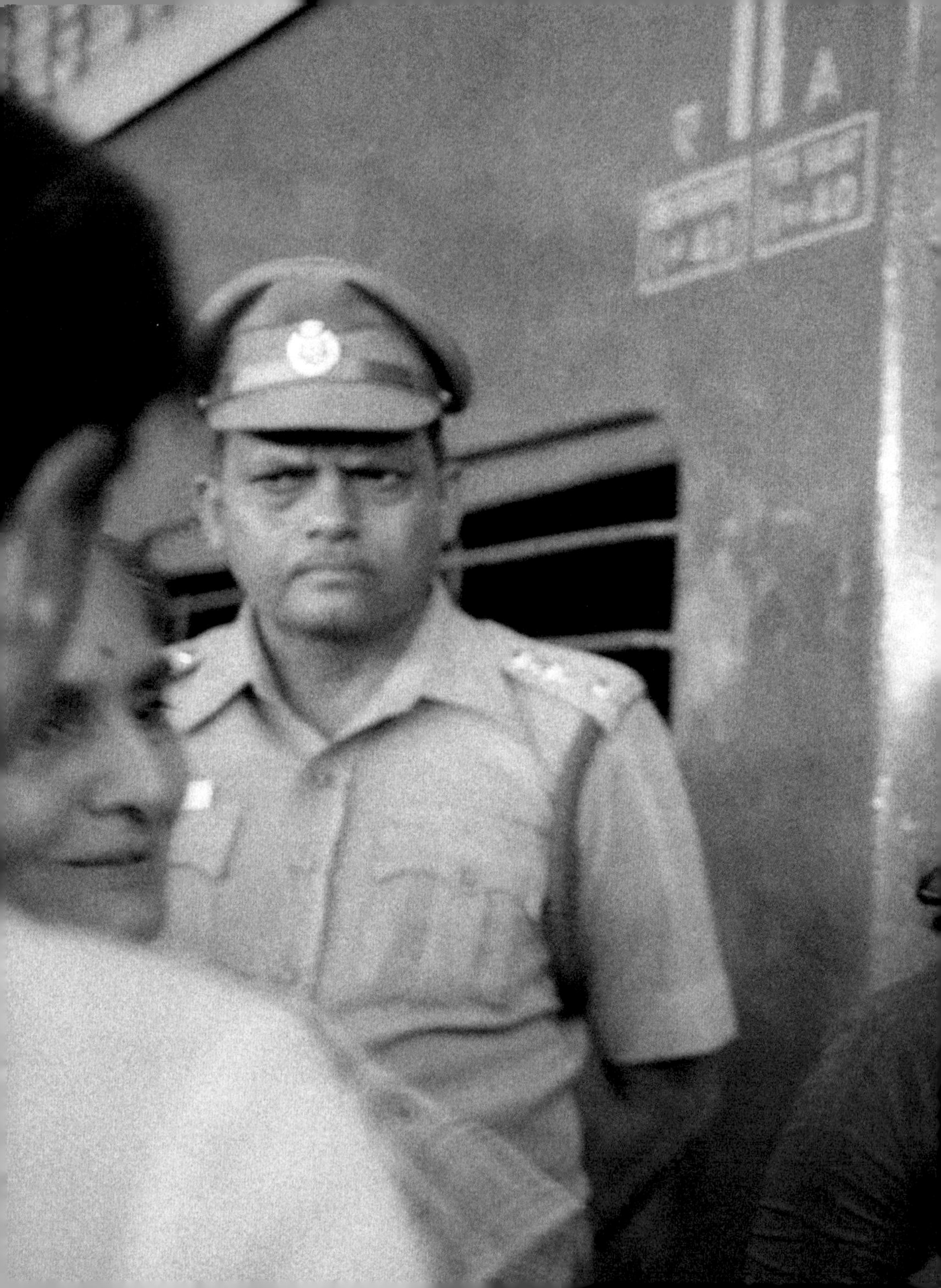

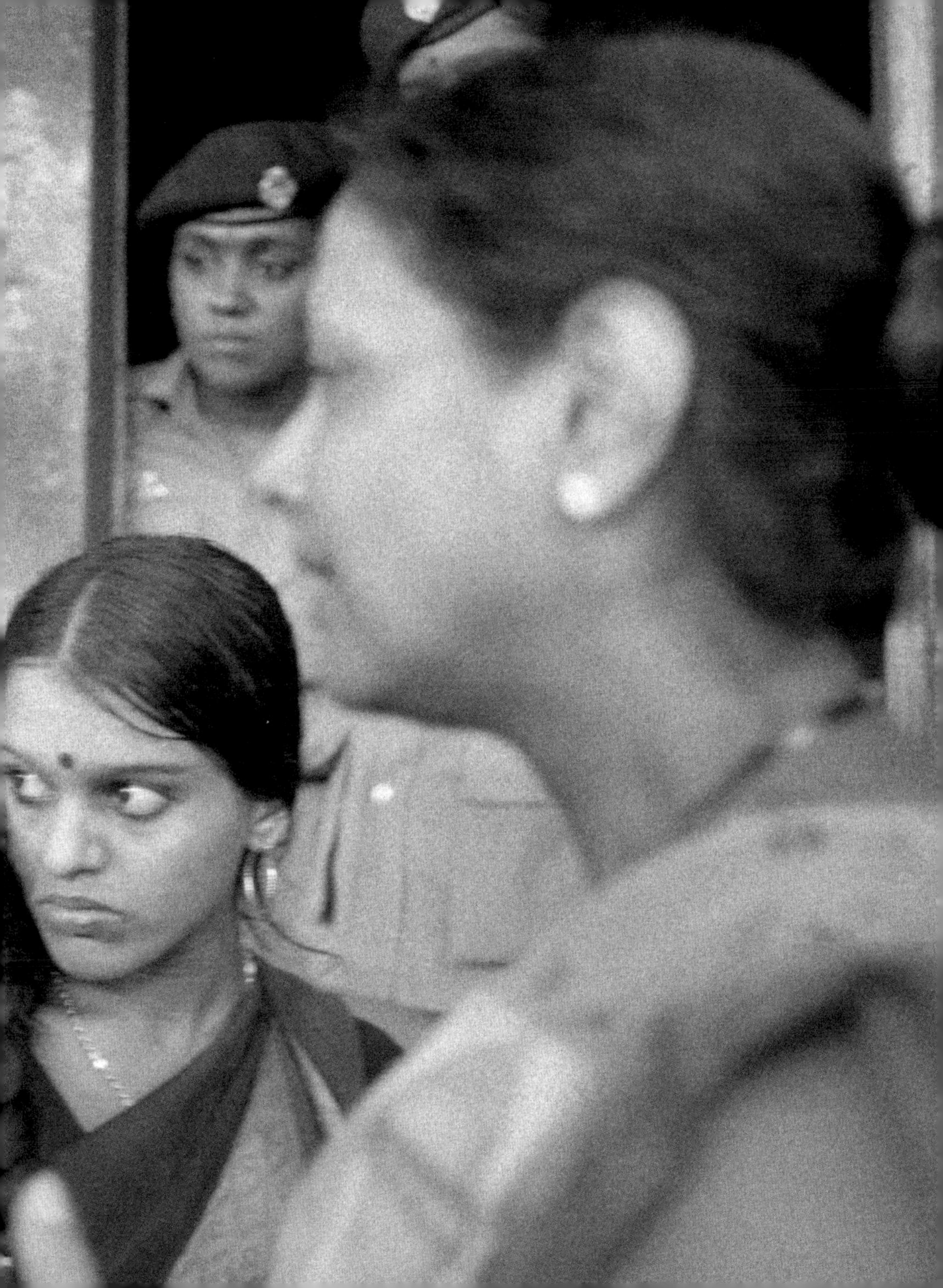

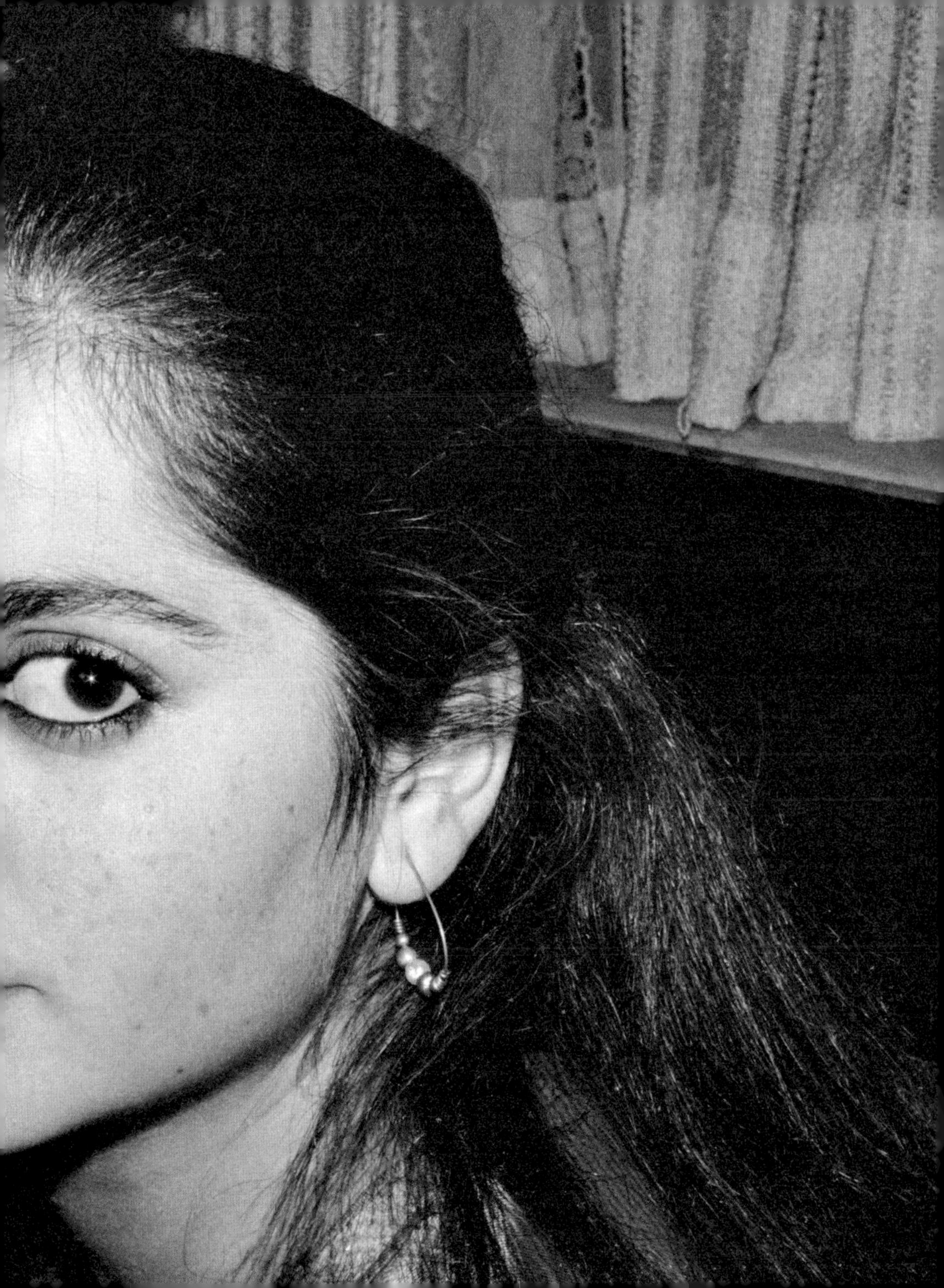

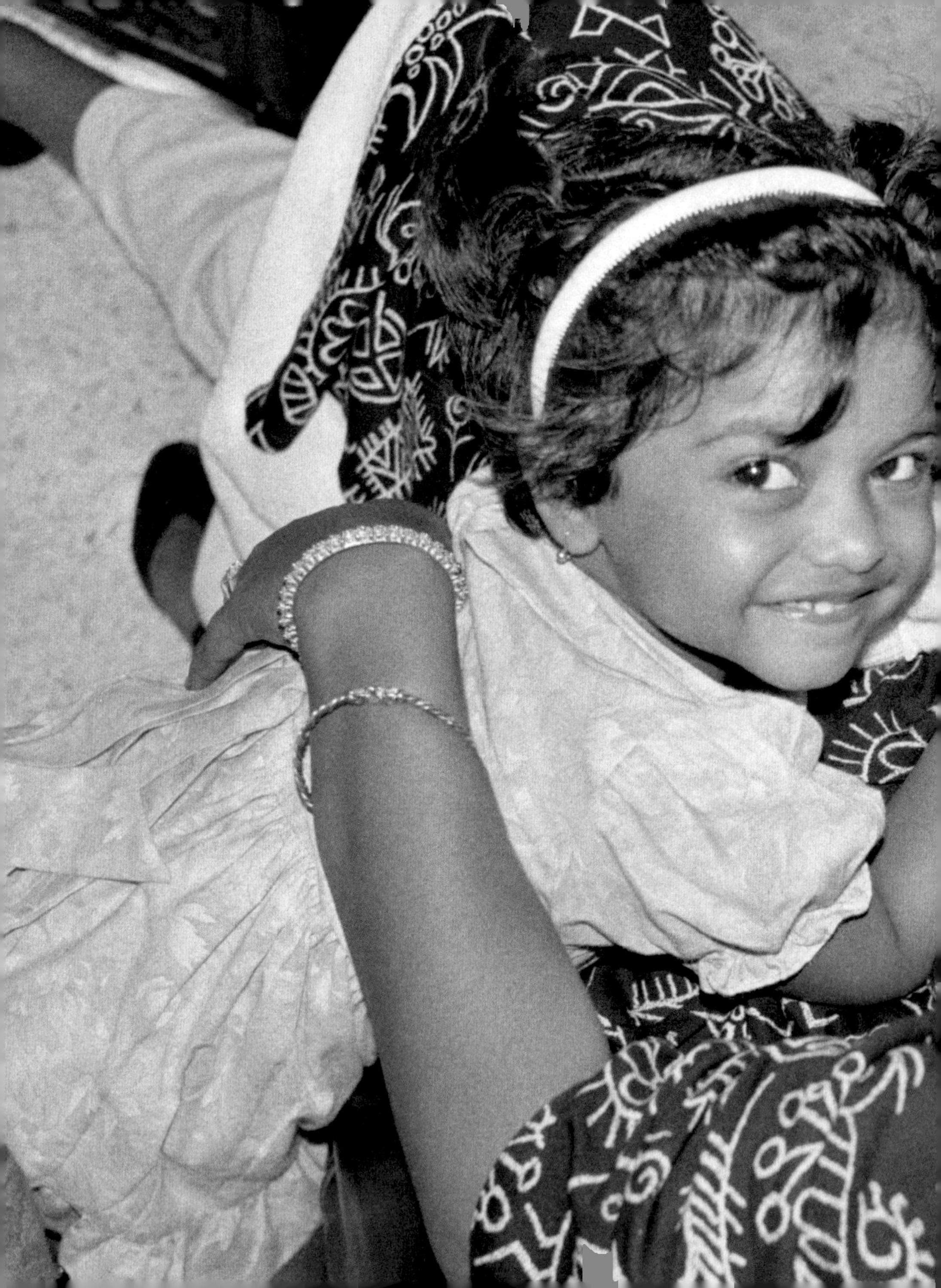

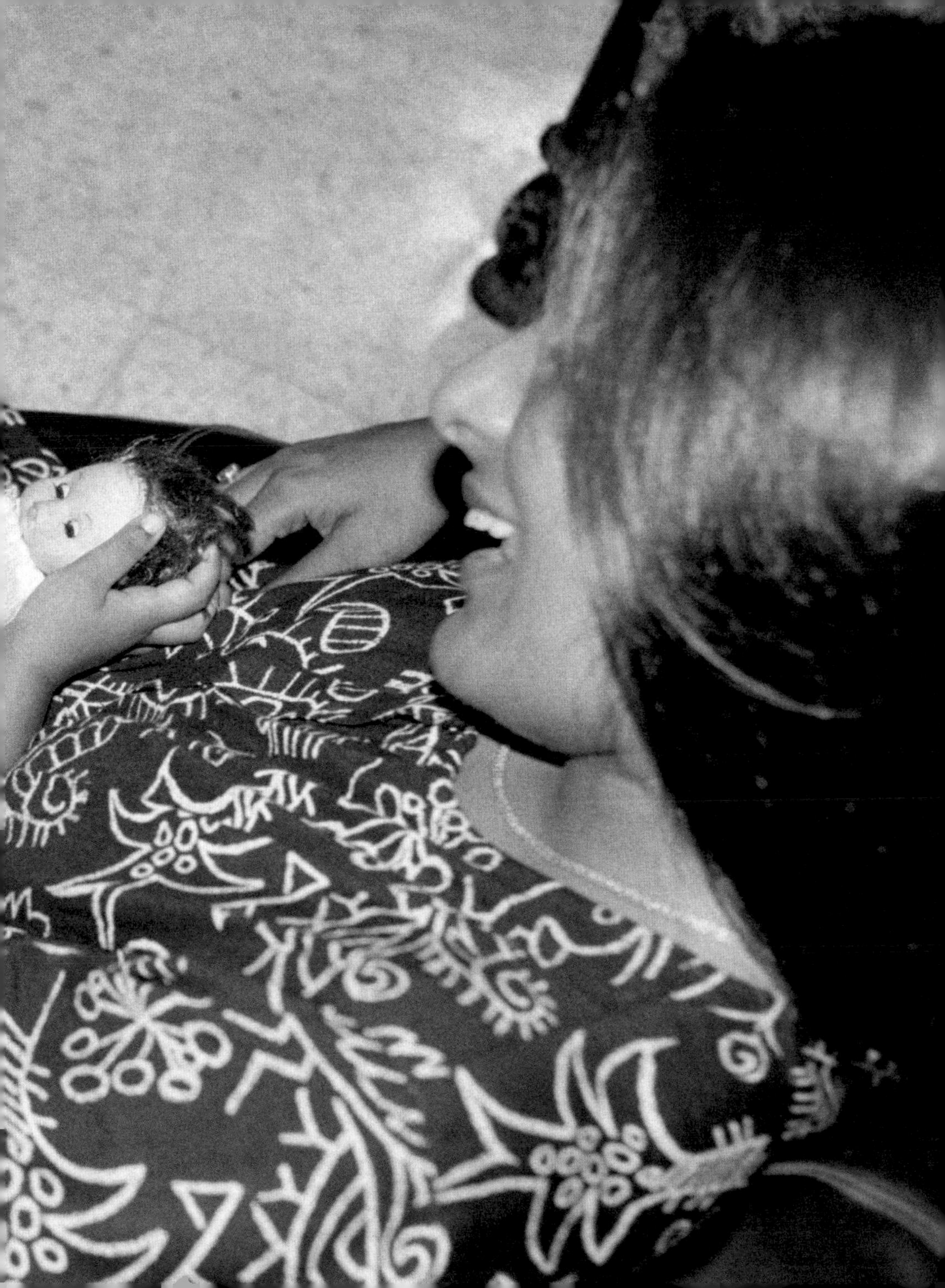

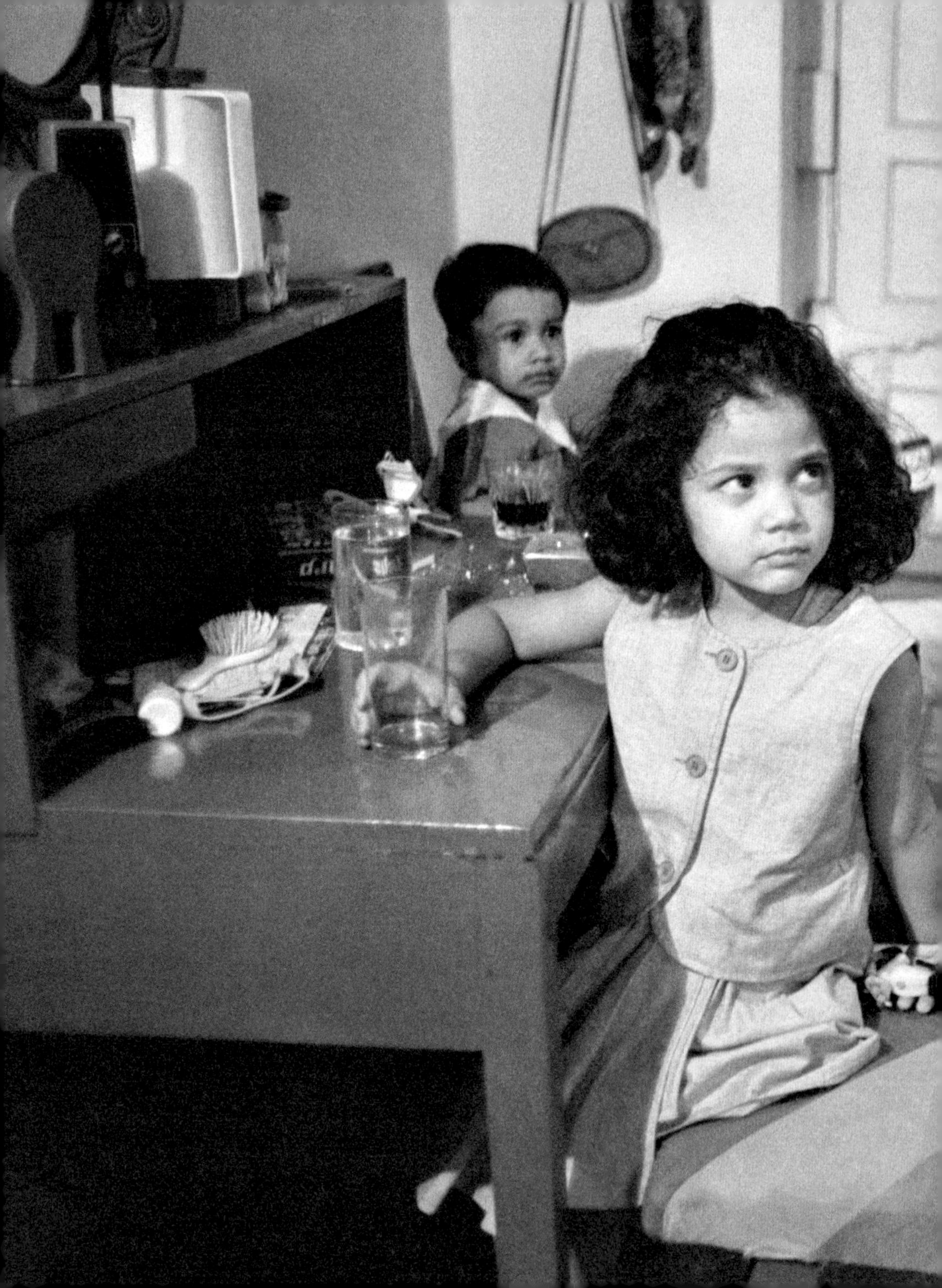

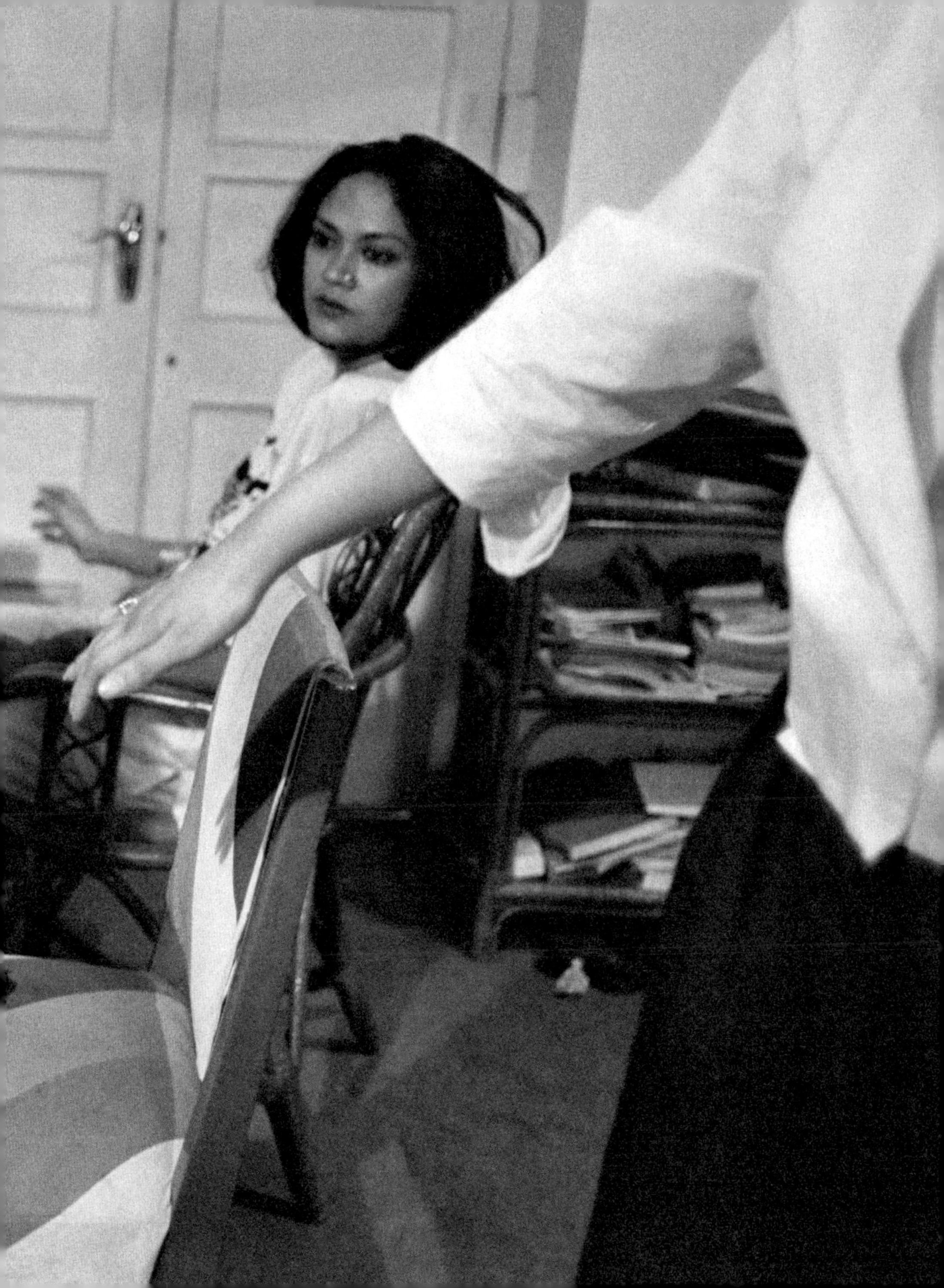

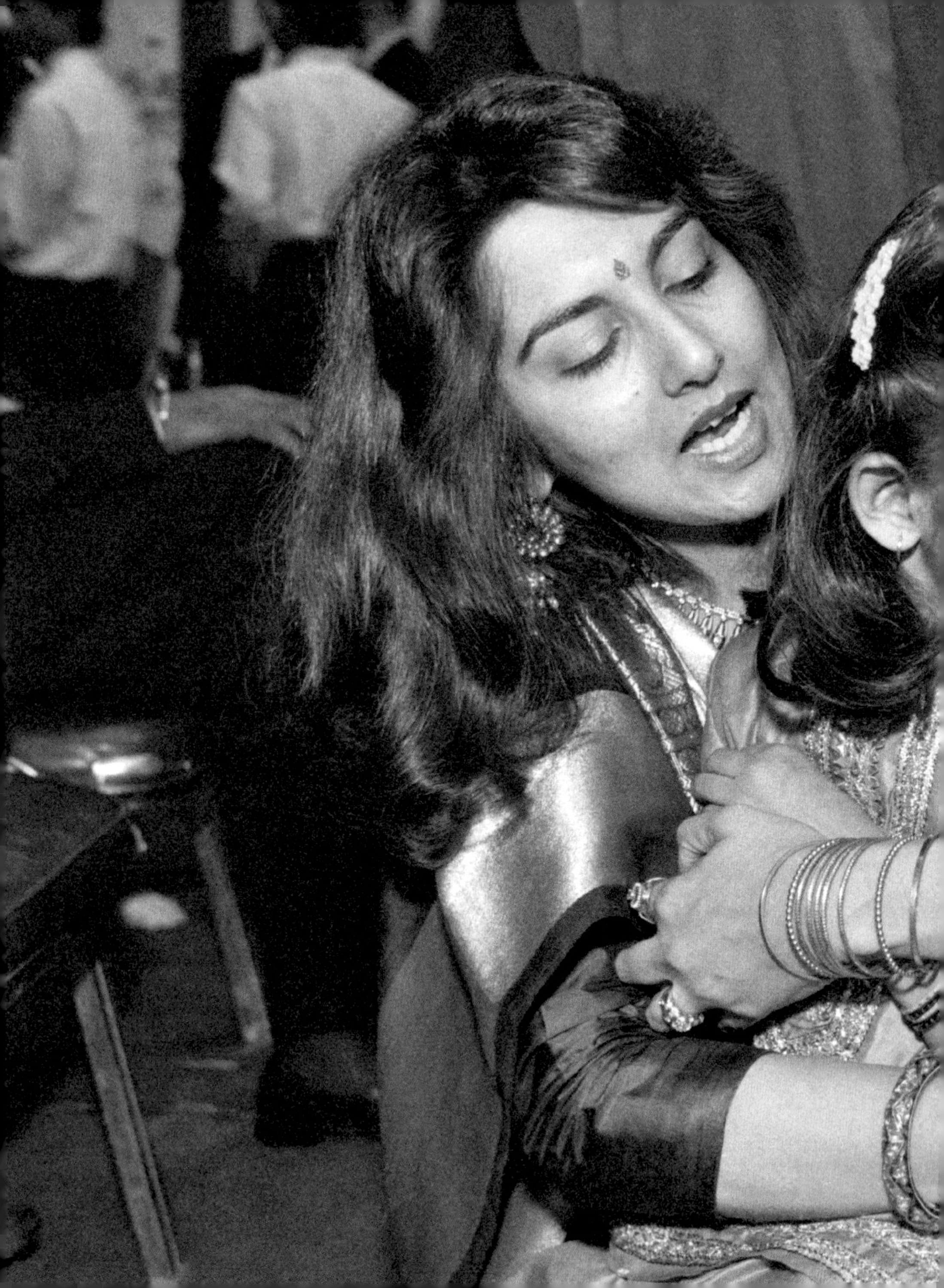

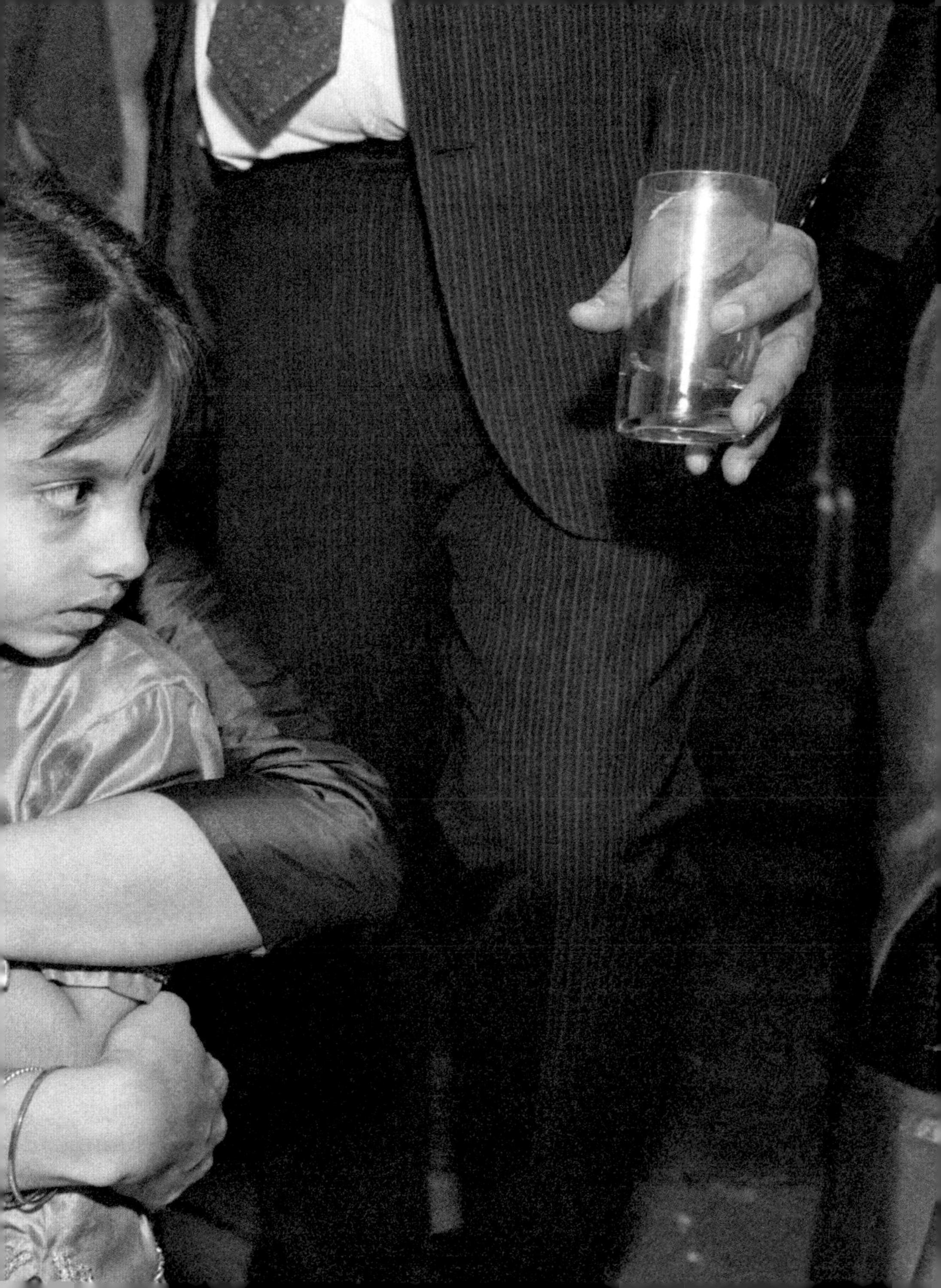

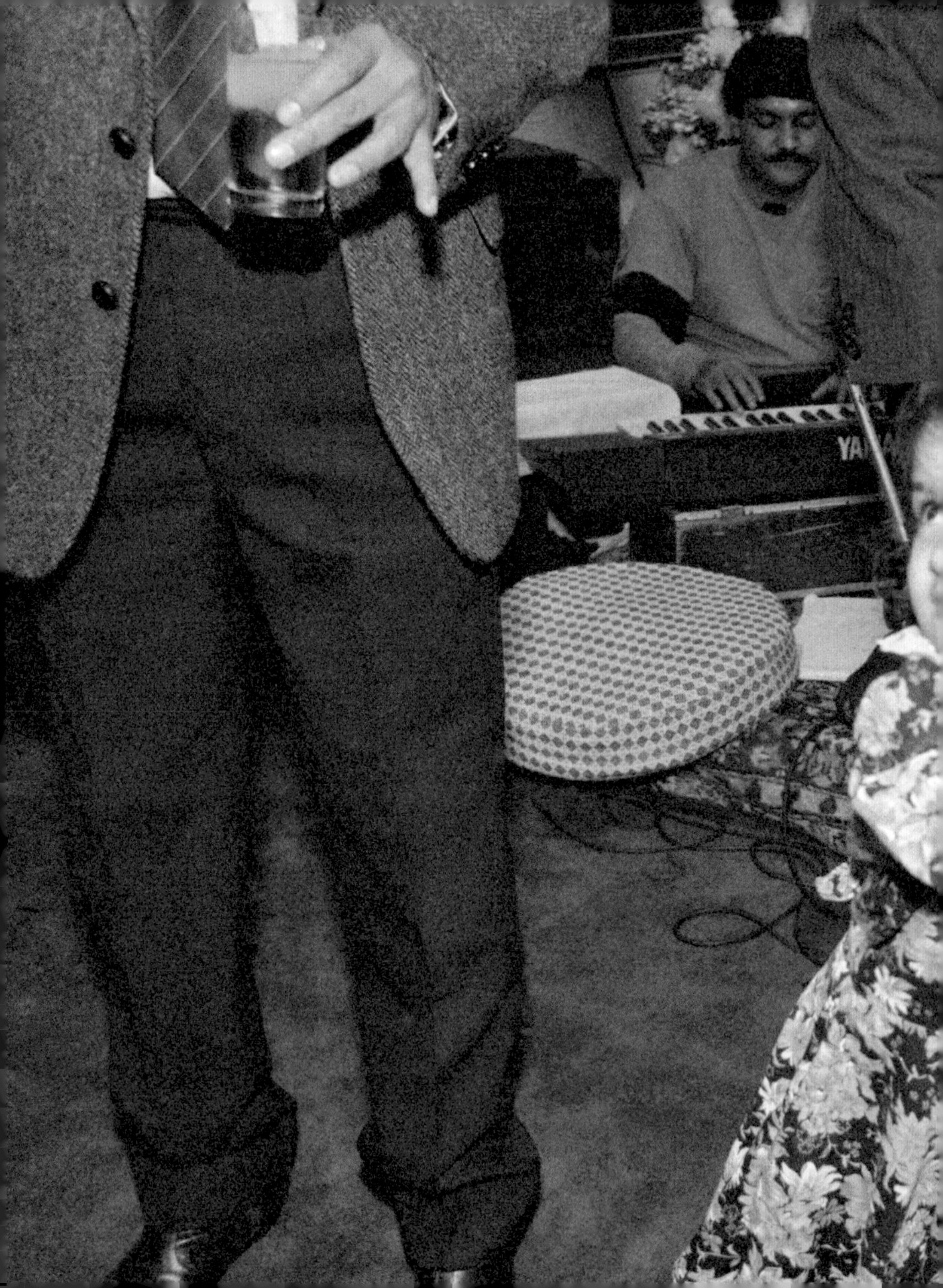

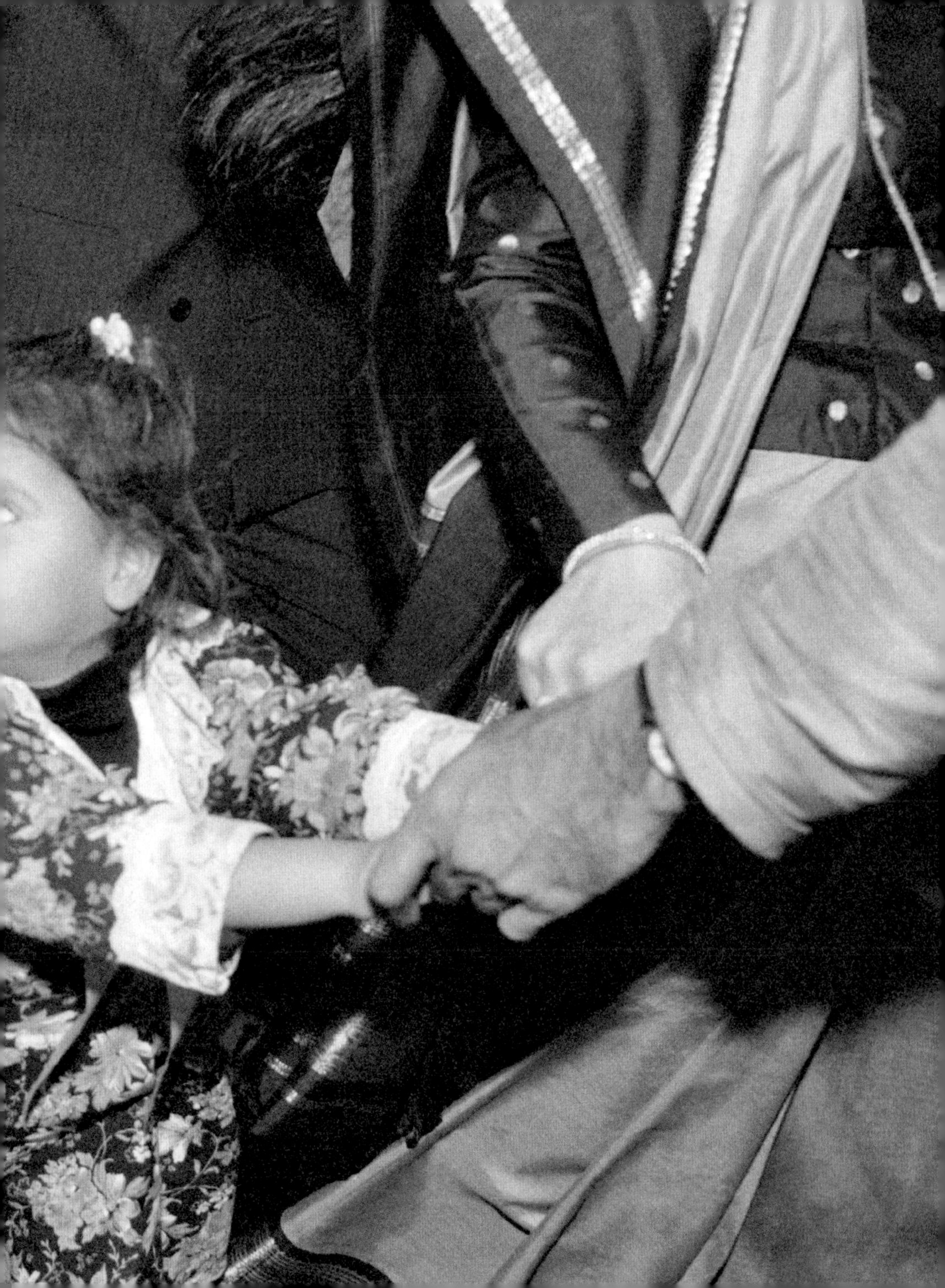

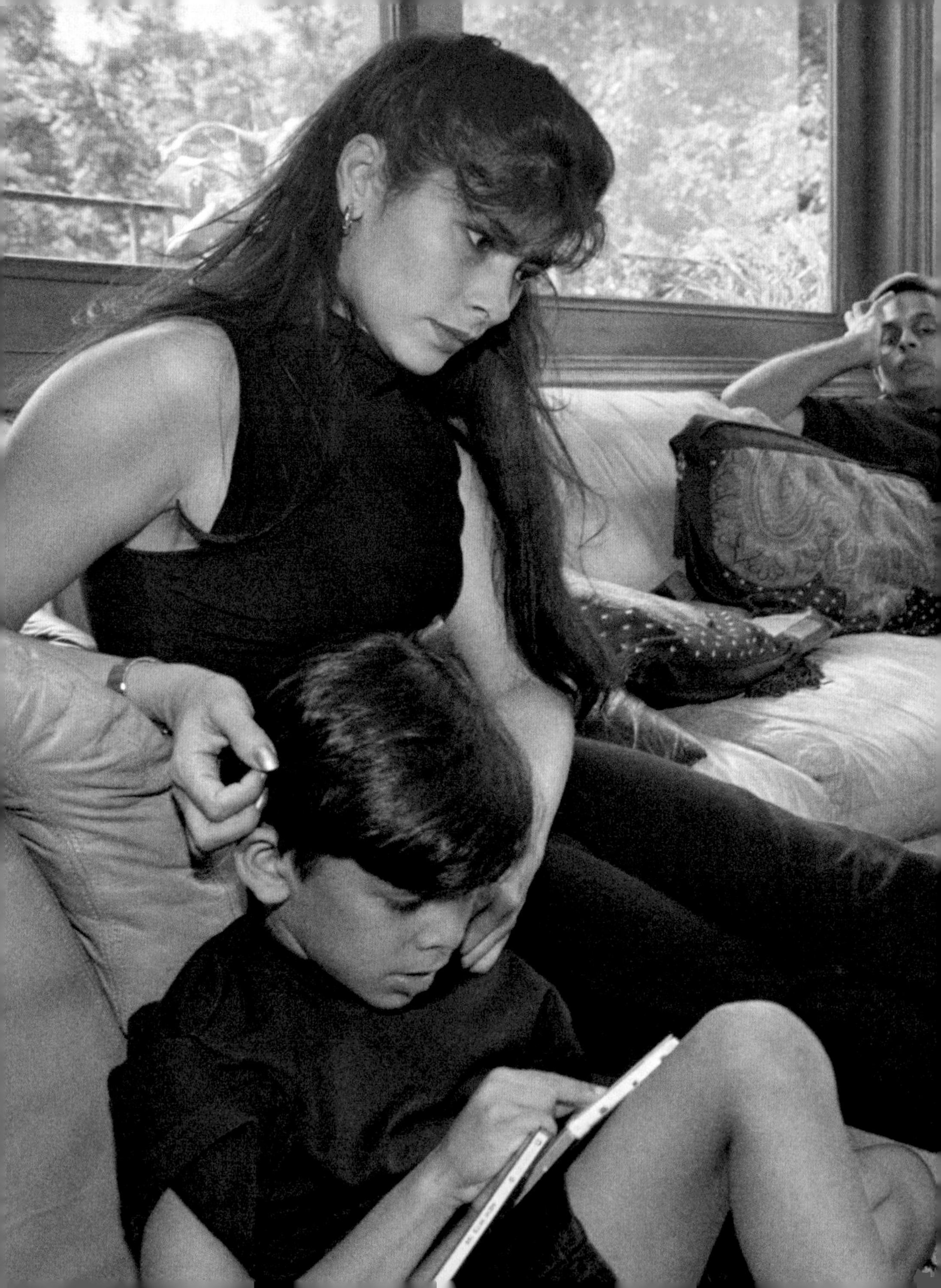

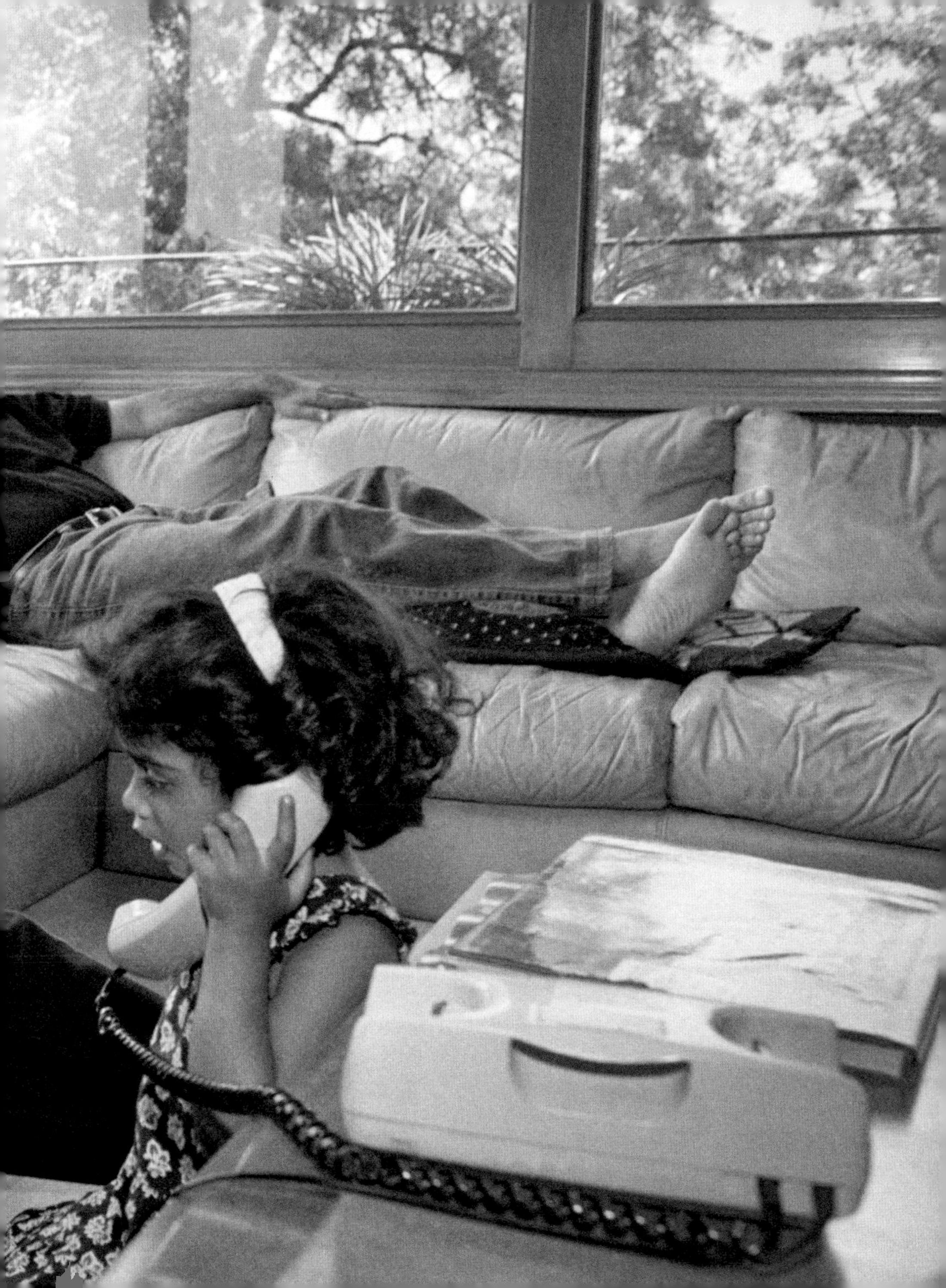

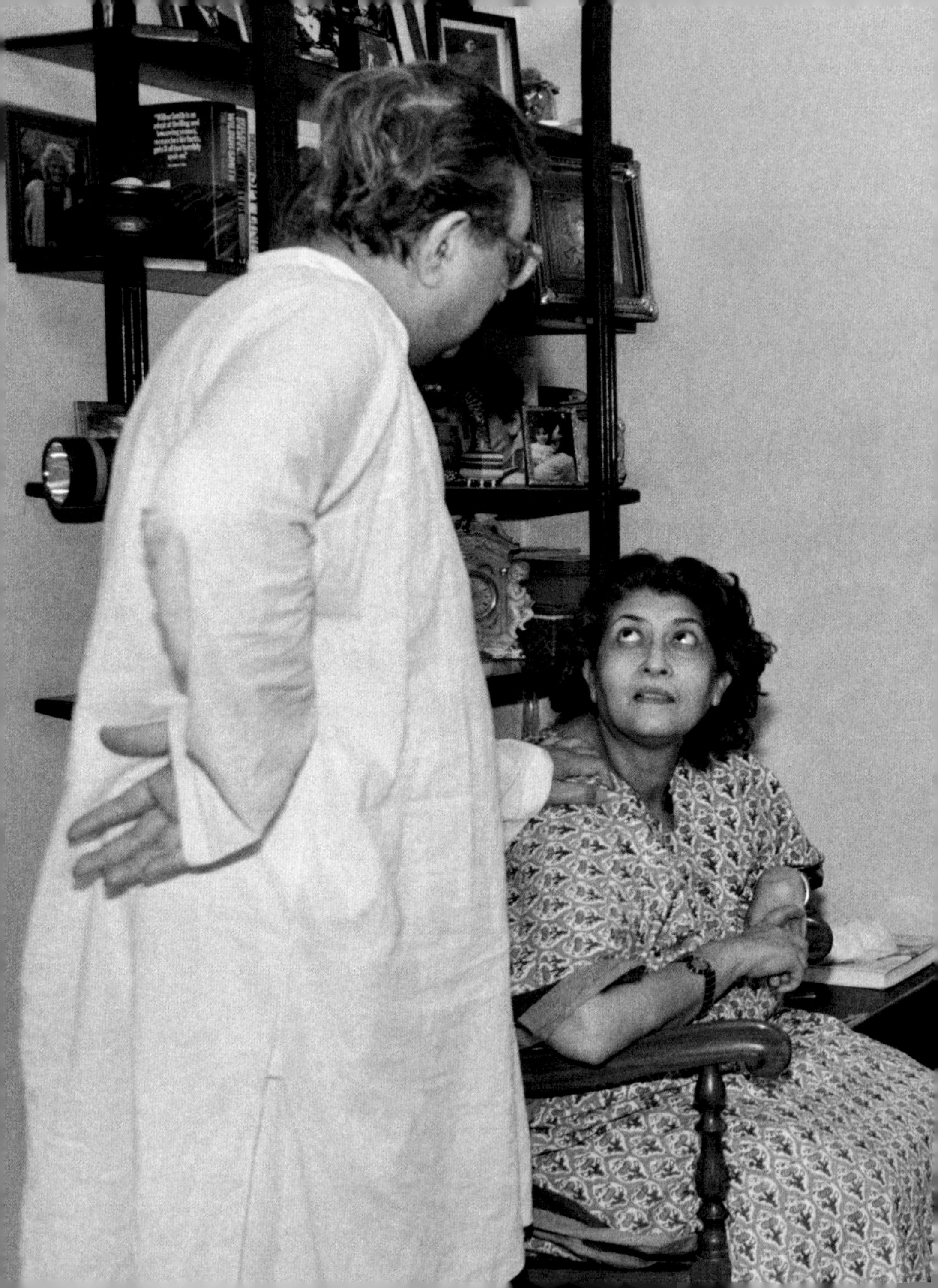

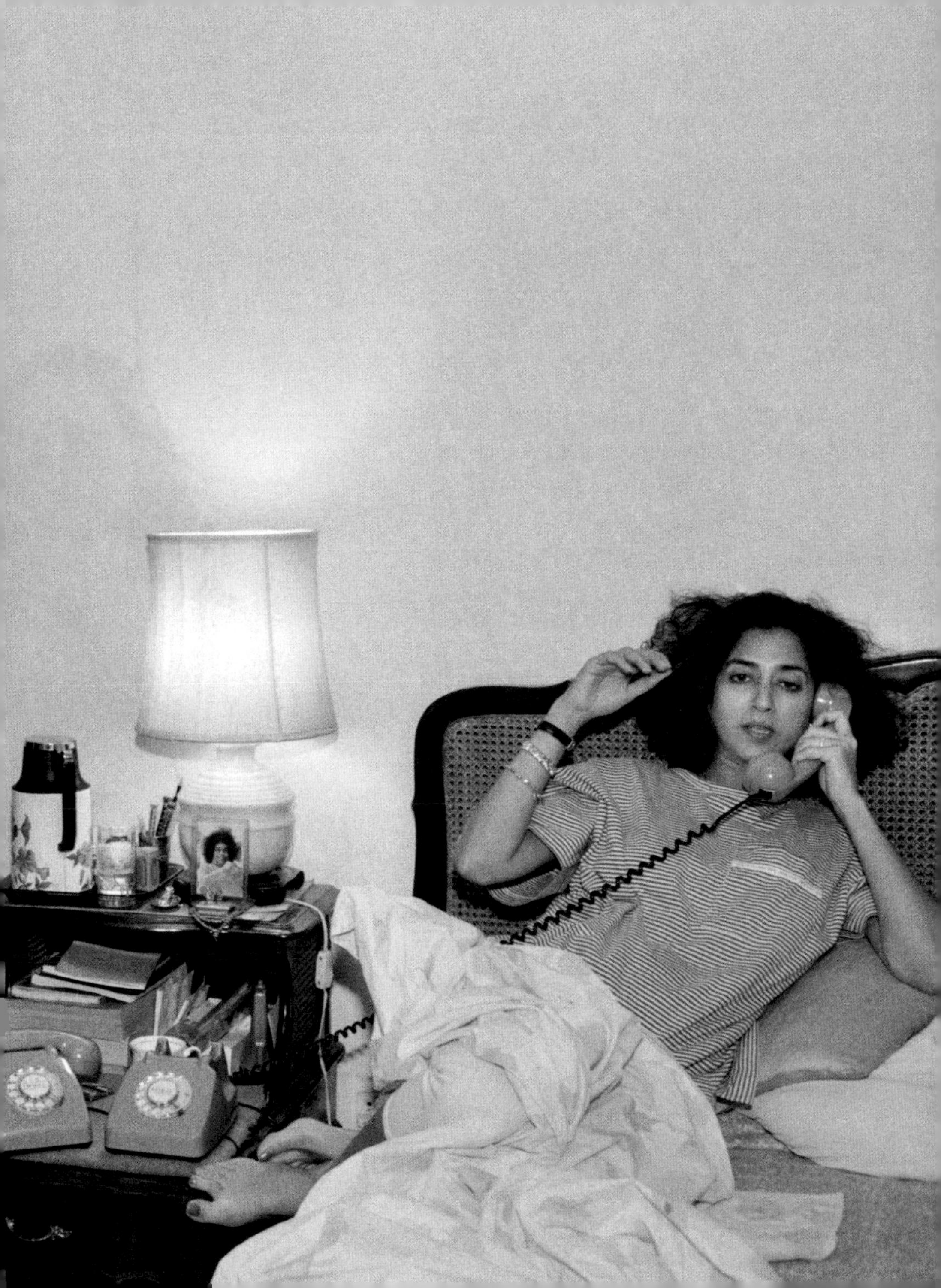

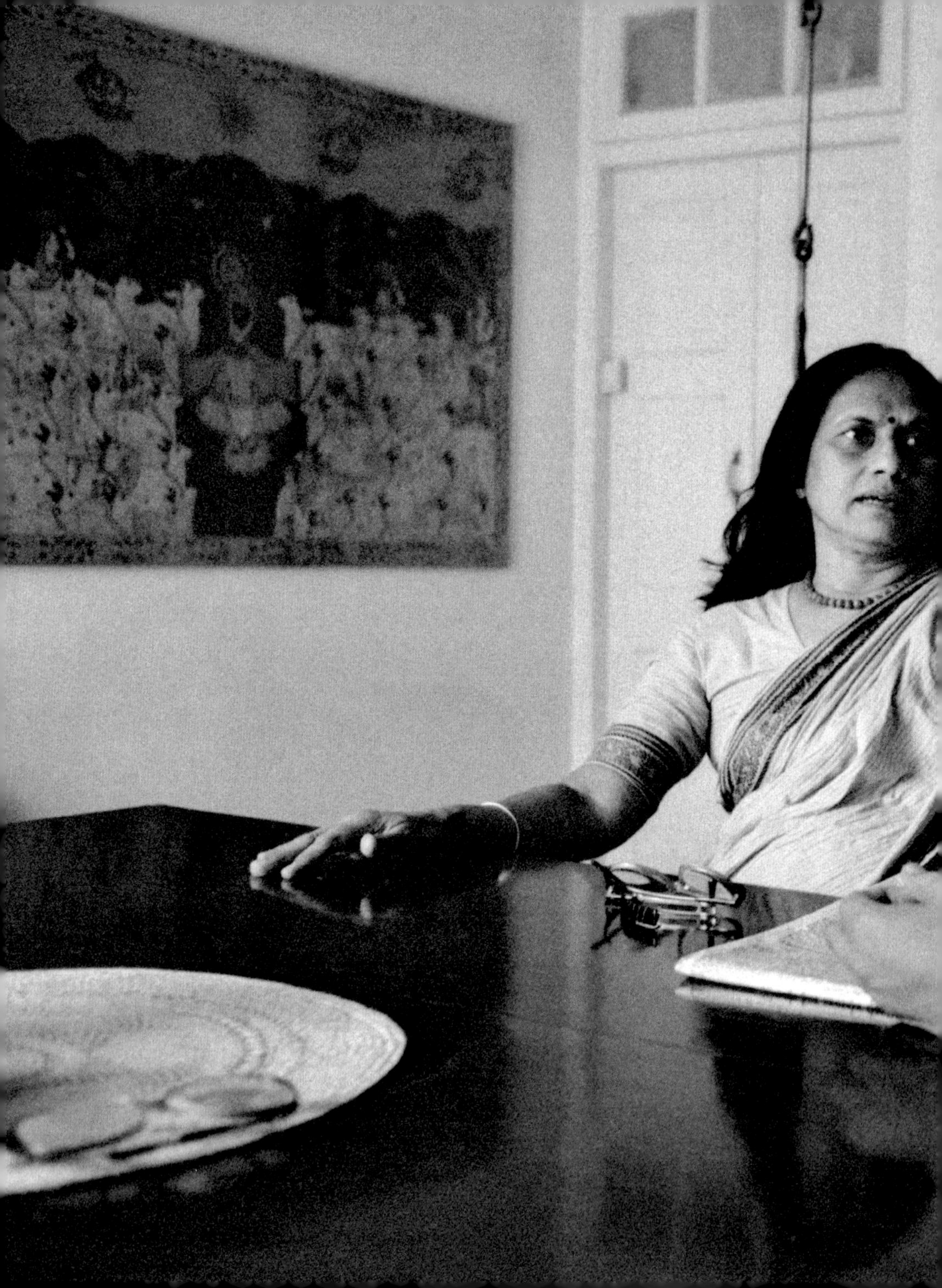

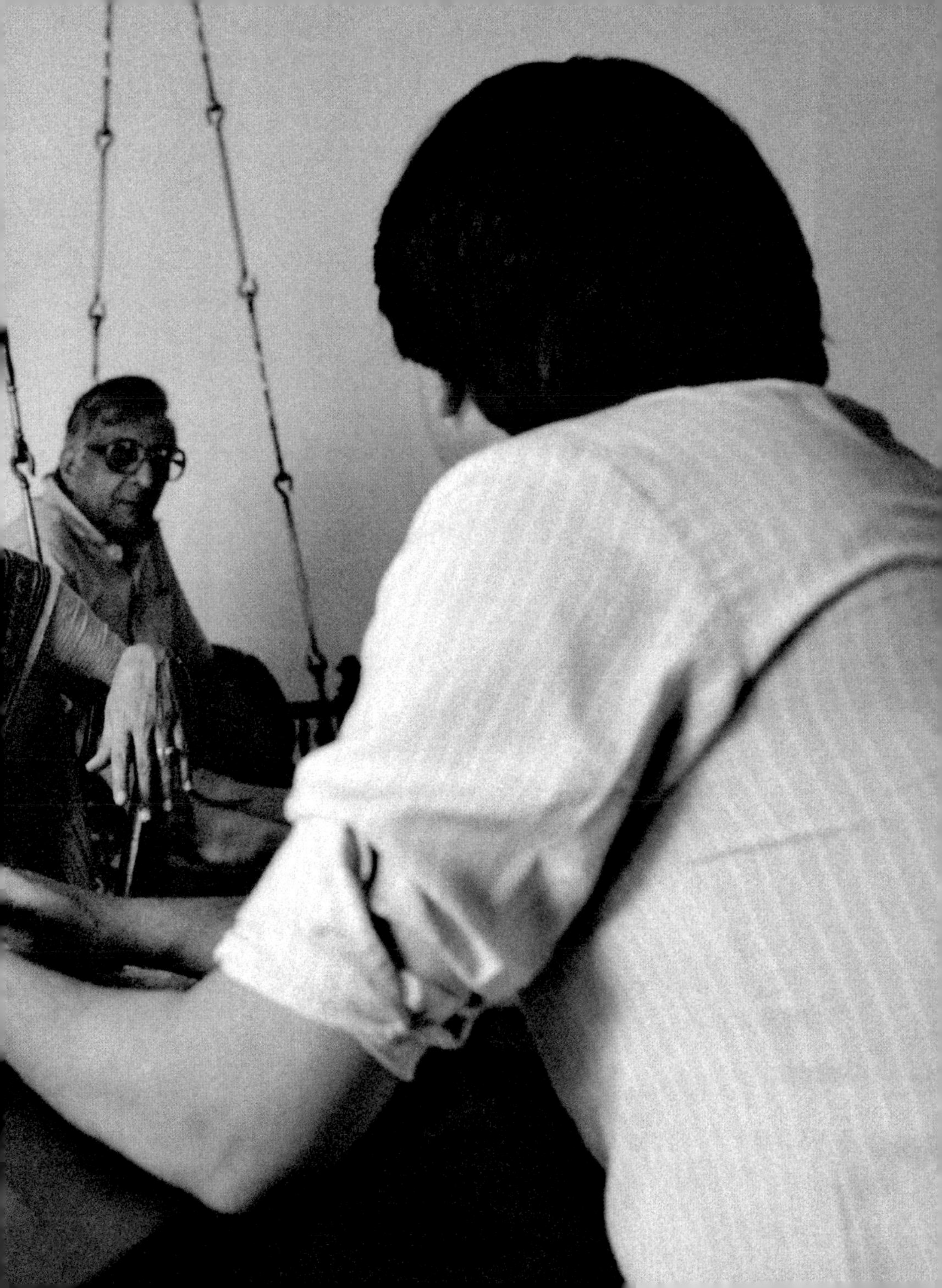

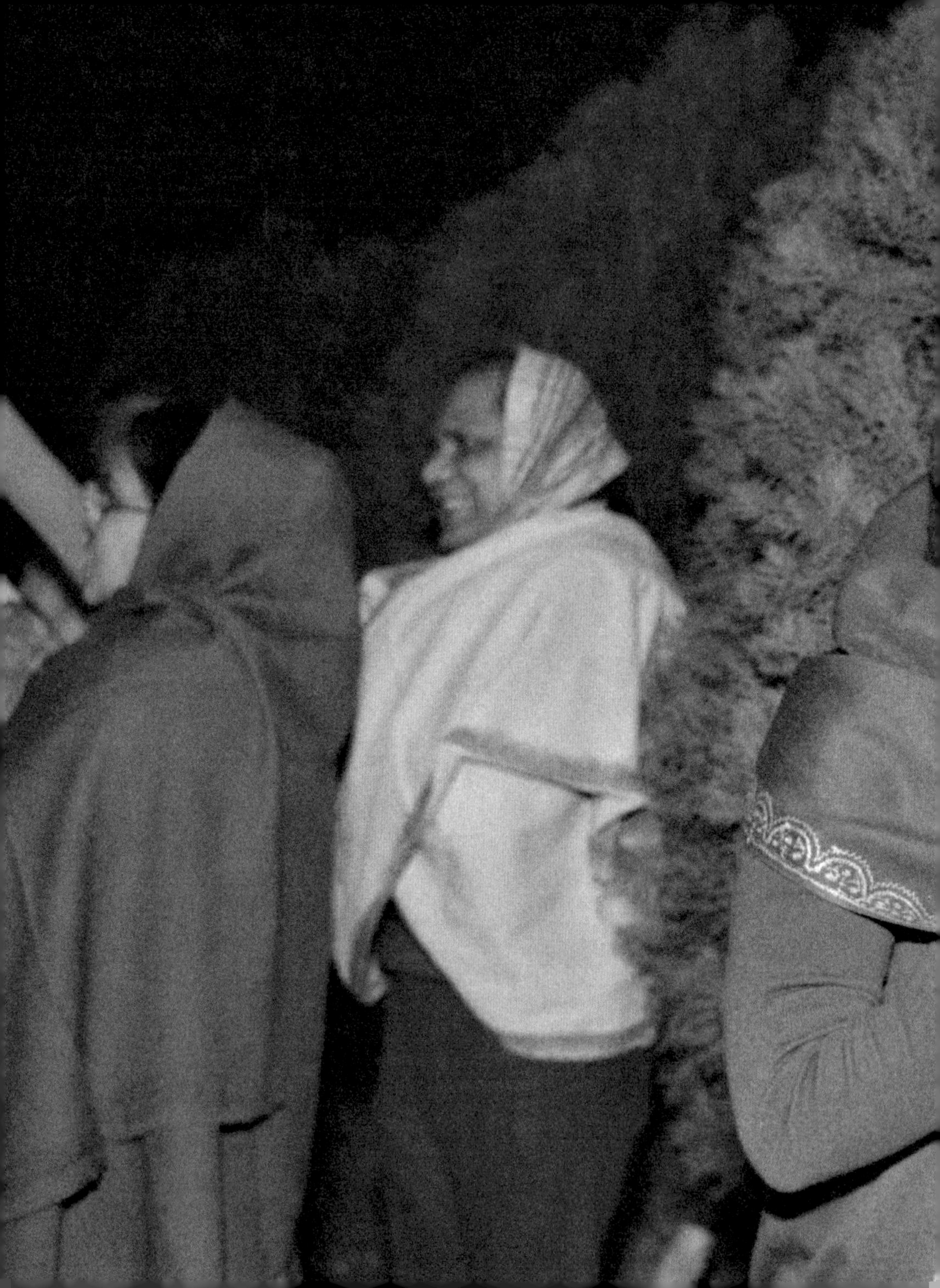

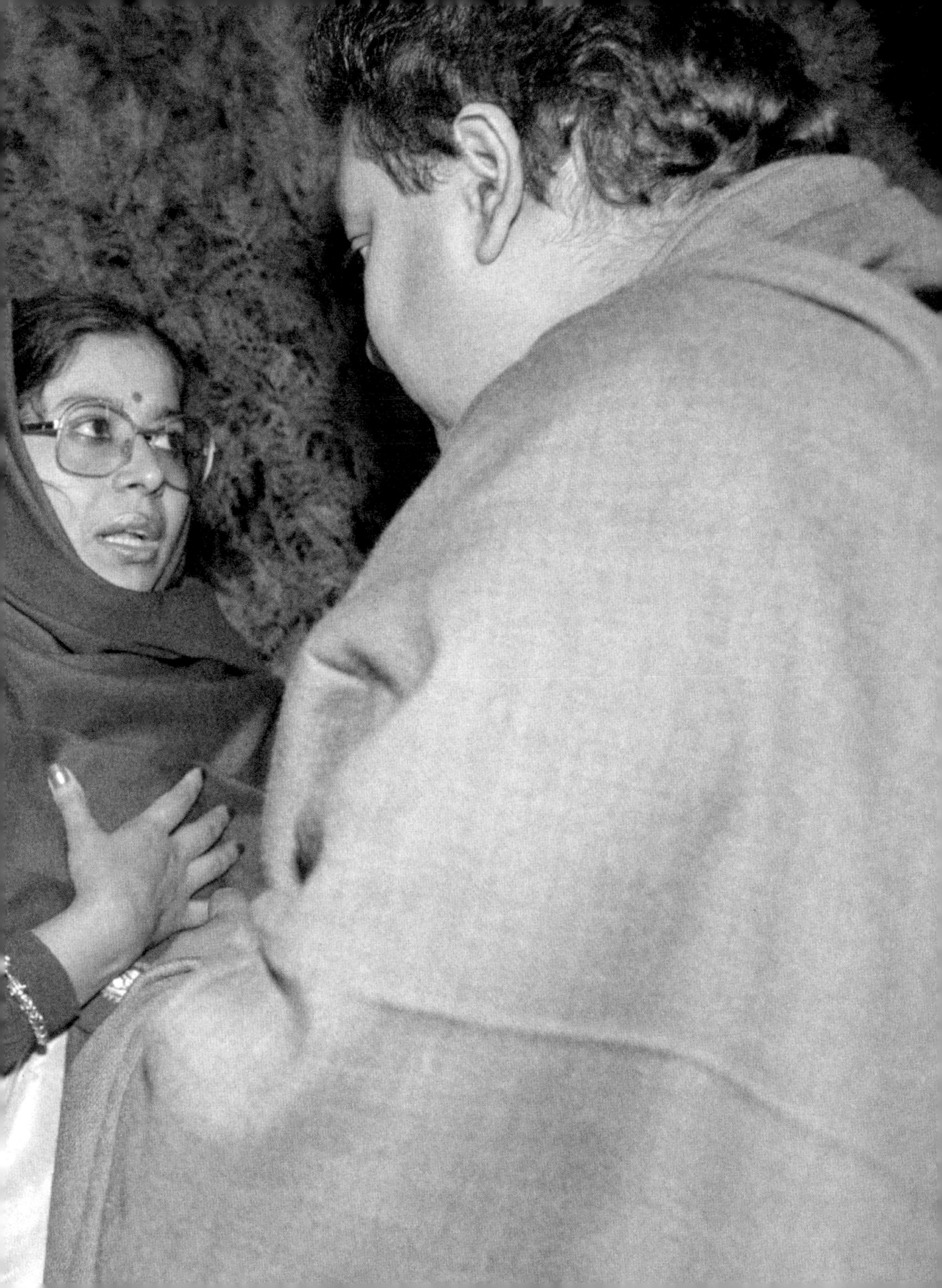

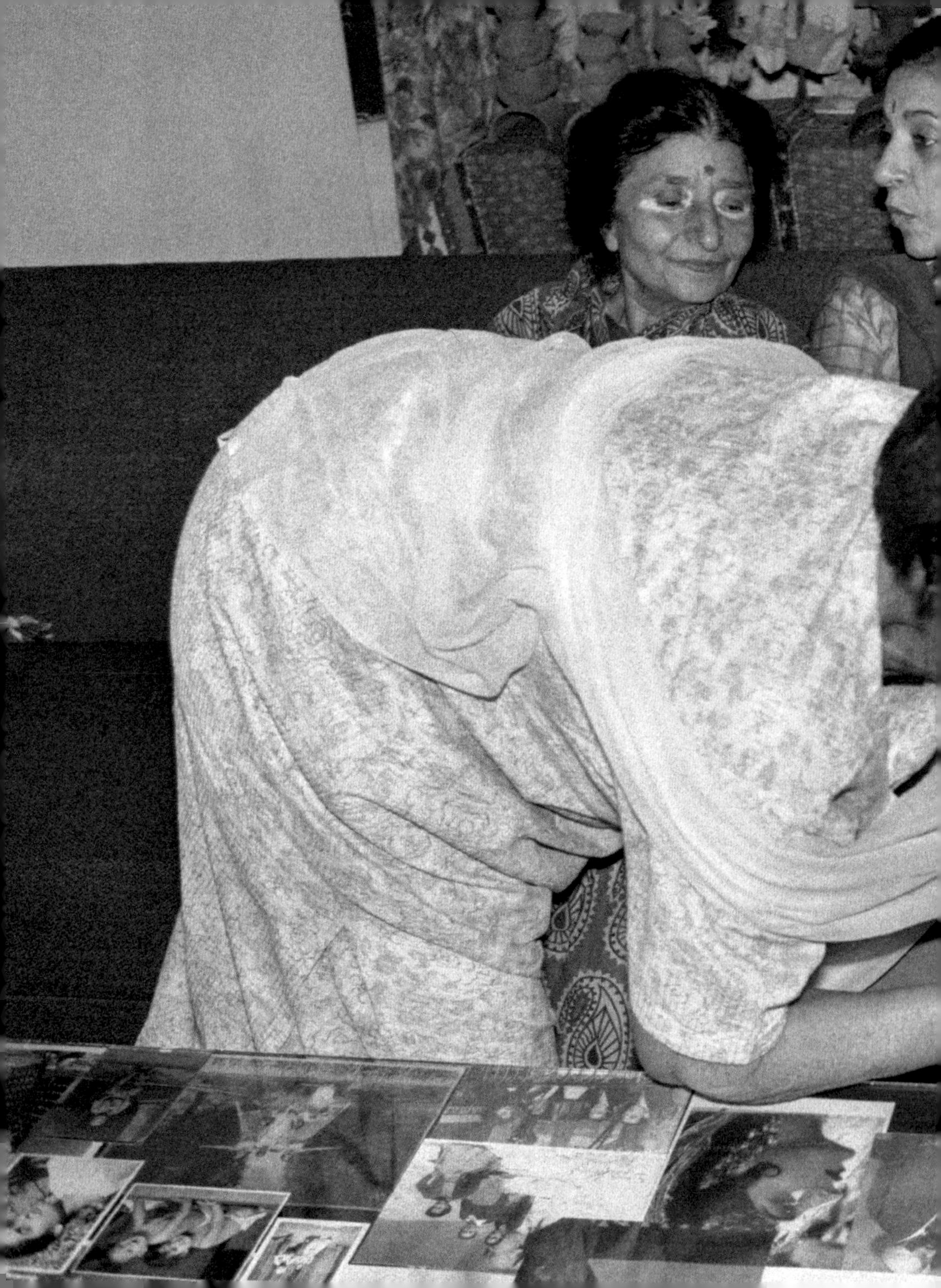

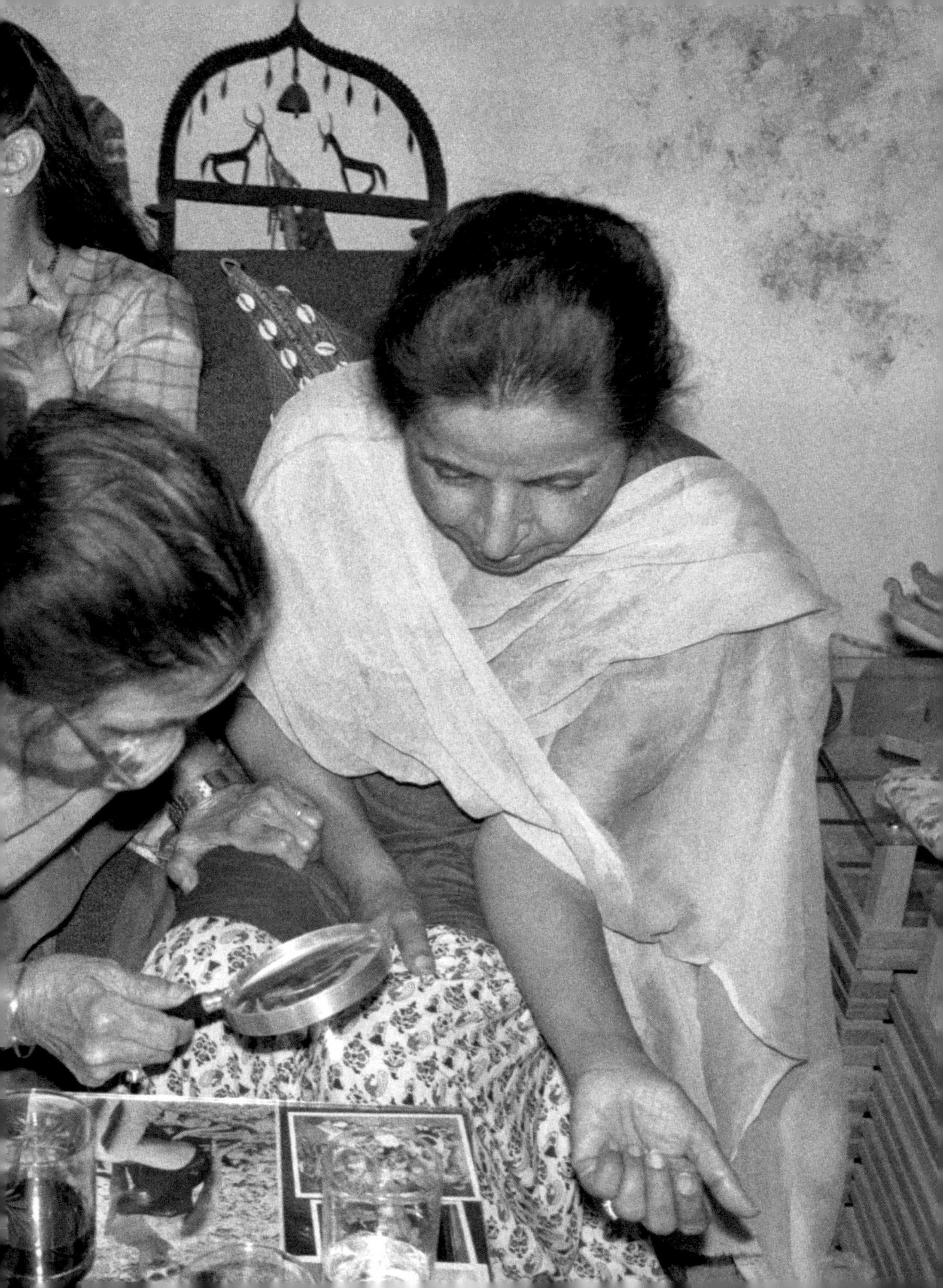

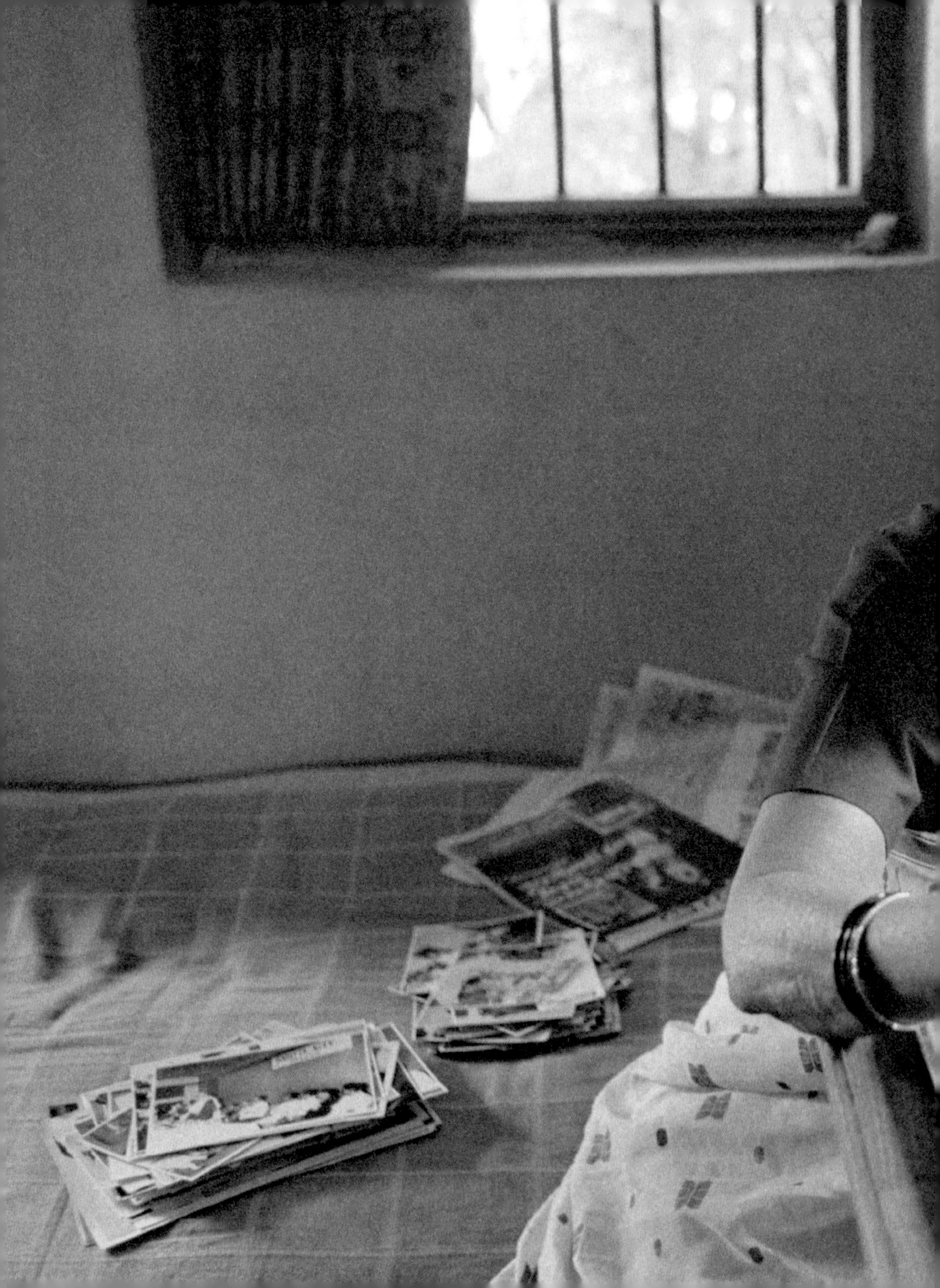

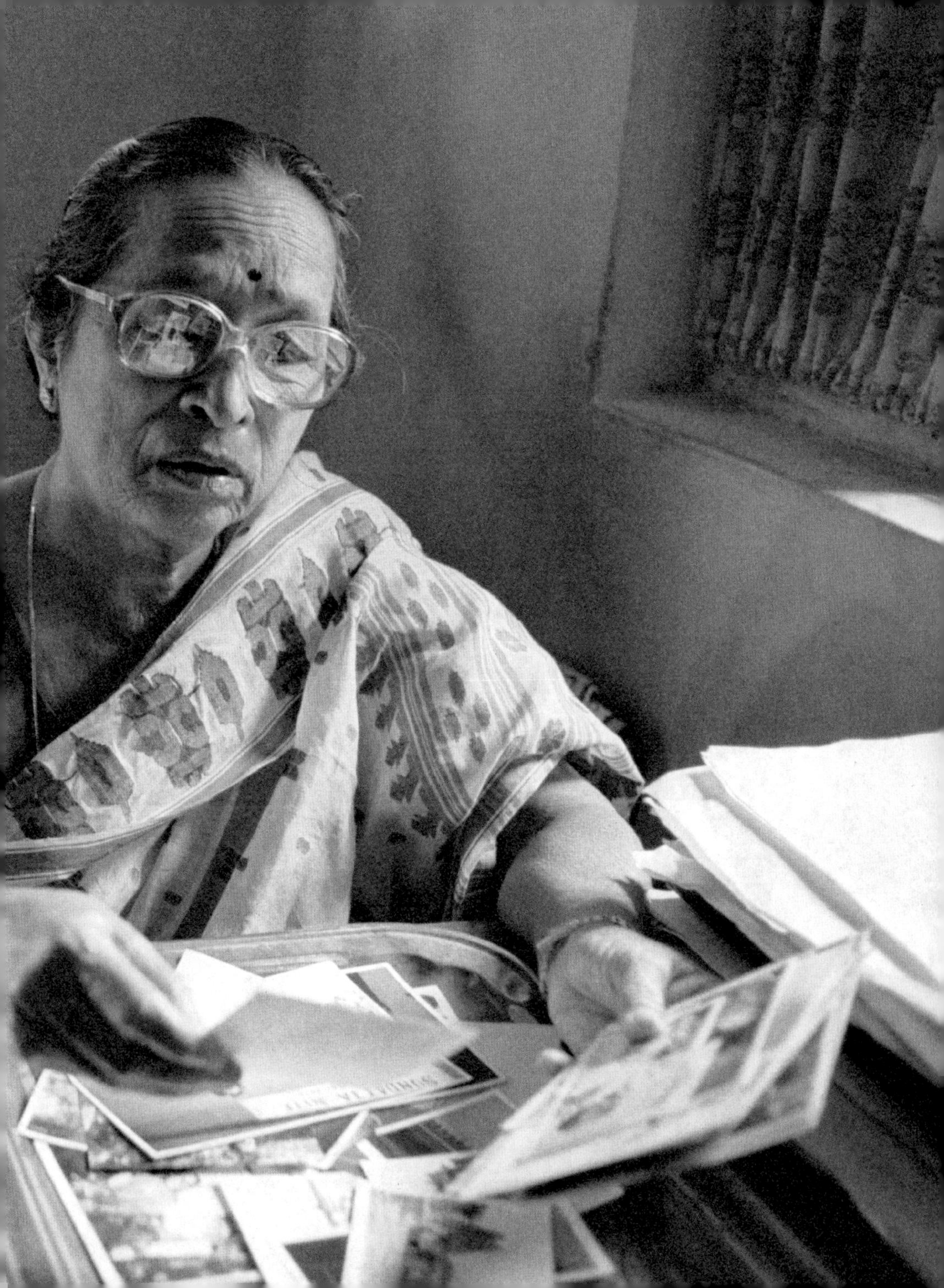

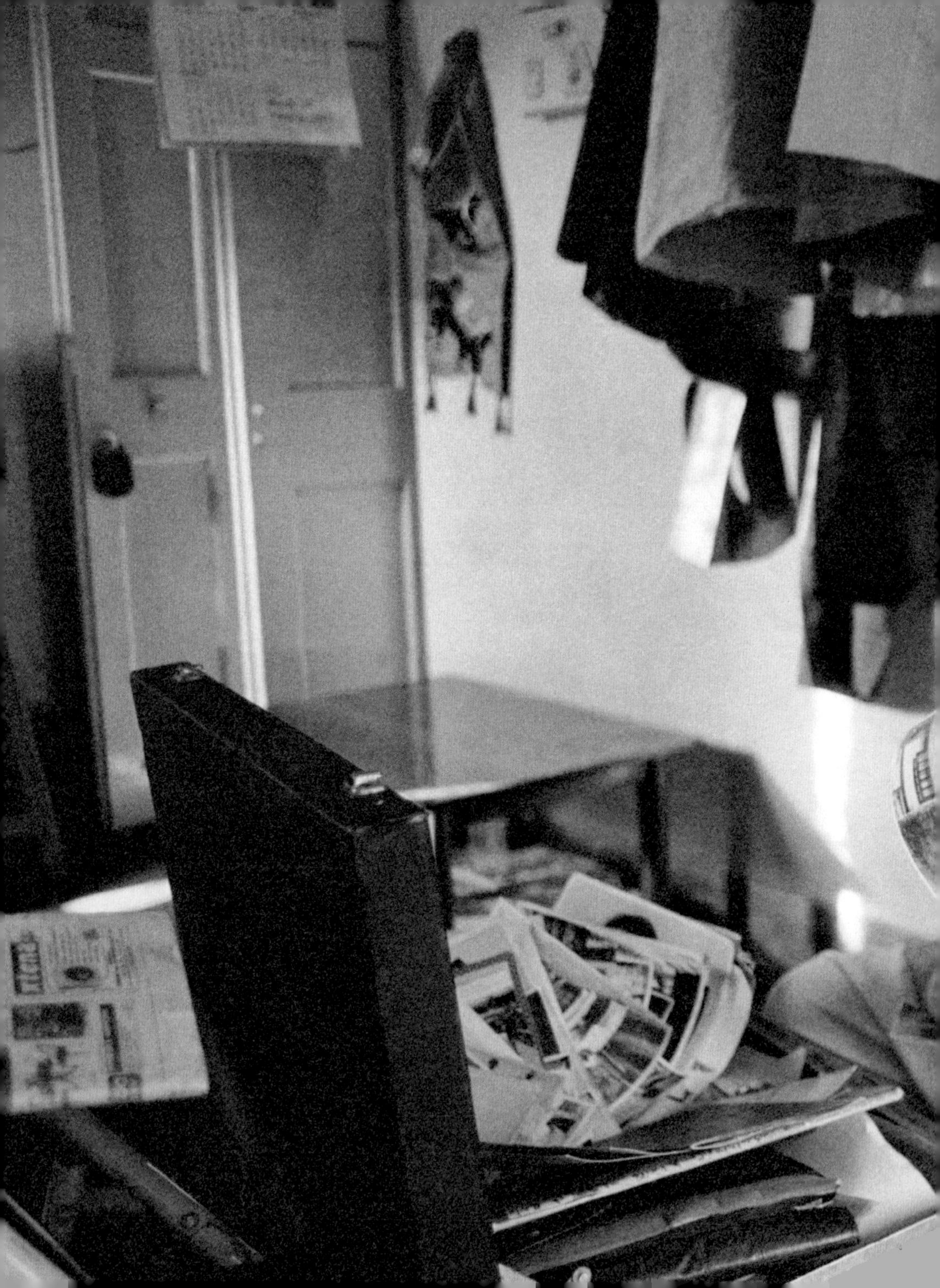

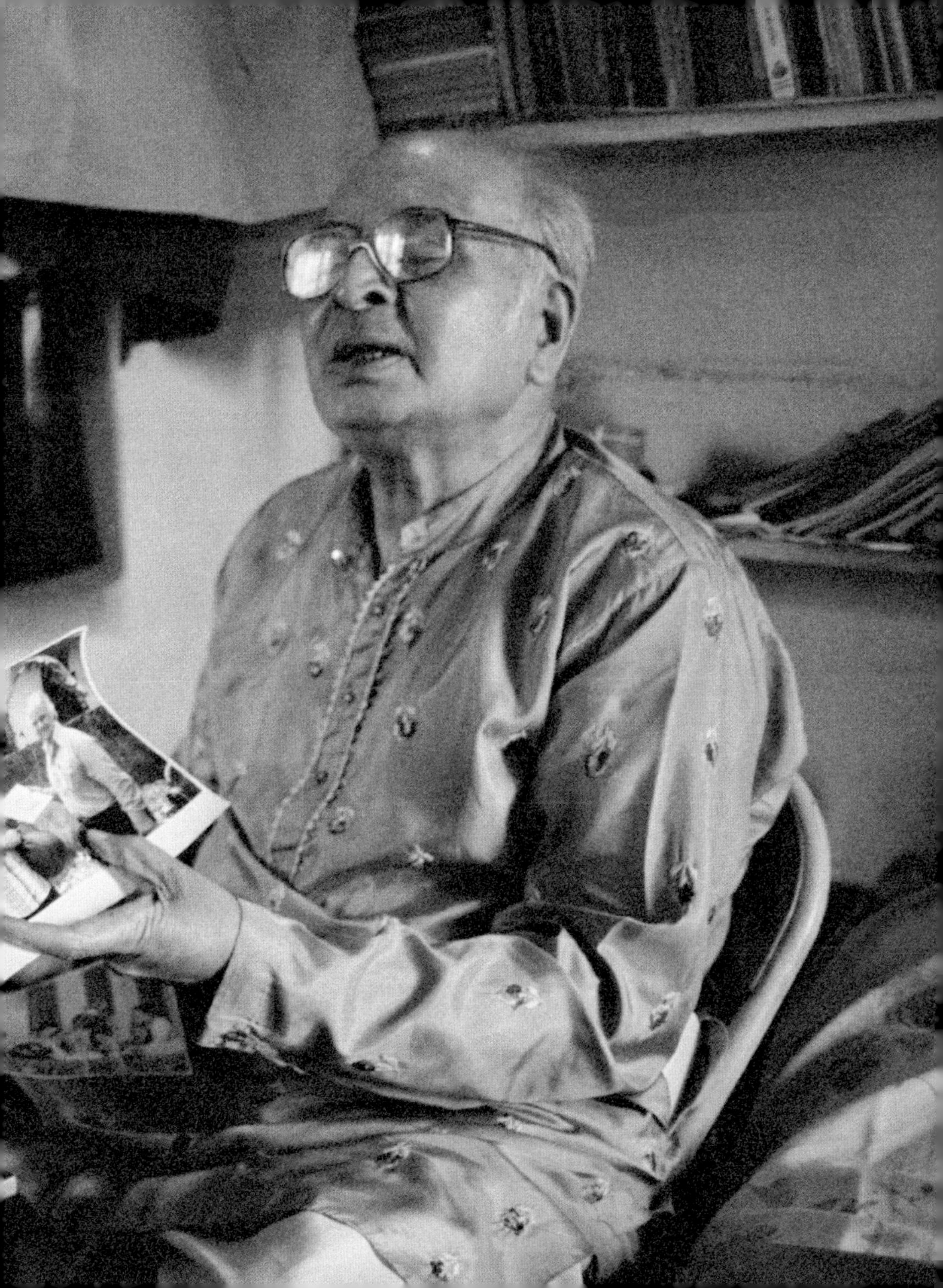

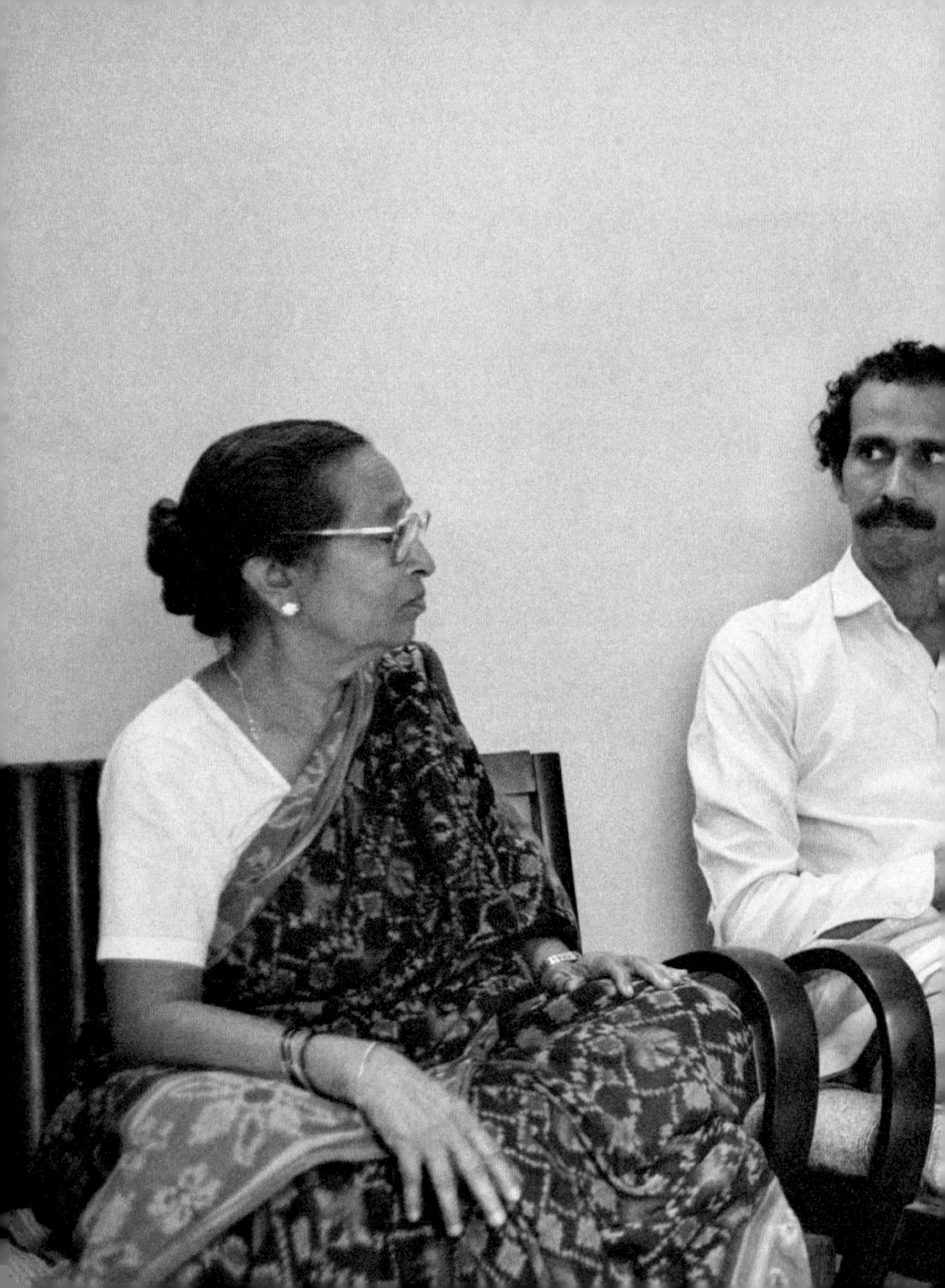

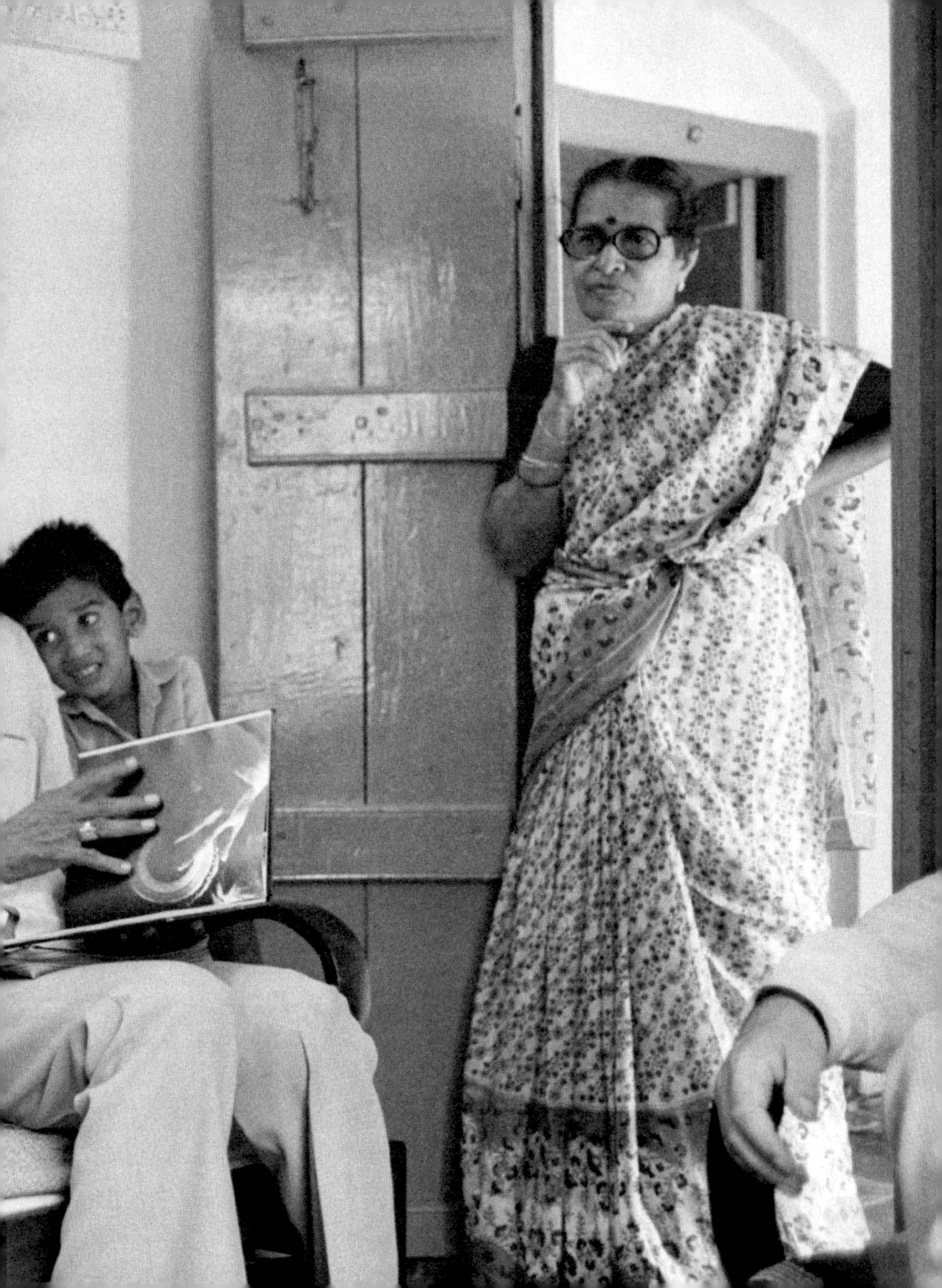

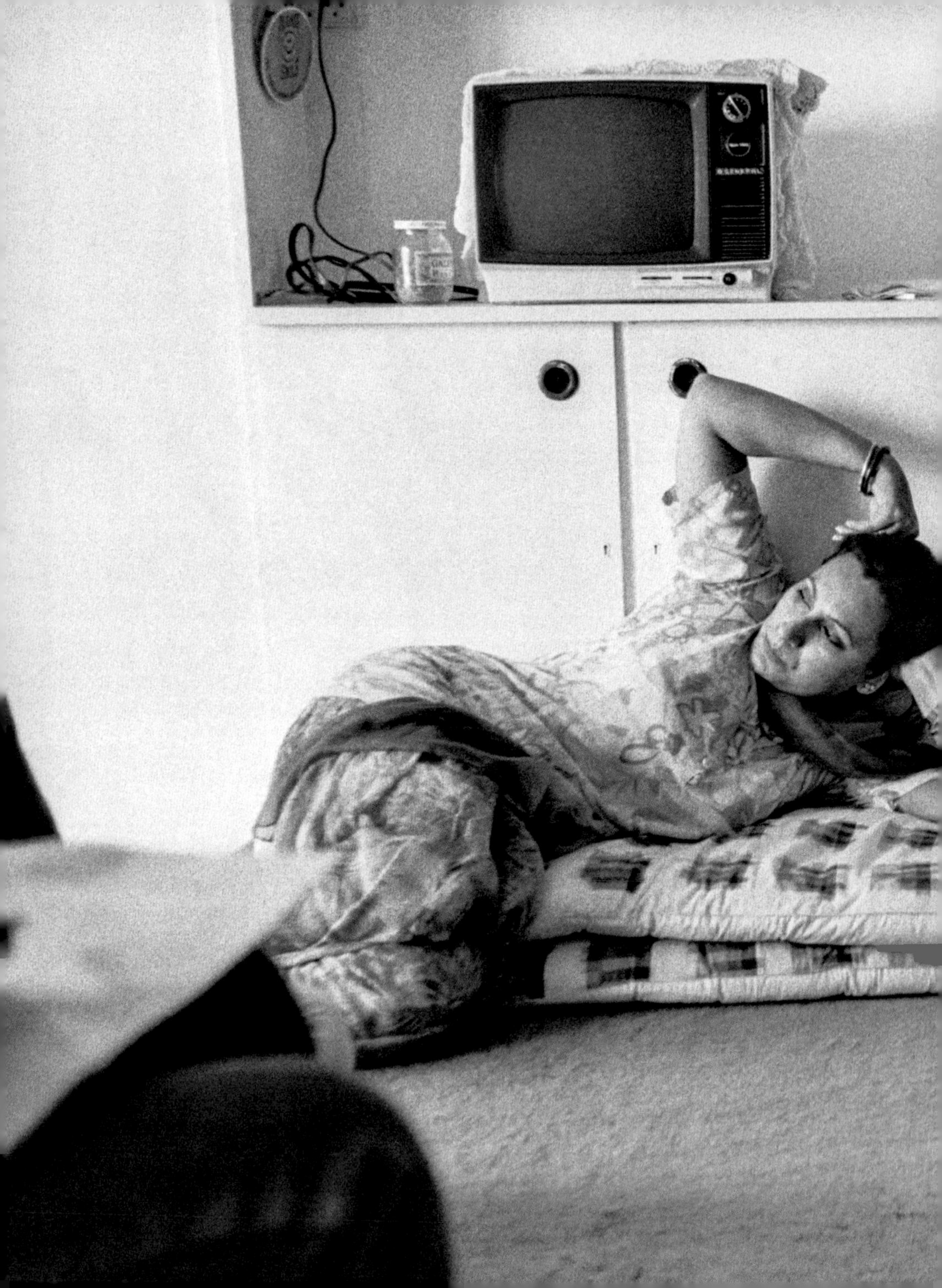

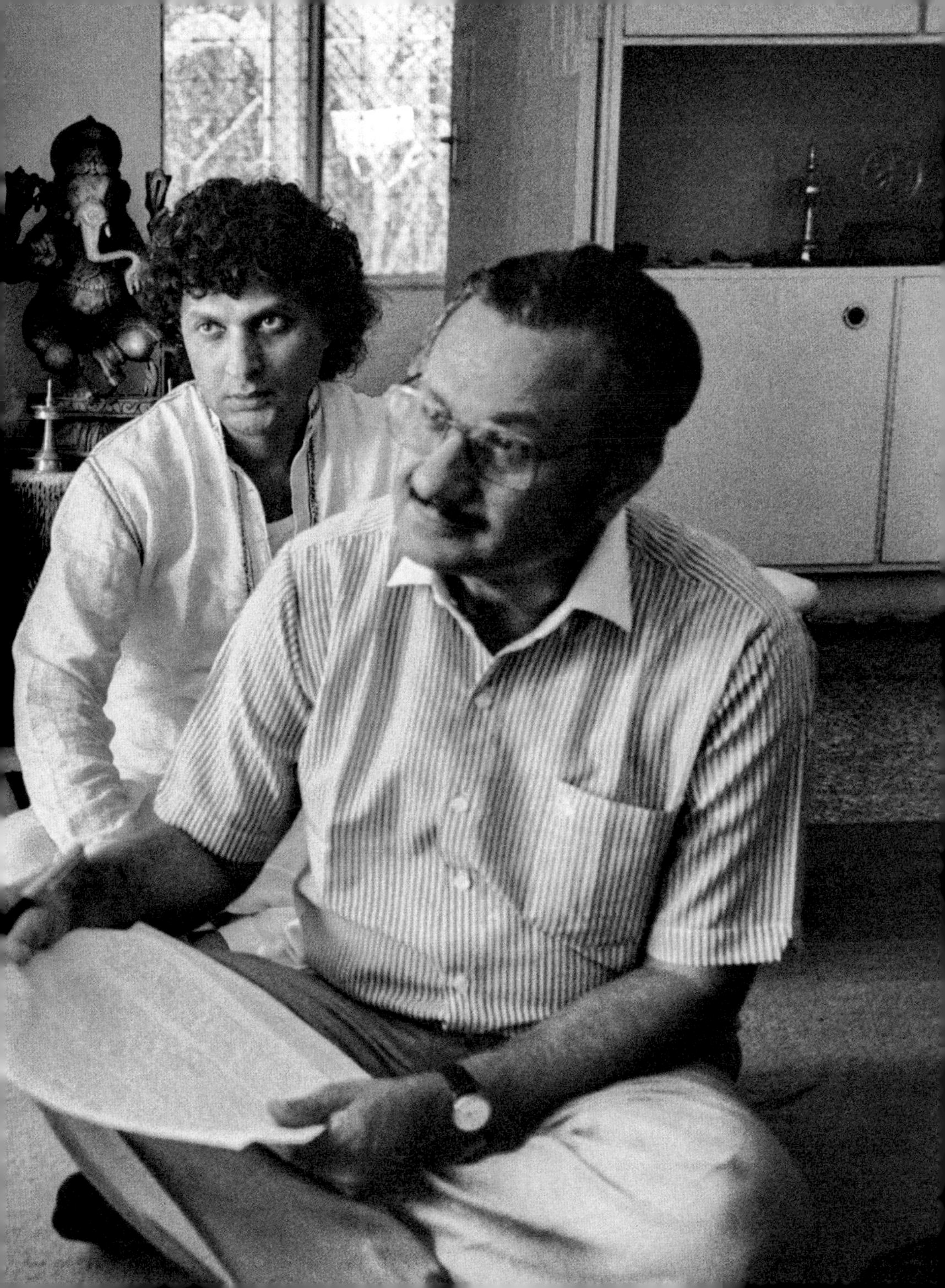

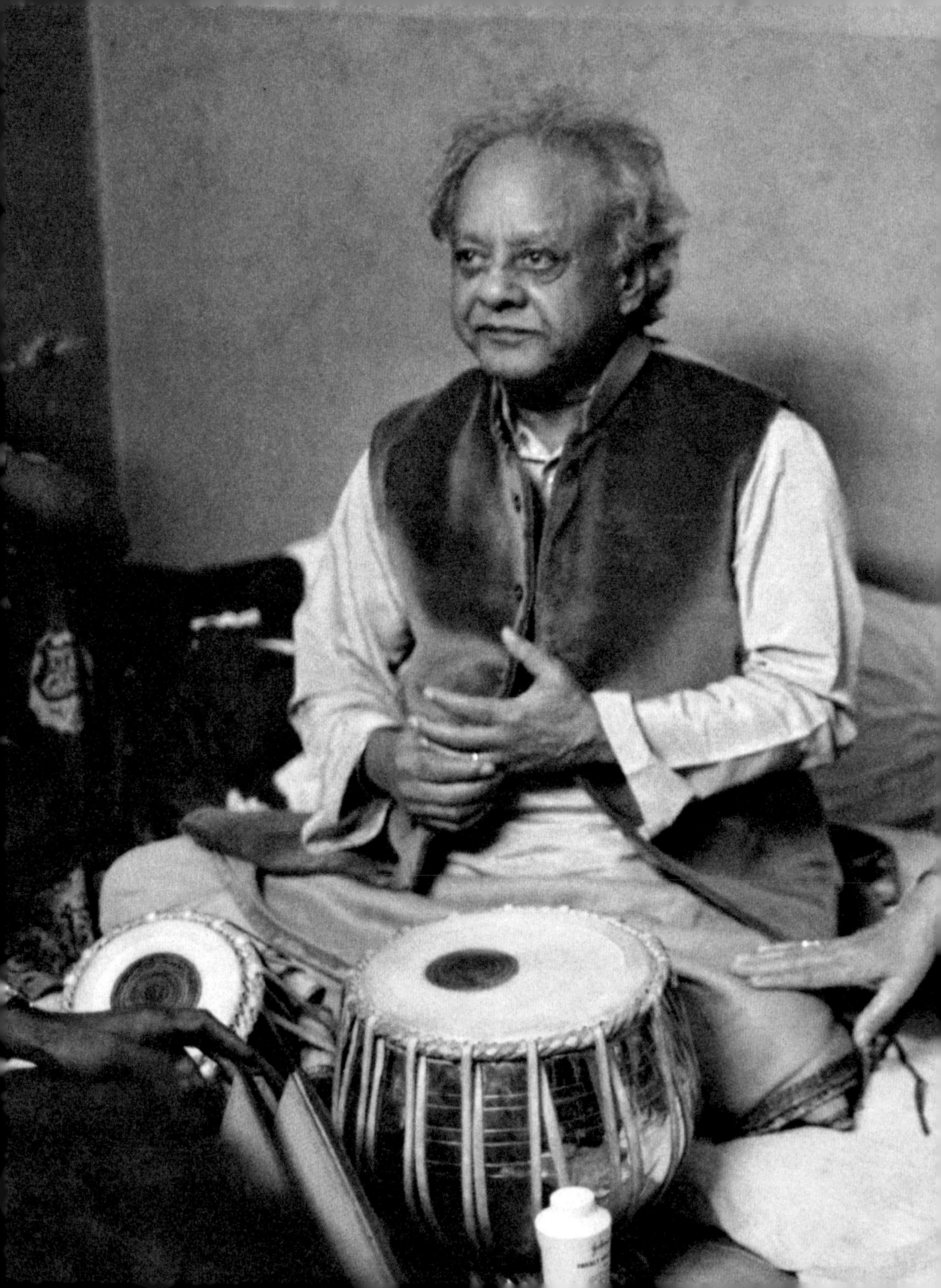

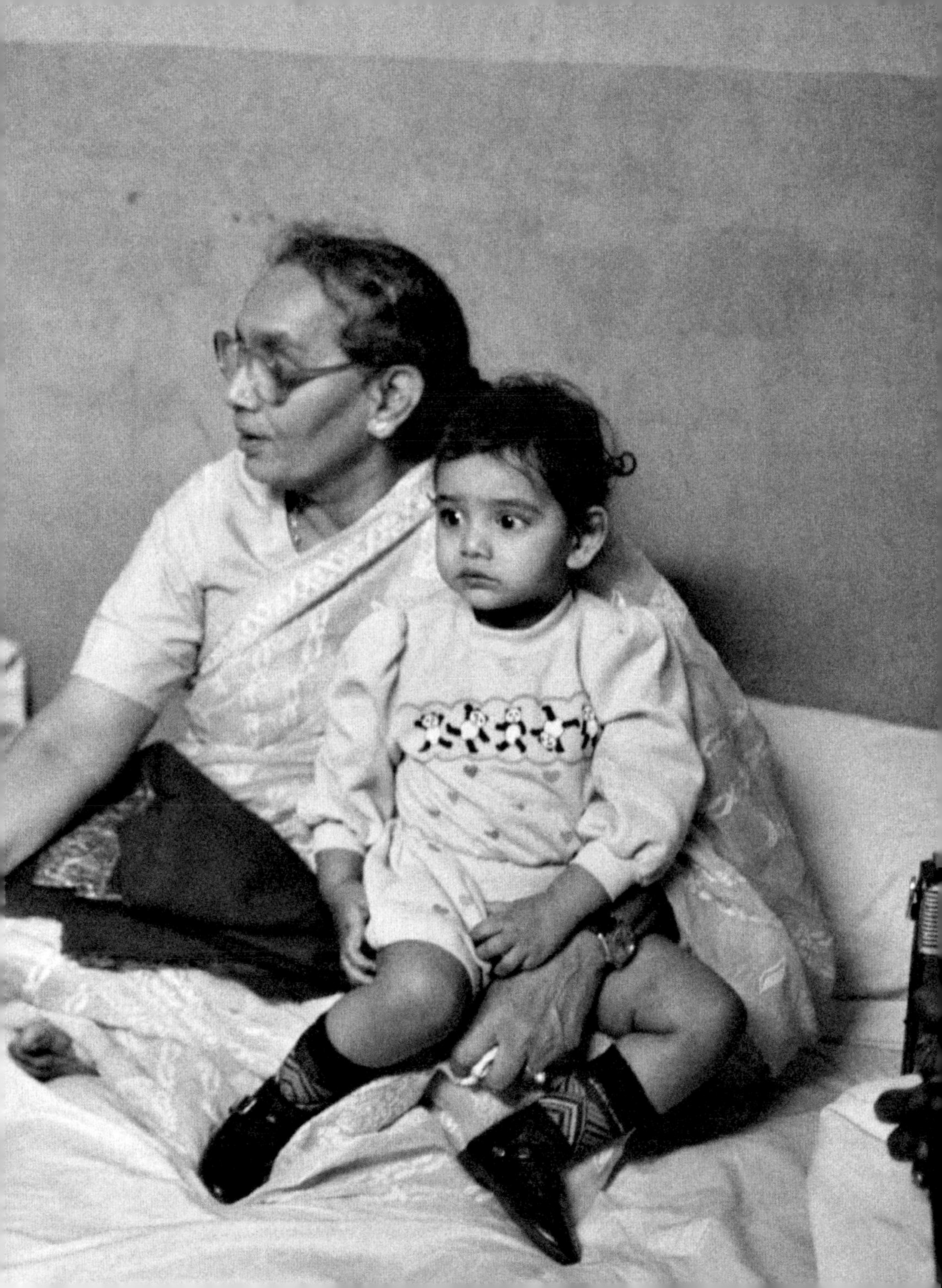

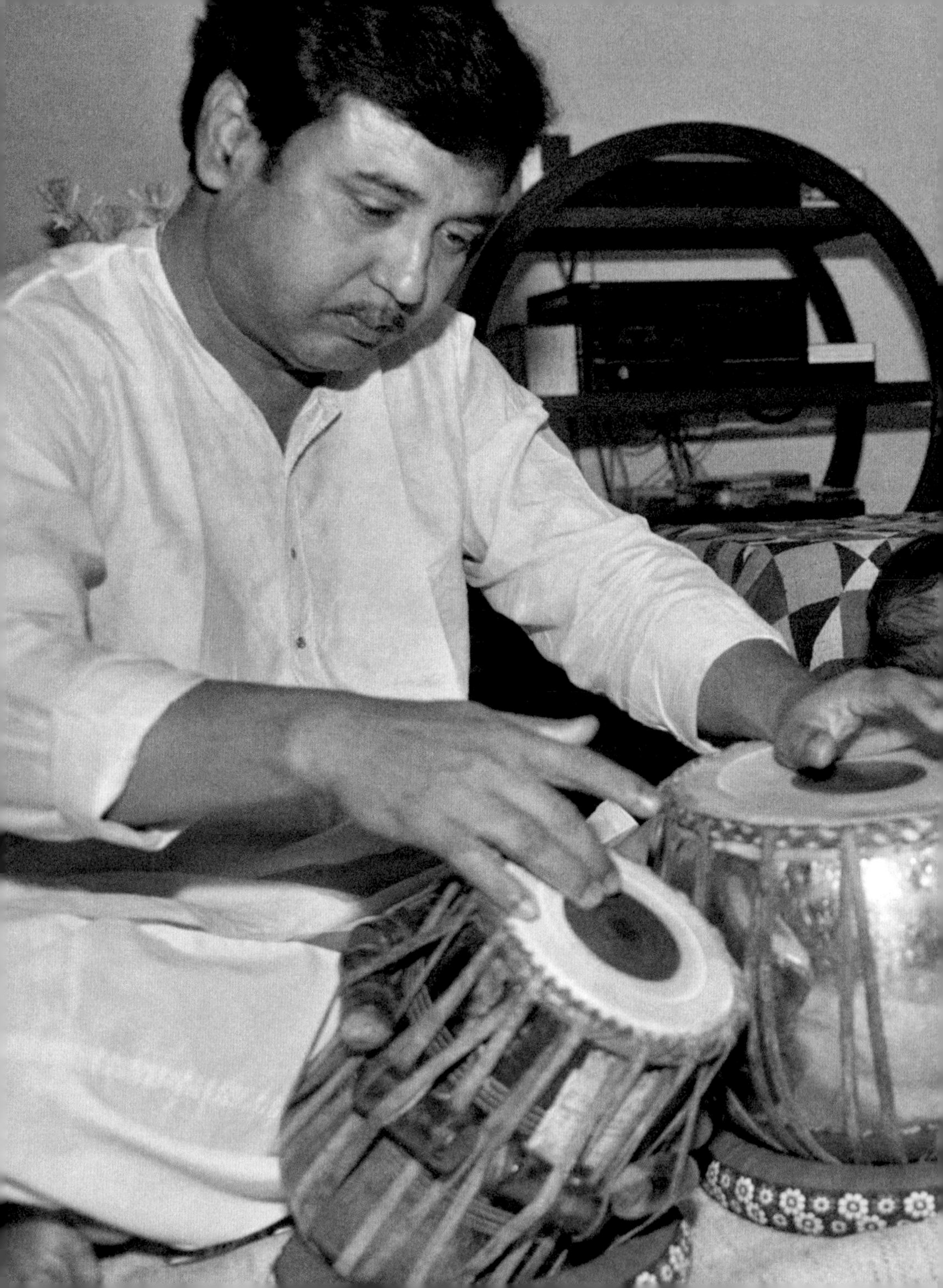

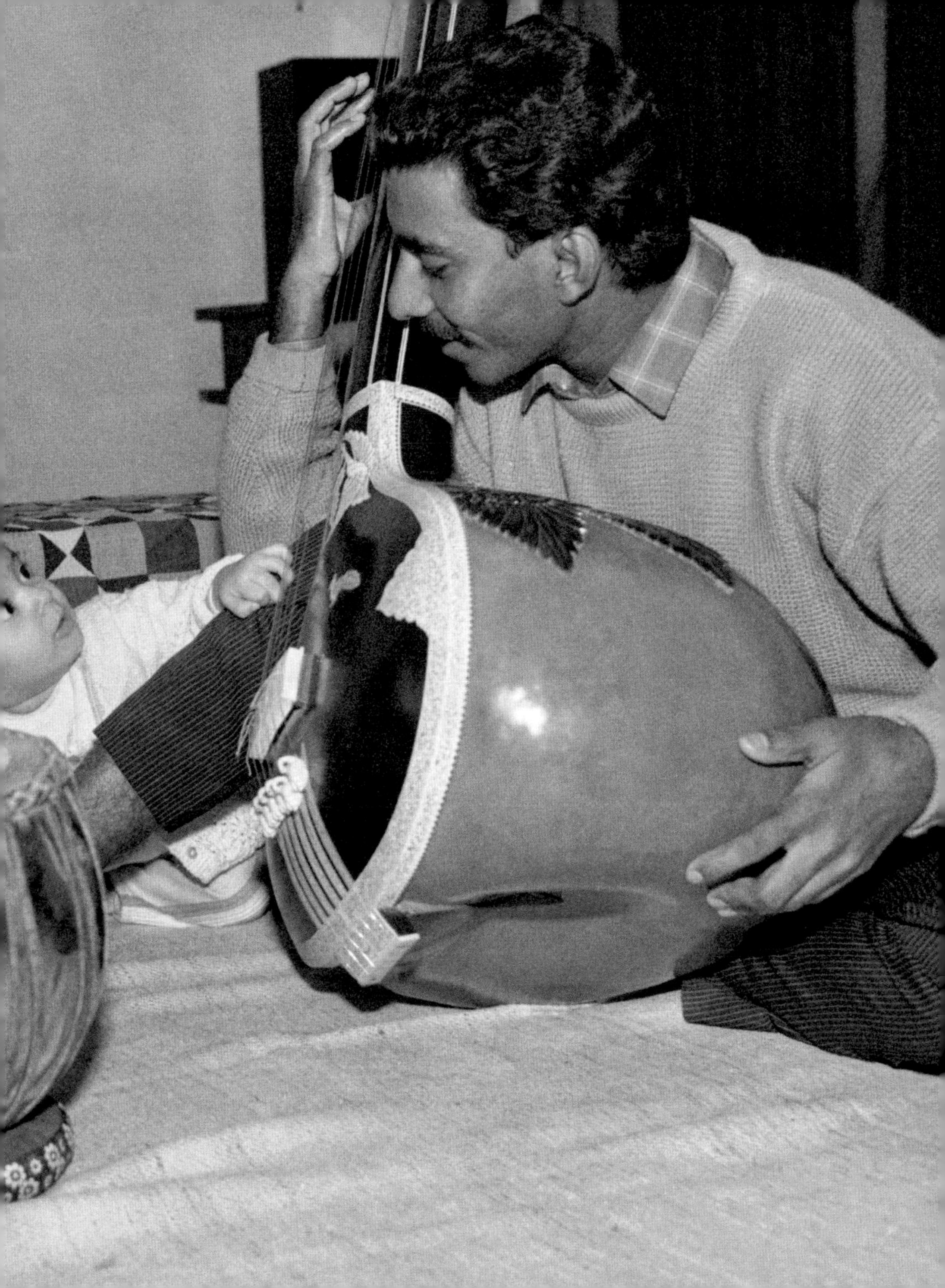

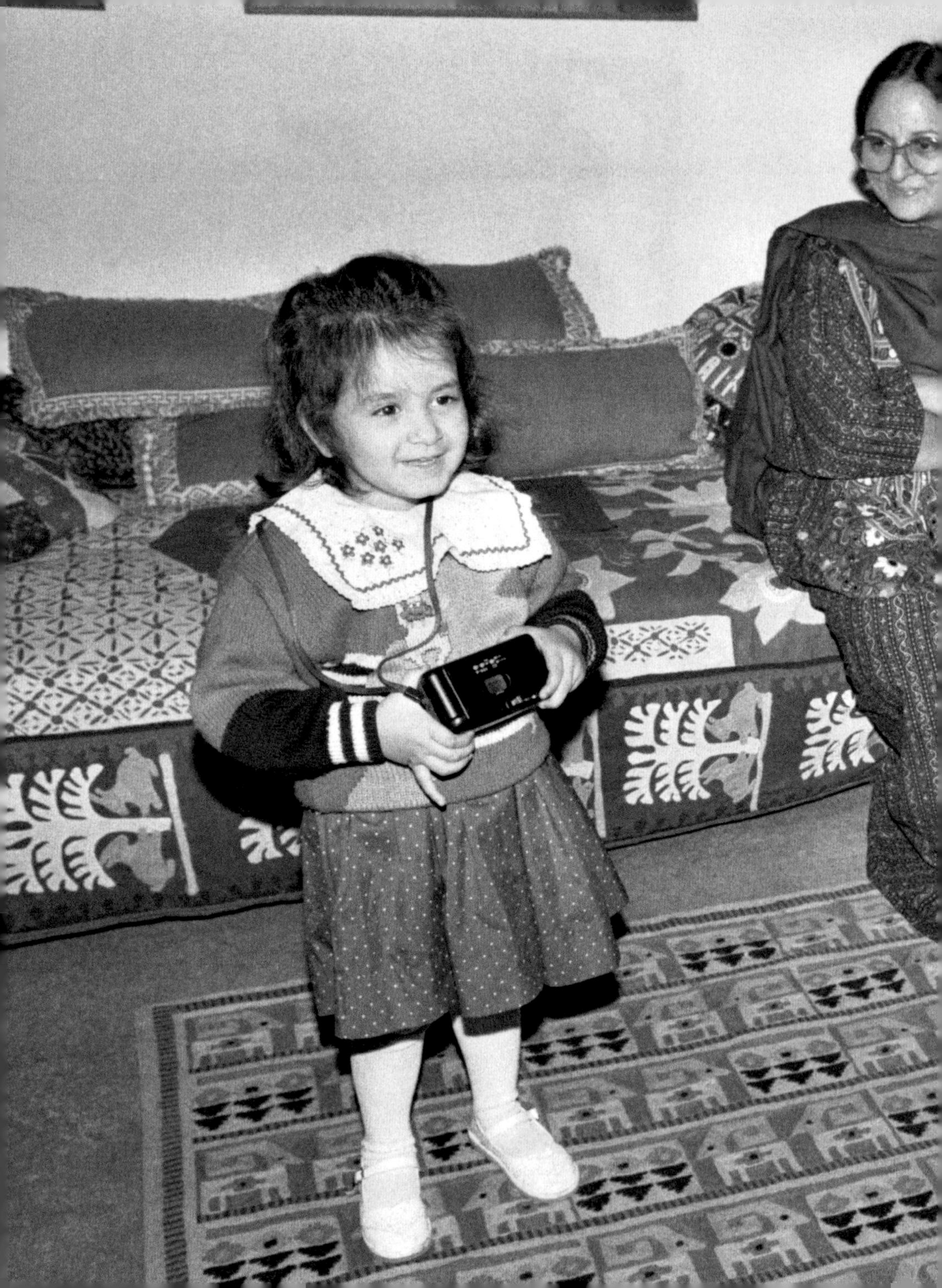

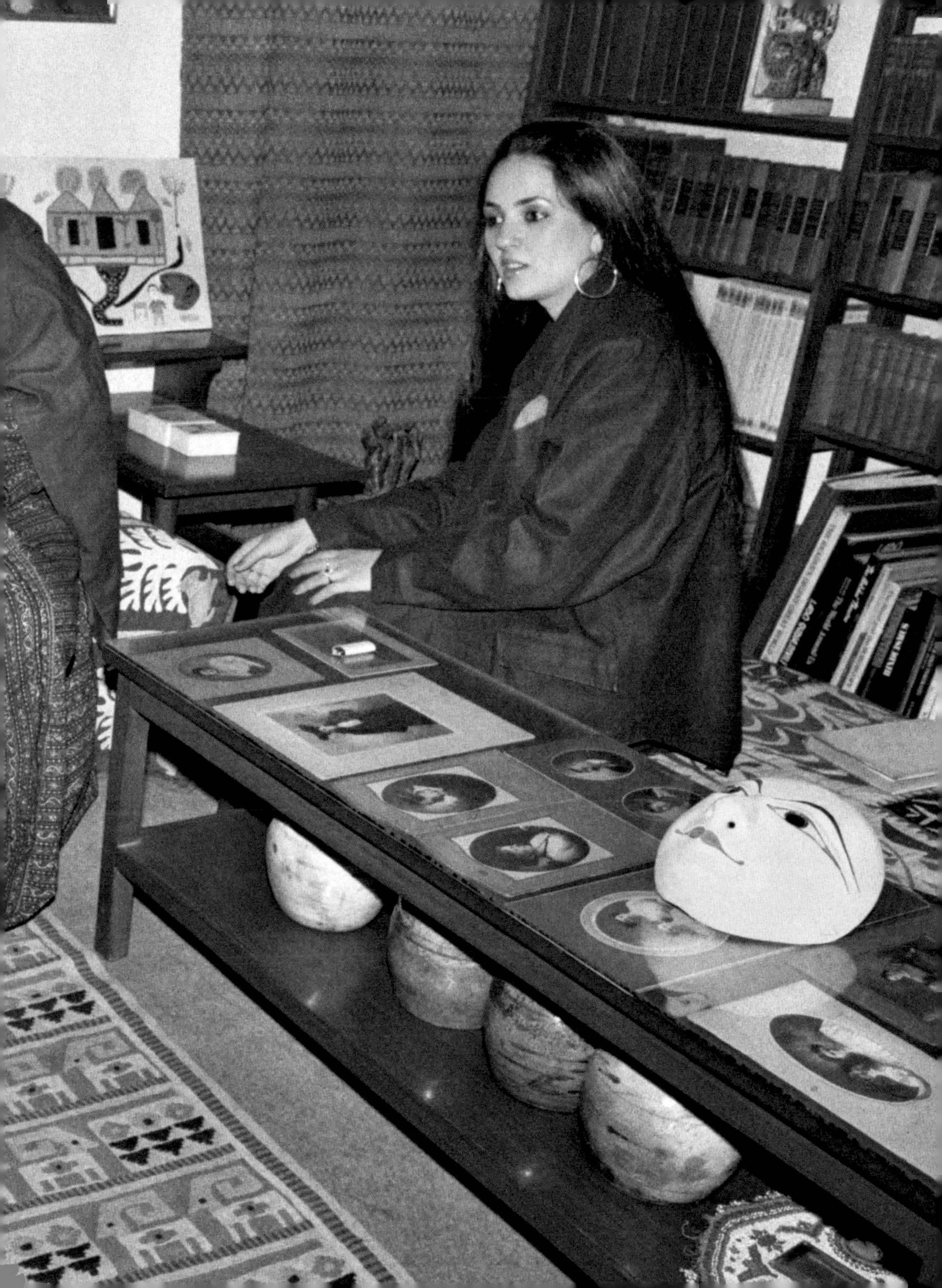

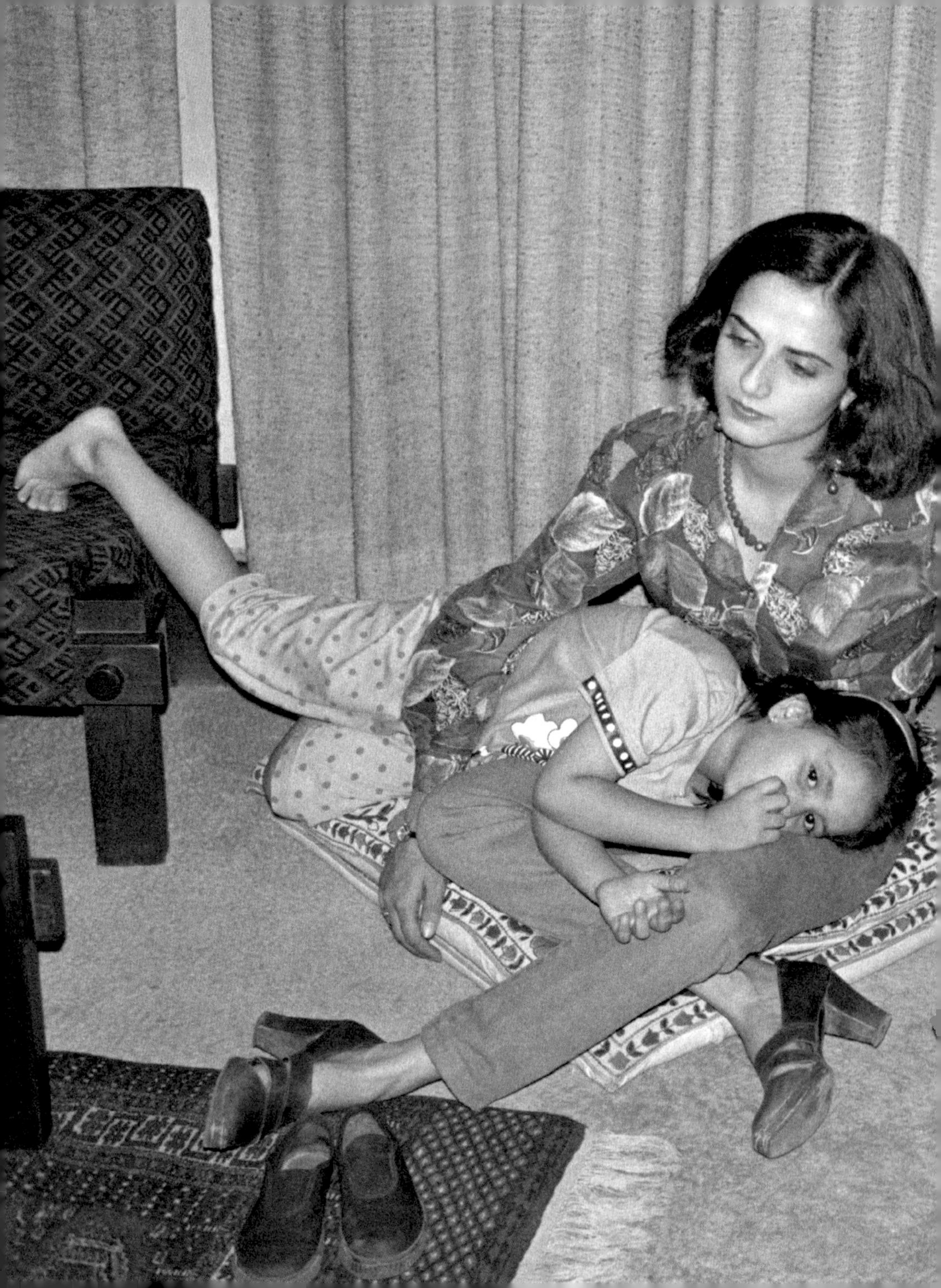

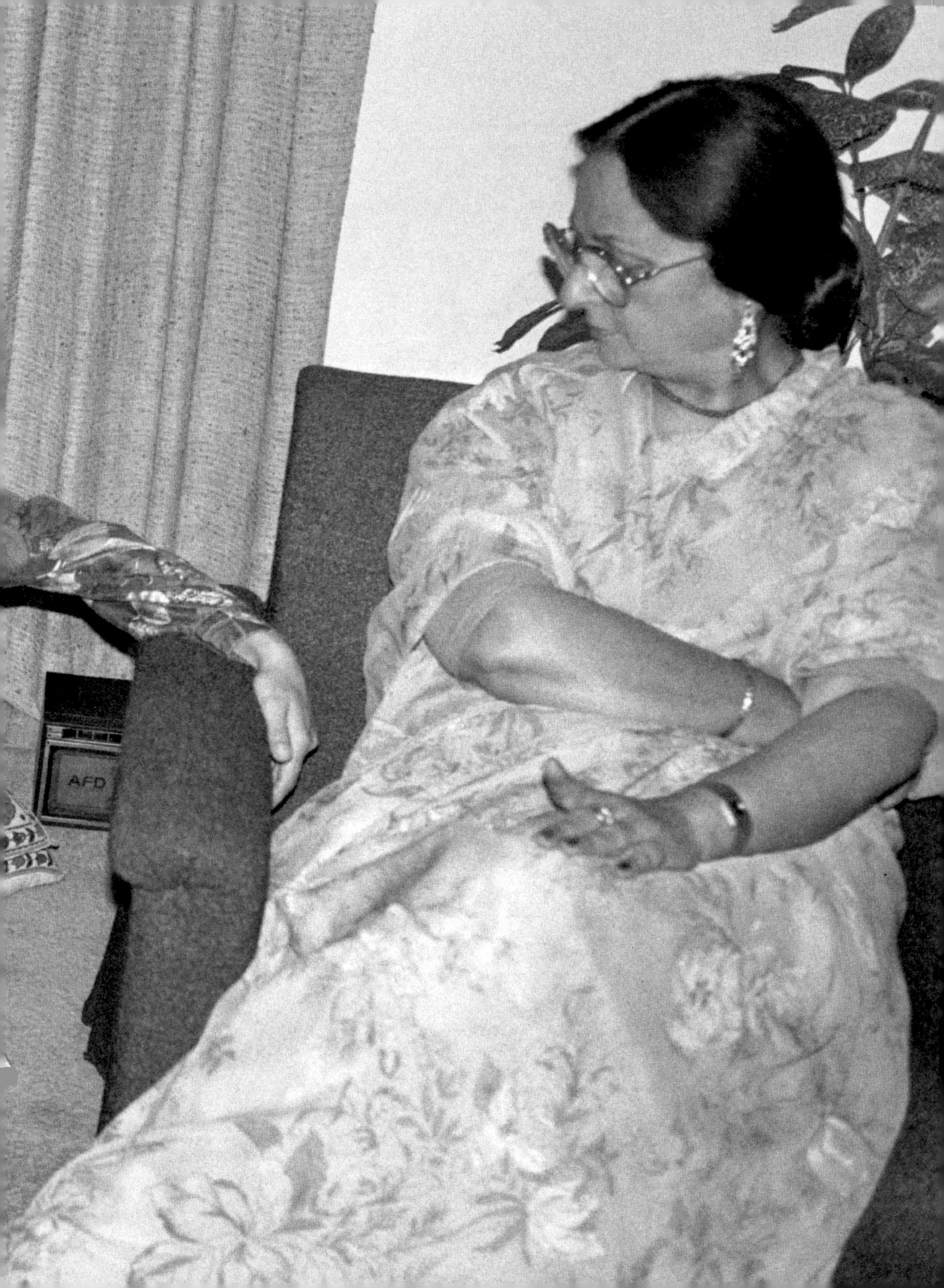

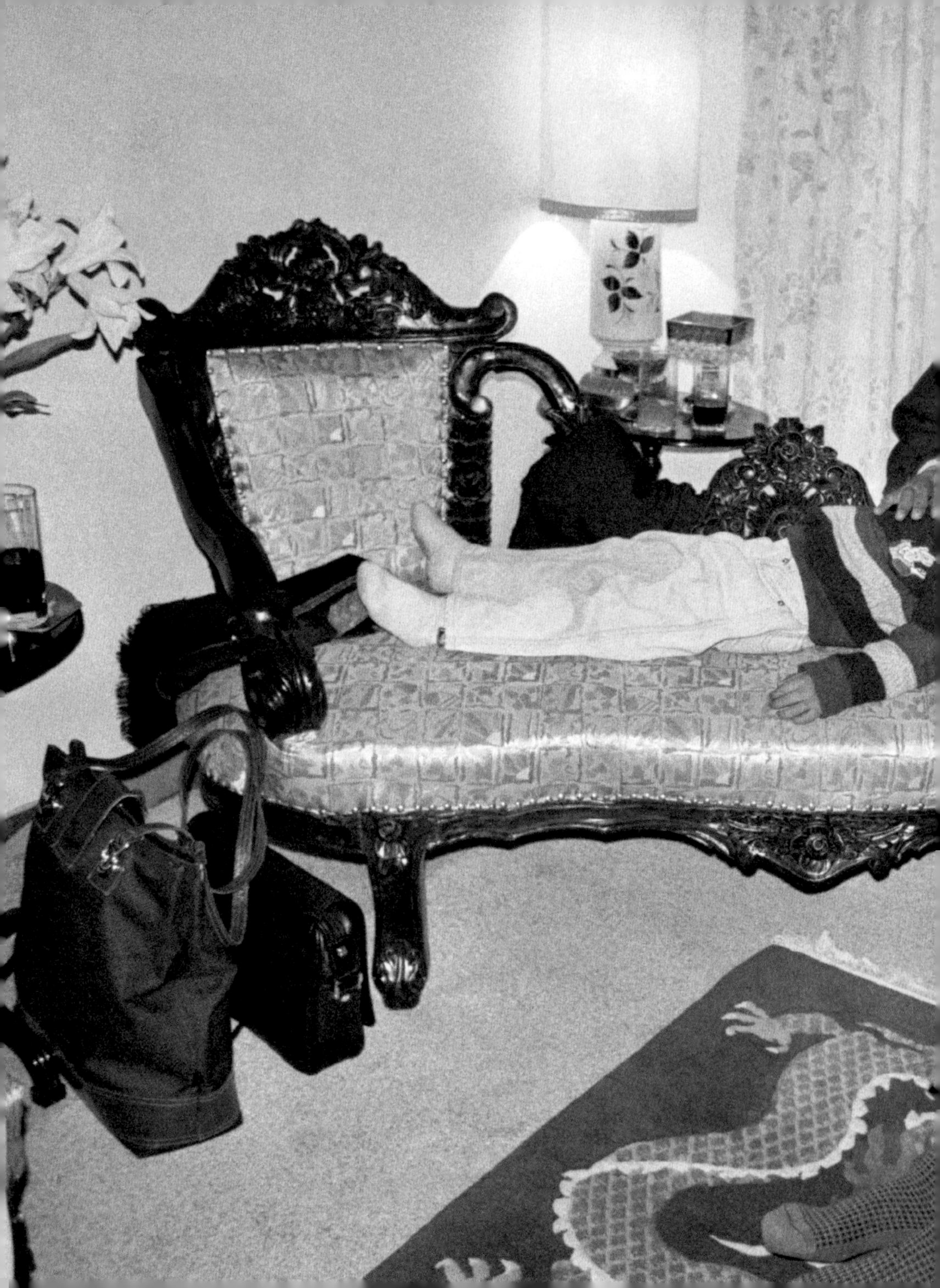

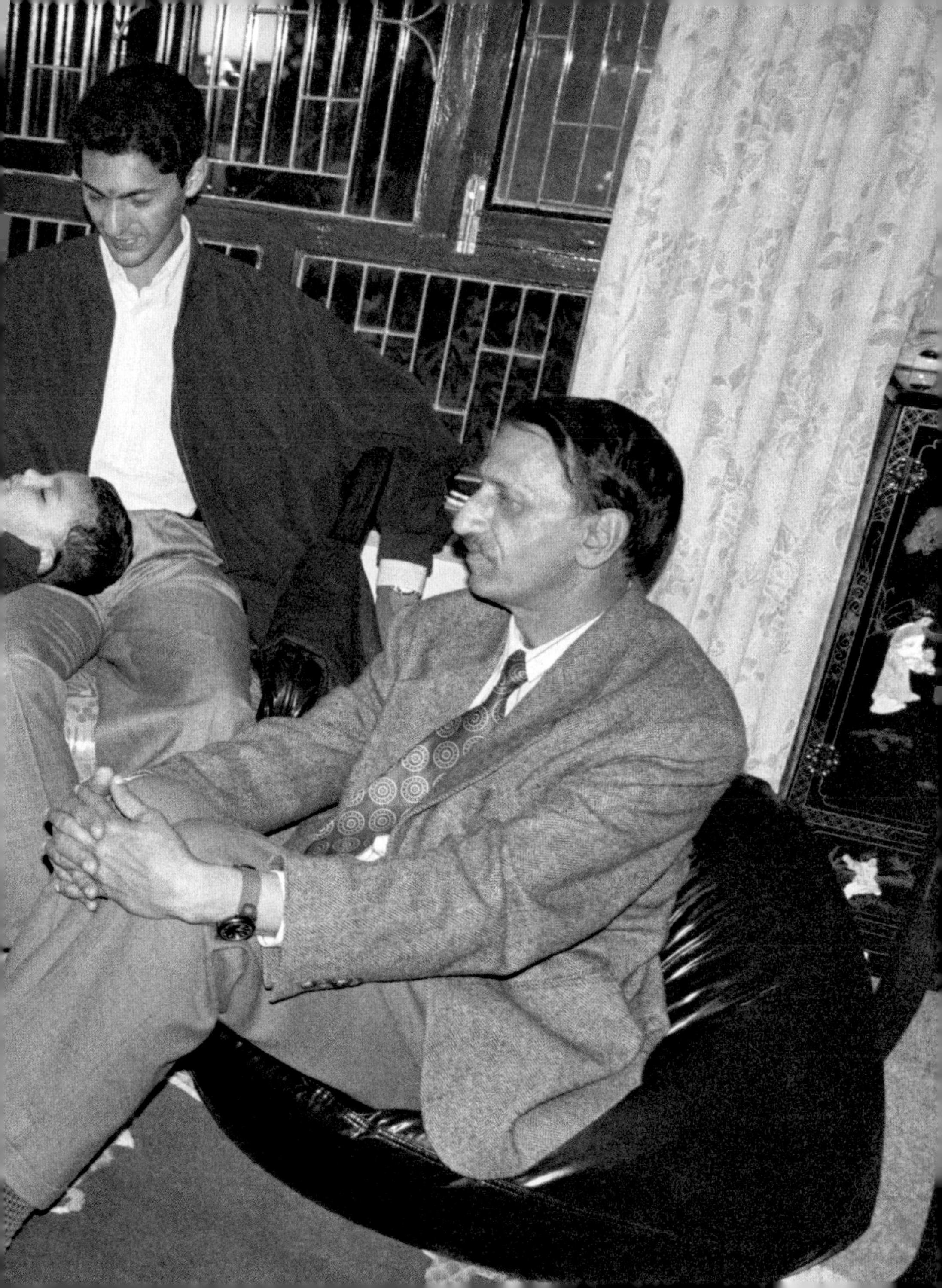

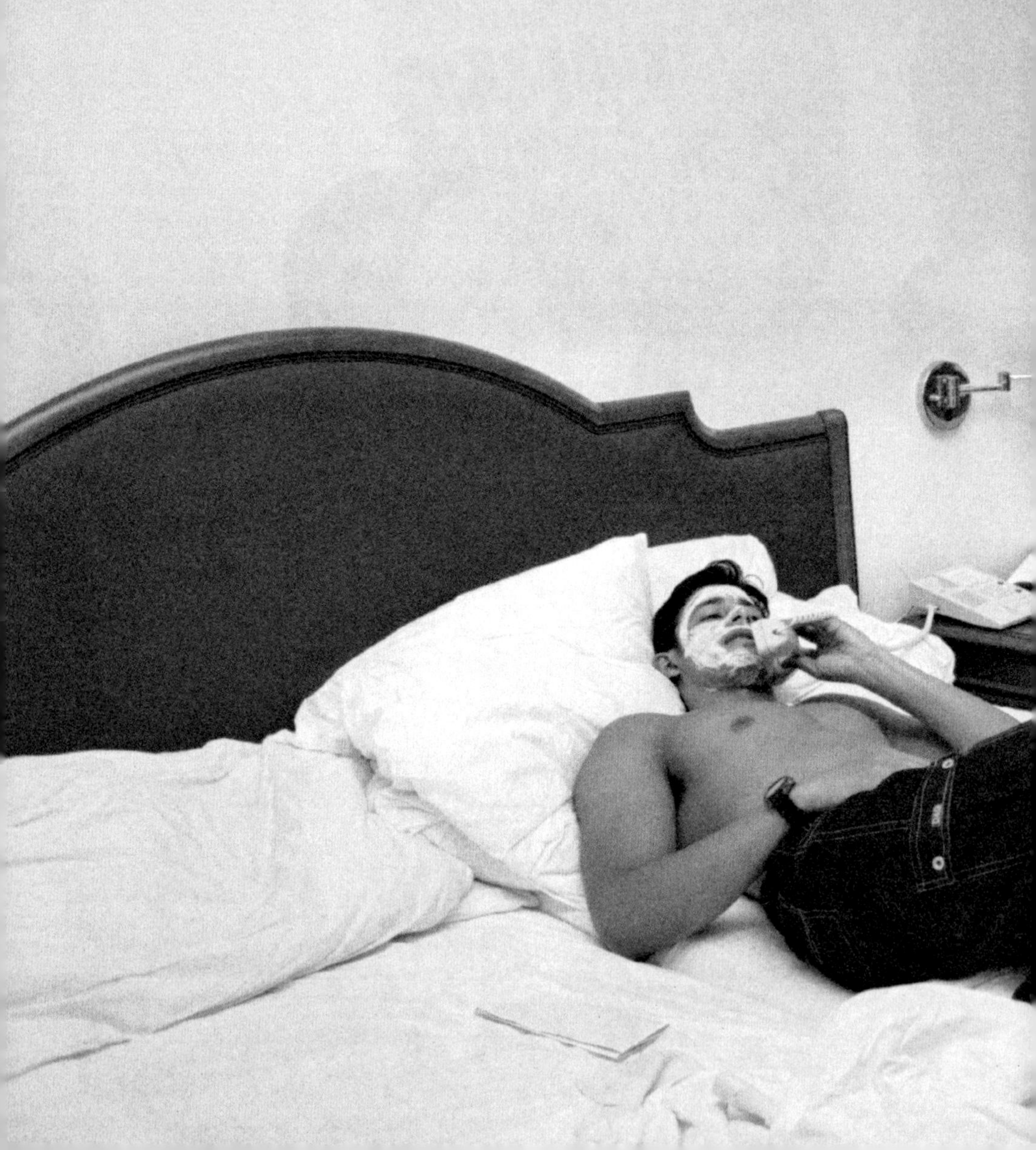

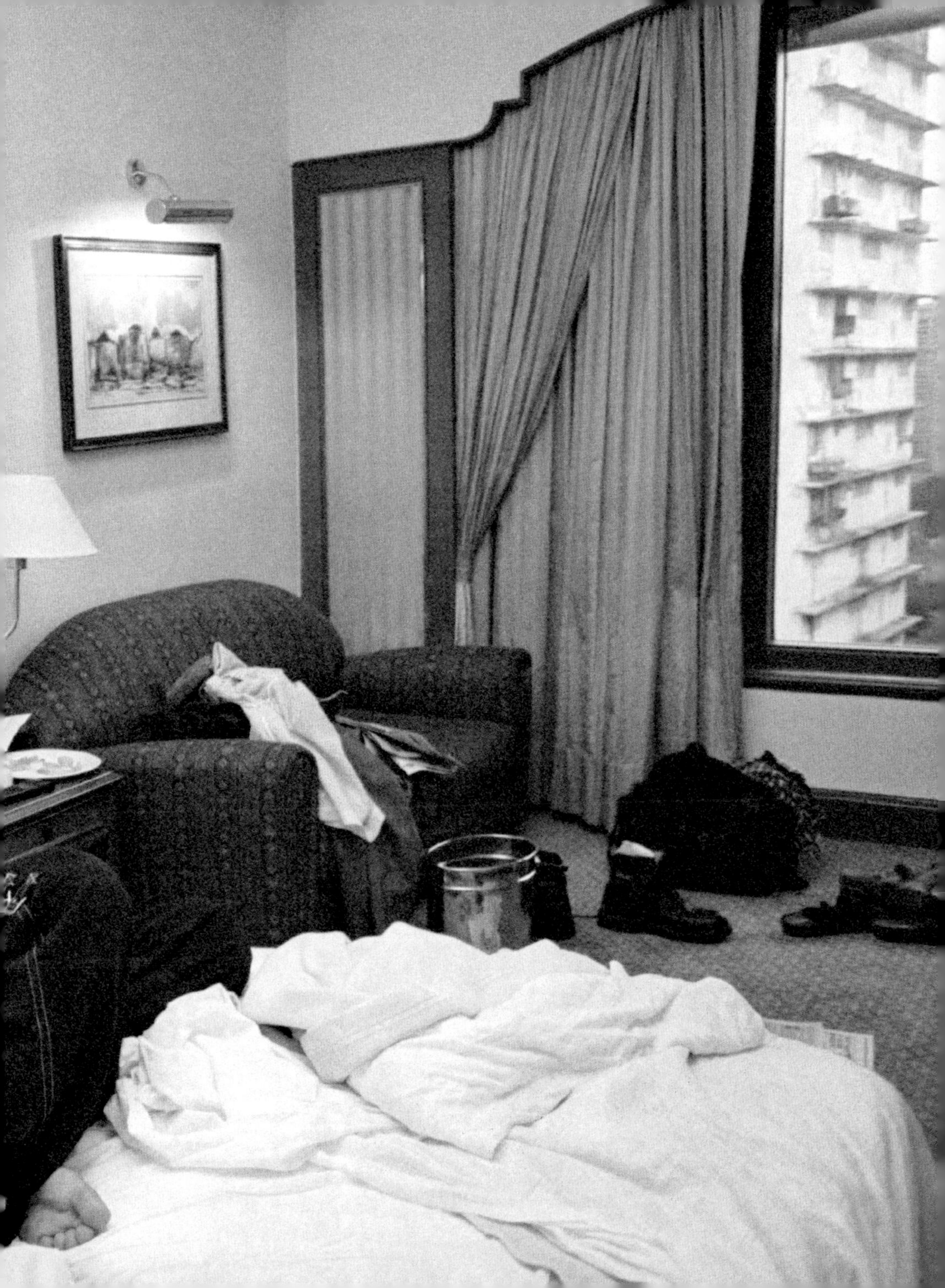

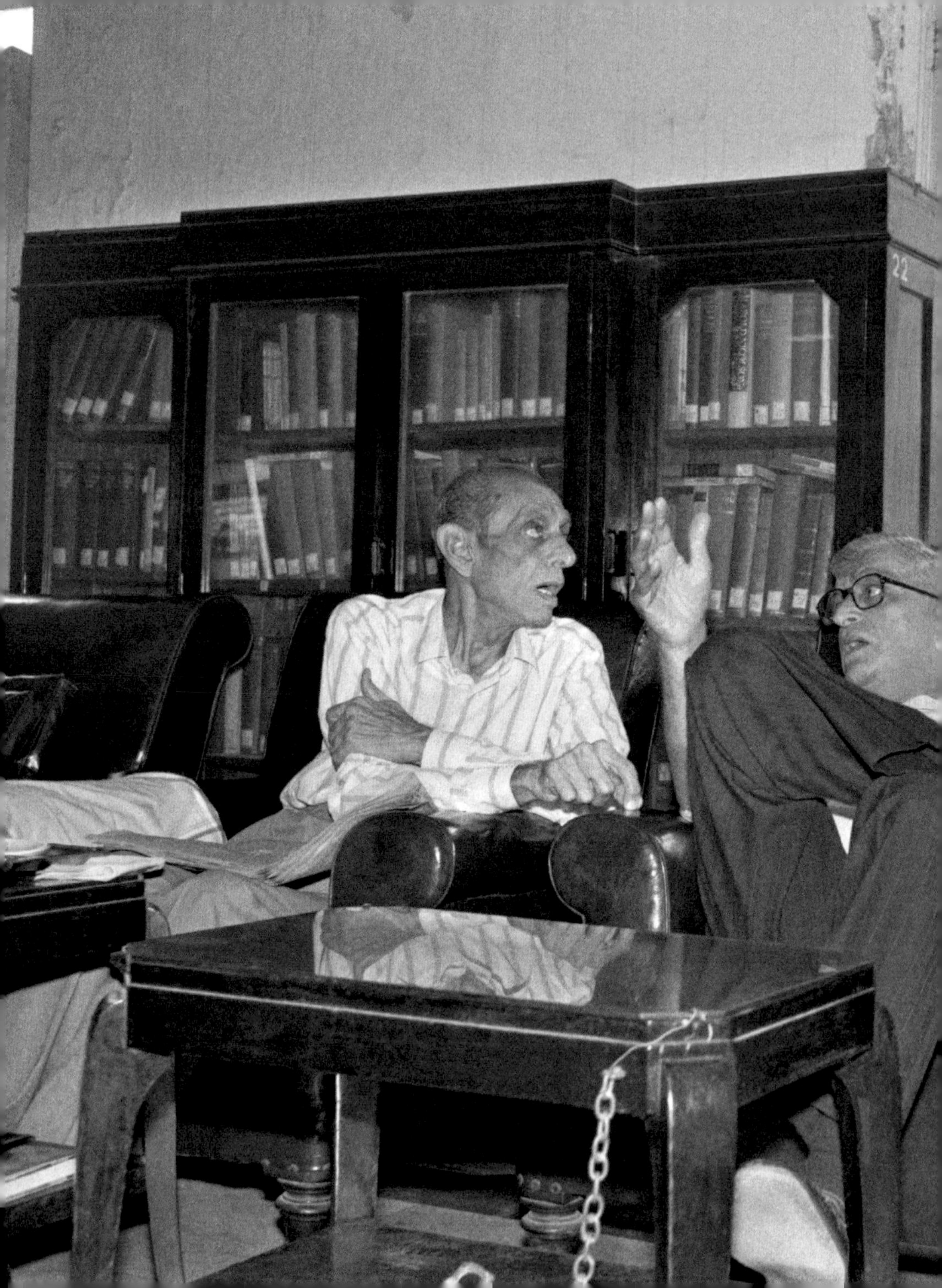

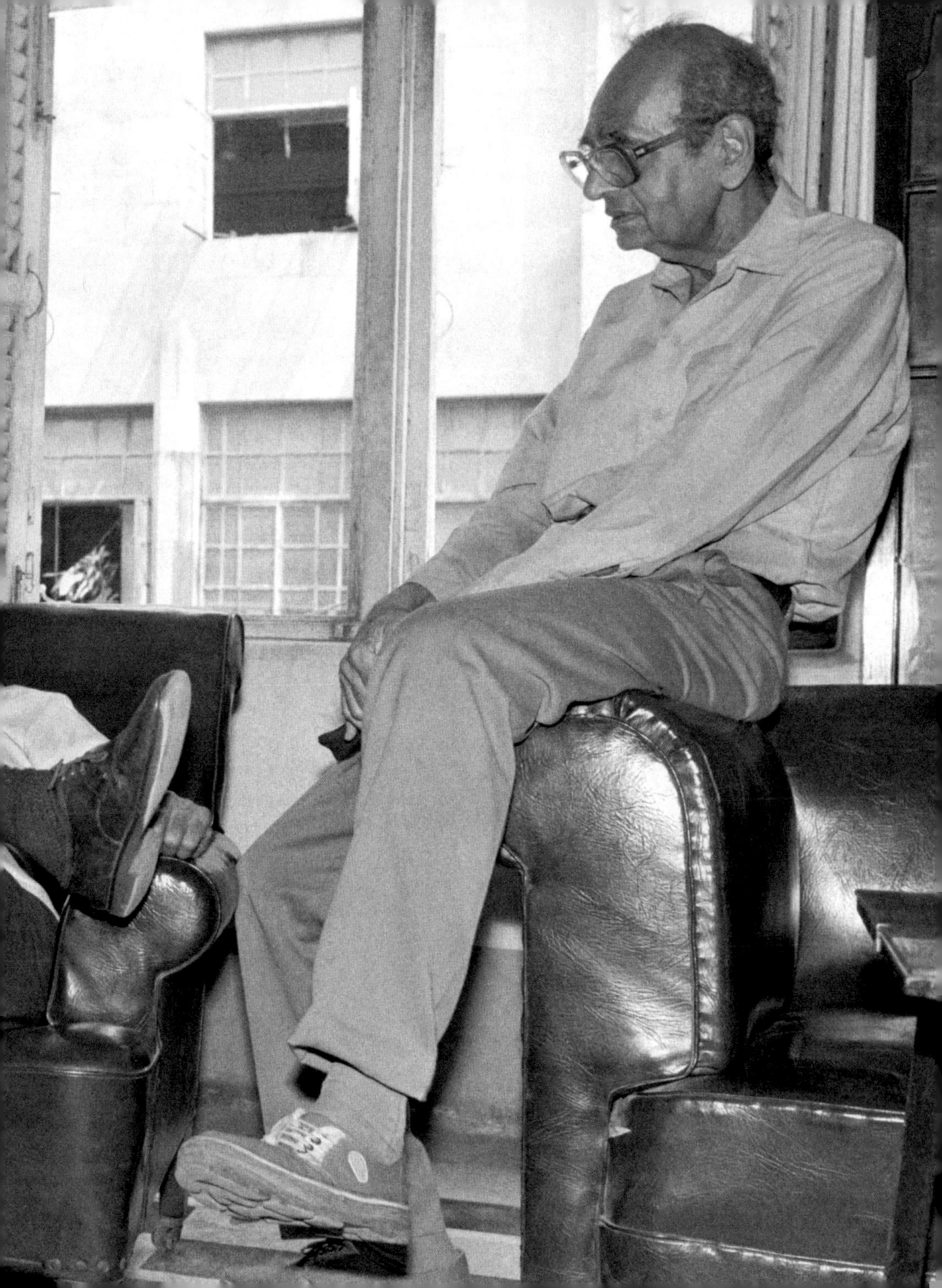

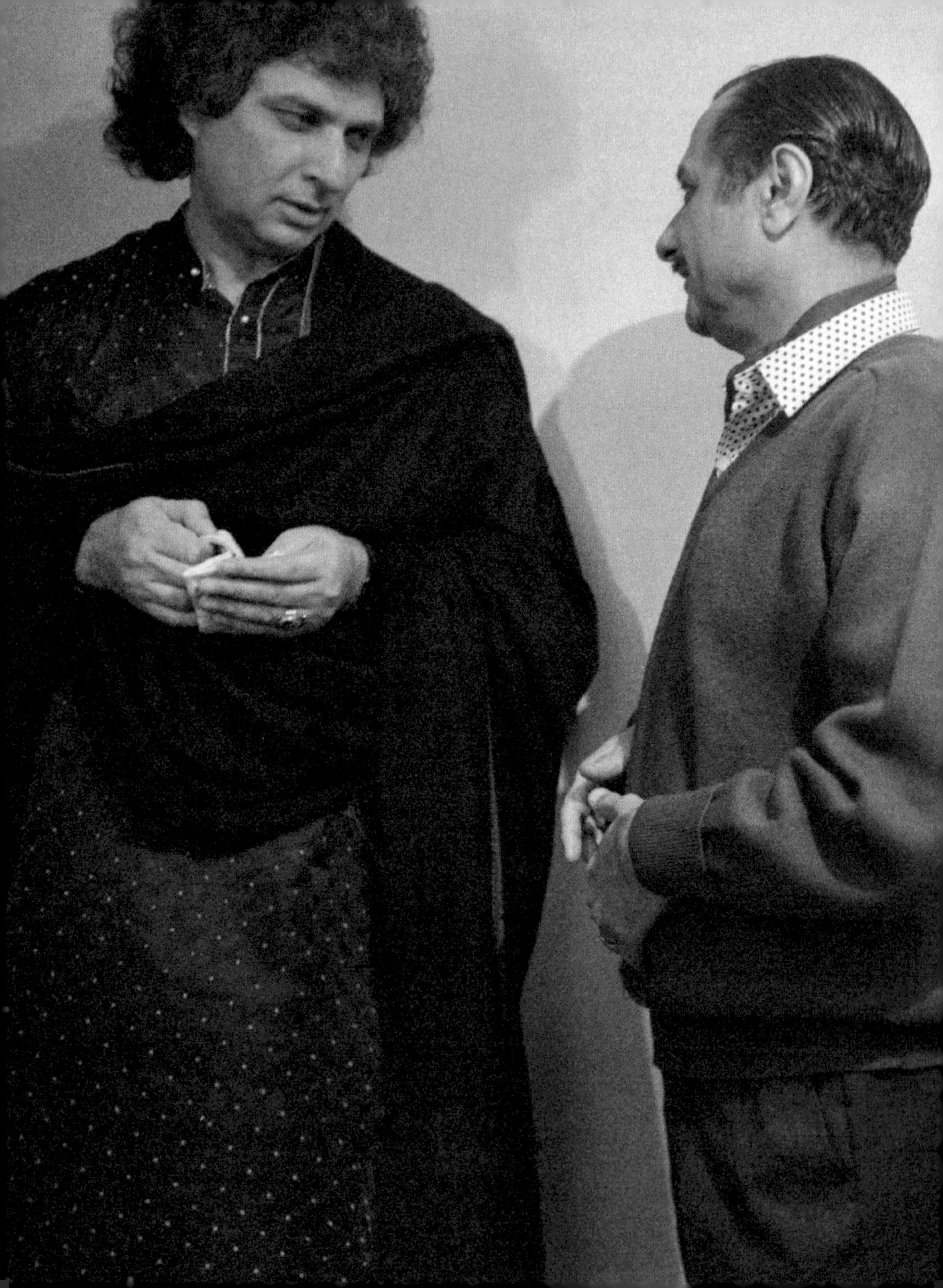

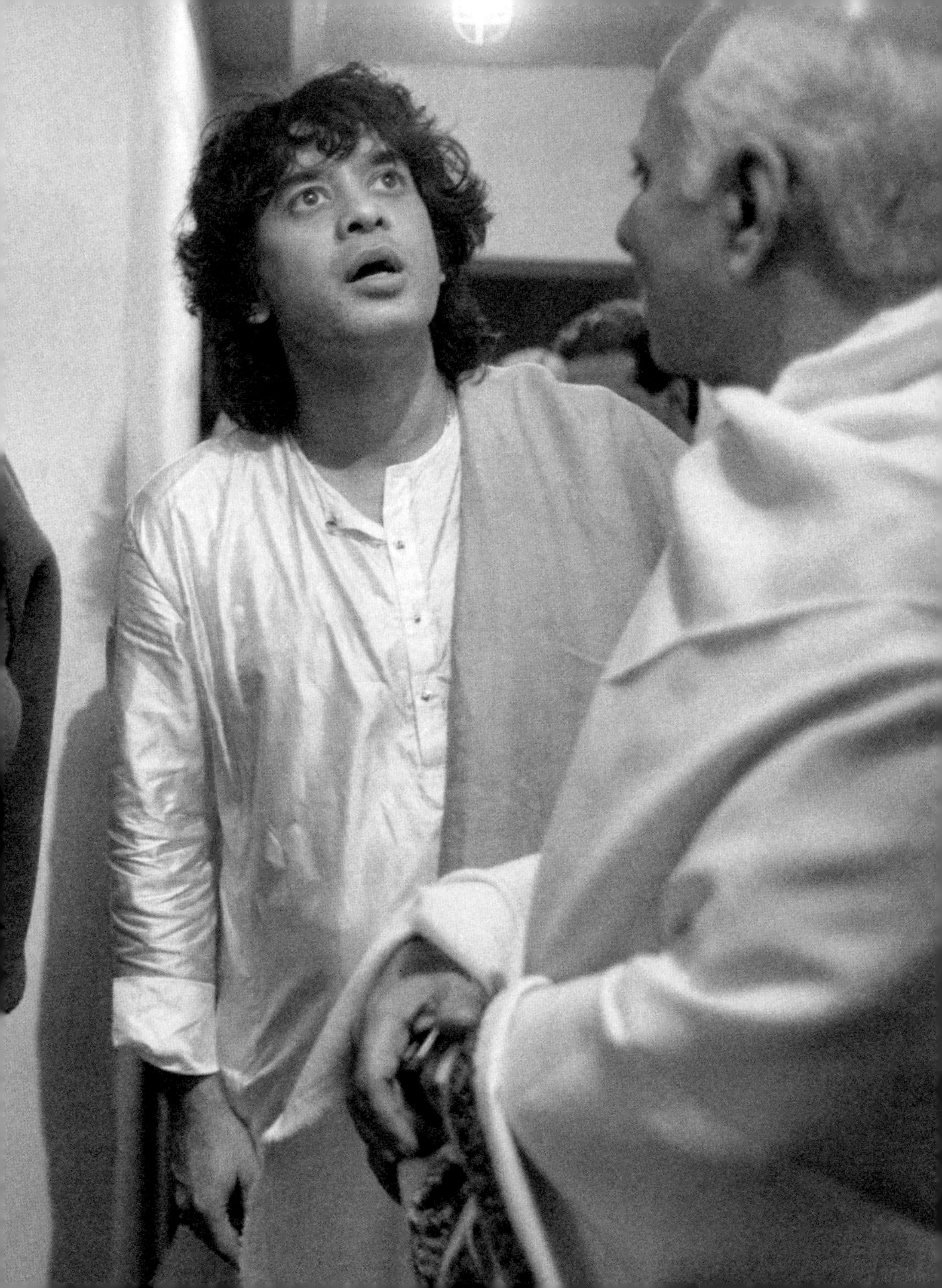

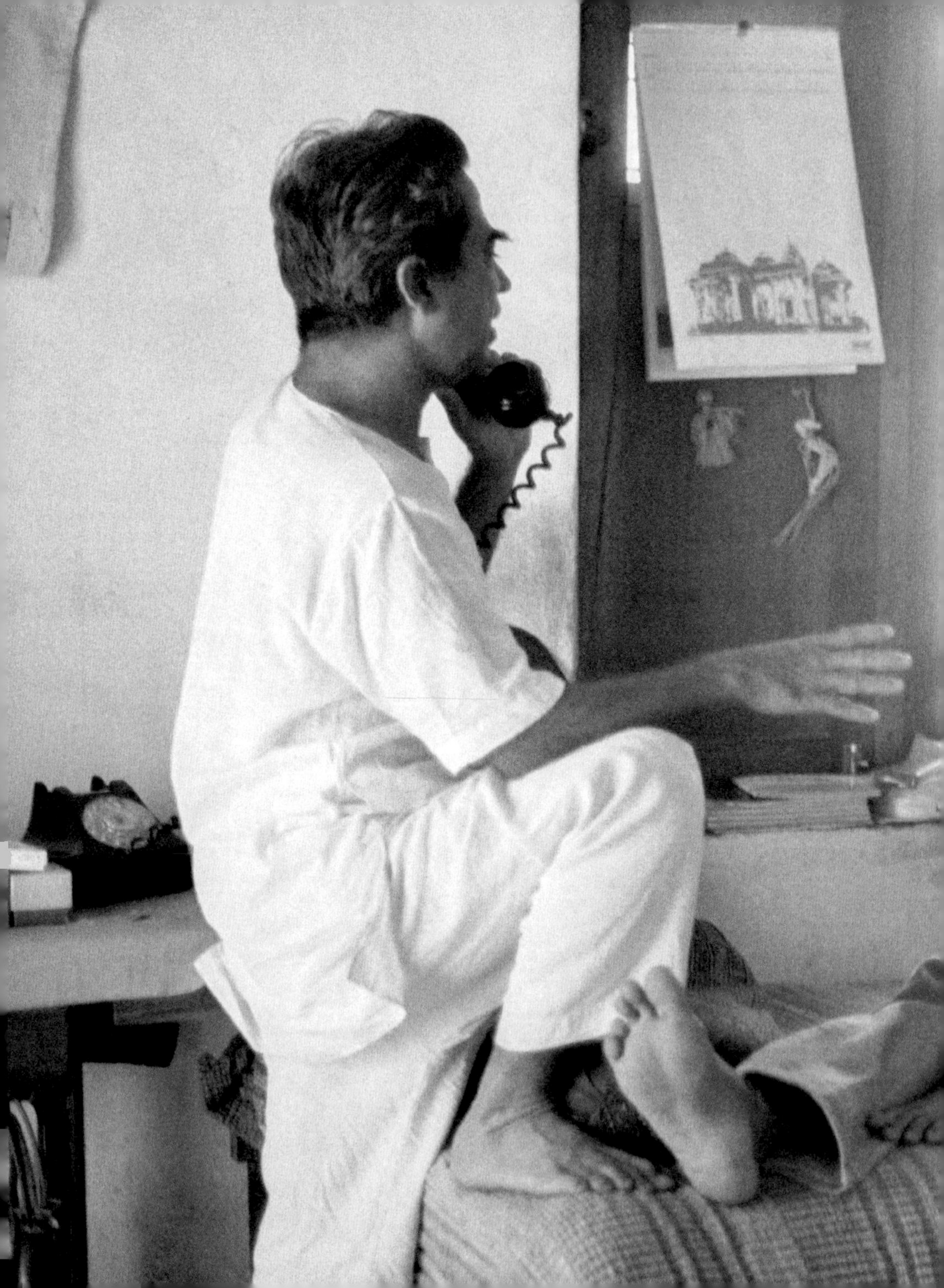

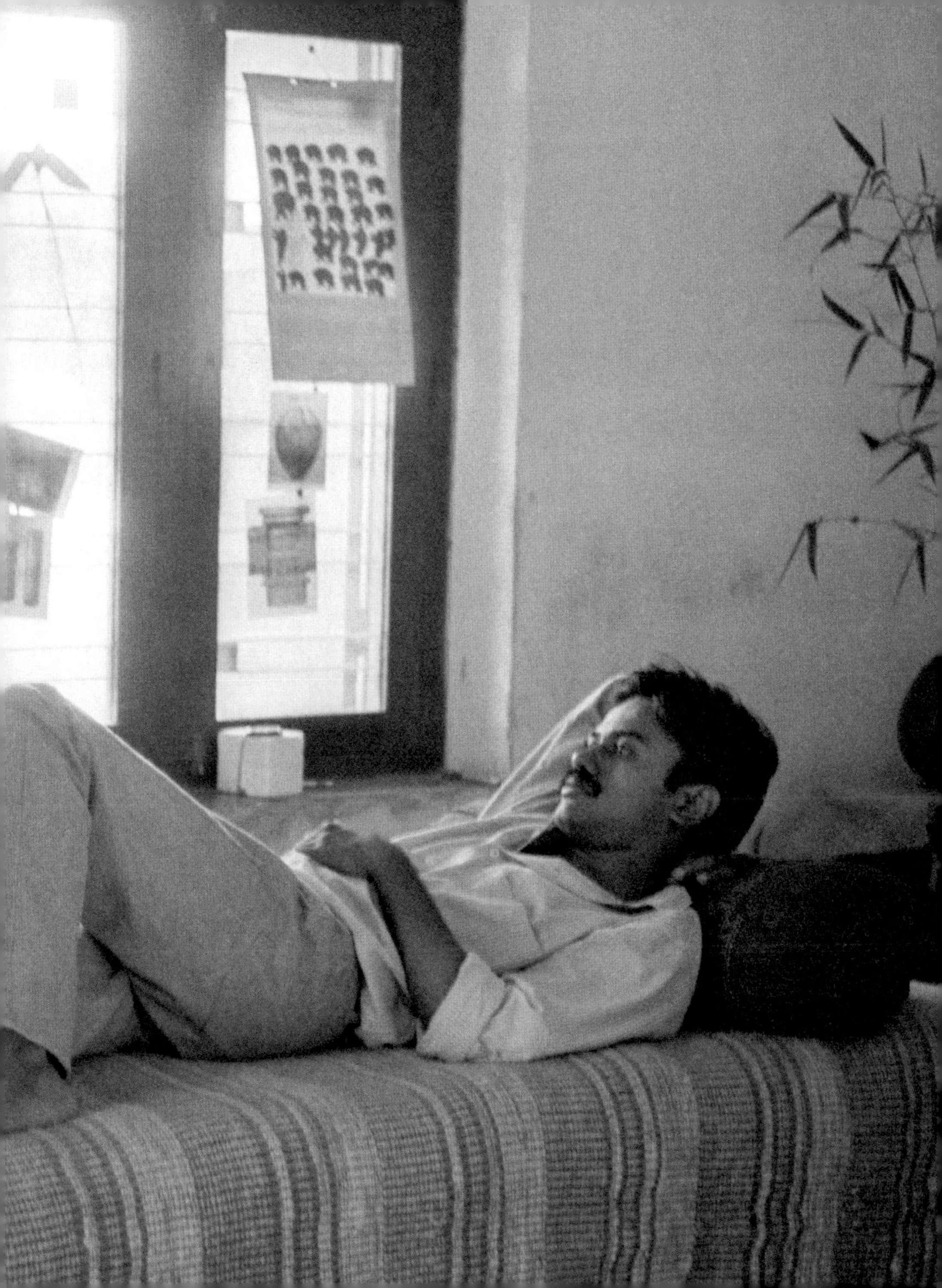

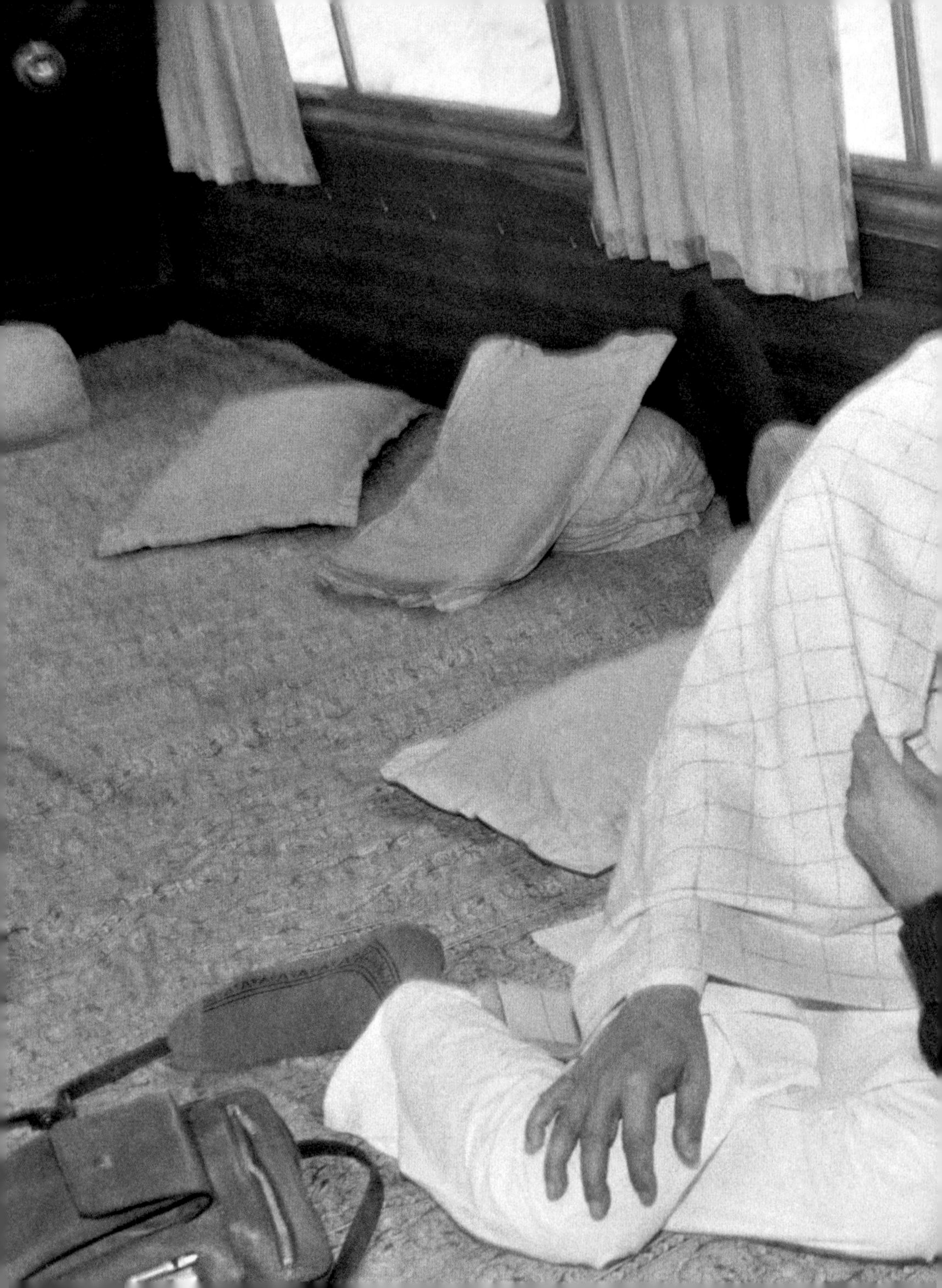

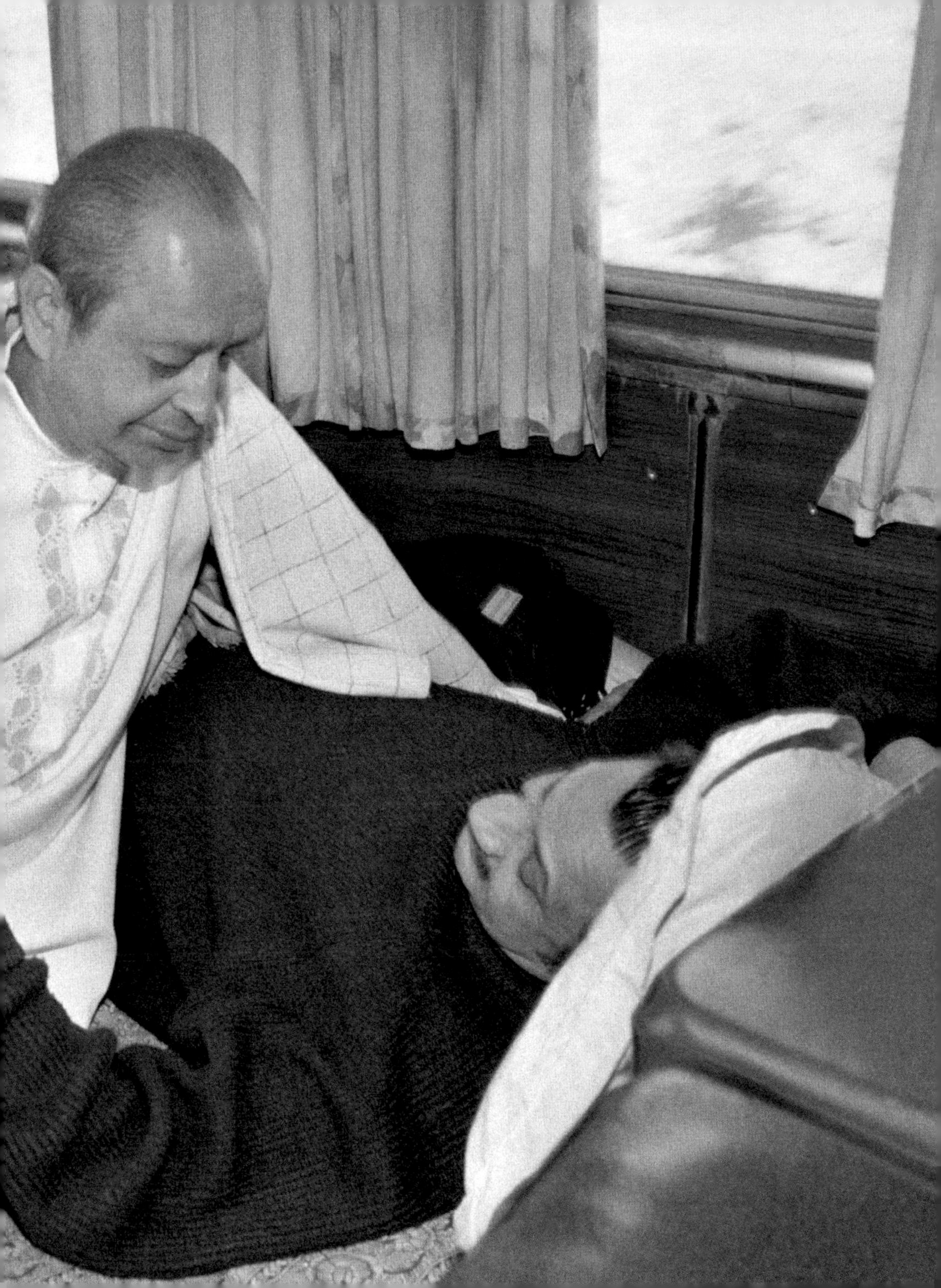

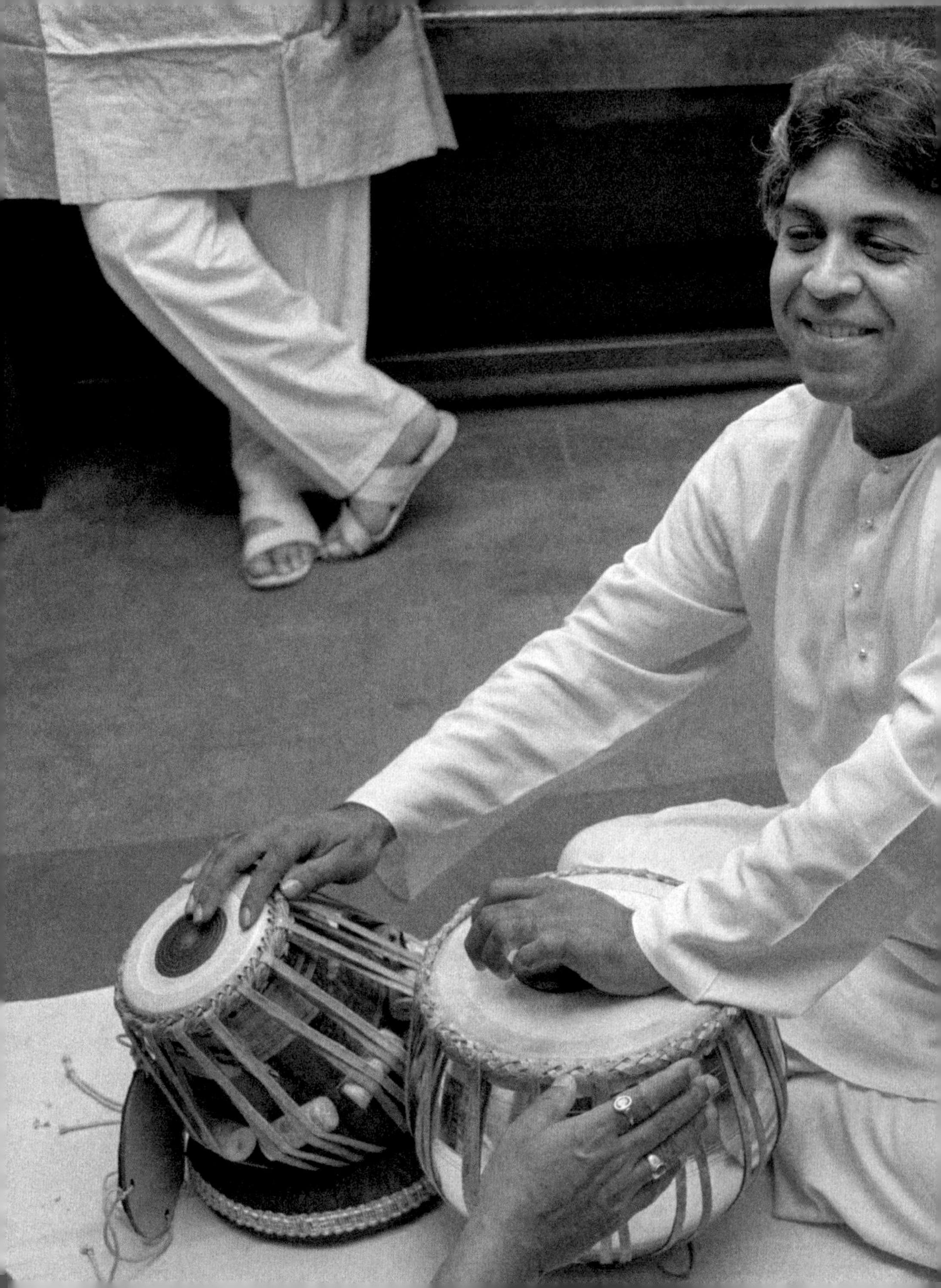

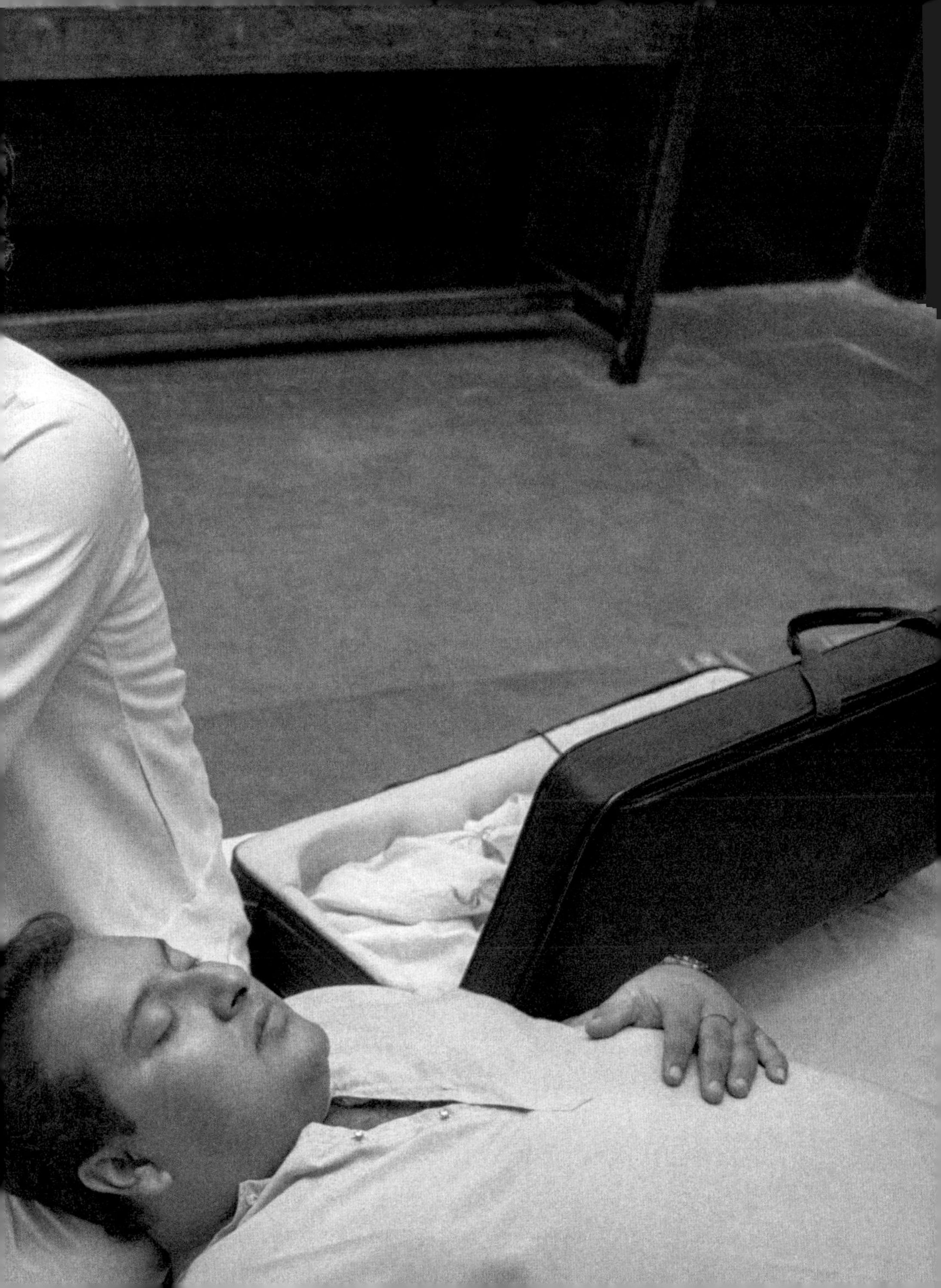

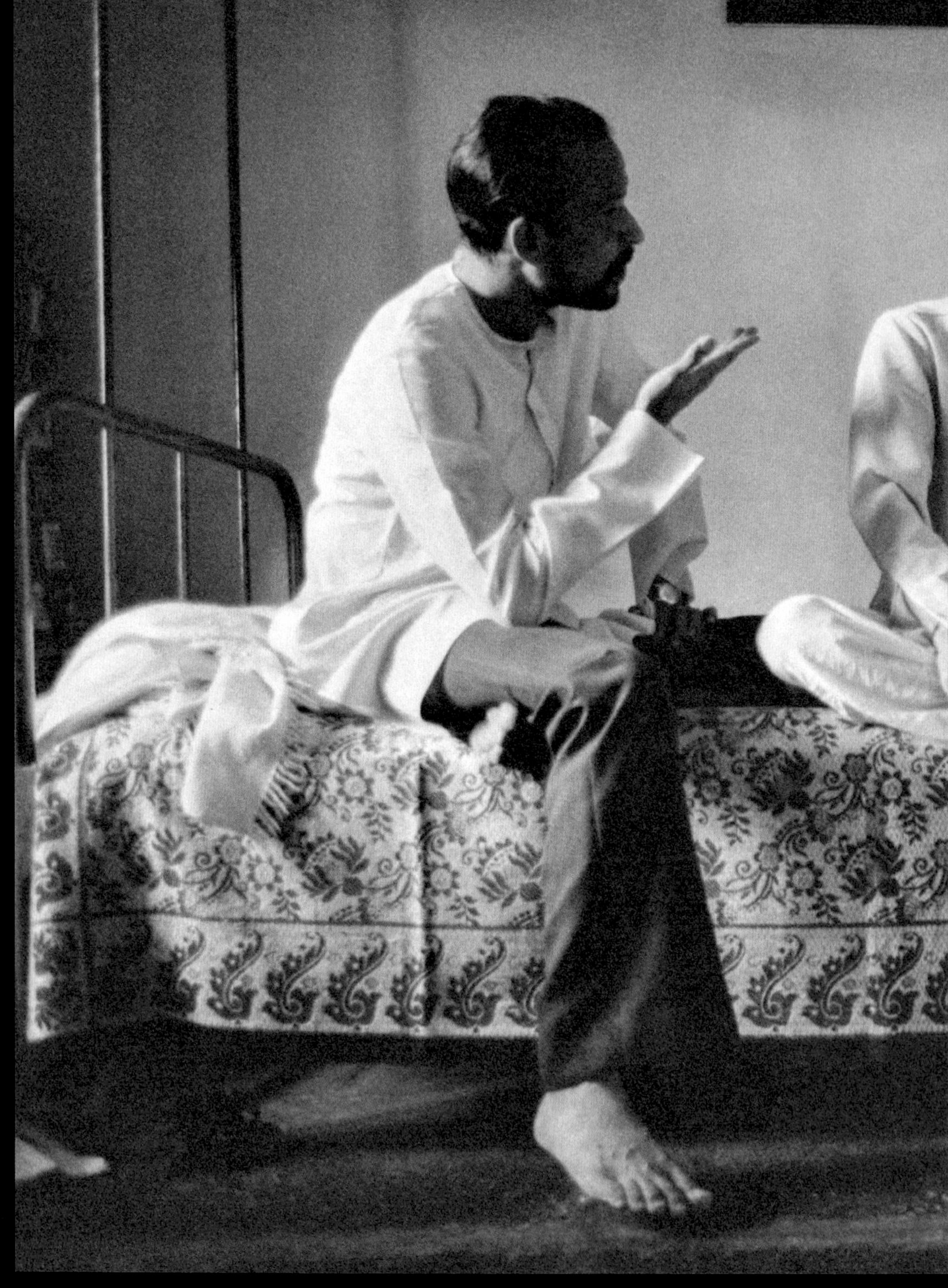

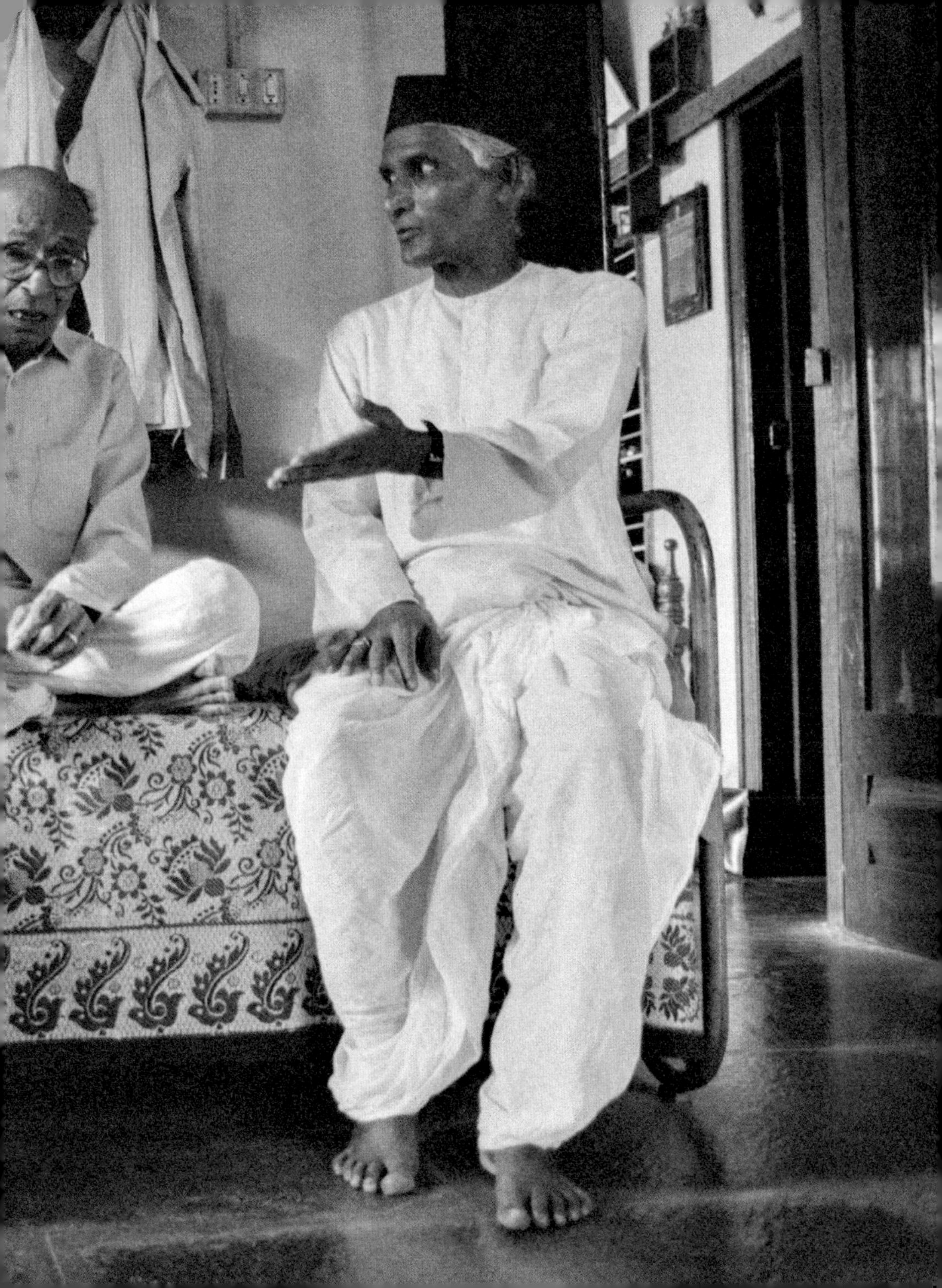

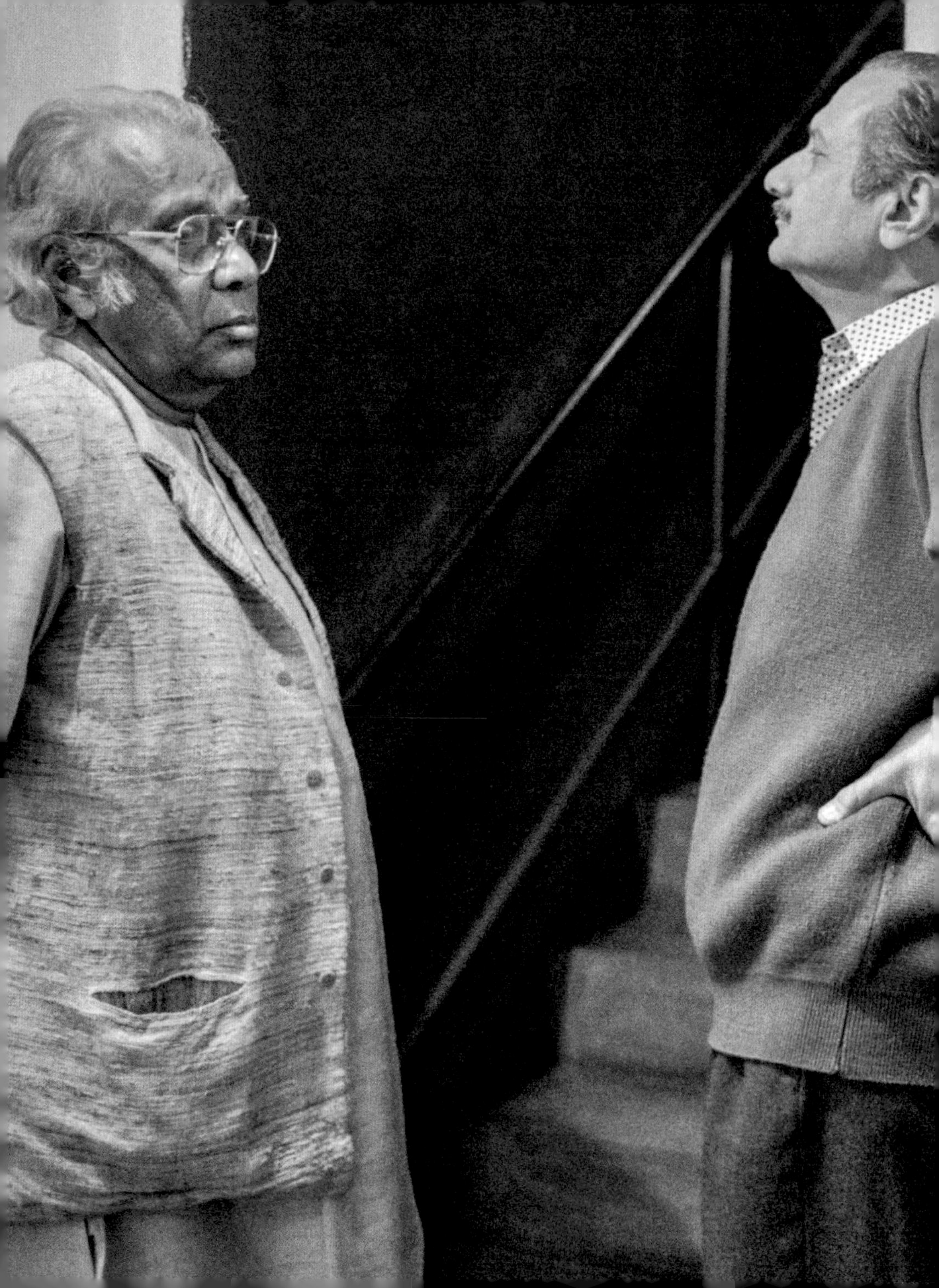

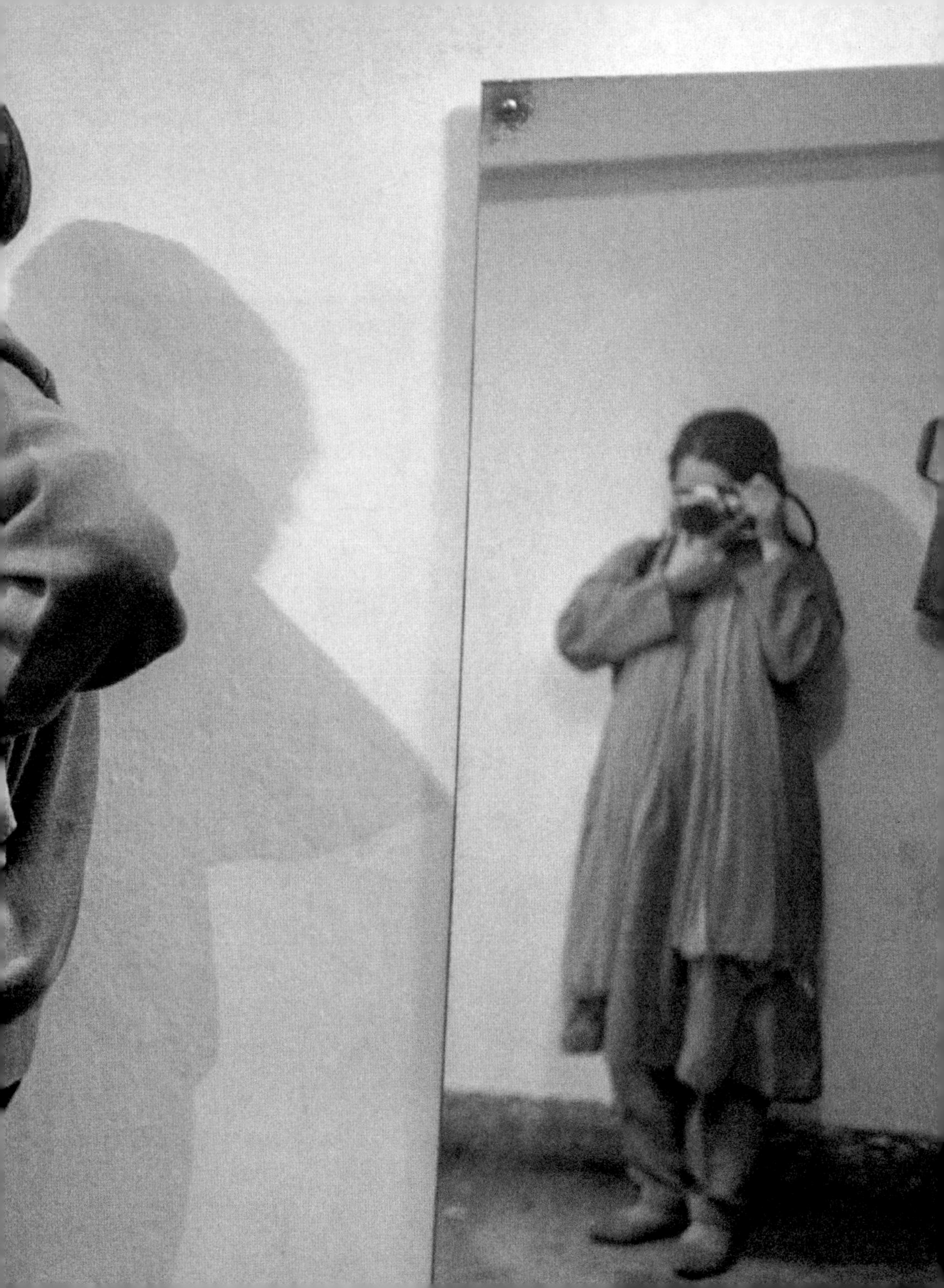

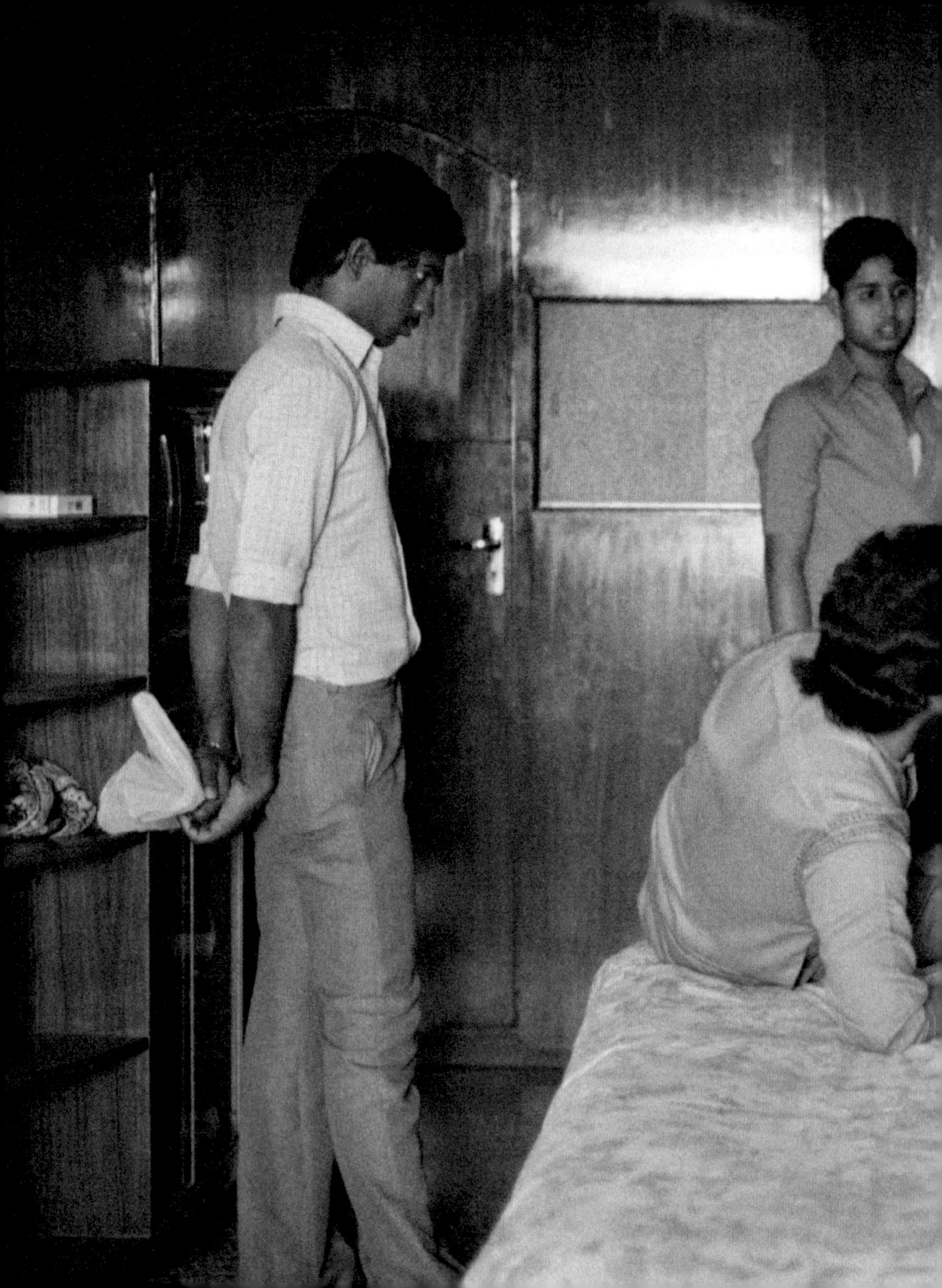

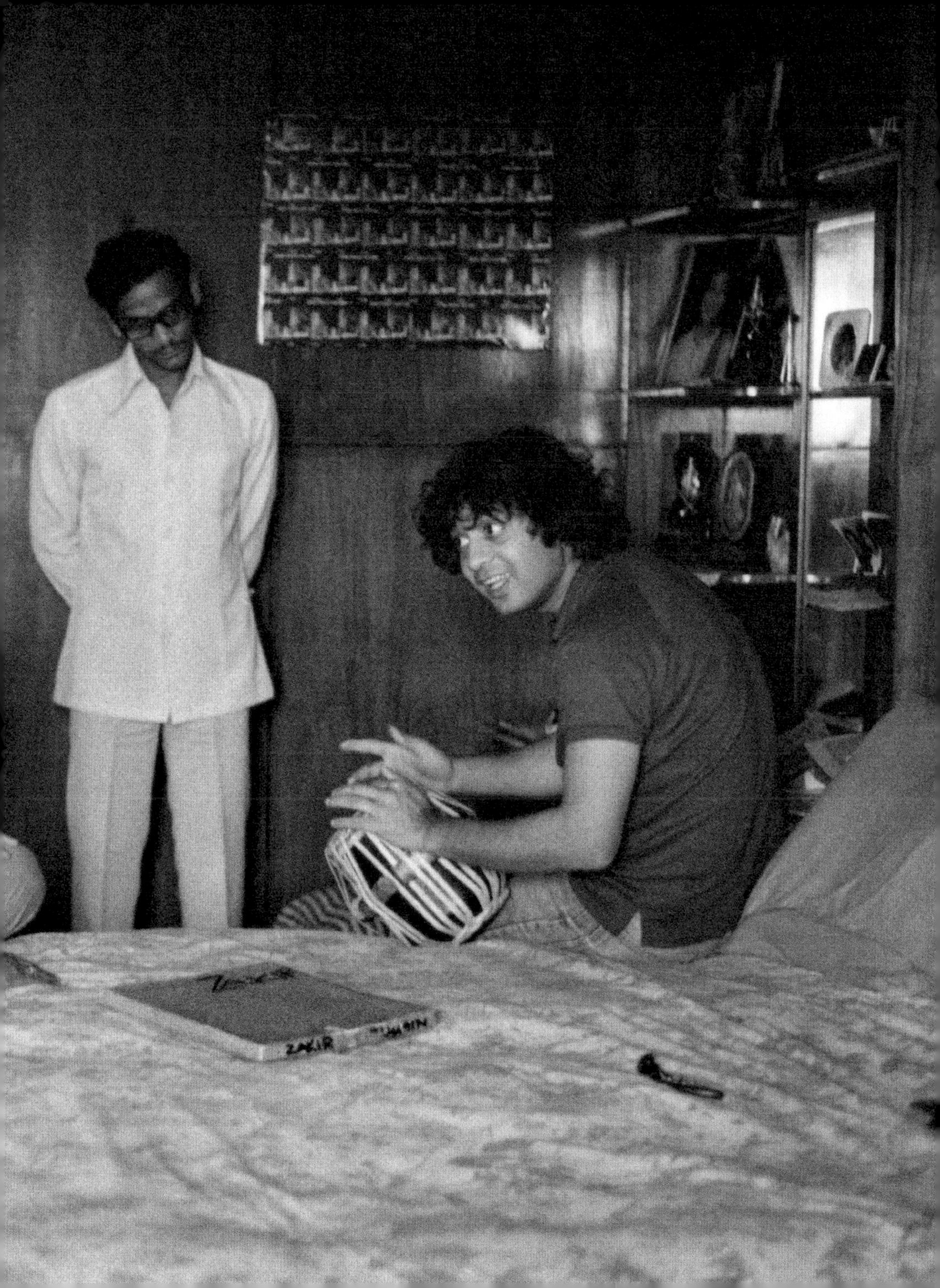

ZAKIR
ZAKIR HUSAIN

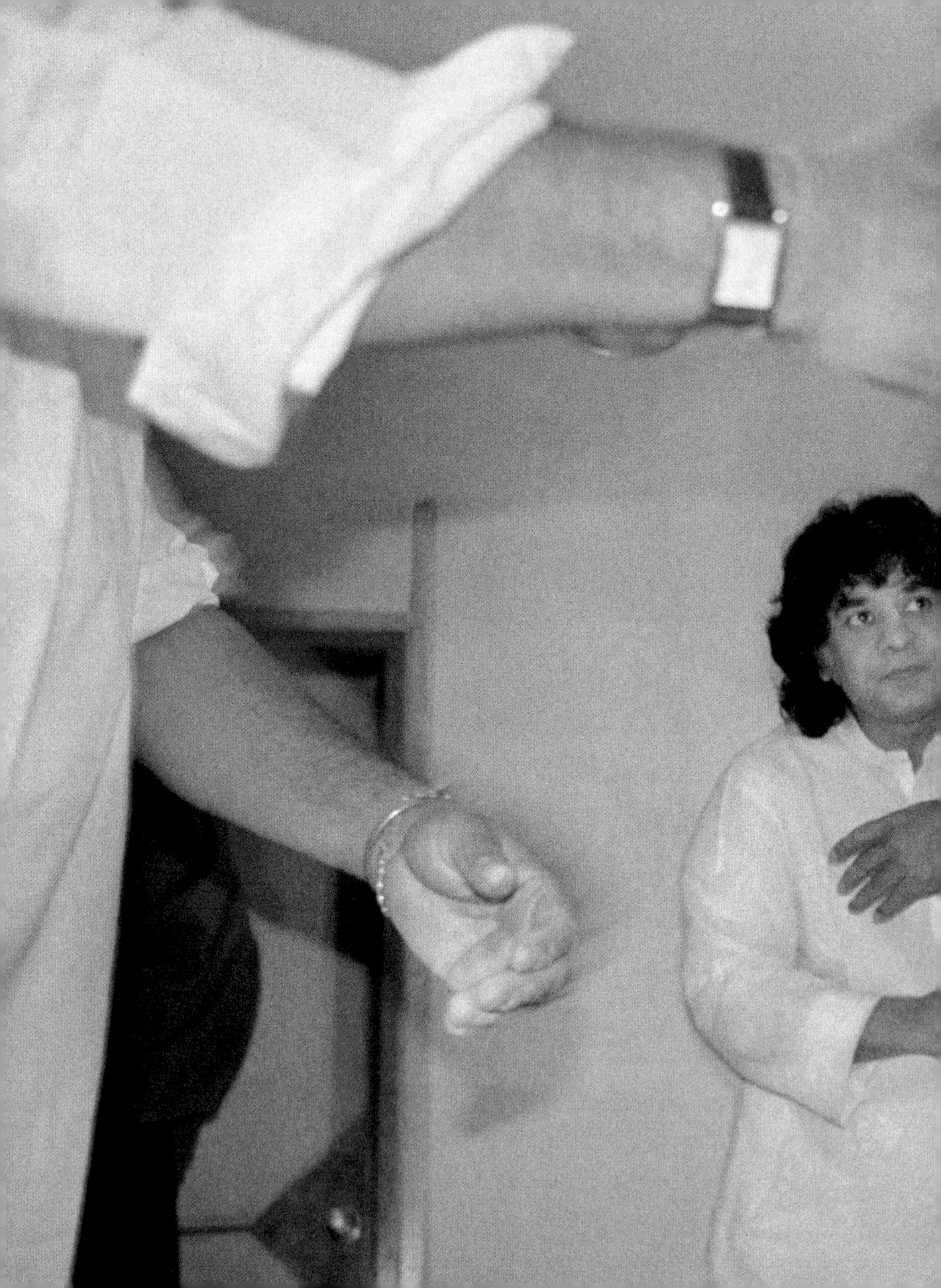

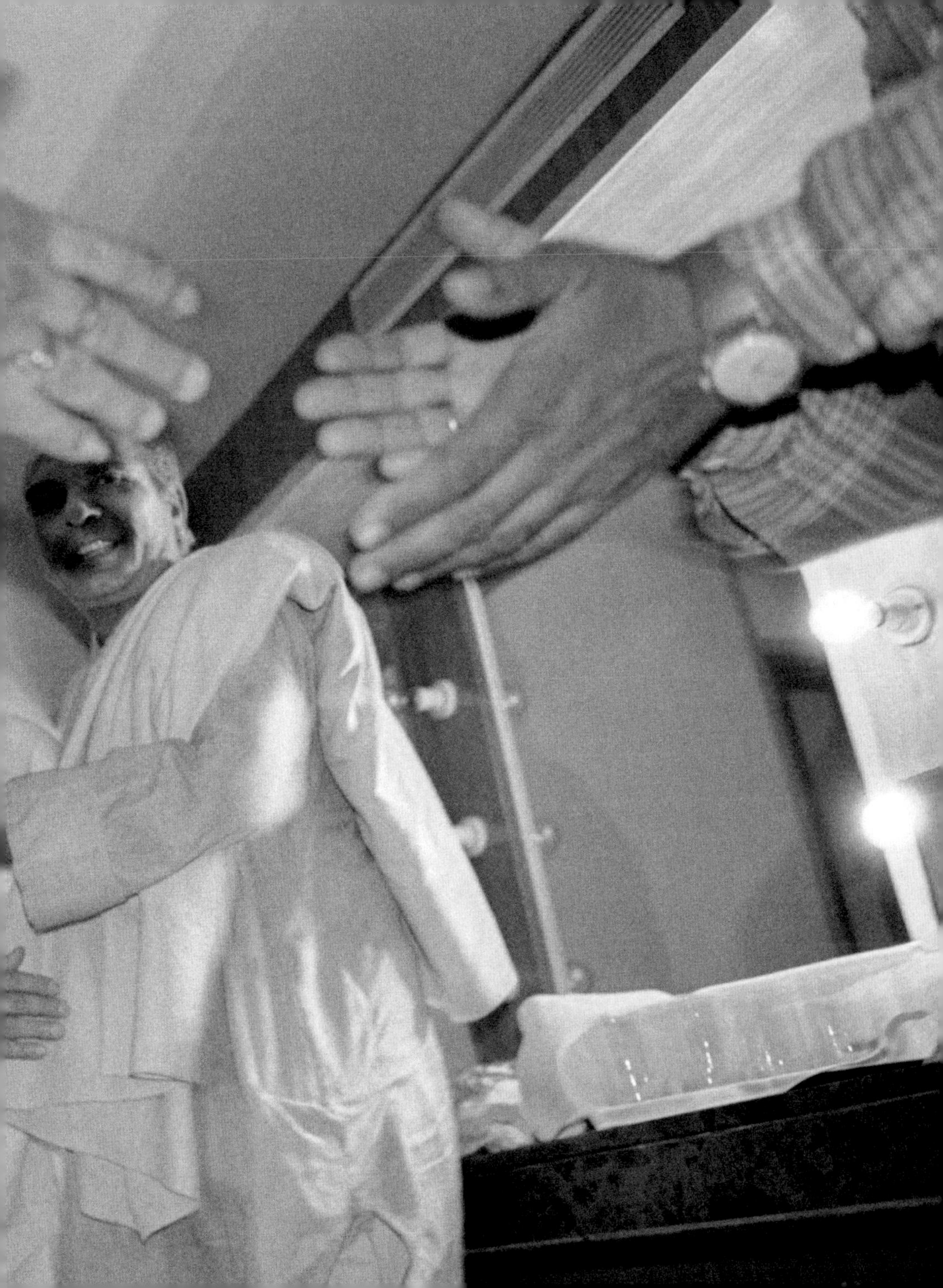

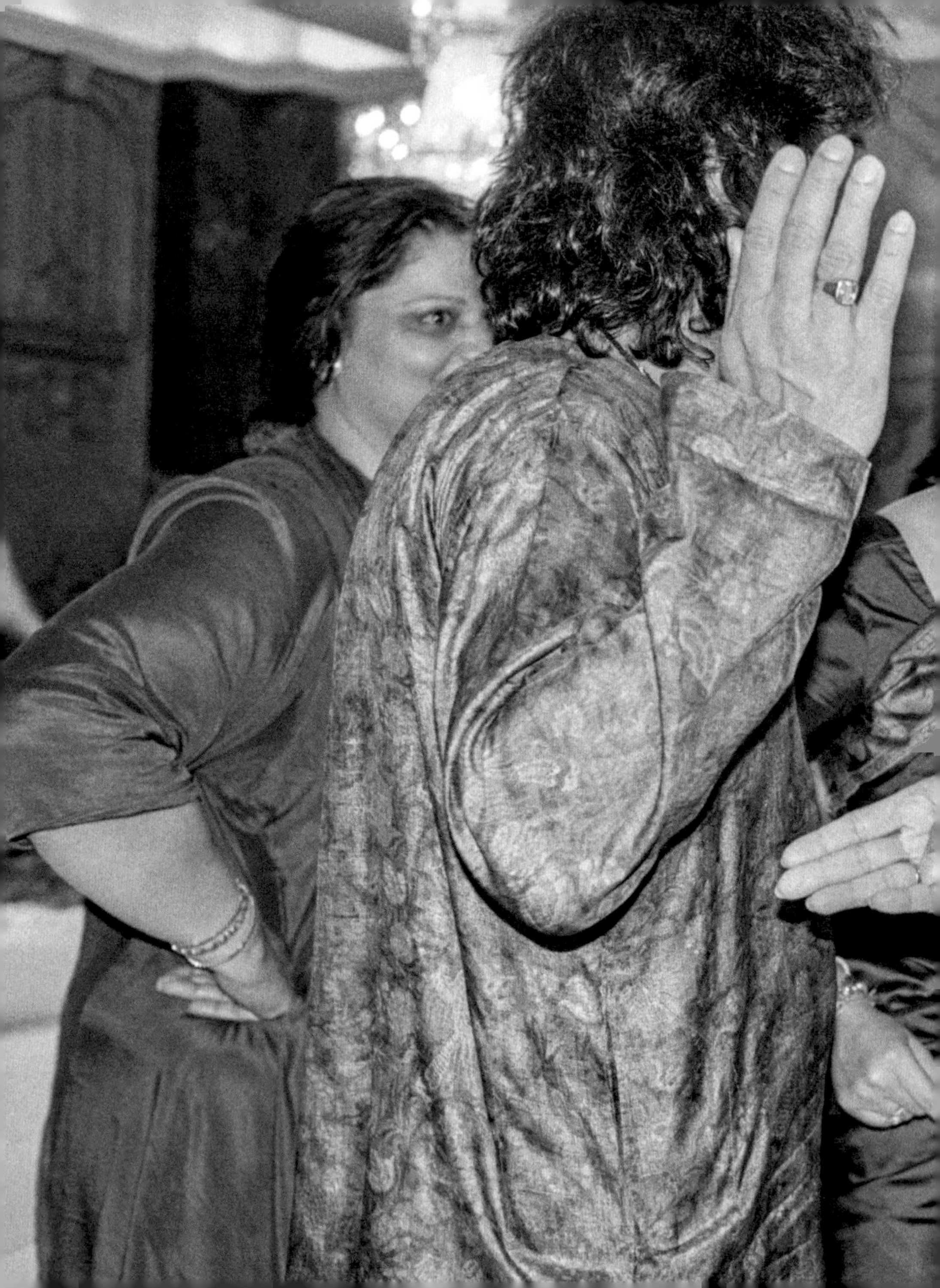

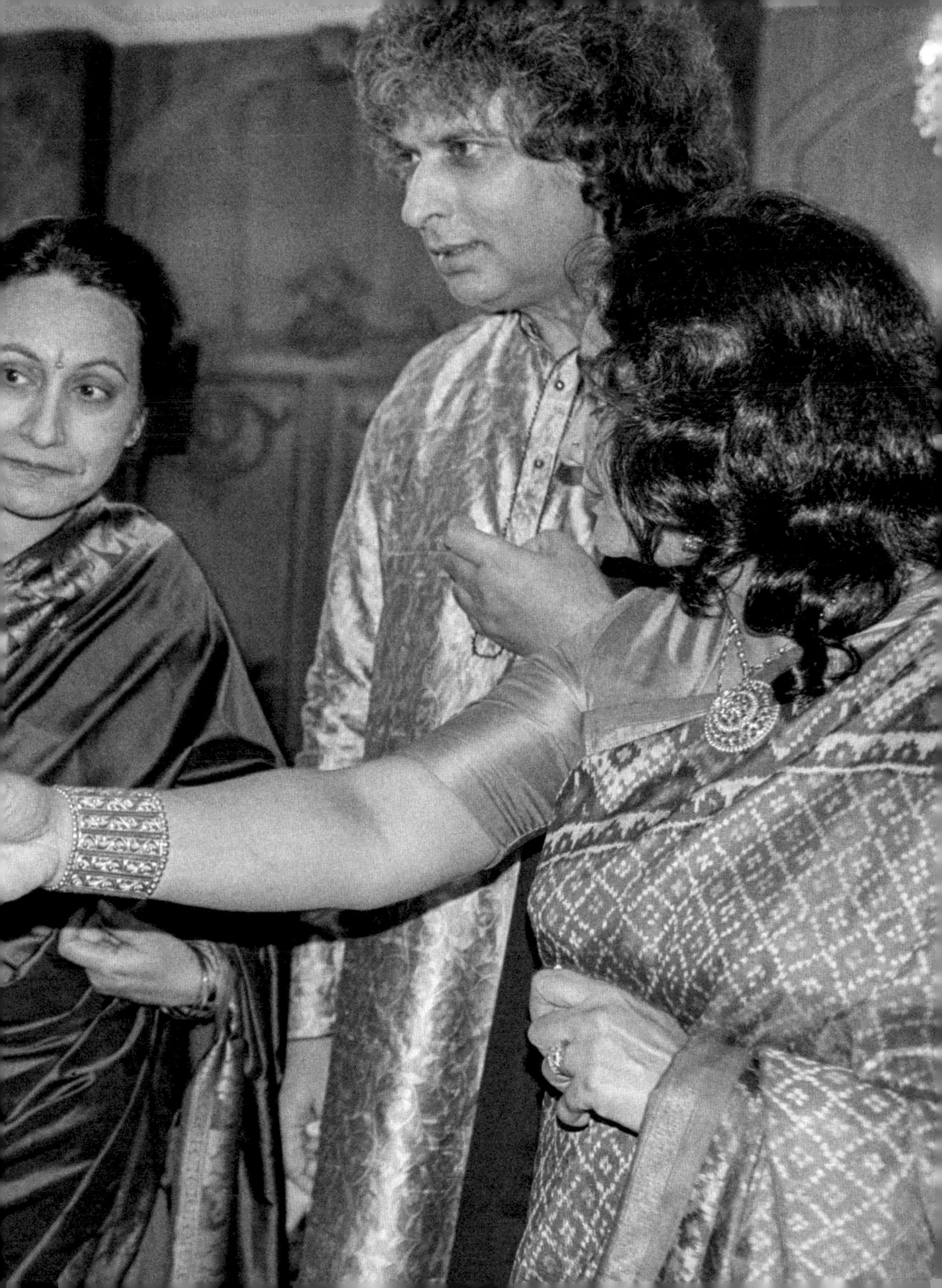

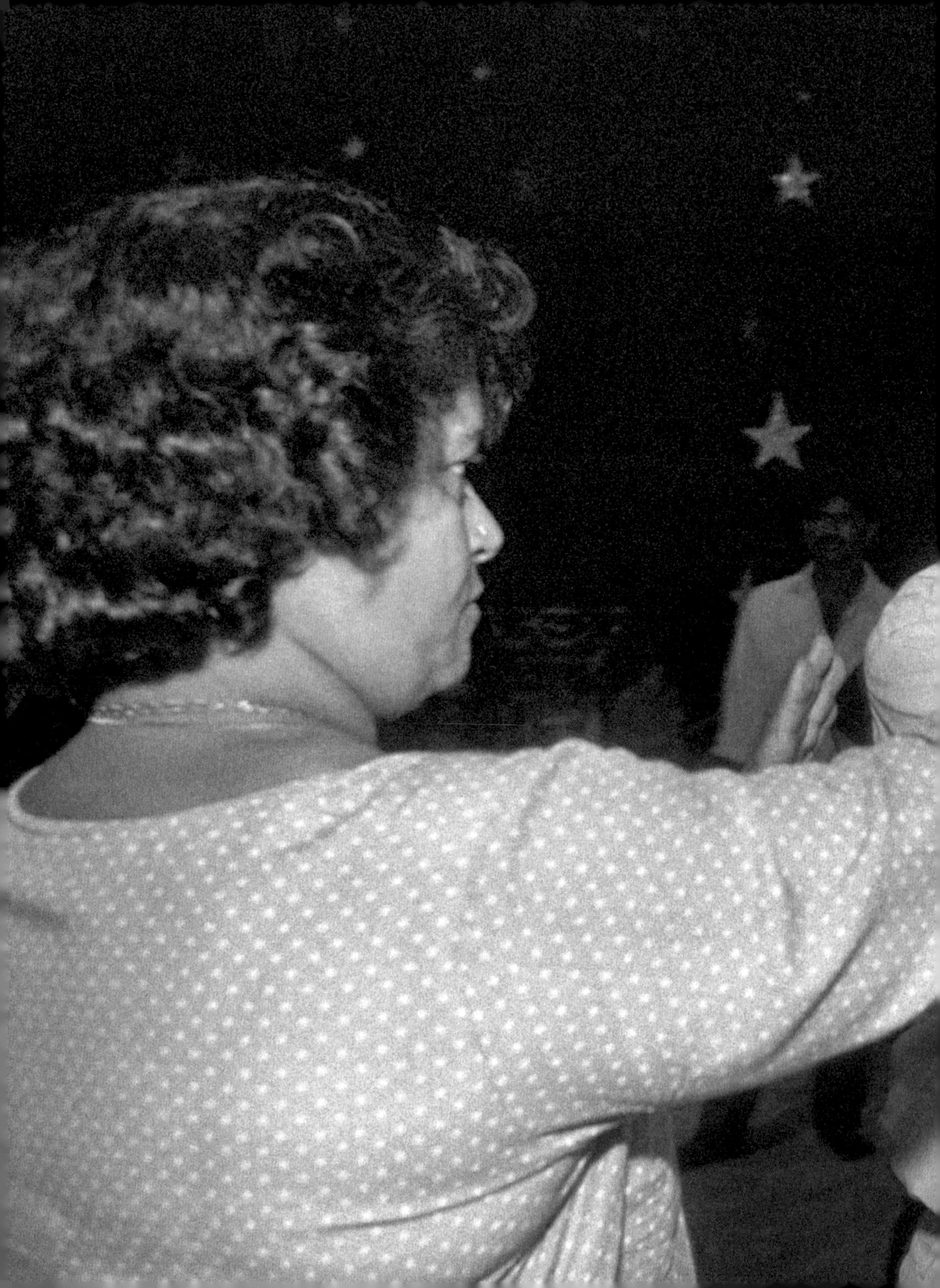

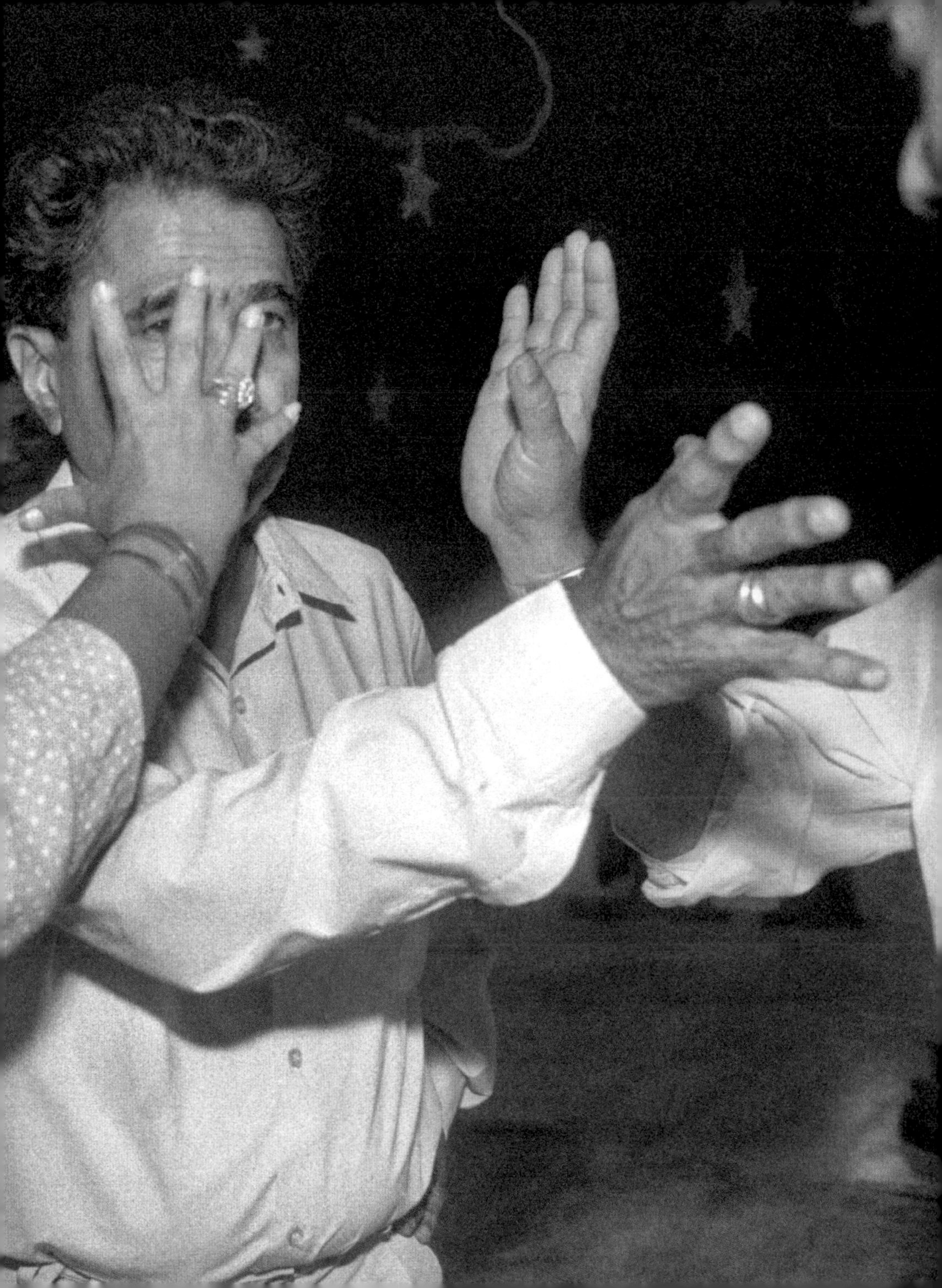

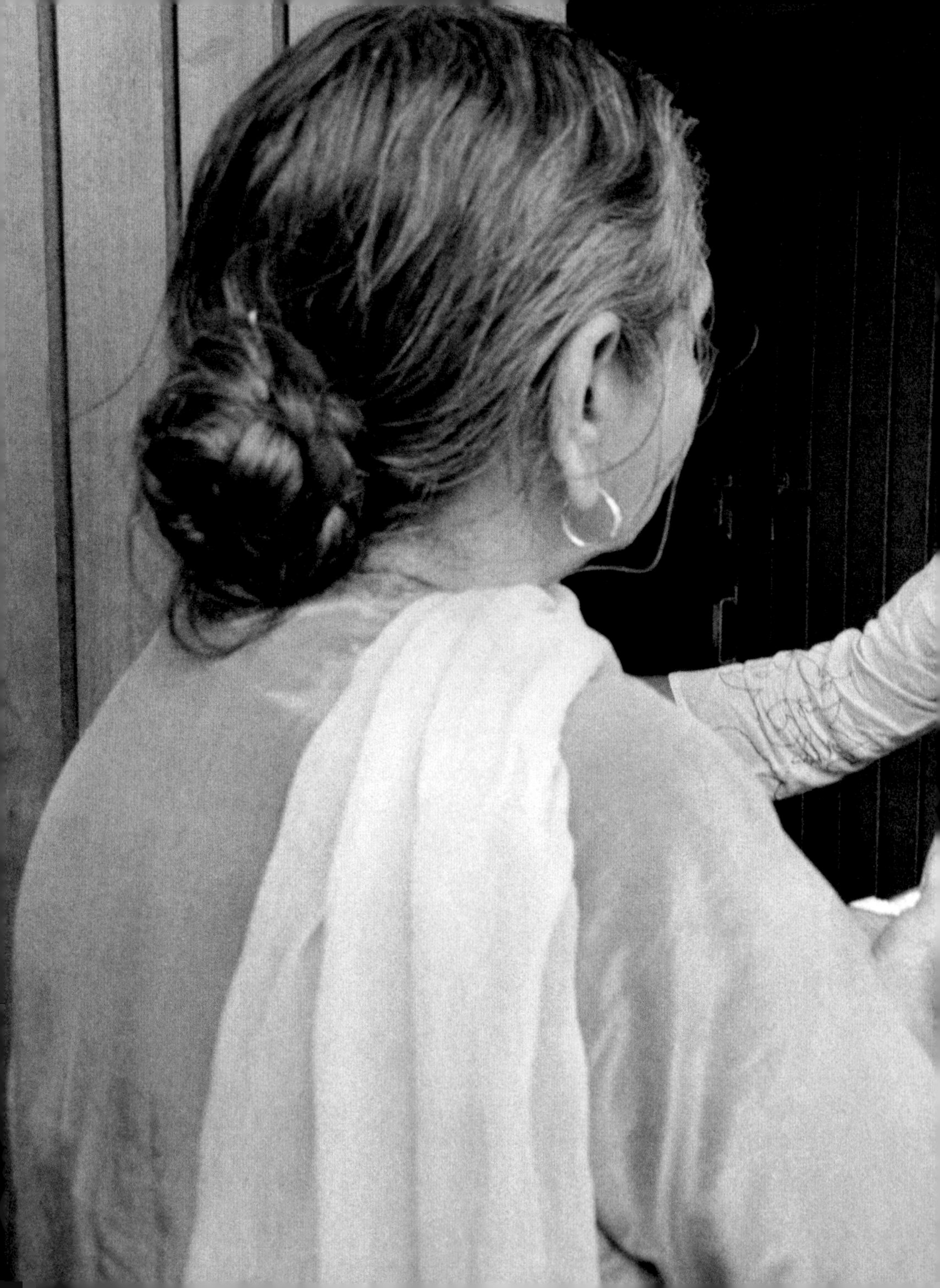

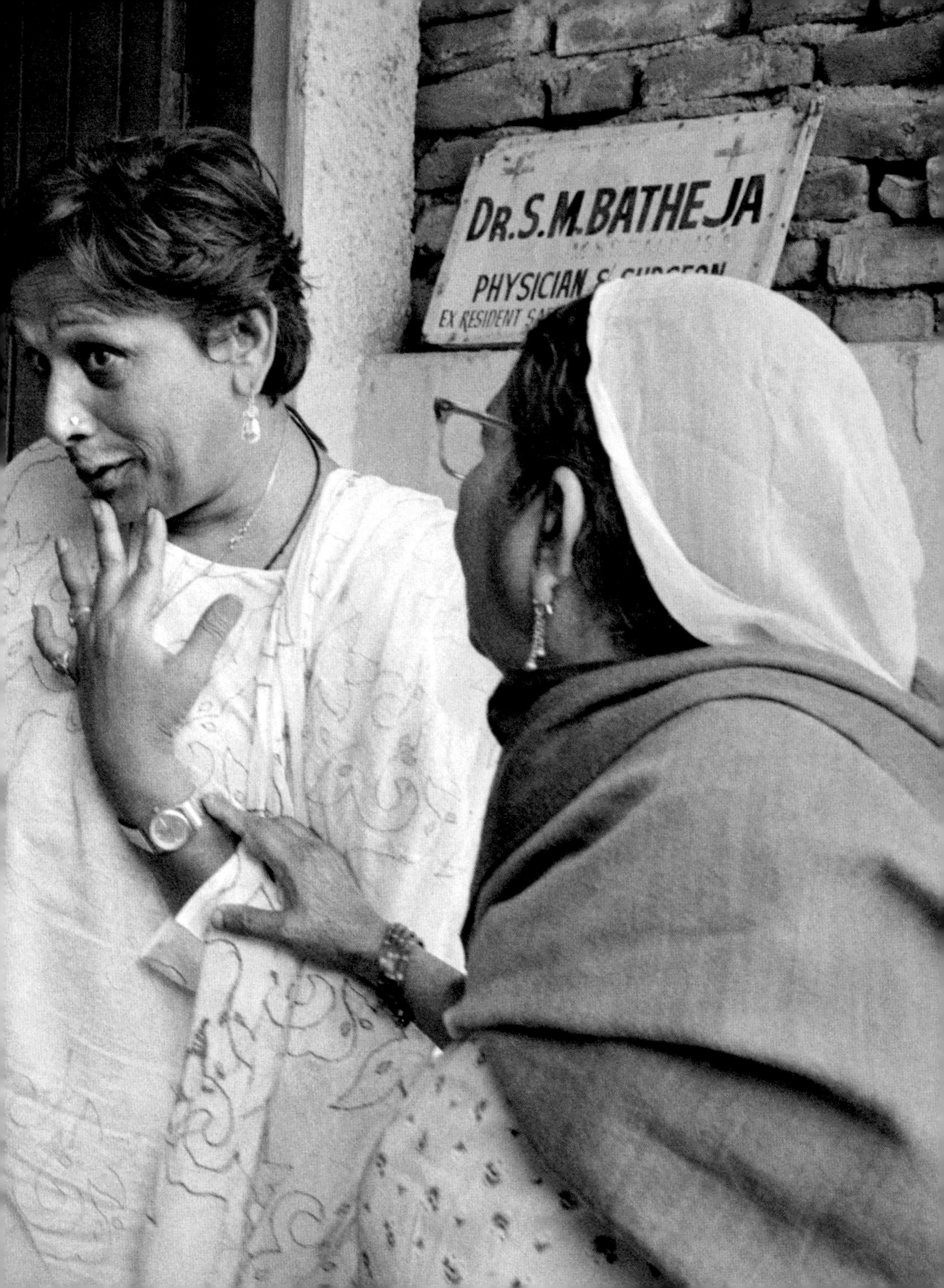

Dr. S. M. BATHEJA
PHYSICIAN & SURGEON
EX RESIDENT SA

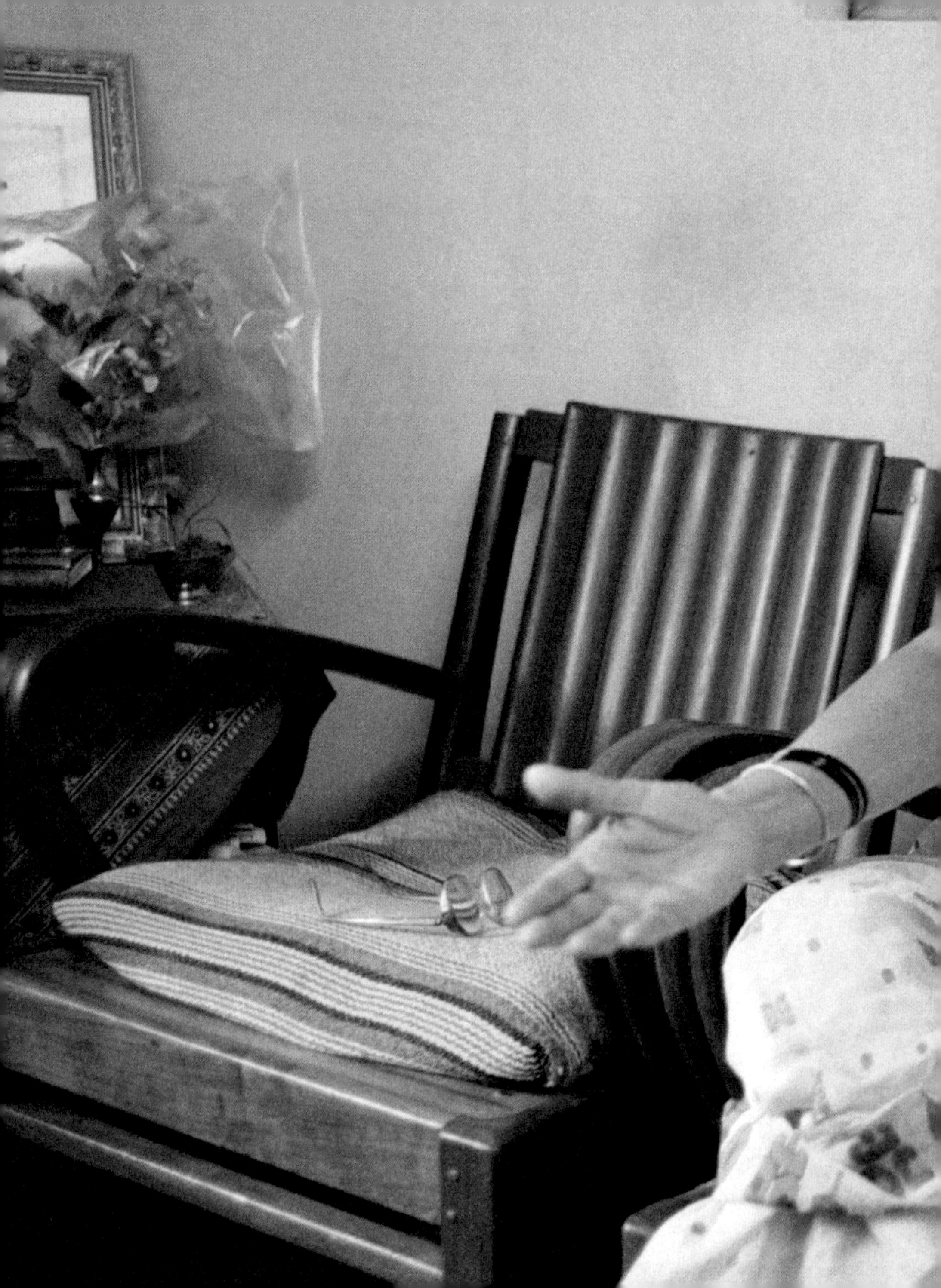

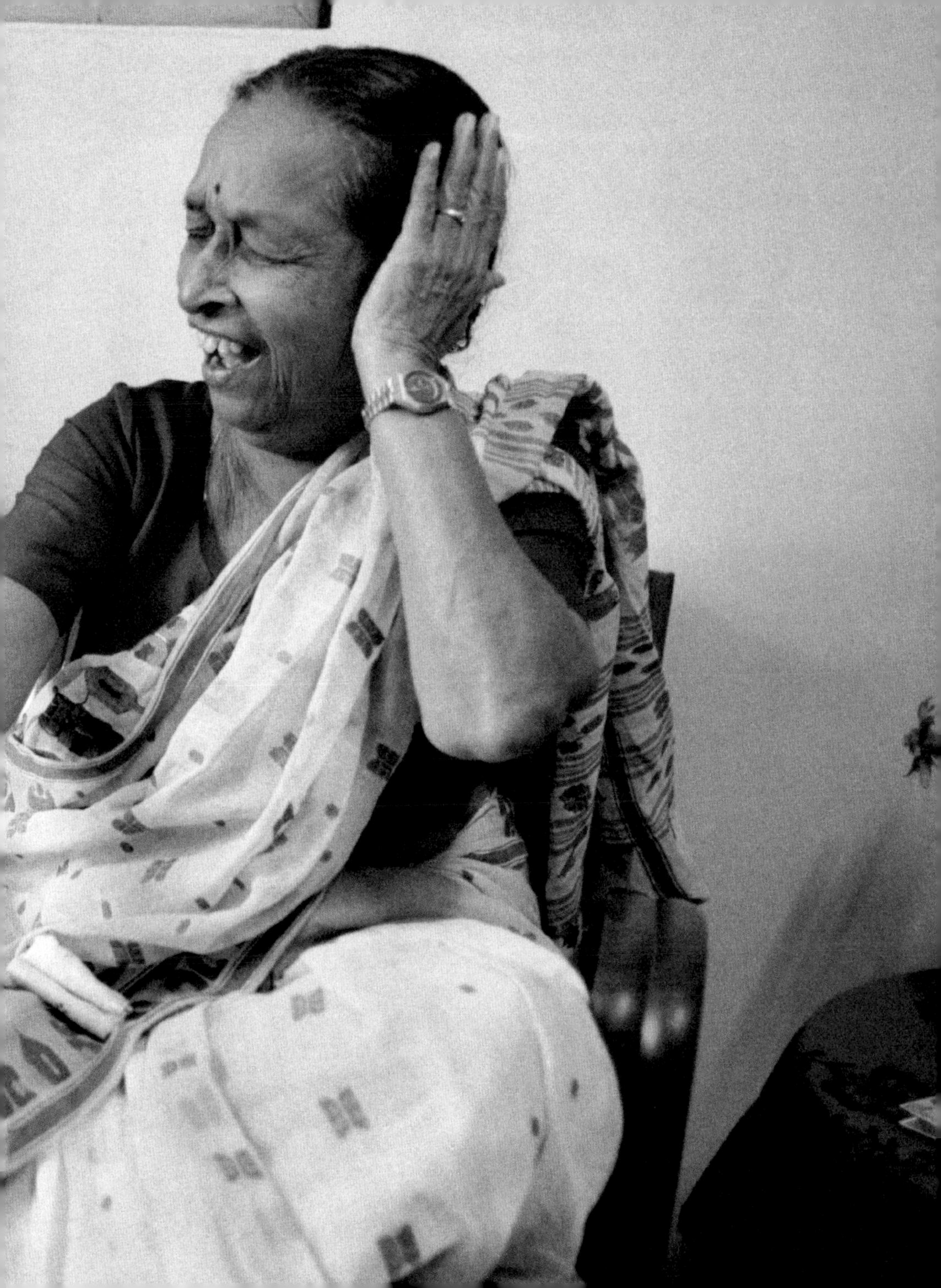

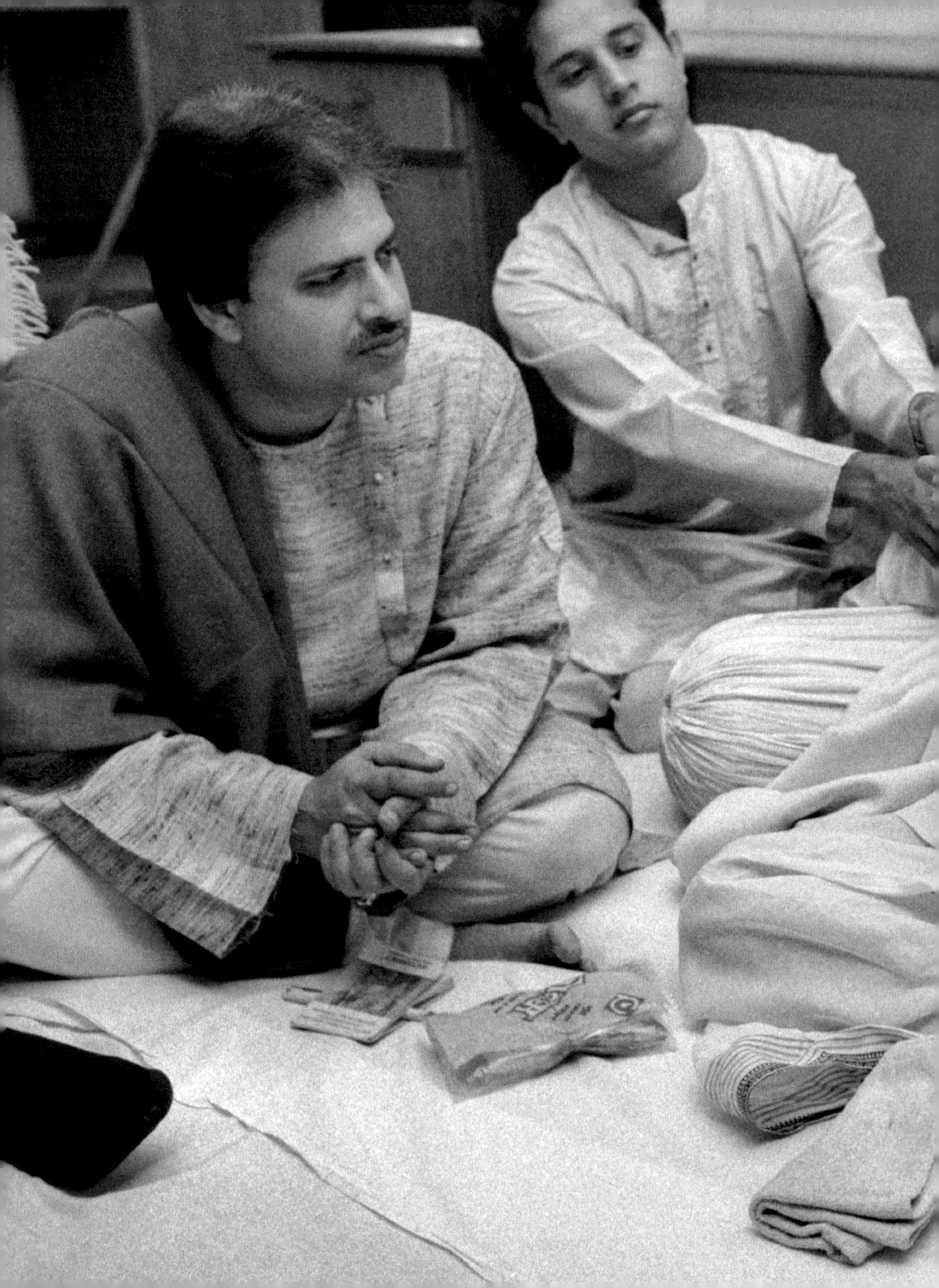

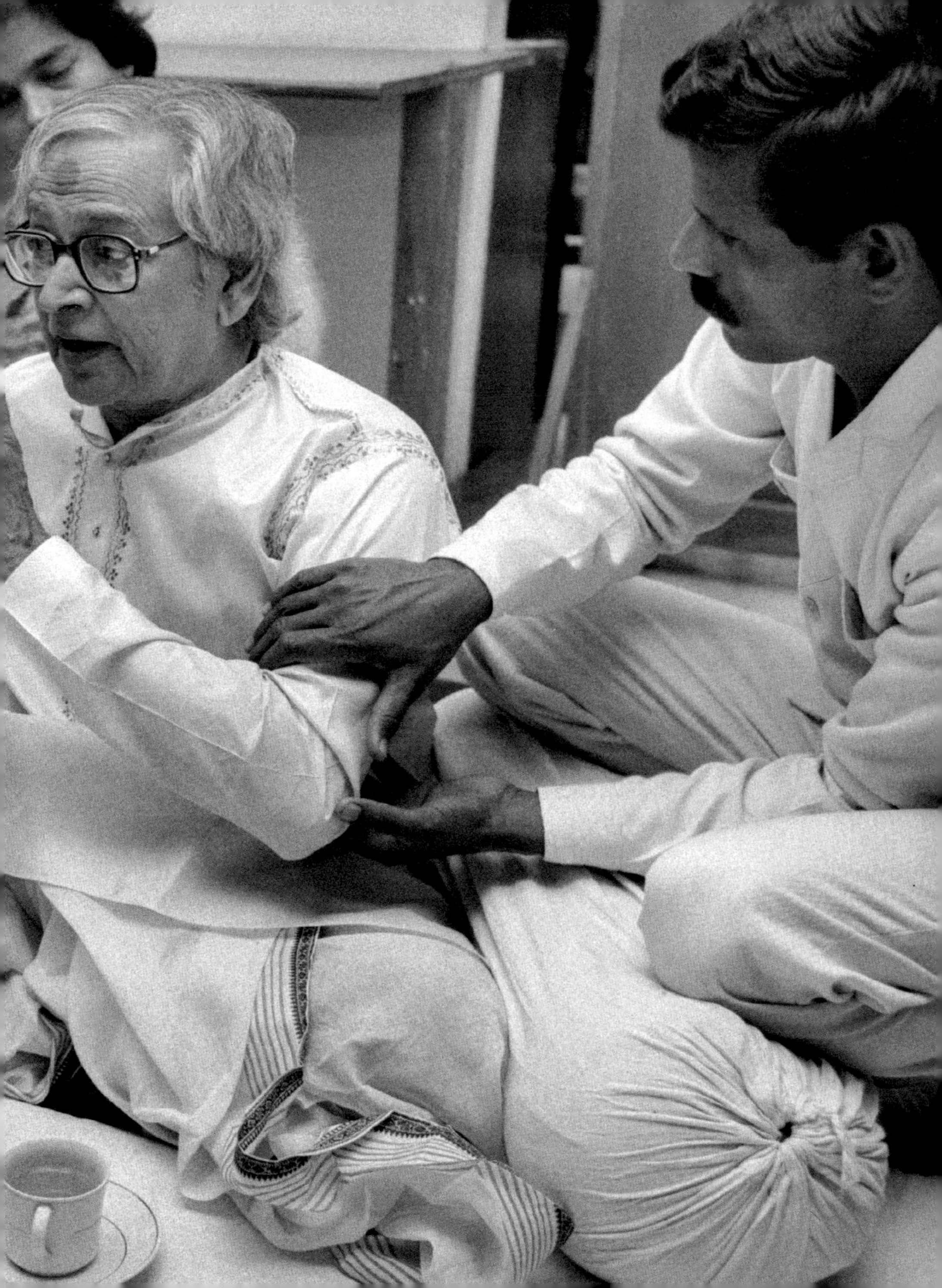

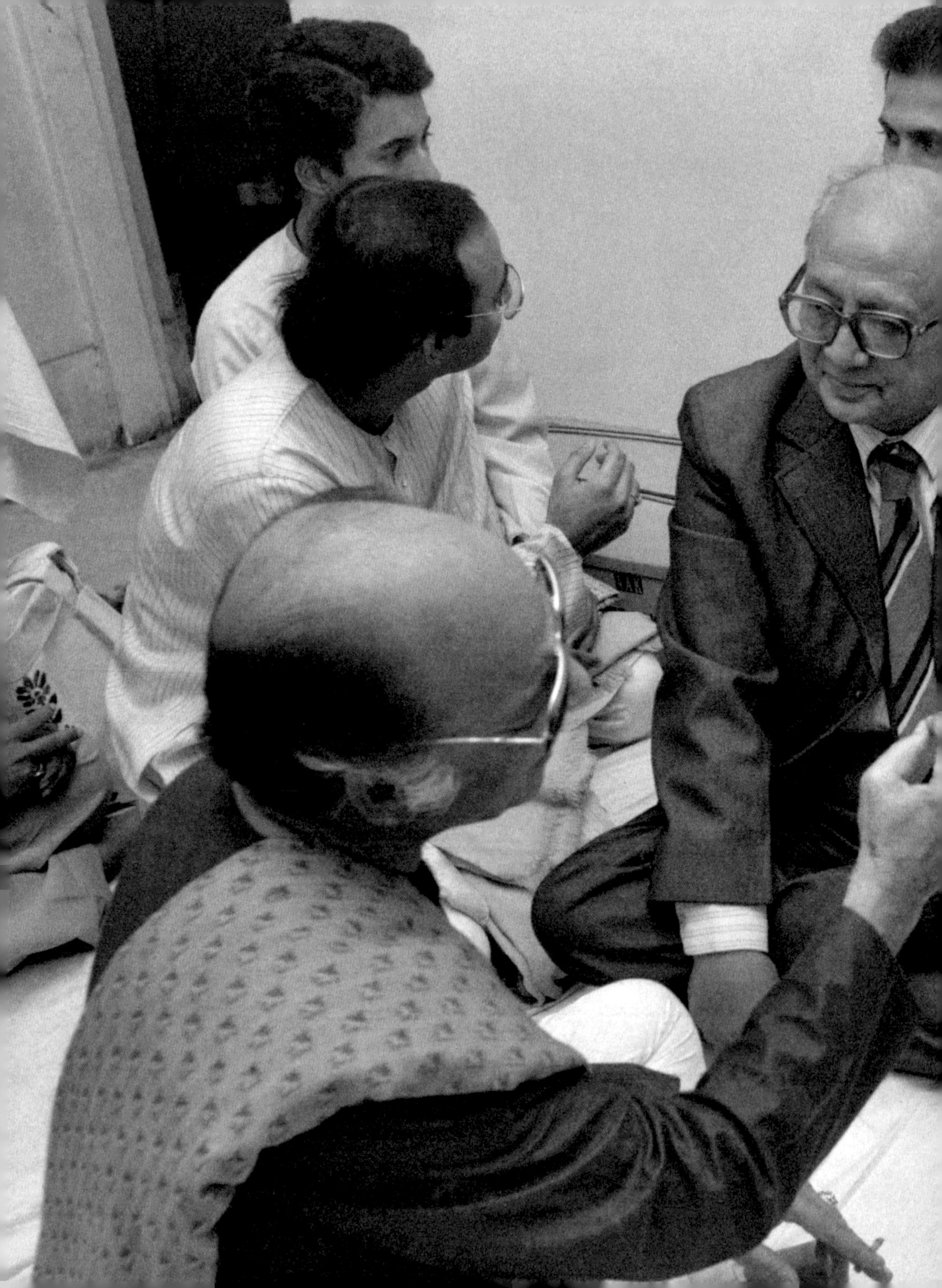

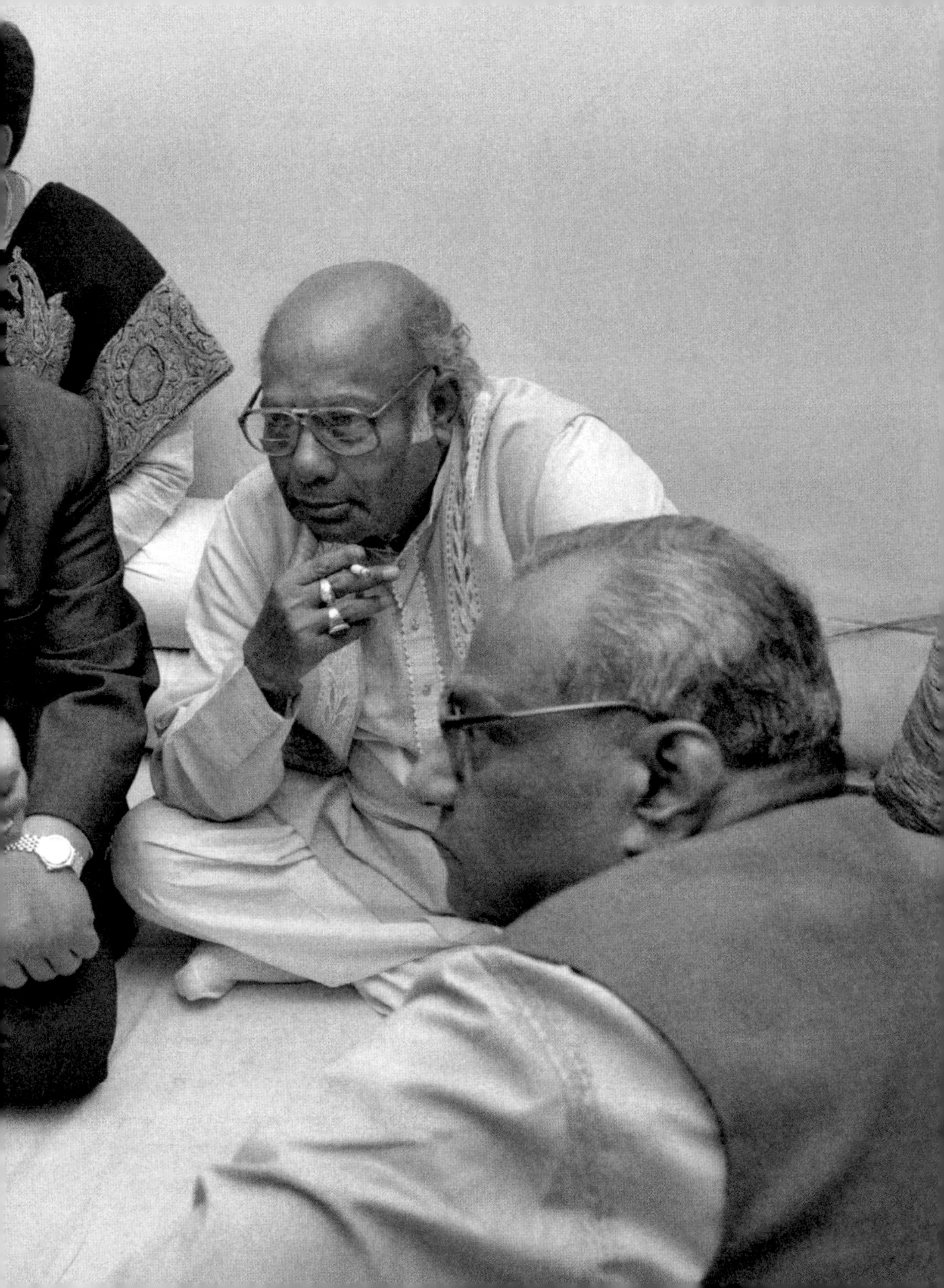

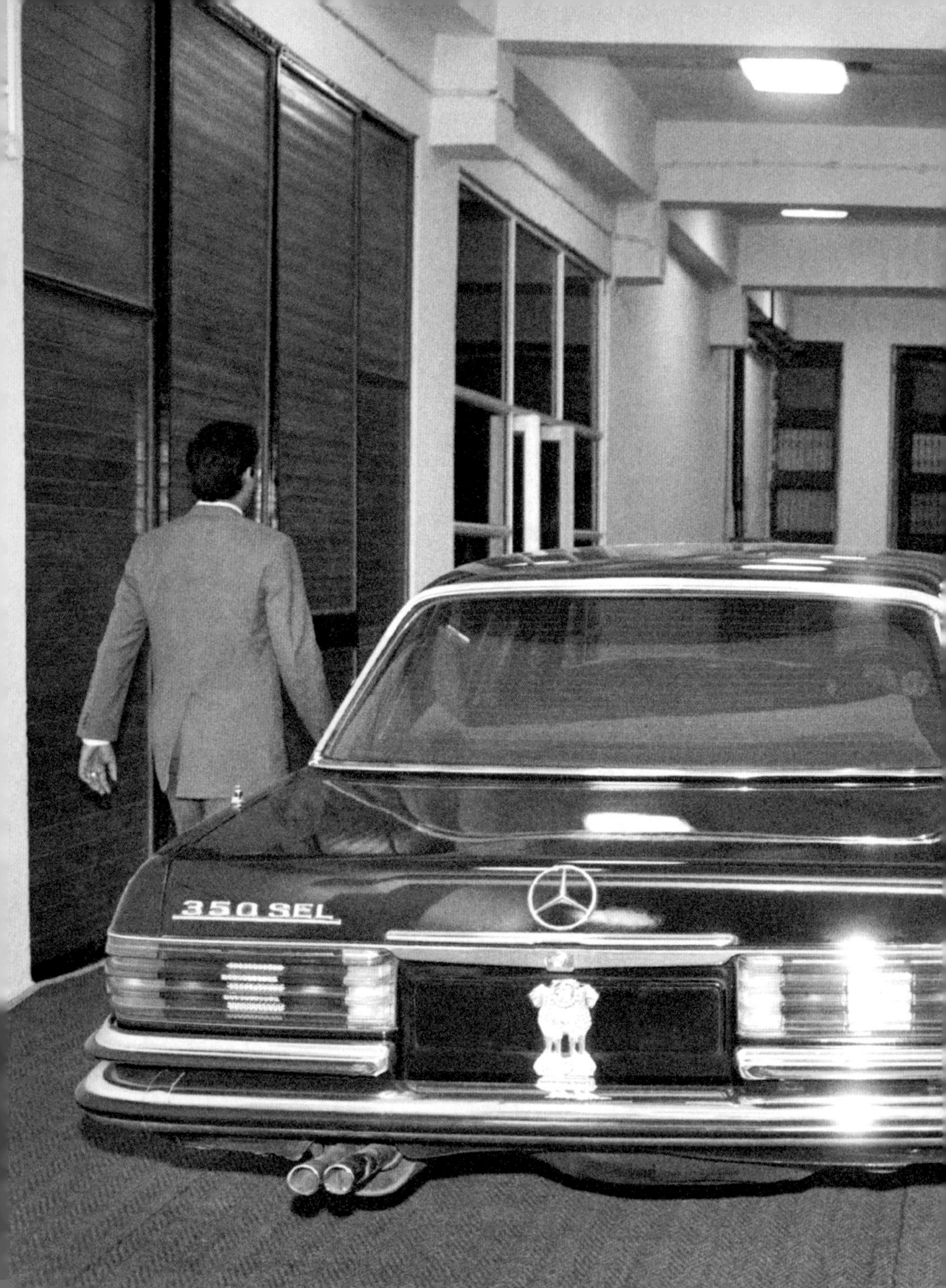

350 SEL

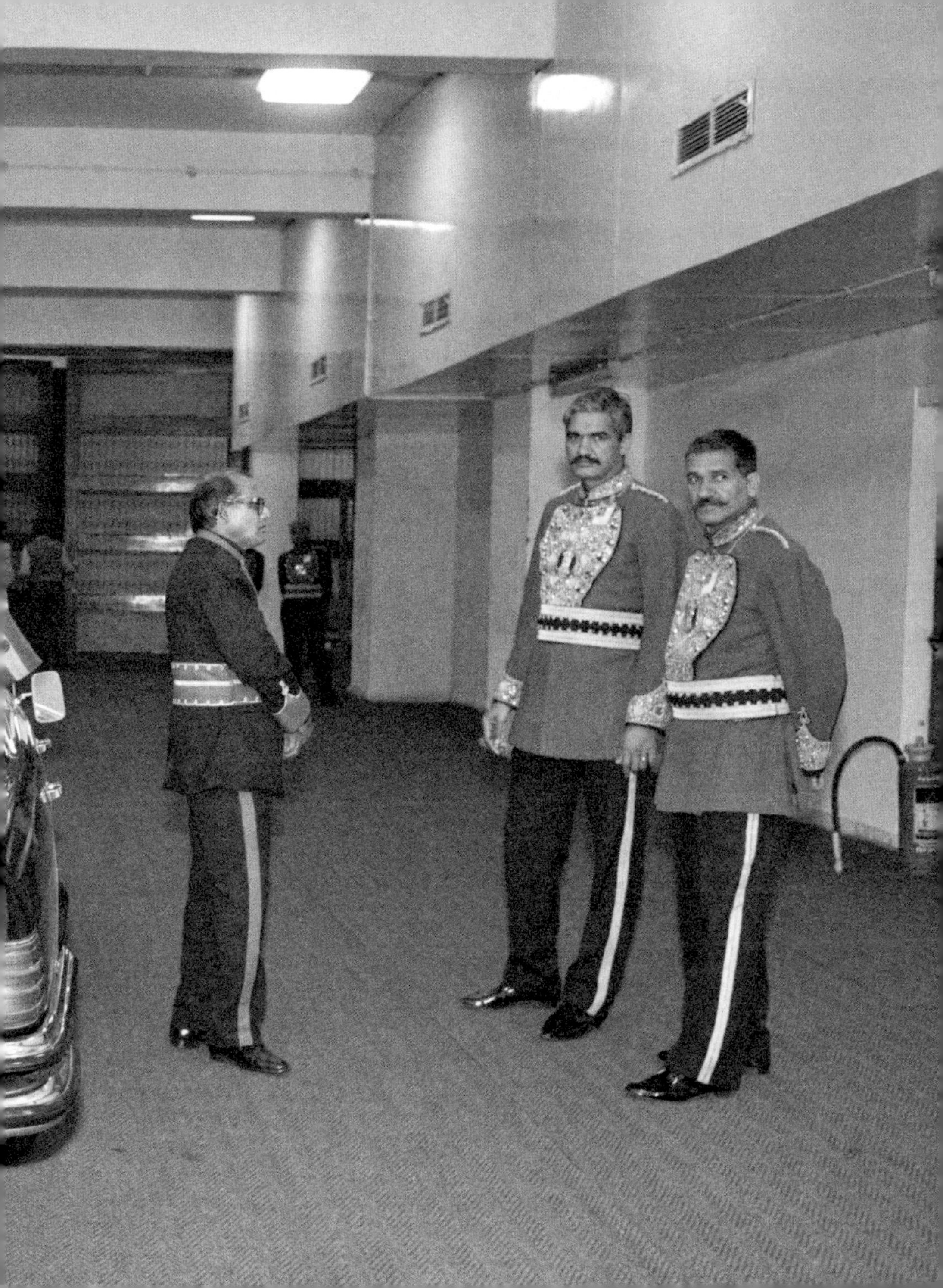

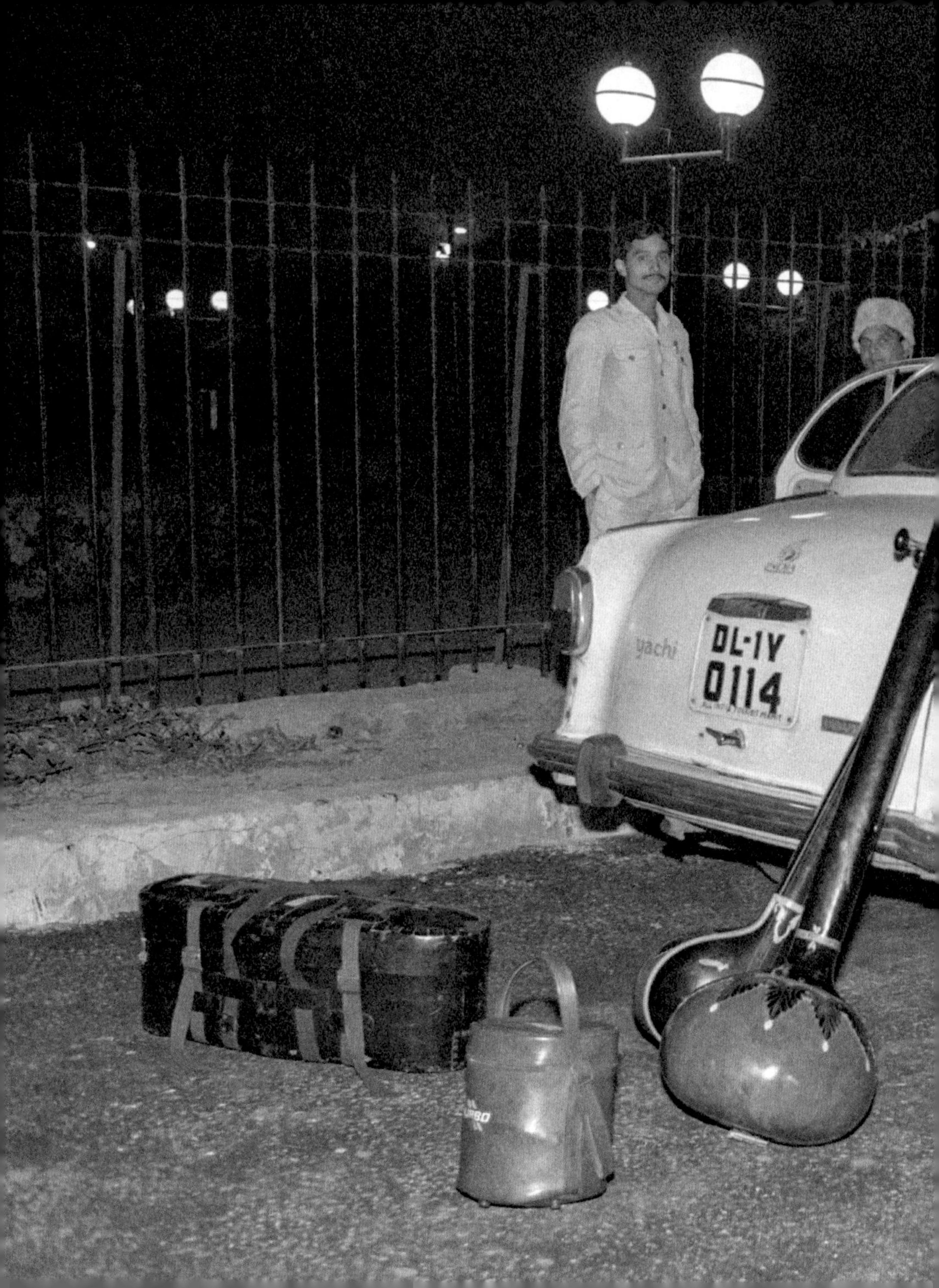

yachi
DL-1Y
0114

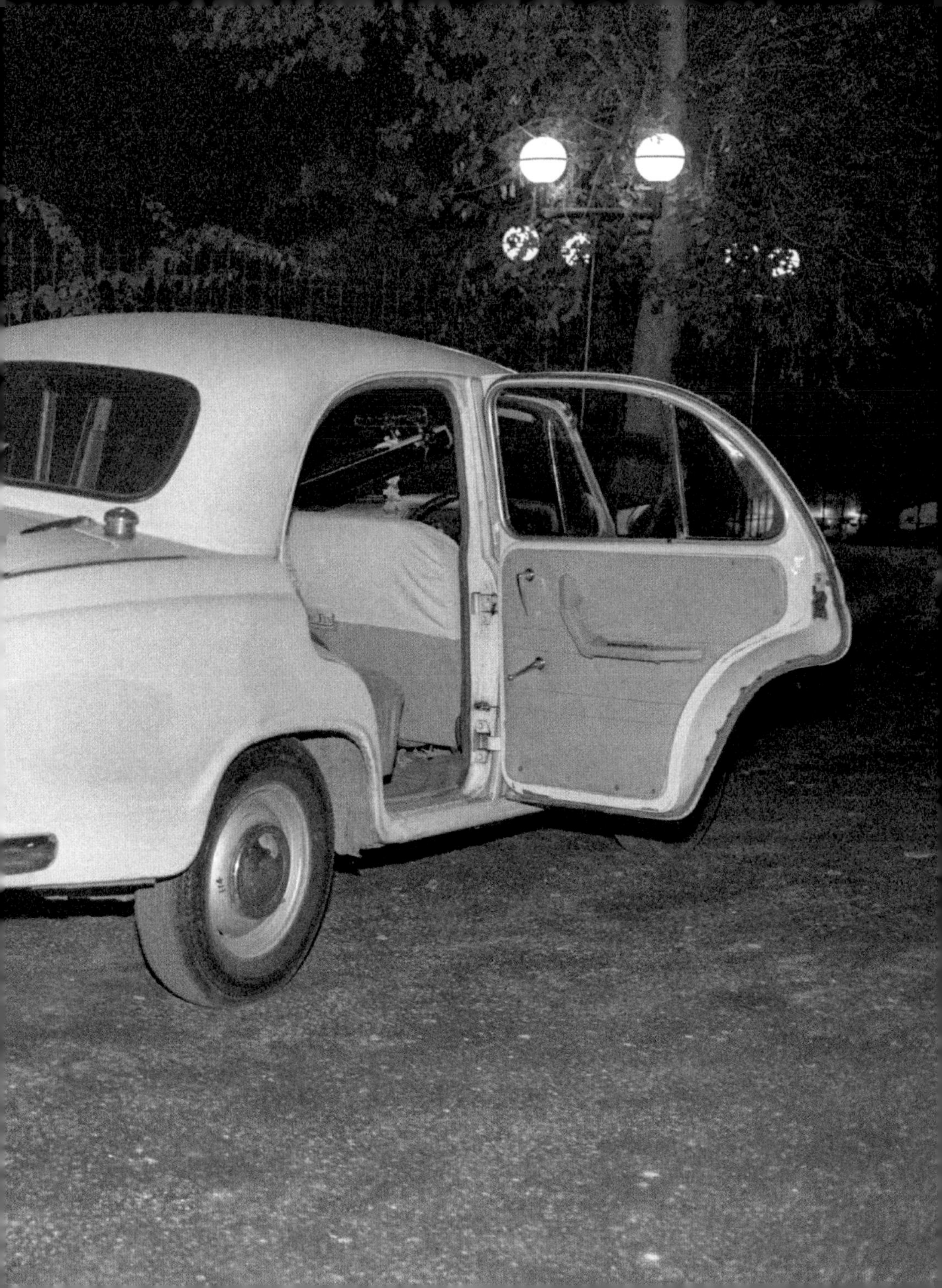

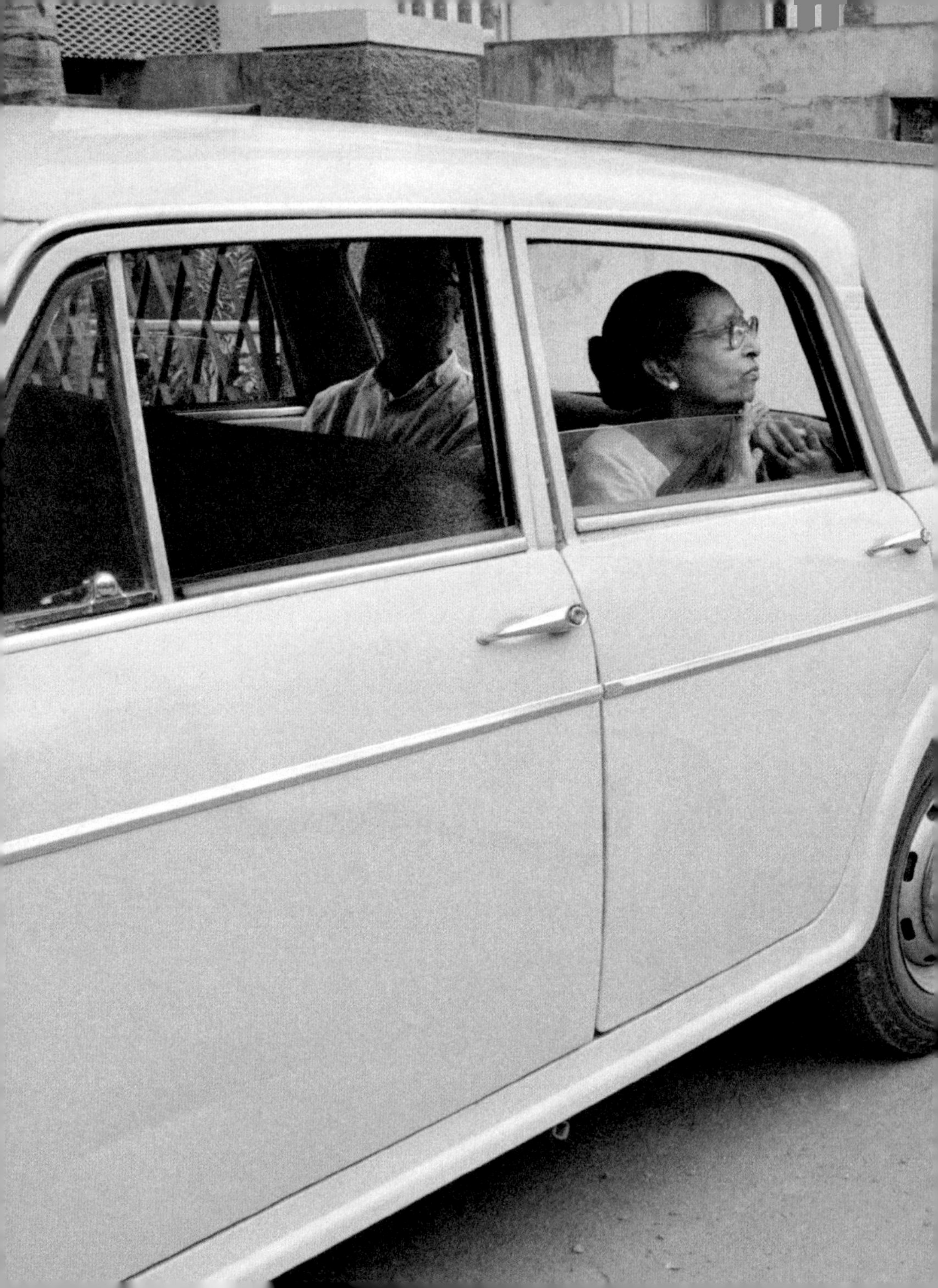

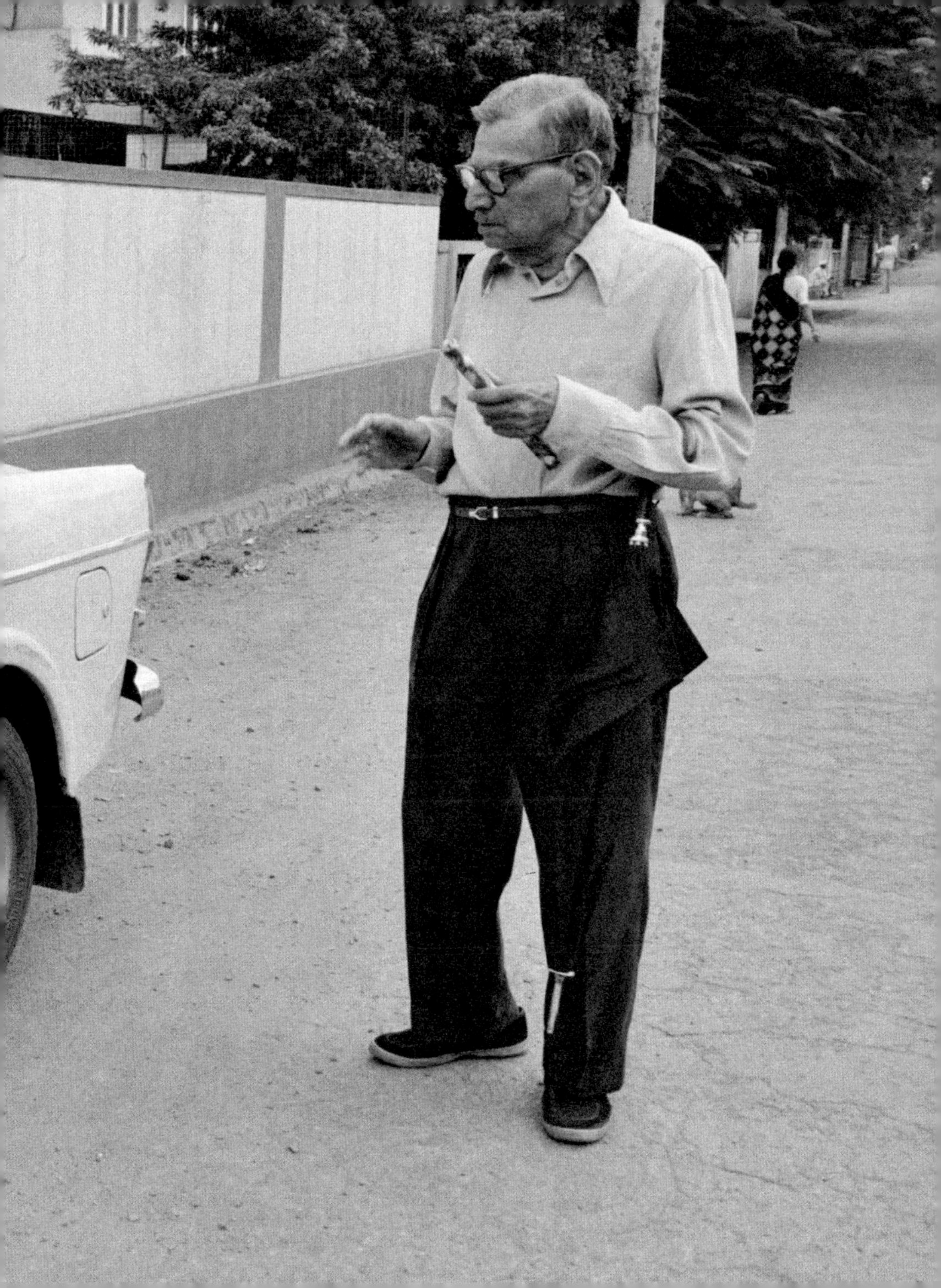

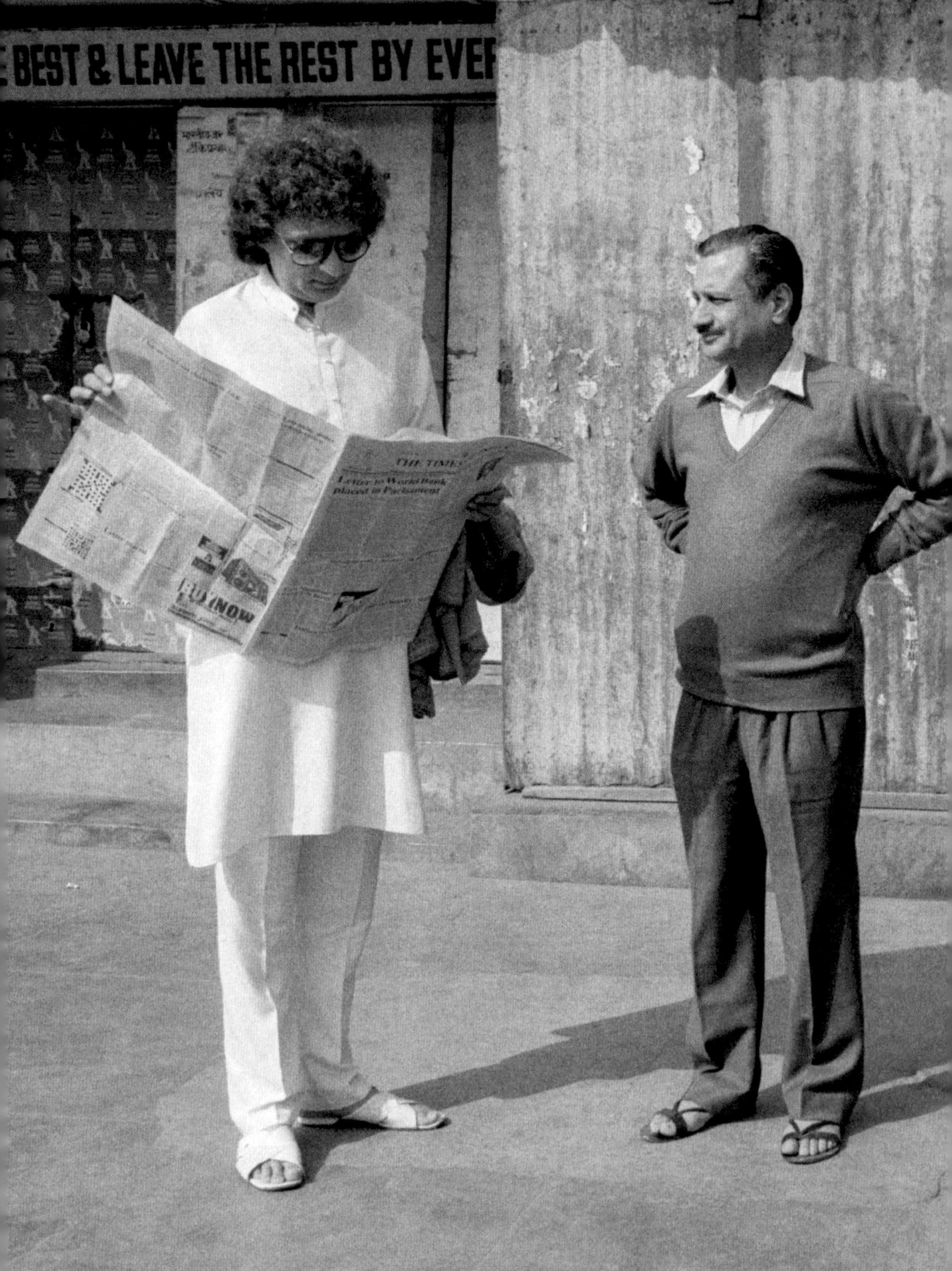
E BEST & LEAVE THE REST BY EVER
THE TIMES
Letter to World Bank
placed in Parliament
BUY NOW

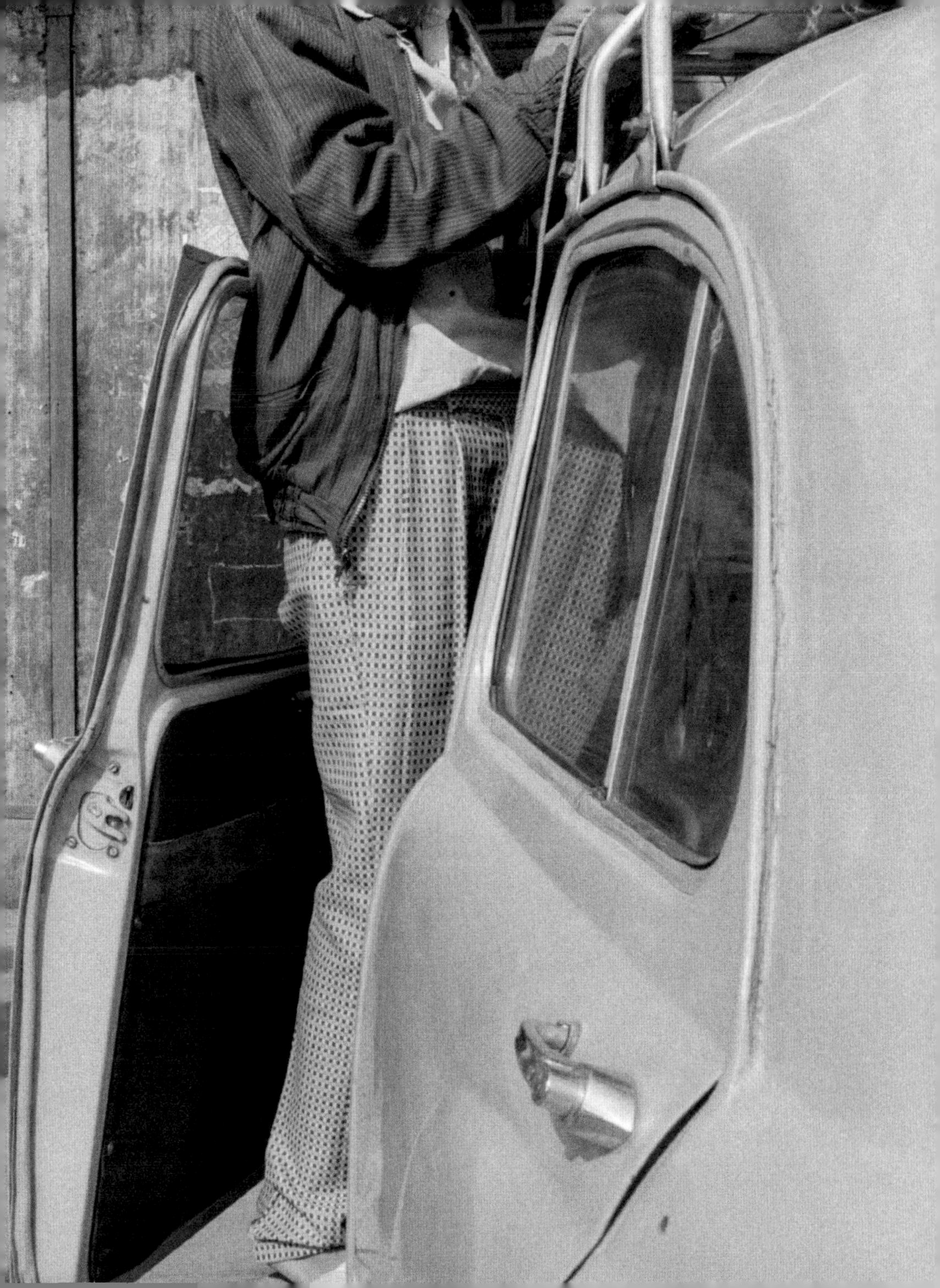

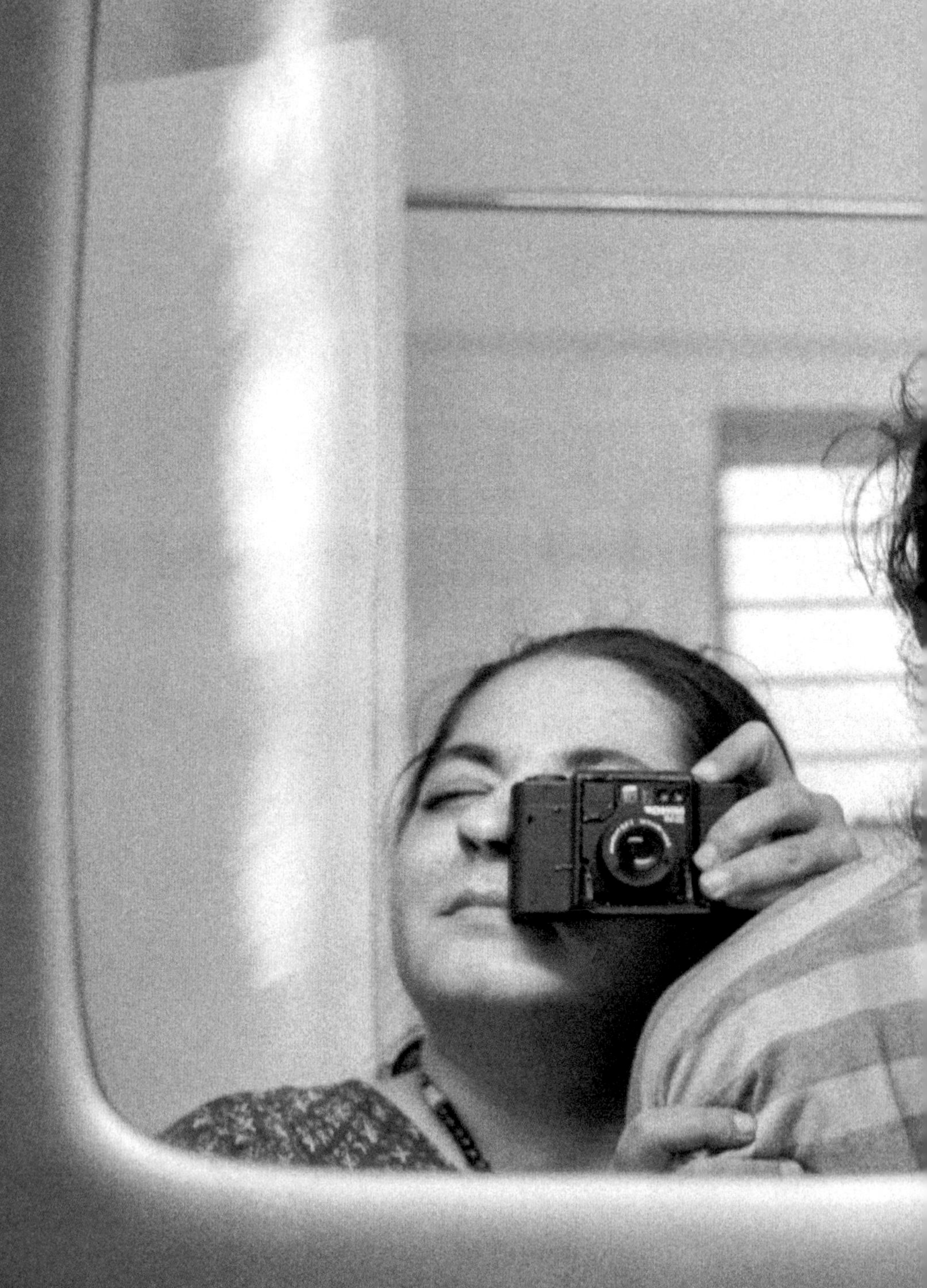

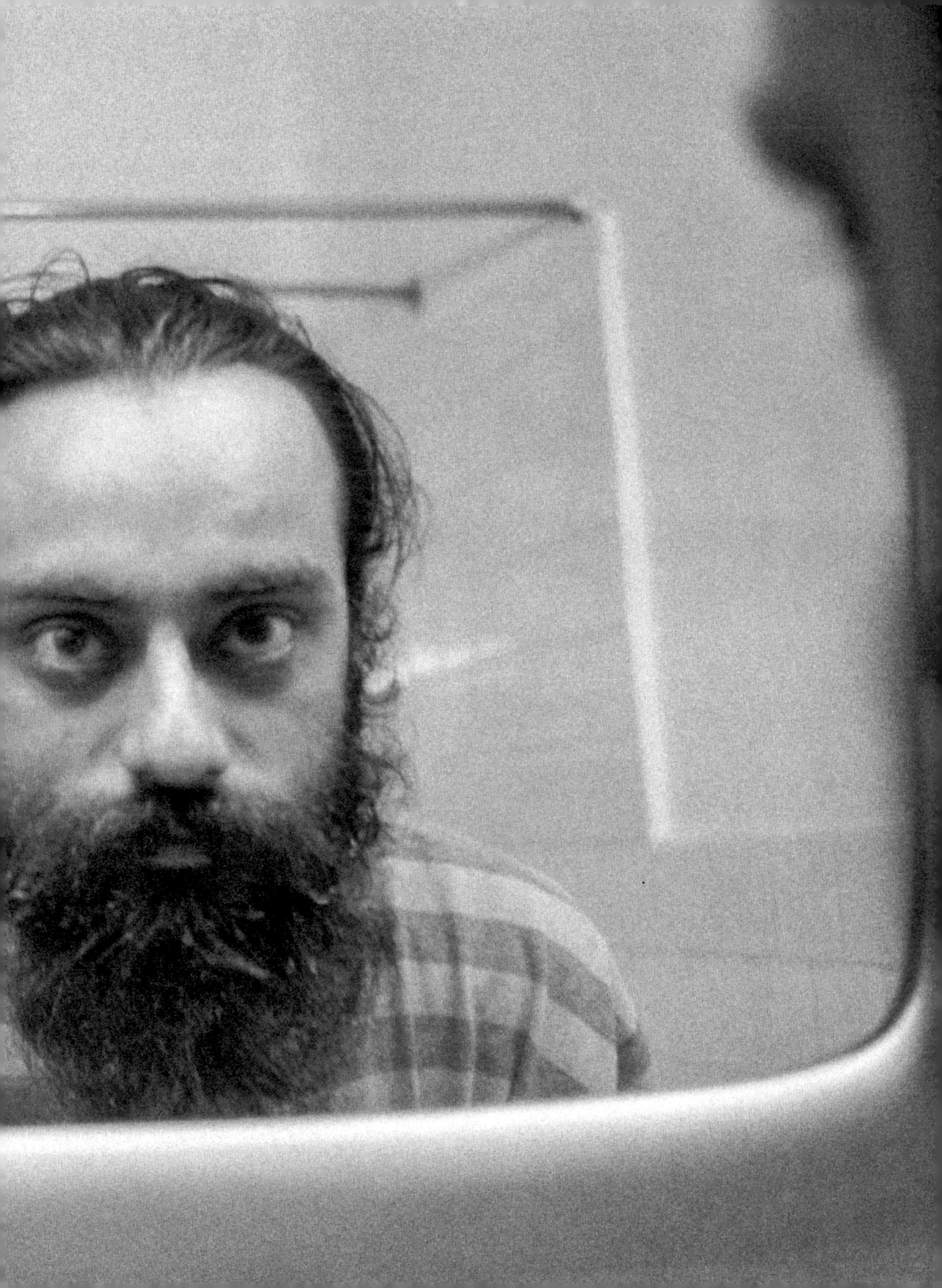

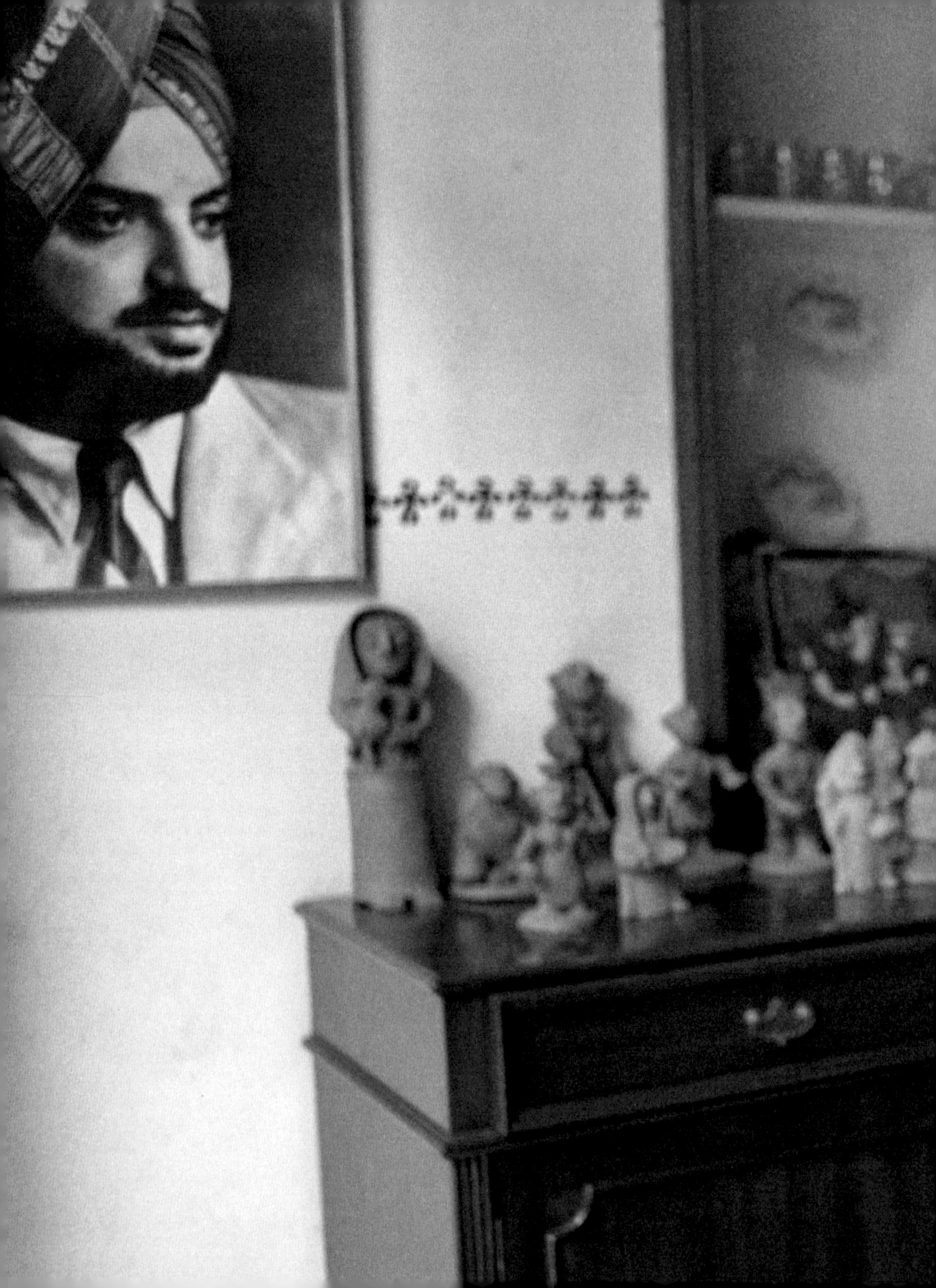

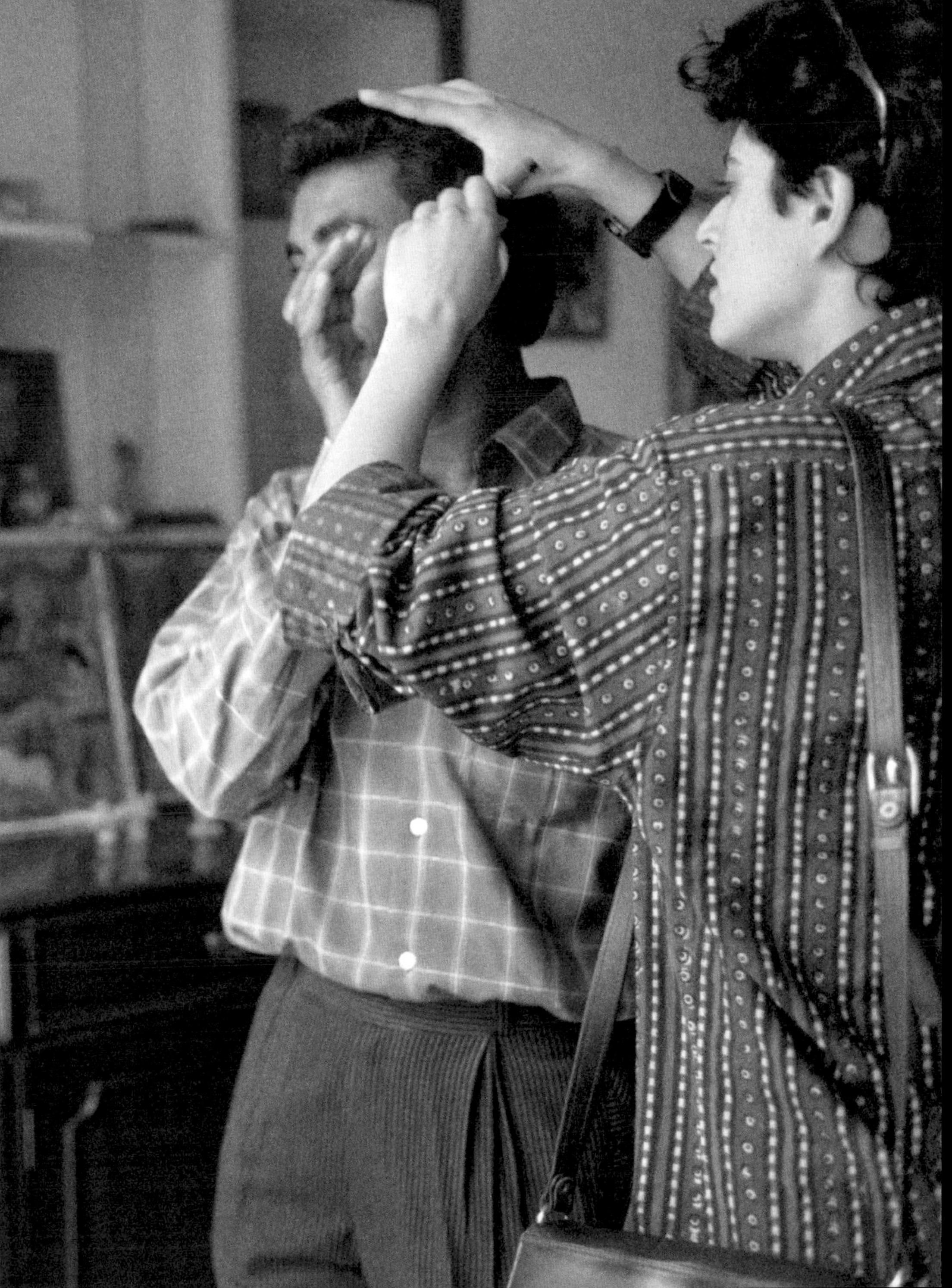

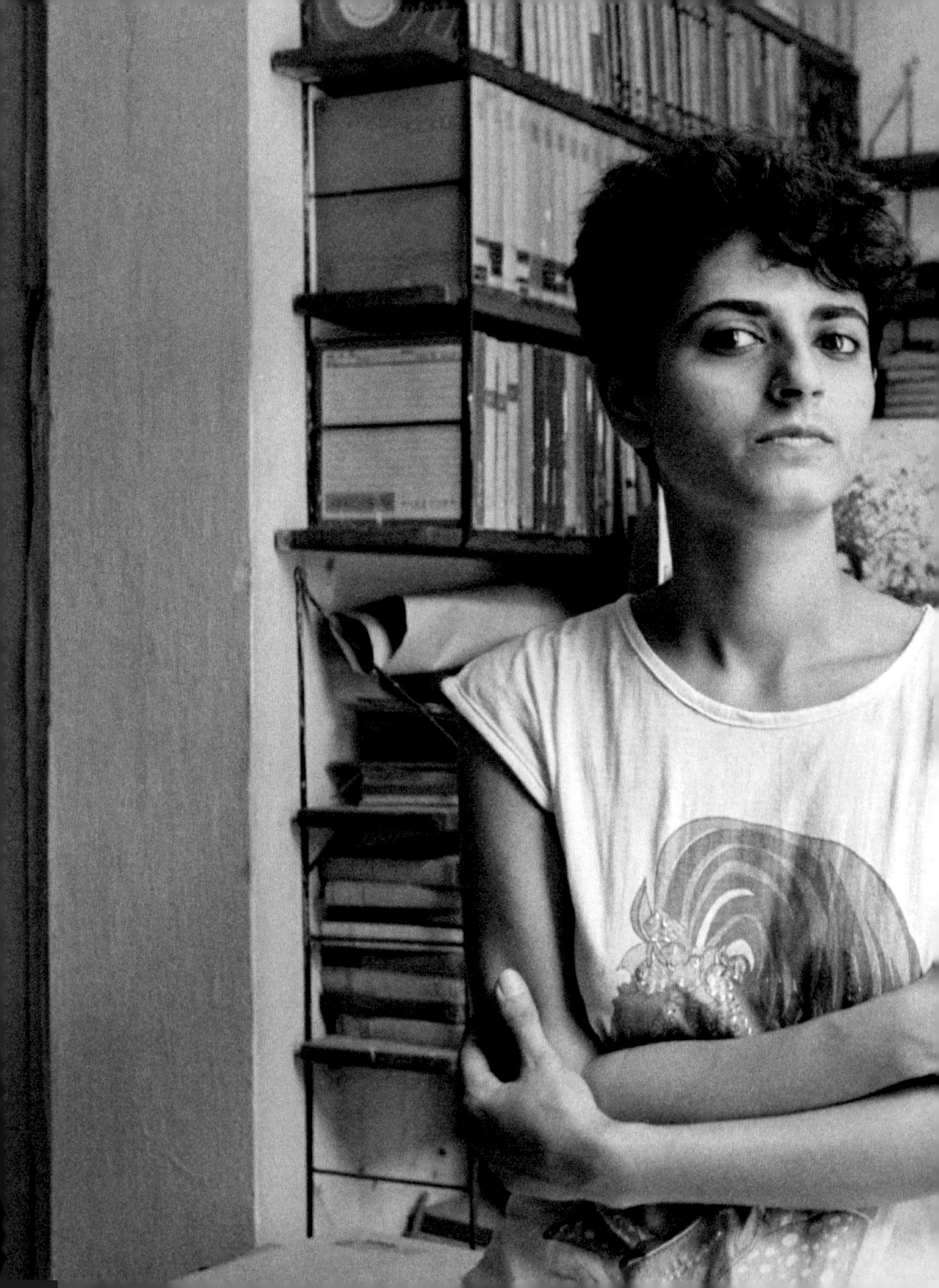

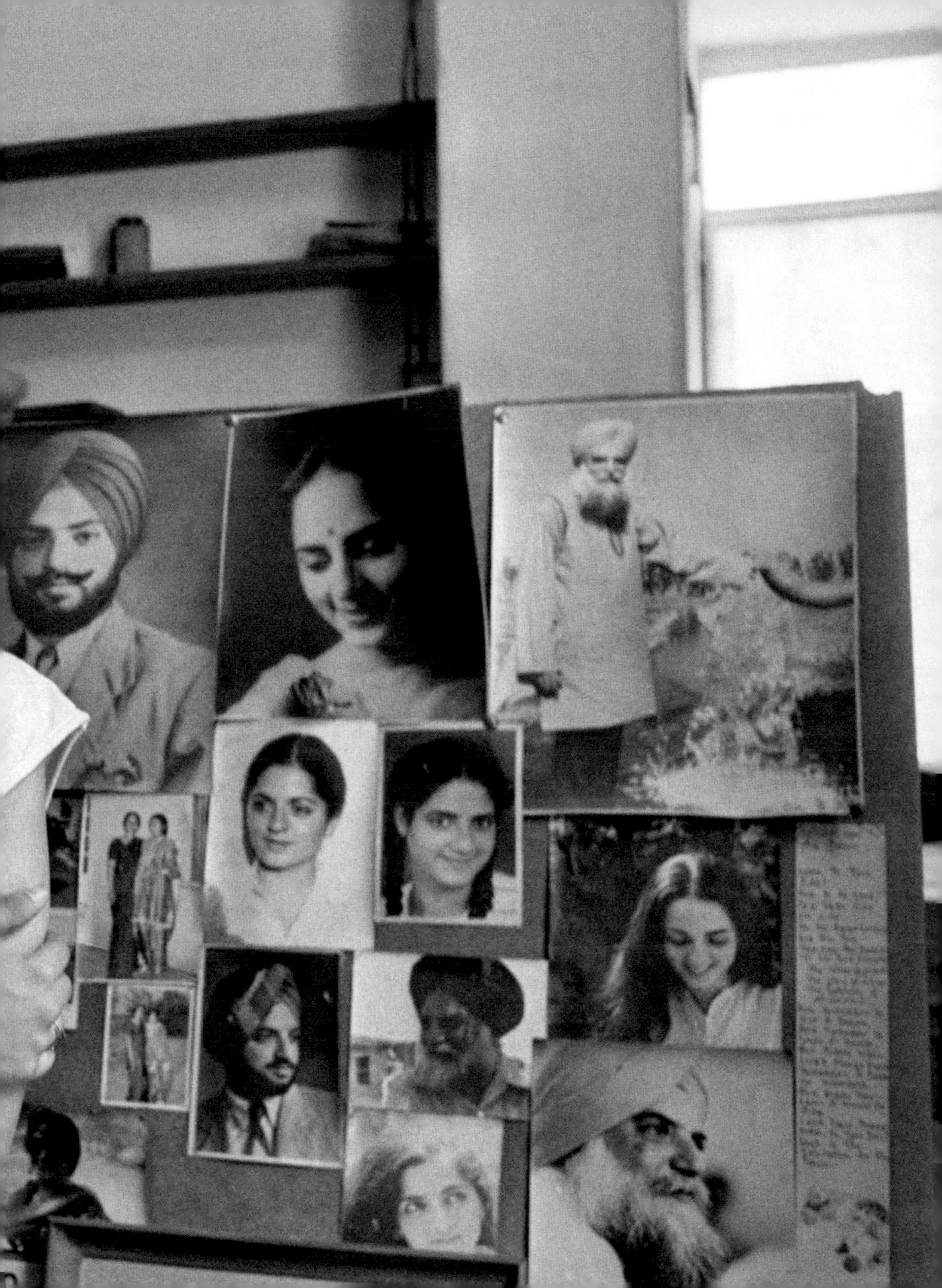

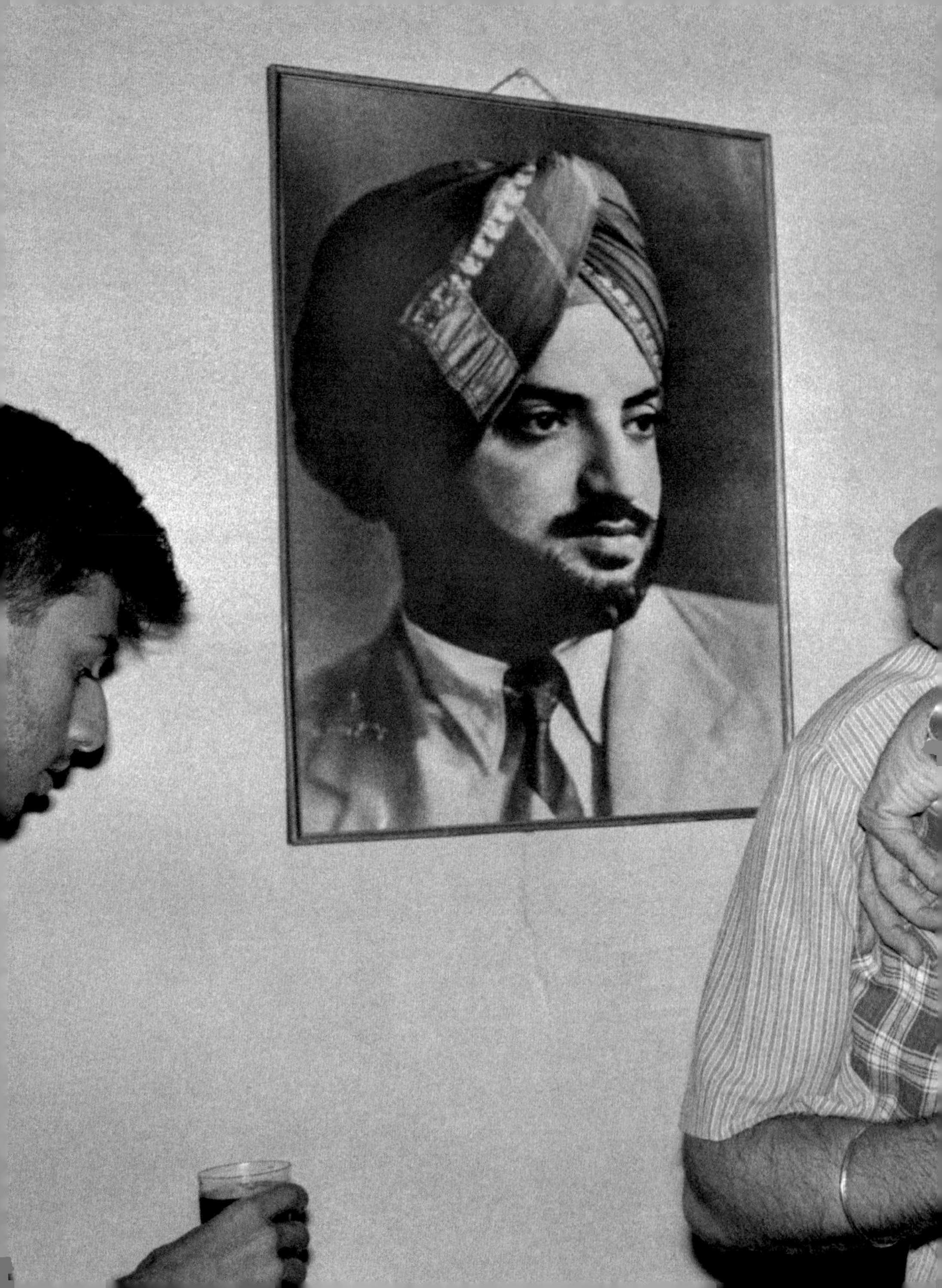

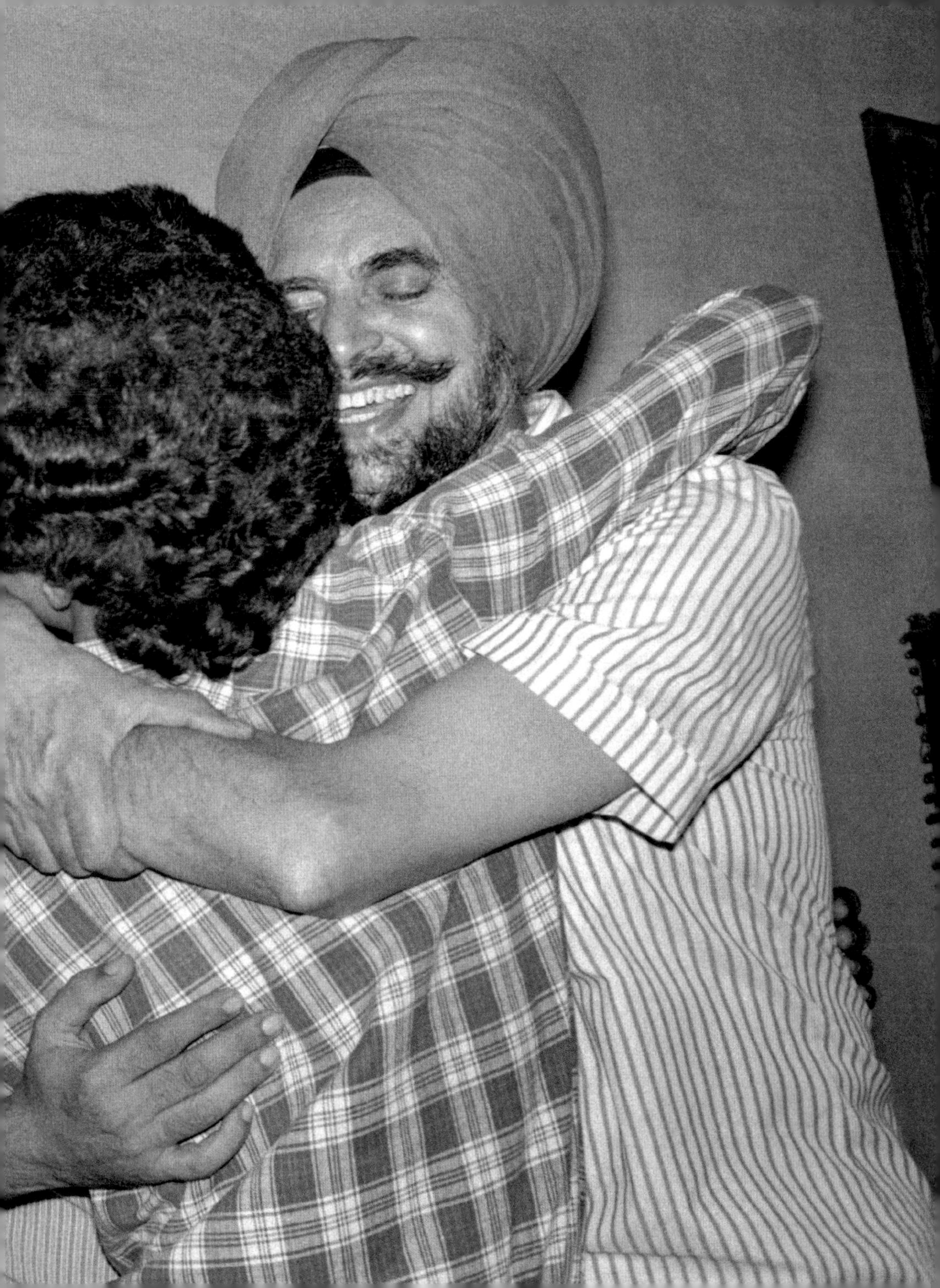

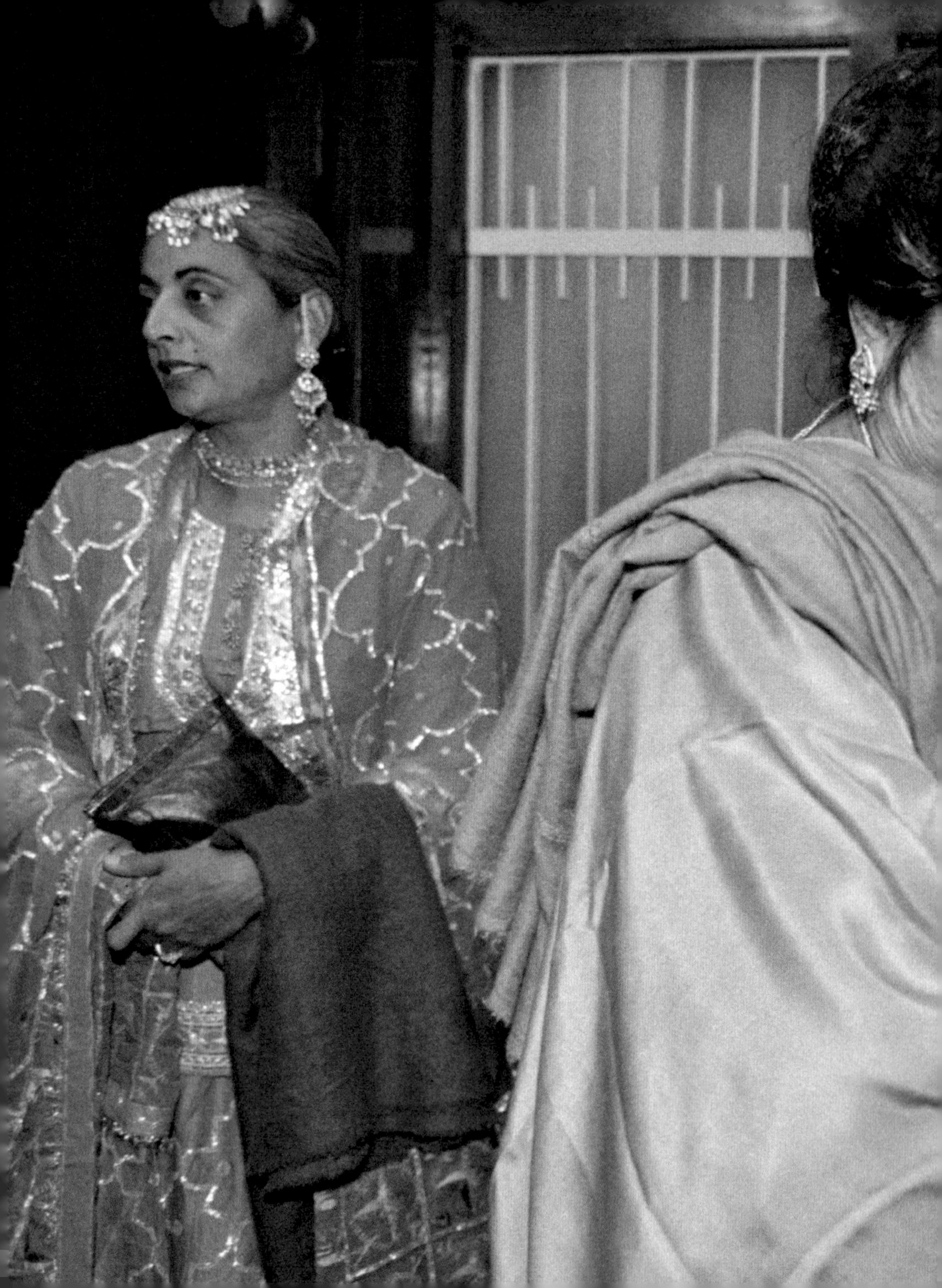

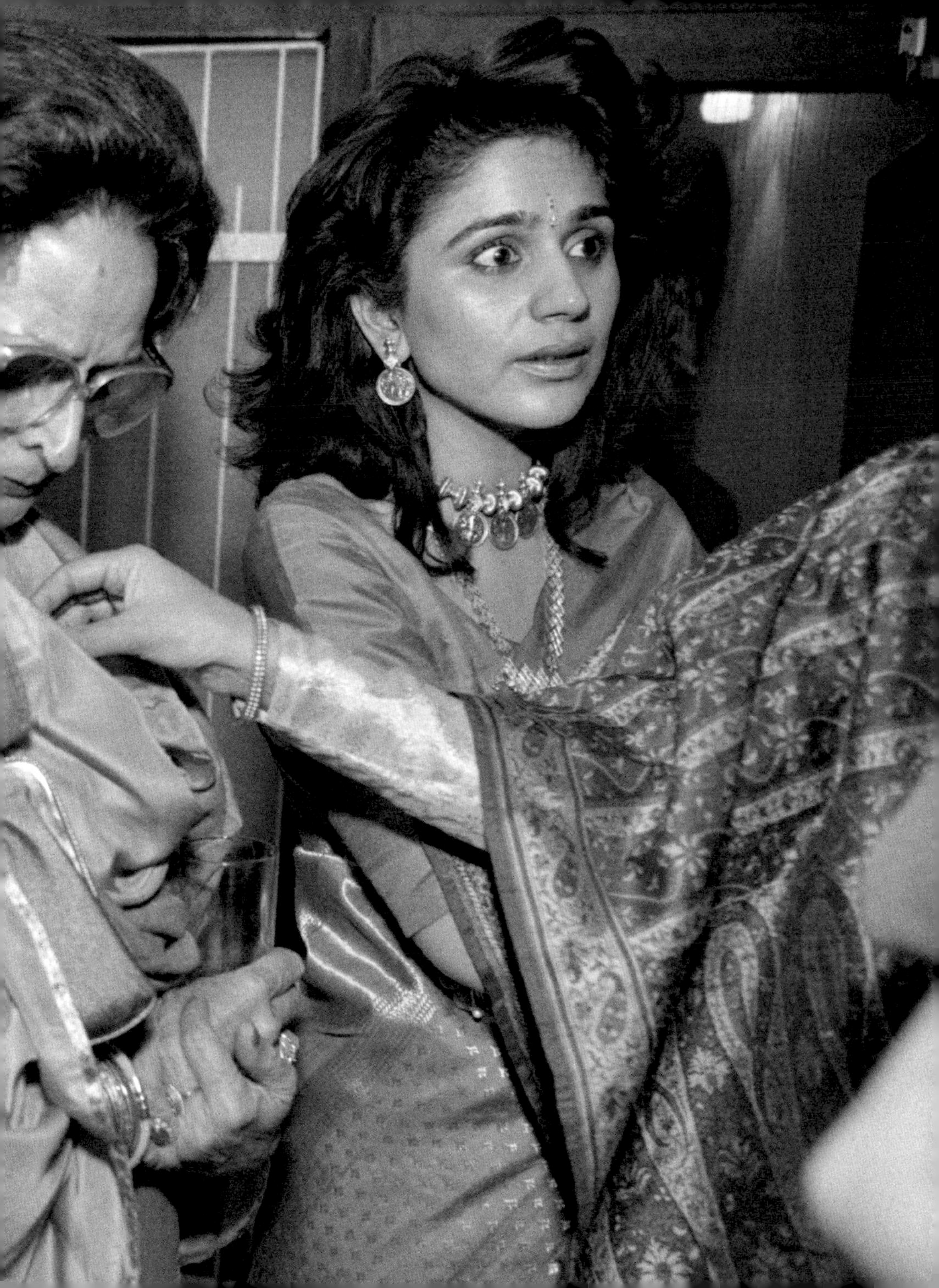

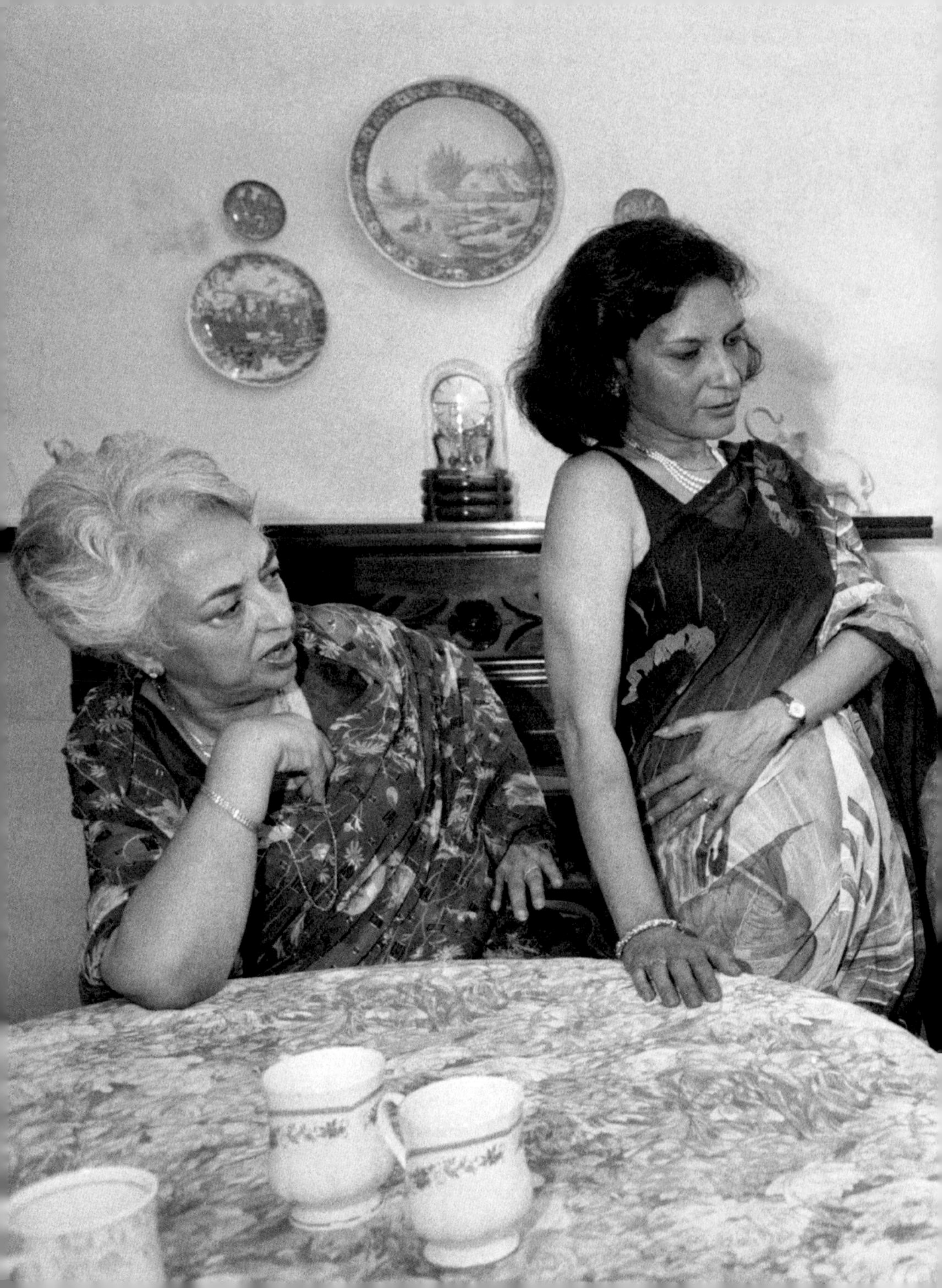

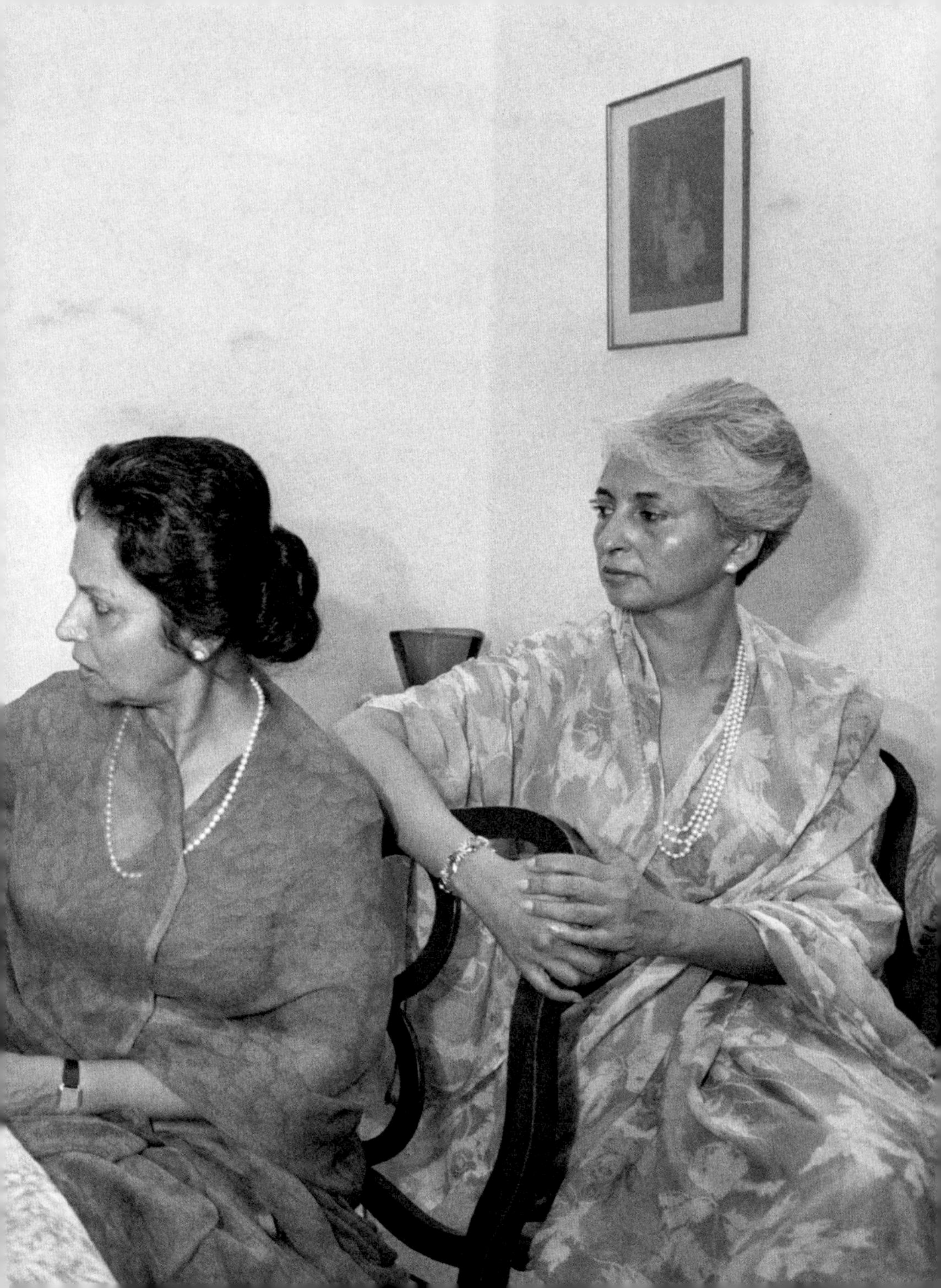

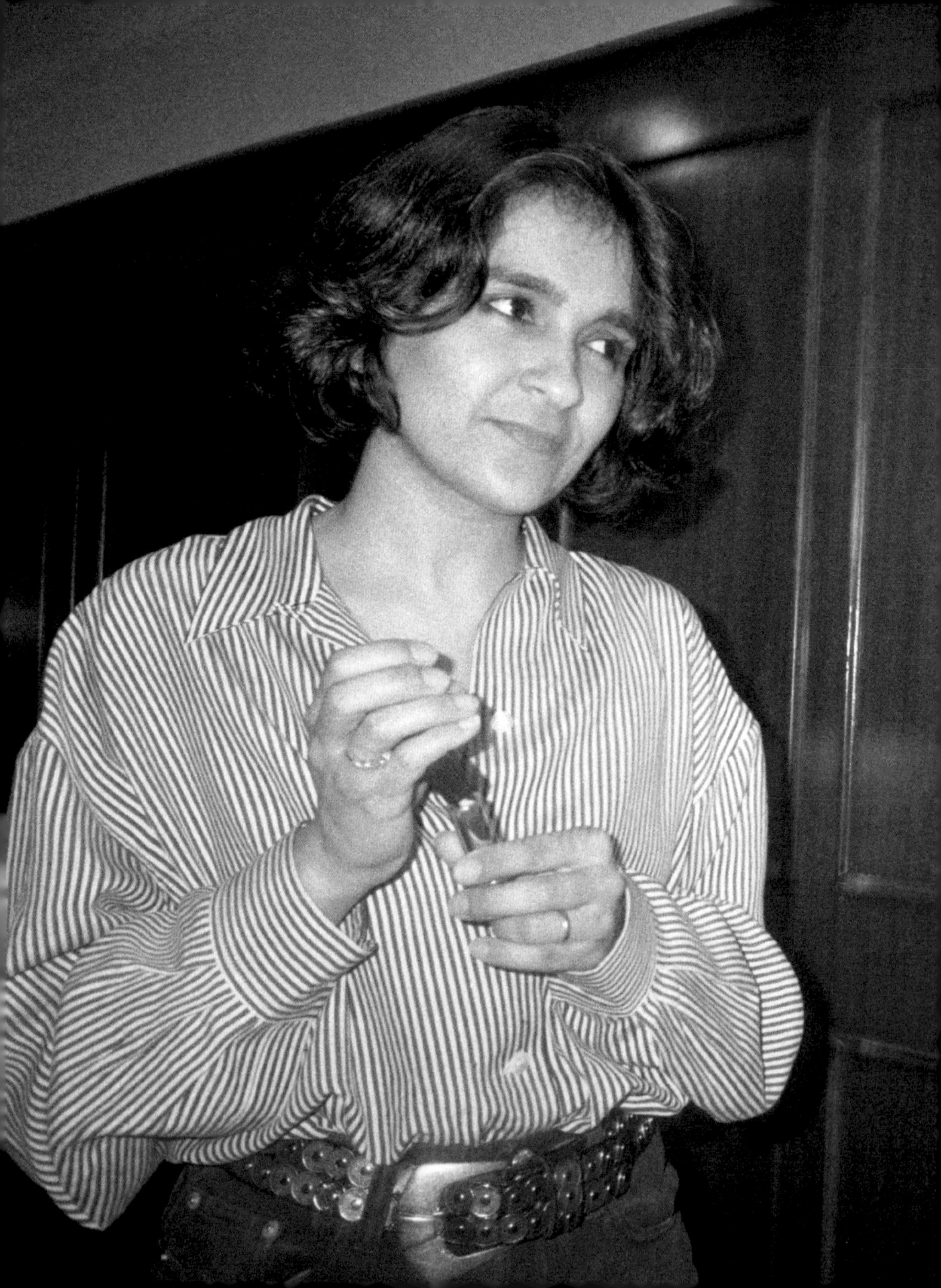

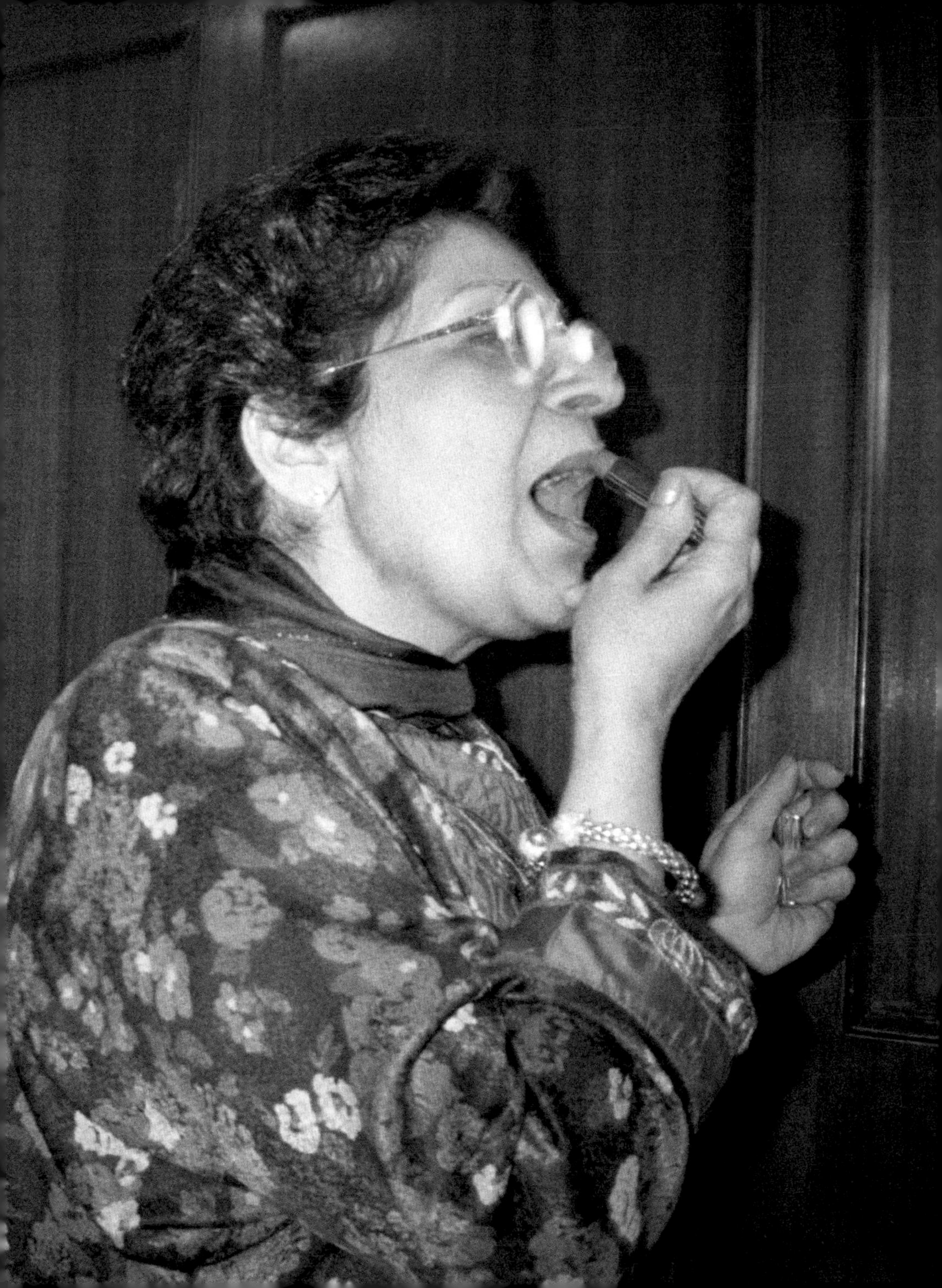

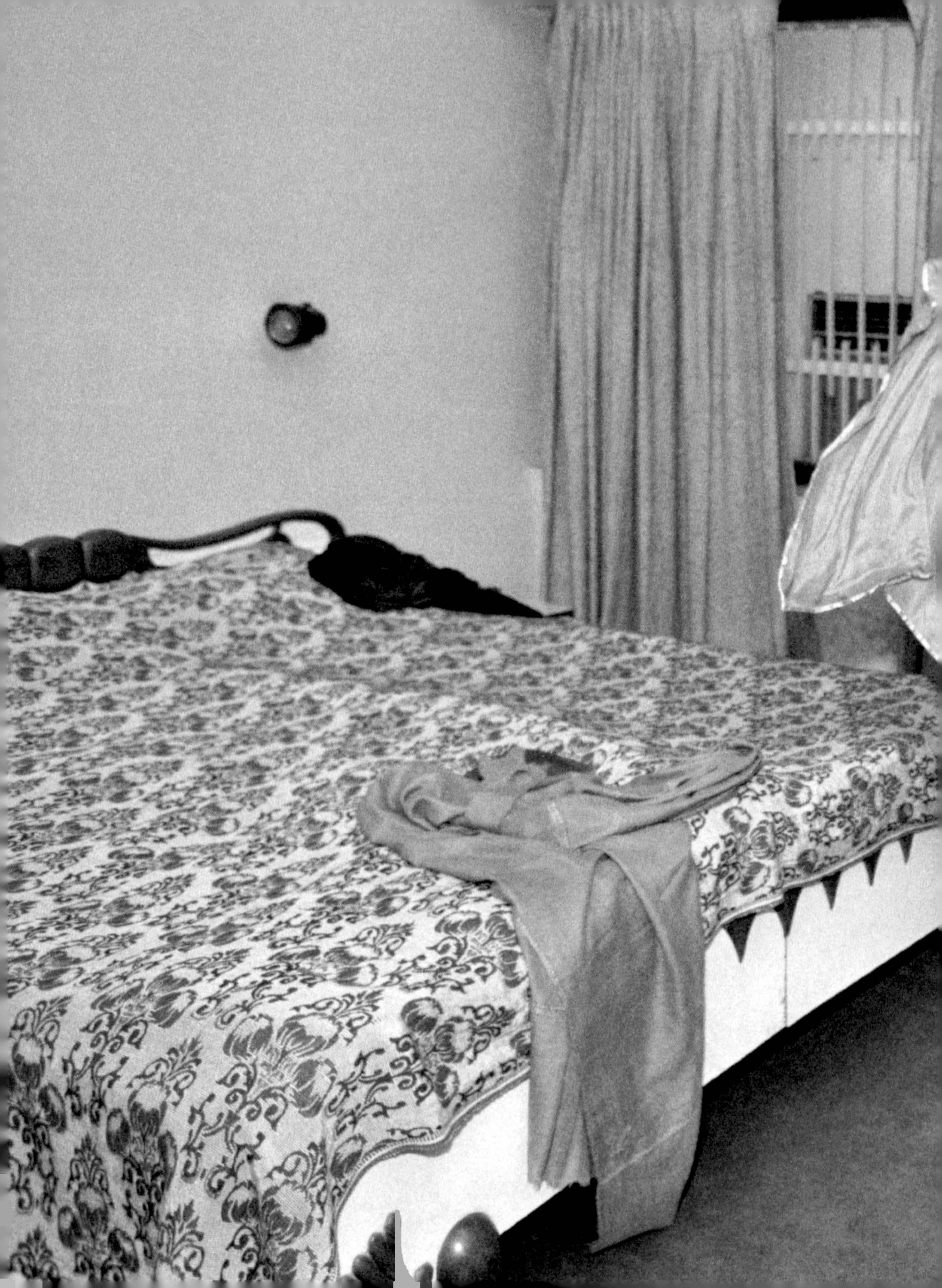

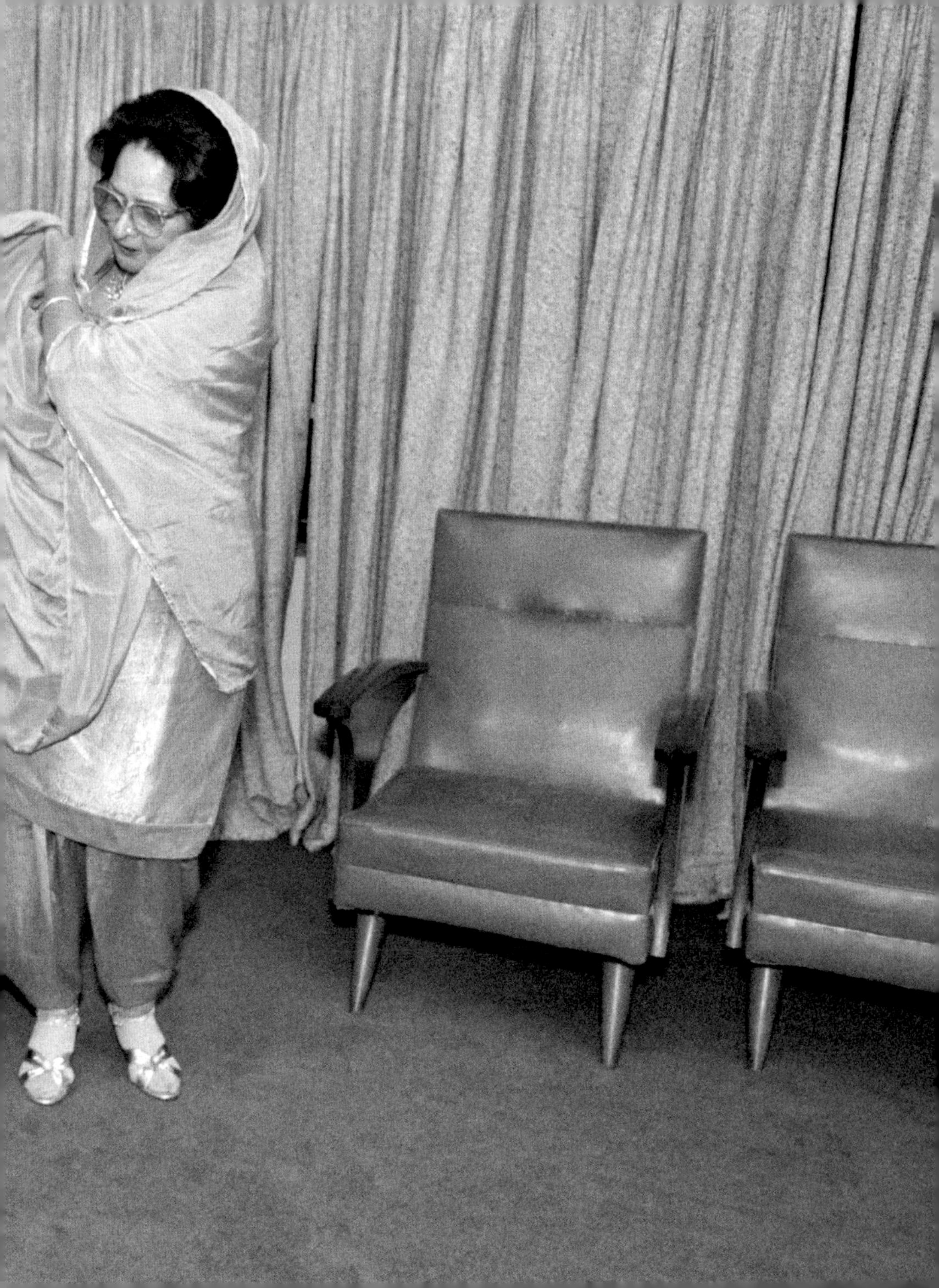

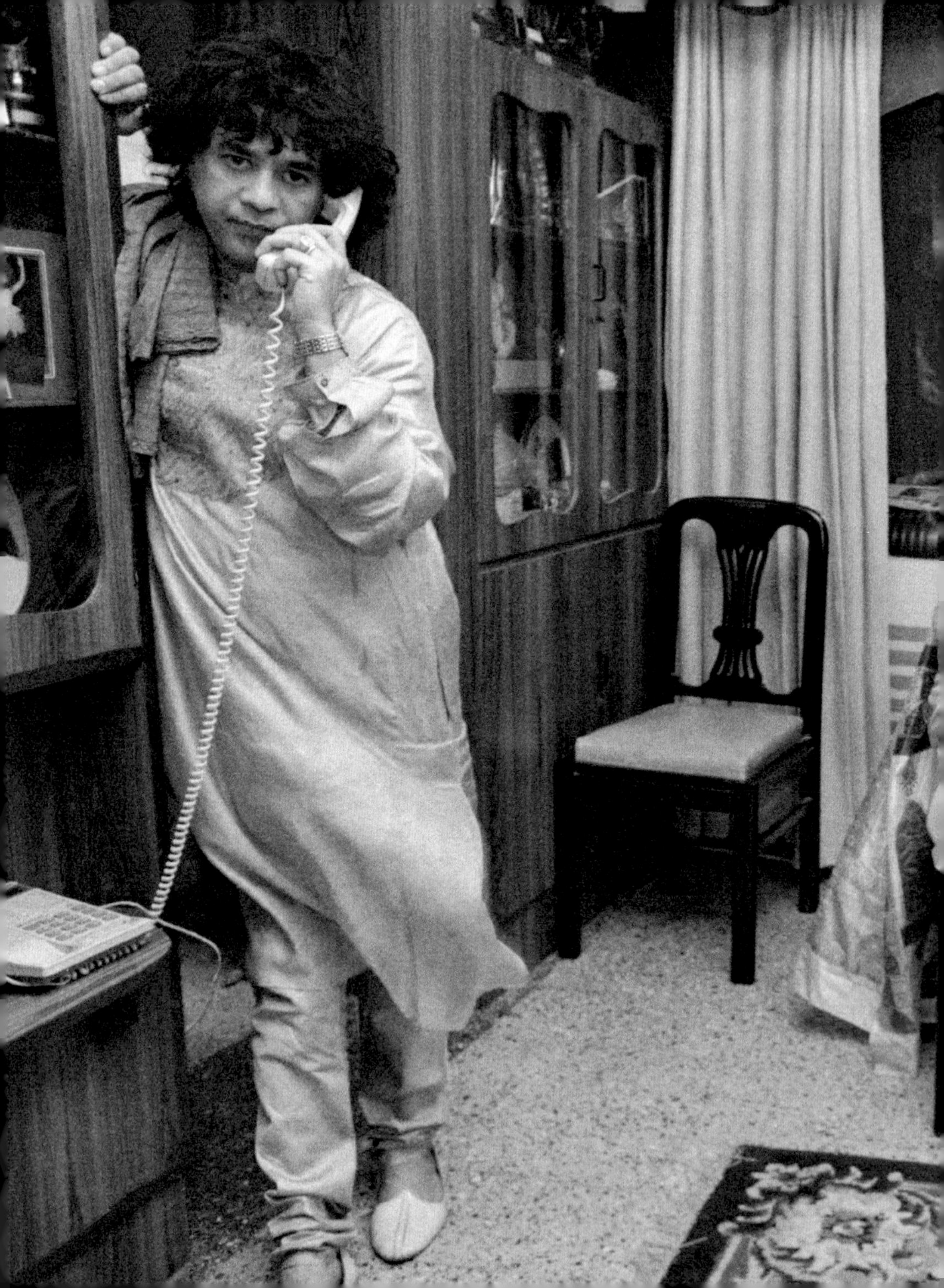

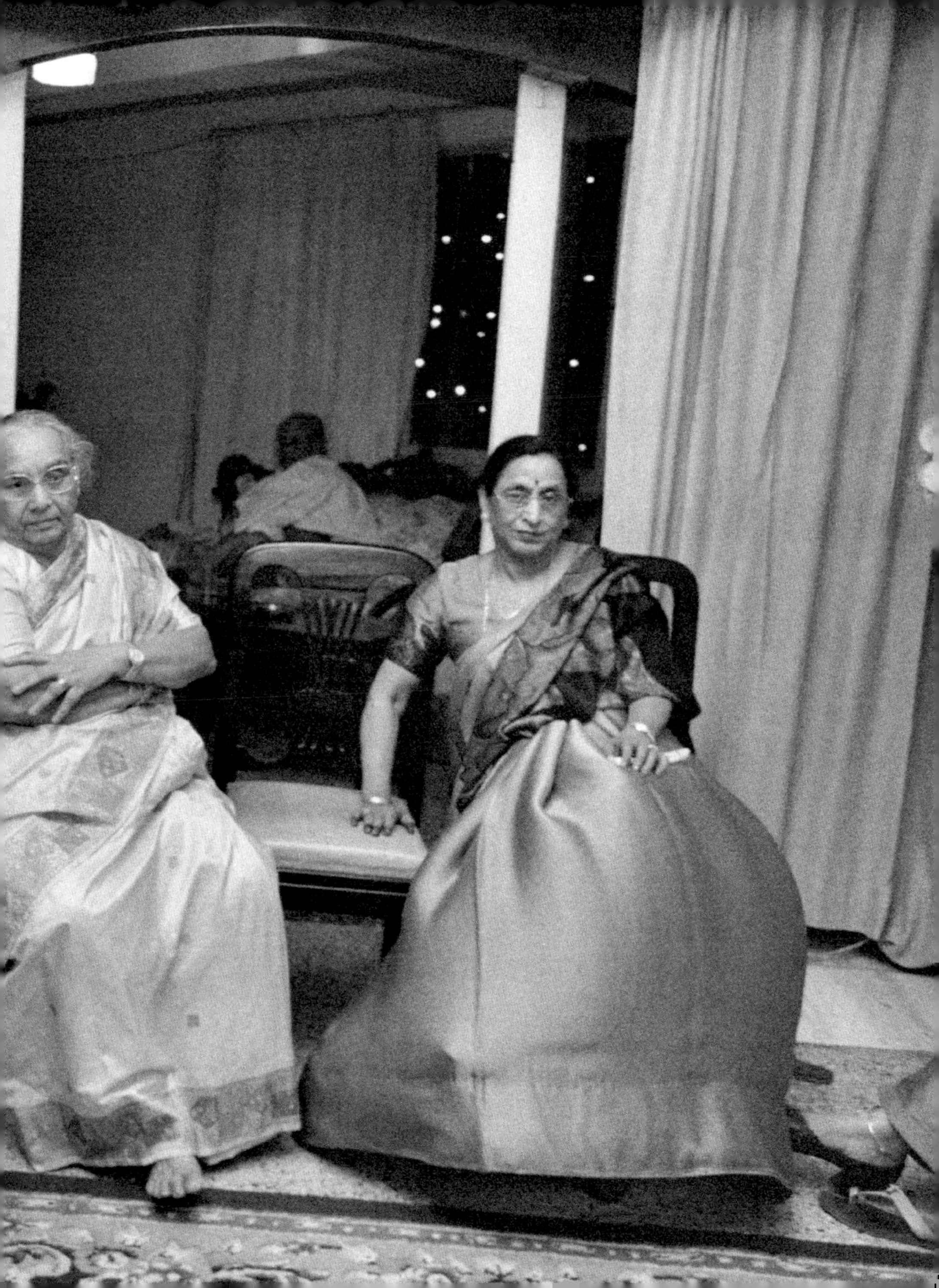

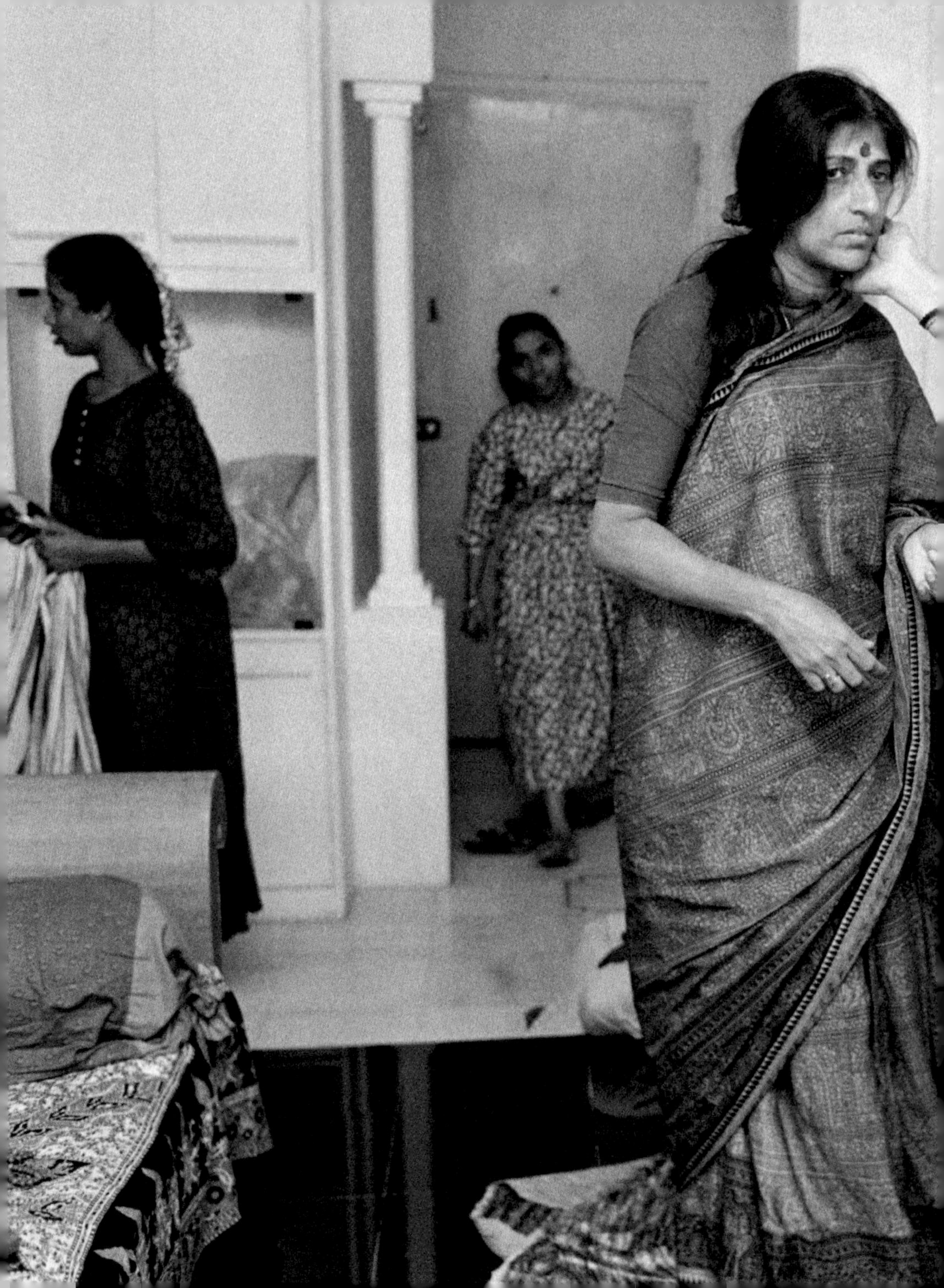

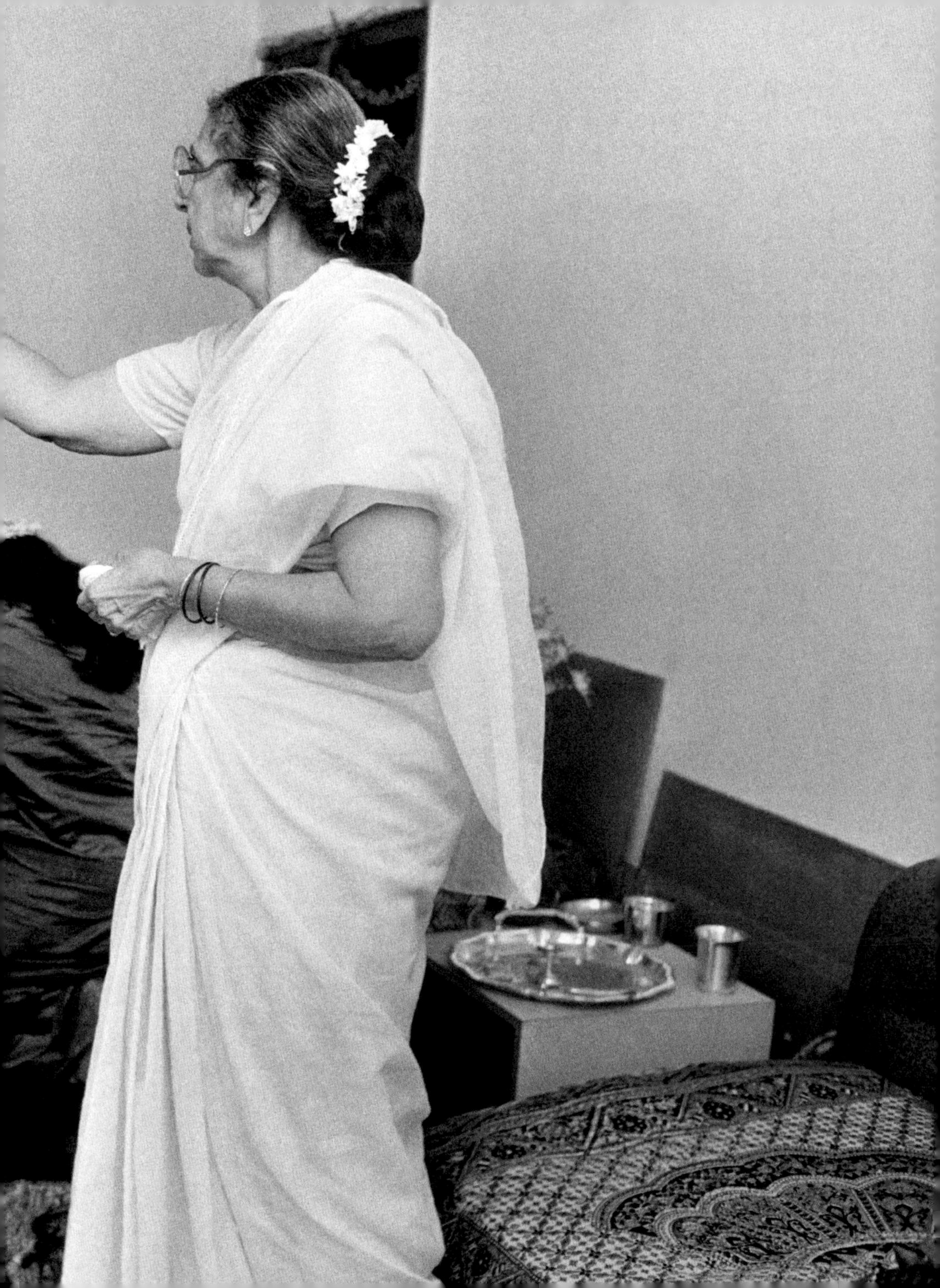

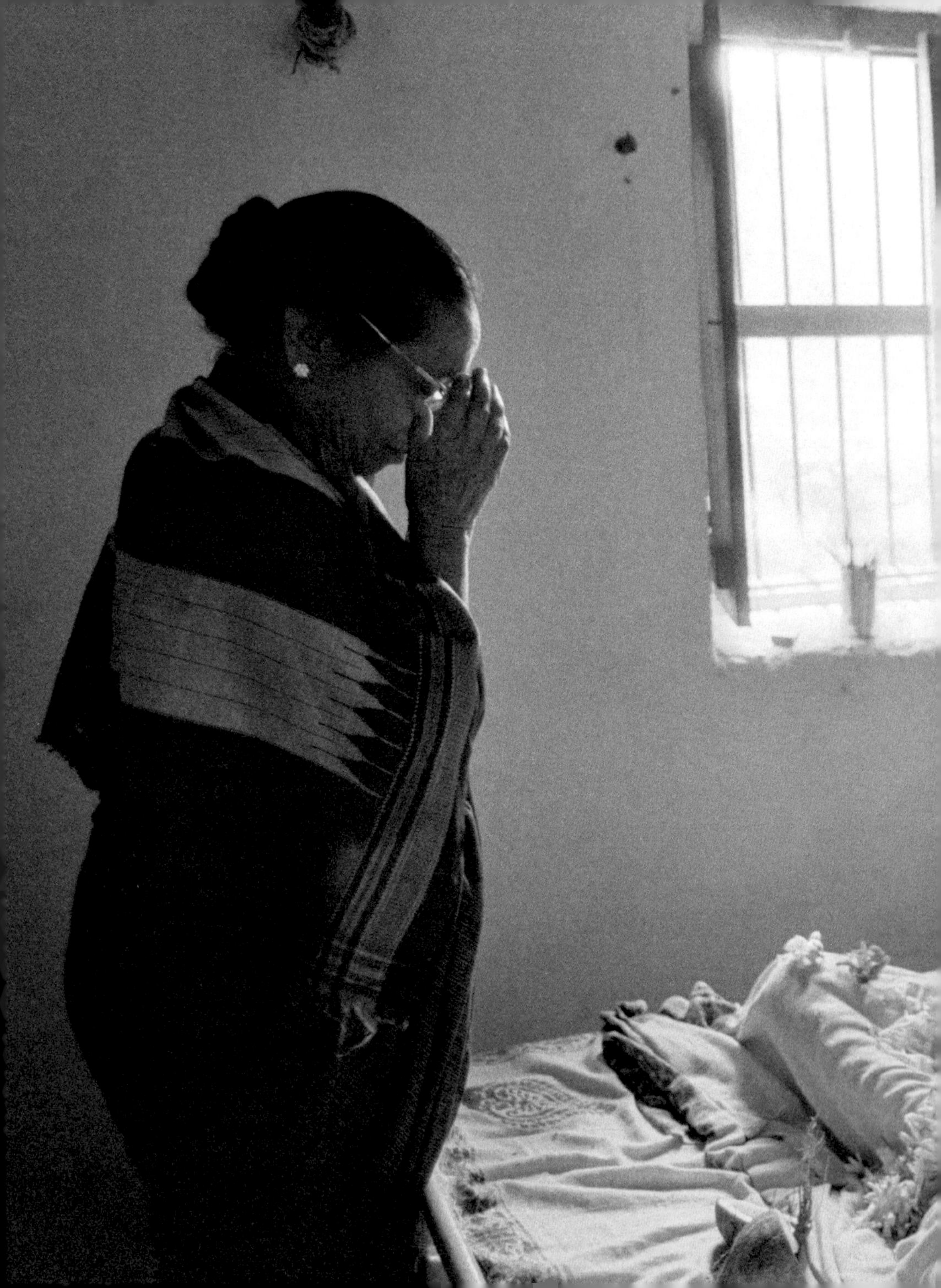

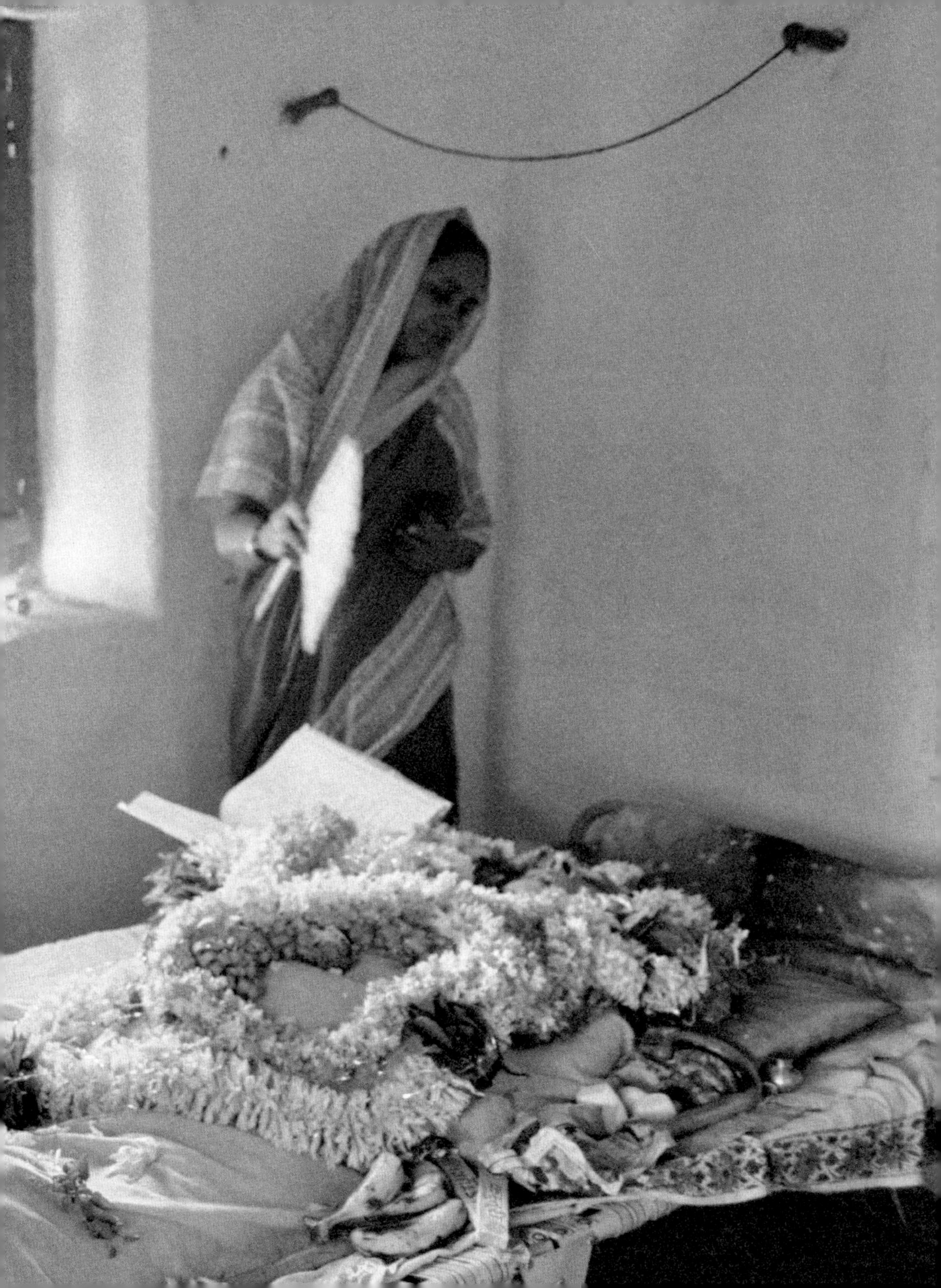

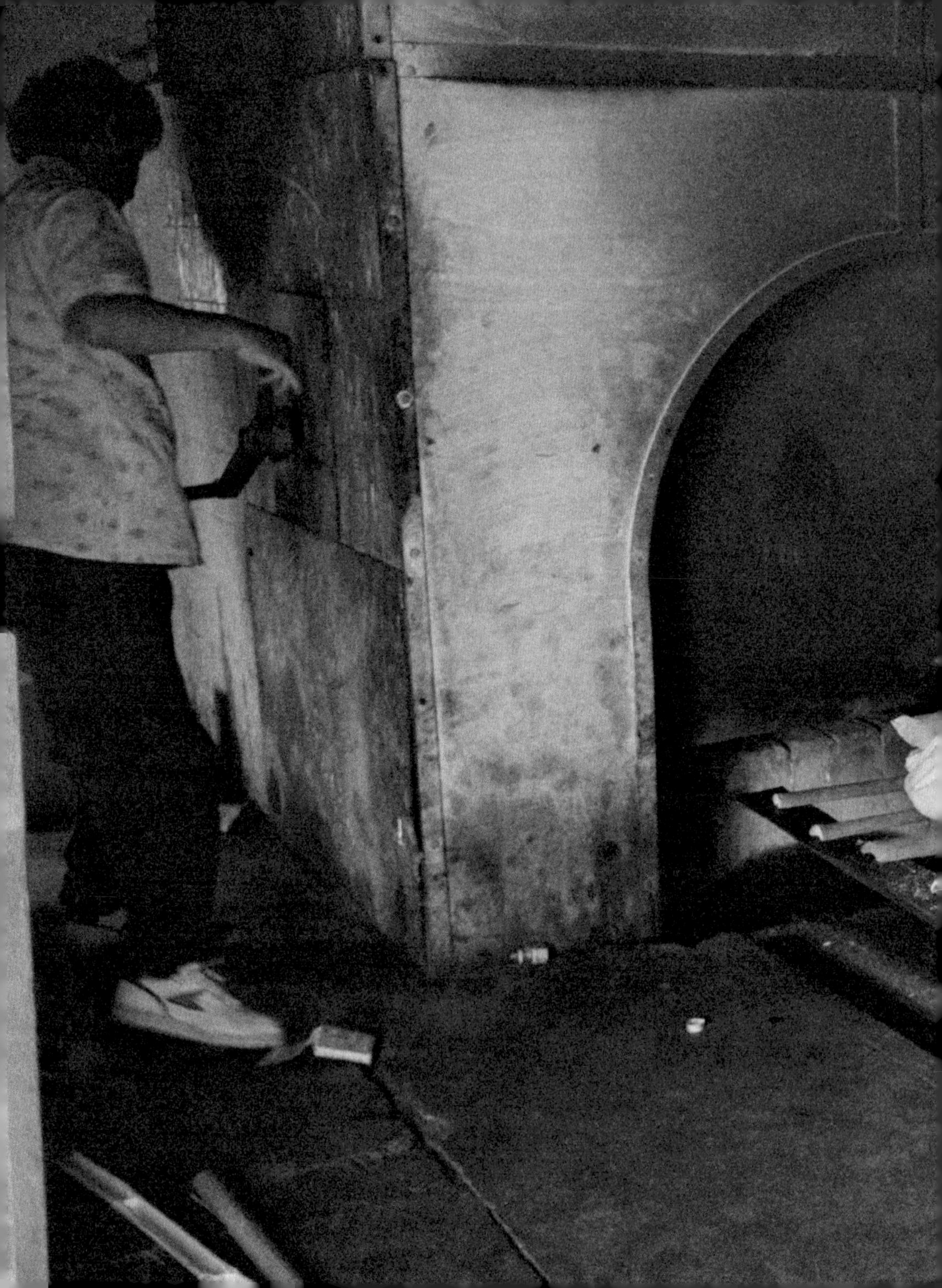

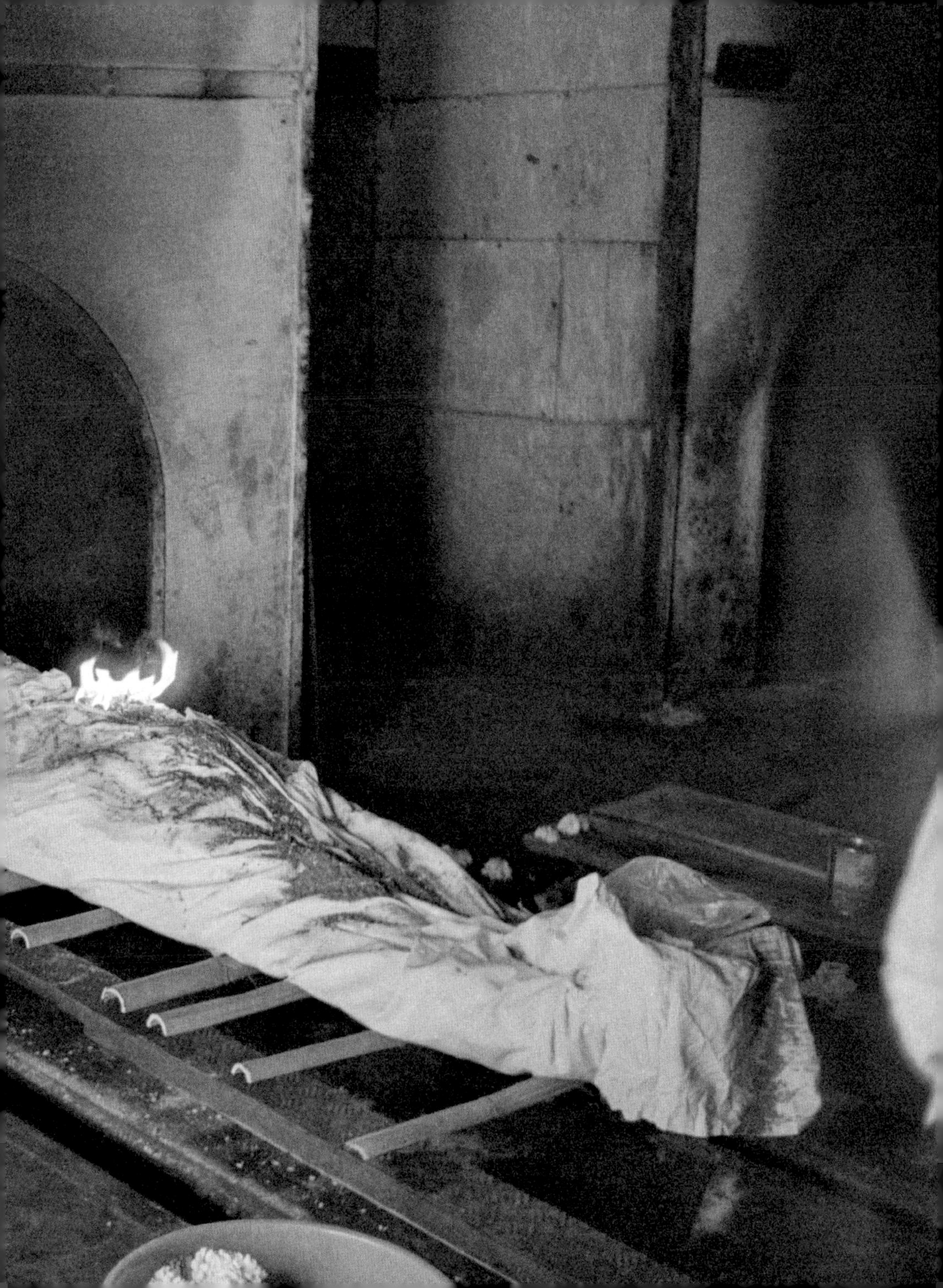

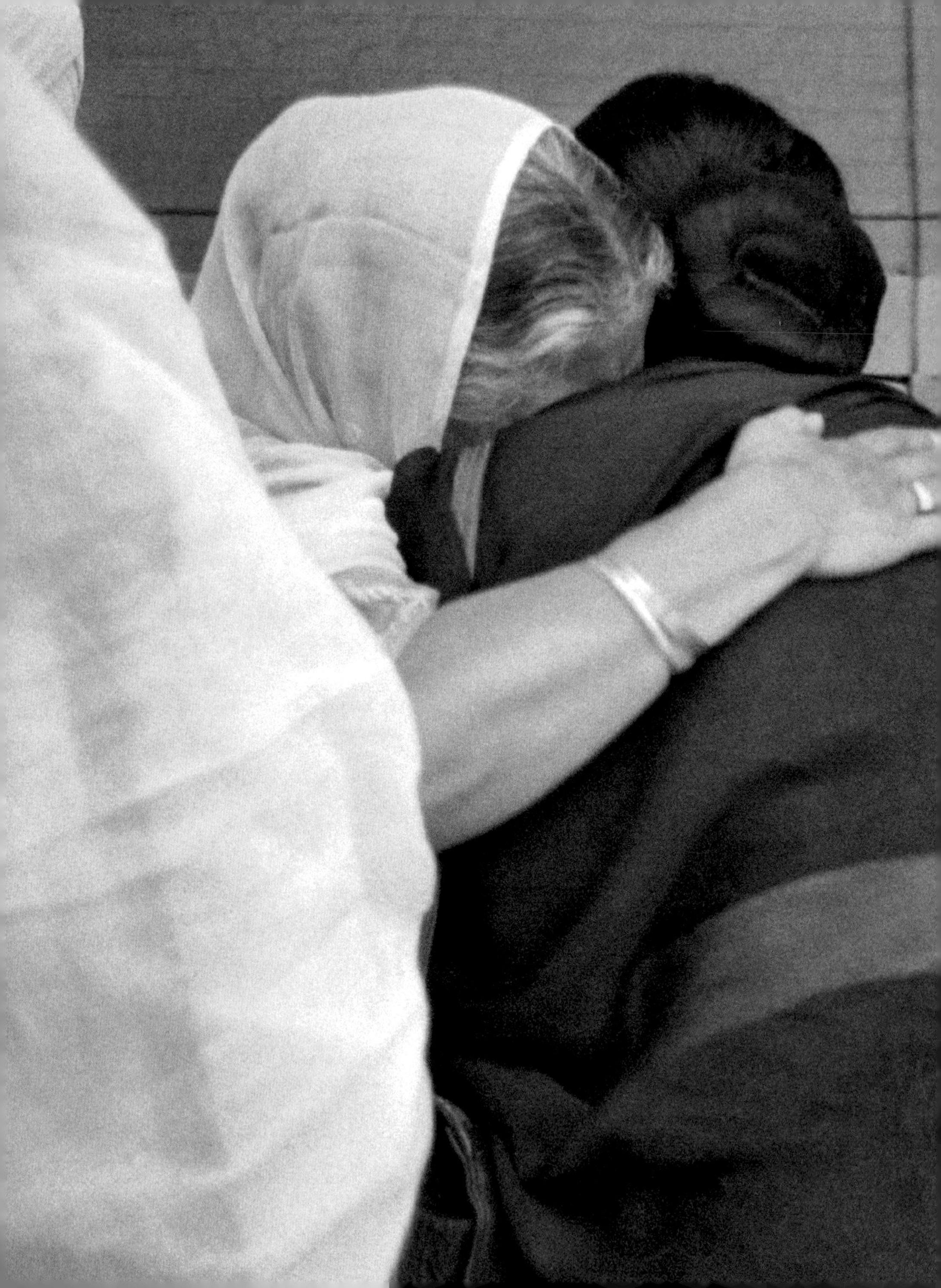

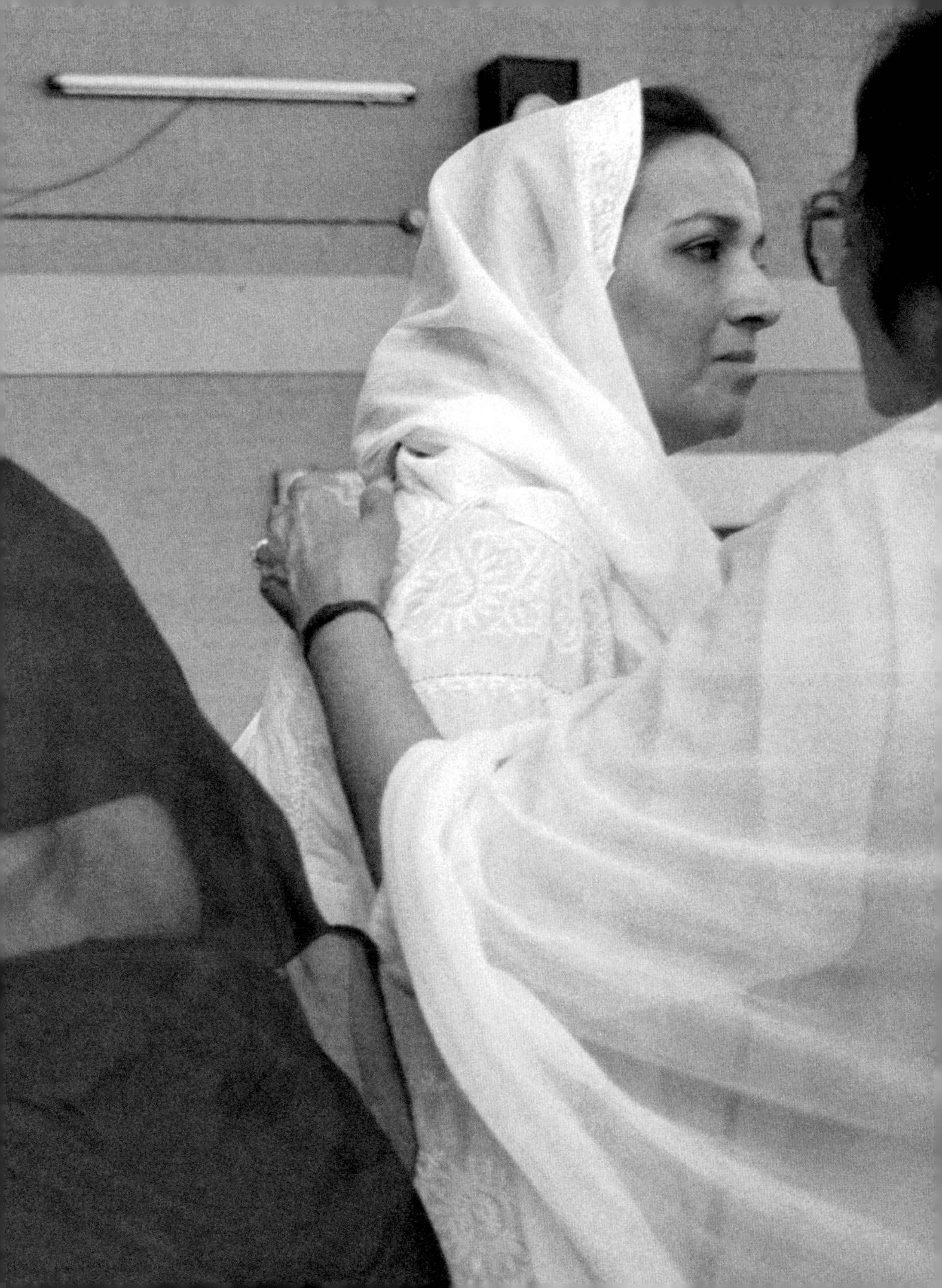

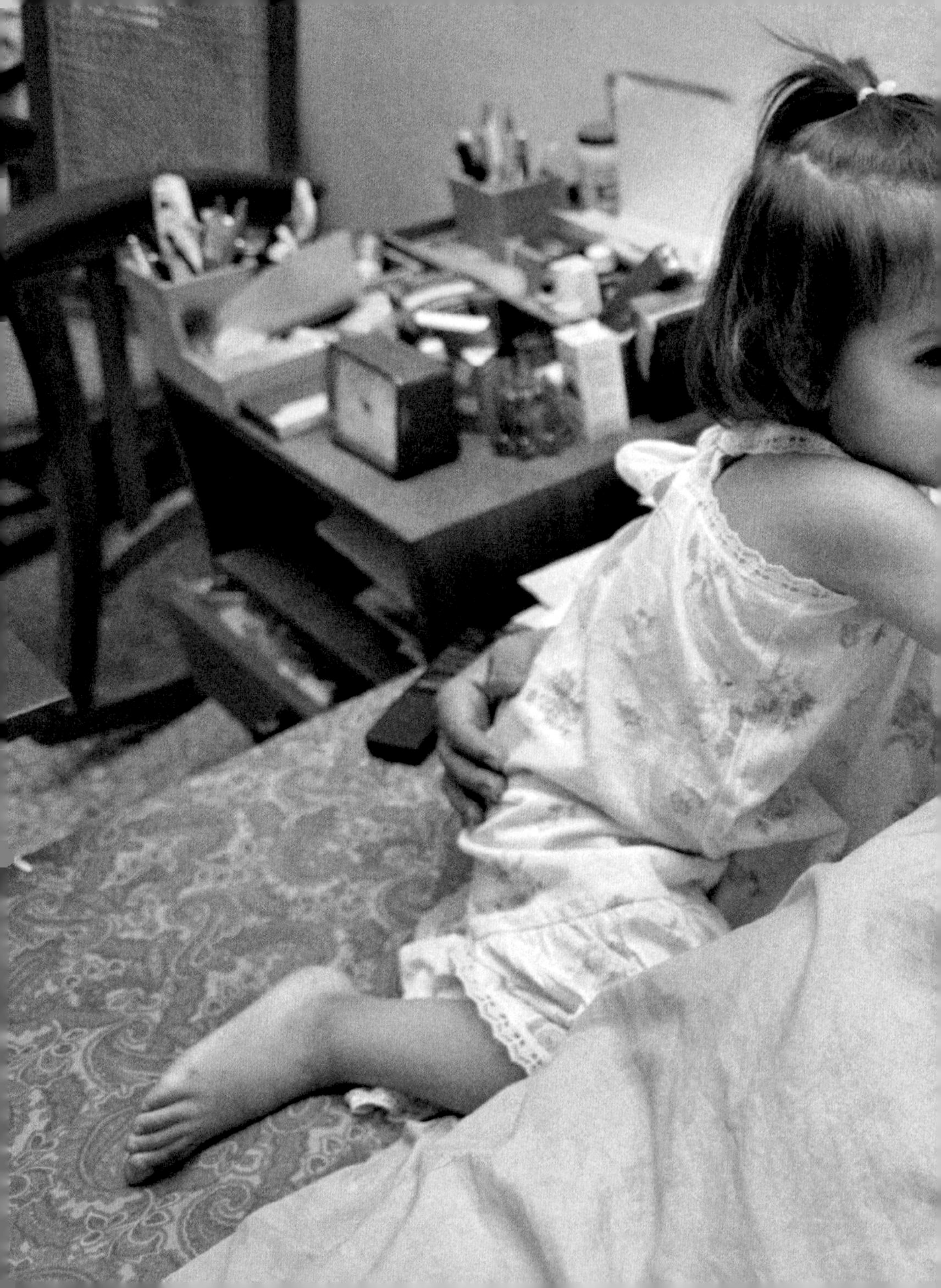

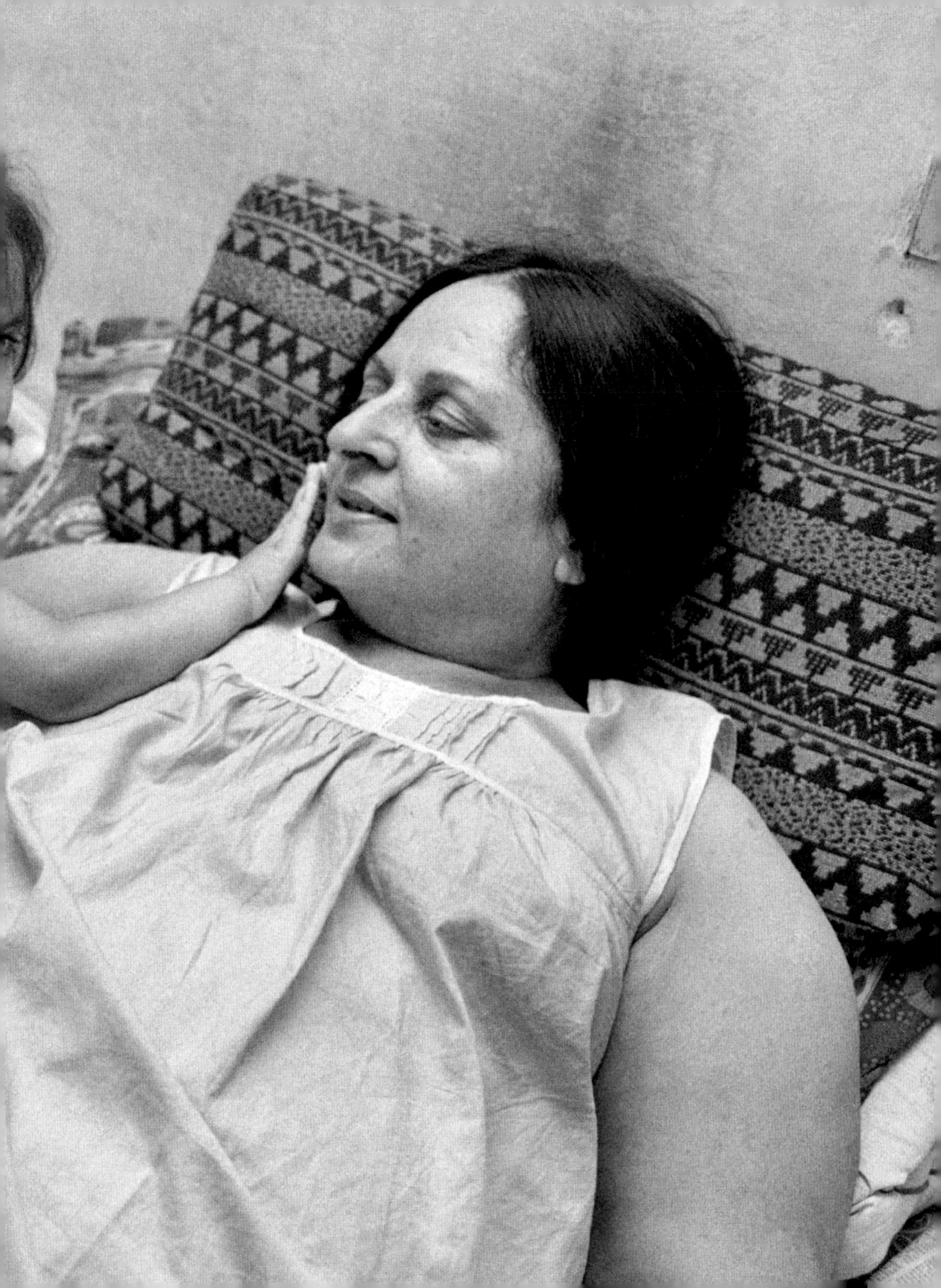

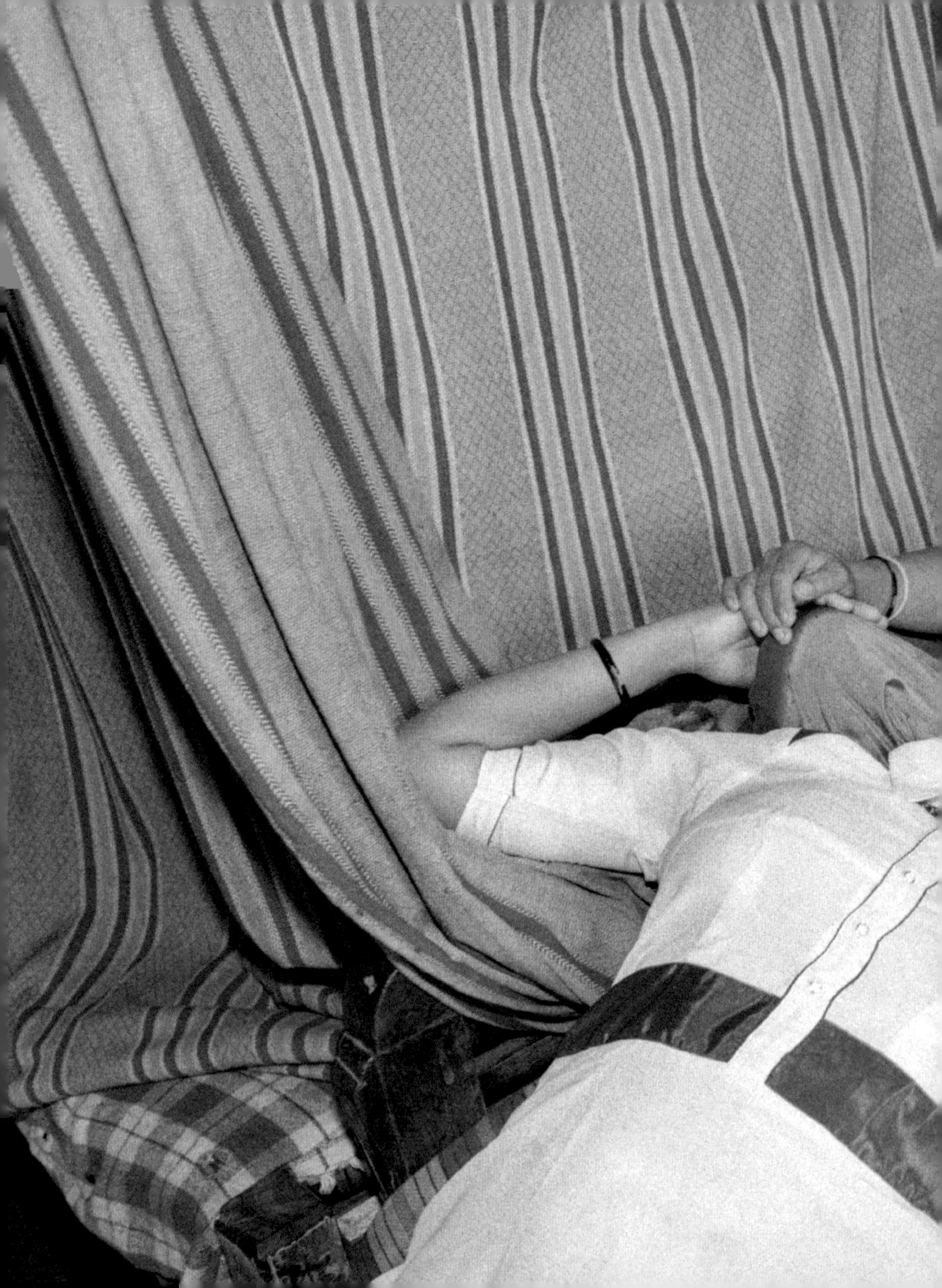

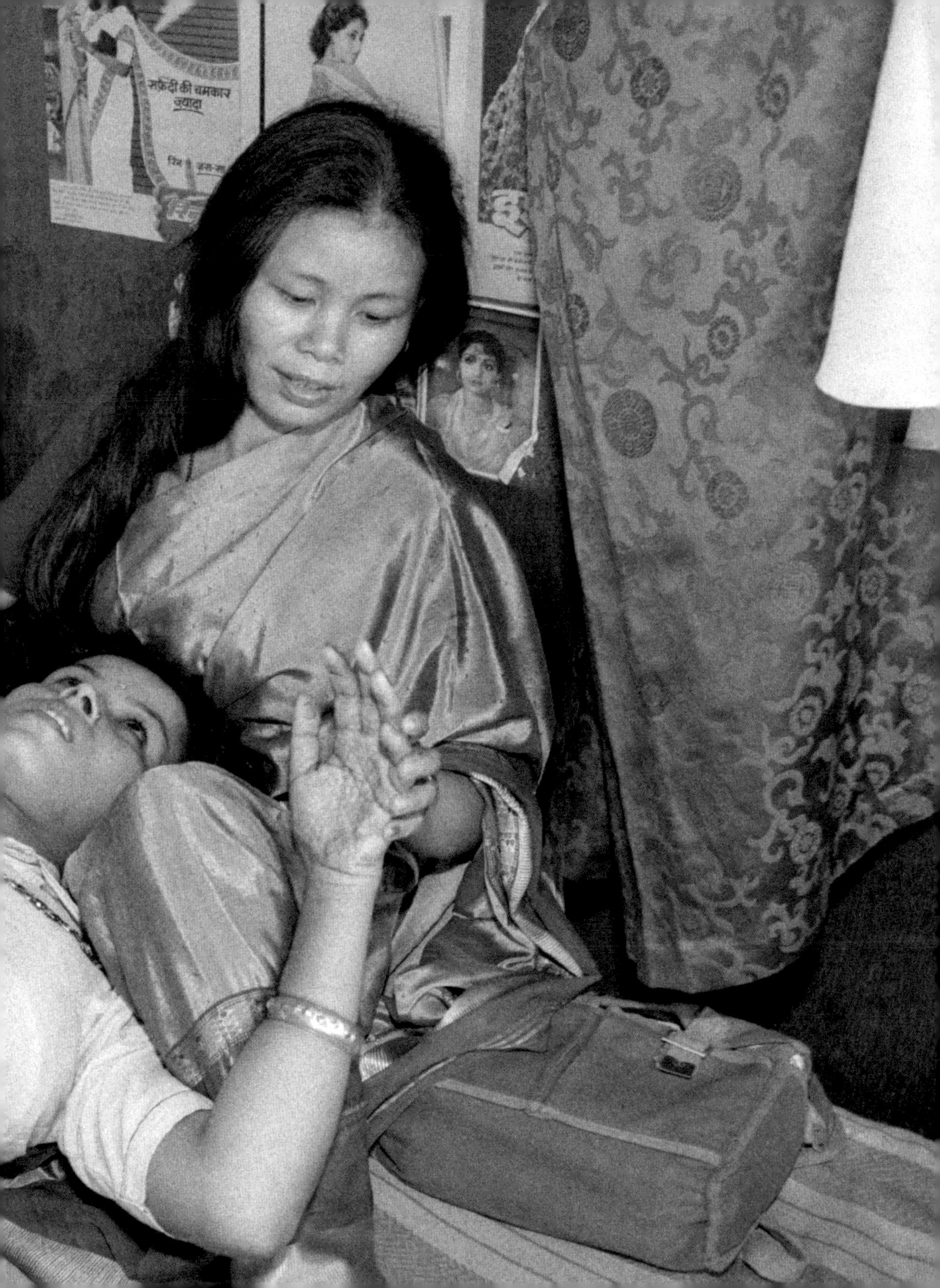

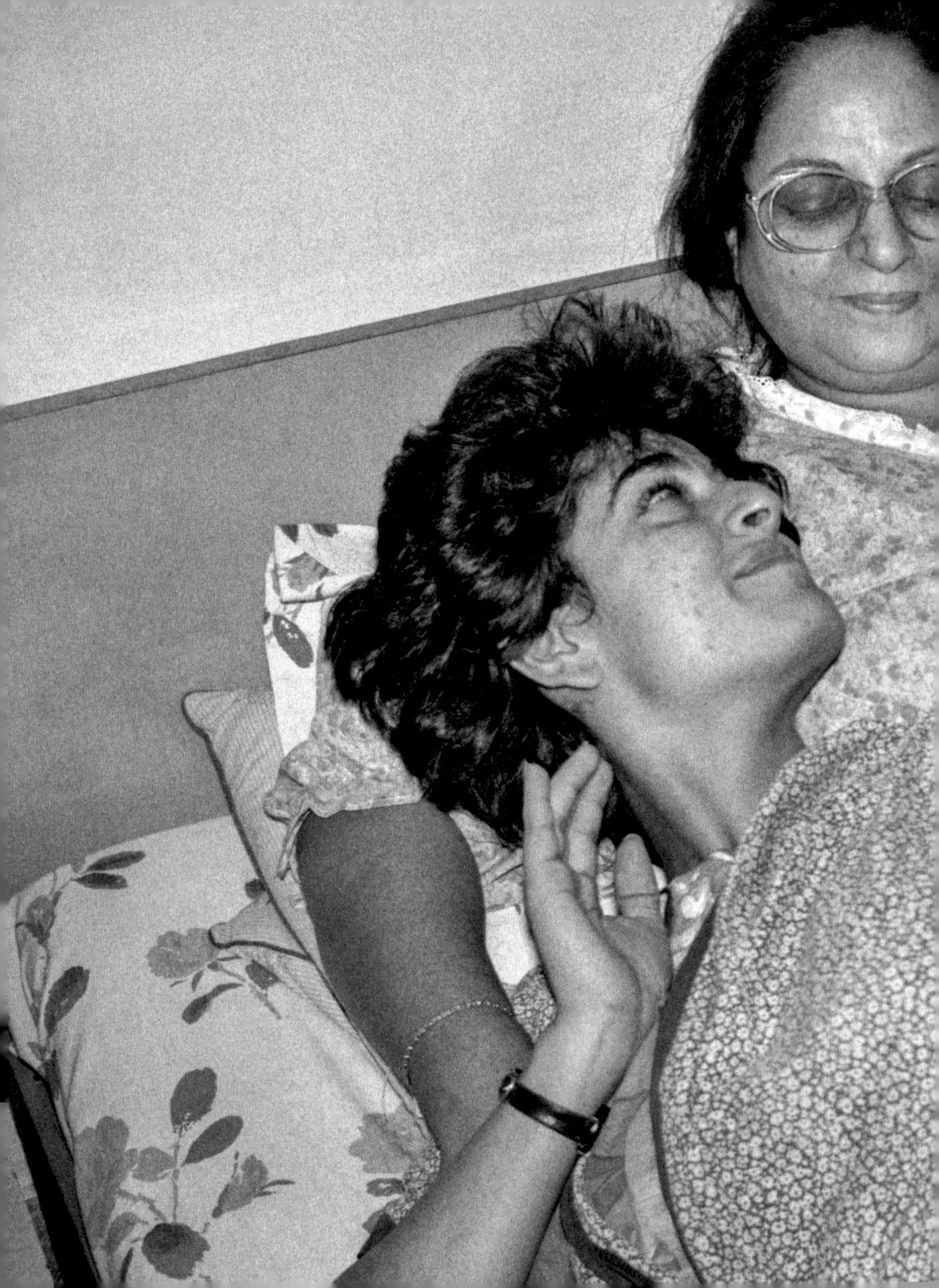

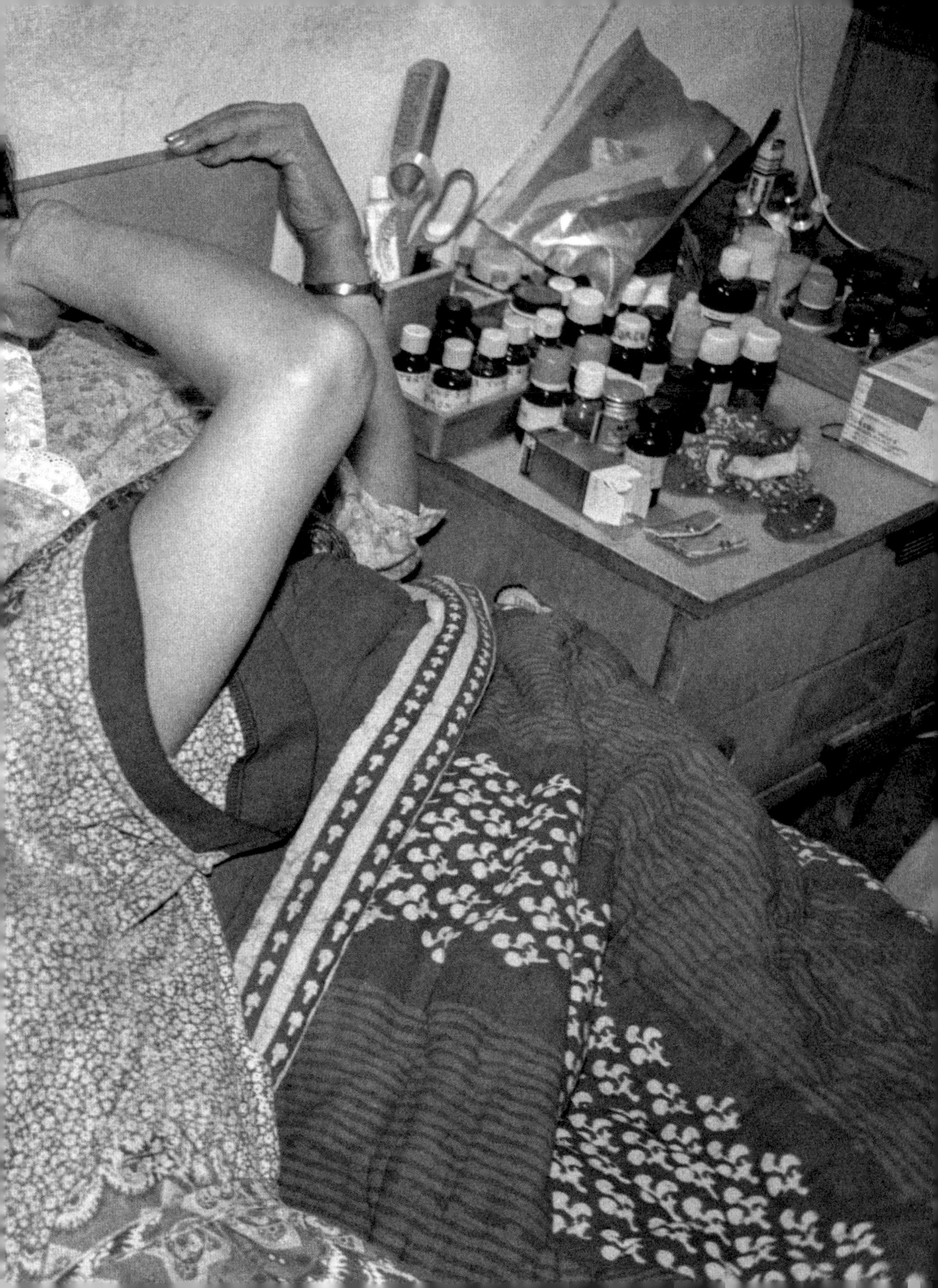

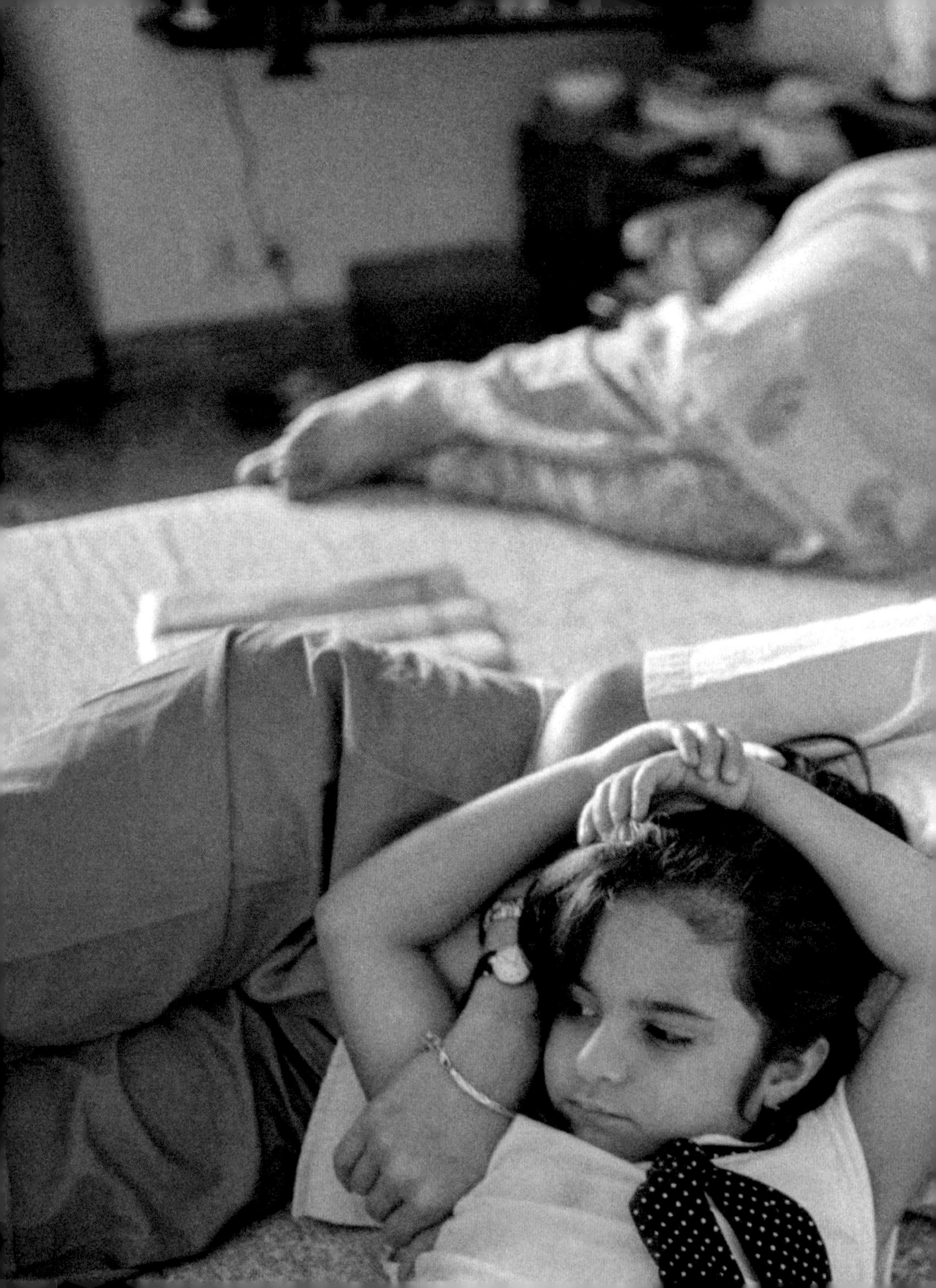

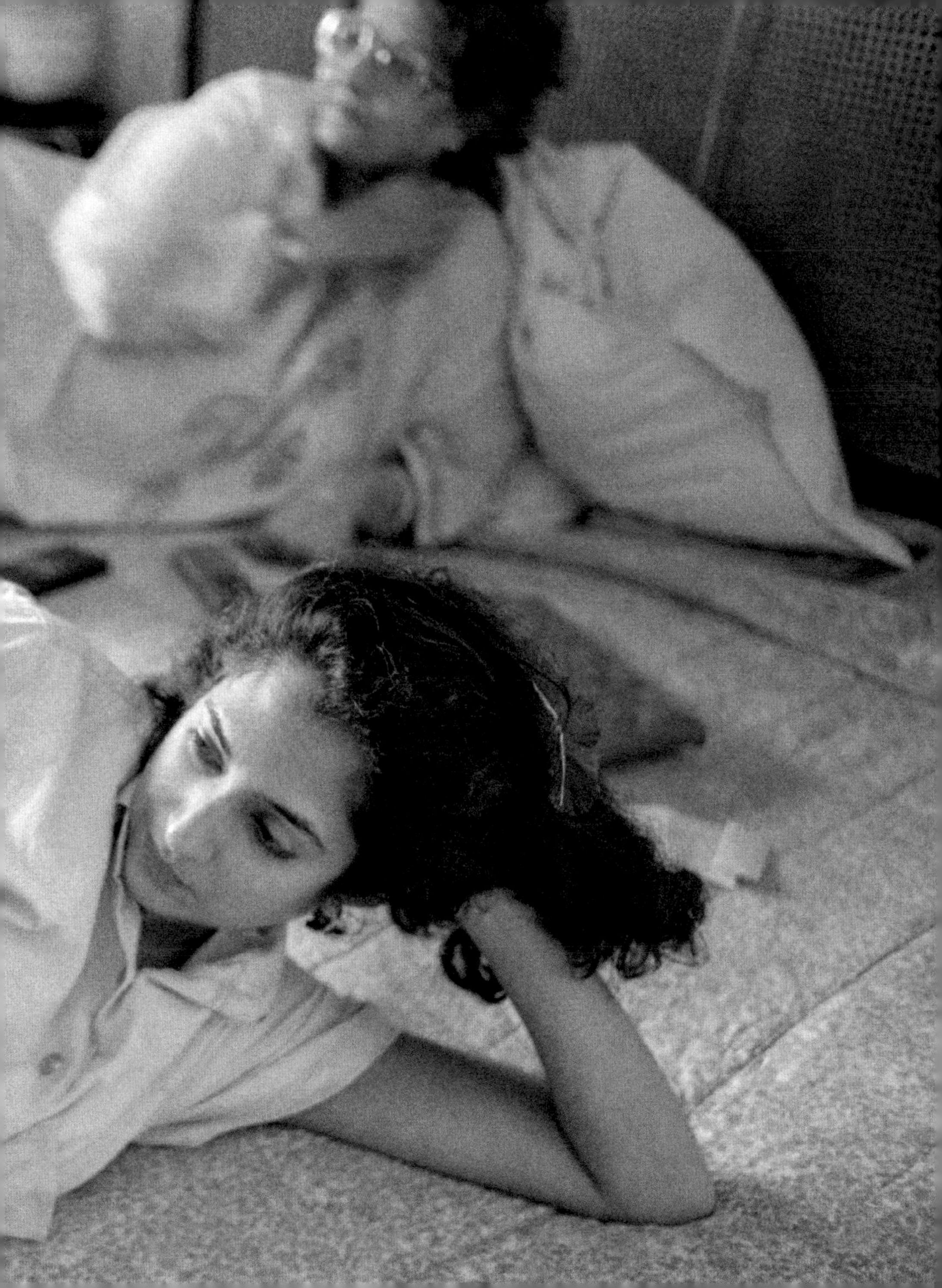

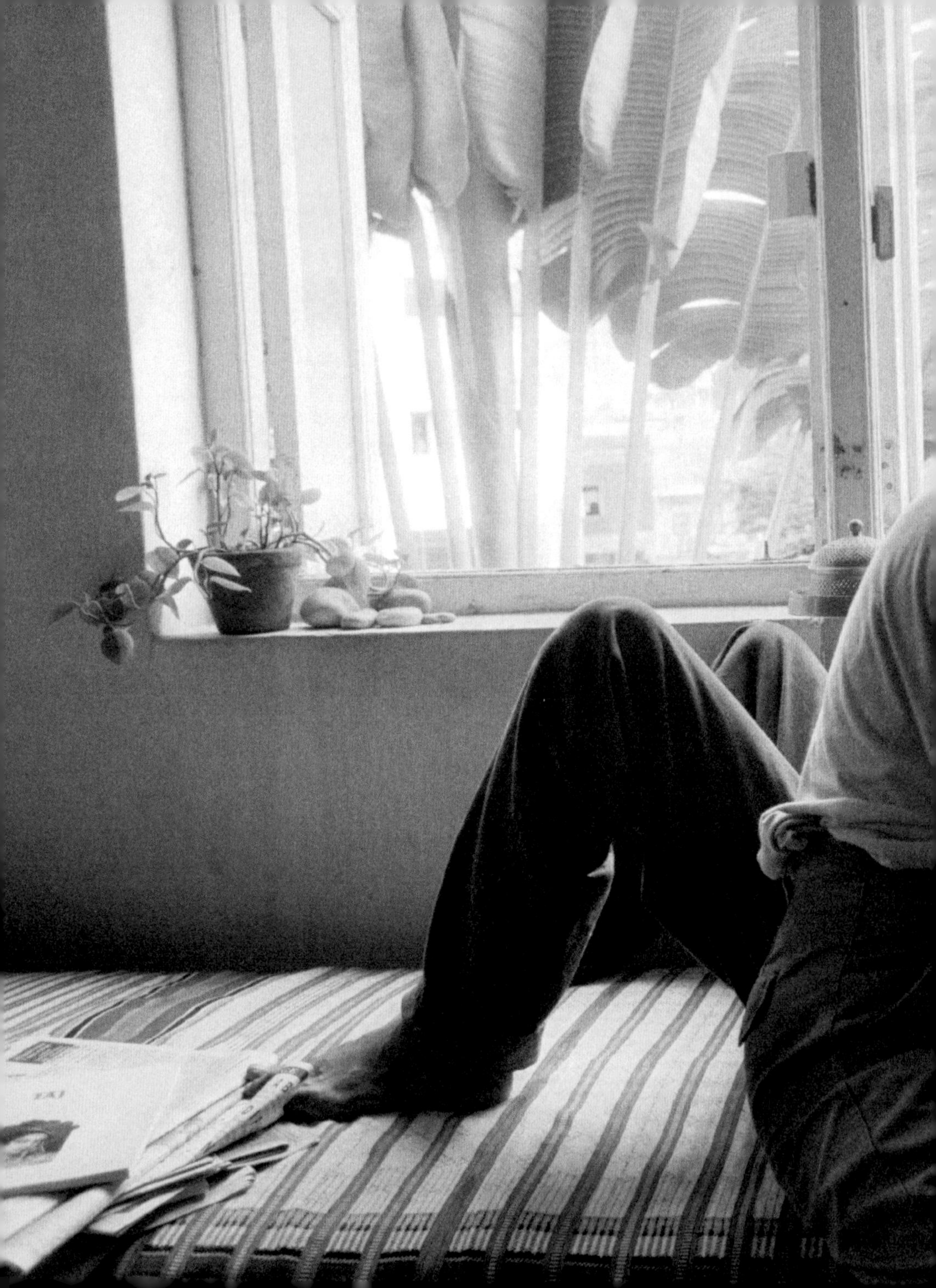

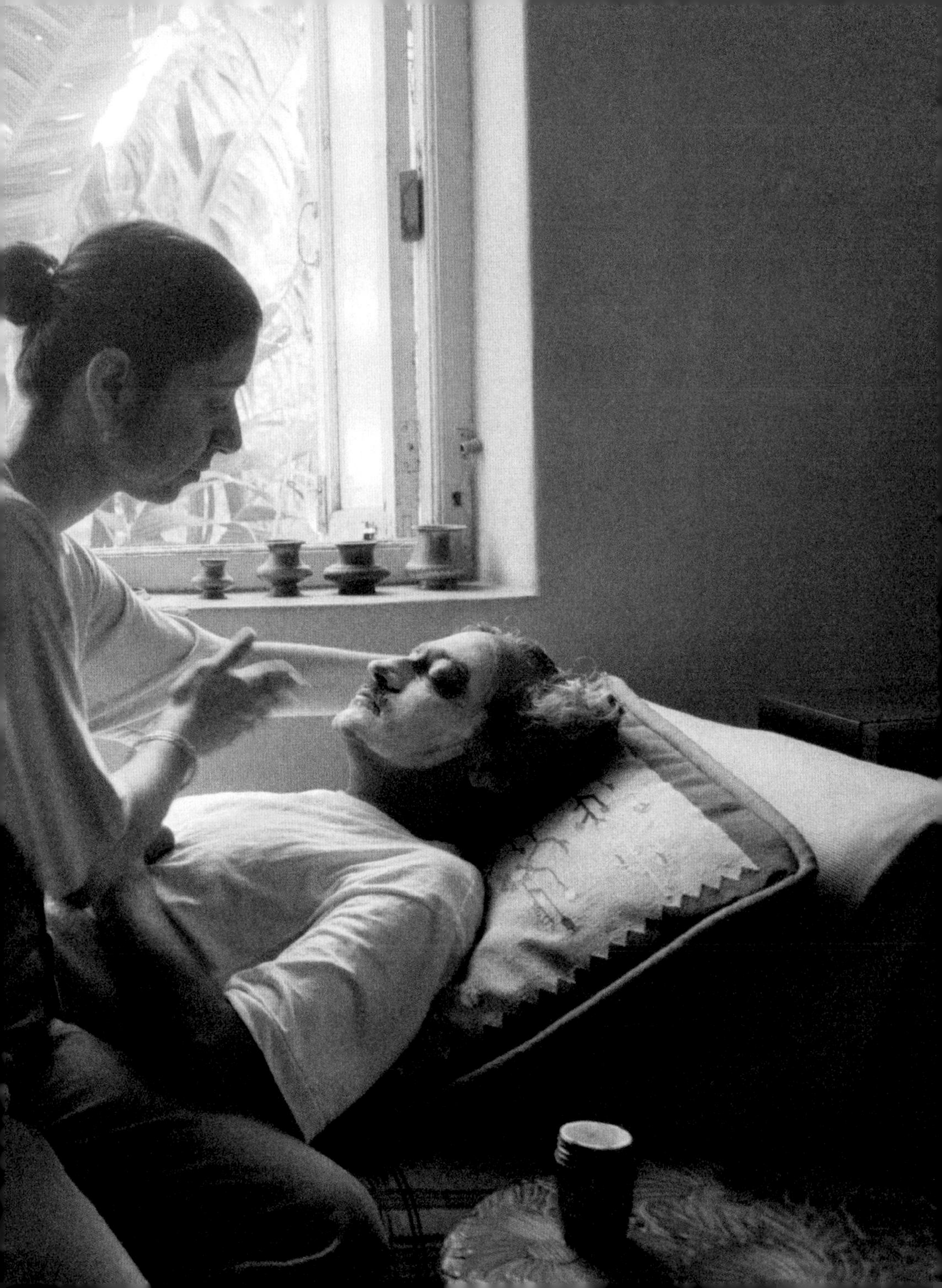

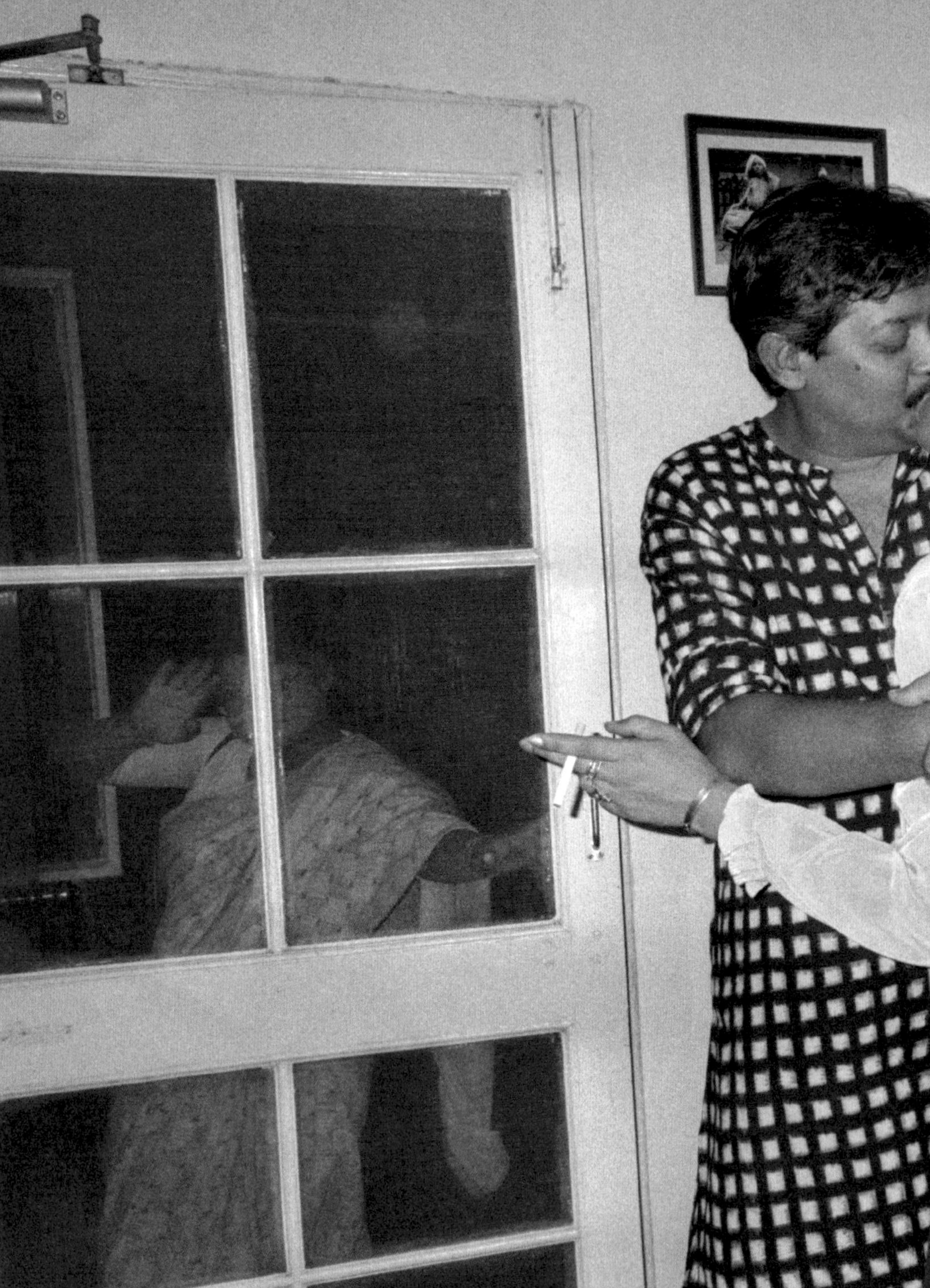

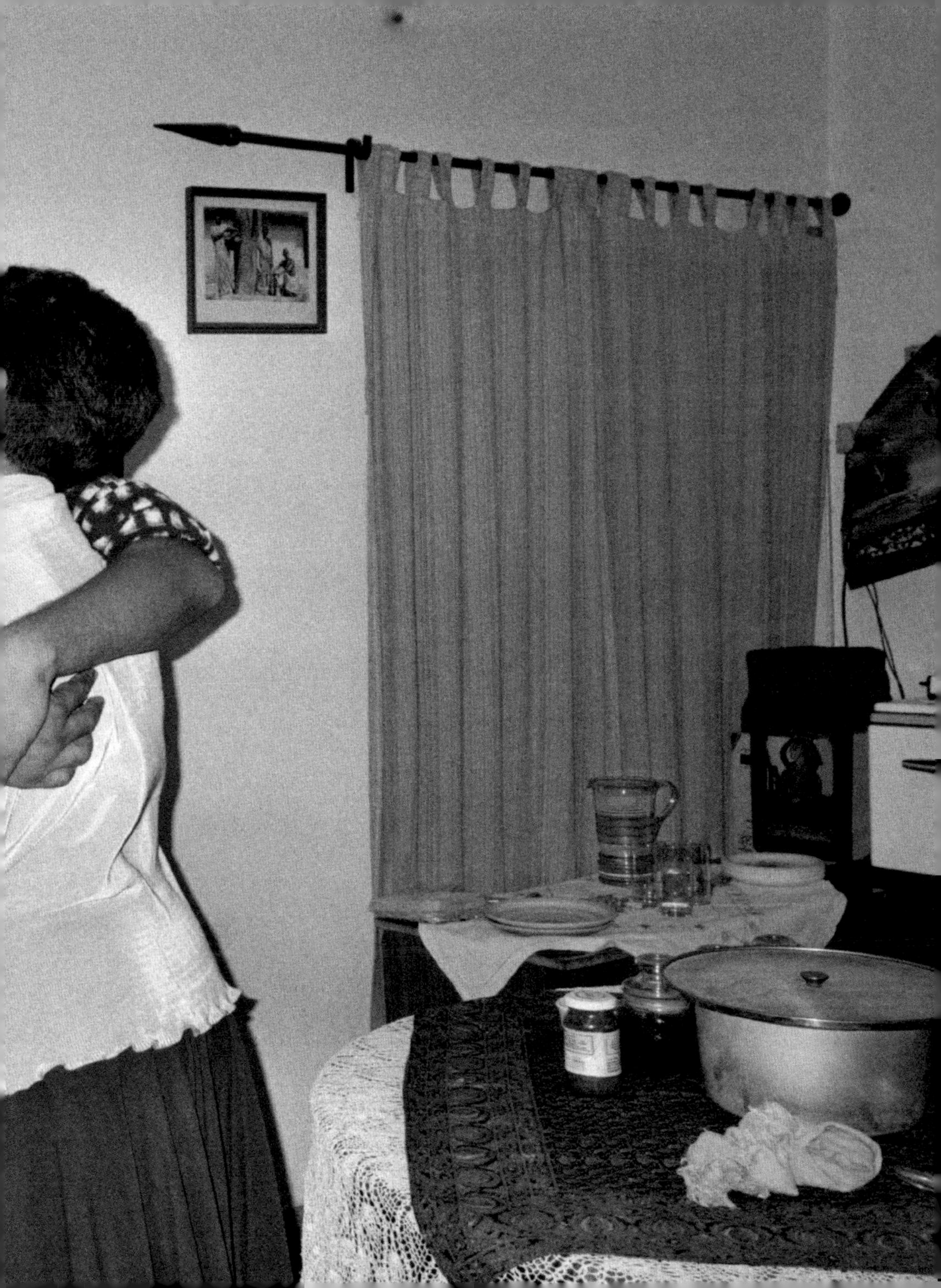

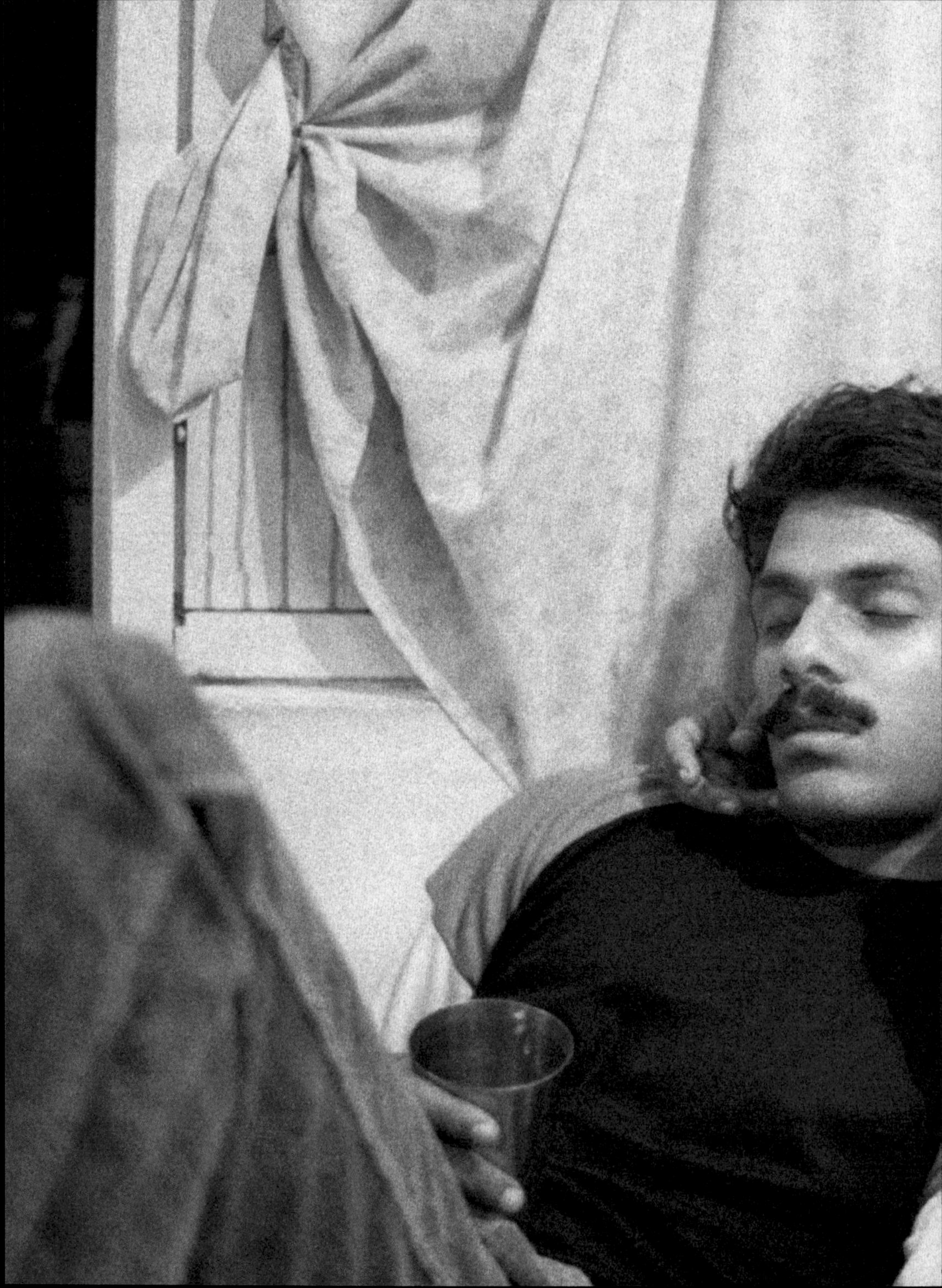

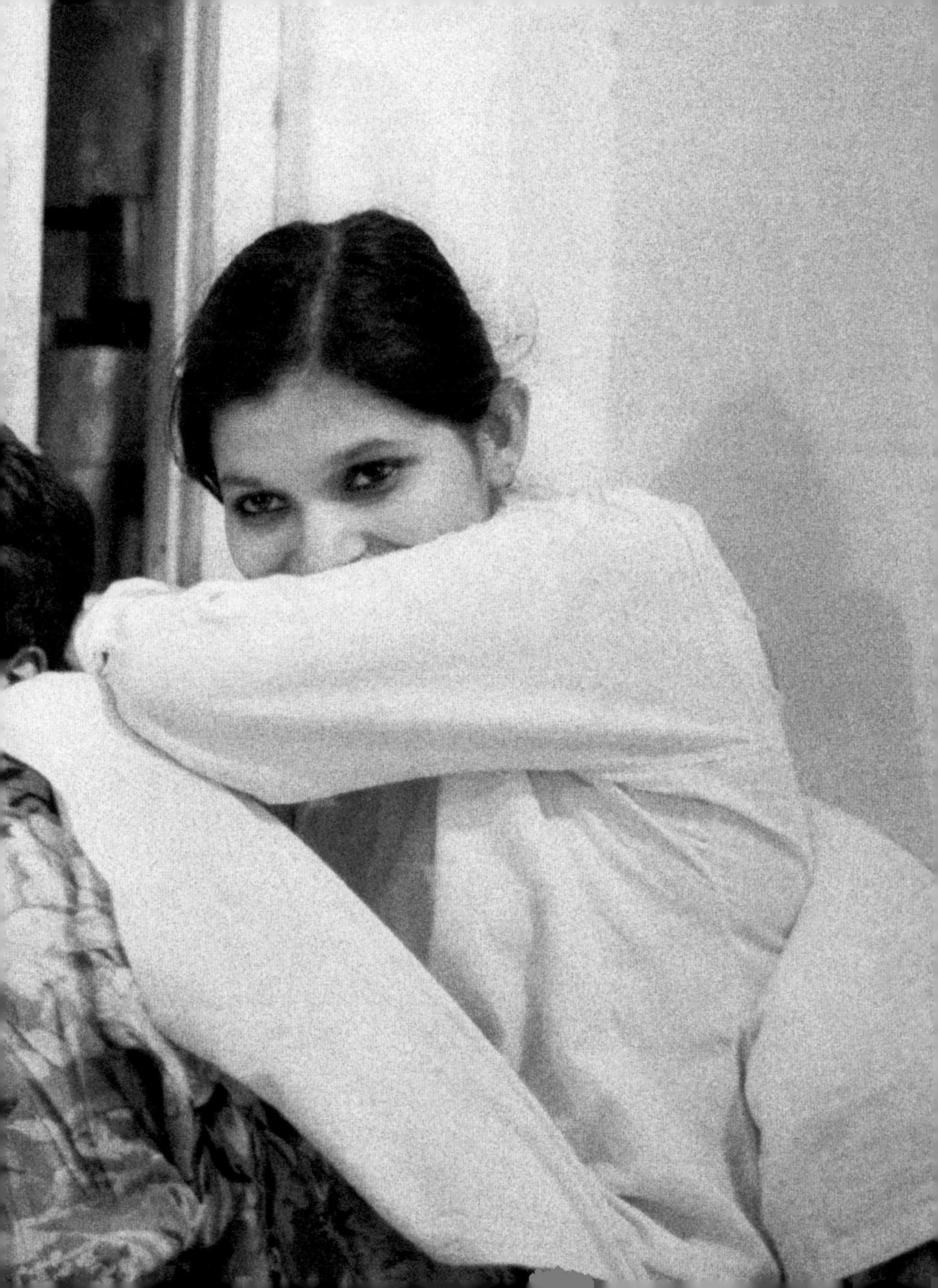

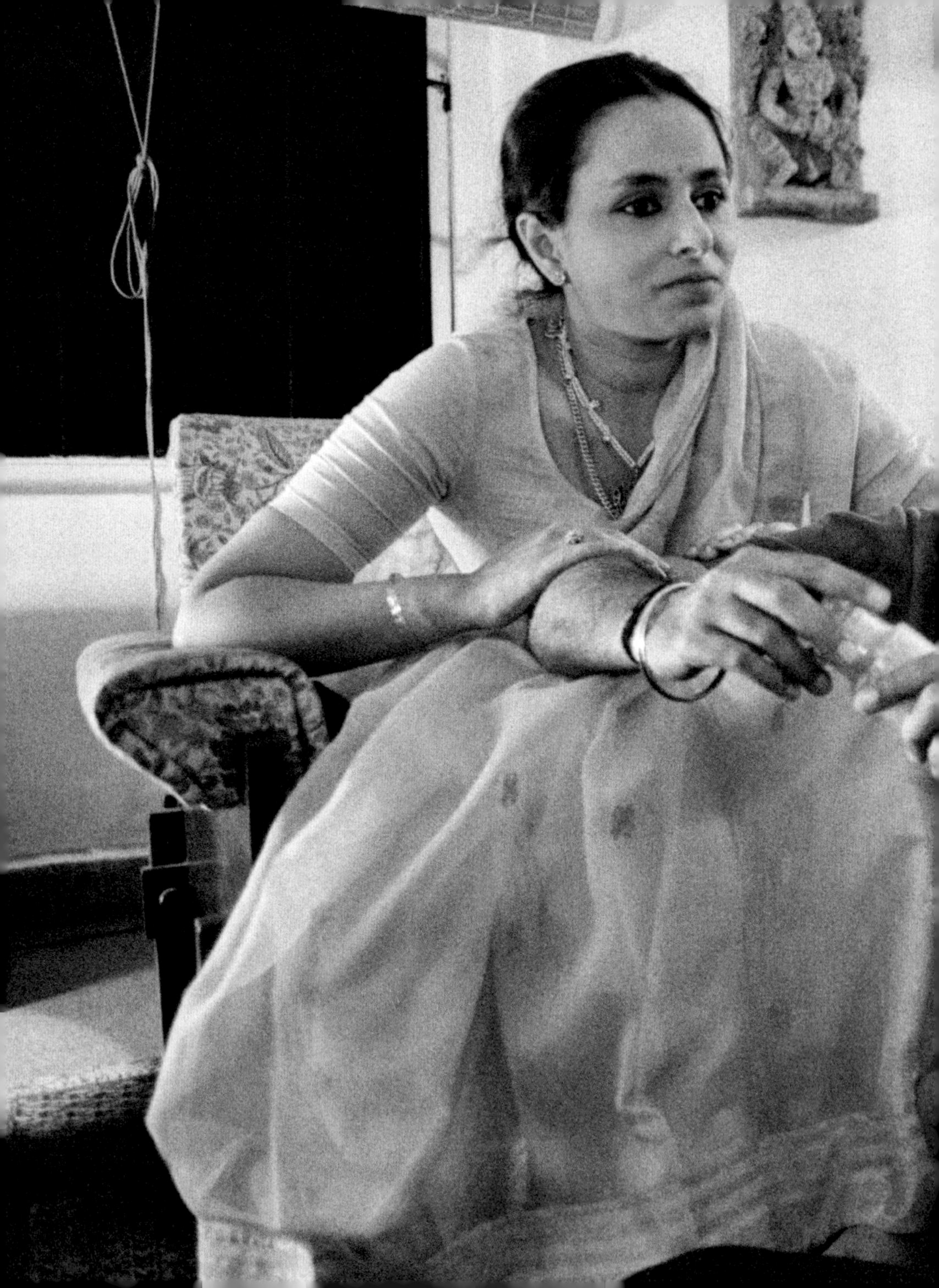

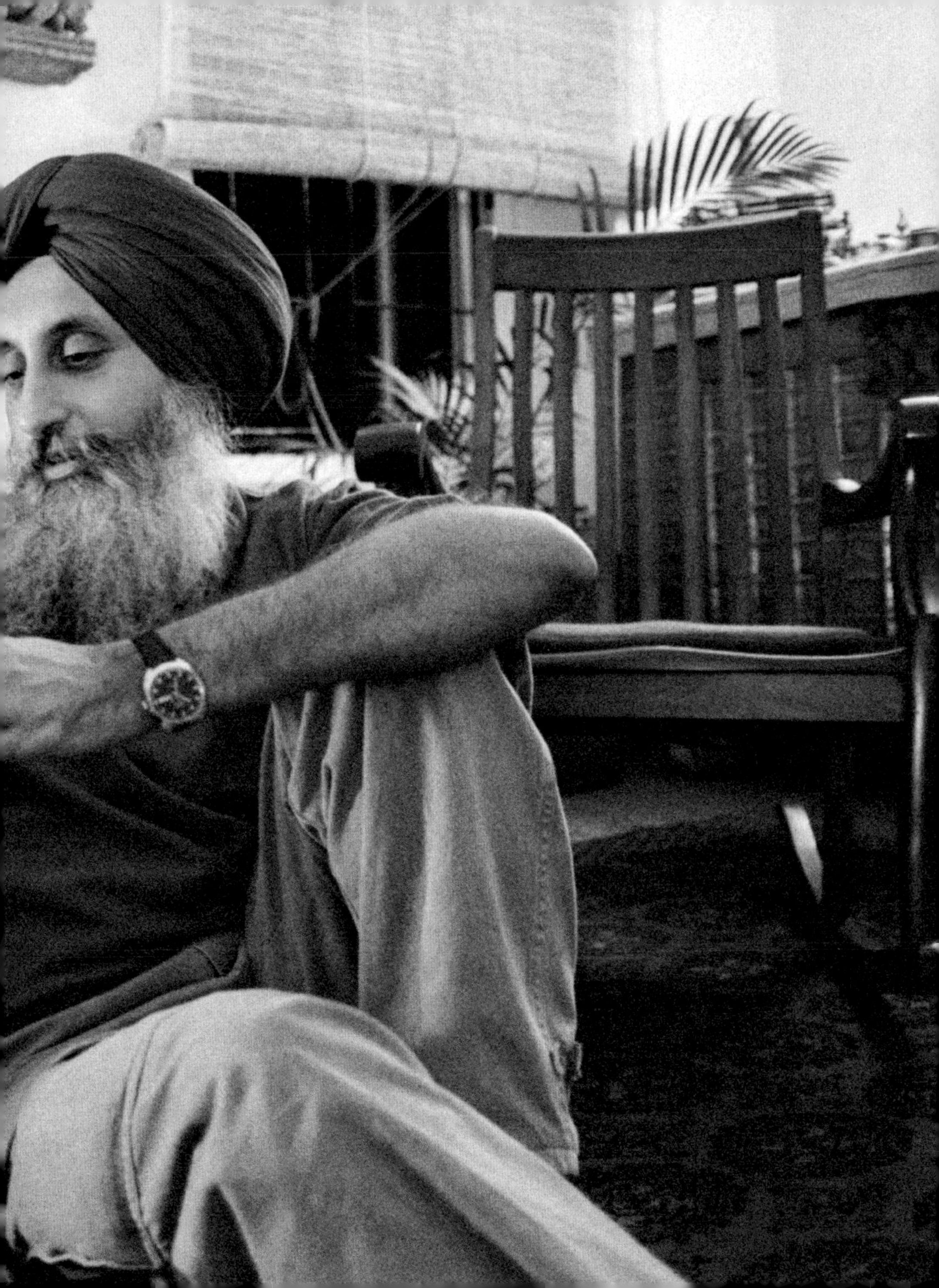

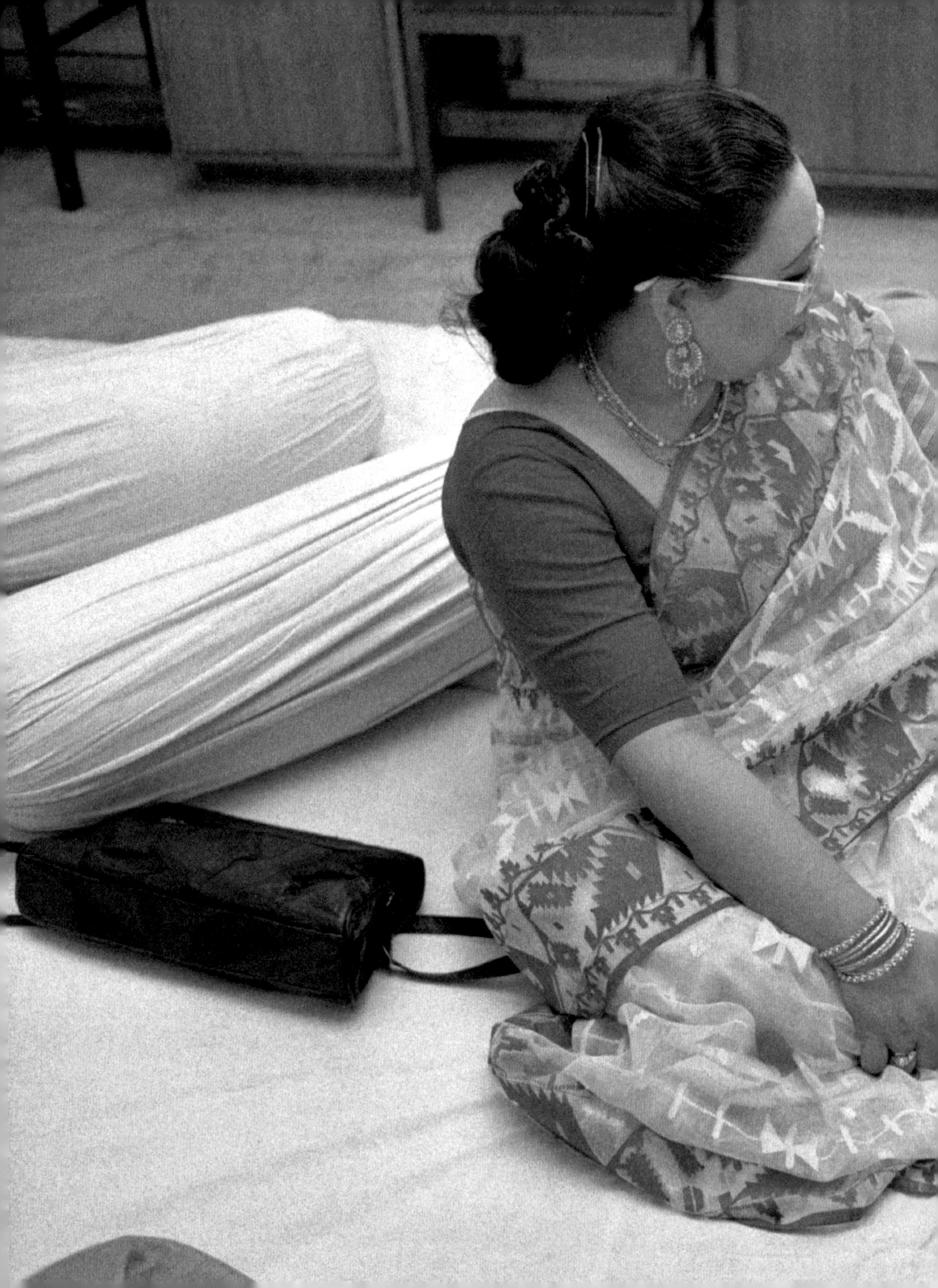

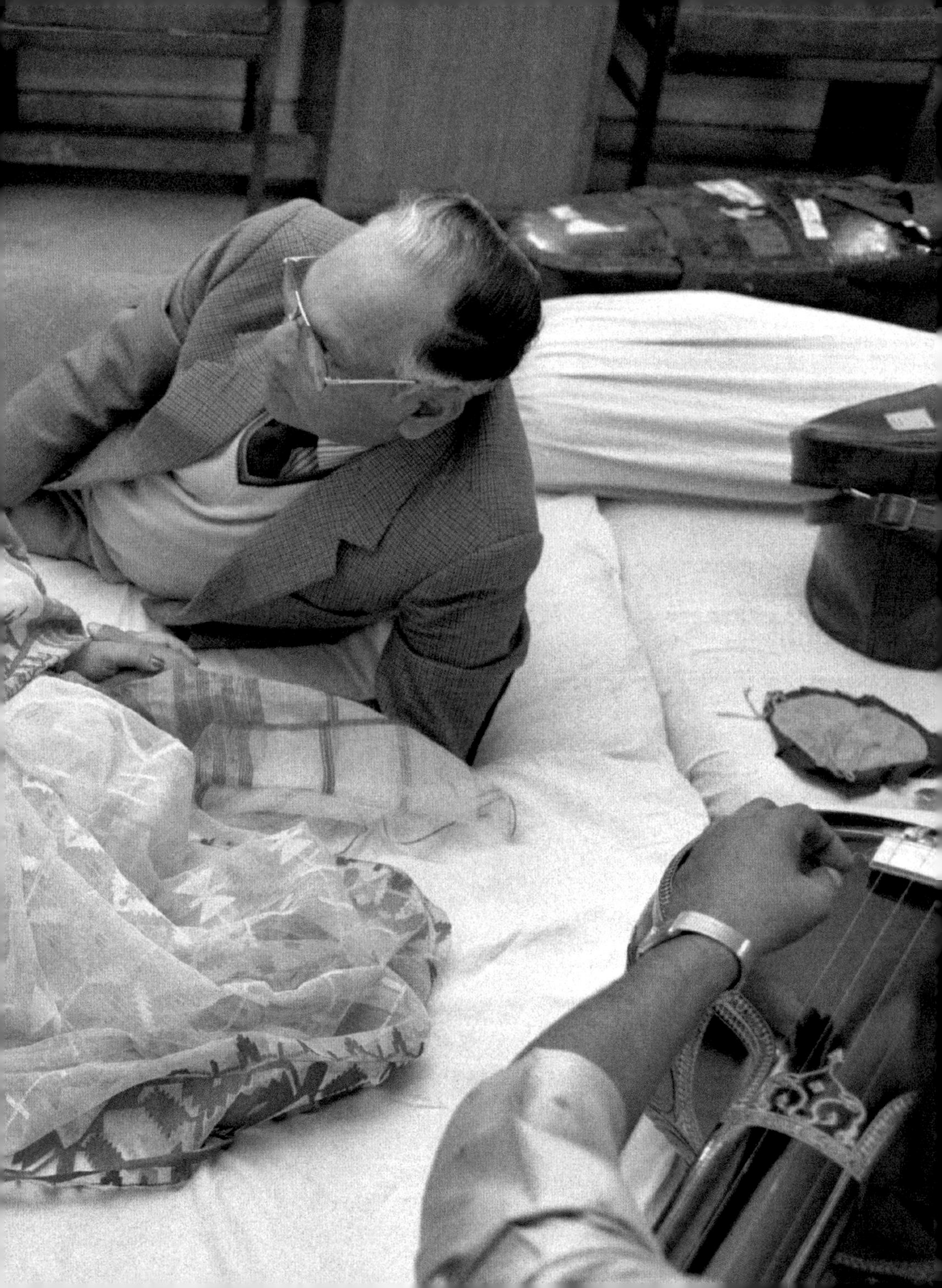

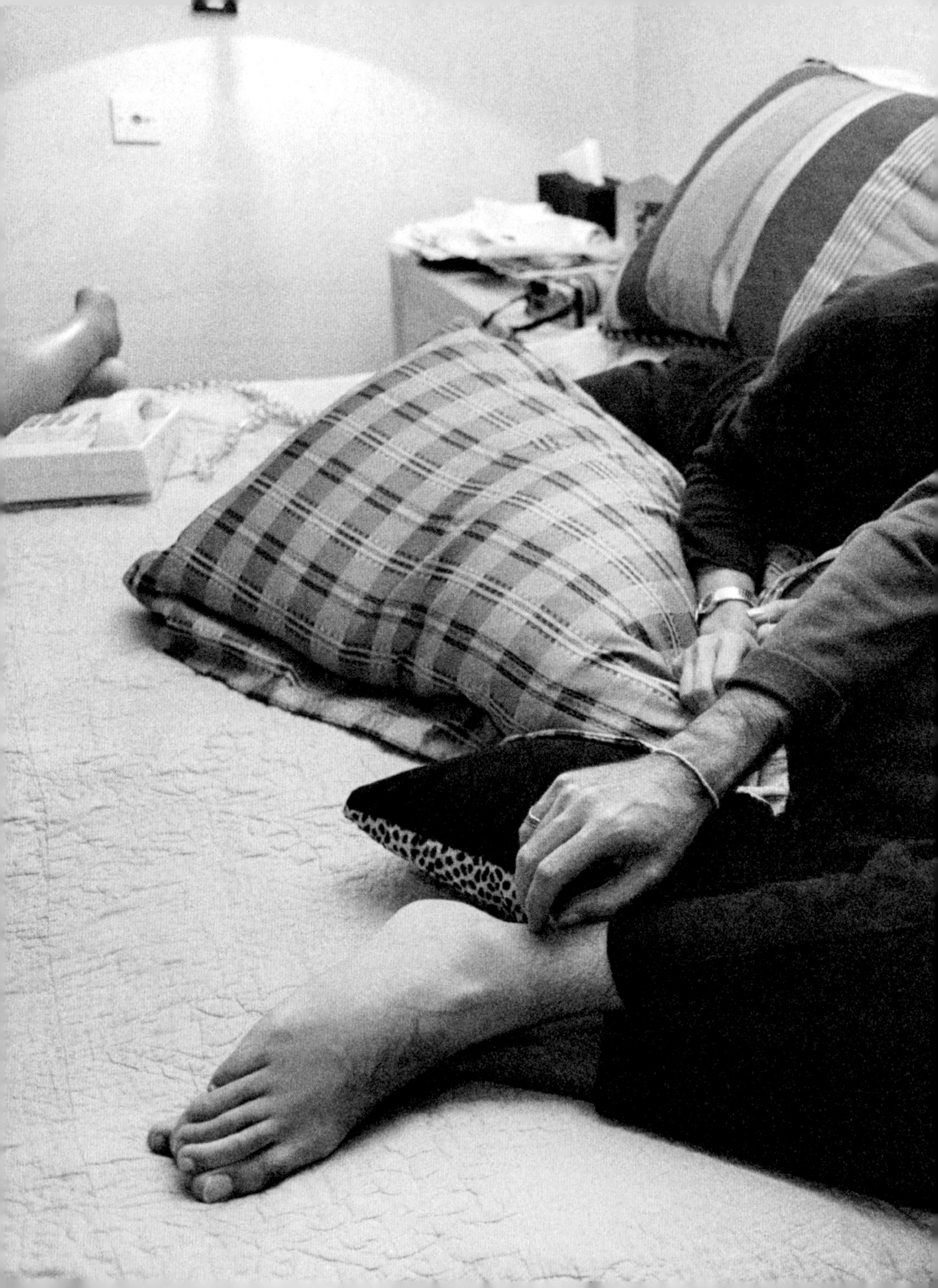

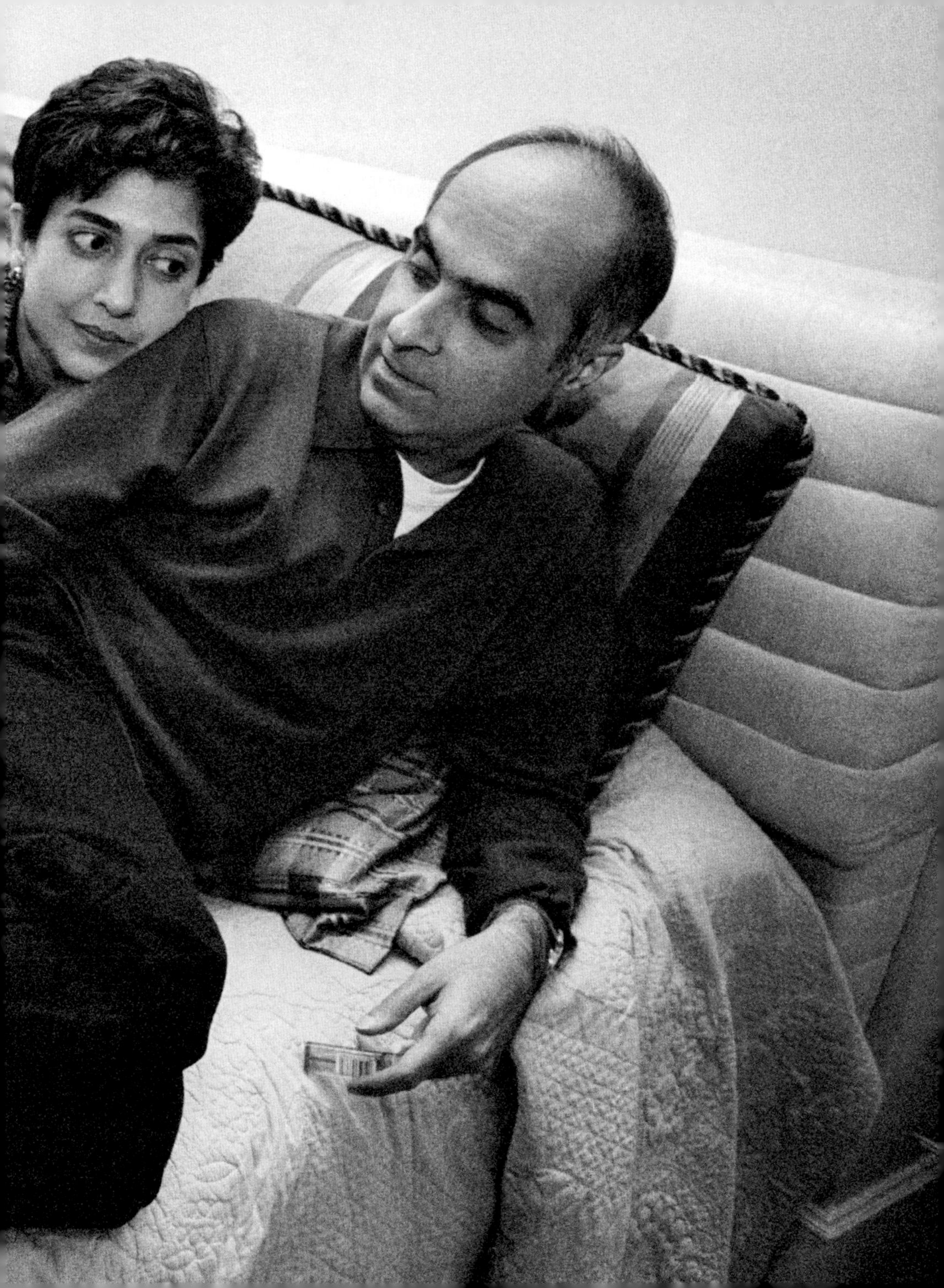

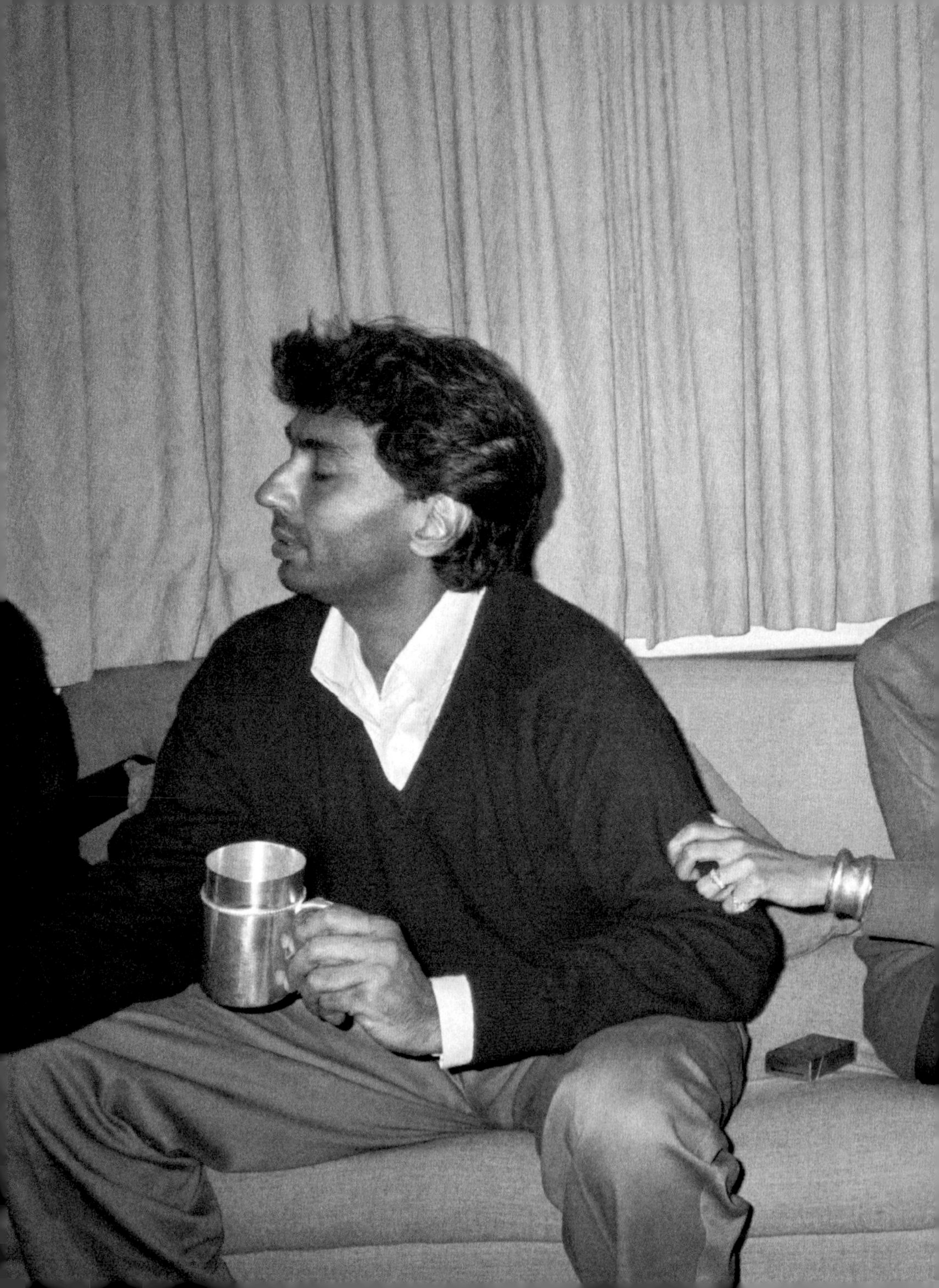

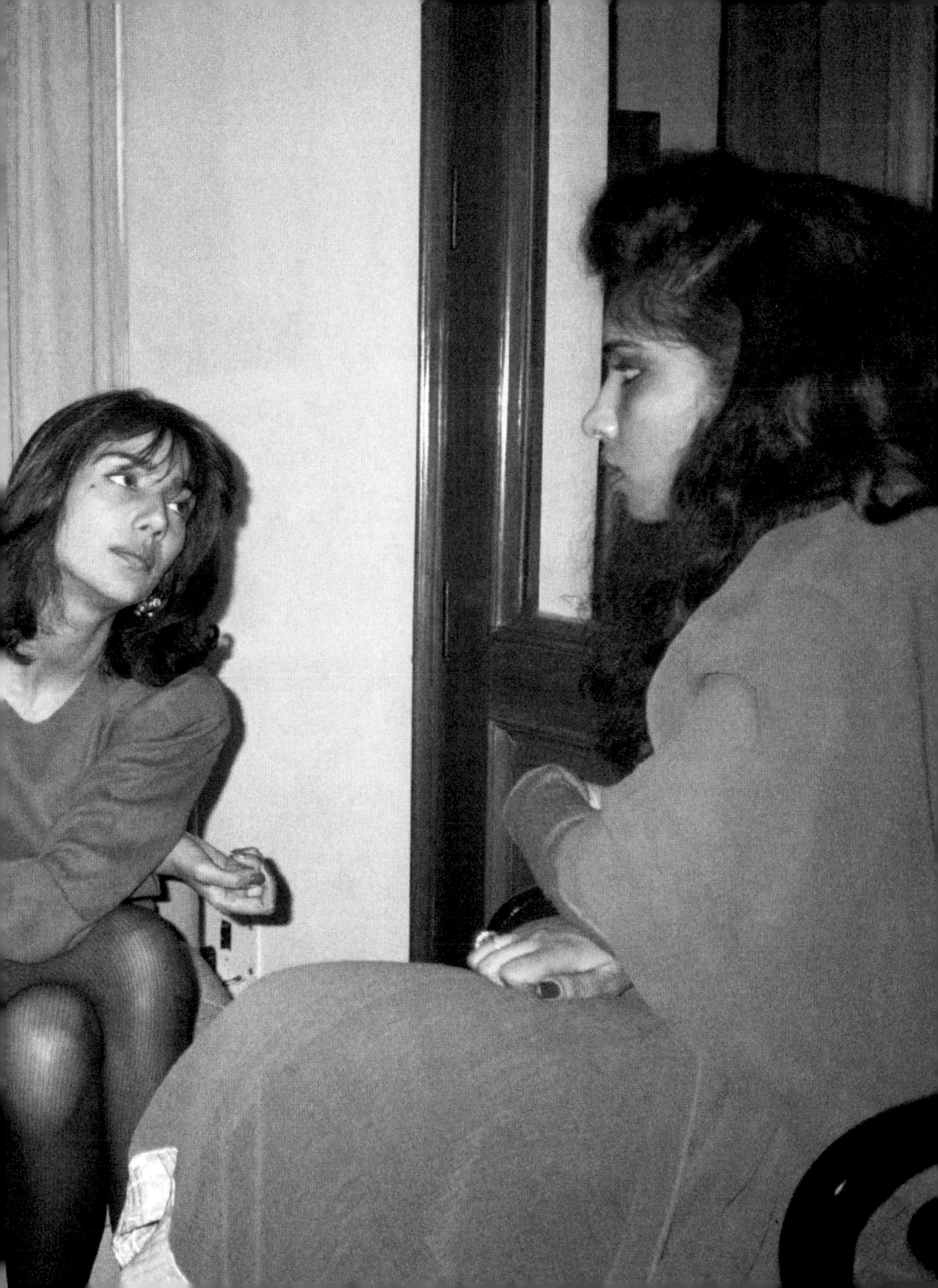

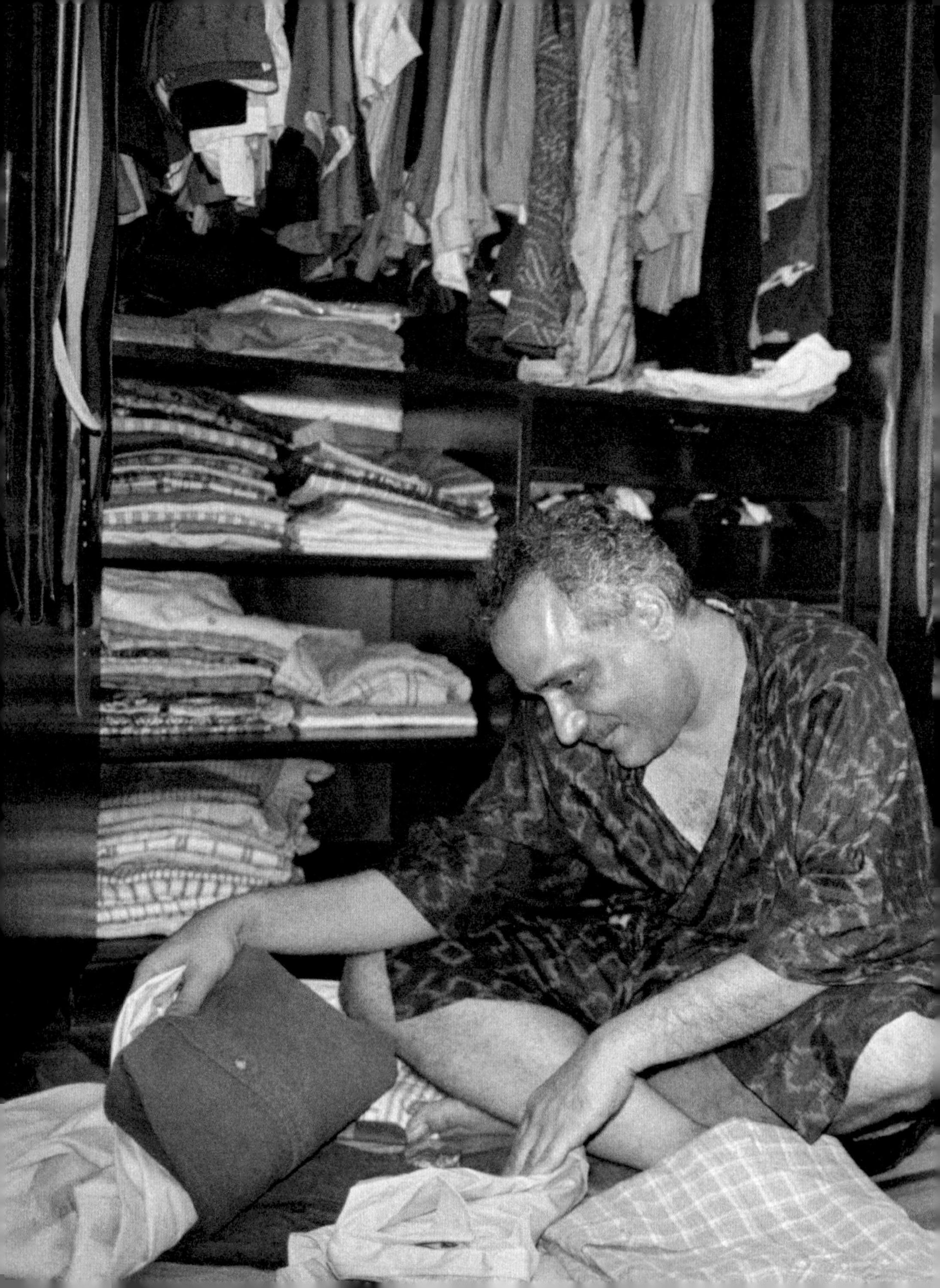

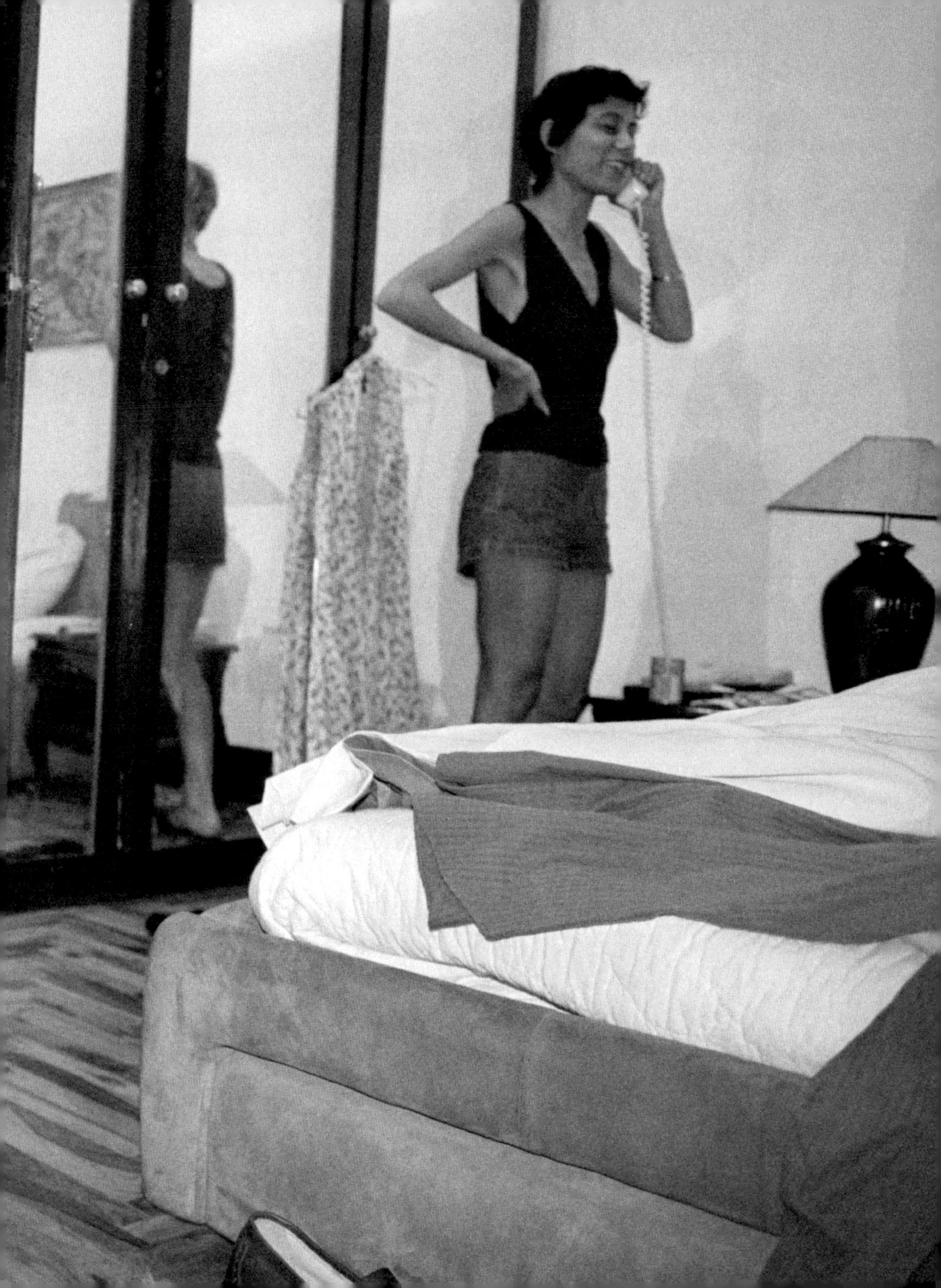

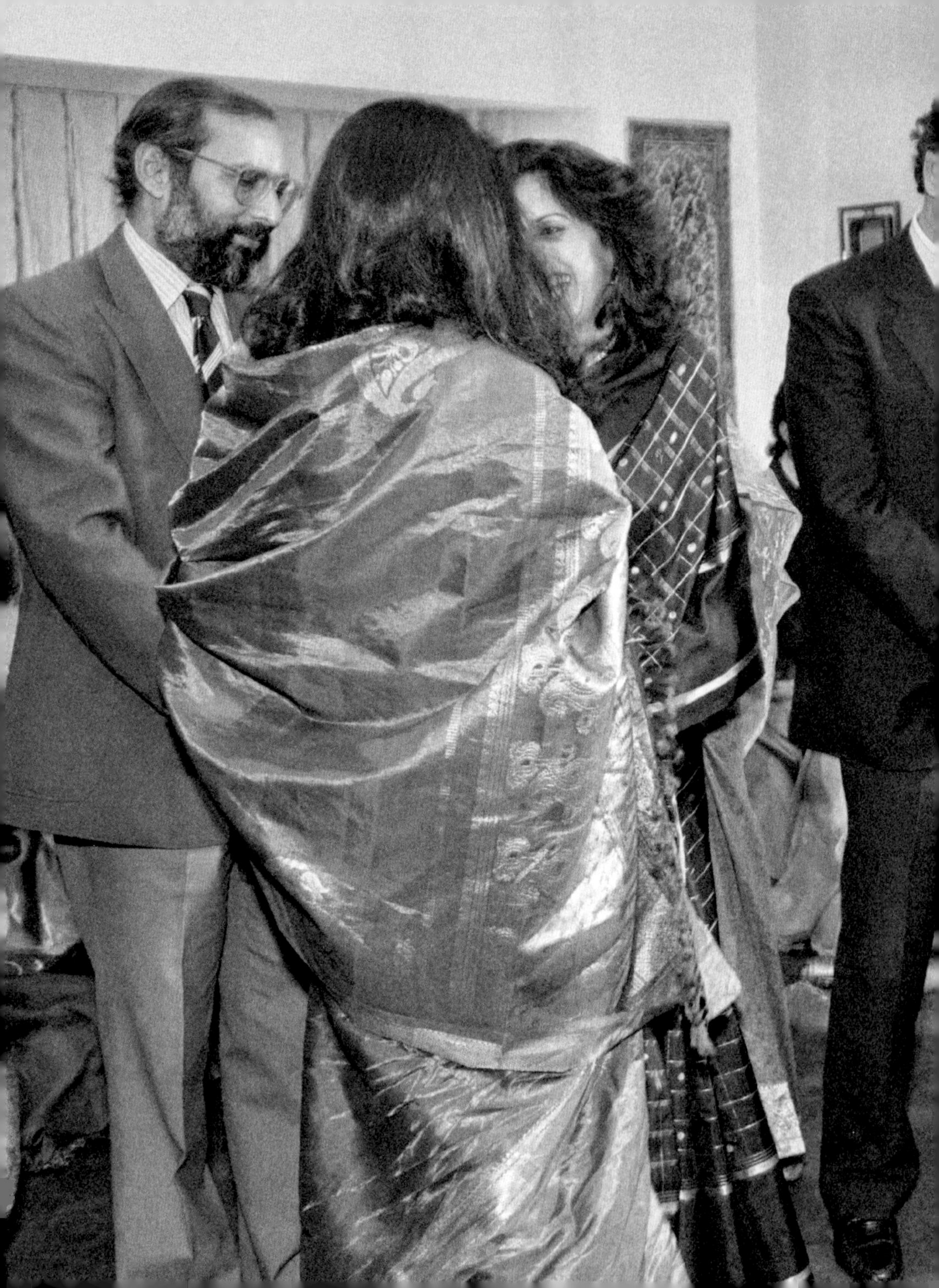

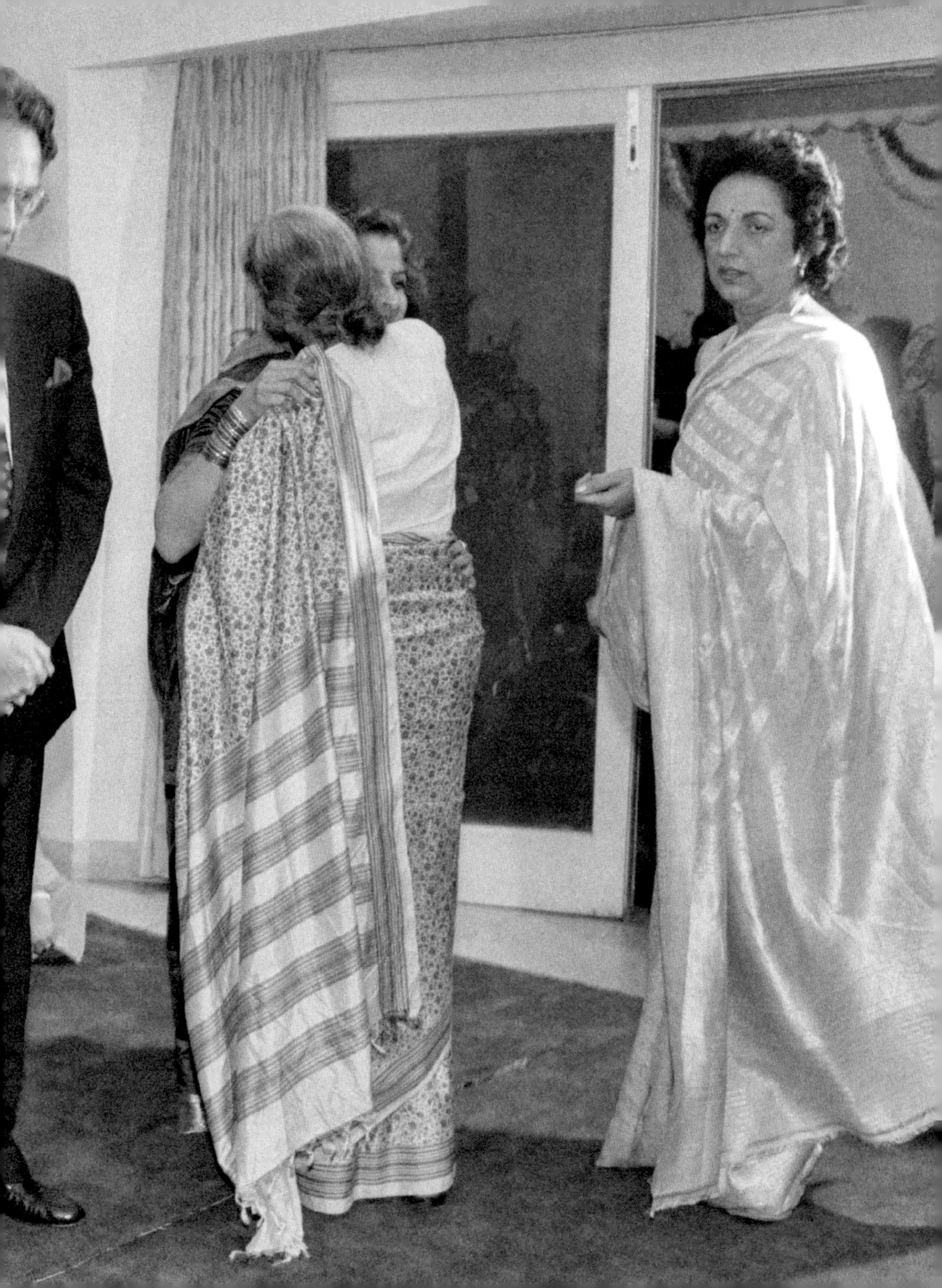

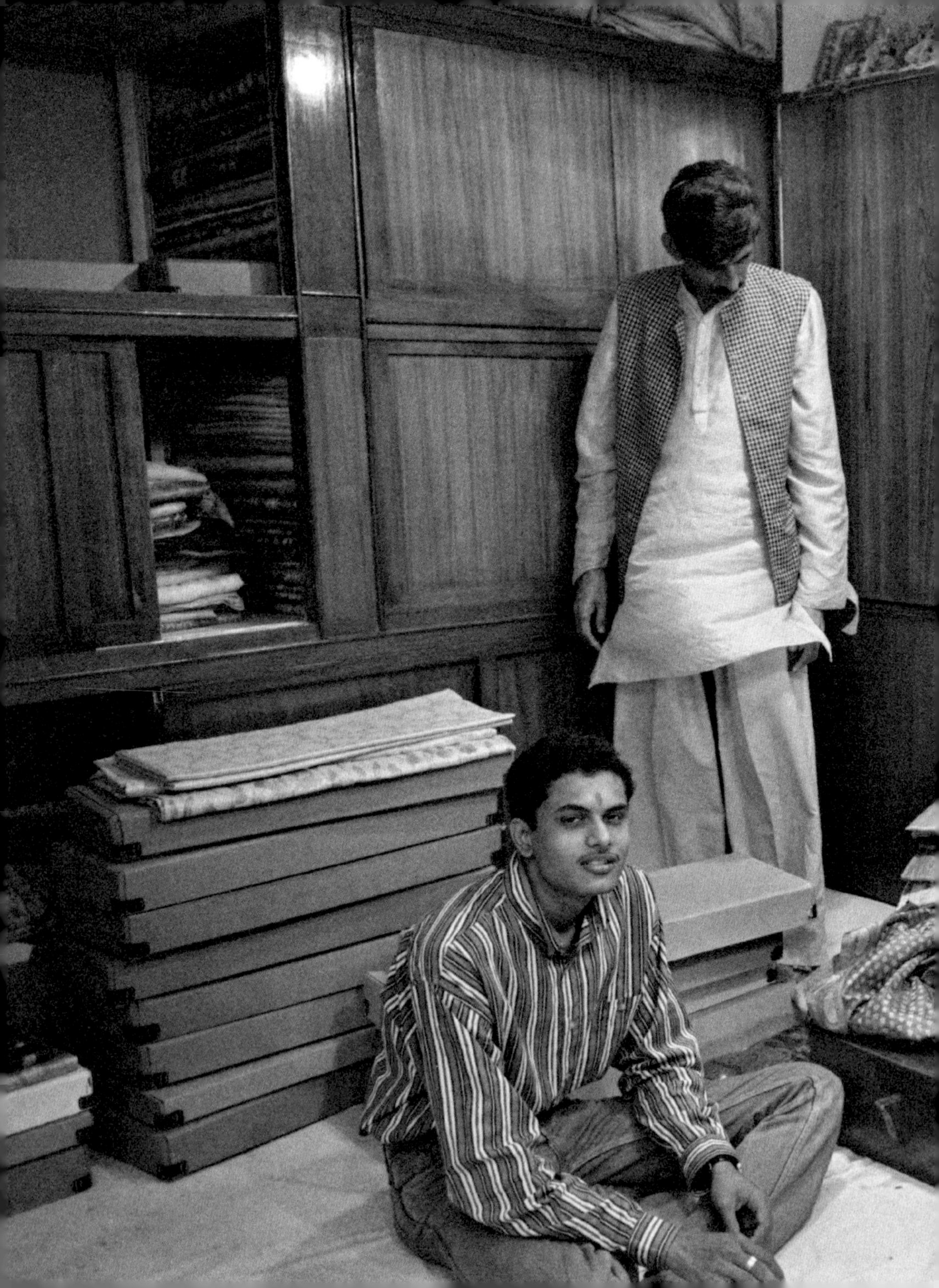

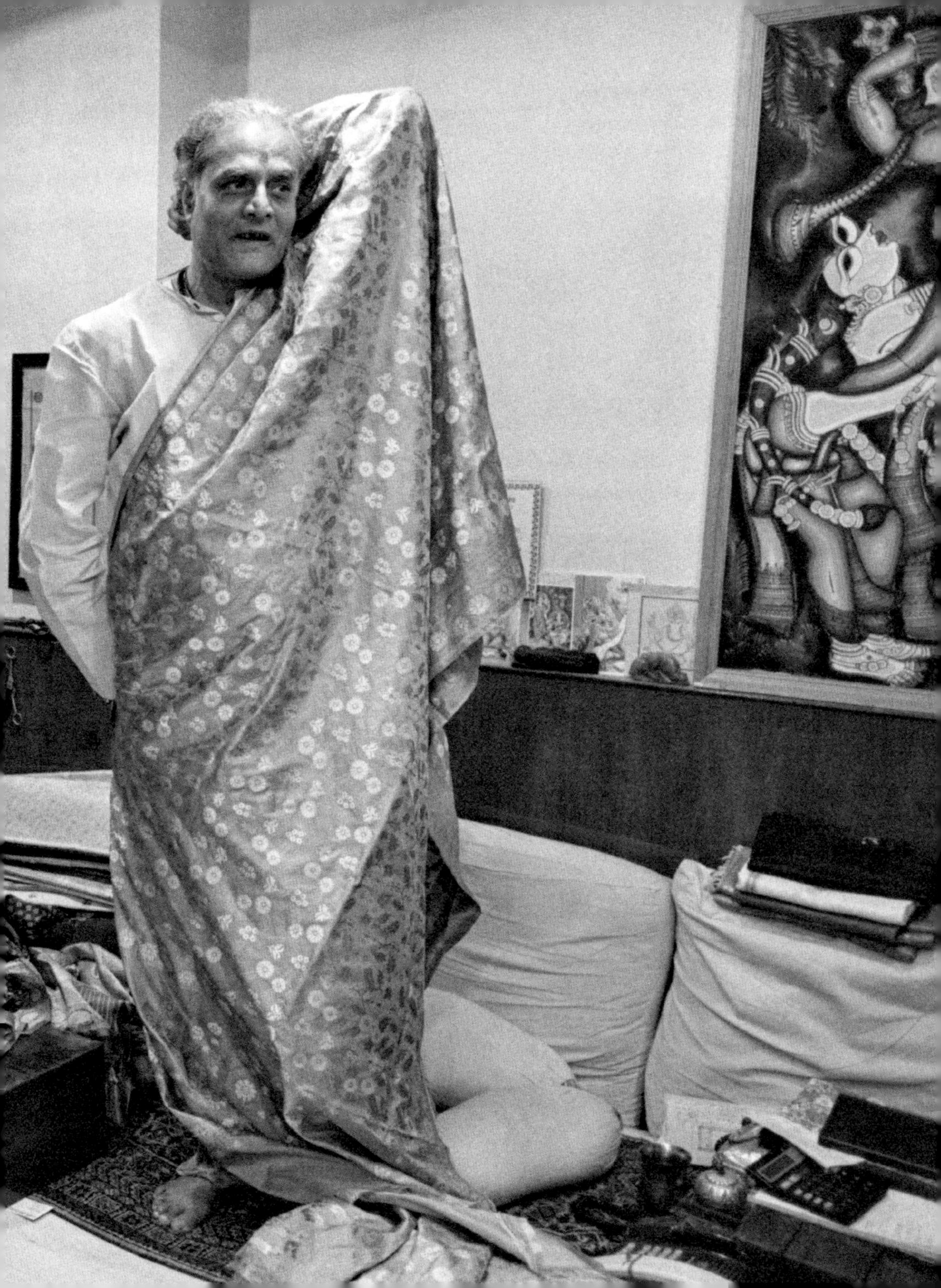

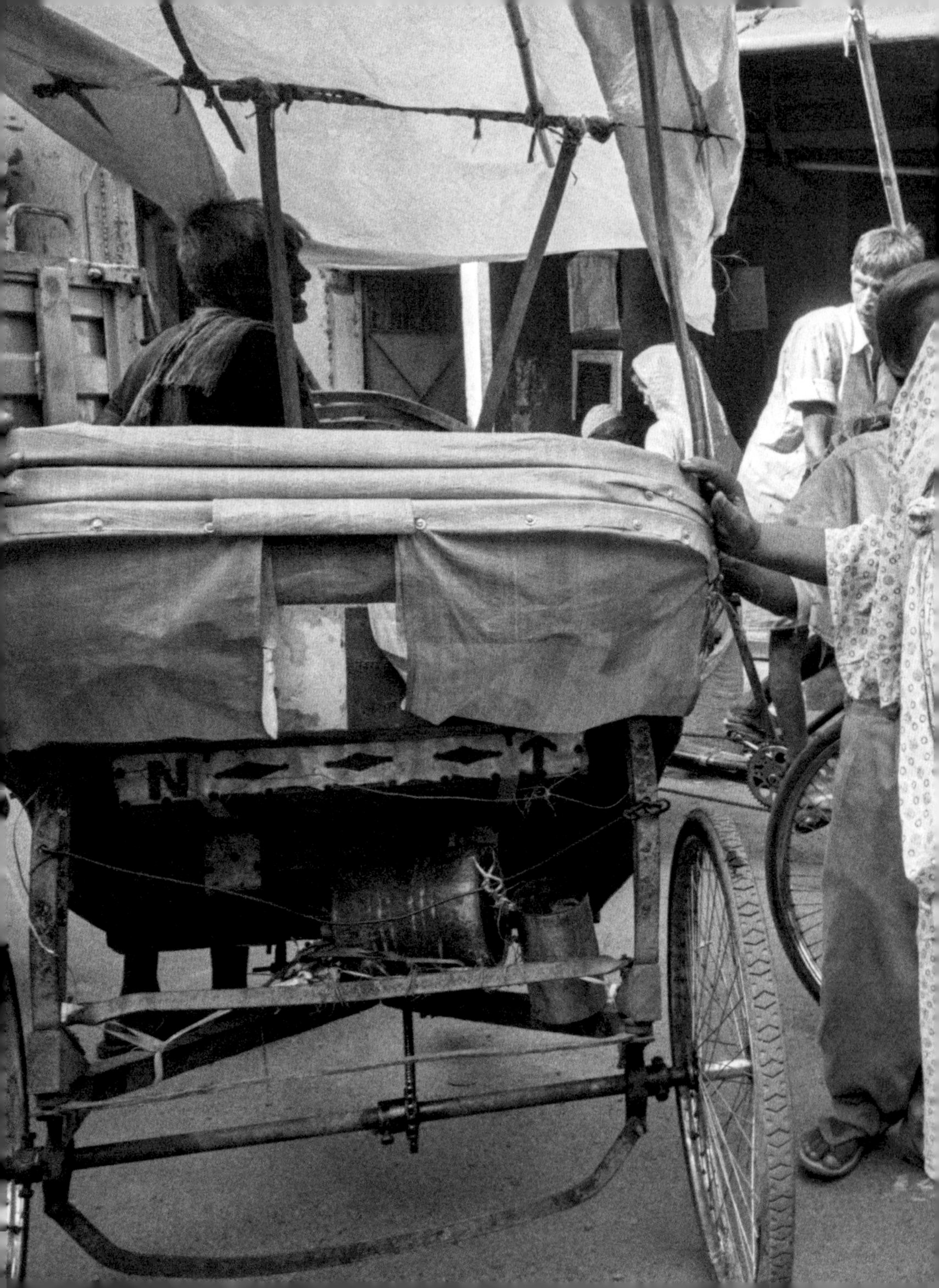

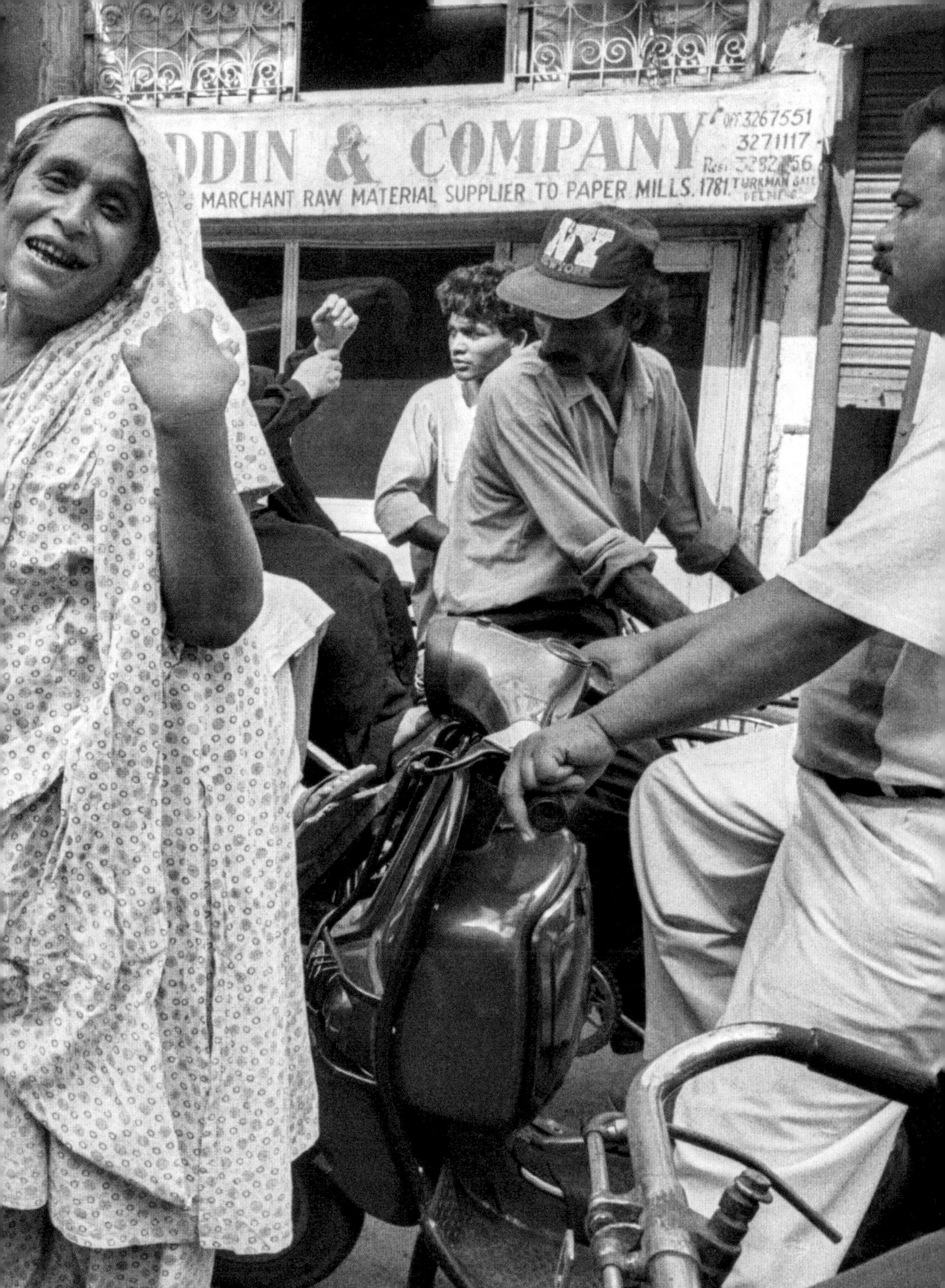
DDIN & COMPANY
Off. 326 7551
327 1117
Resi. 328 2756
MARCHANT RAW MATERIAL SUPPLIER TO PAPER MILLS. 1781. TURKMAN GATE
DELHI-6
NY
NEW YORK

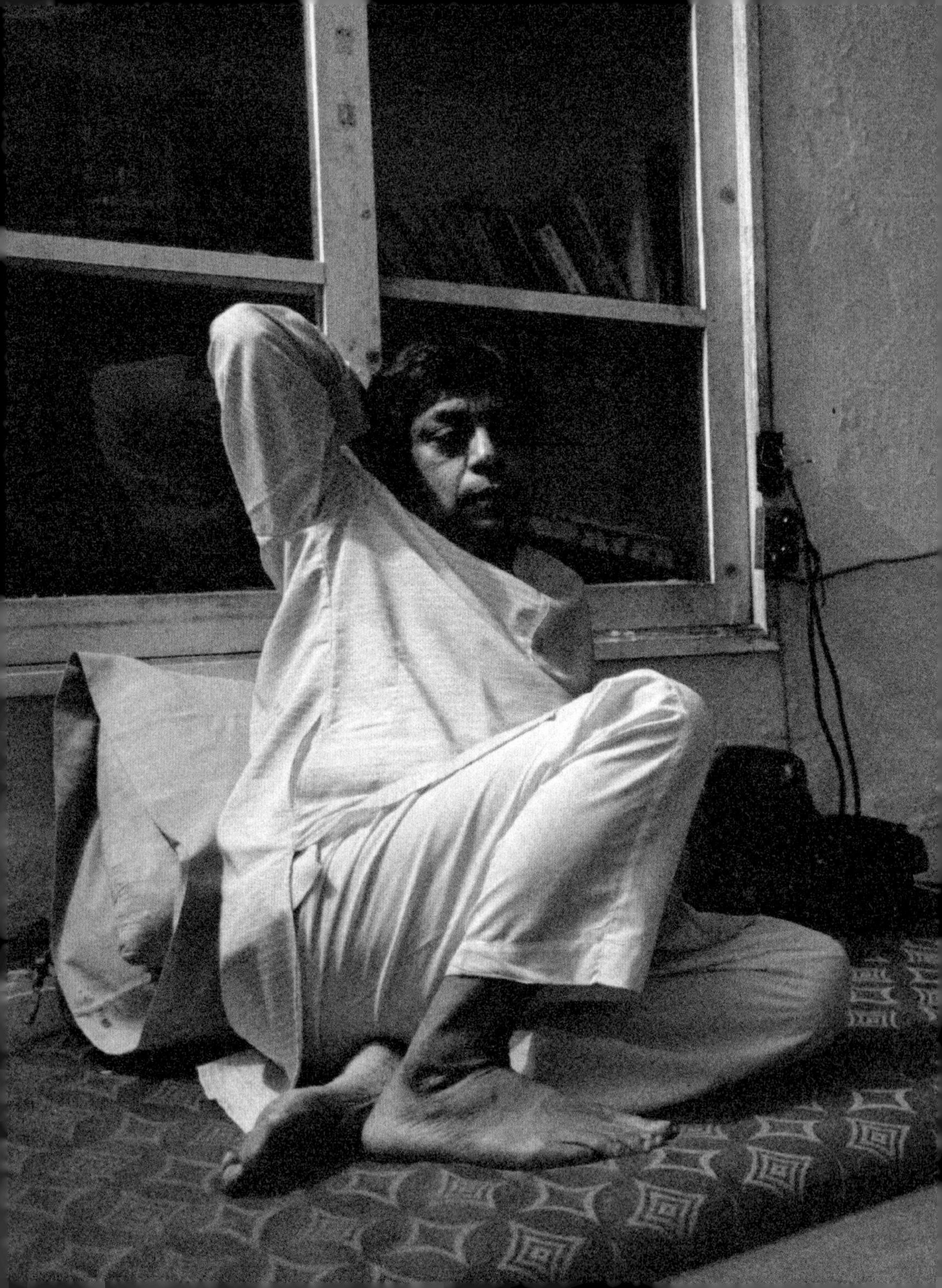

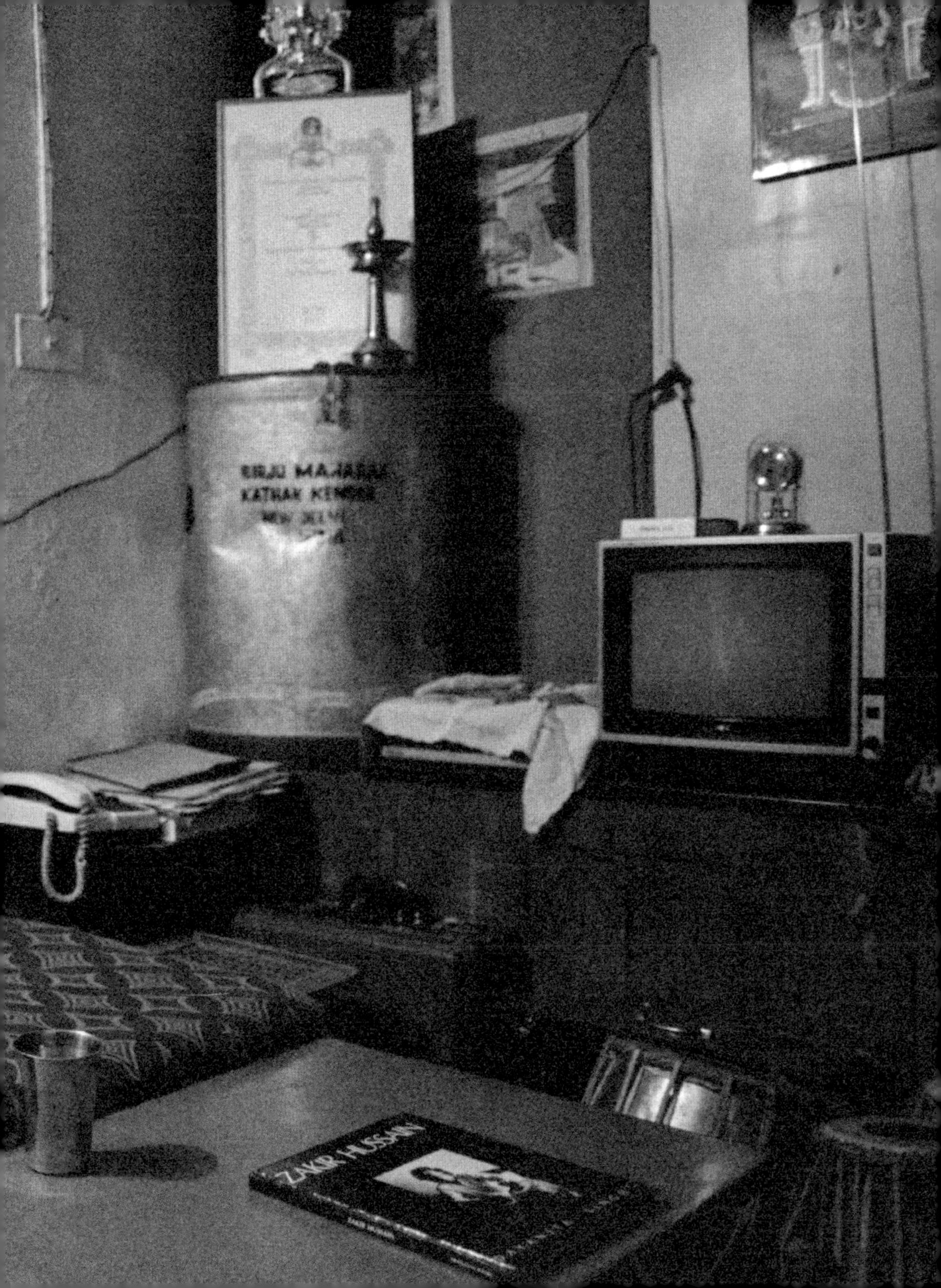

BIRJU MAHARAJ
KATHAK KENDRA
NEW DELHI
ZAKIR HUSSAIN

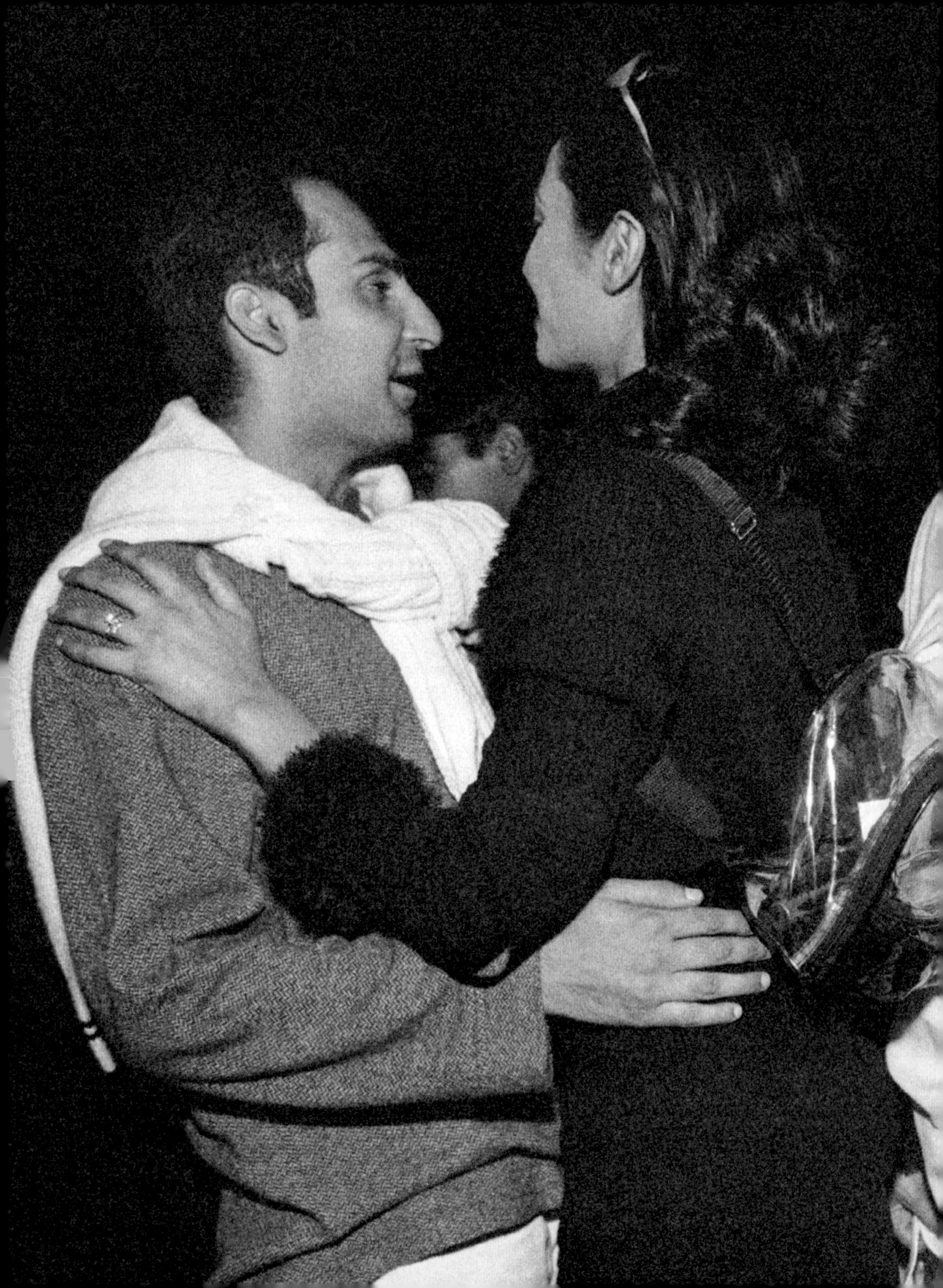

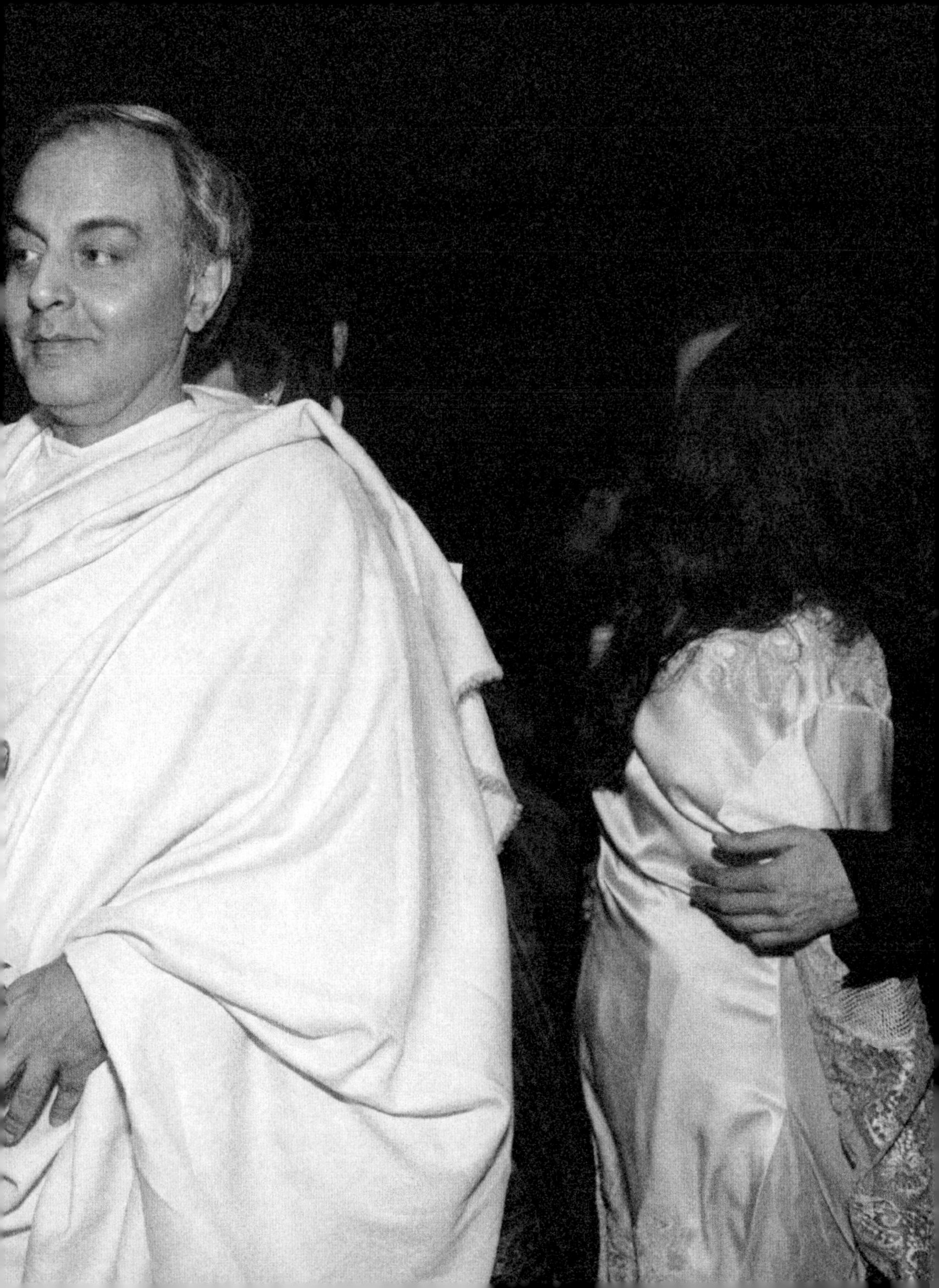

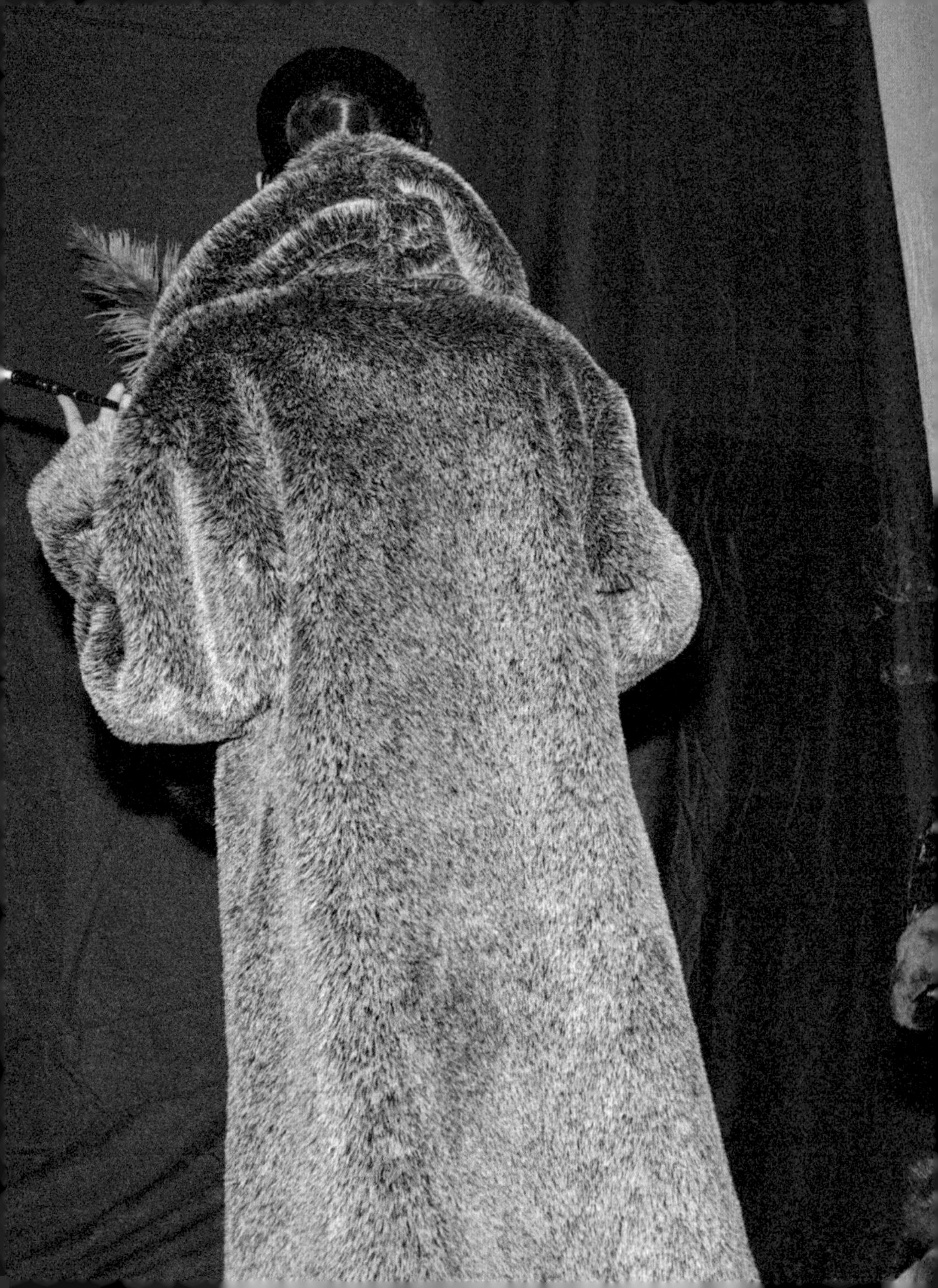

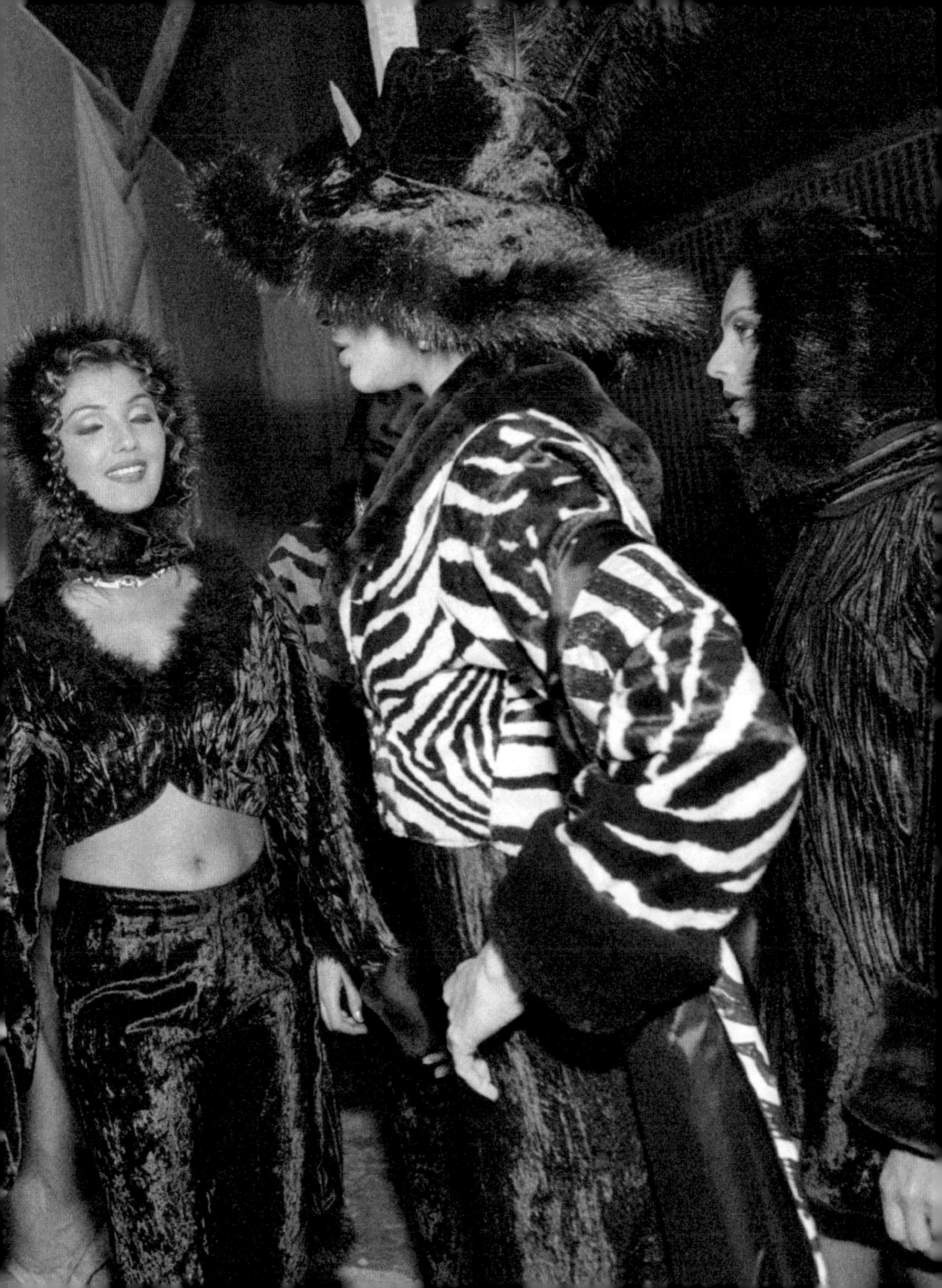

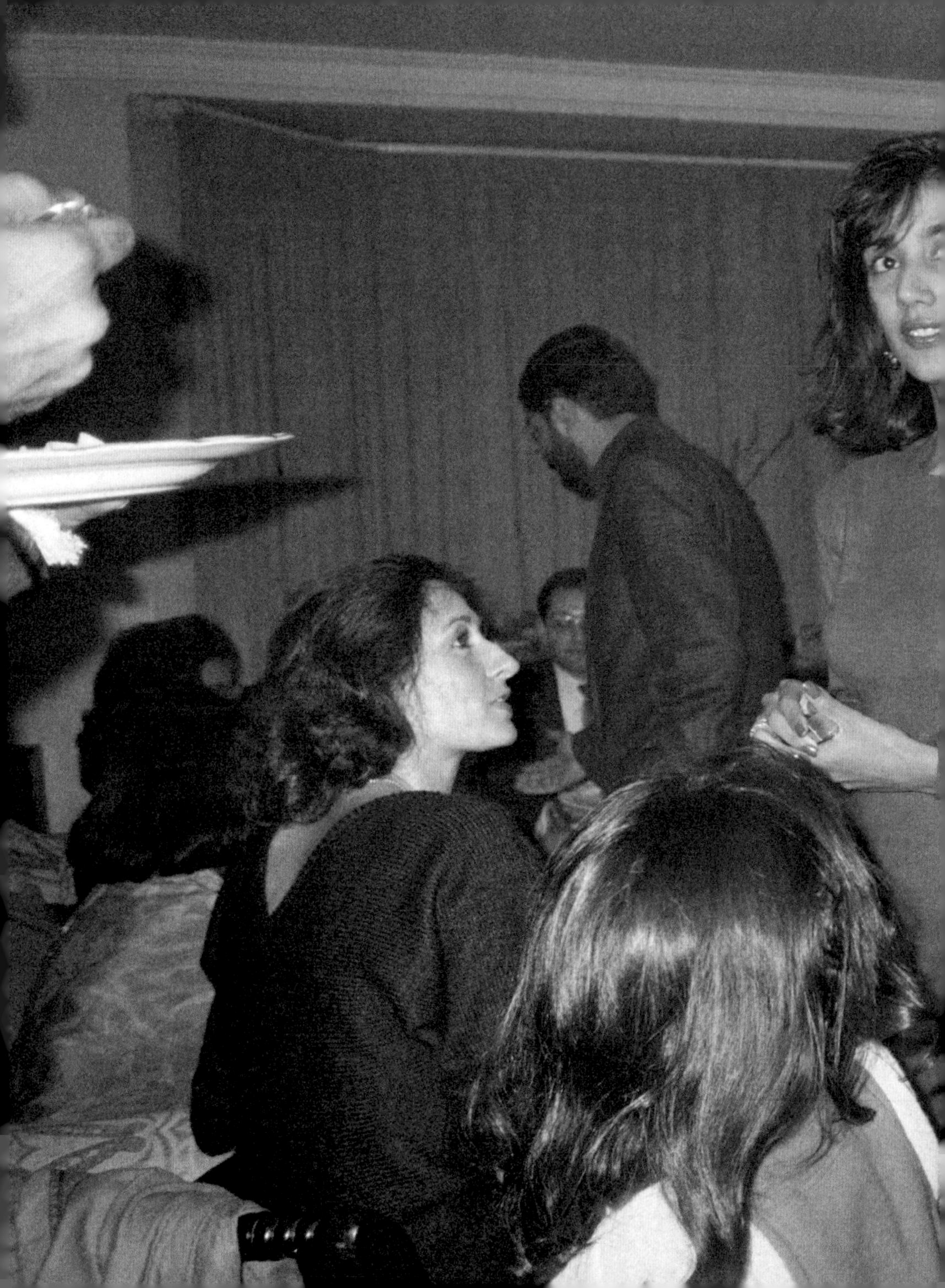

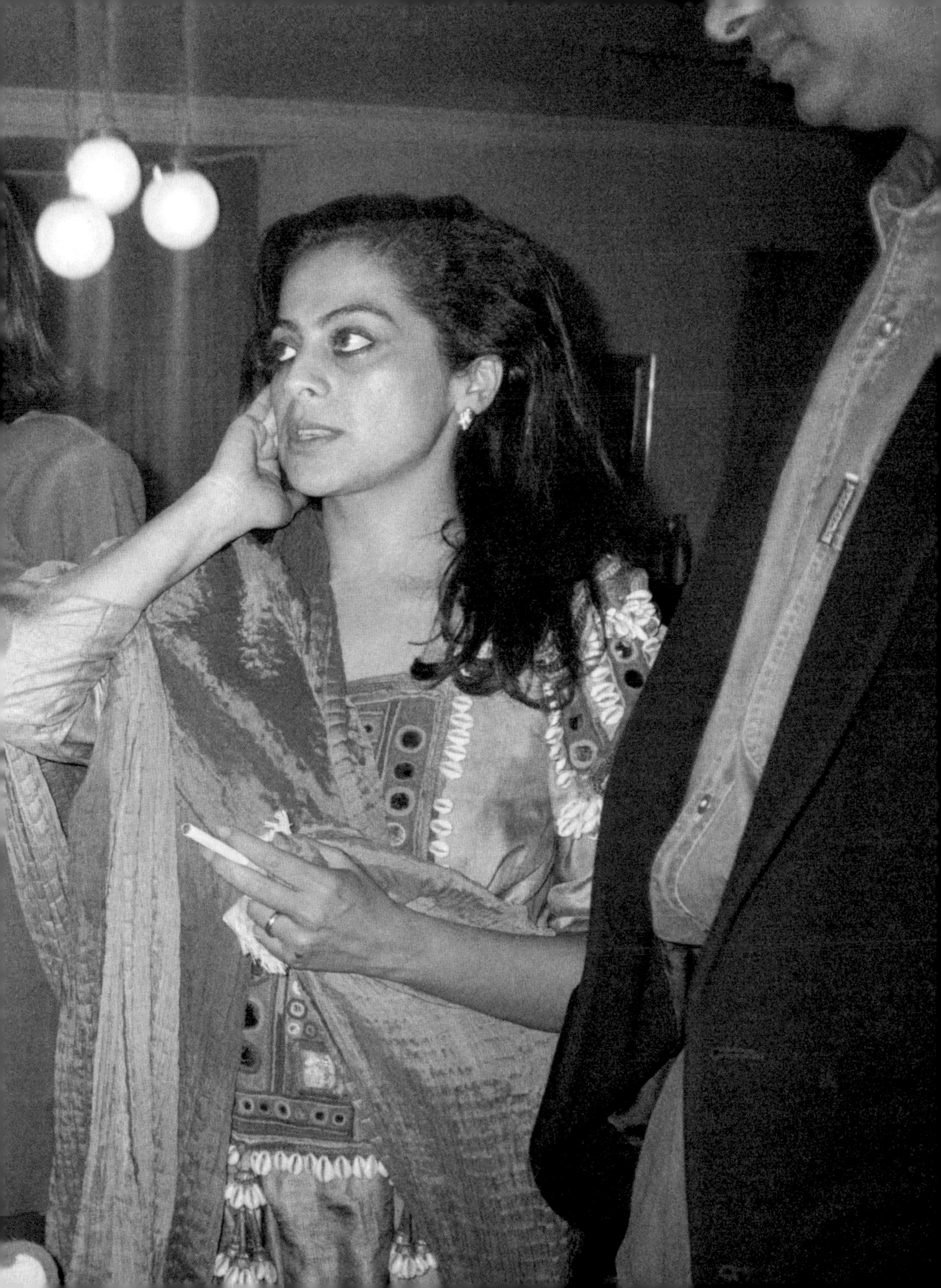

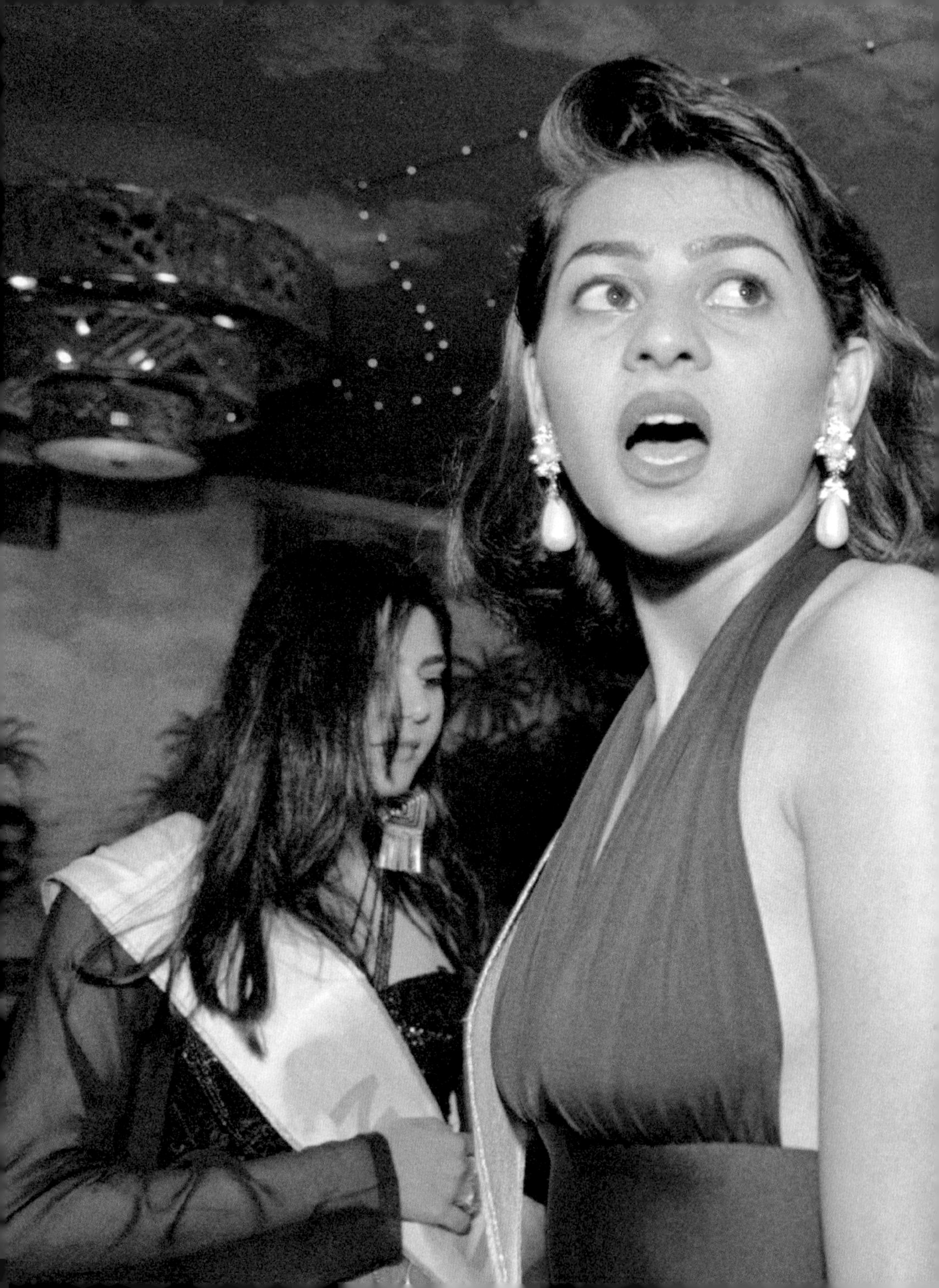

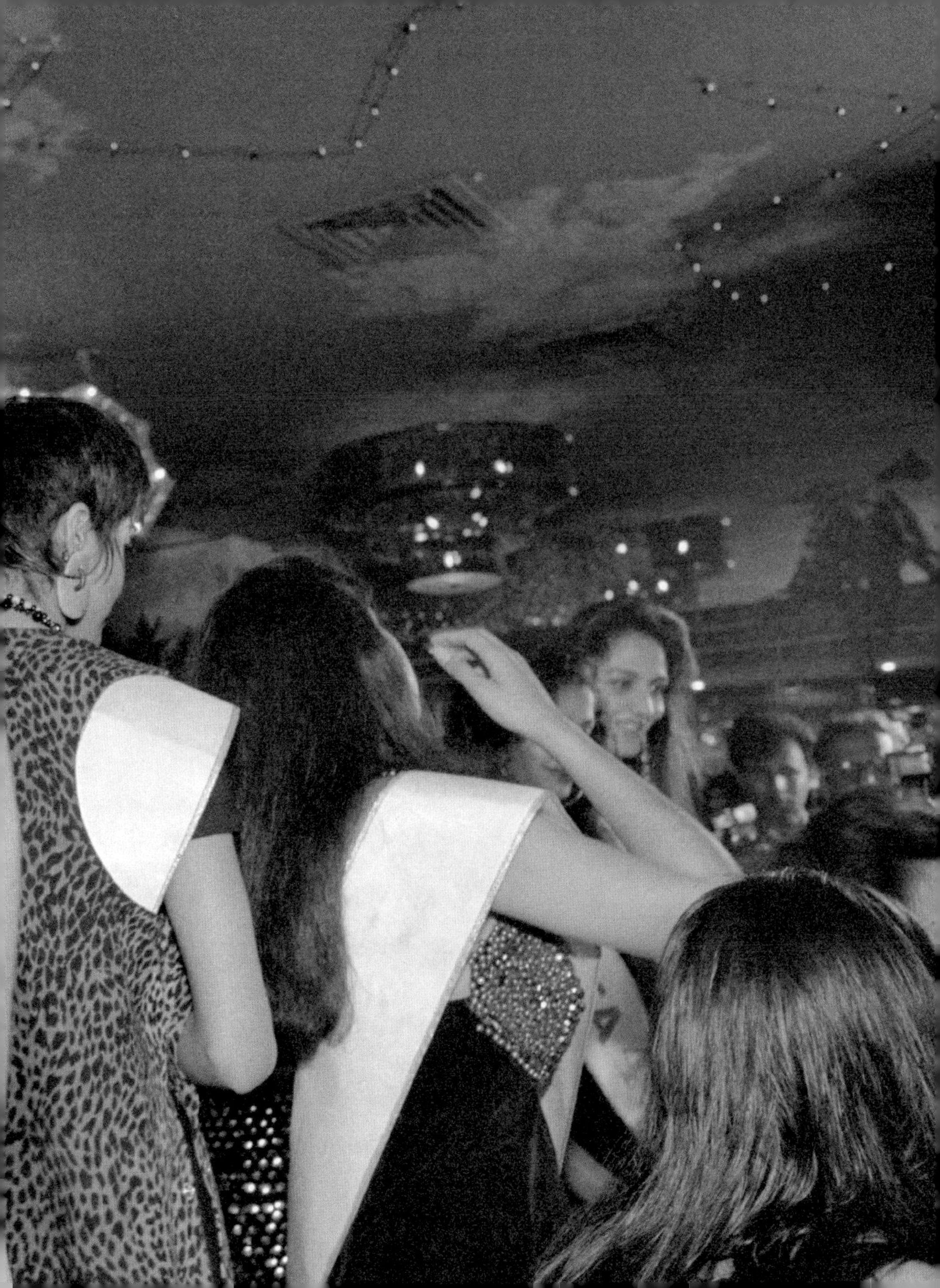

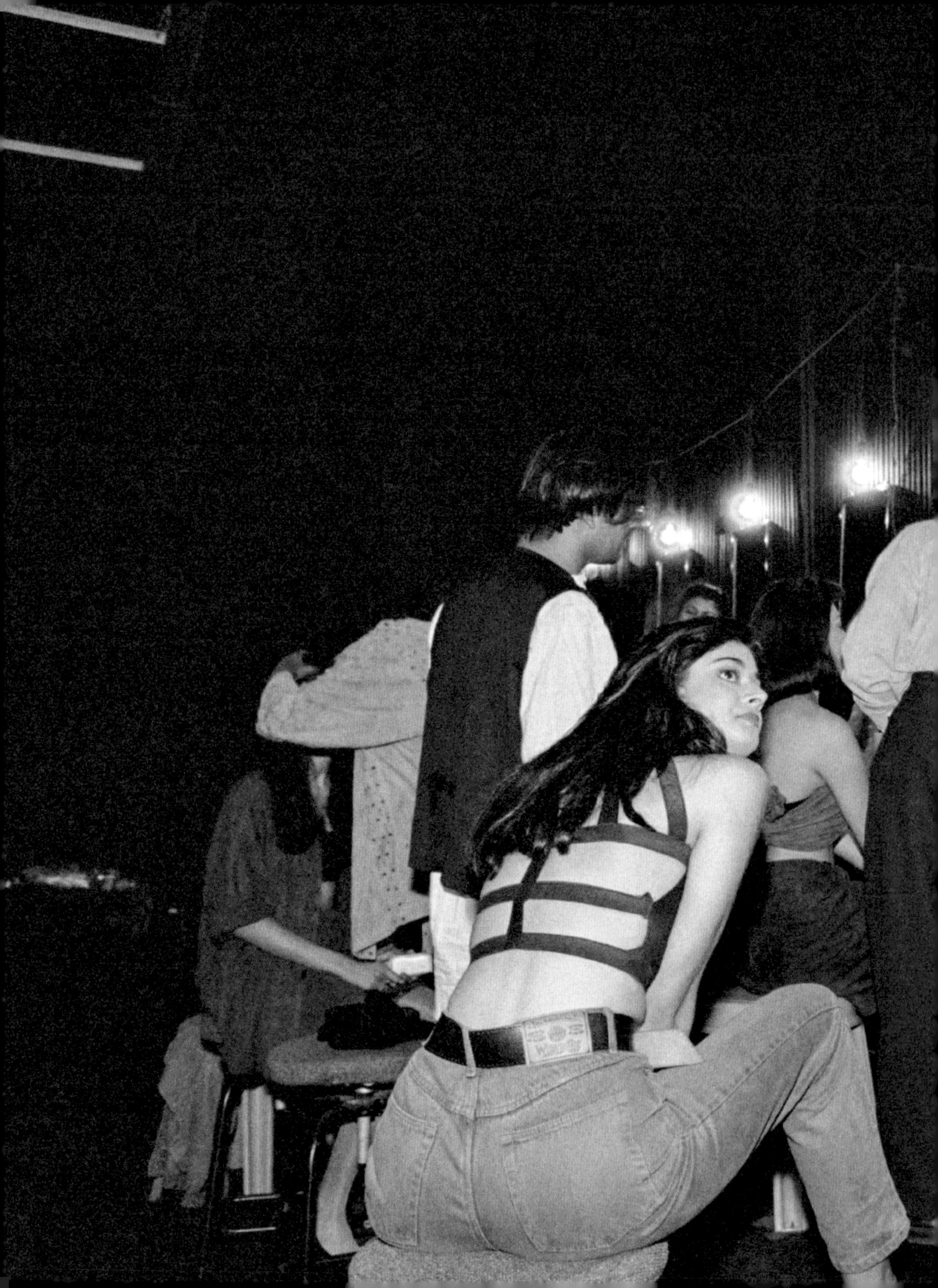

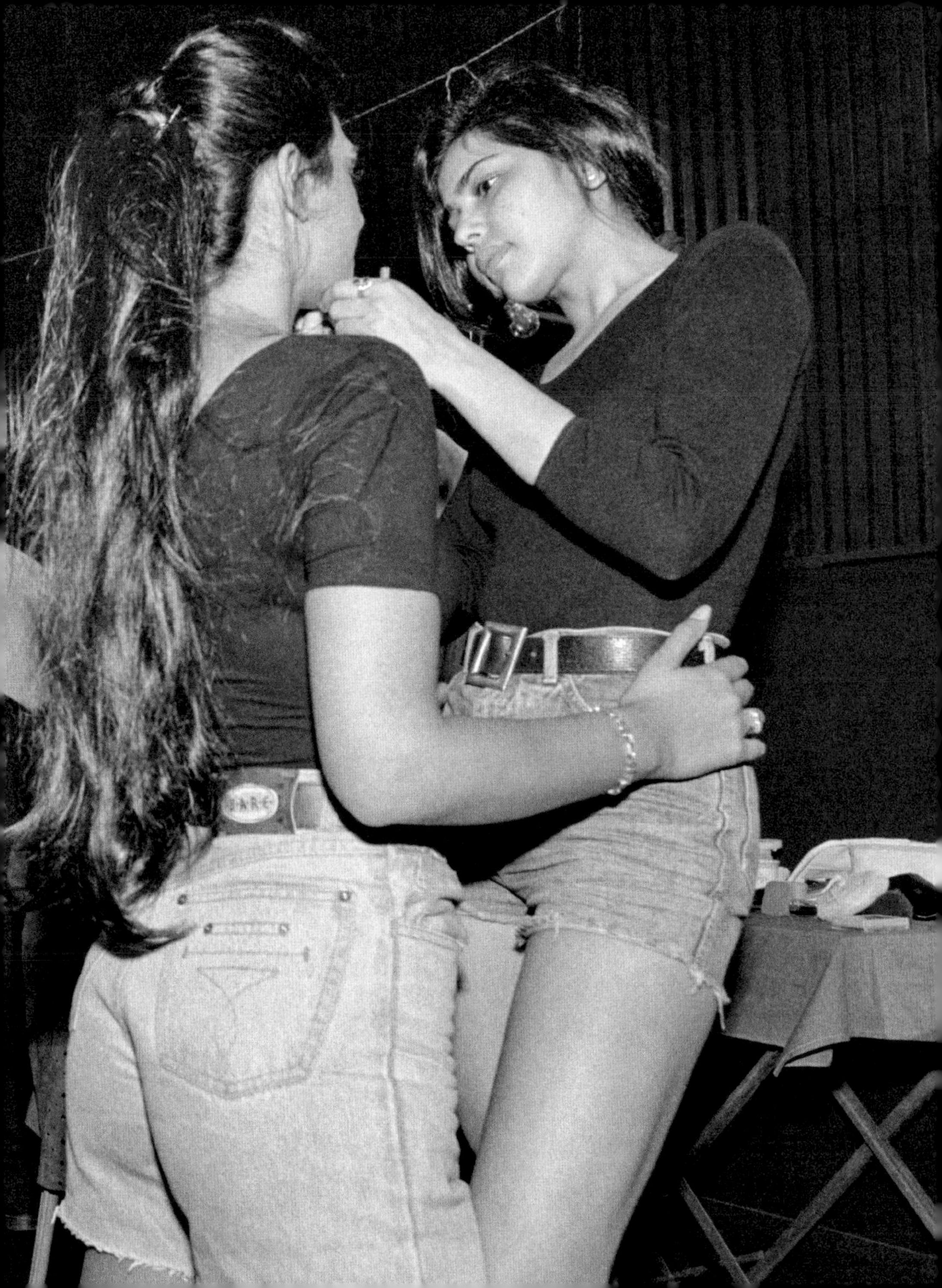

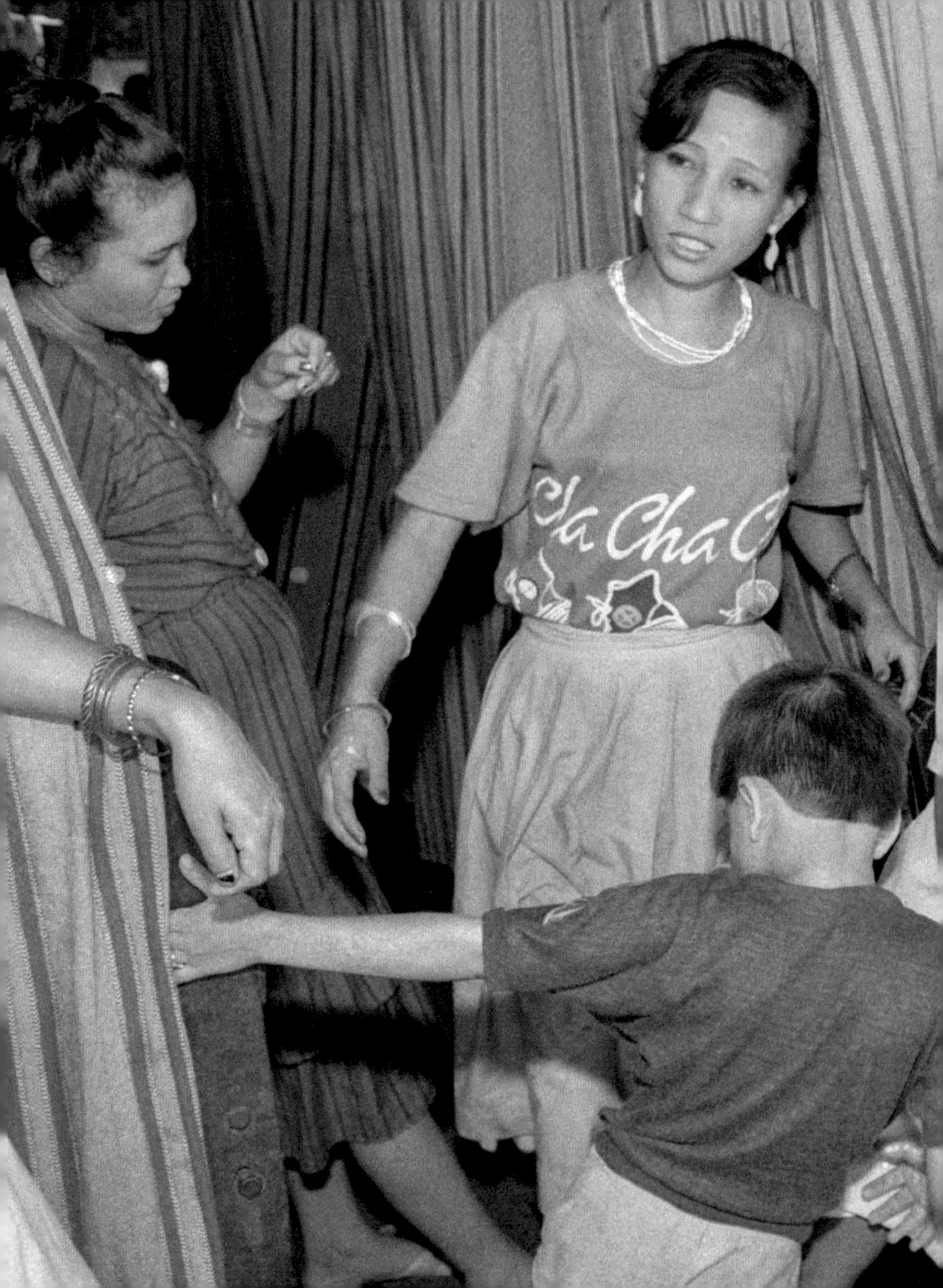

a Cha C

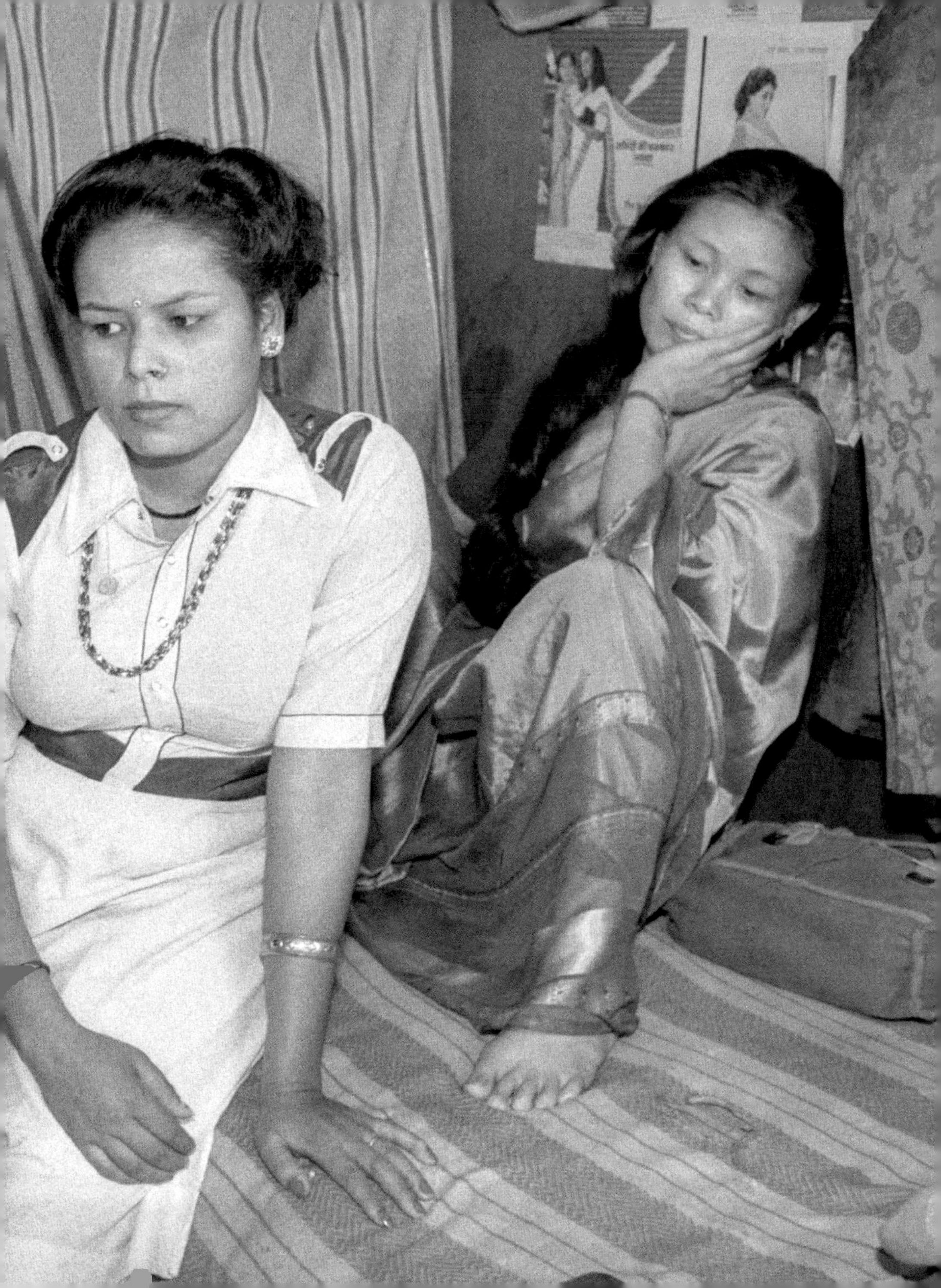

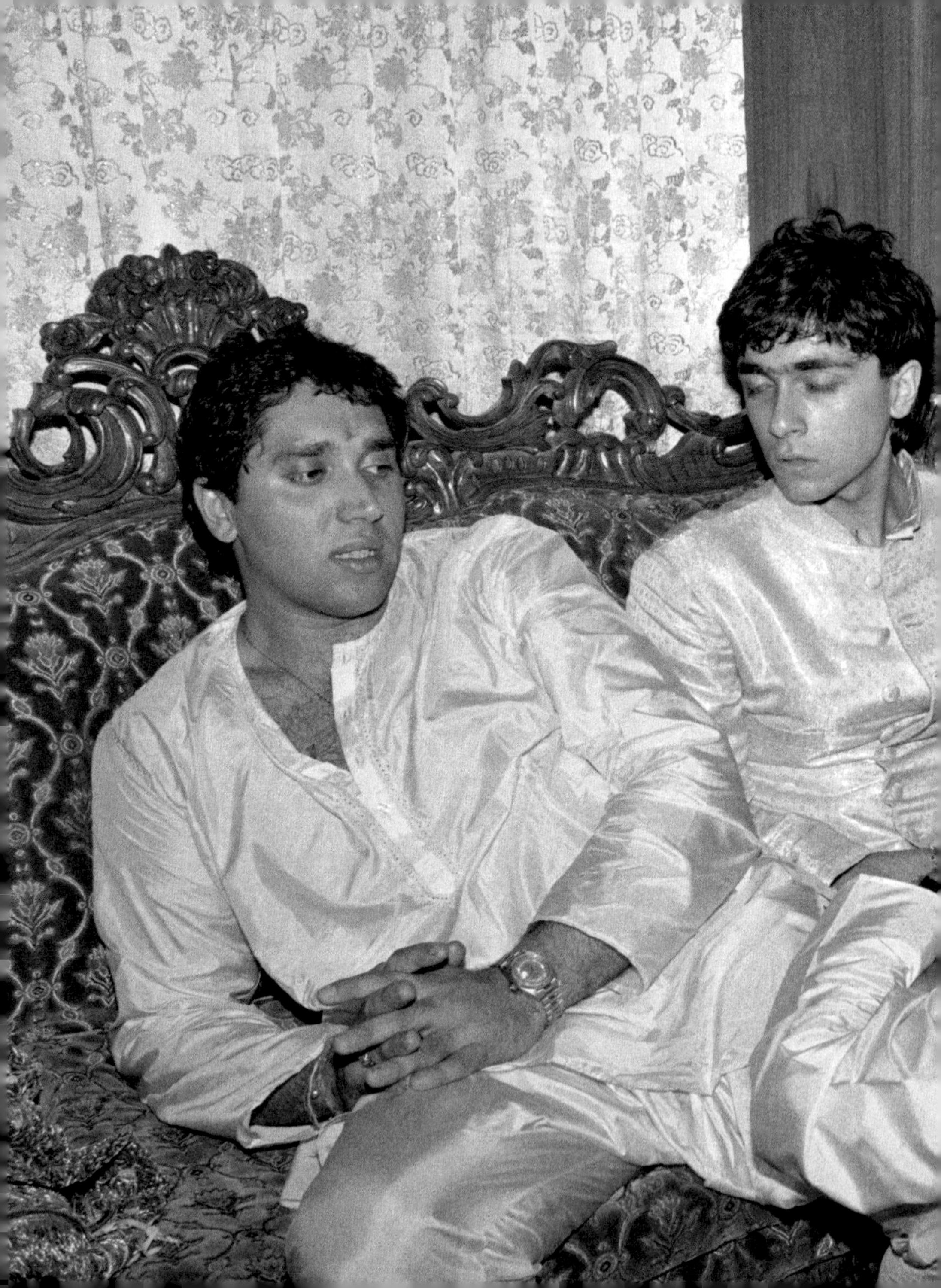

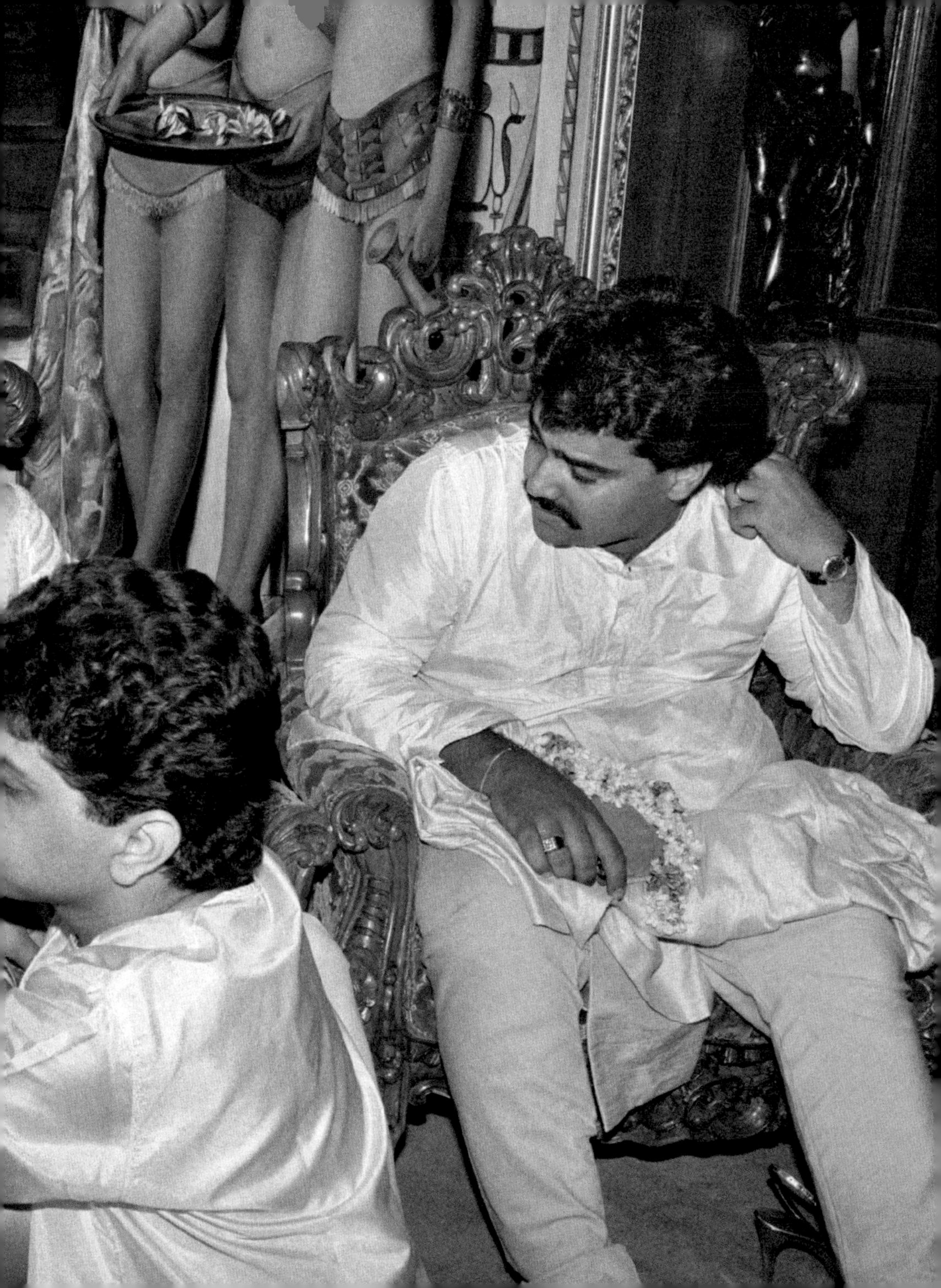

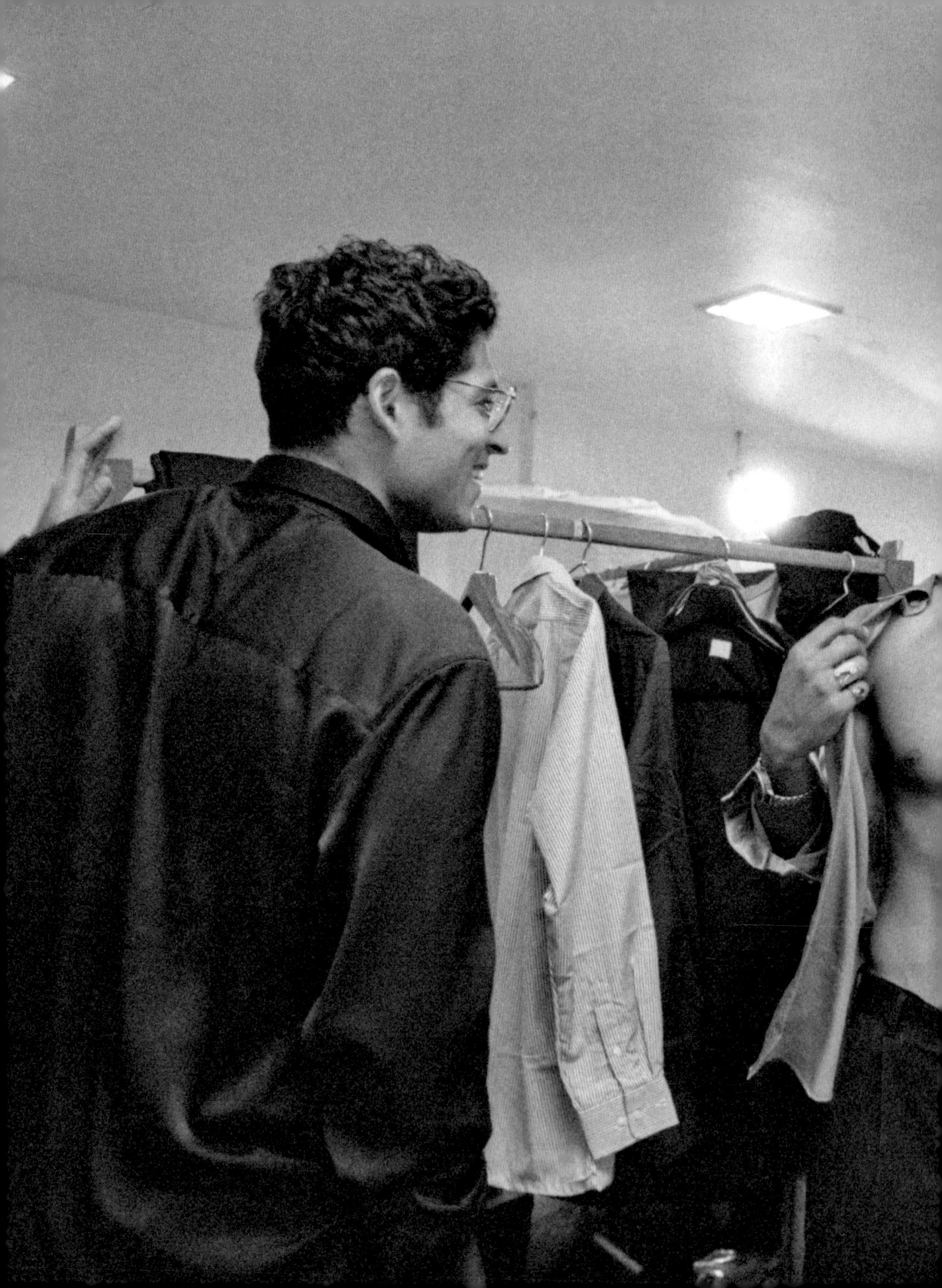

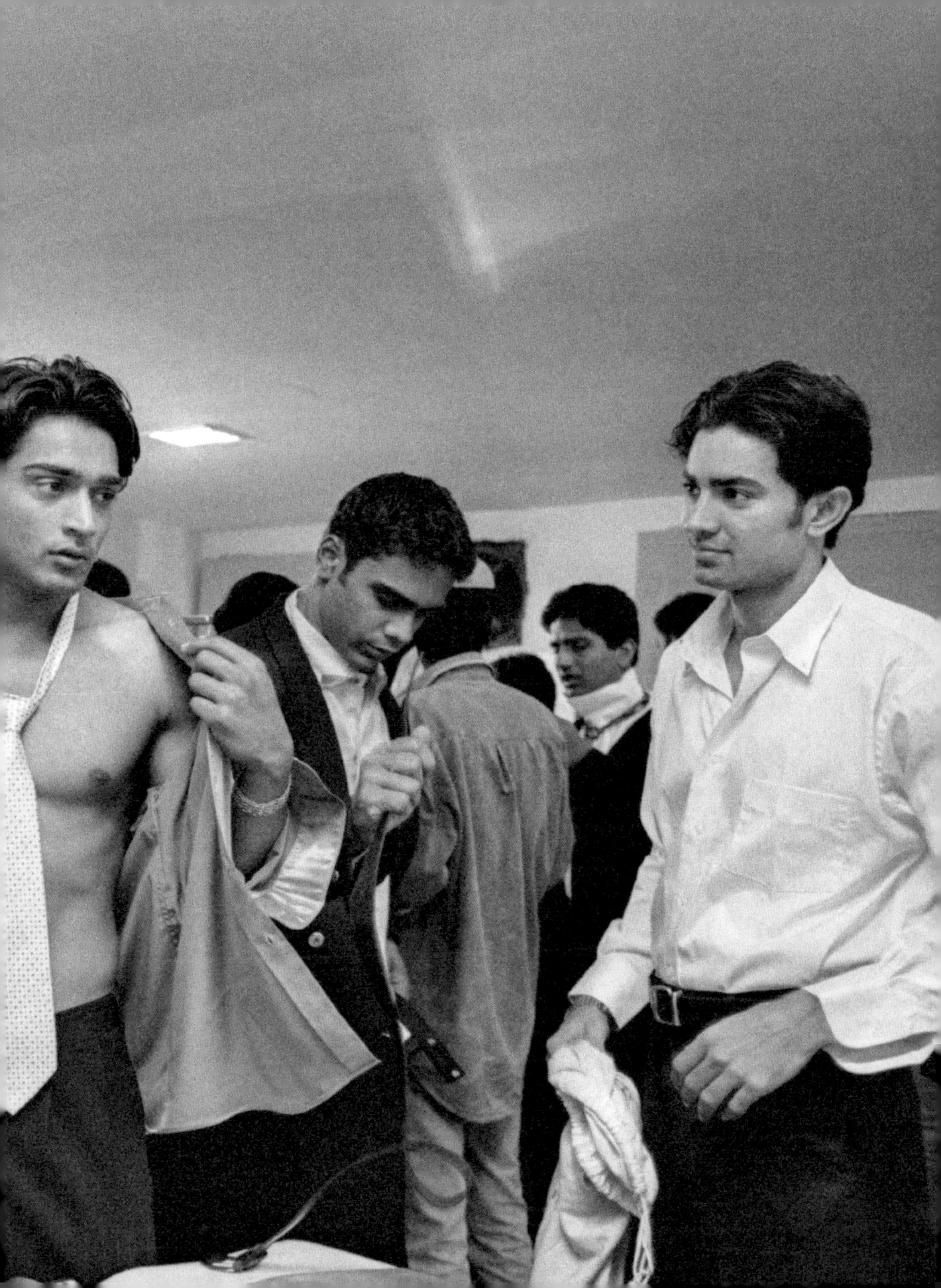

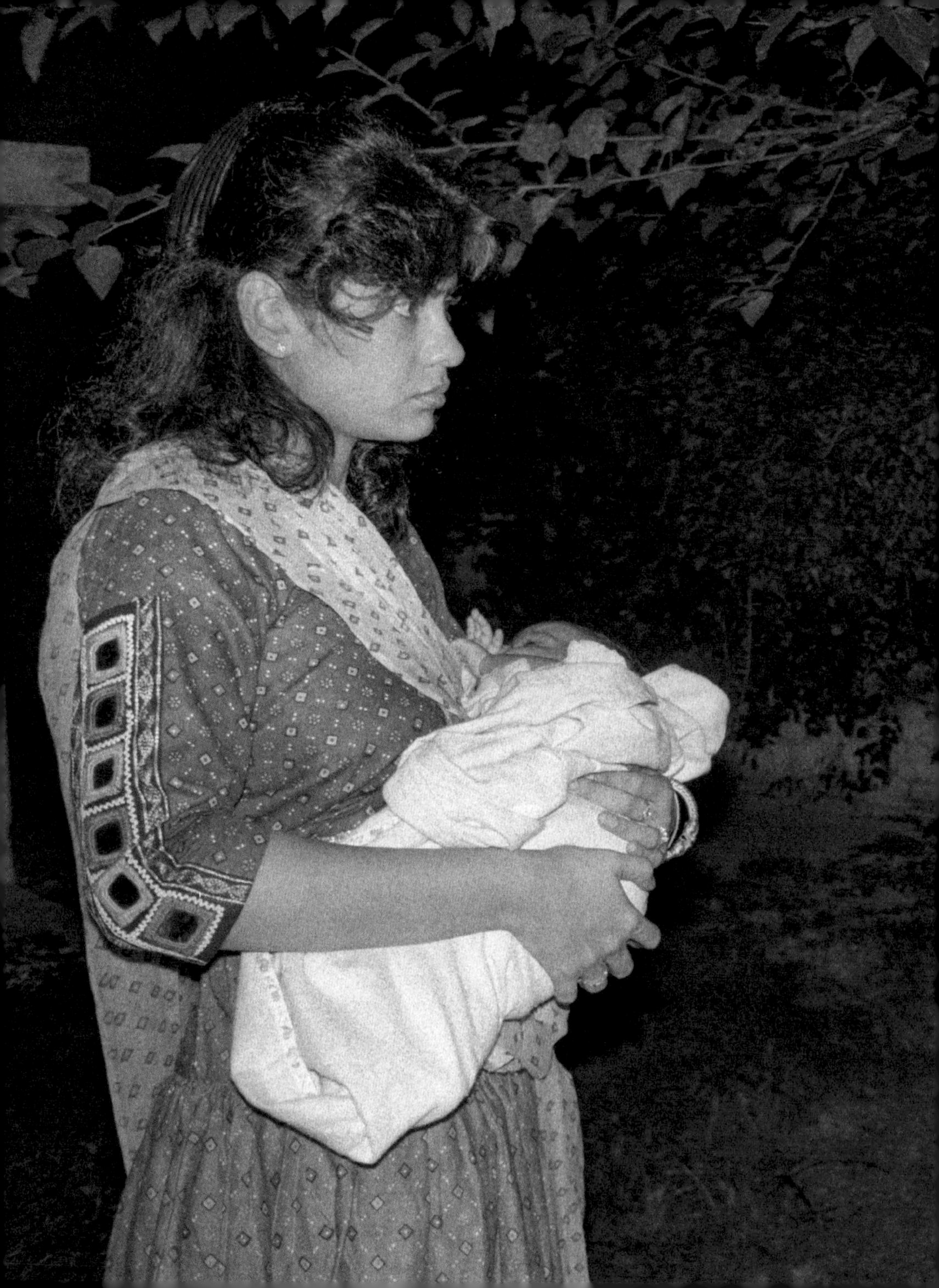

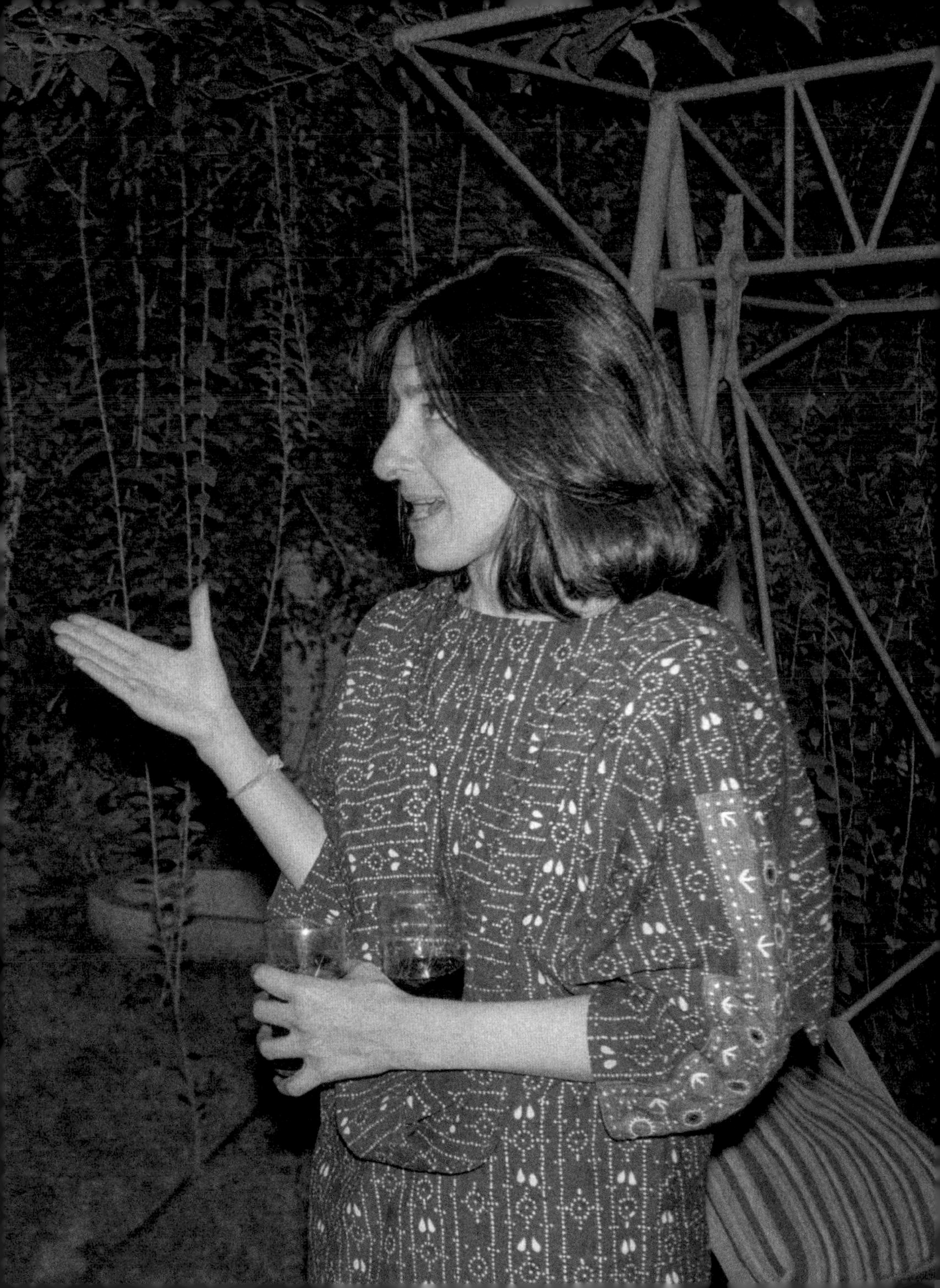

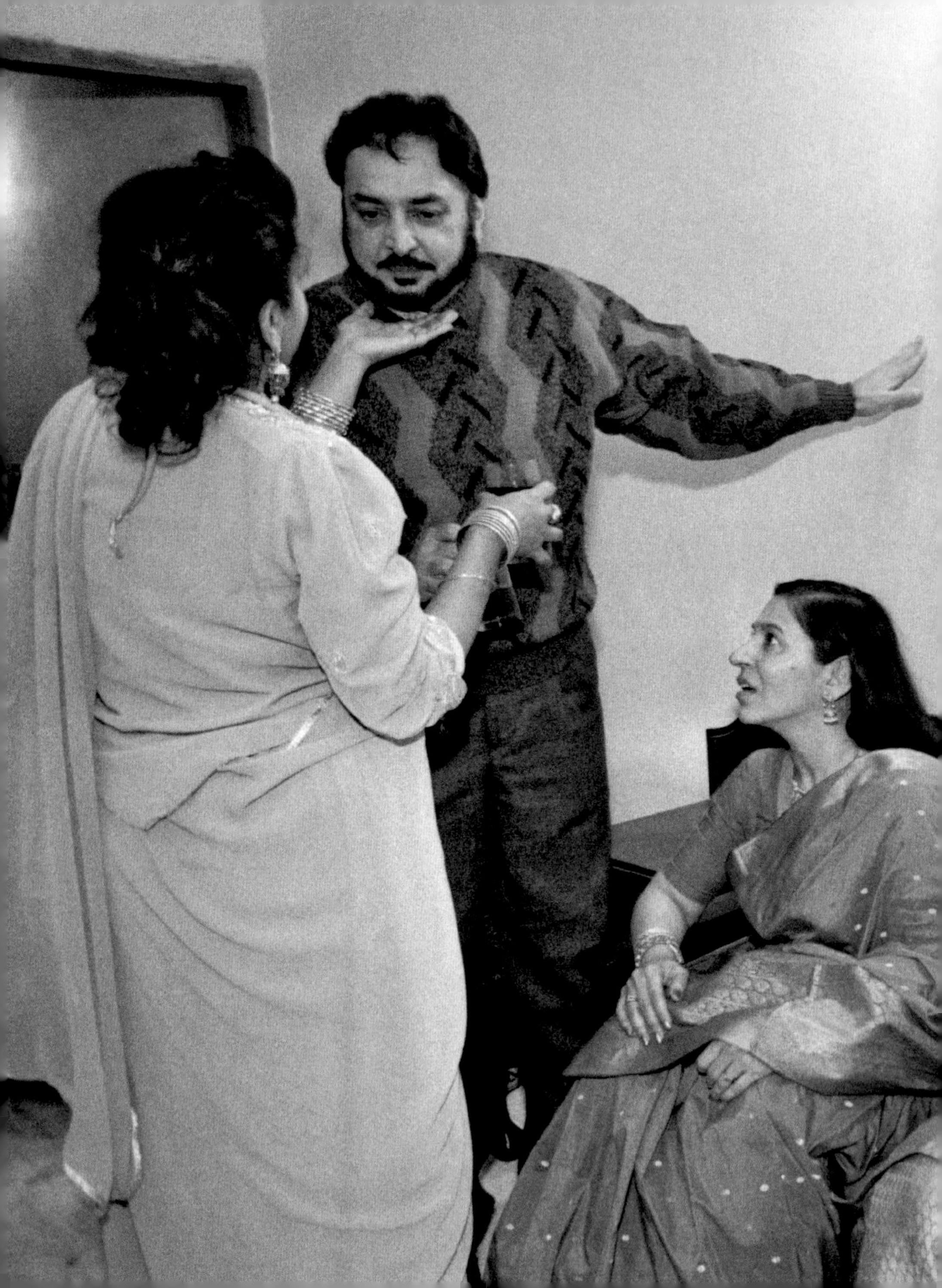

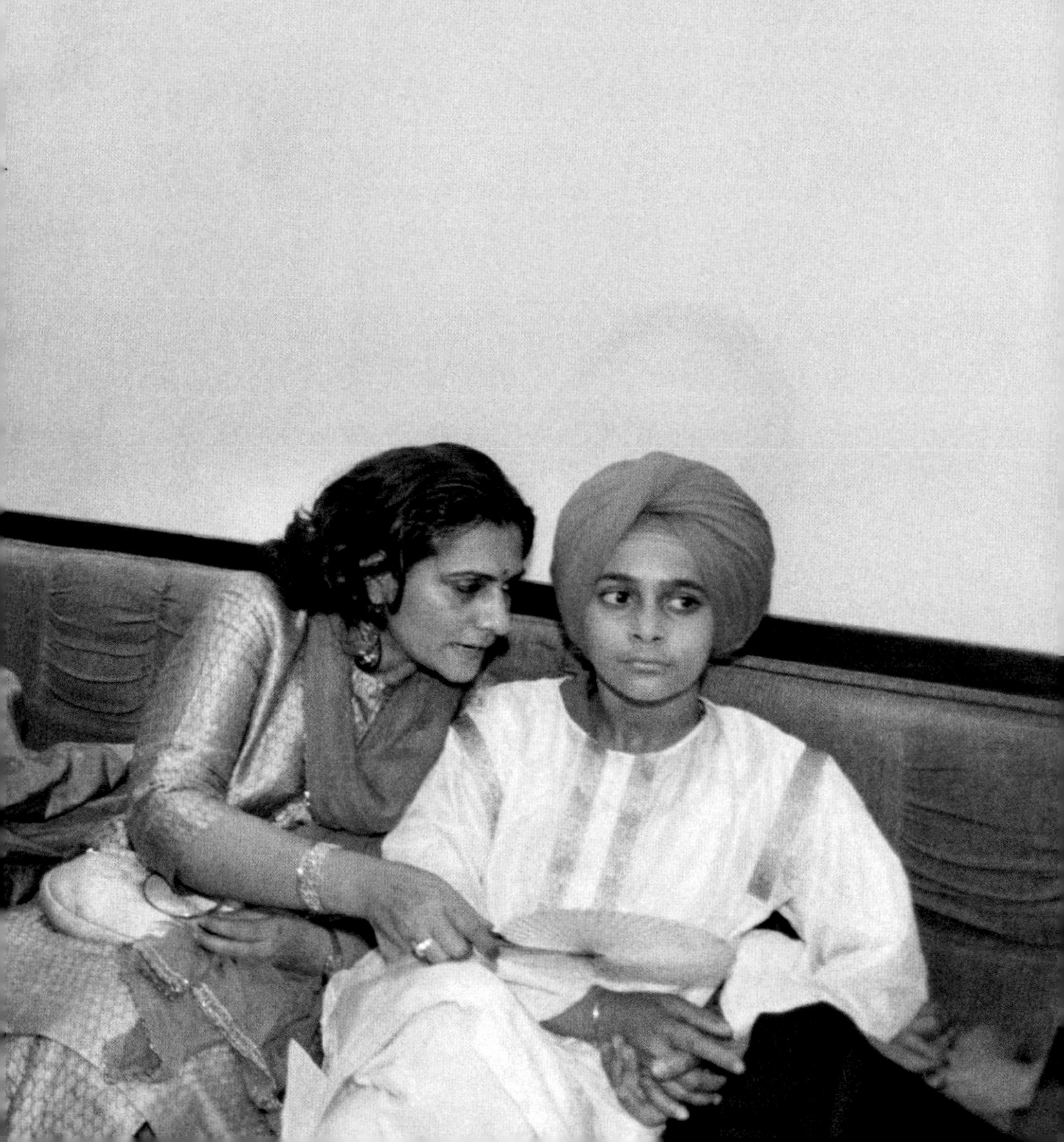

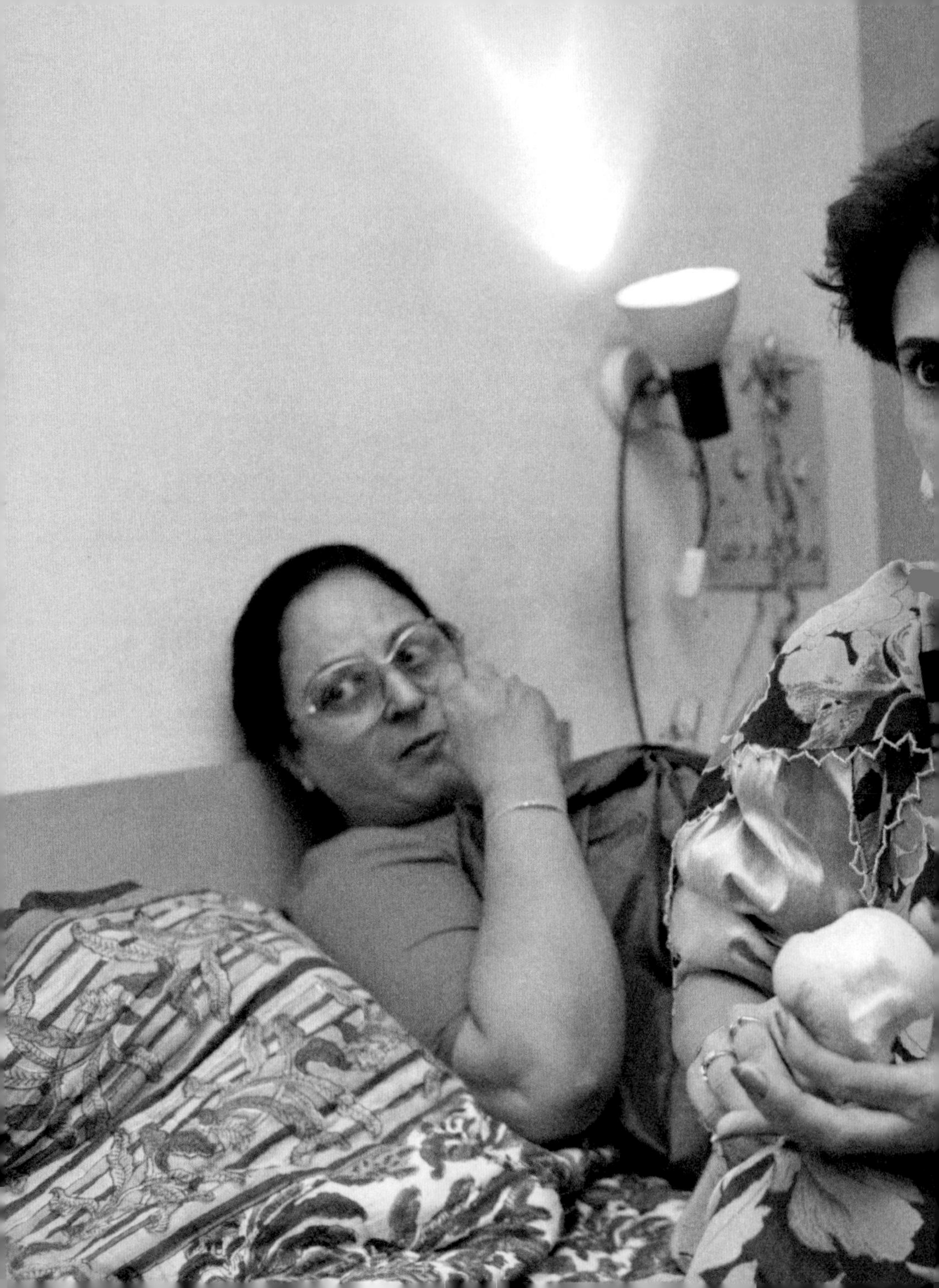

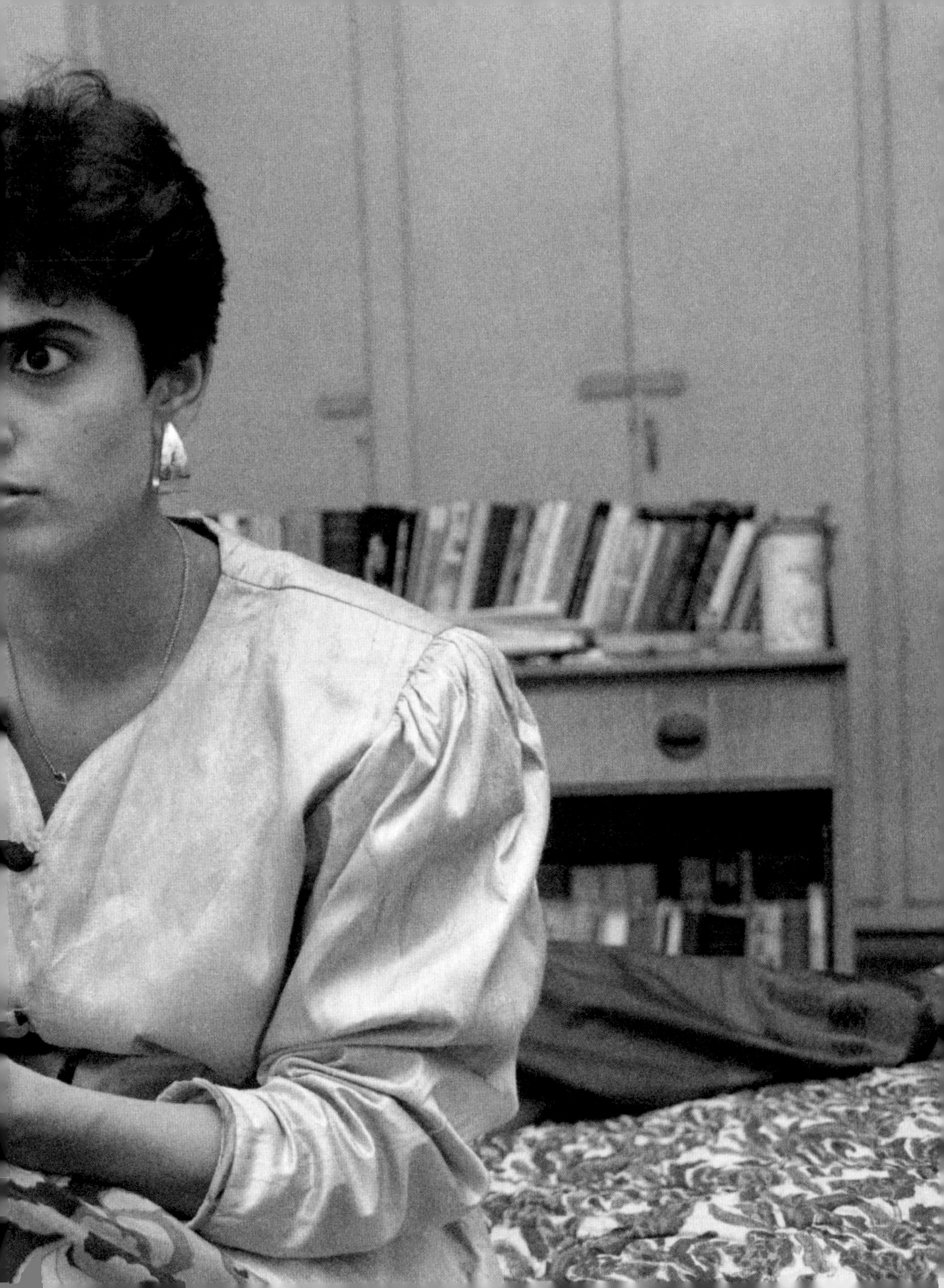

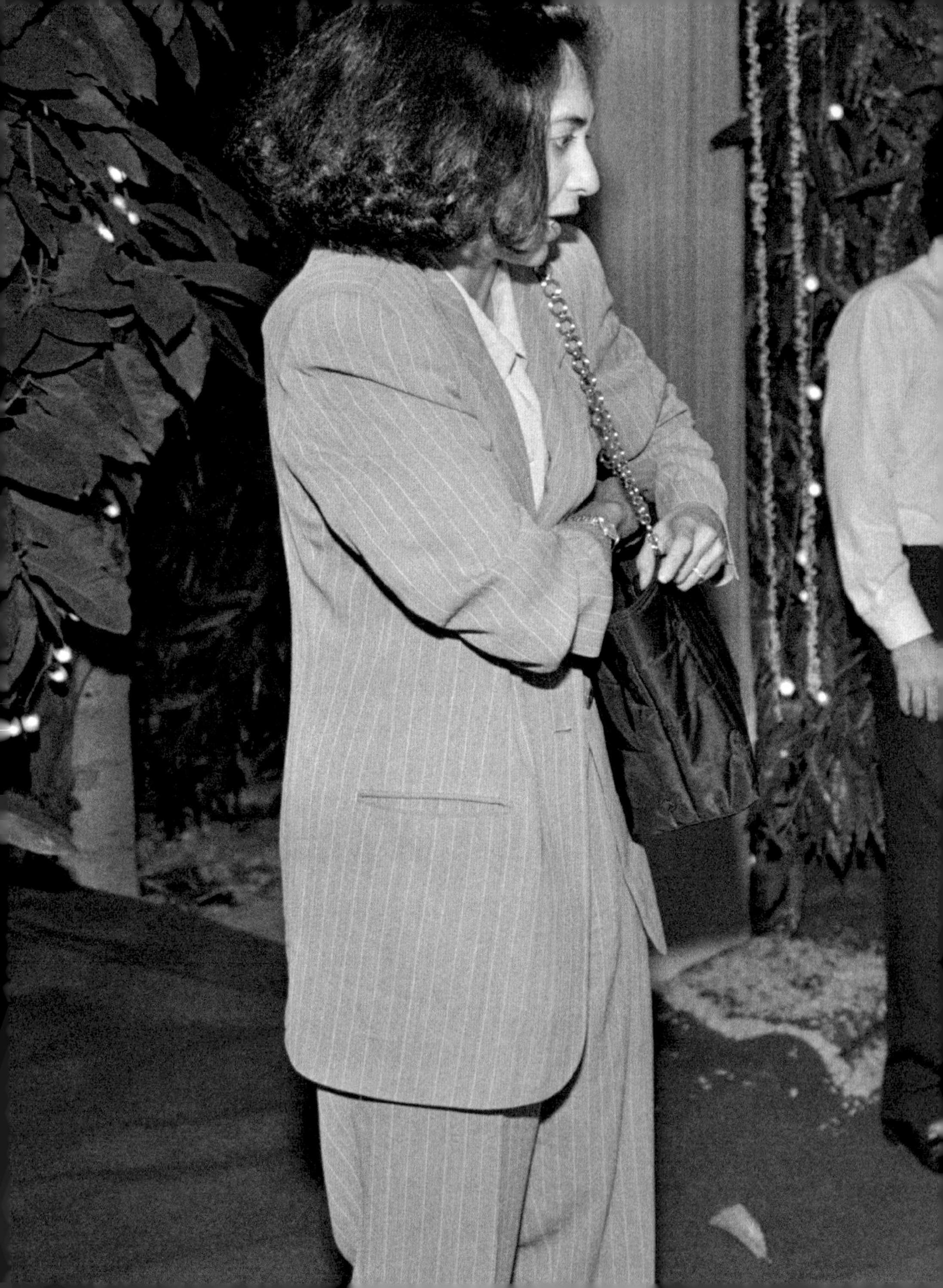

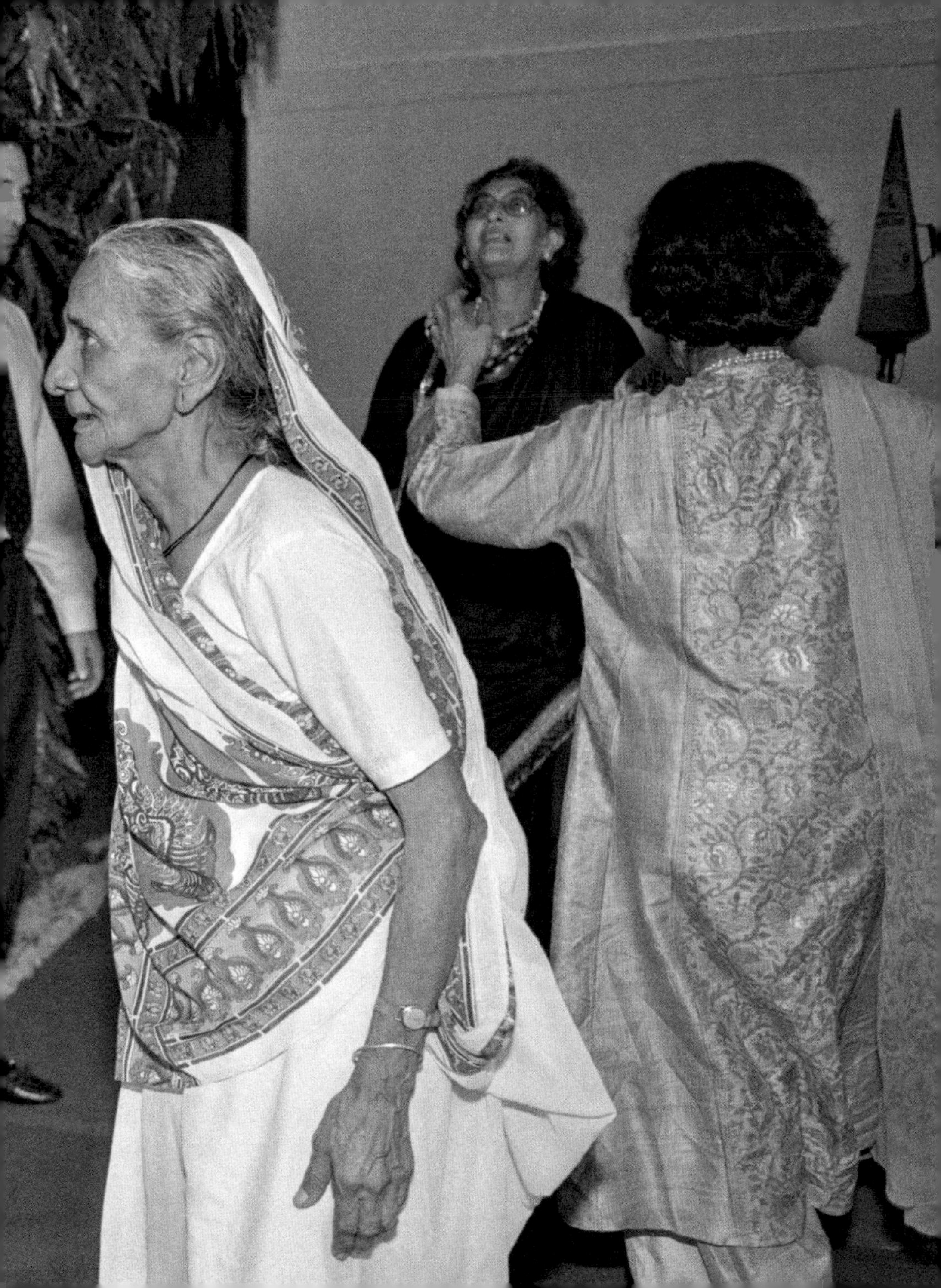

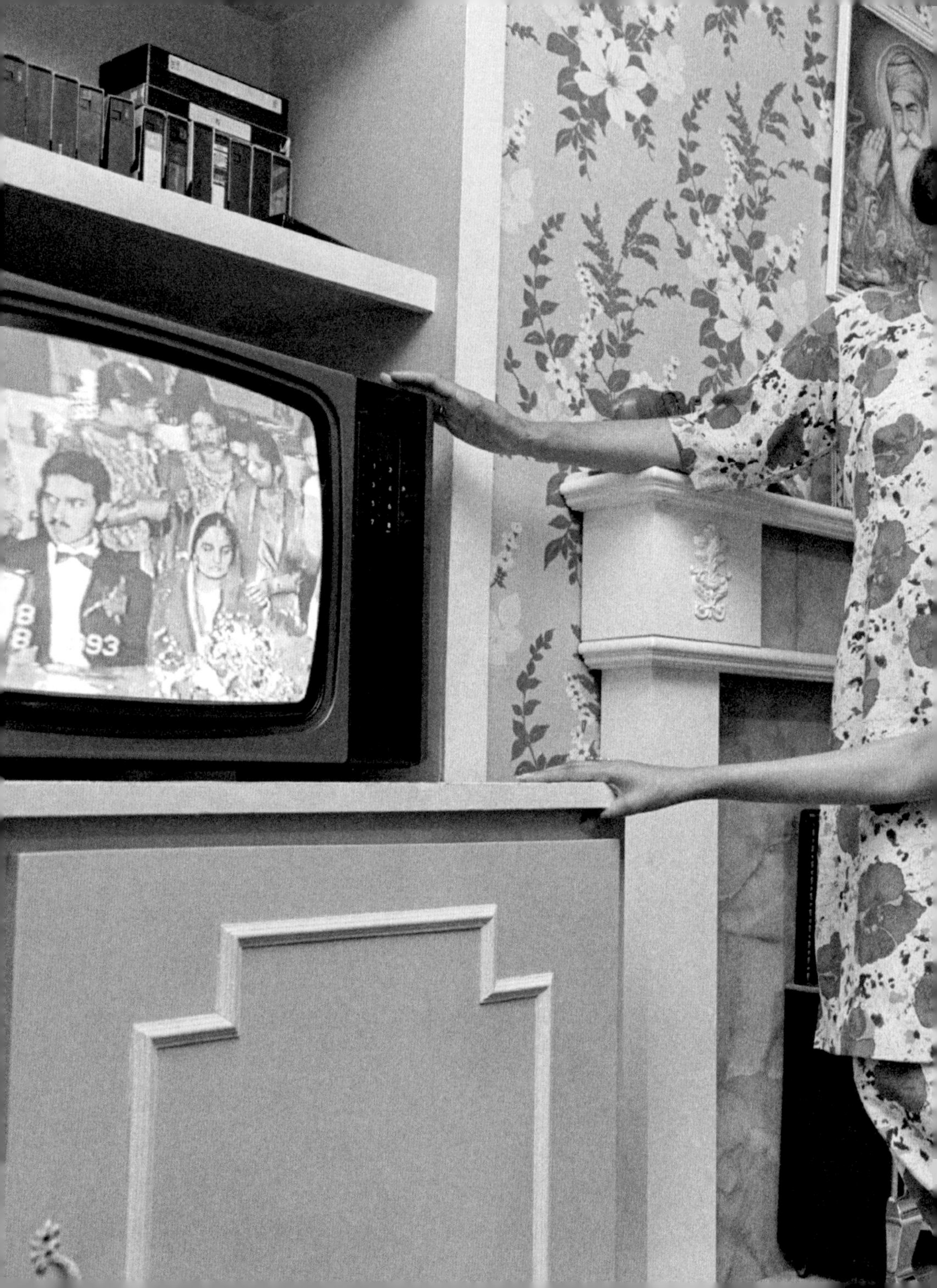

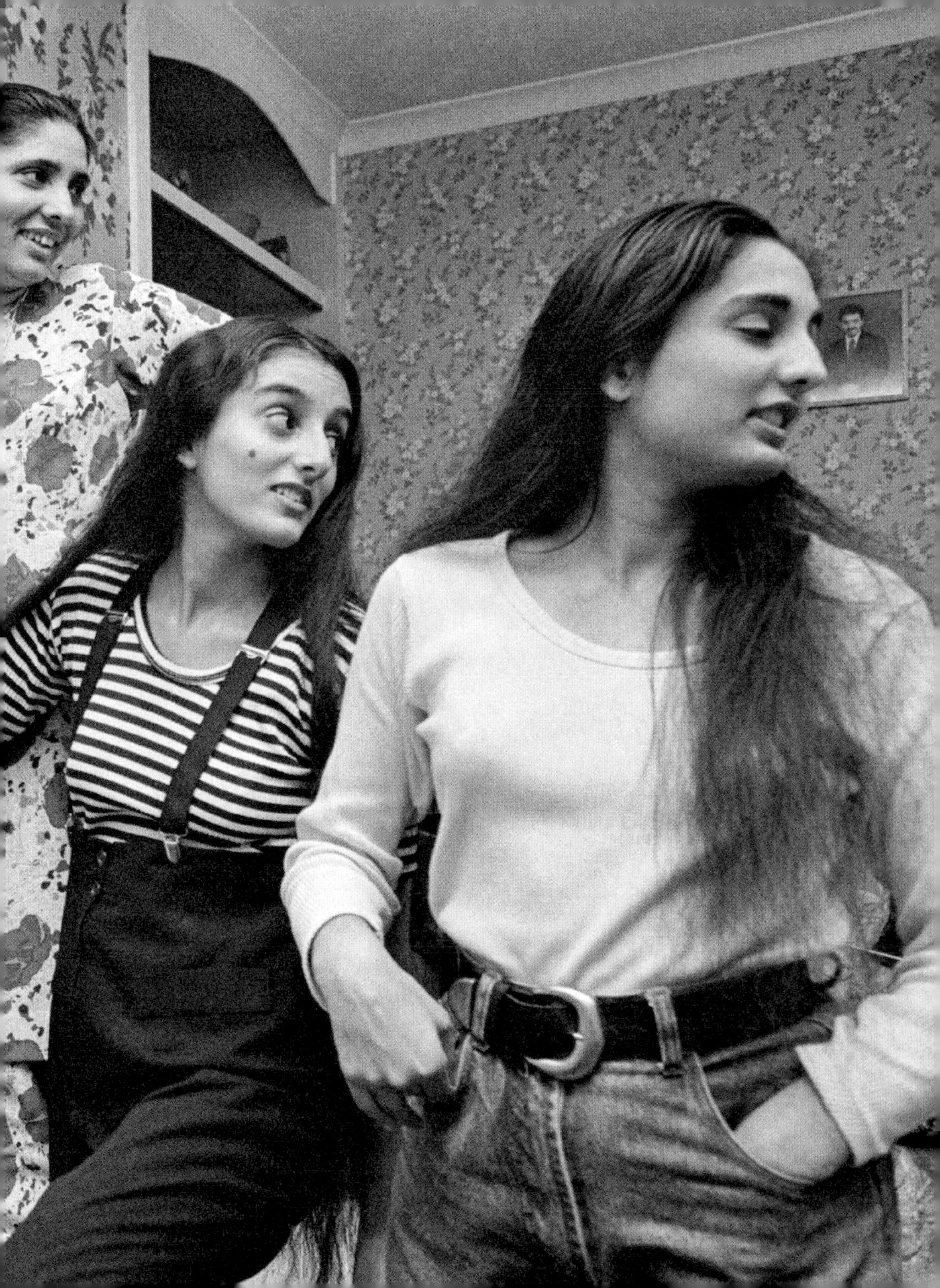

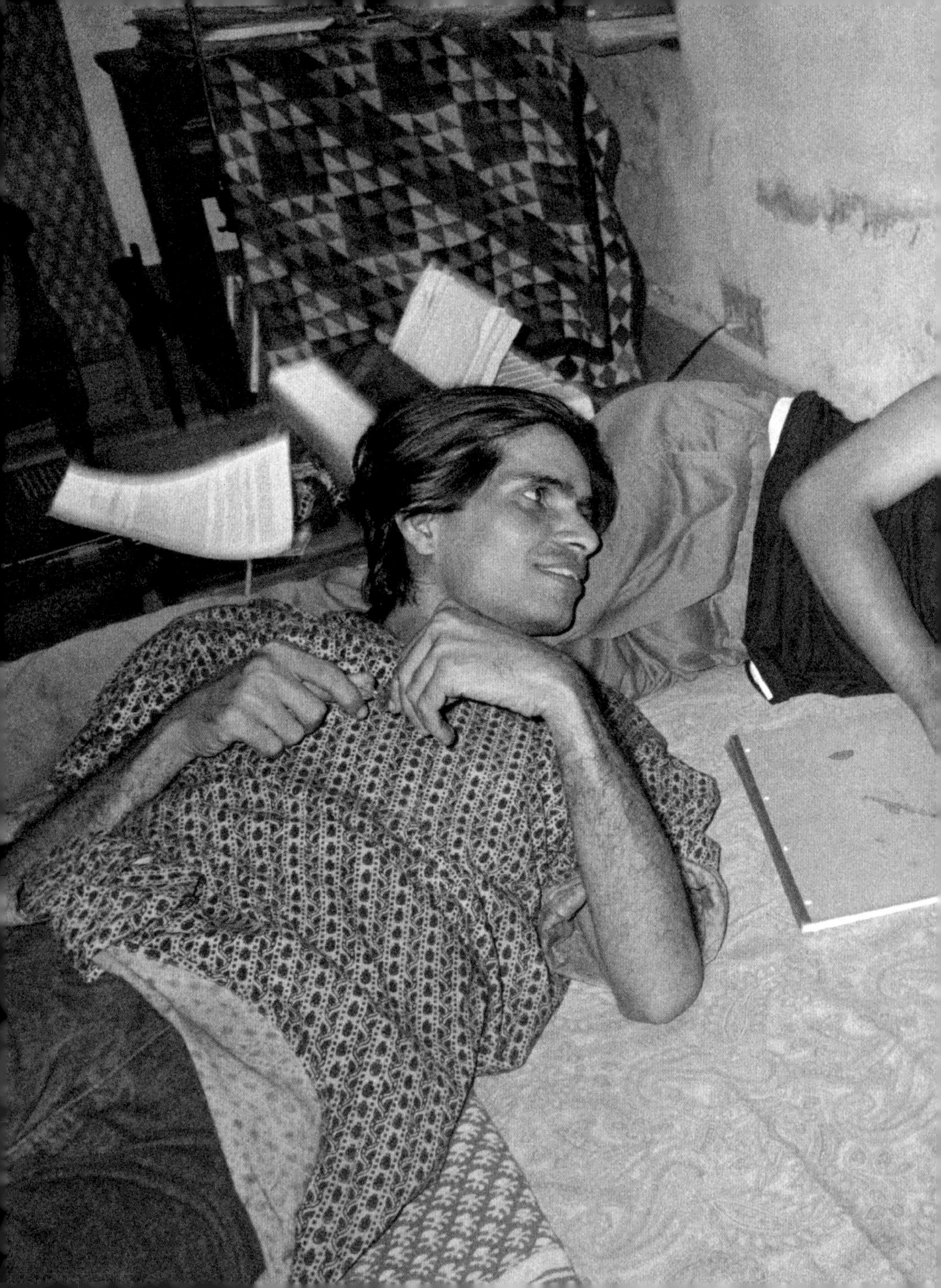

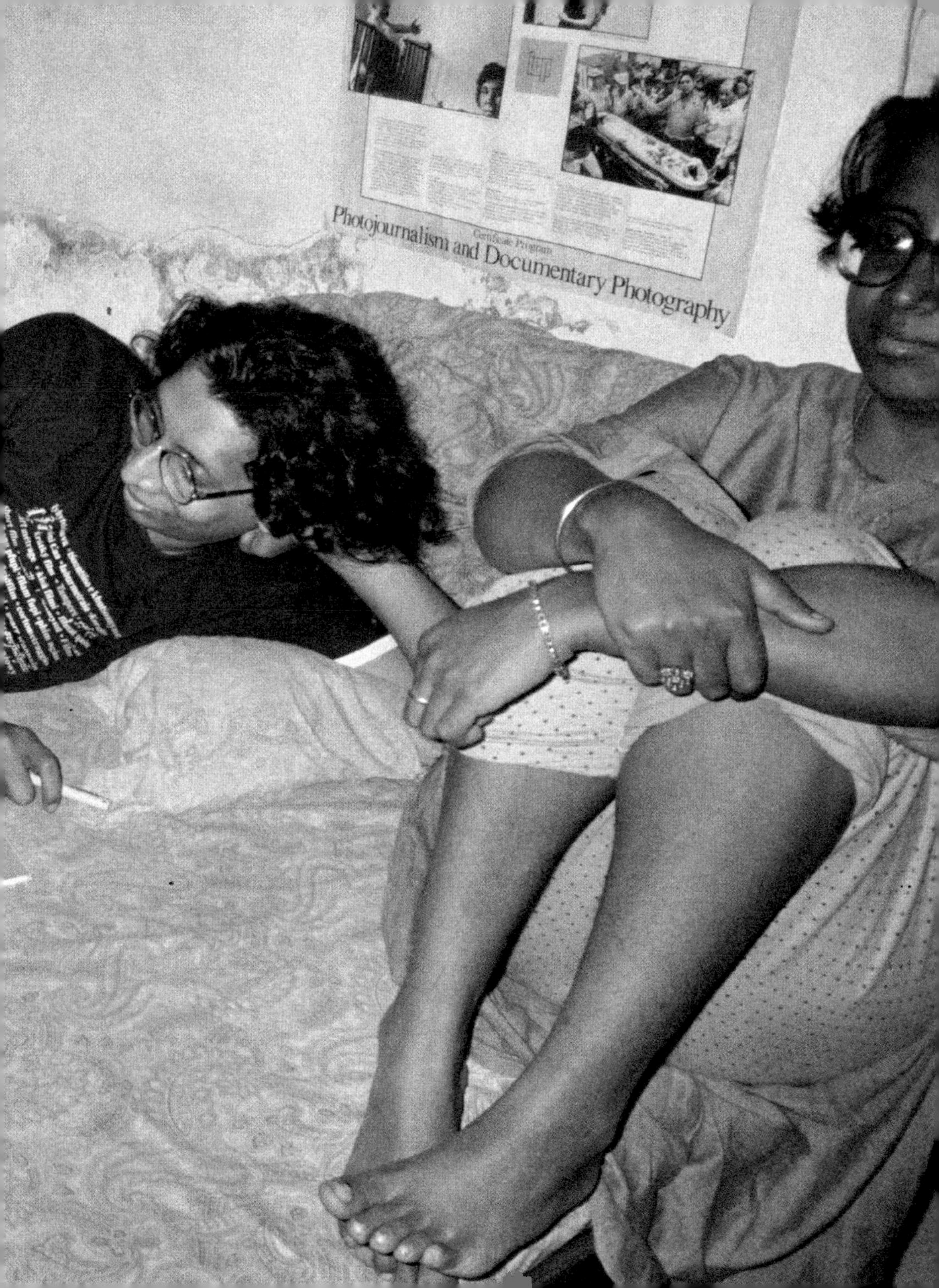

Certificate Program
Photojournalism and Documentary Photography

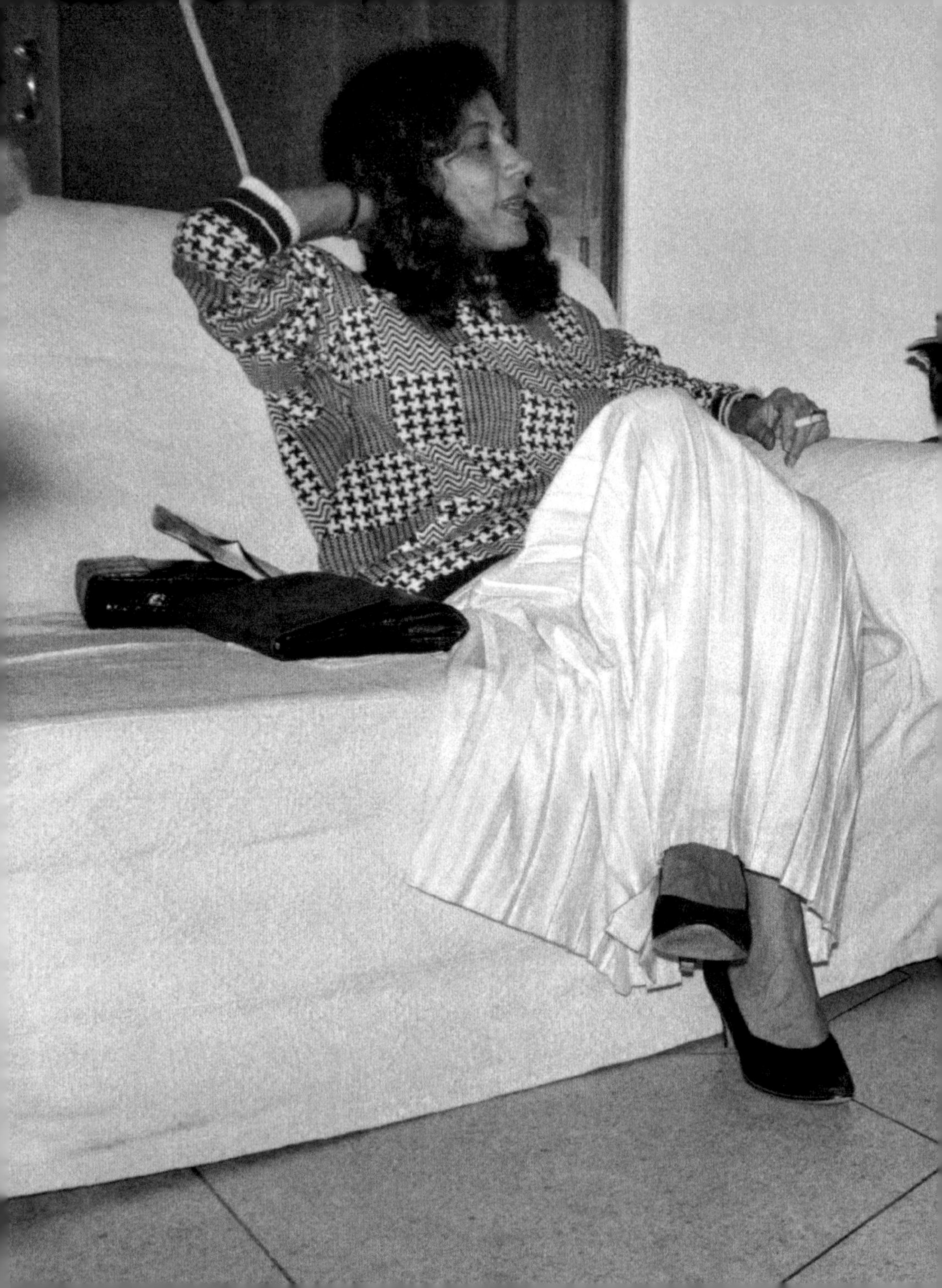

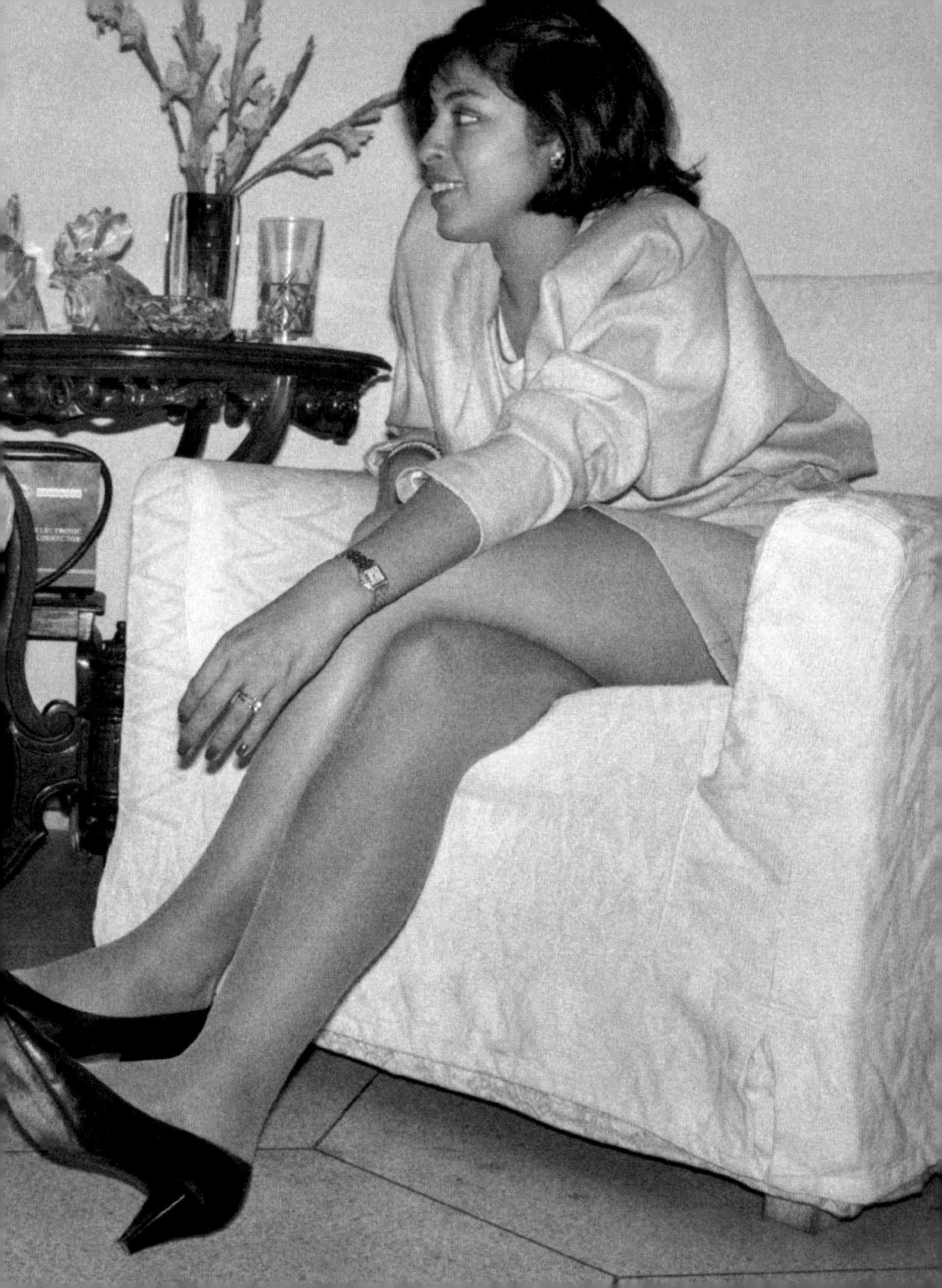

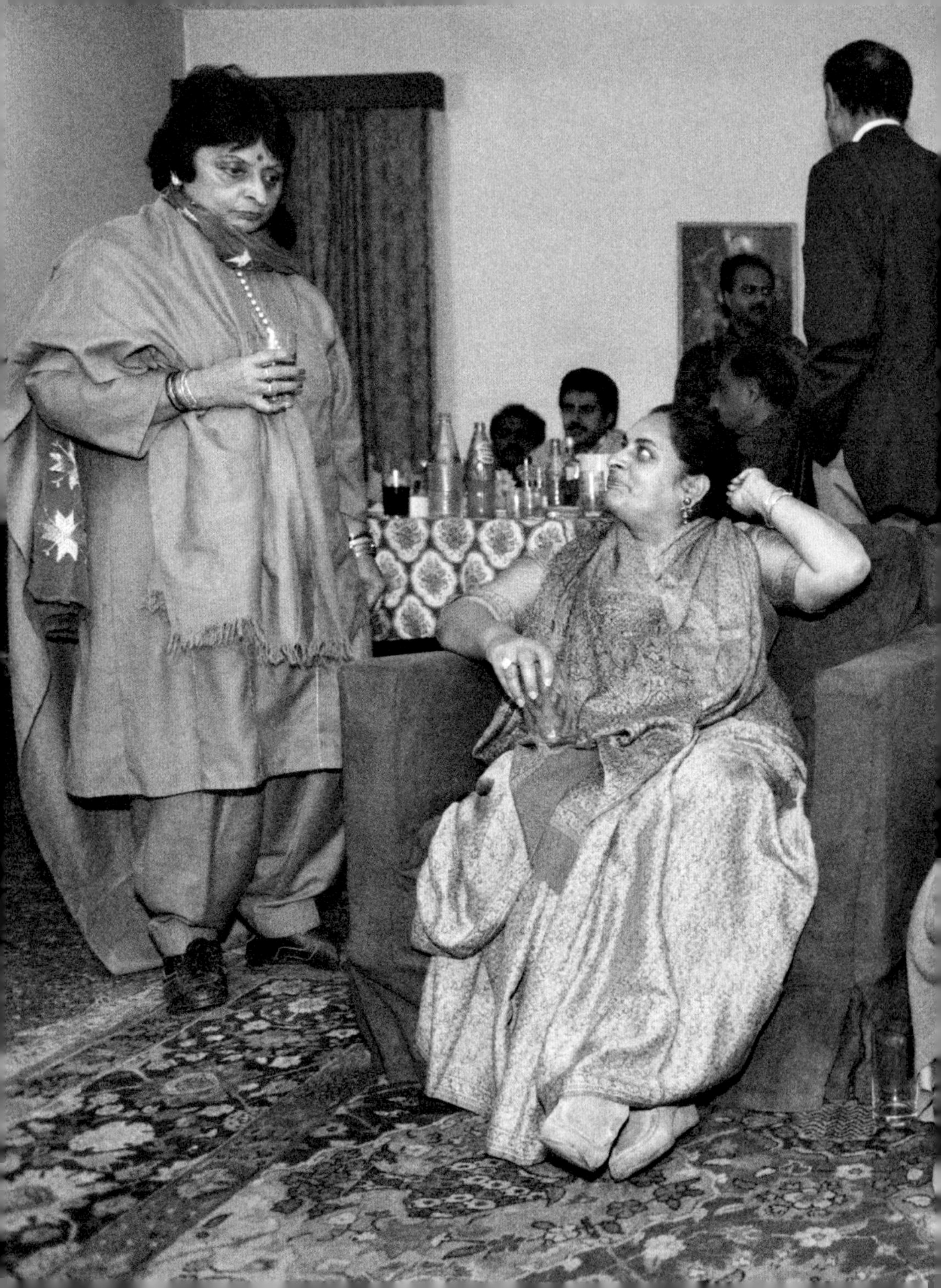

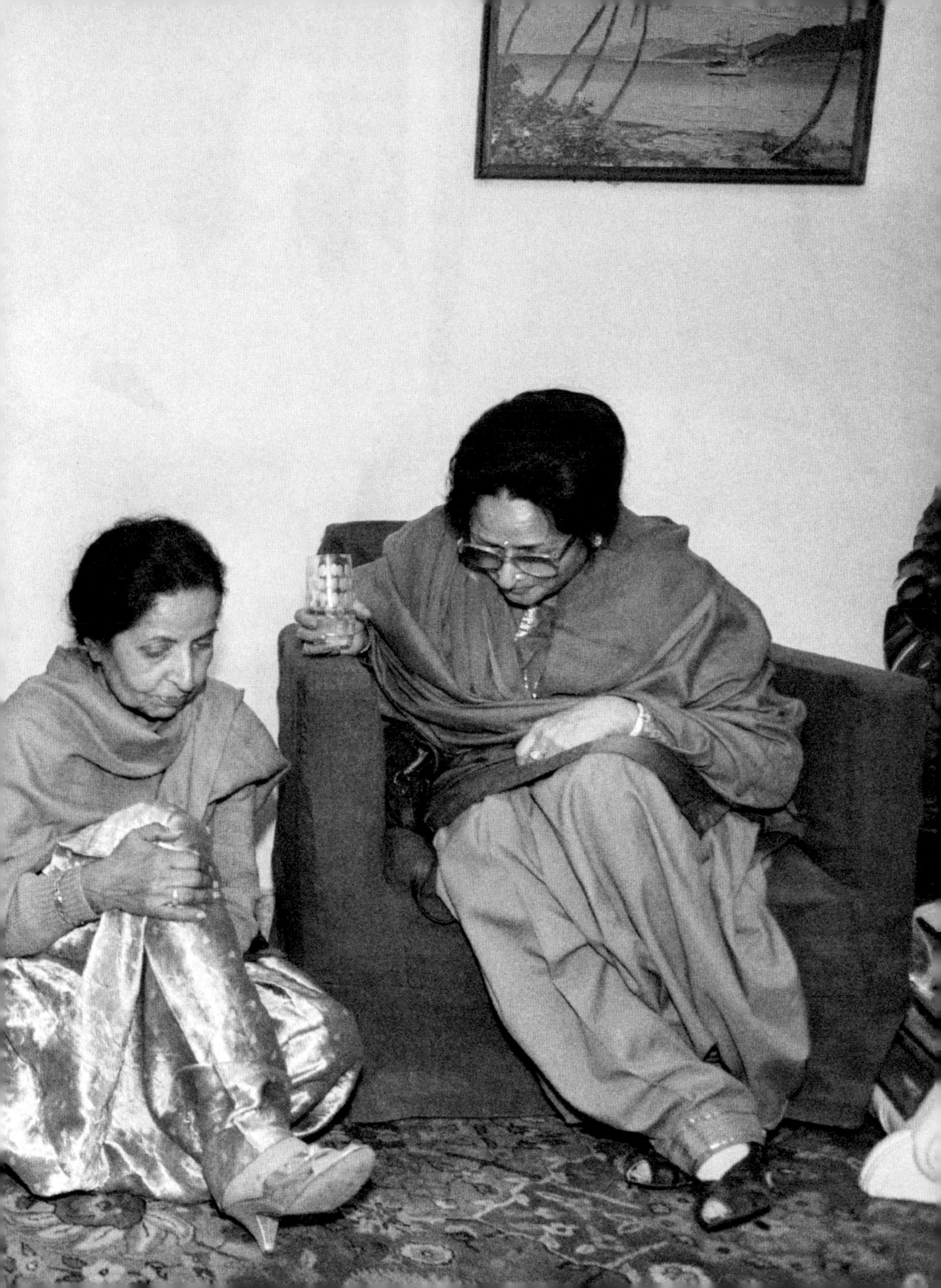

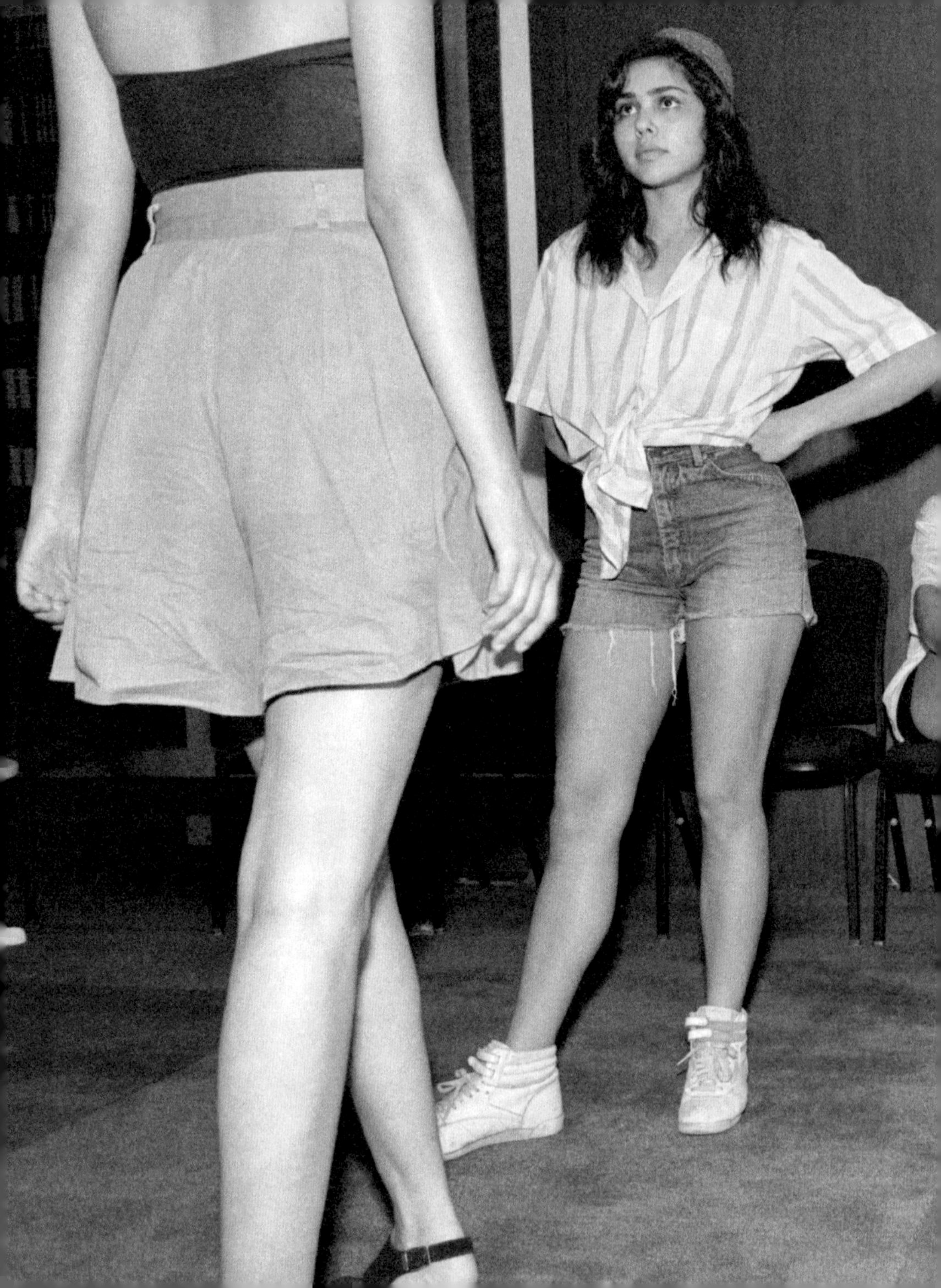

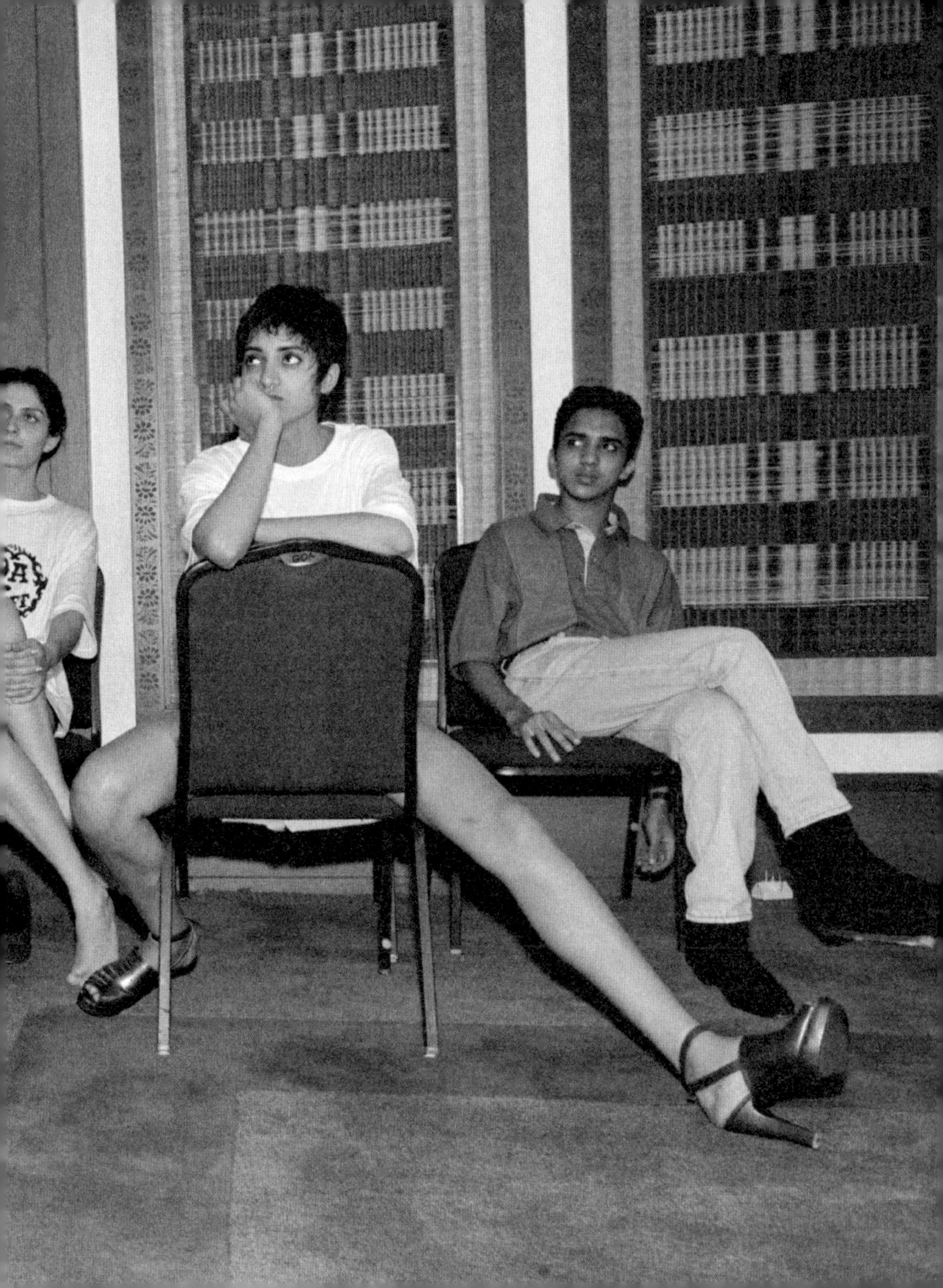

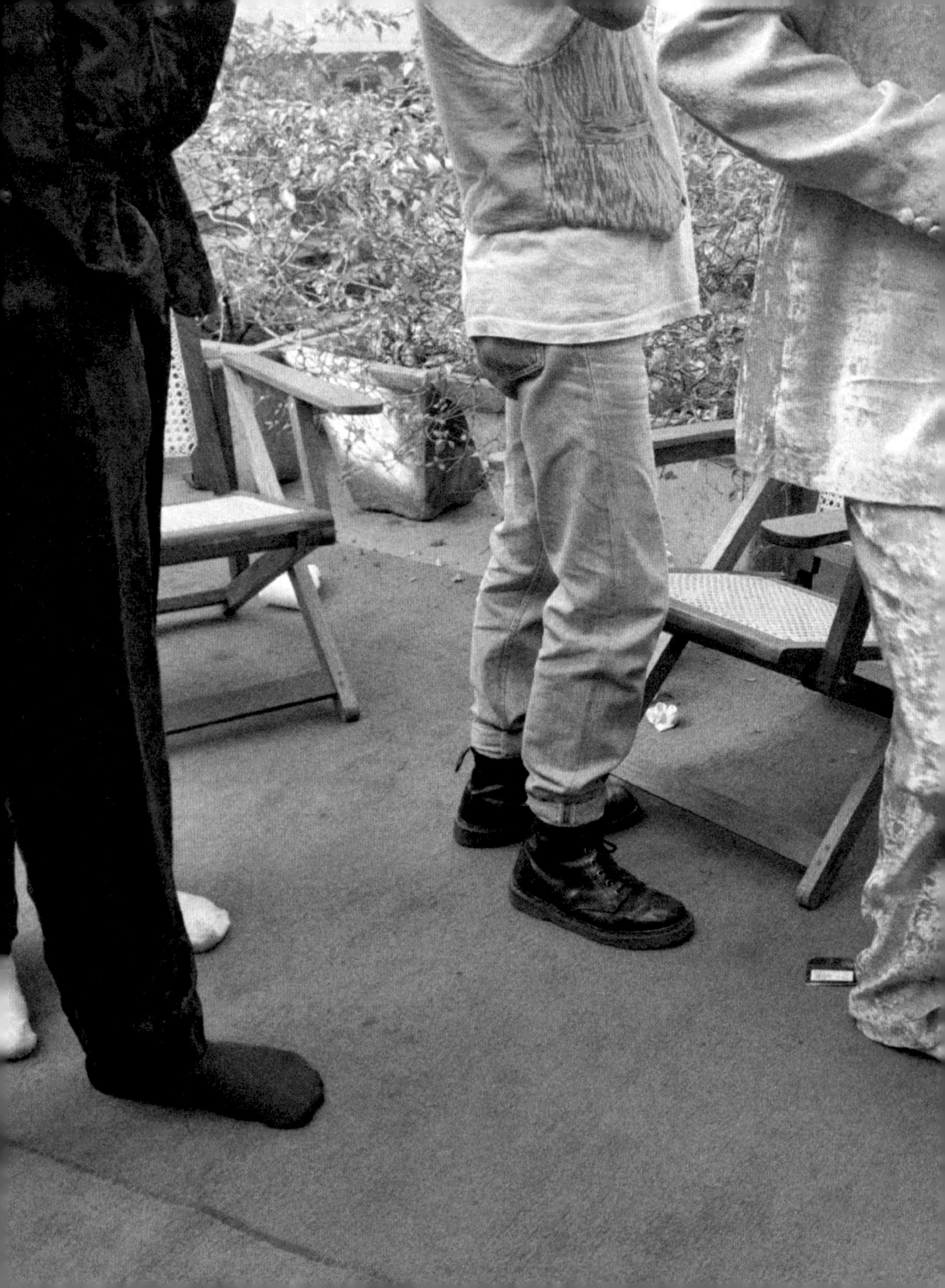

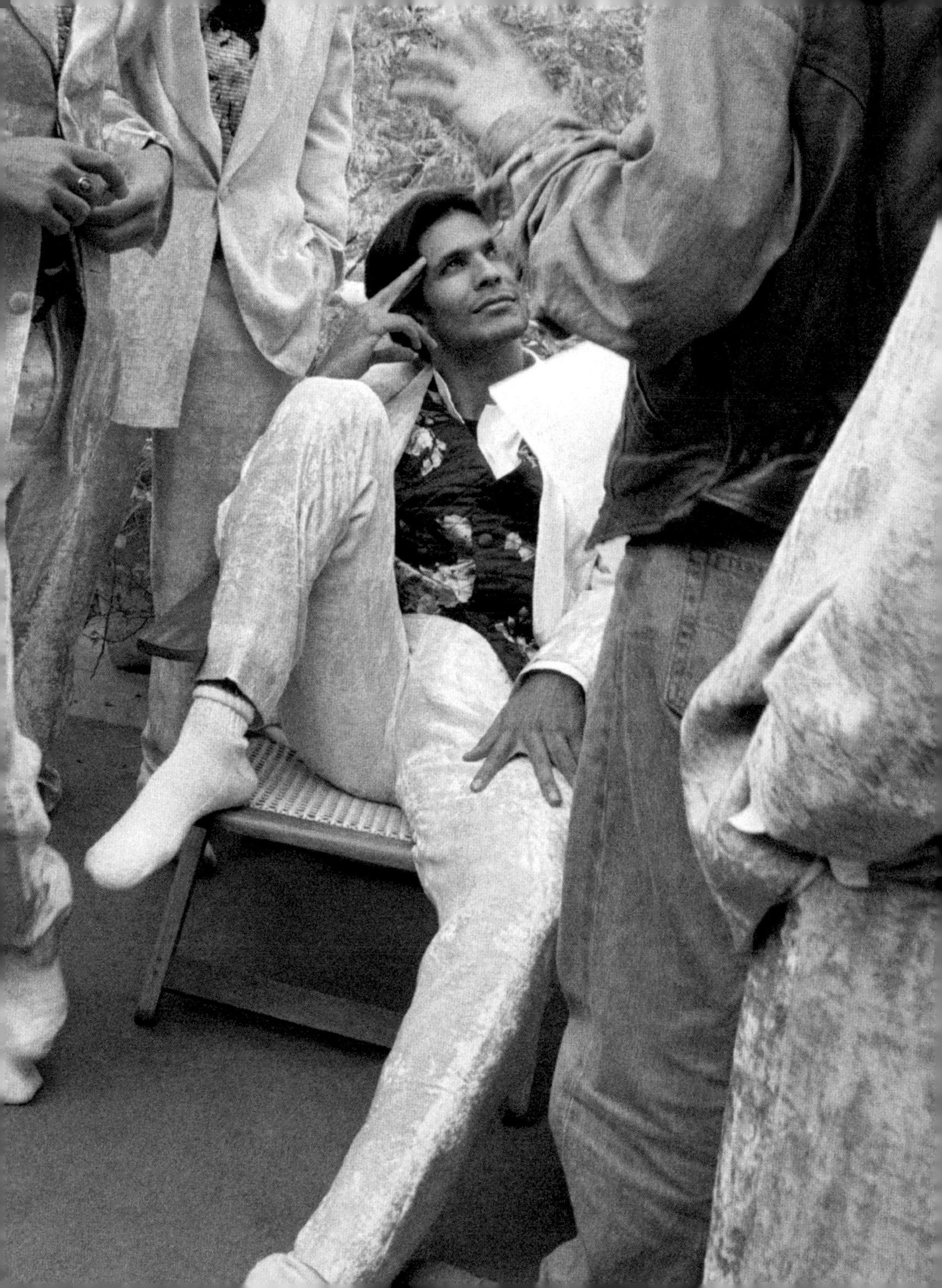

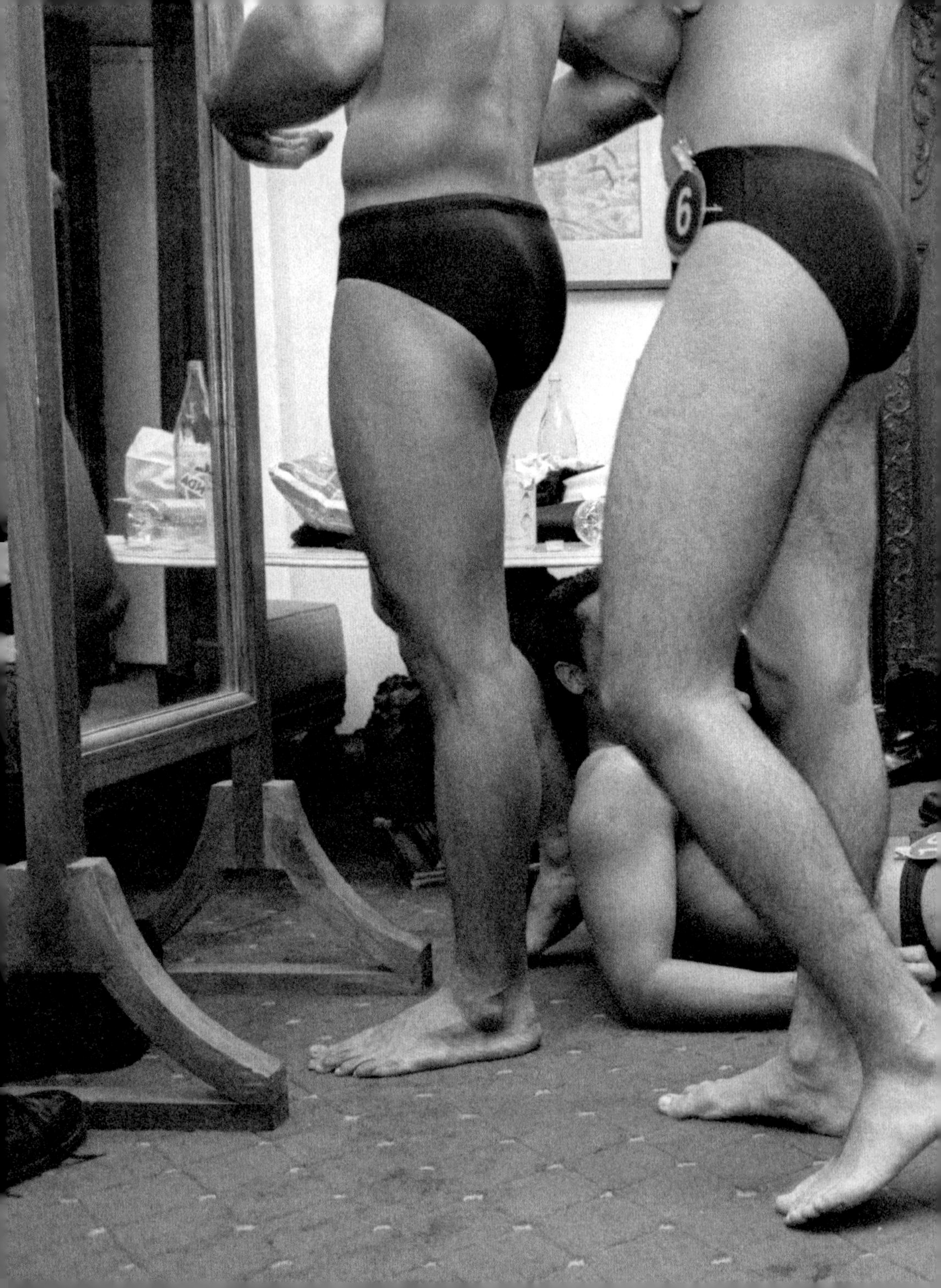

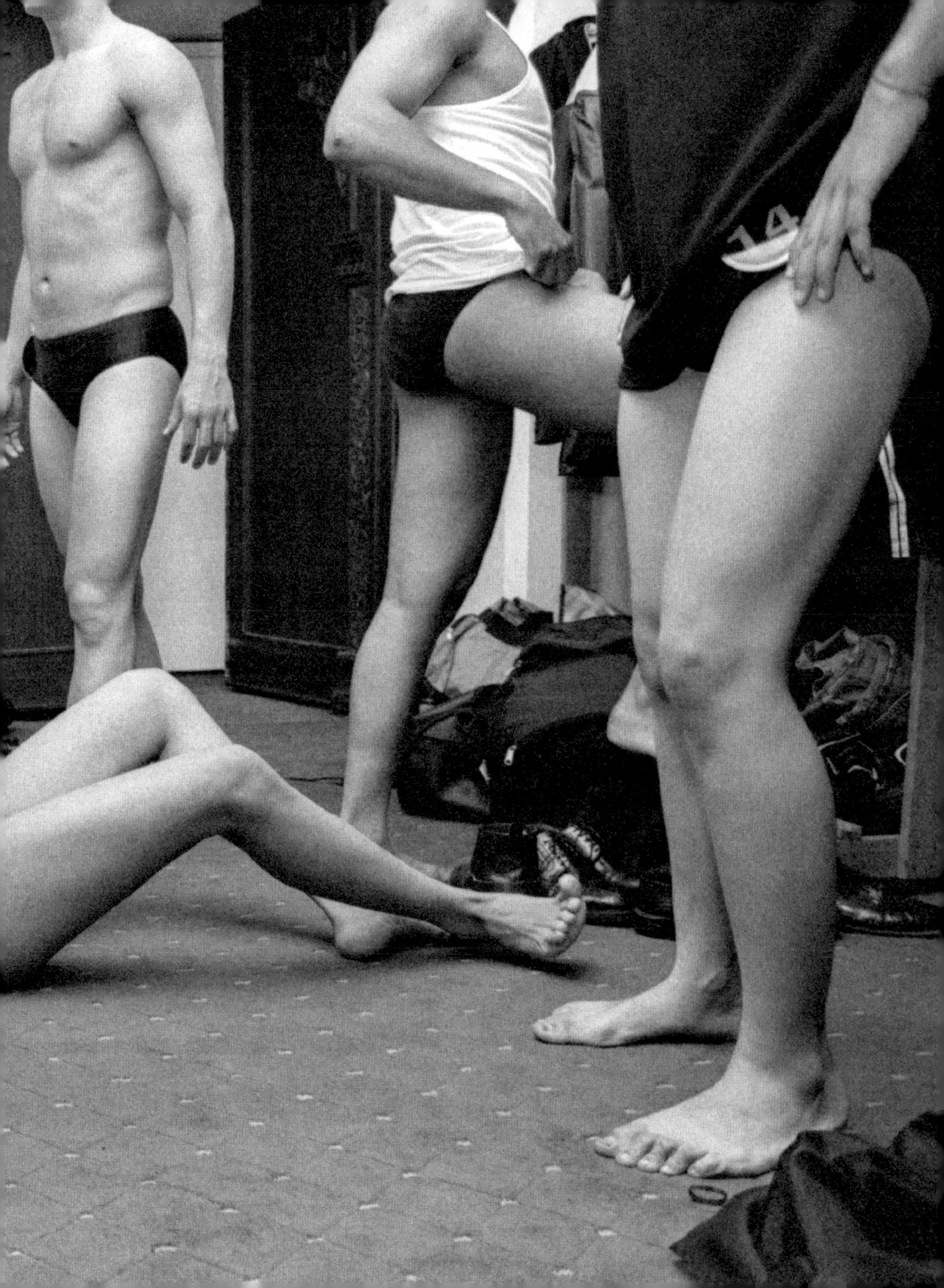

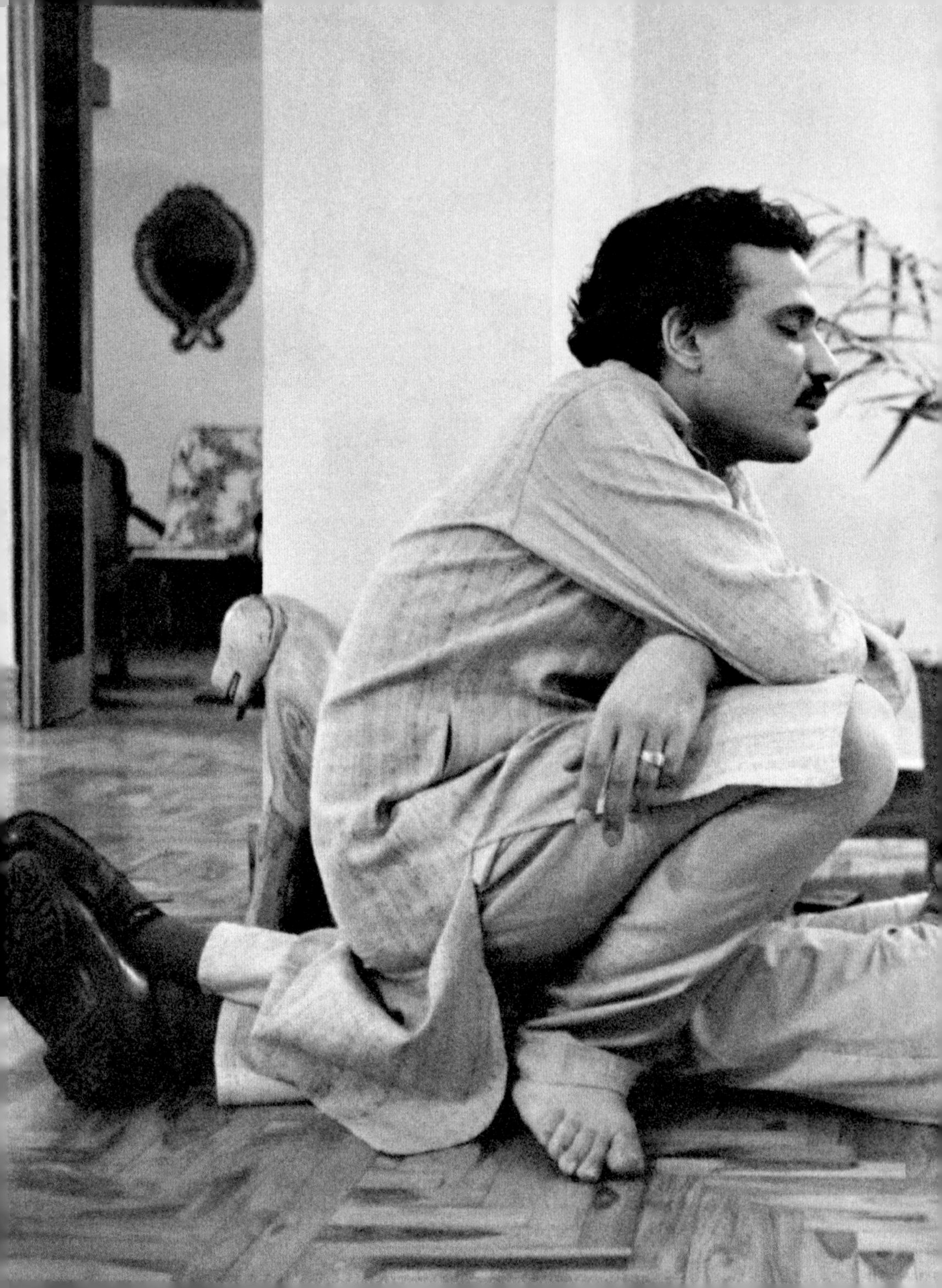

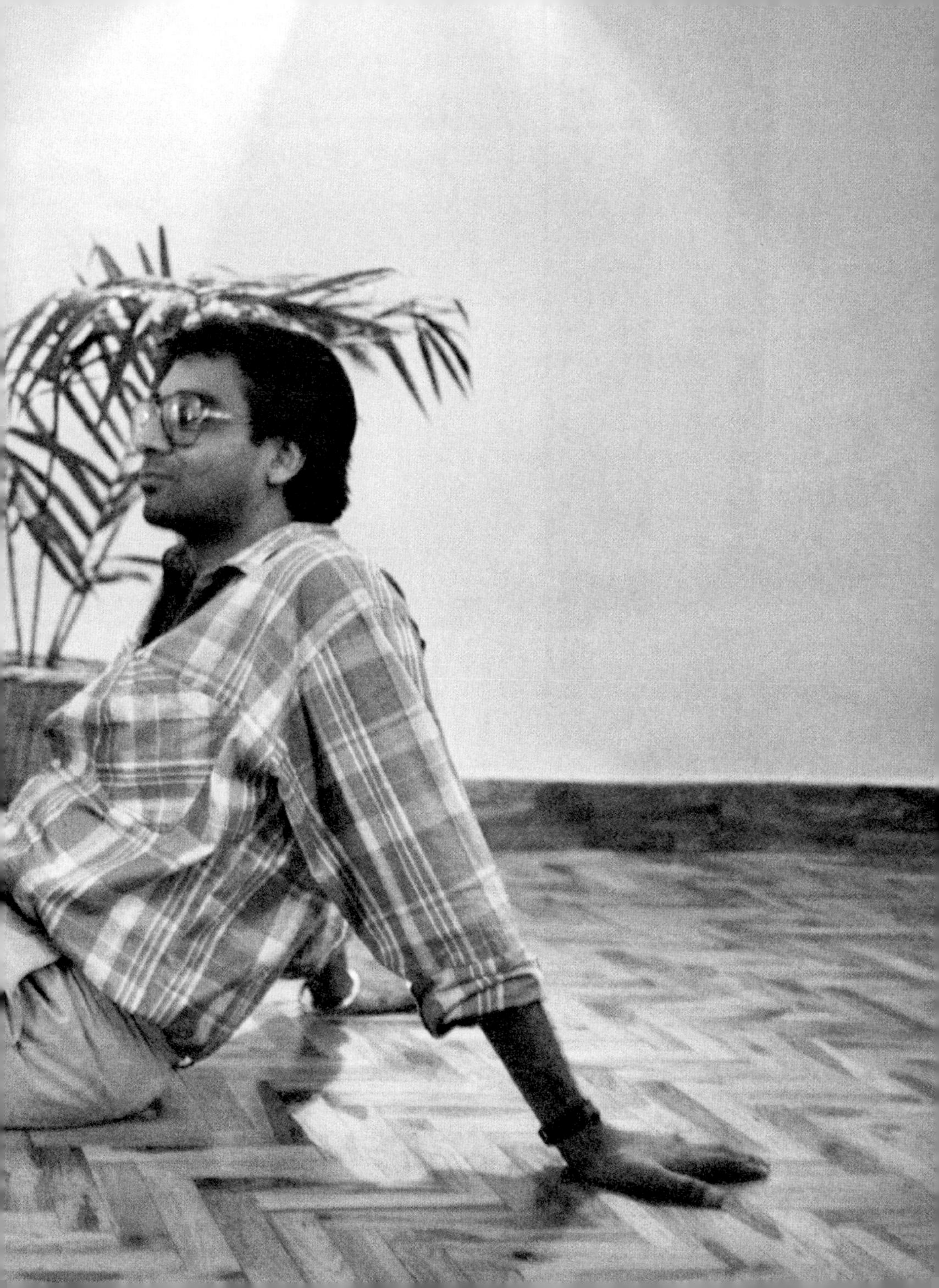

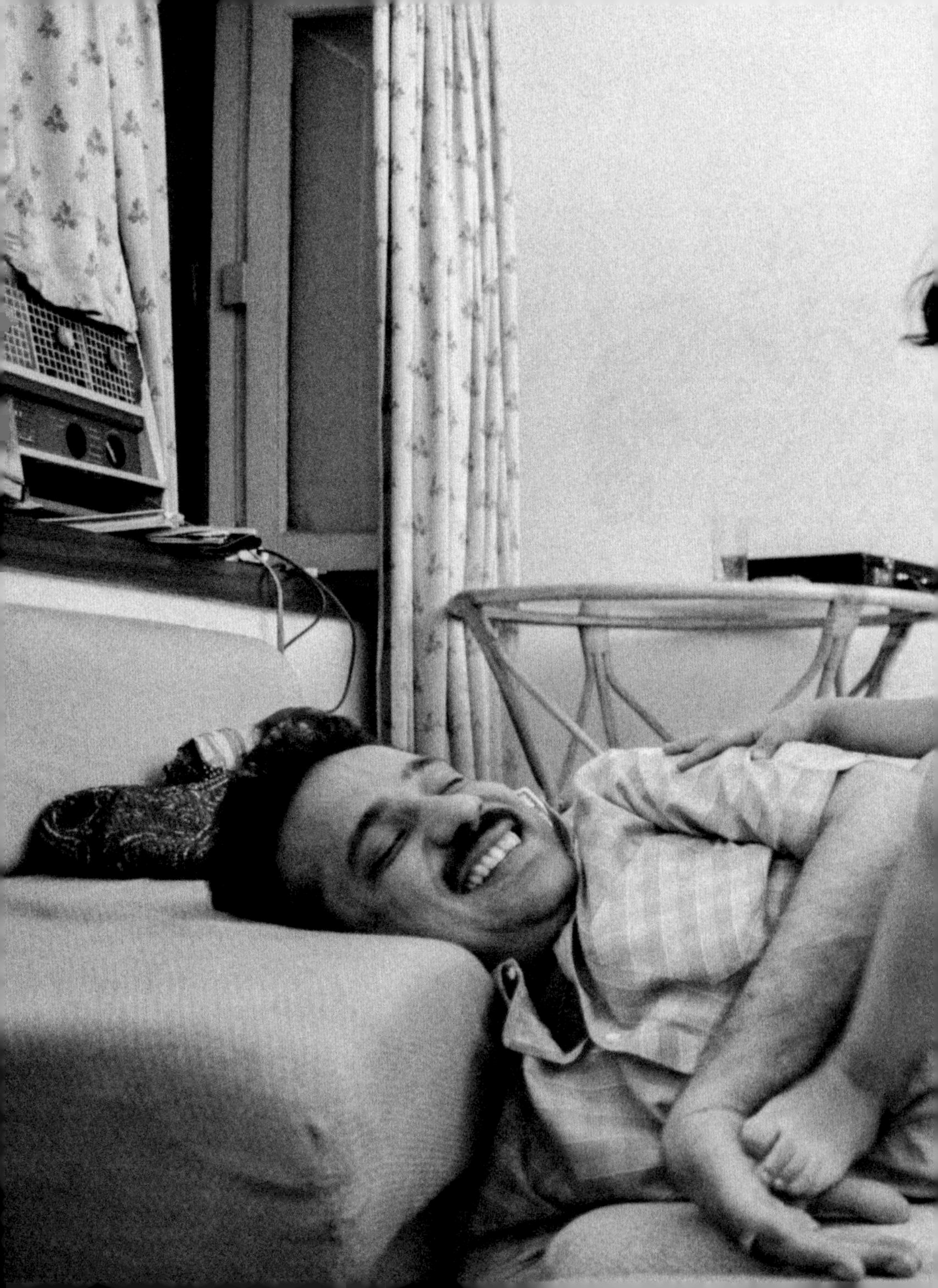

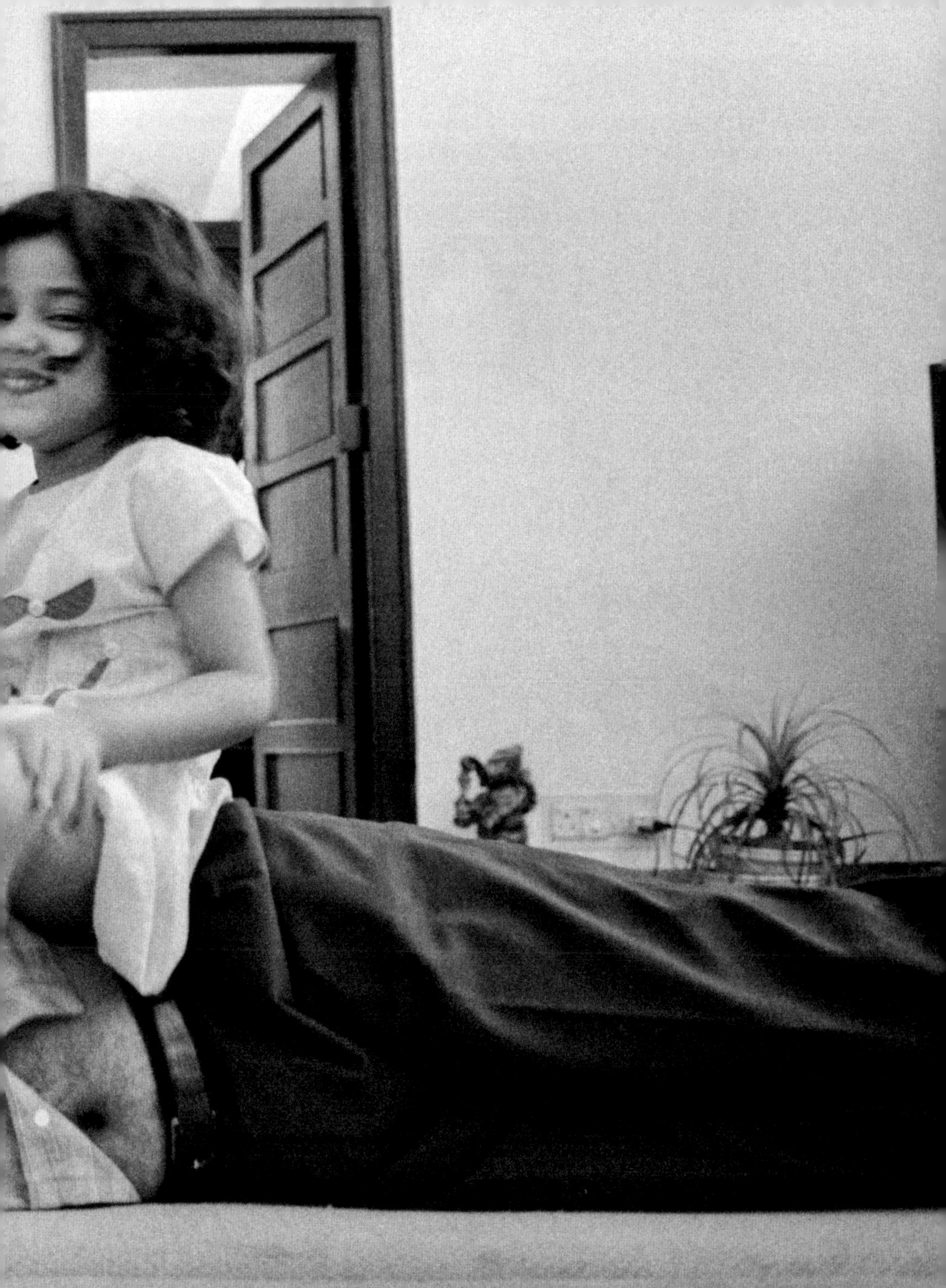

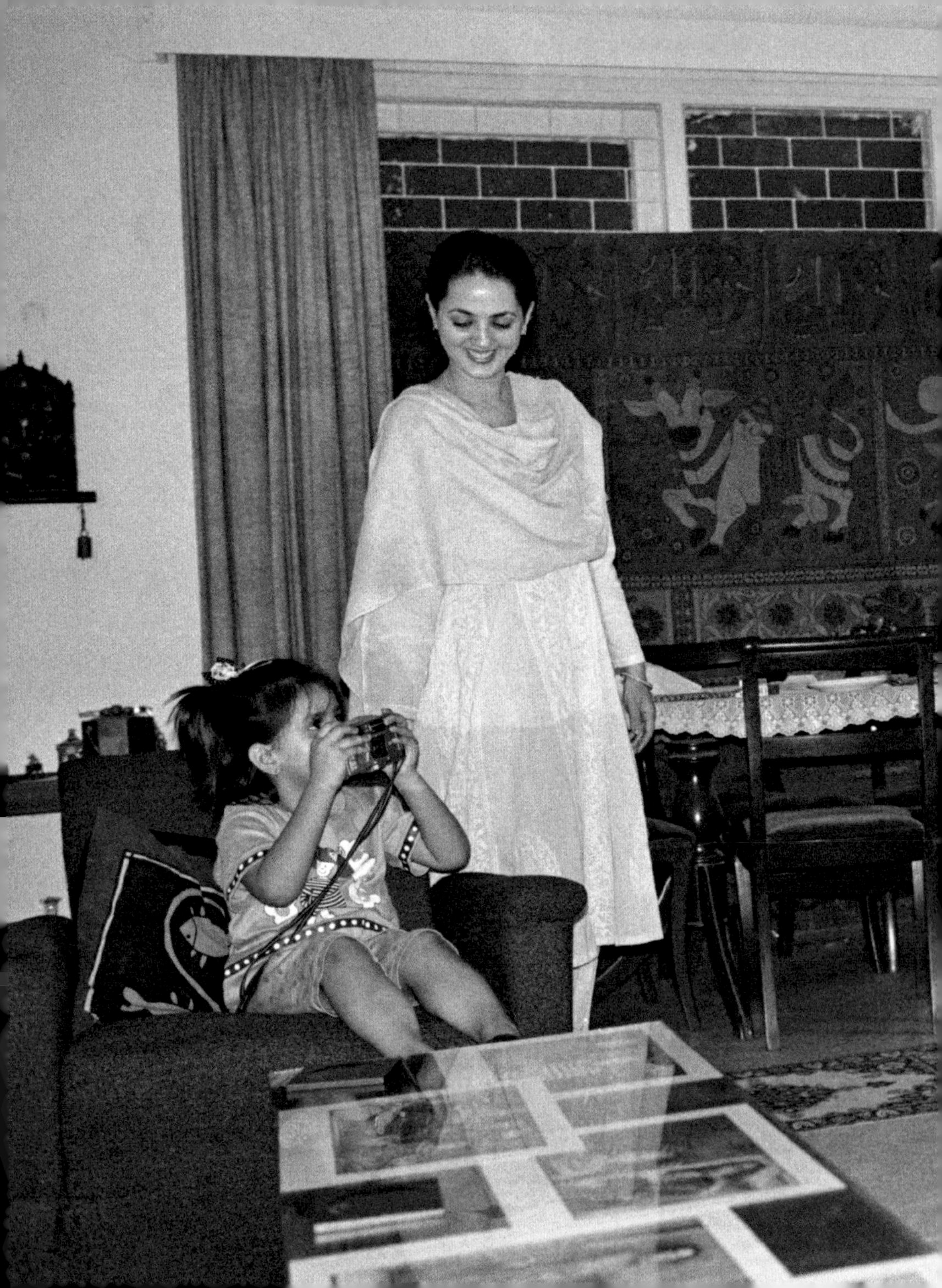

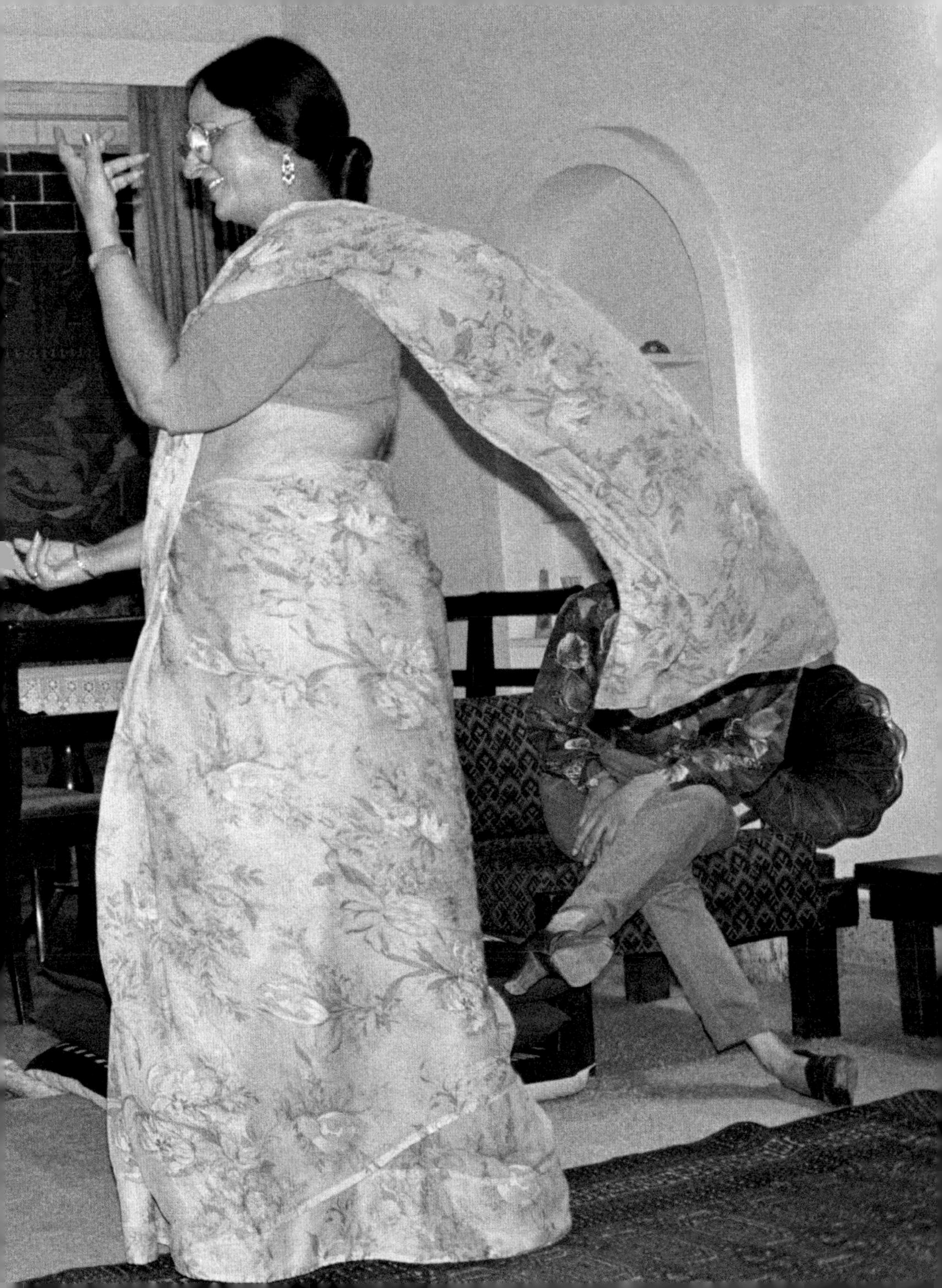

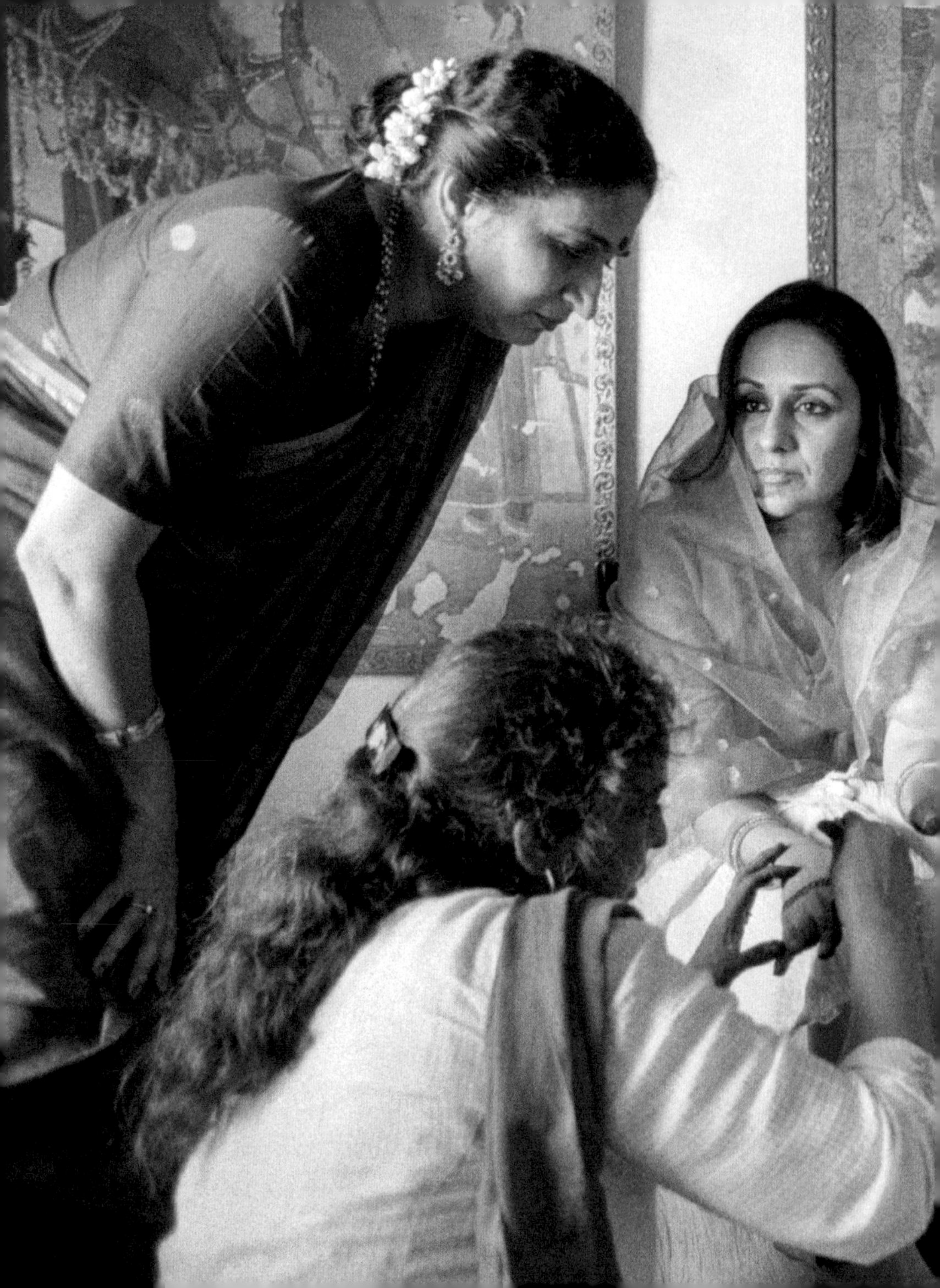

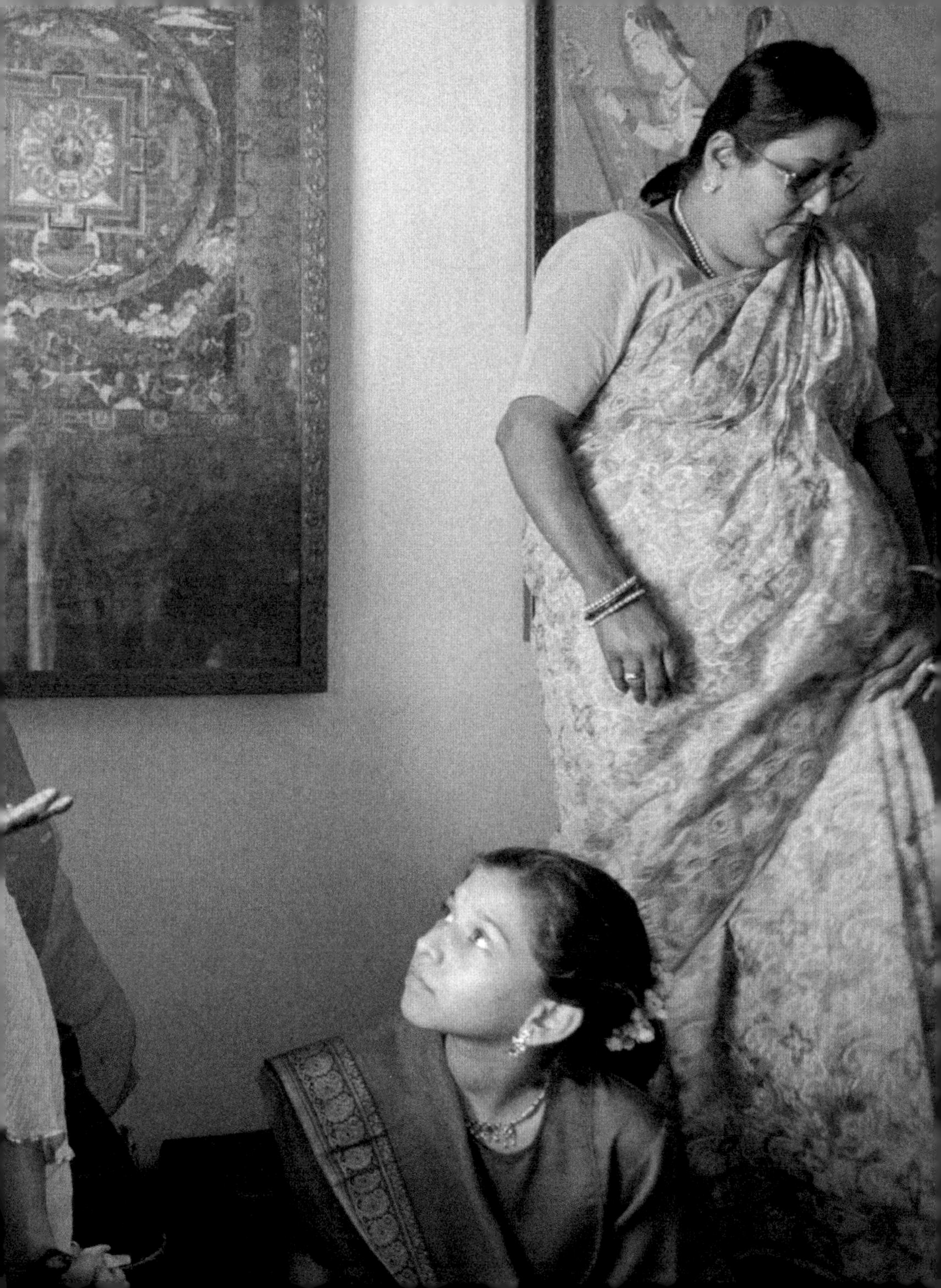

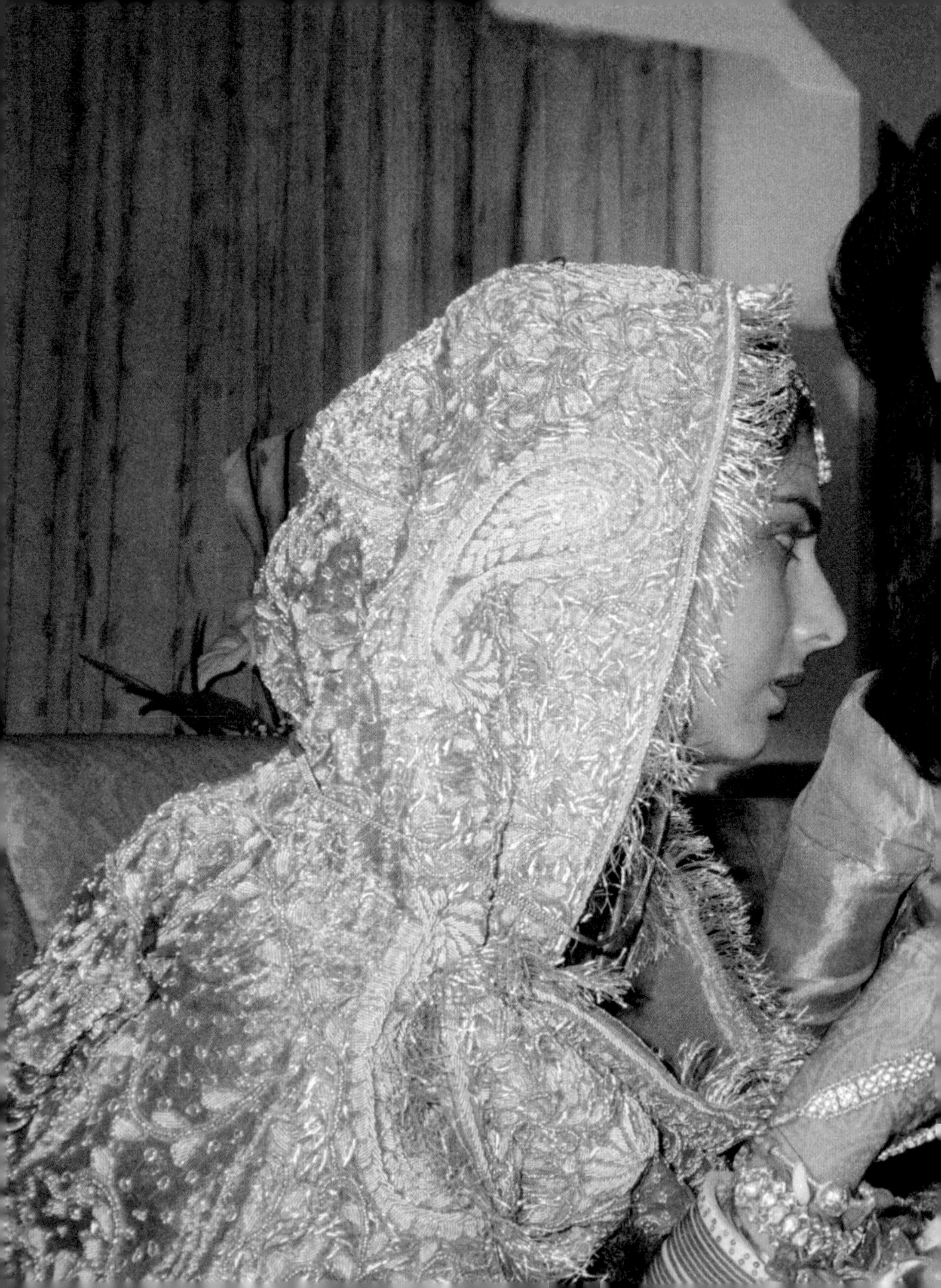

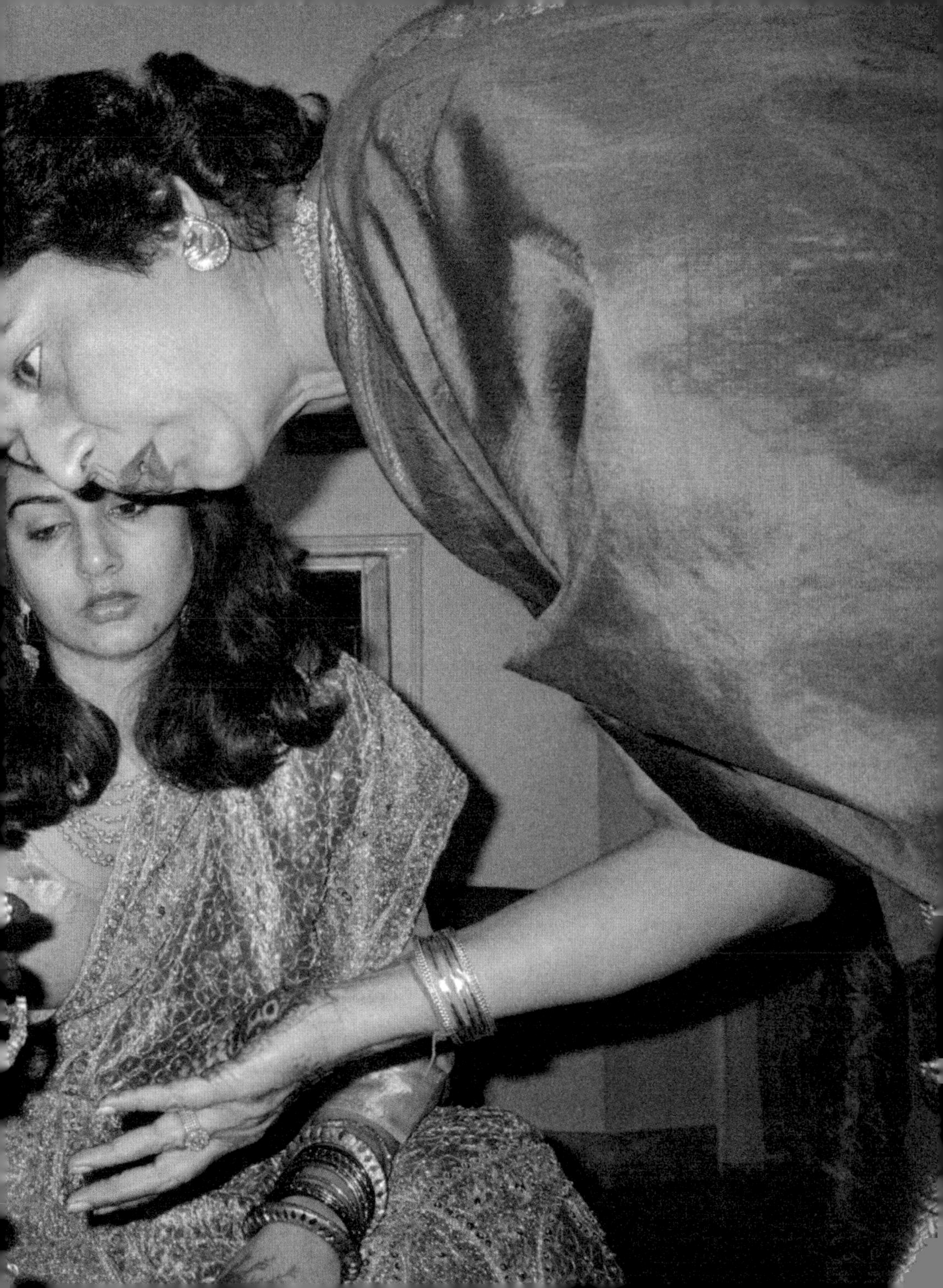

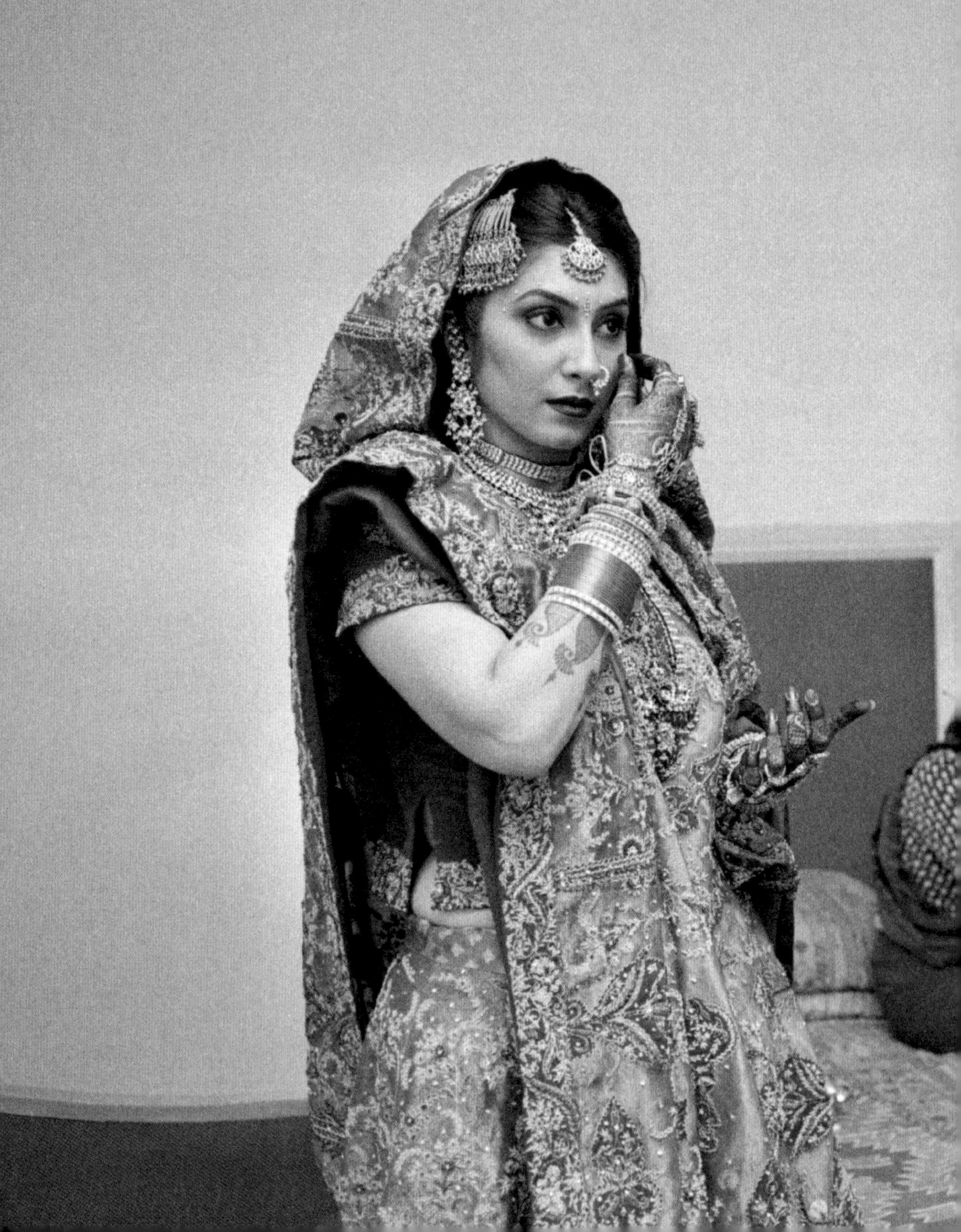

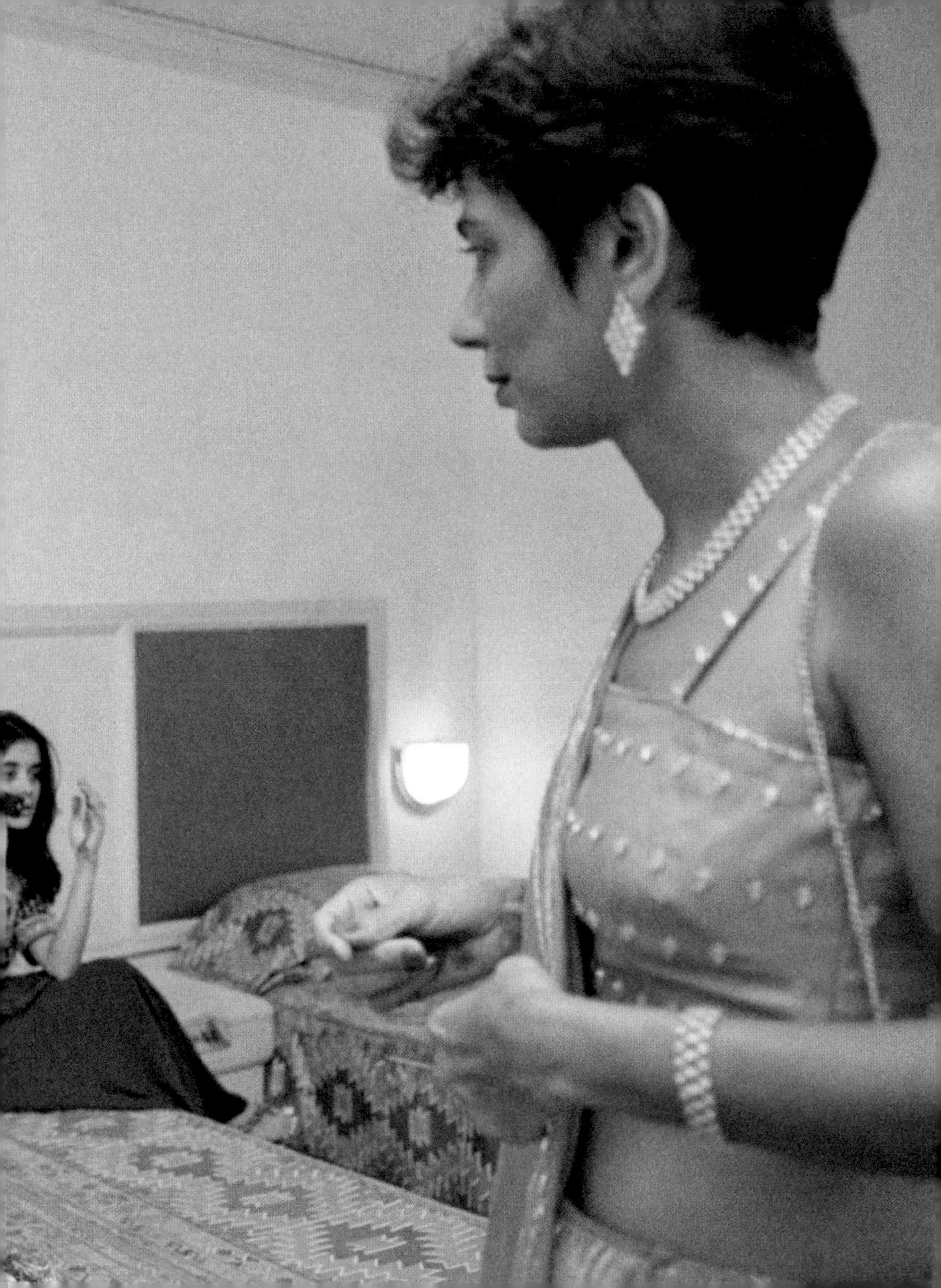

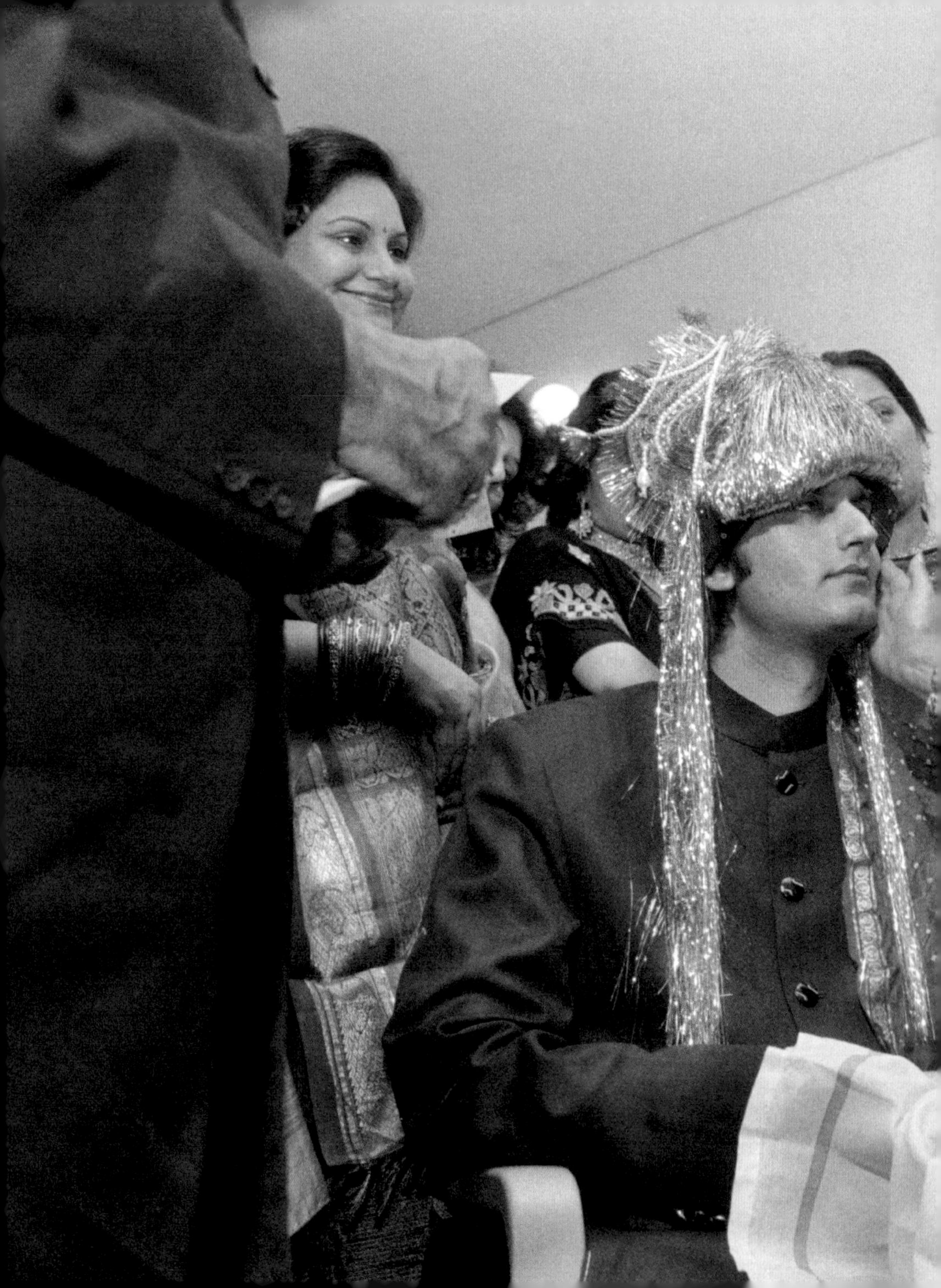

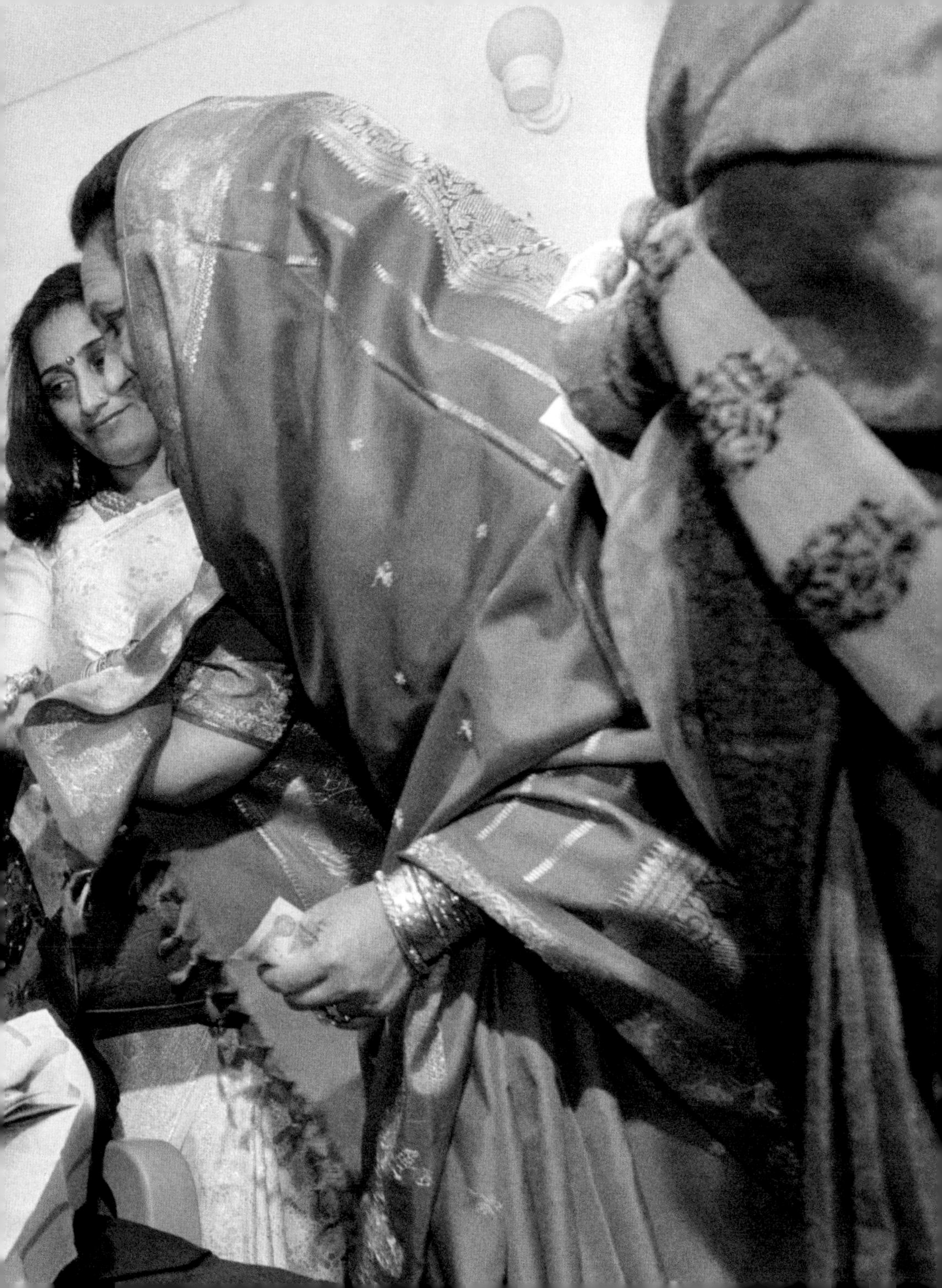

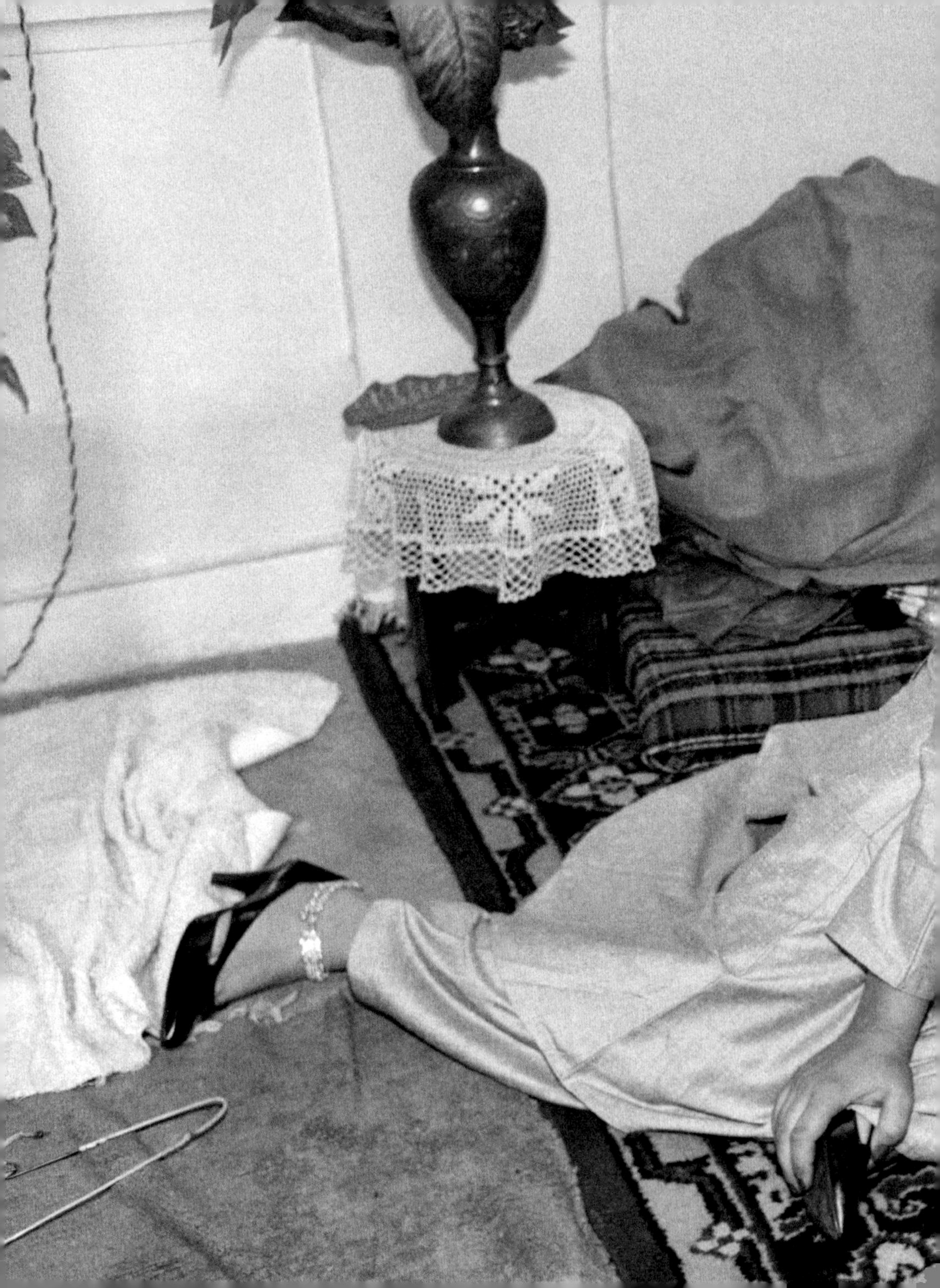

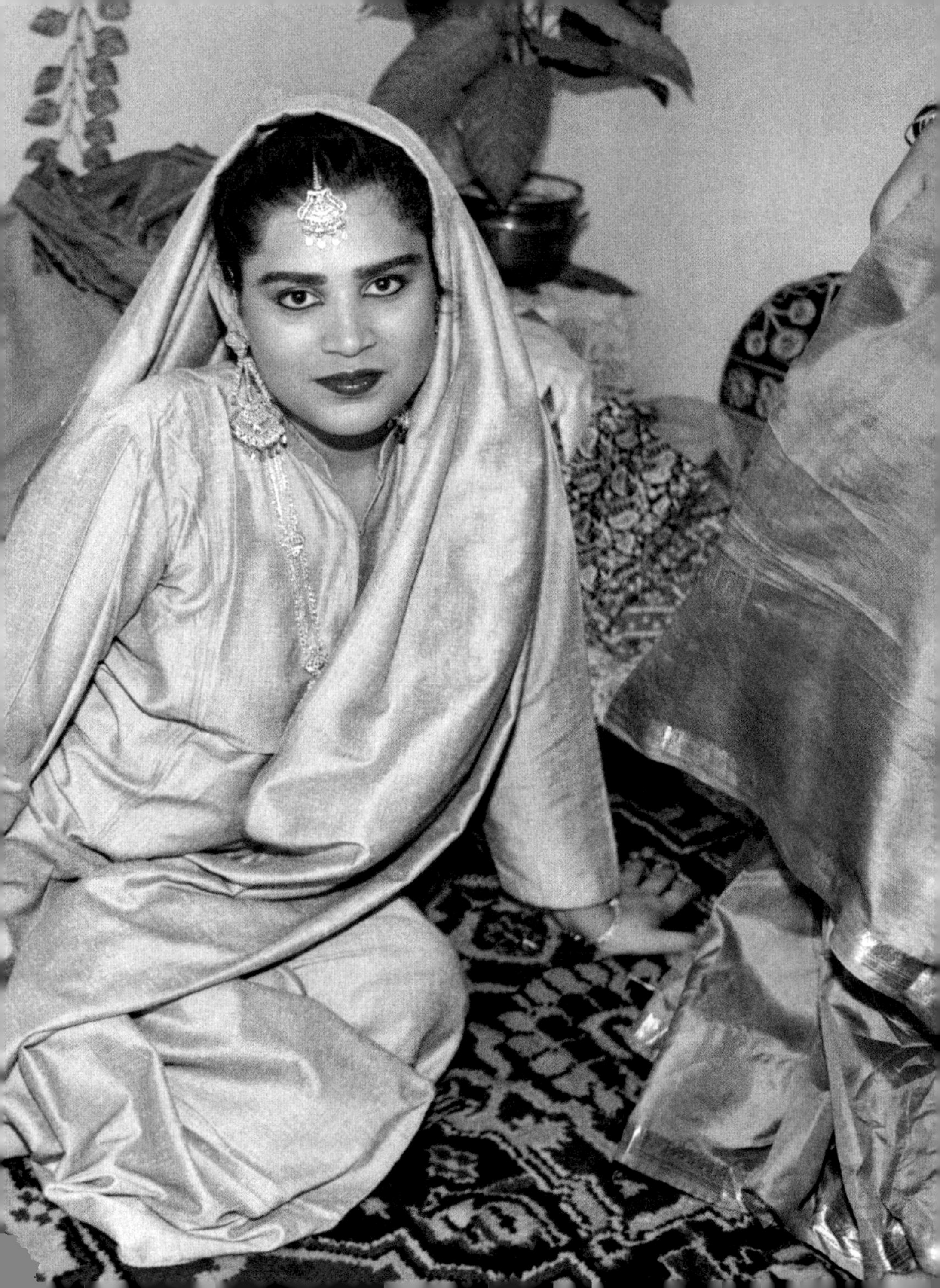

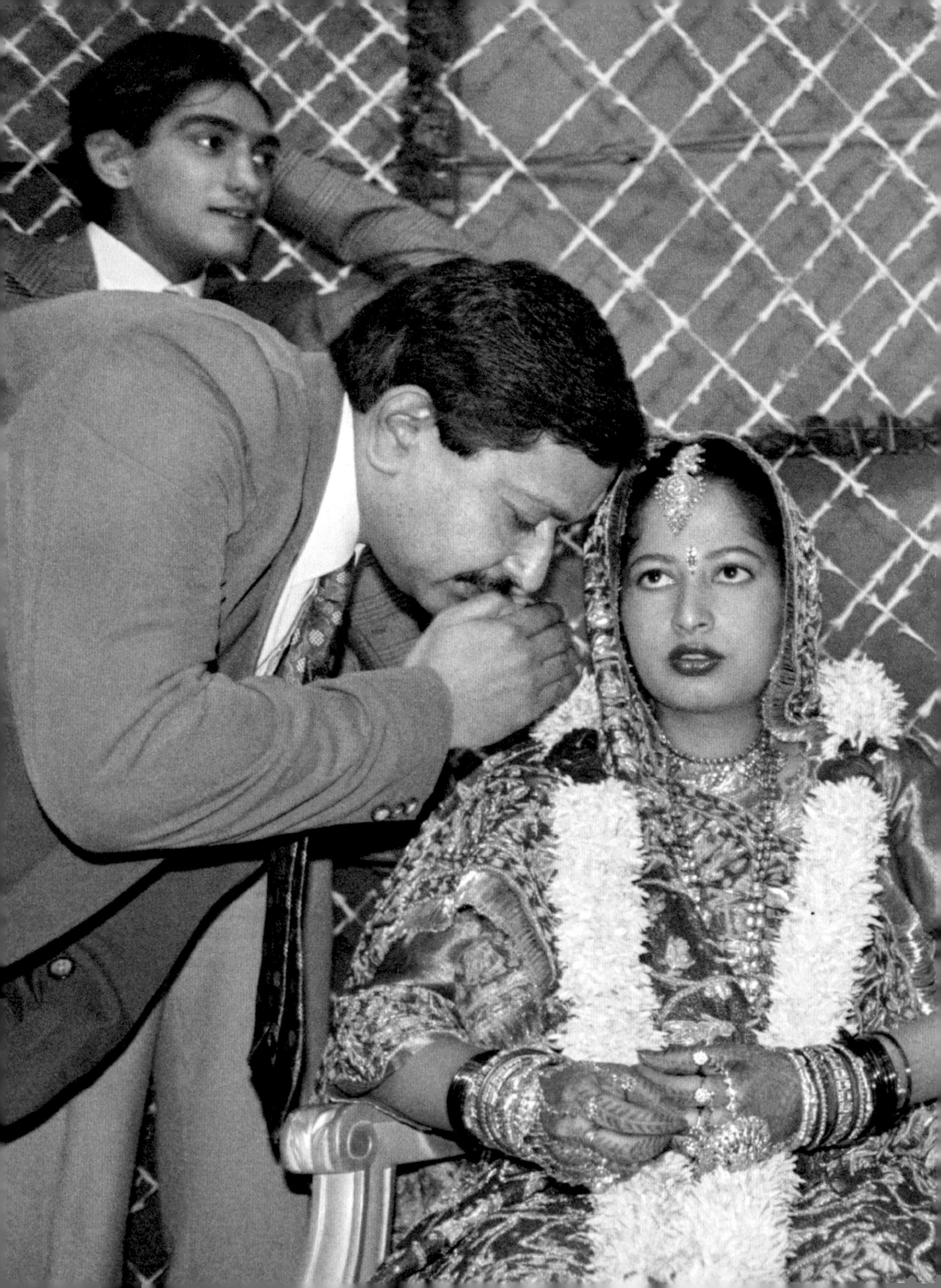

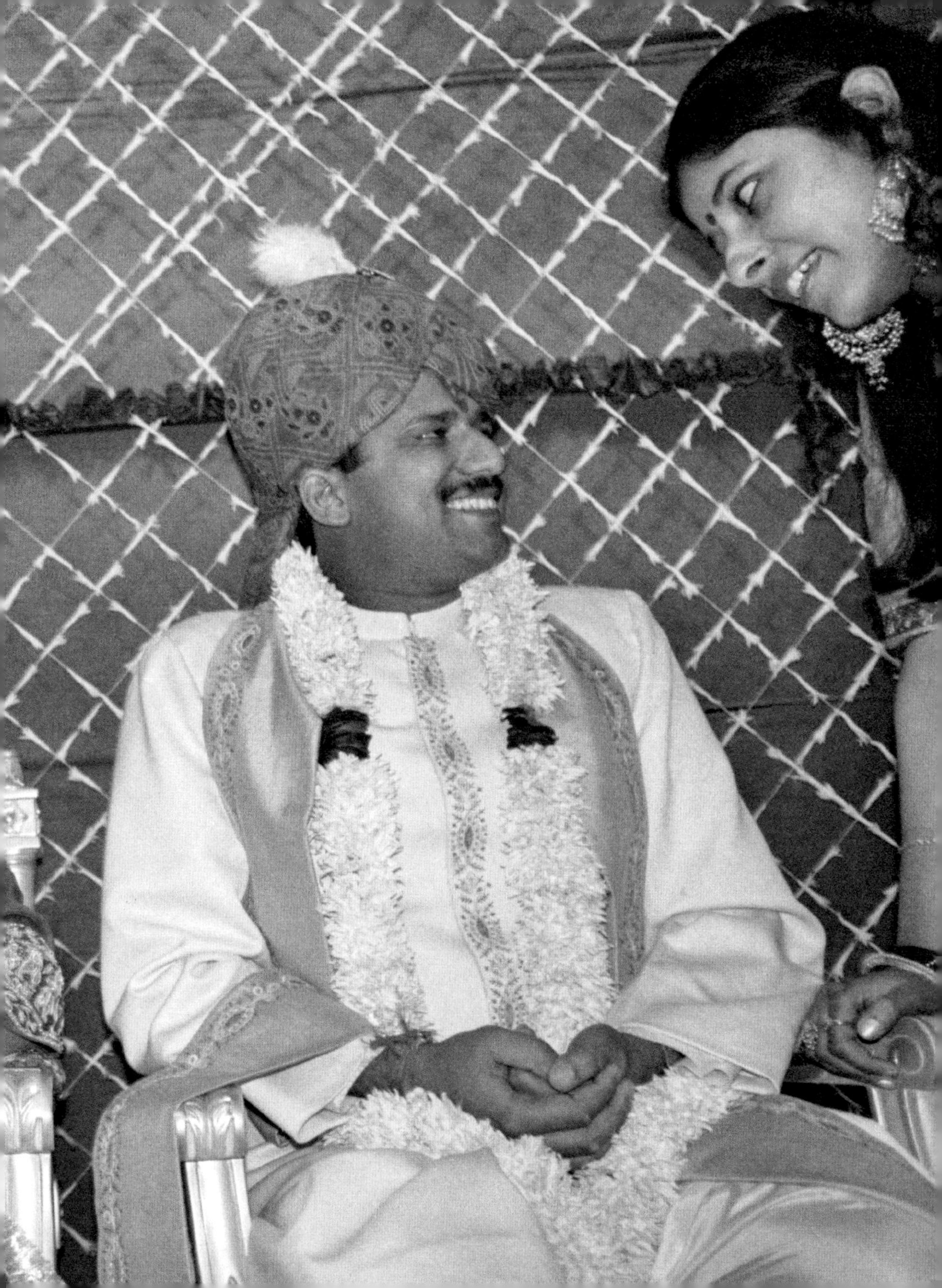

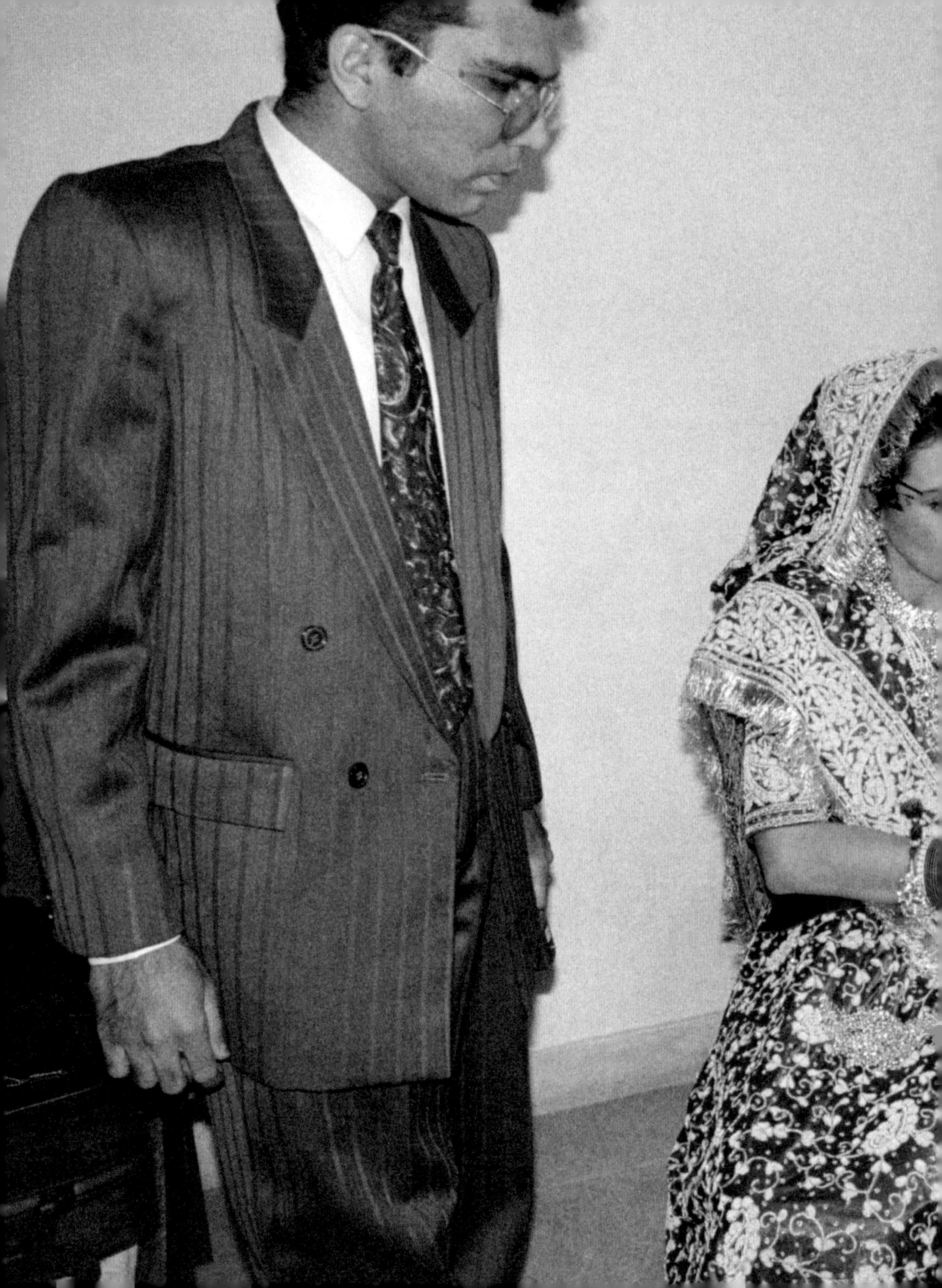

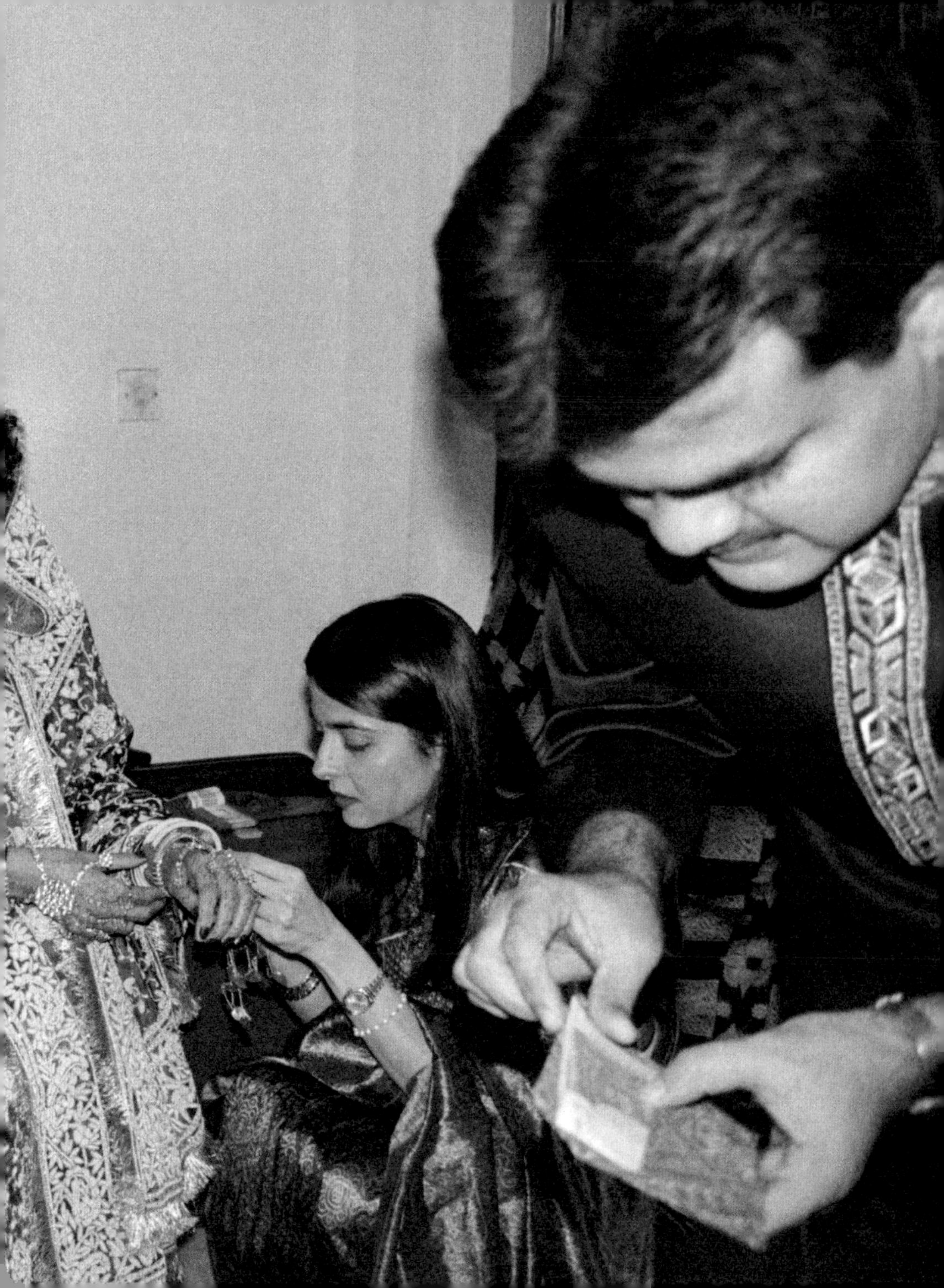

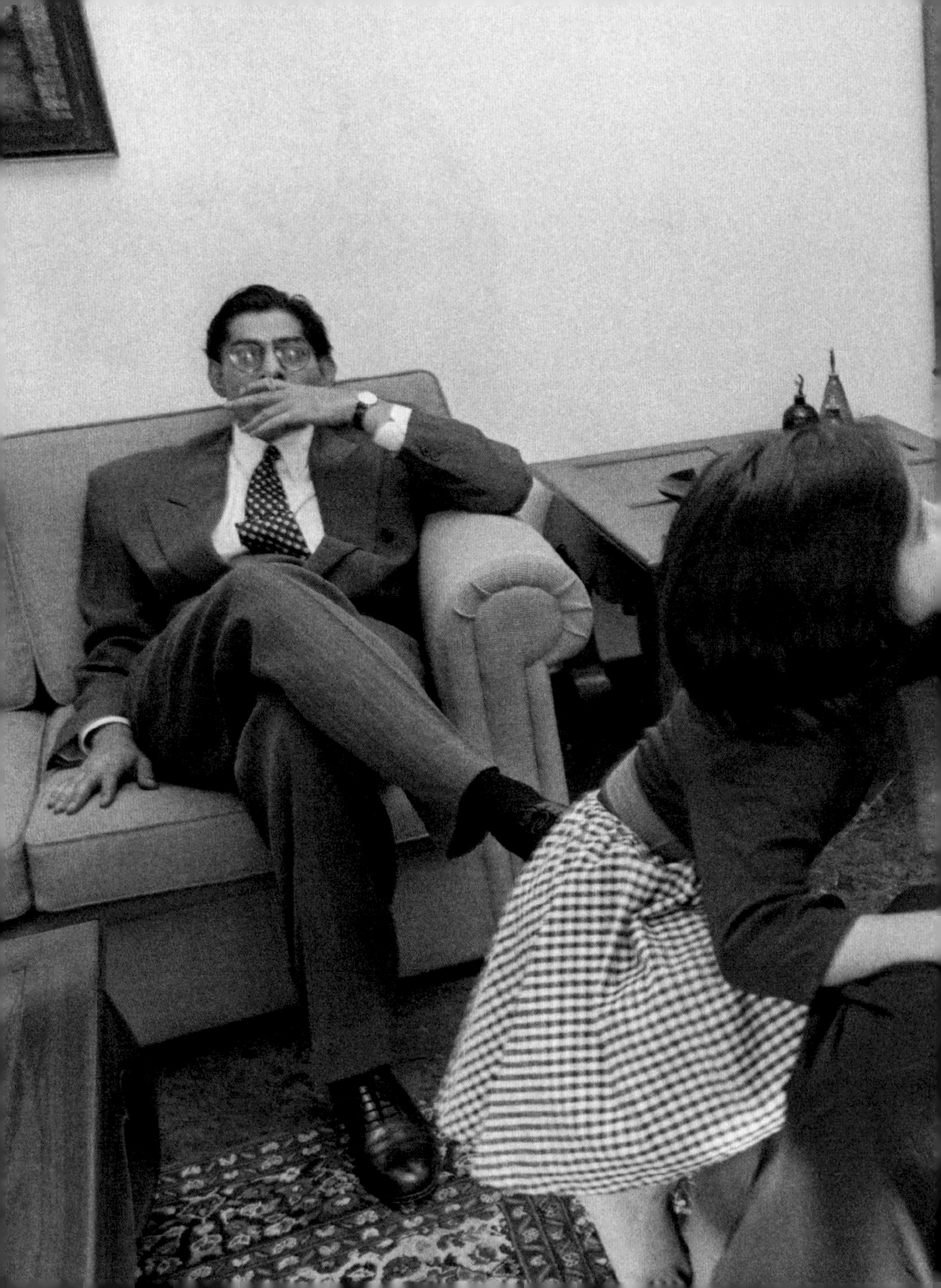

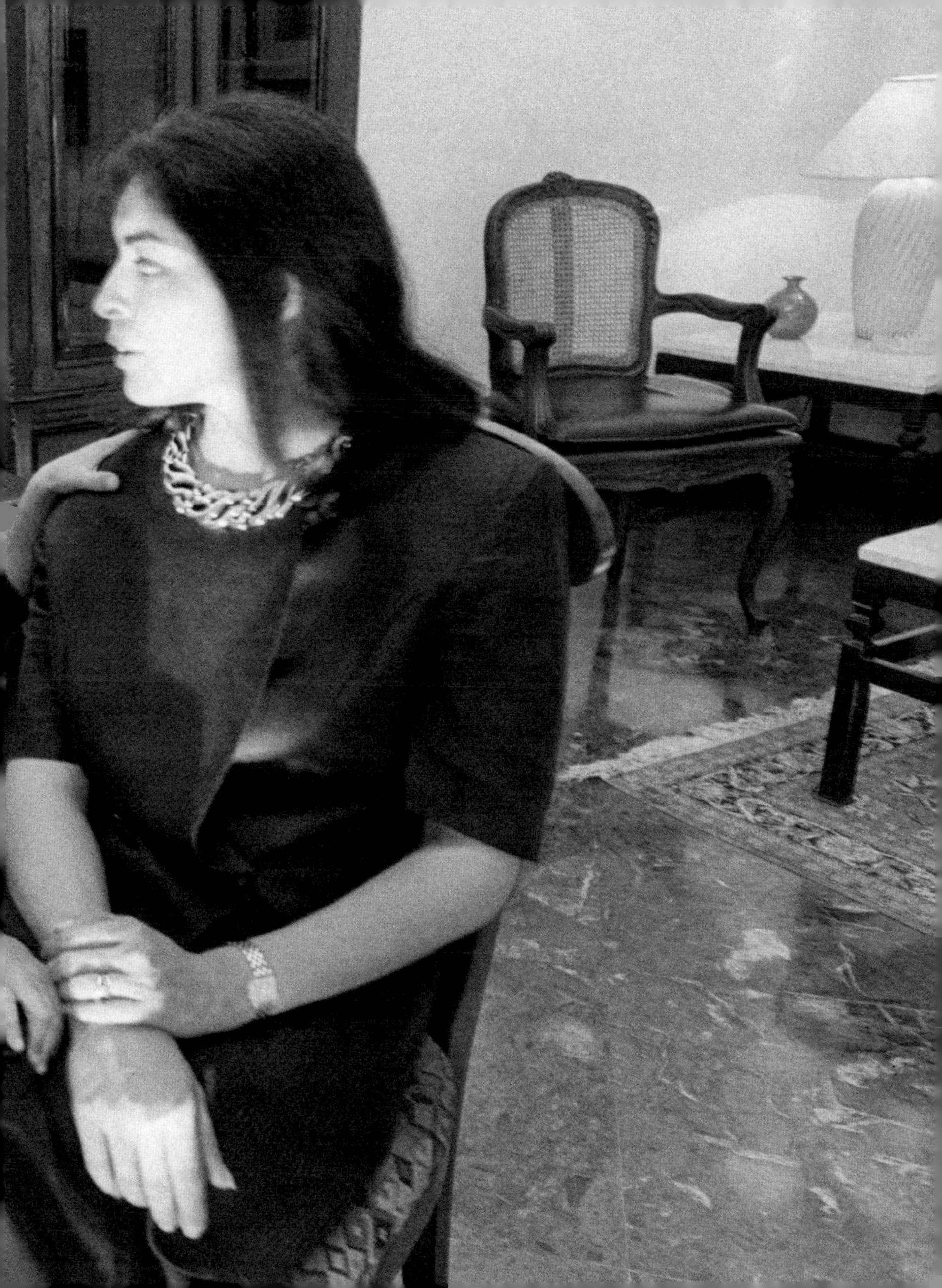

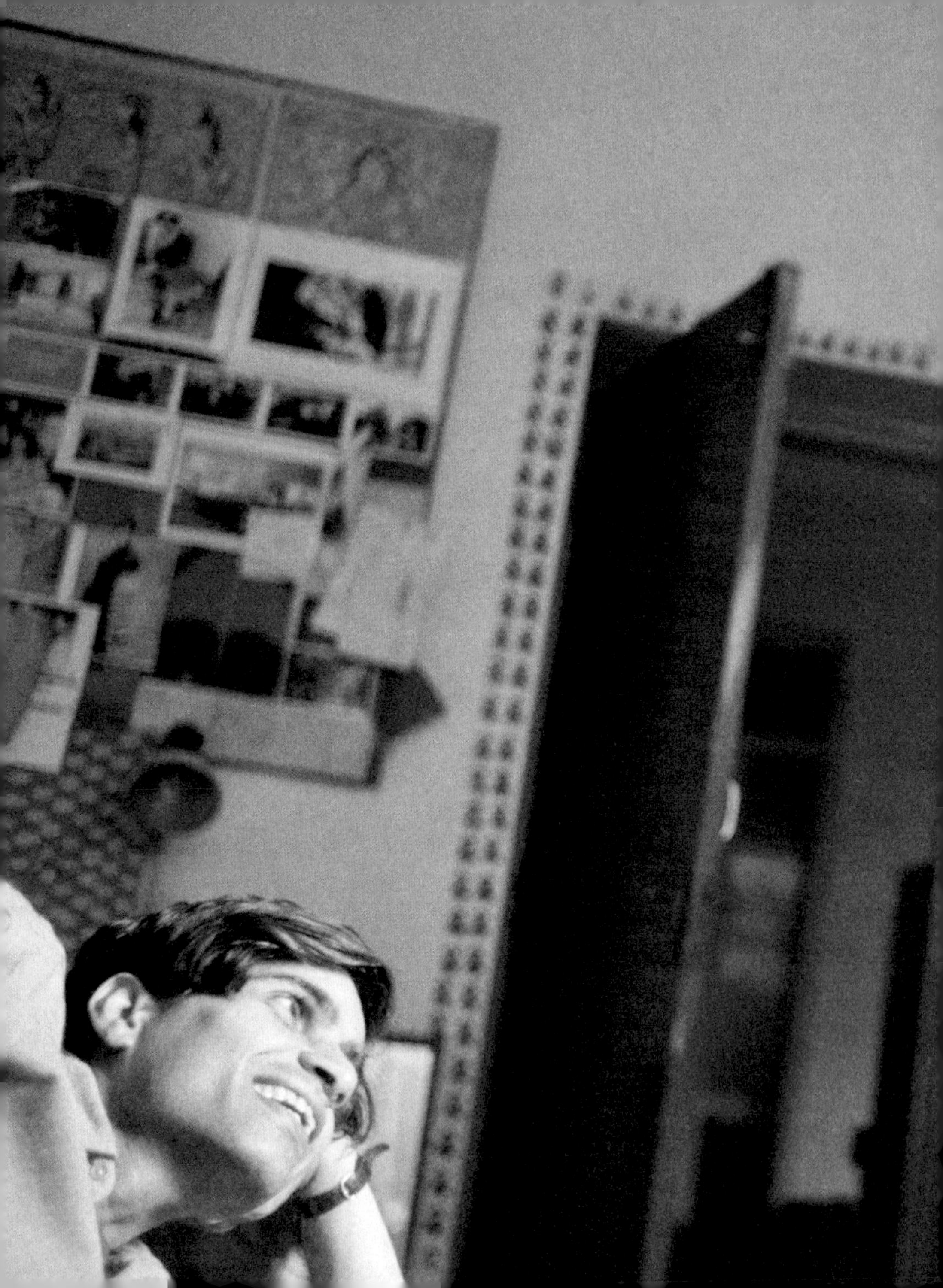

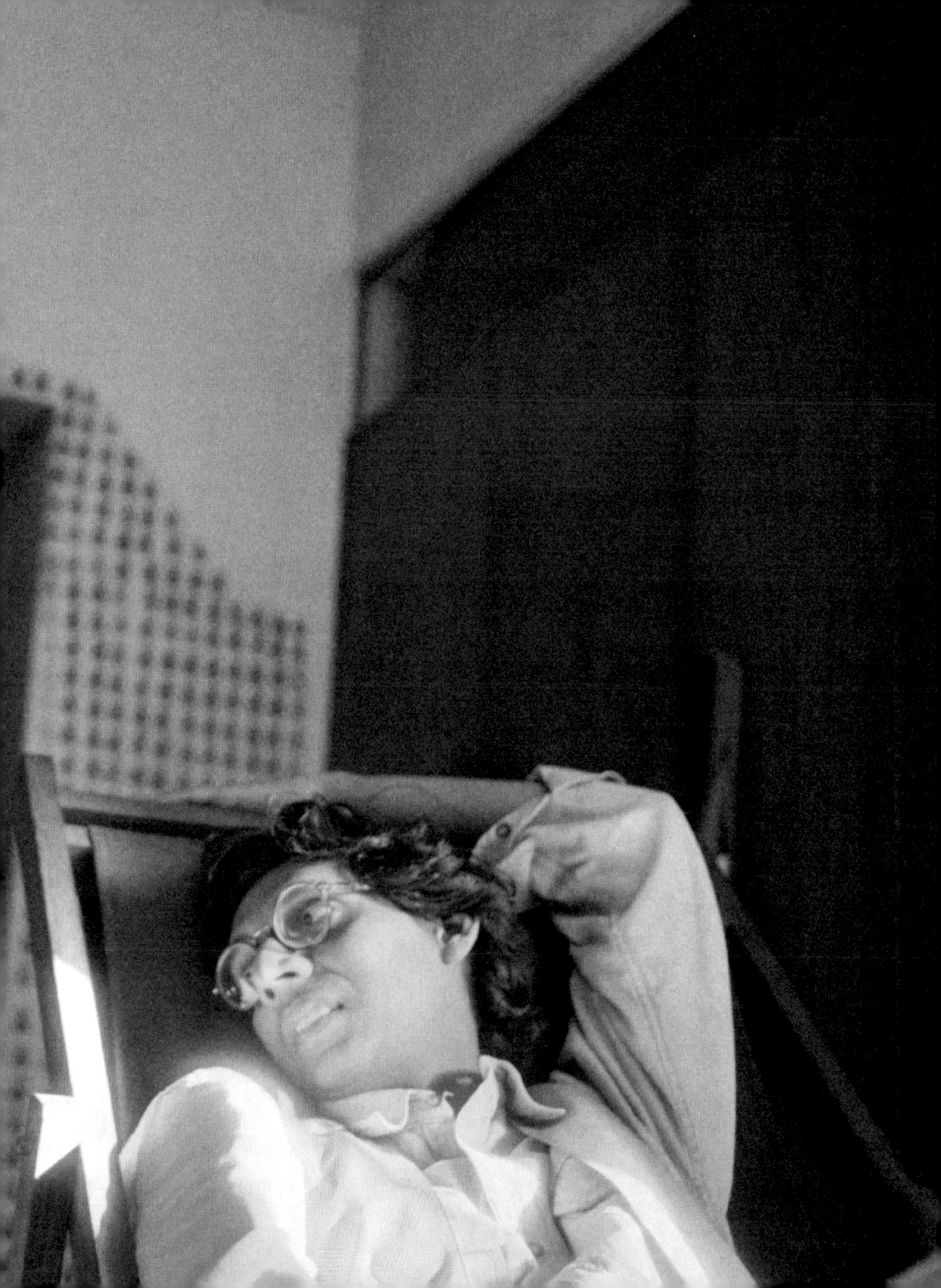

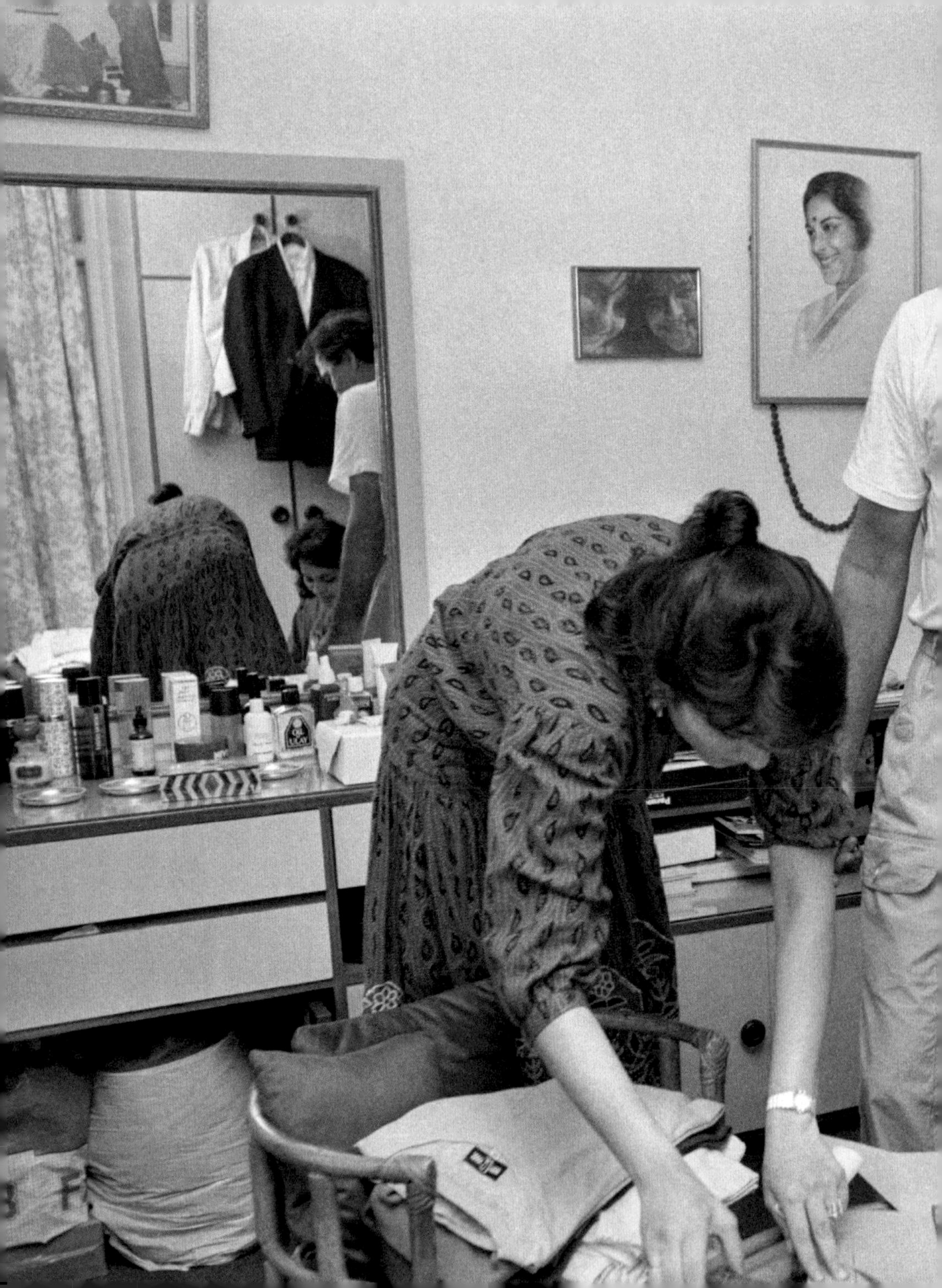

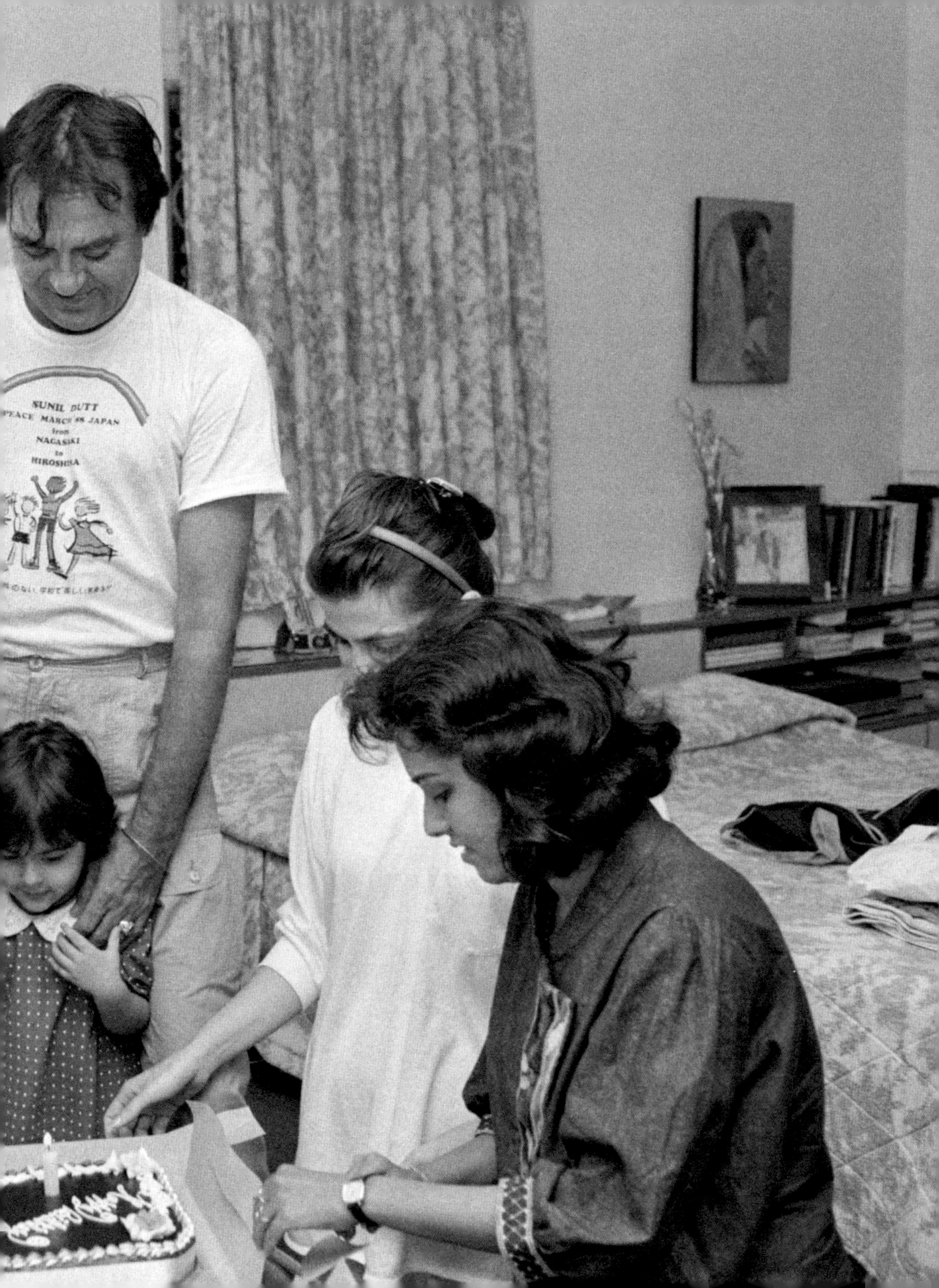
SUNIL DUTT
PEACE MARCH '88 JAPAN
from
NAGASAKI
to
HIROSHIMA

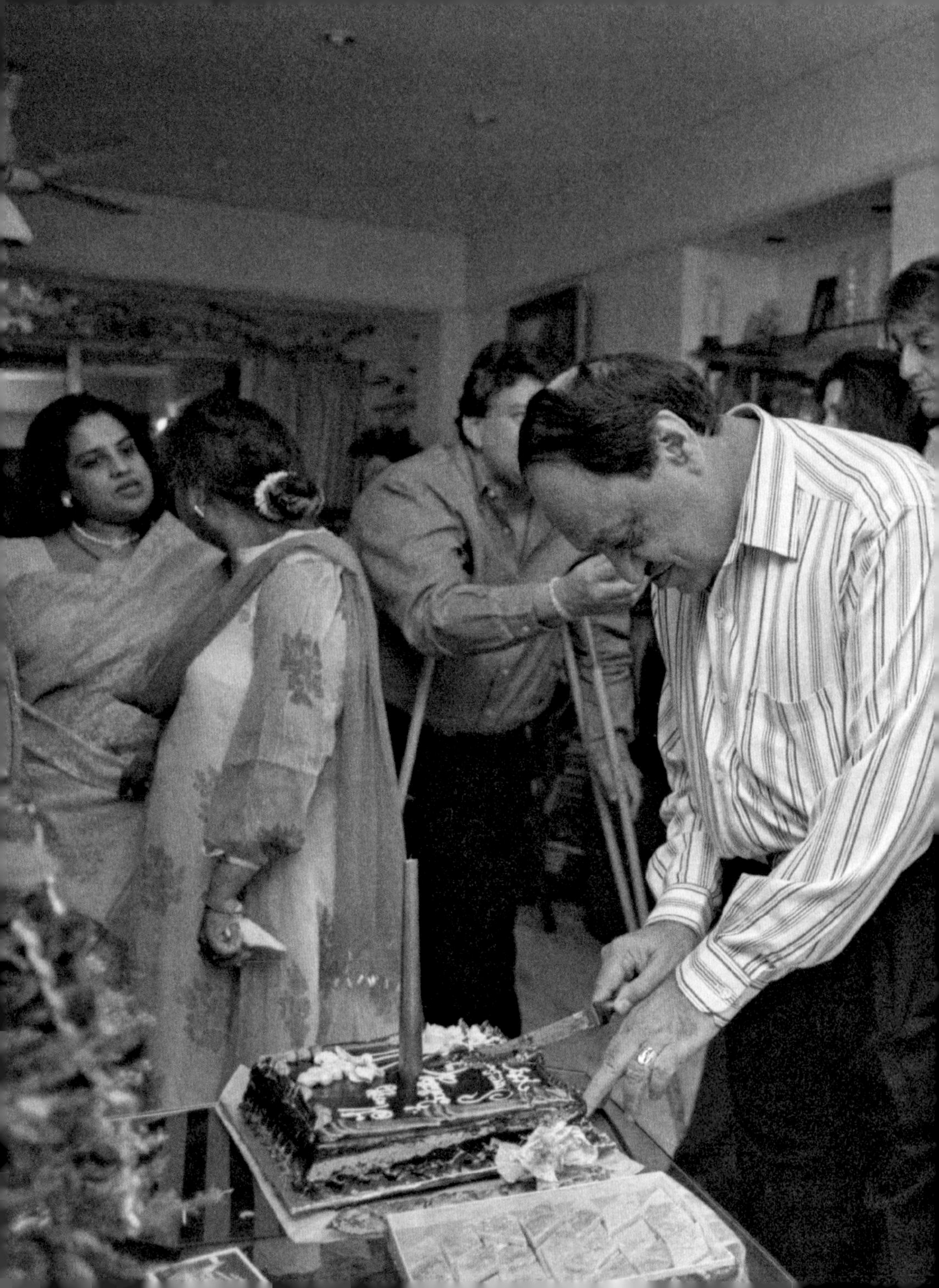

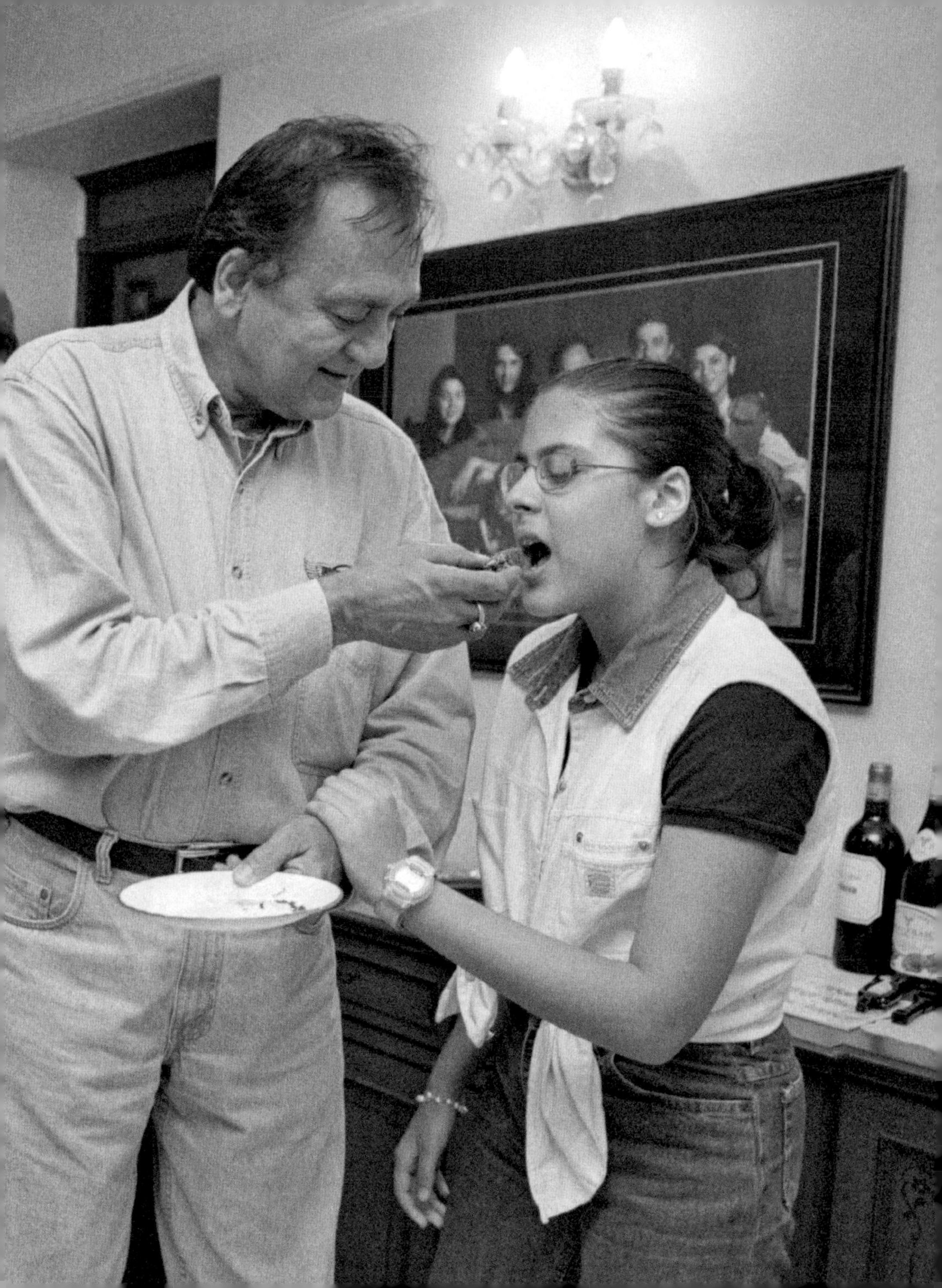

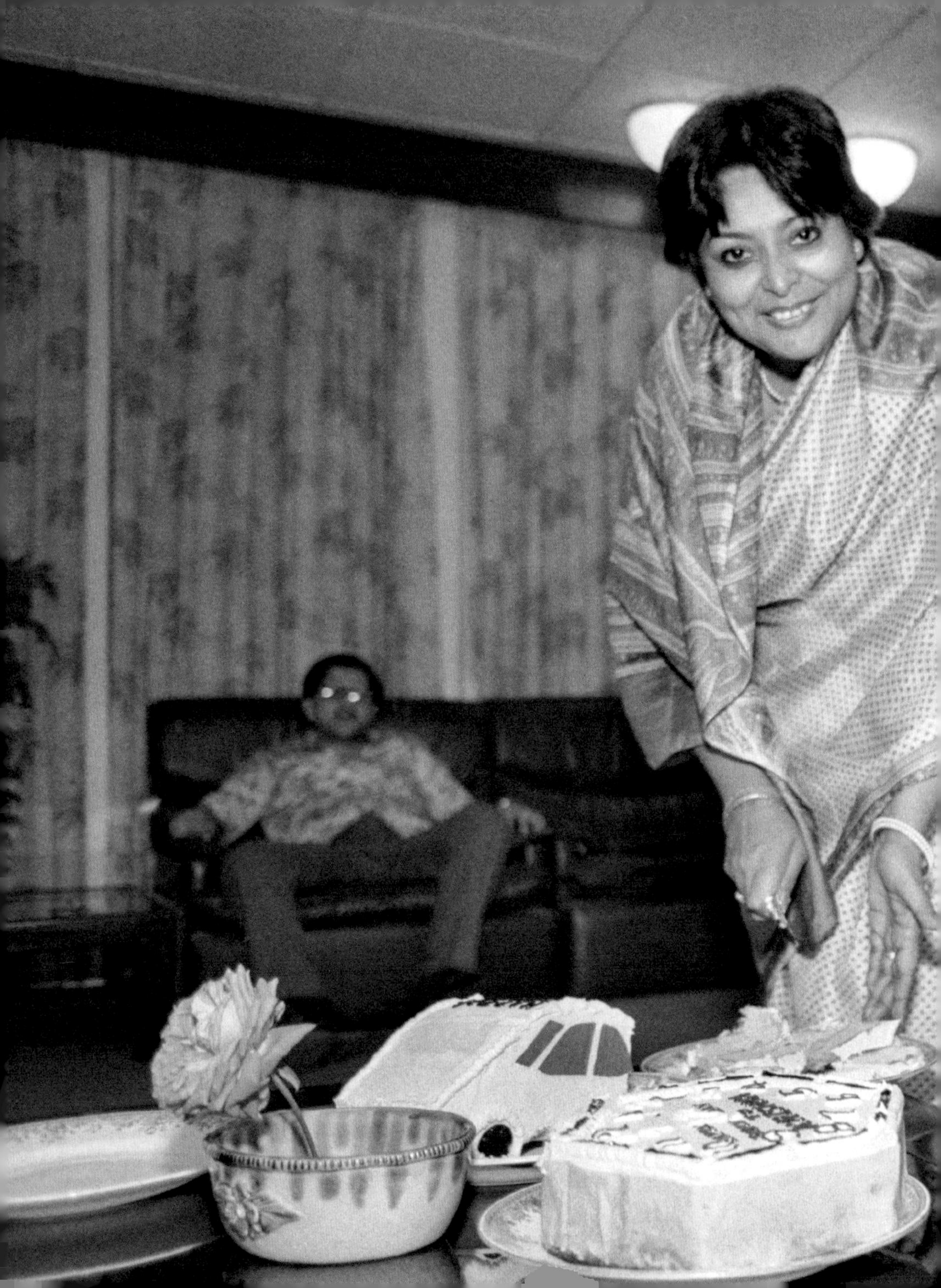

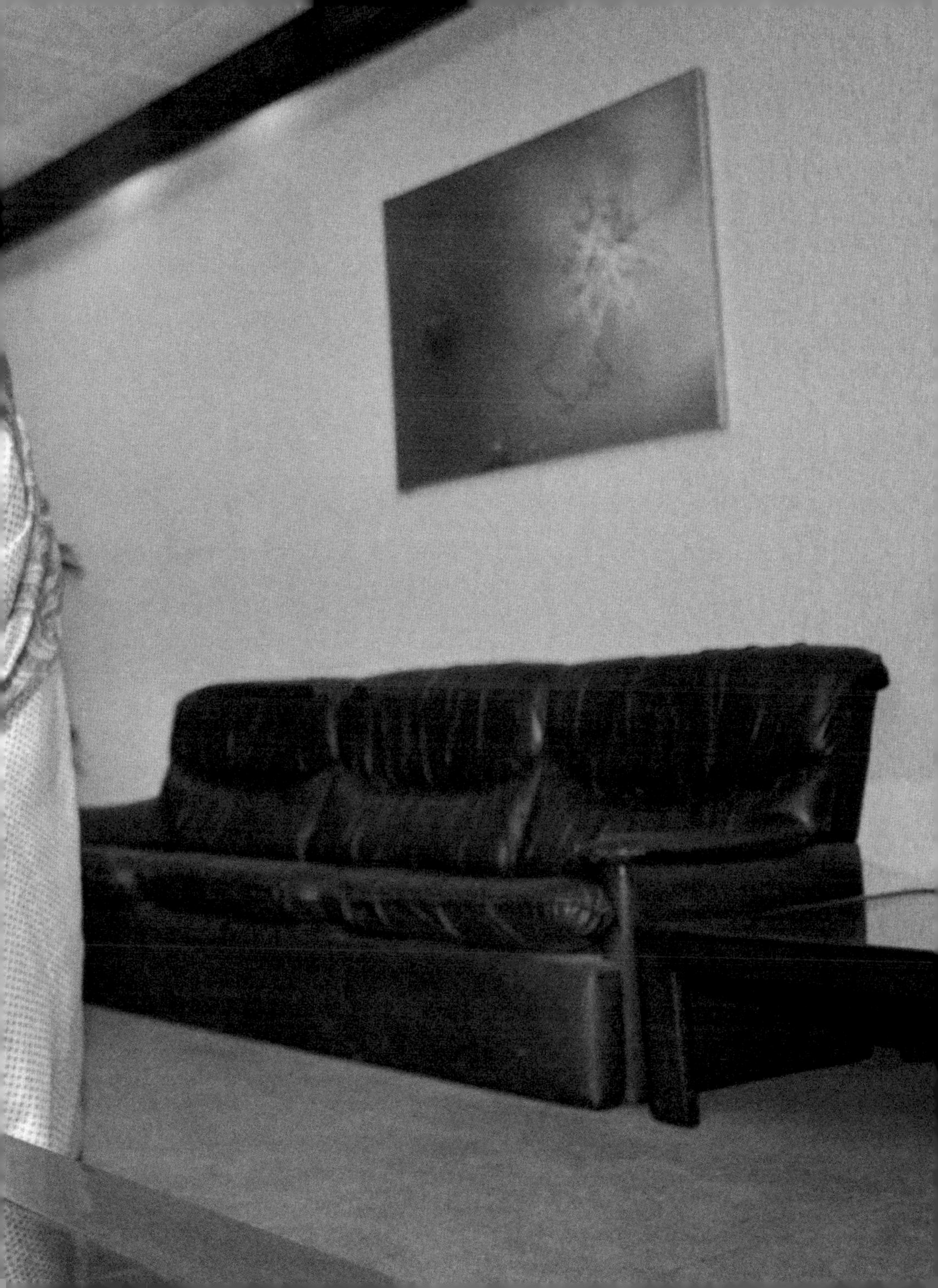

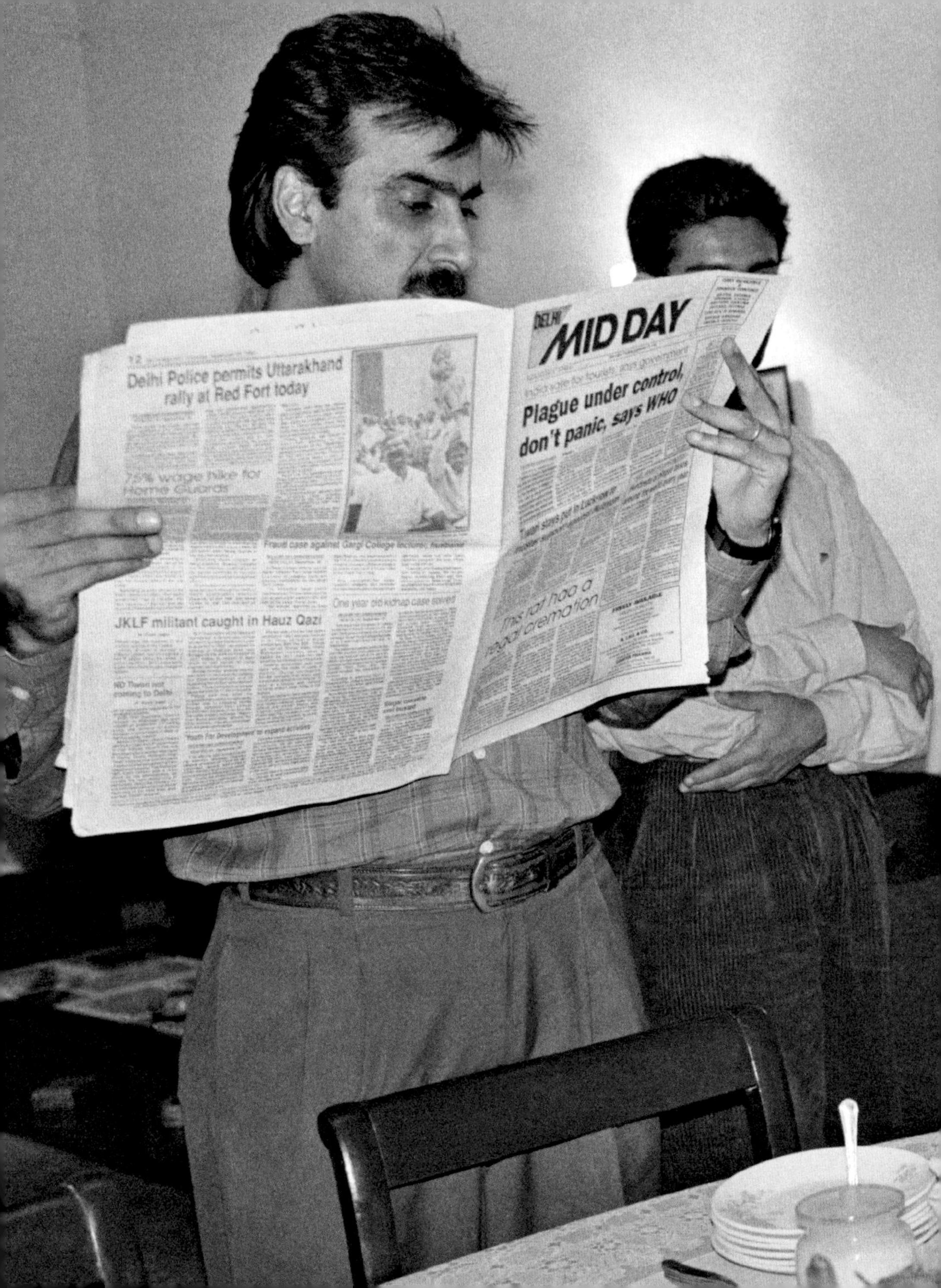
12
Delhi Police permits Uttarakhand
rally at Red Fort today
75% wage hike for
Home Guards
Fraud case against Gargi College lecturer, husband
One year old kidnap case solved
JKLF militant caught in Hauz Qazi
ND Tiwari not coming to Delhi
DELHI MID DAY
Plague under control,
don't panic, says WHO

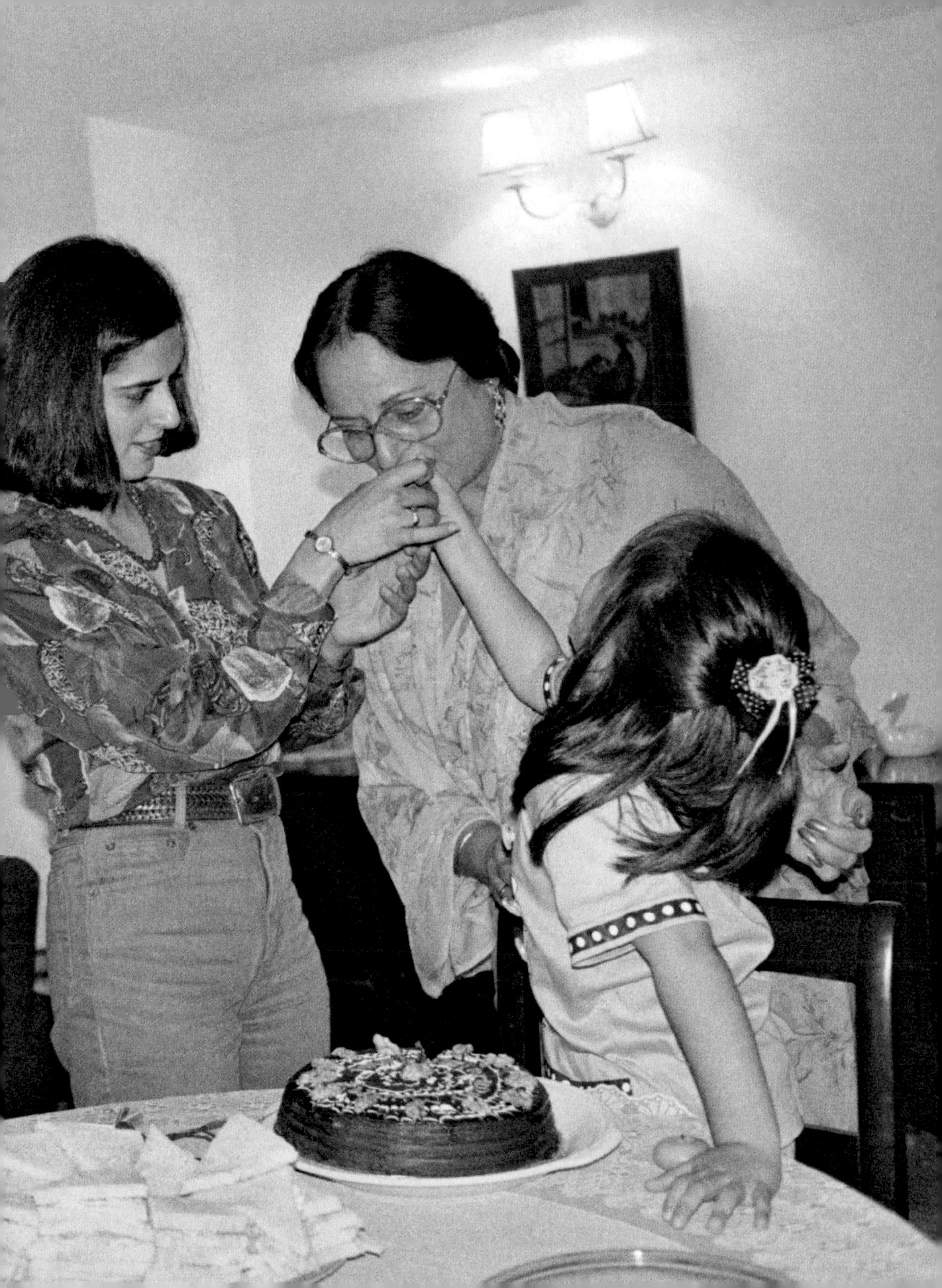

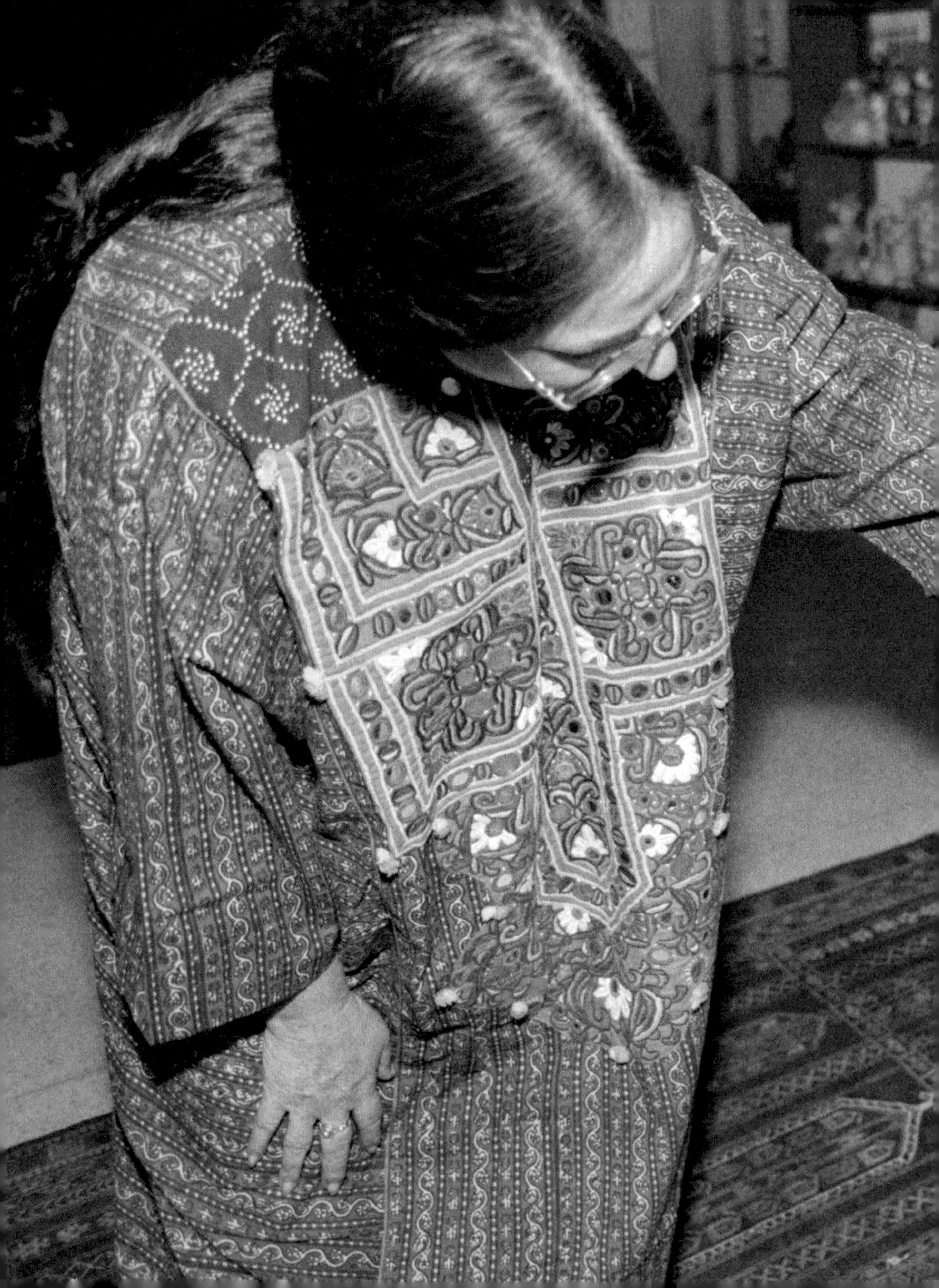

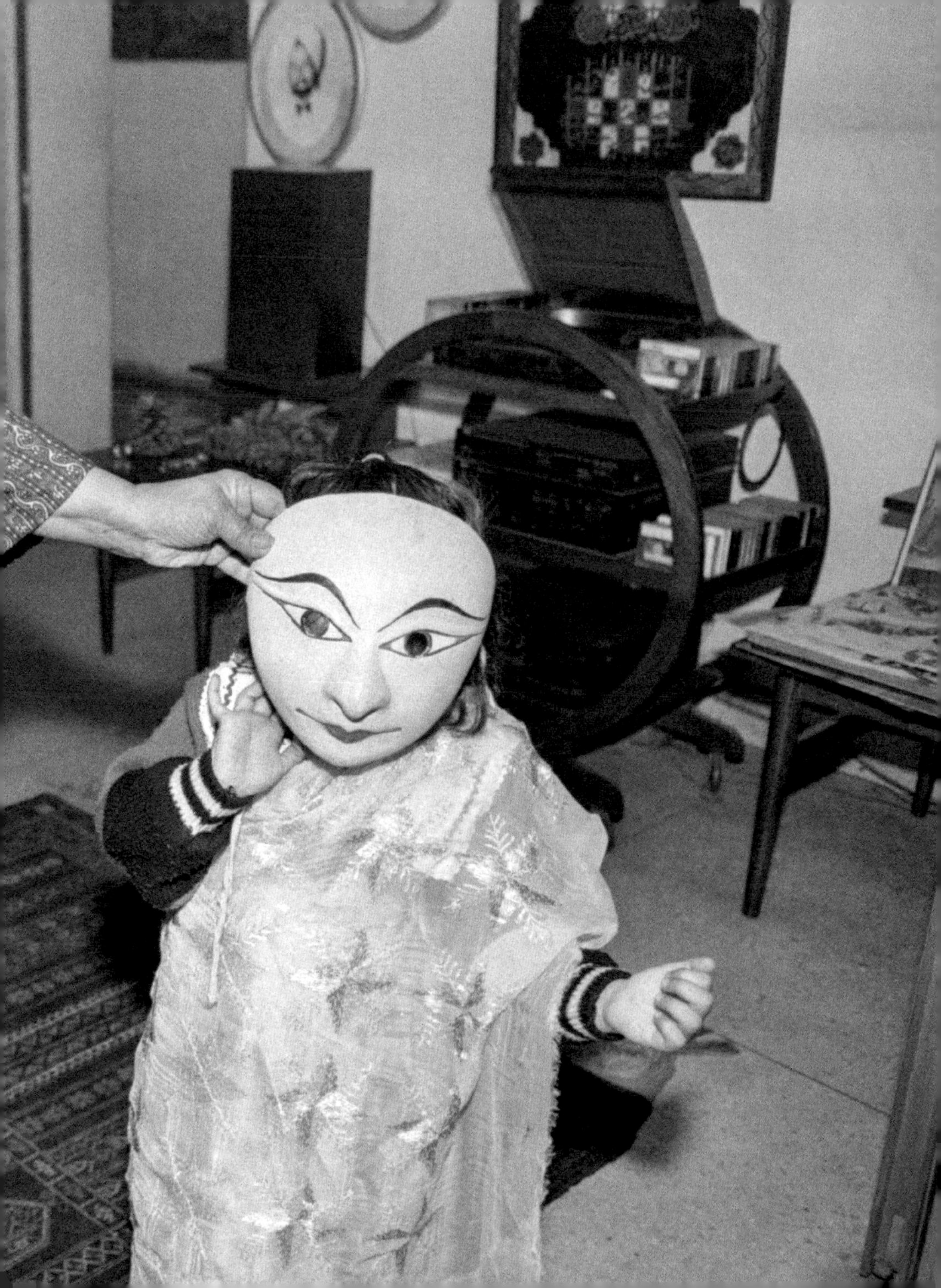

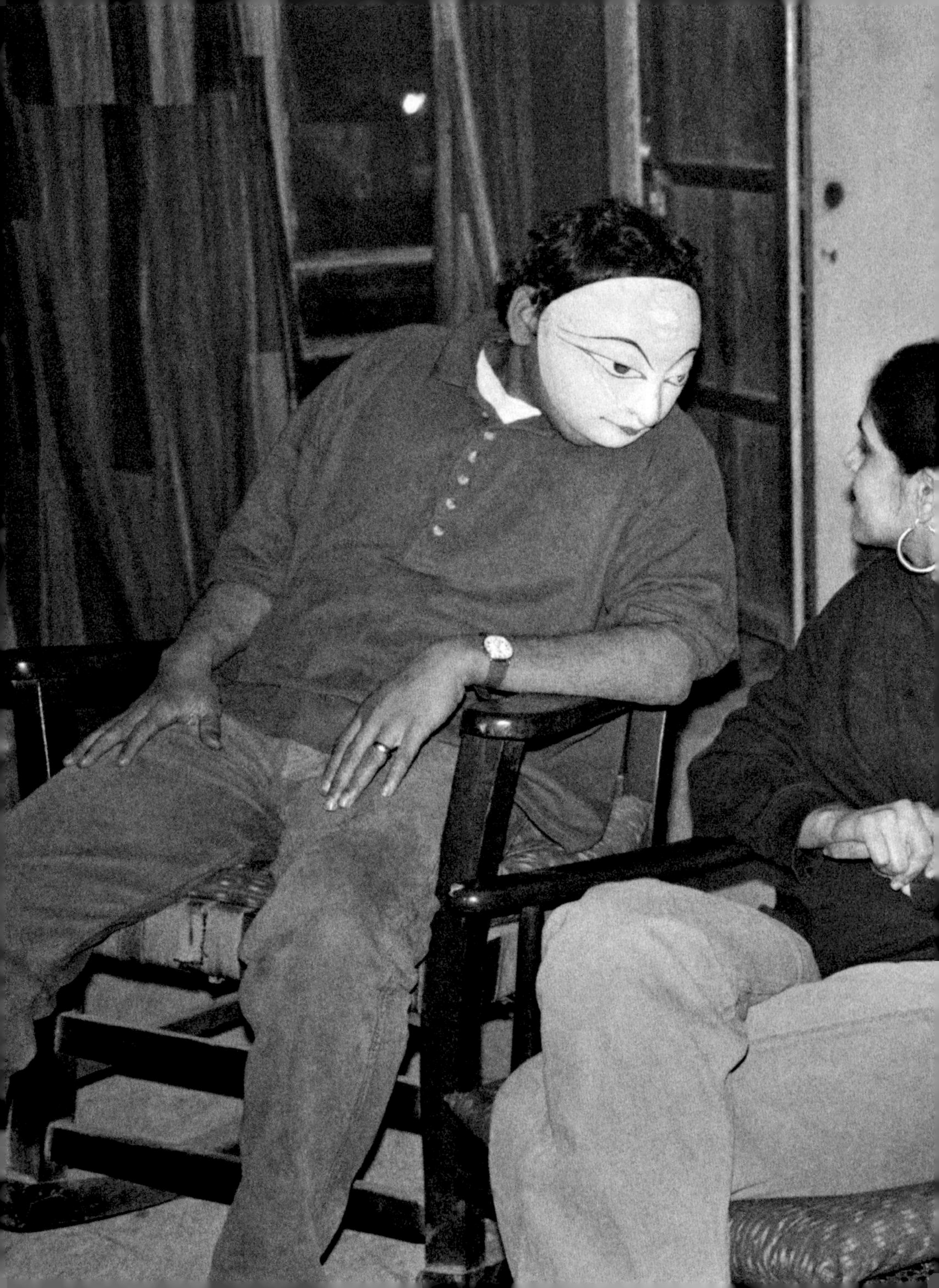

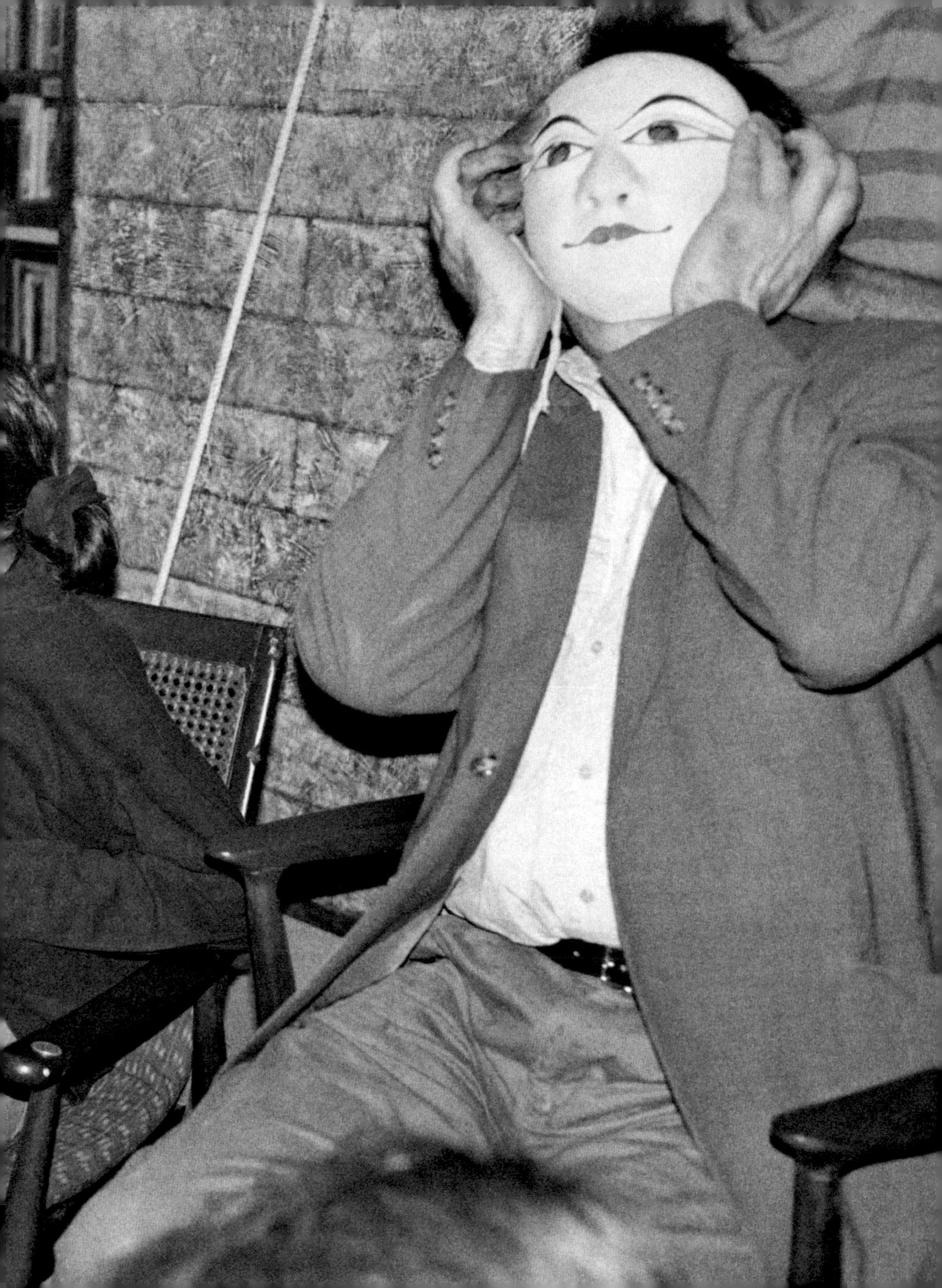

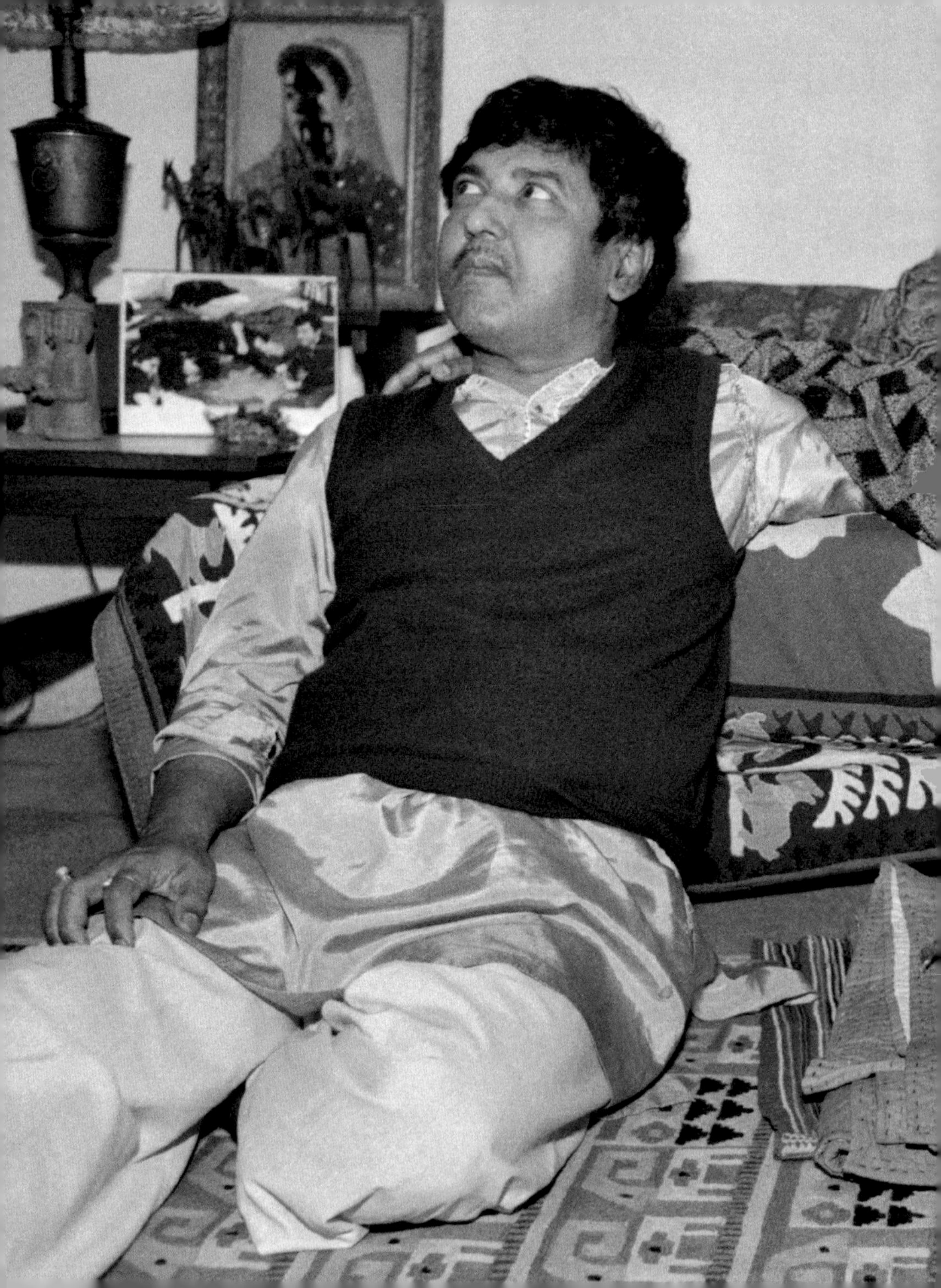

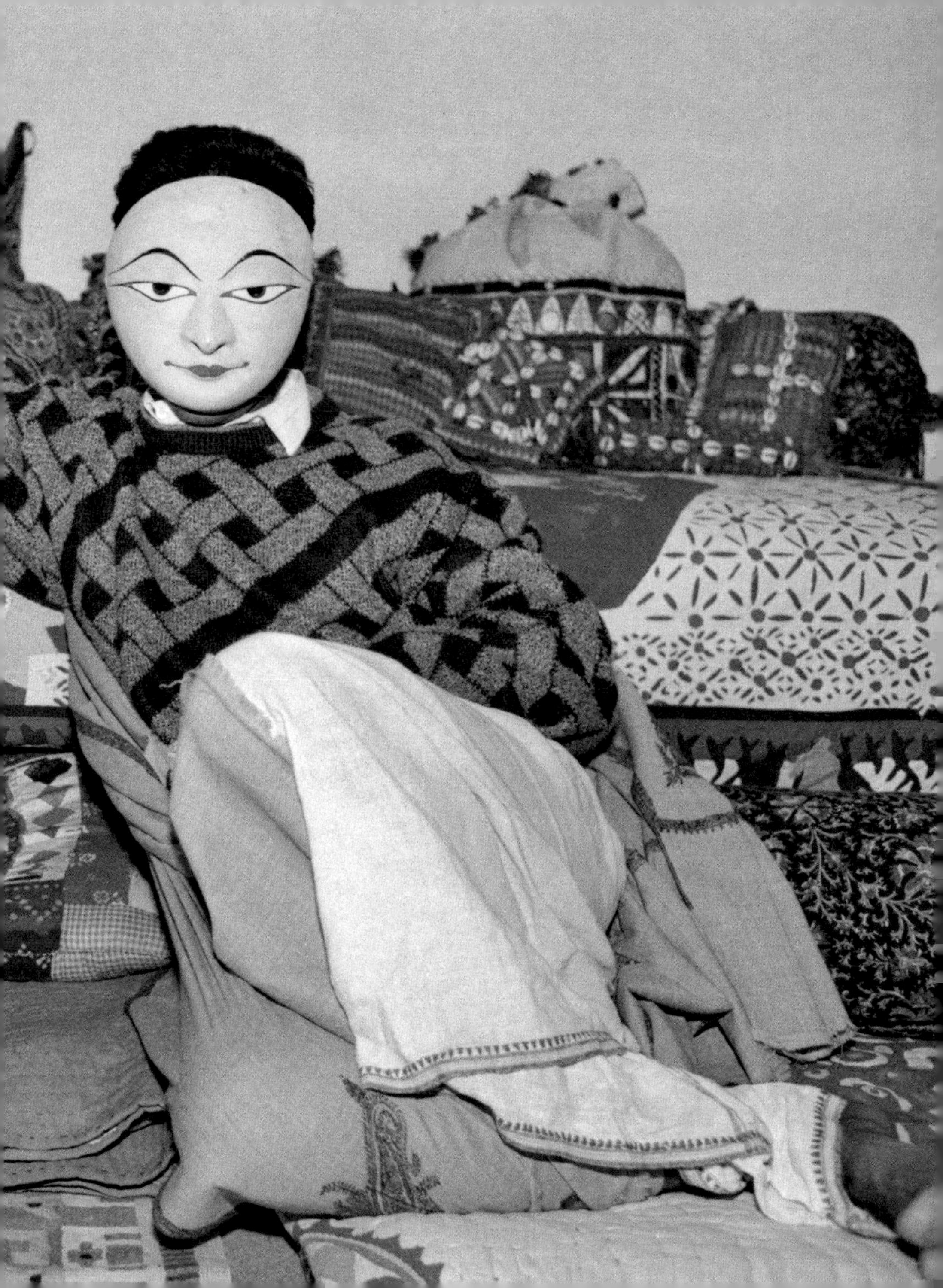

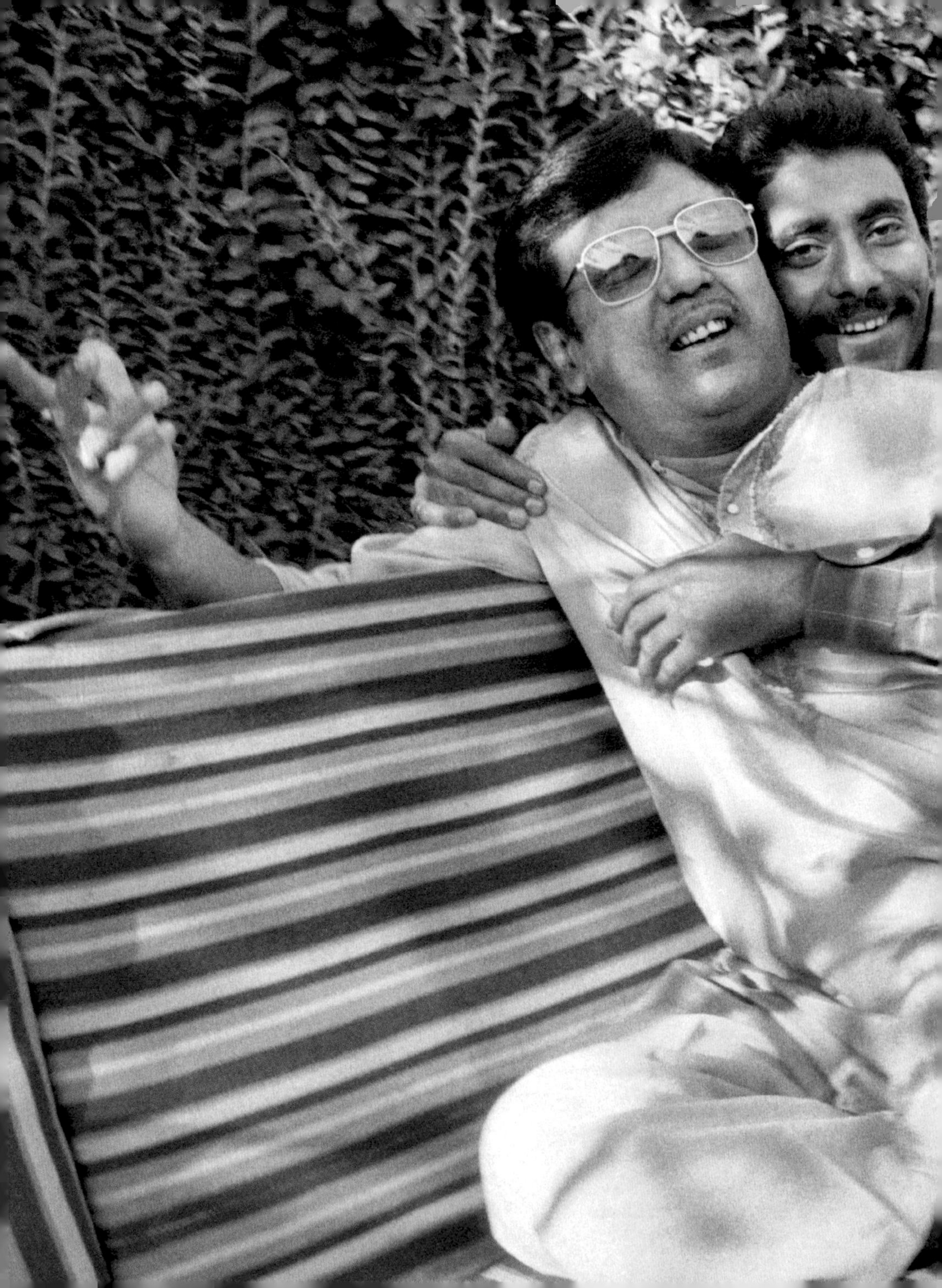

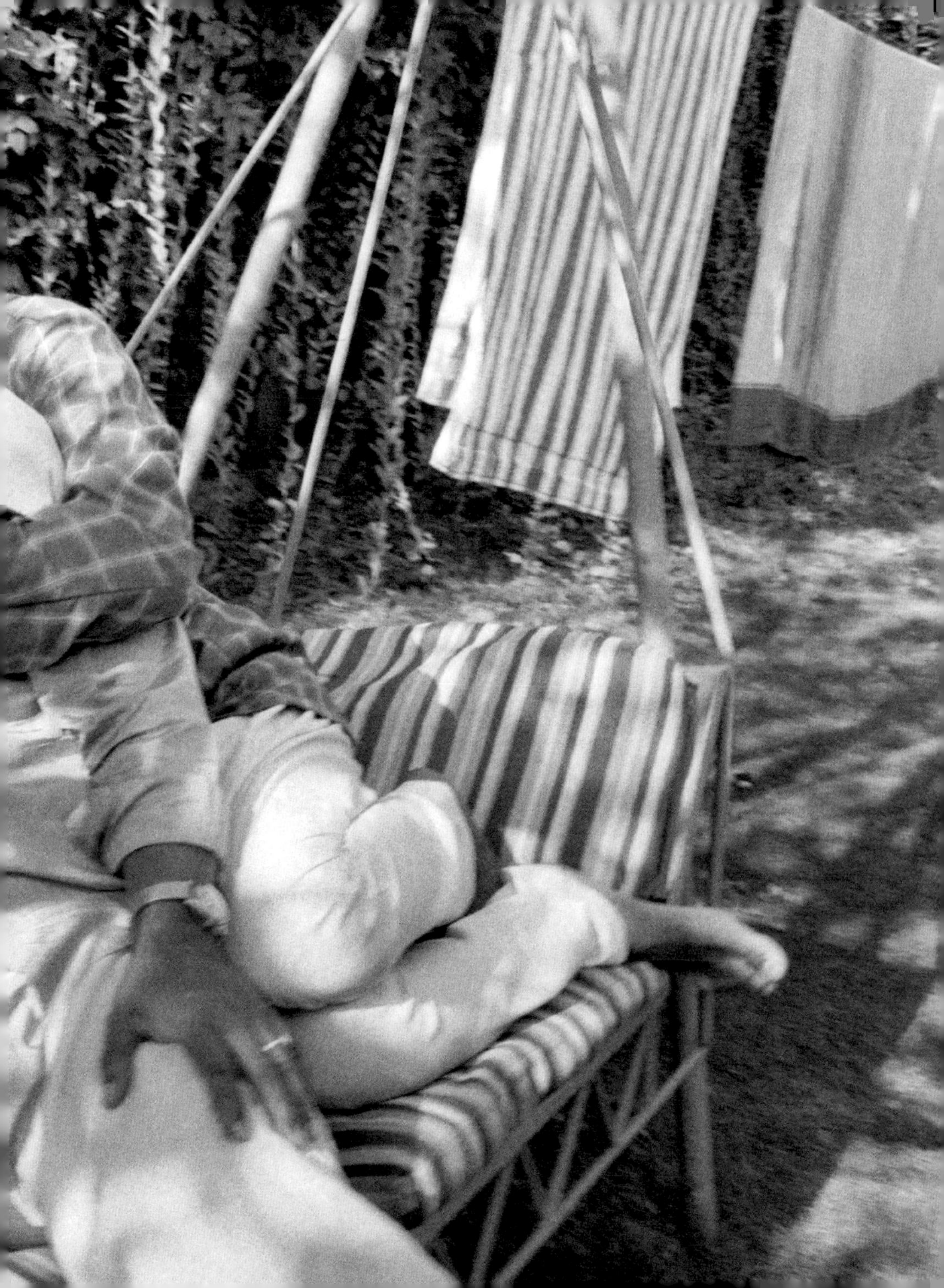

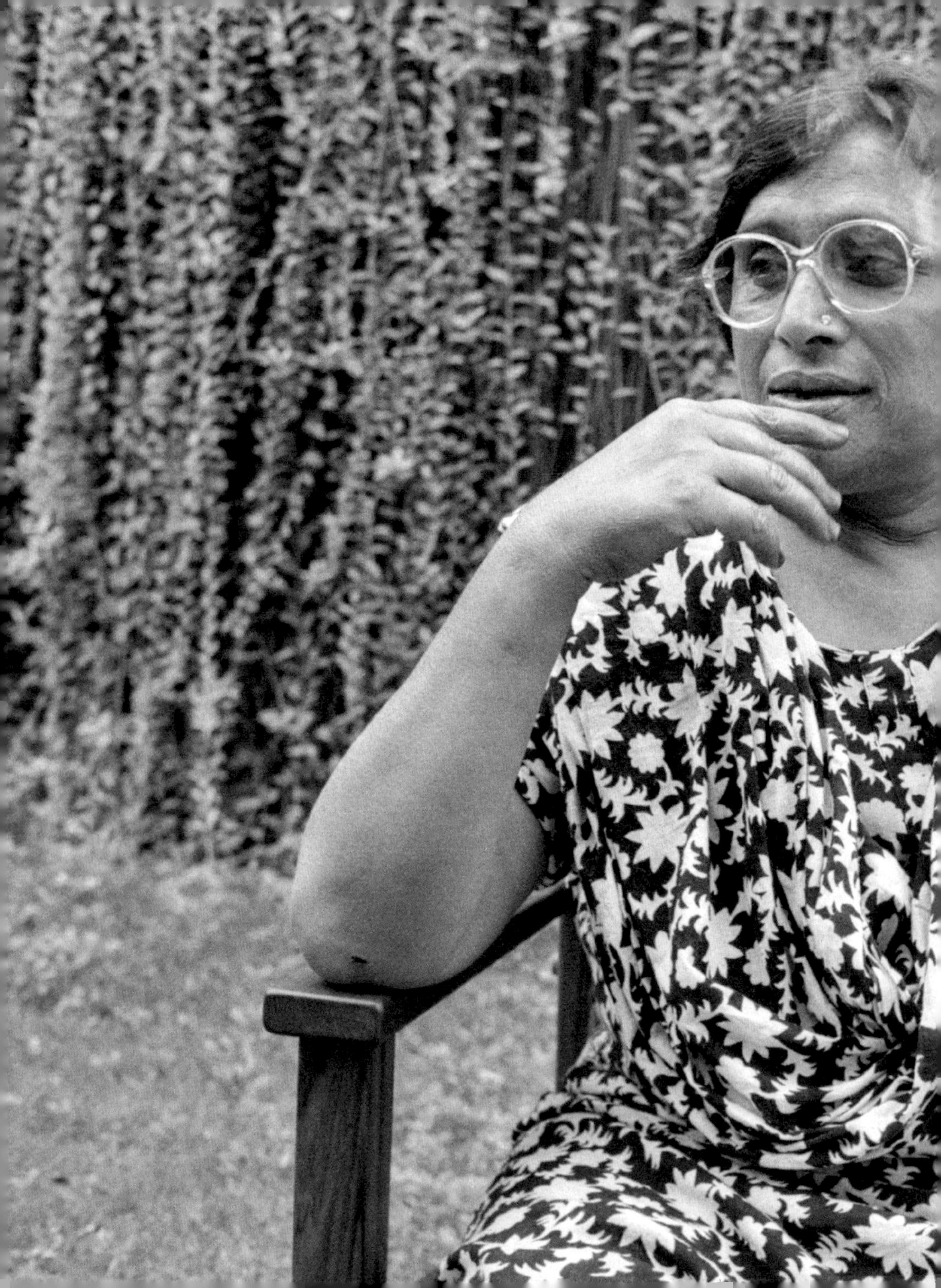

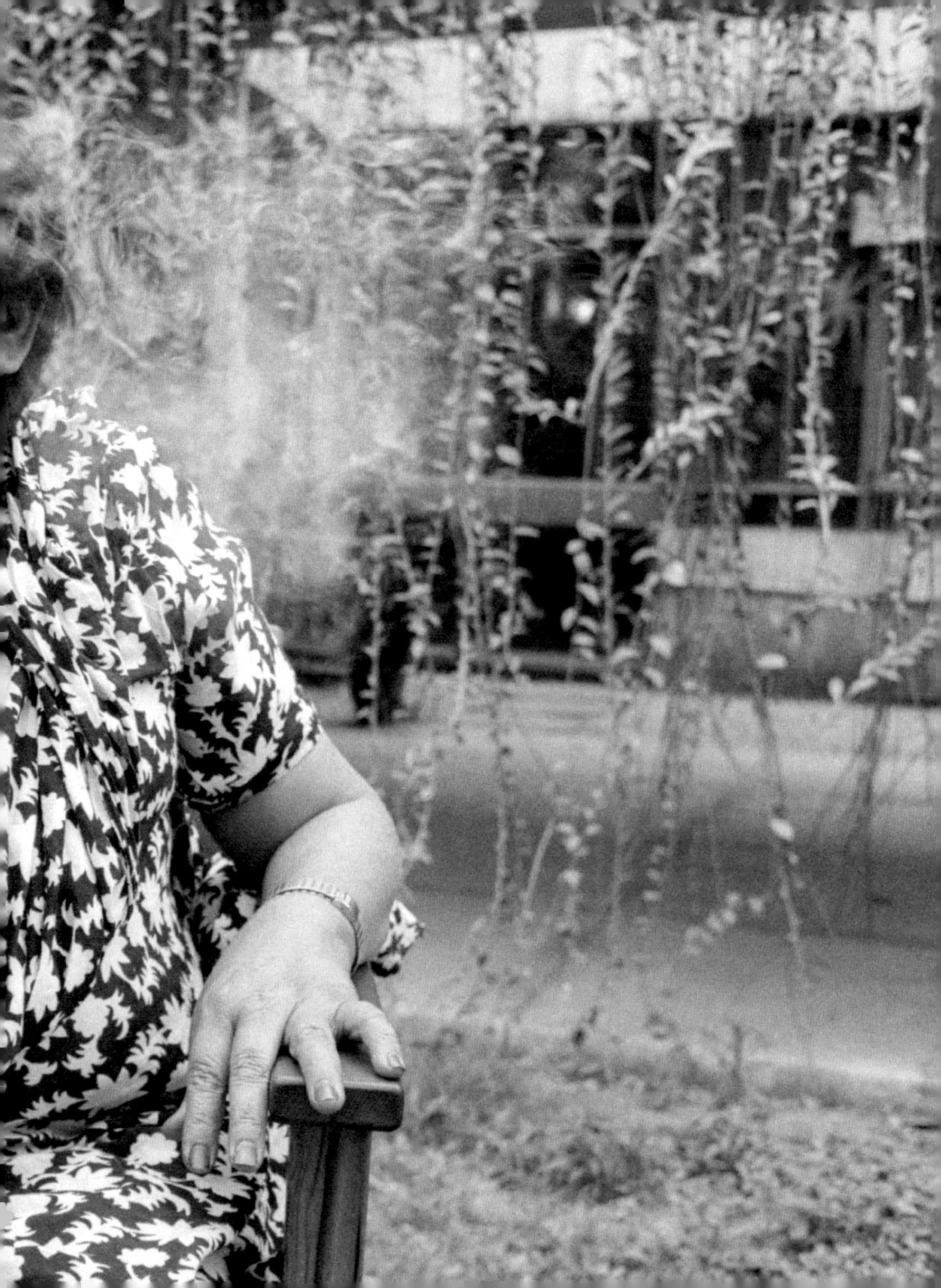

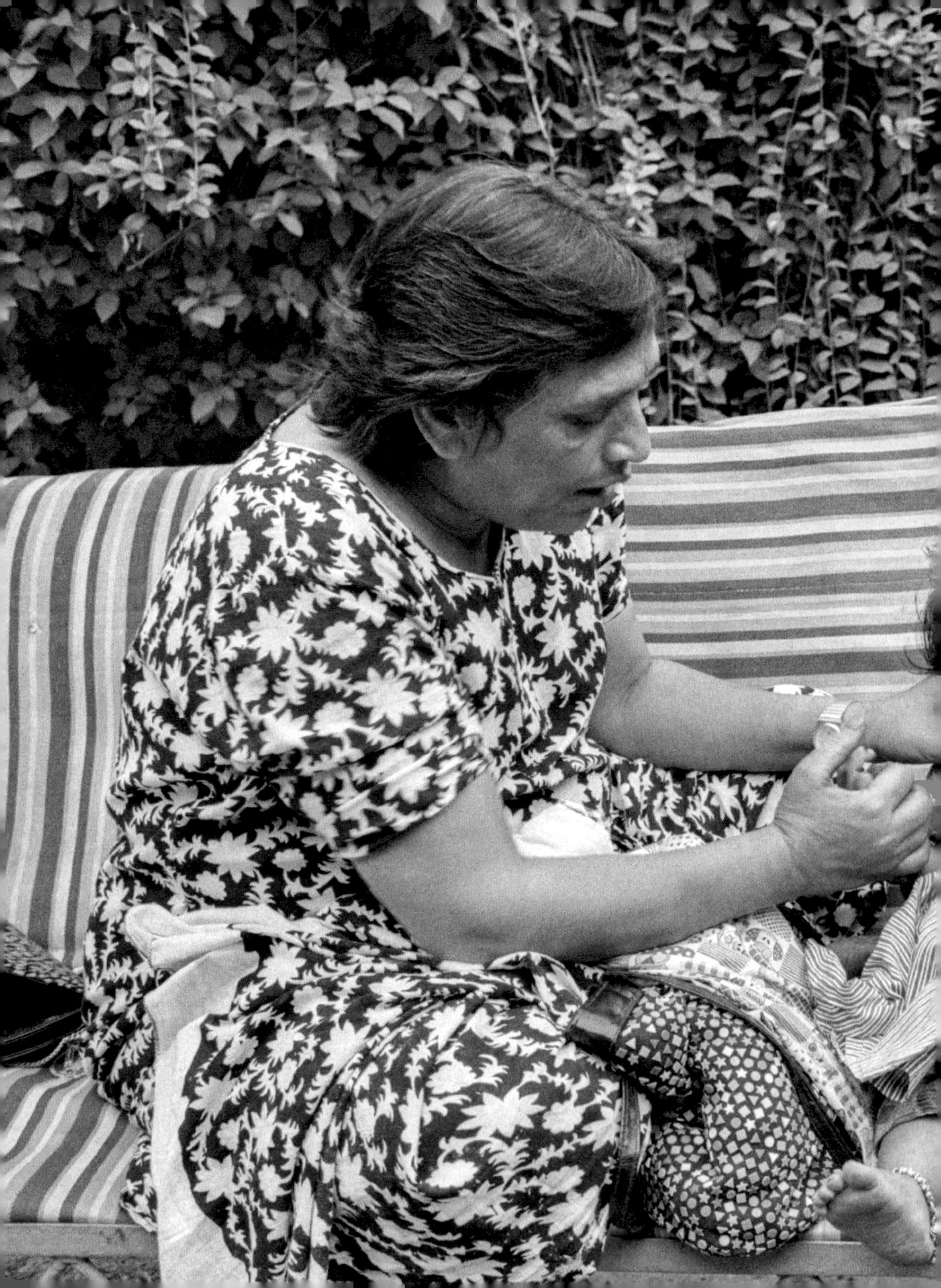

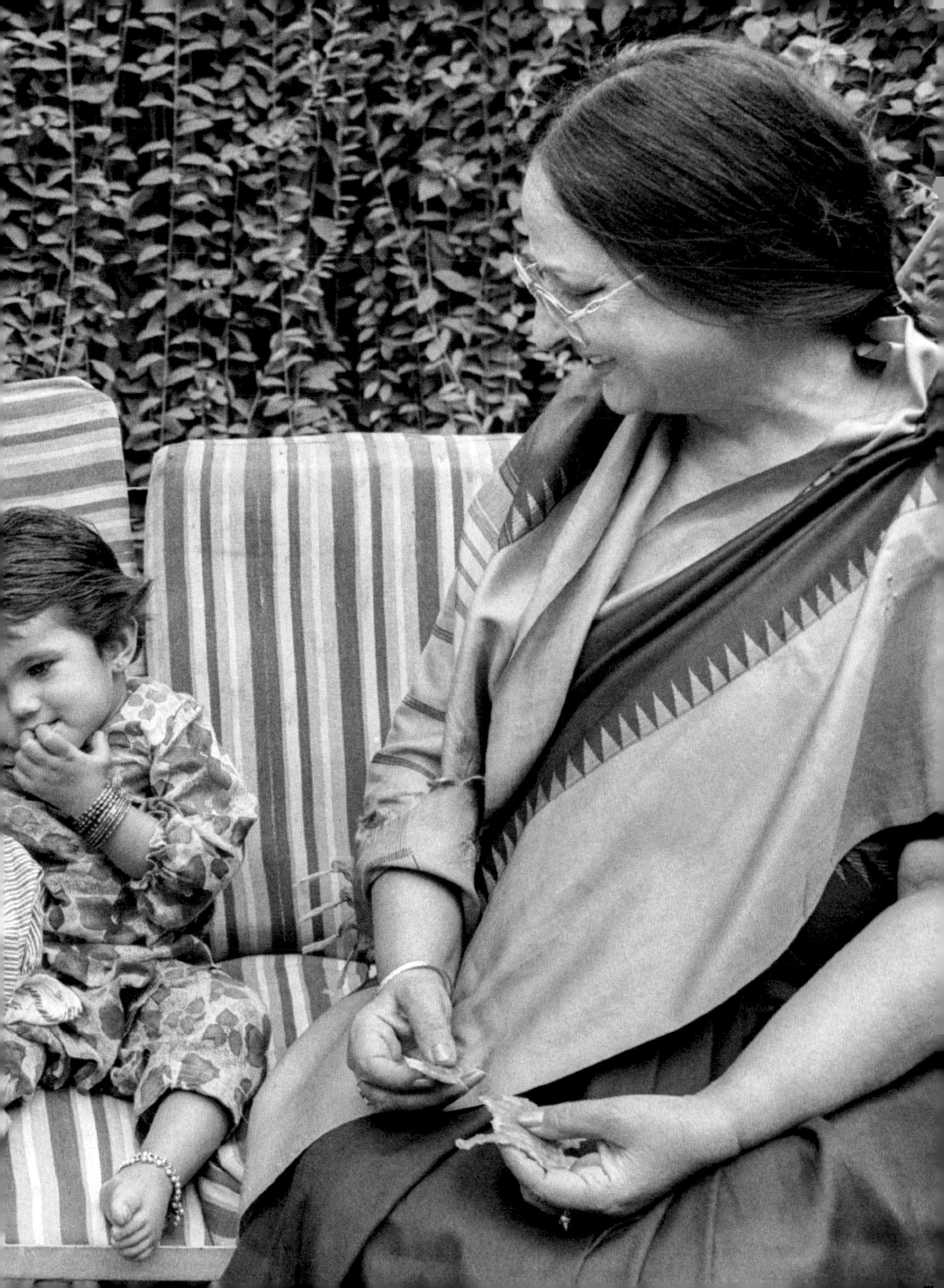

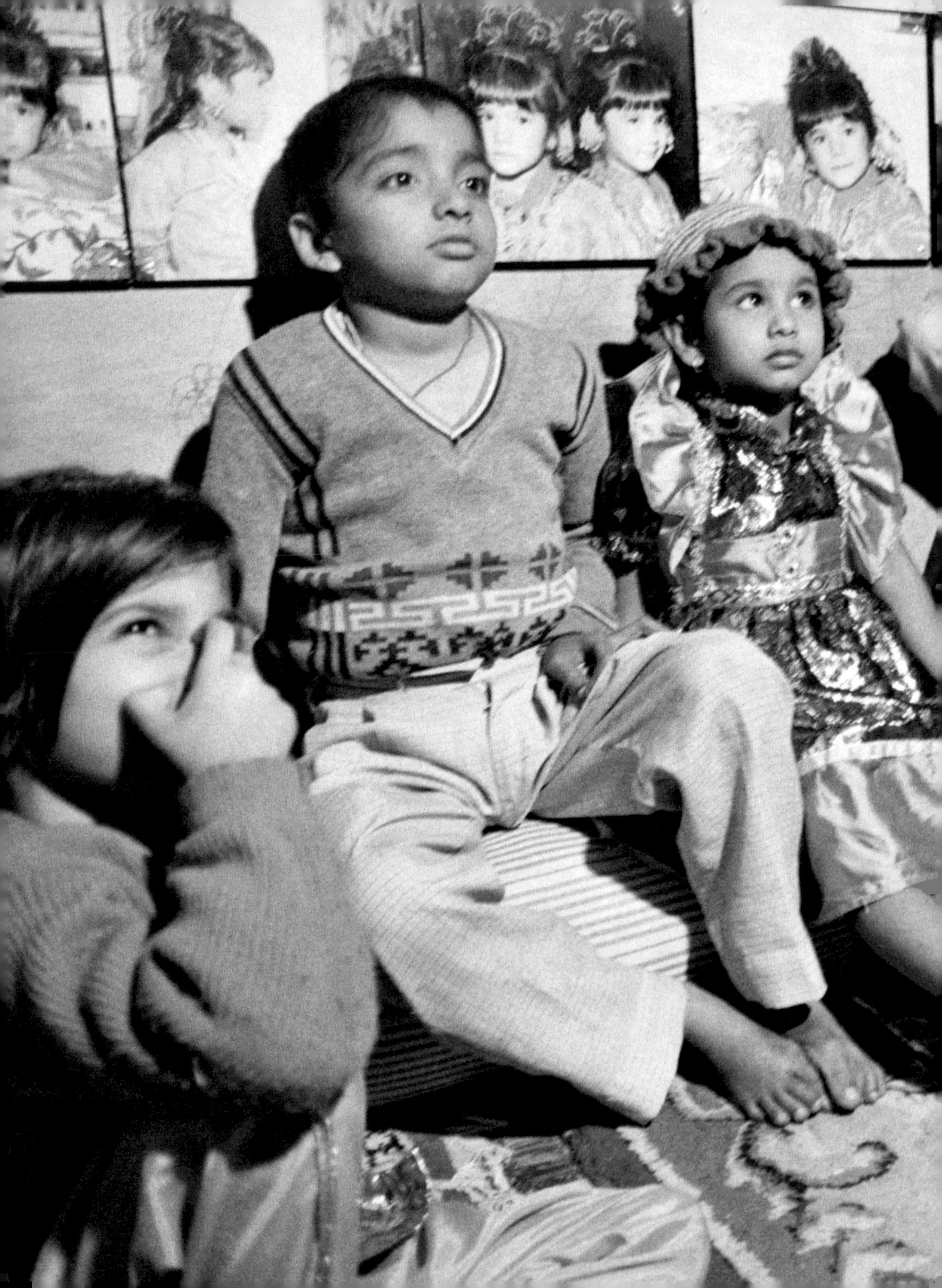

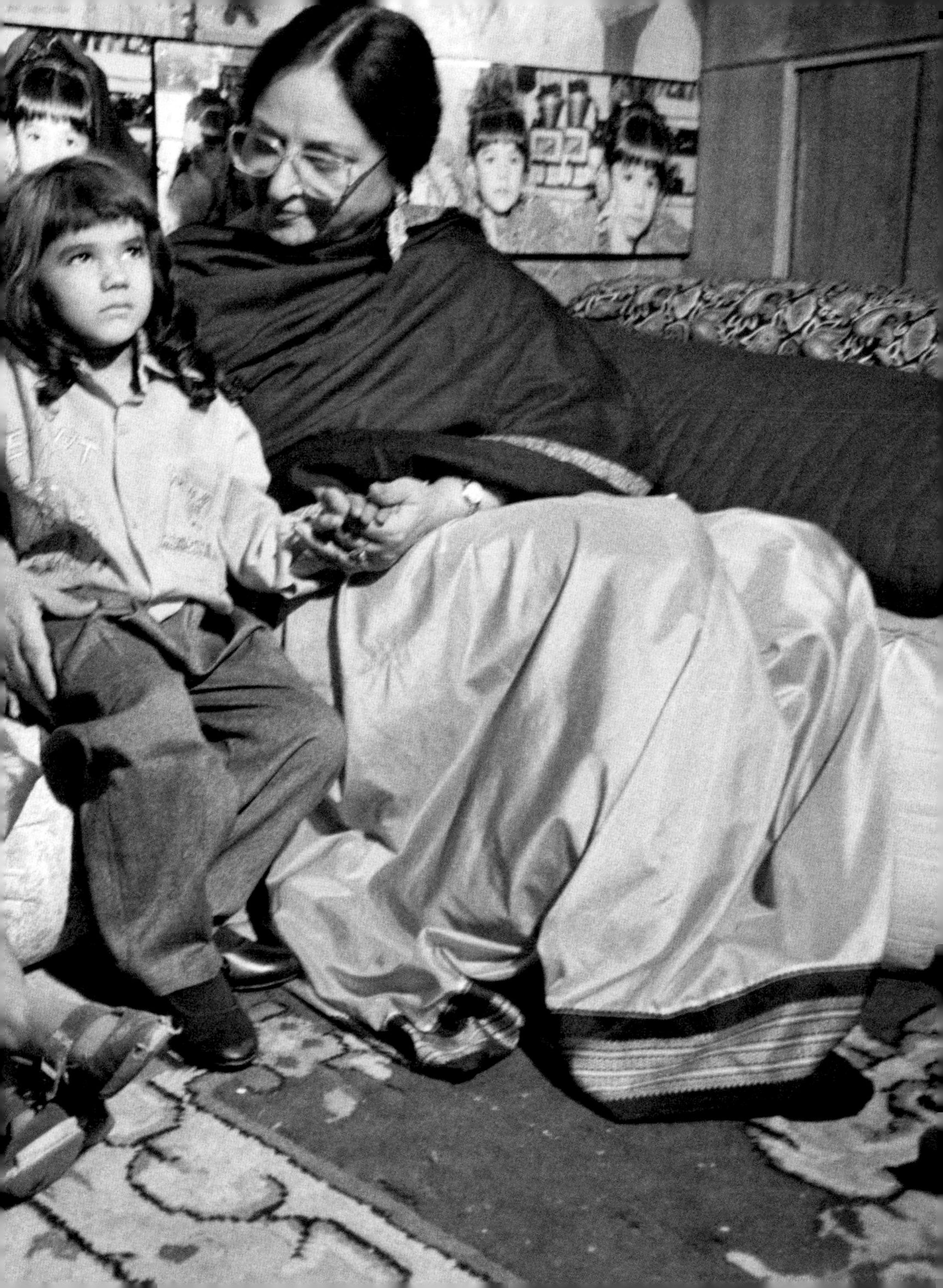

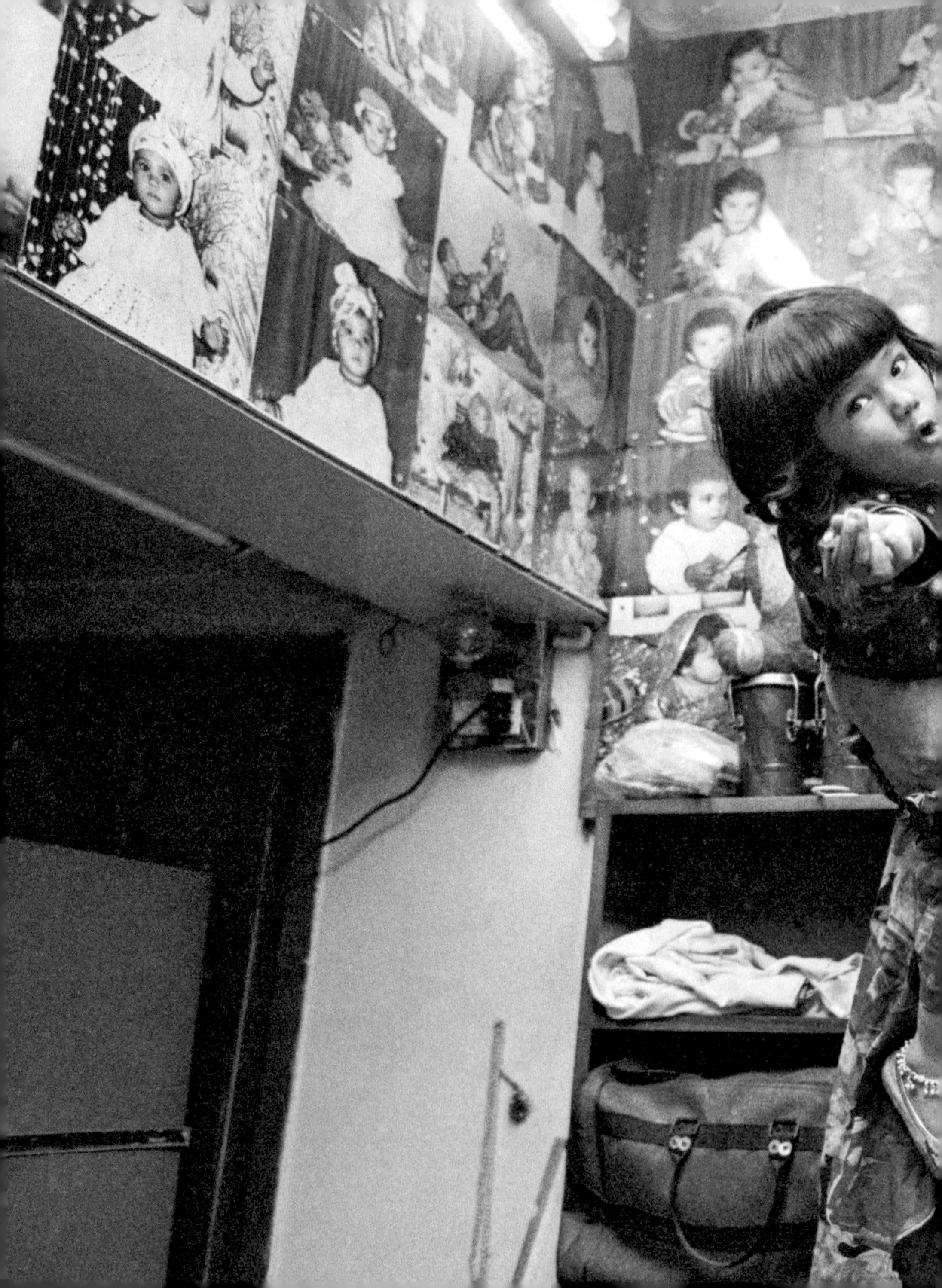

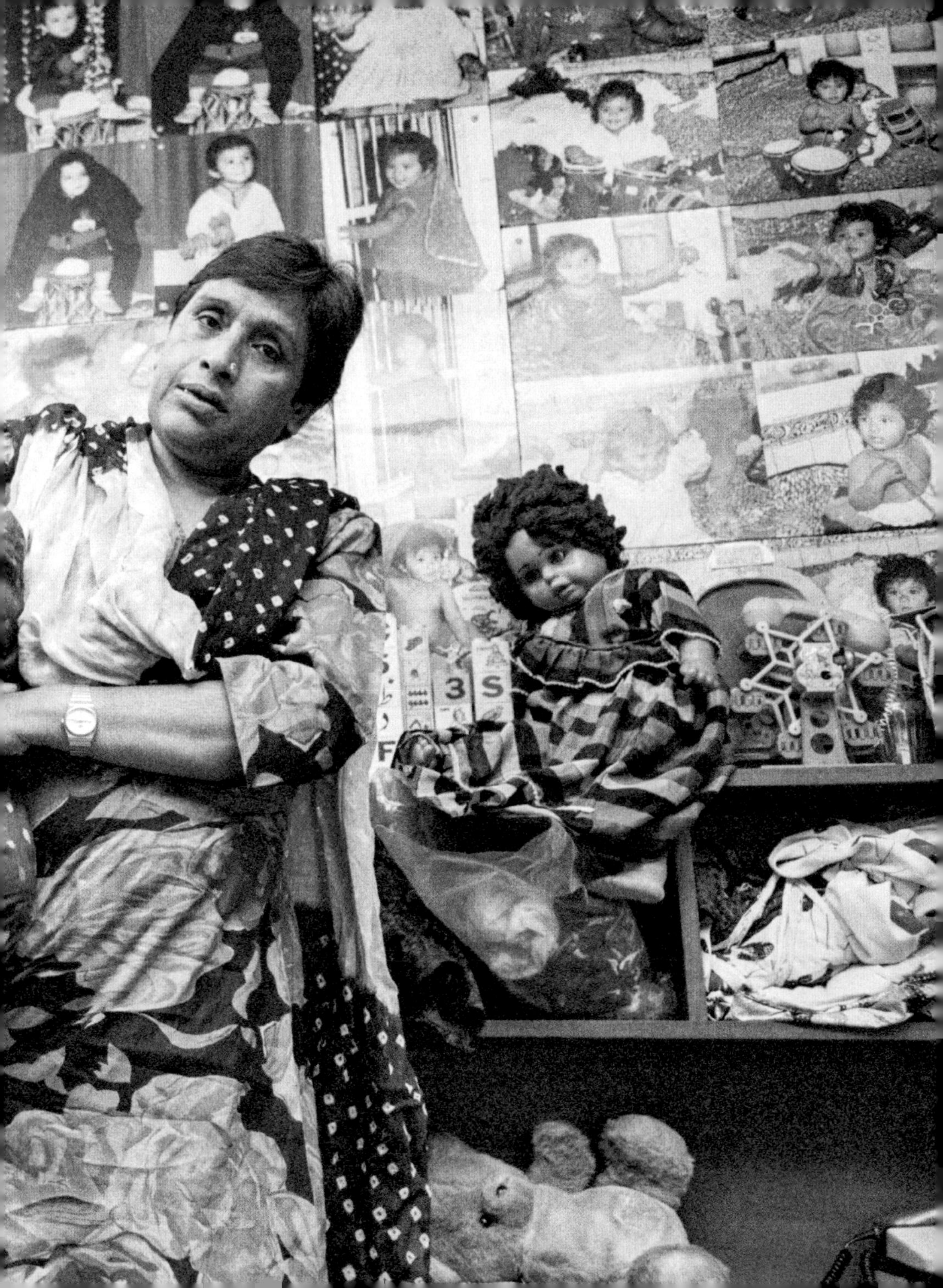

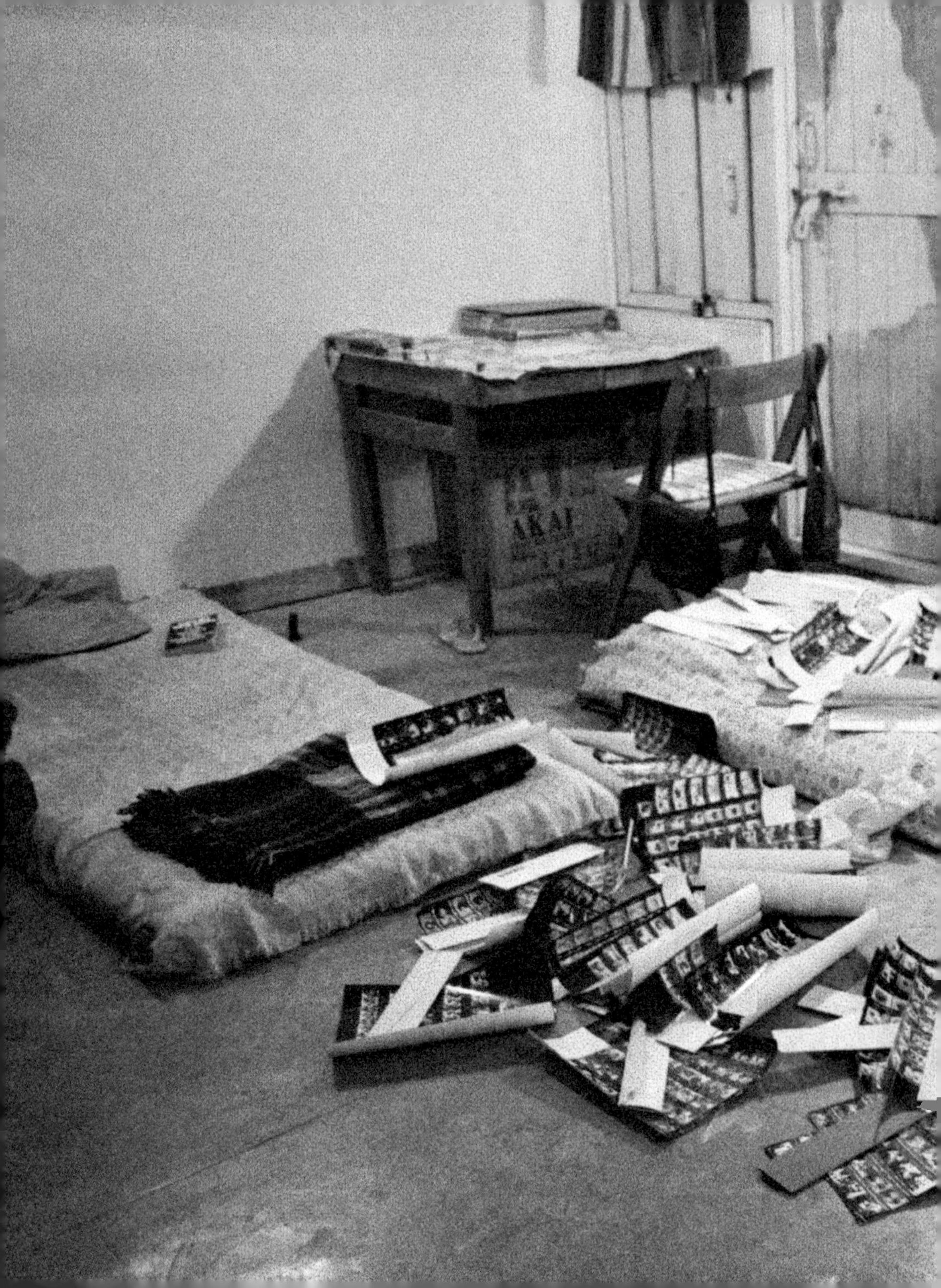